GIRLHOOD

The Rutgers Series in Childhood Studies

The Rutgers Series in Childhood Studies is dedicated to increasing our understanding of children and childhoods, past and present, throughout the world. Children's voices and experiences are central. Authors come from a variety of fields, including anthropology, criminal justice, history, literature, psychology, religion, and sociology. The books in this series are intended for students, scholars, practitioners, and those who formulate policies that affect children's everyday lives and futures.

Edited by Myra Bluebond-Langner, Distinguished Professor of Anthropology, Rutgers University, Camden, and founding director of the Rutgers University Center for Children and Childhood Studies

Advisory Board
  Joan Jacobs Brumberg, Cornell University
  Perri Klass, New York University
  Jill Korbin, Case Western Reserve University
  Bambi Schiefflin, New York University
  Enid Schildkraut, American Museum of Natural History and Museum
    for African Art

GIRLHOOD

A Global History

EDITED BY

JENNIFER HELGREN AND
COLLEEN A. VASCONCELLOS

WITH A FOREWORD BY

MIRIAM FORMAN-BRUNELL

RUTGERS UNIVERSITY PRESS
New Brunswick, New Jersey, and London

Library of Congress Cataloging-in-Publication Data

Girlhood : a global history / edited by Jennifer Helgren and Colleen A. Vasconcellos ; with a foreword by Miriam Forman-Brunell.

p. cm. — (The Rutgers series in childhood studies)

Includes bibliographical references and index.

ISBN 978-0-8135-4704-6 (hbk. : alk. paper) — ISBN 978-0-8135-4705-3 (pbk. : alk. paper)

1. Girls. 2. Girls—Social conditions. I. Helgren, Jennifer, 1972– II. Vasconcellos, Colleen A., 1973–

HQ798.G5255 2010

305.23082—dc22

2009016182

A British Cataloging-in-Publication record for this book is available from the British Library.

Visit our Web site: http://rutgerspress.rutgers.edu

Manufactured in the United States of America

For all the girls in the world

Contents

Foreword
MIRIAM FORMAN-BRUNELL —— xi

Acknowledgments —— xv

Introduction
JENNIFER HELGREN AND COLLEEN A. VASCONCELLOS —— I

Toward Political Agency for Girls: Mapping the
Discourses of Girlhood Globally
JACKIE KIRK, CLAUDIA MITCHELL, AND JACQUELINE
REID-WALSH —— 14

Part I Girls' Cultures and Identities · · · · · · · · · · · · · · · 31

1 American Jewish Girls and the Politics
   of Identity, 1860–1920
   MELISSA R. KLAPPER —— 33

2 Growing Up in Colonial Algeria: The Case
   of Assia Djebar
   CHRISTA JONES —— 49

3 Immigrant Girls in Multicultural Amsterdam:
   Juggling Ambivalent Cultural Messages
   MARION DEN UYL AND LENIE BROUWER —— 65

4 Feminist Girls, Lesbian Comrades: Performances
   of Critical Girlhood in Taiwan Pop Music
   FRAN MARTIN —— 83

Part II The Politics of Girlhood · · · · · · · · · · · · · · · · · · 103

5 Girlhood Memories and the Politics of Justice in Post-Rosas
   Argentina: The Restitution Suit of Olalla Alvarez
   JESSE HINGSON —— 105

6 "A Case of Peculiar and Unusual Interest": The Egg
   Inspectors Union, the AFL, and the British Ministry
   of Food Confront "Negro Girl" Egg Candlers
   JAN VOOGD —— 124

7   "Life Is a Succession of Disappointments": A Soviet Girl
    Contends with the Stalinist Dictatorship
    E. THOMAS EWING ⸺ 142

8   Fragilities and Failures, Promises and Patriotism:
    Elements of Second World War English and
    American Girlhood, 1939–1945
    LISA L. OSSIAN ⸺ 162

9   Holy Girl Power Locally and Globally: The Marian
    Visions of Garabandal, Spain
    JESSAMY HARVEY ⸺ 179

10 Rebels, Robots, and All-American Girls:
    The Ideological Use of Images of Girl Gymnasts
    during the Cold War
    ANN KORDAS ⸺ 195

Part III   The Education of Girls   215

11 Palestinian Girls and the British Missionary Enterprise,
    1847–1948
    NANCY L. STOCKDALE ⸺ 217

12 "The Right Kind of Ambition": Discourses of Femininity
    at the Huguenot Seminary and College, 1895–1910
    S. E. DUFF ⸺ 234

13 Stolen Girlhood: Australia's Assimilation Policies and
    Aboriginal Girls
    CHRISTINE CHEATER ⸺ 250

14 Fathers, Daughters, and Institutions: Coming of Age
    in Mombasa's Colonial Schools
    CORRIE DECKER ⸺ 268

15 Mothers of Warriors: Girls in a Youth Debate of
    Interwar Iraq
    PETER WIEN ⸺ 289

16 "'Homemaker' Can Include the World": Female Citizenship
    and Internationalism in the Postwar Camp Fire Girls
    JENNIFER HELGREN ⸺ 304

Part IV   Girls to Women: Work, Marriage,
          and Sexuality   323

17 From Chattel to "Breeding Wenches": Abolitionism,
    Girlhood, and Jamaican Slavery
    COLLEEN A. VASCONCELLOS ⸺ 325

18 Girls, Labor, and Sex in Precolonial Egypt, 1850–1882
    LIAT KOZMA ⸺ 344

19 Defiant Daughters and the Emancipation of Minors
in Nineteenth-Century Mexico
KATHRYN A. SLOAN ——— 363

20 The Shifting Status of Middle-Class Malay Girlhood:
From "Sisters" to "Sinners" in One Generation
PATRICIA SLOANE-WHITE ——— 382

Contributors ——— 403
Index ——— 407

Foreword

MIRIAM FORMAN-BRUNELL

The copious collection of girls included in *Girlhood: A Global History* stirred recollections of my girlhood, especially of the exquisitely dressed costume dolls I collected in the early 1960s. That was long before we understood that the clothing sewn onto the dolls' bodies signified female identities as immutable, uniform, and uncomplicated by gender, age, race, religion, nationality, sexuality, ethnicity, class, power, and the like. The realization that girlhood is a constructed, changing, and contested category of both experience and expectations only became apparent in the late 1980s and early 1990s as scholars began to chart the history of American girls. Since then historians and other scholars studying children and youth have been teaching, researching, writing monographs, editing journals, and compiling anthologies that place girls at the center of scholarly inquiry. The unprecedented scope of *Girlhood: A Global History*, however, makes it the first work to illuminate how vast, varied, and intricate girlhood is.

This essay collection is noteworthy for its infinite variety across all axes from the methodological to the topical, the disciplinary to the definitional. While some scholars use the diaries, memoirs, and semiautobiographical works of women to reconstruct girlhood, others make use of questionnaires and oral histories of girls themselves. Some essays rely on traditional historical evidence (e.g., archival material, interviews, official records) and qualitative research, whereas others "read" the body as a historical text. The volume also includes an enormous variety of girl-centered subjects (e.g., cultures, politics, love, sexuality, education, clothes, music, parties, dances, diary writing, talking, family, friends) and sites of study (e.g., churches, synagogues, mosques, temples, boarding schools, youth meetings, community clubs and centers, the streets, and shopping centers).

Vastly expanding the field of study across borders and boundaries, over time, and around the world, this collection, with its broad focus, also challenges standard definitions and traditional assumptions about girlhood as a uniform category of experience and expectation. By examining girls as students, citizens, sexual beings, and workers, and in numerous other social roles, the essays in this pioneering collection are significant for the opportunities they provide for the transnational study of girls. The numerous regional studies of girls from Mexico to Malaysia illuminate not only the multiplicity of girlhoods but their complexity as well. Principally written by the most recent generation of girlhood scholars in the United States, United Kingdom, and around the world, these historical examinations make visible the continuities, changes, and challenges of girlhoods.

The contributors analyze varieties of girls' experiences and the range of girlhood ideals within numerous and new historical contexts. Represented here are many different "dominant" or "mainstream" cultures ("decent culture") shaped by racial, national, ethnic, and religious elites with varying cultural ideals, expectations, and hegemonic strategies. Girlhood is also examined within religious (Jewish, Muslim, Catholic), ethnic, class, and political contexts. The use of a girl-focused lens permits examination of varieties of girlhoods under an array of systems from slavery to colonialism and dictatorships to democracies. Moreover, these essays provide opportunities to examine changes in the social construction of girlhood over time and place. For instance, in one essay we learn how the Great War politicized African American workers who became actors on larger political stages and in broader labor conflicts. The Second World War similarly led girls in the United States and the United Kingdom to assume new social roles. A handful of essays focus on the politicization of girlhoods by investigating ordinary girls as well as exceptional ones. One essay examines the gendering of Soviet celebrity gymnasts in a broader international arena.

While Soviet gymnasts symbolized the superiority of nationalist ideals, other girls manifested more heterogeneous identities. Shaped by an assortment of racial, religious, class, ethnic, and national influences, many girls laid claim to such complex identities as Arab Muslim, Arab Christian, Surinamese Dutch, French Algerian, and African Caribbean. For many, the intersections and contradictions made girlhood a particularly distinctive as well as disputed category. For Muslim girls such as Assia Djebar, her French colonial education isolated her from her cousins and other female peers with different girlhood principles and practices. Despite the differences among girls, there are striking similarities among those who struggled to construct independent identities. From the Soviet Union to the United States, girls negotiated among conflicting cultural scripts and indigenous codes as they shaped their own identities and collective subcultures. For many, personal empowerment, autonomy, individuality, was frequently achieved through diaries, books, and music often with feminist themes.

Unlike mute and immobile costume dolls, the girls from Argentina to Zimbabwe included in this collection exhibit enormous personal agency. Many contested the limitations of their gender and age by creating opportunities and claiming space. While repressive regimes often proved perilous, wars, revolutions, and immigration provided girls with greater chances for mobility, both spatial and monetary. Through numerous acts of resistance and the creation of autonomous spaces, spirited girls resisted confinement and militant ones challenged containment. Girls' many transgressive acts represented here include writing secret love letters, swinging to see over confining walls, using their voices, or suing the state. Whether enslaved or colonized, real or representations, girls used a variety of strategies to correct injustices and protect themselves from cruelty and coercion. Girls resisted indoctrination, exploitation, and commercialization as they claimed their rights and struggled for redemption, restitution, and self-determination.

Amid the diversity of cultural practices, religious beliefs, and languages, however, similarities between girls' subcultural practices are evident in the many different counternarratives that serve as sources of evidence. Whether playing, singing, dancing, dating, reading, romancing, learning, or writing (especially in diaries), girls such as those in nineteenth-century Palestine, interwar Iraq, and colonial Mombassa made the most of practices that served mediating functions. Heterosexual, bisexual, and lesbian girls carved out protected spaces, shaped interests, and constructed identities. At the end of the twentieth century, girls in Taiwan resisted the homogenization of globalized popular culture and created a hybridized subculture and sexual identity.

In ongoing tension with the changes are continuities in notions of girlhood and girls' lived experiences across time and place. While feminine training empowered American, Arab, African, and Australian Aboriginal female youth, it also served to impose severe limitations. Everywhere girls of different ages, ethnicities, and races faced discrimination because they were young females. Studies of schools (mission and public), clubs, seminaries, camps, colleges, and movements in different local contexts reveal that social institutions often served as sites of traditional female socialization and aggressive assimilation to dominant colonial cultures in Palestine, India, Mombassa, and Australia. A familiar cast of characters often hindered and sometimes helped the transformation of girlhood worldwide. These included families (nuclear and matrifocal), parents (Arab, Indian, African, Muslim, and Christian fathers), teachers, reformers, missionaries, and girlfriends. While some adults discouraged girls' defiance, and others fostered girls' negotiation among dominant, indigenous, and subcultural values, many encouraged girls' independence.

By focusing historical inquiry on girls from a global perspective, *Girlhood: A Global History* provides those in the fields of girls' studies, youth studies, children's studies, and women's studies with fresh opportunities to reevaluate and recenter girlhood, the notion long assumed to be uniform and unchanging.

Acknowledgments

Creating this book has been a long and winding road, one that began in the summer of 2005 amid conversations at the global-themed conferences of the Society for the History of Children and Youth and the Berkshire Women's History Conference. It goes without saying that a project of this magnitude had many contributors outside of those whom you will meet in the following pages. We take a minute to acknowledge all of them. Before we do so, however, the deepest of thanks go to those contributors whose essays make up this anthology on global girlhood.

We also thank Miriam Forman-Brunell, who not only took the time to contribute the foreword in the midst of her demanding schedule but also offered valuable advice on obtaining funding. At Rutgers University Press, specifically Marlie Wasserman, Adi Hovav, Beth Kressel, and Myra Bluebond-Langner: we thank you for your support and guidance and for the opportunity to publish this collection of essays. Kendra Boileau, previously at Rutgers University Press and now at the University of Illinois Press, worked with us during the early stages of the project, helping us refine our vision into a workable book. Paula Fass also encouraged this project when it was in its infancy, lending her name and wisdom to its genesis. Jay Mechling's careful reading of the manuscript was instrumental in this volume's progress, and his detailed comments and suggestions helped strengthen the transnational and comparative lens of the anthology. We also thank Kathryn Gohl for her careful copyediting and keen eye for detail. Thank you also to Andreea Boboc and Marcia Hernandez for your insights on improving the introduction. Tom Ewing, whose essay appears here, went beyond the role of contributor. His advice on putting together a volume, the terrific "Girls and Girlhood in Global History" panel that he organized for the 2008 American Historical Association meeting, and his efforts to secure funding from Virginia Tech made our job as editors much smoother.

We are also grateful to those institutions that saw the value in a project on girls' history and provided the funding to see it through to its completion, especially, the history department and the College of the Pacific at the University of the Pacific, and Virginia Tech.

On a personal note, we thank our families and friends.

COLLEEN VASCONCELLOS

I first thank my husband, John Wilson, for his unwavering support, patience, and abilities as a sounding board. It doesn't seem like enough to just say thank you, but thank you for everything. To my parents: you are the reason I am where I am today; "hang in there" means so much. To Aimee Erhard, my best friend and partner in crime, thank you for the "text support" and for the fun weekends with just us girls. And last, but certainly not least, I thank Jennifer Helgren, my coeditor, for inviting me to work with her on this project. It's been a lot of work, but I have loved every single minute of it.

JENNIFER HELGREN

My family, especially little Thomas, who waited a week to be born so that I could finish editing the first manuscript draft, and my husband, partner, and best friend Erik Helgren deserve my deepest thanks for always supporting my pursuits. My parents, too, have been stalwart supporters. Coeditor Colleen, this project truly would not have happened without you. Not only did you bring an additional network and outstanding editing skills, but also your sense of humor helped put many of its challenges in perspective.

GIRLHOOD

Introduction

JENNIFER HELGREN

COLLEEN A. VASCONCELLOS

In response to globalization and the fracturing of nation-states since the end of the Cold War, historians have increasingly turned toward international perspectives and comparisons. No longer are themes of international conflict, ethnic tension, and the migrations of peoples and ideas across borders simply the realm of international studies. In fact, over the last several years, social and cultural historians are adopting global frameworks to bring new insights and analytical methods to their research. This global study of girlhood furthers their efforts by presenting a complex study of girls within their national settings and by adding to this comparative global project. Furthermore, this collection critically explores the nexus of the two fields of children's and women's history so that we may begin to understand the history of girlhood in international and transnational contexts.

Accordingly, the scholars represented here are an interdisciplinary and international group, and their essays help to develop cross-disciplinary and cross-national perspectives and methodologies in the history of gender, children, and youth. By breaking down regional boundaries that often limit scholarly inquiries, transnational and international scholarship asks new questions and reframes old ones with new insights. In the chapters that follow, we examine the centrality of girlhood in shaping women's lives by studying how age and gender, along with a multitude of other identities, work together to influence the historical experience. This volume is a significant step in building the scholarship of international comparison and transnational inquiry, a step that is necessary for understanding girls in the world and one that we hope will inspire further research in the field.

The chapters in this volume cover a broad time frame, from 1750 to the present, to illuminate the various continuities and differences in girls' lives across cultures and across time. The regional scope of these chapters is similarly broad, and girls on all continents except Antarctica are represented. Although the current state of the field of girlhood studies has prompted us to give slightly greater representation to twentieth-century experiences as well as to girls in North America and Europe, readers will also find chapters about girls from nations in which the study of girls' history has been ignored until now. Drawing on national and local case studies, the authors assess how girls in specific localities were affected by historical developments such as colonialism, political repression, war, modernization, shifts in labor markets, migrations, and the rise of consumer culture. We have placed regionally diverse essays together in thematic sections to encourage global comparisons among girls' experiences in various locales, giving the local more recognition as part of a larger global narrative. These chapters, therefore, show how local events such as the establishment of schools for girls reflect a larger international process of change such as modernization and the formation of youth culture. More important, these chapters show how the ideas and activities of girls within these contexts had international and transnational implications.

In these essays the terms "international" and "transnational" overlap but are not synonymous. By using the term "international," we refer to developments, events, and ideas that are global in scale. International events such as the wars that Jan Voogd and Lisa Ossian detail in their chapters, as well as the shifting labor markets noted by Patricia Sloane-White in hers, may affect multiple nation-states and societies simultaneously, although their impacts may be uneven. More important, the chapters in this collection, through specific case studies, examine how such historical developments, events, and ideas shaped and influenced girlhood and how girls created or modified their cultural identities. The usage of "transnational" addresses the crossing of boundaries, such as those that separate nations and cultures. Transnational studies include the penetration or exchanges of ideas, reform networks, images, technologies, markets, and goods as well as people. Nation-based studies informed by international and transnational concerns are global in their nature. In fact, they reveal the interconnections of people worldwide.

Many of the chapters in this volume are local case studies informed by a global perspective, showing how girls responded to and shaped international events. They also show how girls' local identities result from transnational processes. Fran Martin explains, for example, that the cultural identity of the *nütongzhi*, a Taiwanese term for a girl with same-sex desires, has evolved as a locally specific phenomenon made possible by the broader context of international feminism and gay rights and evidenced by the global pop-music industry. Similarly, the girls in Iraq who were included in the youth movement al-Futuwwa as future patriotic mothers received a culturally specific model of feminine citizenship, but the presence of al-Futuwwa was the result of the spread of scouting and other youth organizations across borders. Moreover, the girls' inclusion as patriotic mothers was a theme consistent with the socialization of girls globally. As Jennifer Helgren shows, American girls were also expected to serve the nation through their families.

The objective of adopting a global perspective does not preclude nation-based studies. Just as we do not abandon significant categories of race, ethnicity, class, sexuality, religion, and gender when we think about girls in the world, we do not abandon nationality; as children's historian Paula Fass argues in *Children of a New World*, "a global perspective encourages us to appreciate the role, power, and influence of nationality in the lives of children."[1]

Central to this project is the examination of girlhood as a cultural and historical construct, and the ways the idea of girlhood changes over time. The girls discussed in our volume range in age from early childhood to their midtwenties, but most are in their teens. Chronological age, however, is only one measure of girlhood, and girlhood is a social construct much like gender and race. Collectively the chapters address the ways that the concept of girlhood has been created and changed at different times and in different regions to reflect the political and cultural concerns of societies. In many instances, the definition of girlhood has been imposed on girls. For example, Colleen Vasconcellos shows how Jamaican planters increasingly purchased African girls as "breeding wenches" as the abolition of the slave trade loomed, which shortened these girls' childhood and adolescence considerably. Liat Kozma offers one more interpretation of girlhood's limits when she describes how, in nineteenth-century Egypt, the end of girlhood was variously defined by menarche, defloration, marriage, and chronological age. In S. E. Duff's description of girlhood, however, turn-of-the-century Dutch Afrikaner South African girls readily adopt the terminology of "college girl" to describe a carefree time of relative irresponsibility and college adventure. Similarly, Corrie Decker contends that although, in precolonial Mombasa, girls traditionally entered adulthood upon their marriage, with the advent of modernization and educational opportunities they instead ended girlhood with matriculation or careers.

Girls have mattered across time and place. Until recently, most studies of childhood and youth accepted boys' experiences as normative. This volume contributes to the growth of girls' studies, a field that combats the marginalization of girls. Girls are historically significant as producers and consumers of culture, as future mothers and representatives of the nation-state, and as political and social agents in their own right.[2] Moreover, as Jackie Kirk, Claudia Mitchell, and Jacqueline Reid-Walsh explain, girls can become socially and politically empowered as scholars speak across disciplines. Understanding the past is crucial to taking steps to improve the conditions in which girls today live. Unfortunately we were reminded of the prescience of our topic and the fragility of life when Jackie Kirk was killed in August 2008 by Taliban gunmen in Afghanistan, where she was working to provide children's education through the International Rescue Committee.

Although girls' voices are often difficult to recover in the historical record, the authors here reflect on how girls reacted to and helped shape the ever-changing discourse surrounding their lives. To uncover girls' agency, we are forced to deal with the paucity of sources left behind by children and youth, and especially by girls in cultures where female education was not well established. Although some girls kept diaries or wrote letters, children as a rule are some of history's most silent subjects. In addition to the problem of literacy, children's developmental stages, particularly those of very young children, complicate historical interpretation as we decipher the motives and meanings of those who are growing. Moreover, time further obscures the nature of girls' expressions. Although, for example, European and American children in the eighteenth and early nineteenth centuries expressed themselves in adult terms, their vernacular changed with time. Children's writings from the late nineteenth century onward progressively contain more slang and youthful expressions that may not be understood by adult researchers. Although this complicates historical interpretation of all children's sources, girls were not always privileged to receive the same education as boys, if any, in most societies. Consequently, the cultural and social expectations placed on them by their parents, and to a larger degree by the society in which they lived, often negated any initiative to record their thoughts and feelings in a significant venue. Therefore, scholars who wish to uncover girls' voices must be methodologically creative. Moreover, as Kirk, Mitchell, and Reid-Walsh indicate in their discussion of girls' studies methods in the following chapter, adults may interfere with a girl's free expression. In this volume, scholars make use of traditional written sources such as diaries and memoirs, but they also turn to interviews, fiction, yearbooks, scrapbooks, and court petitions to hear girls speak for themselves. Furthermore, as E. Thomas Ewing, Christa Jones, and others contend, the written word could be a powerful source of personal liberation. Many scholars also turn to adults writing about girls and read against the grain, searching for counternarratives and the subtle girl choices that appear therein.

Historiography

The history of girlhood is a product of the intersection of the emerging field of children's history and the now well-established field of women's history. It is a significant field on its own terms. As Kirk and her coauthors show, research in cultural studies, psychology, education, literature, political science, and other fields provides interdisciplinary insights on definitions of girlhood and girls' roles in different world societies. Both the fields of women's history and children's history have benefited from research on how marginalized groups have been silenced as well as on how these groups have resisted hegemonic cultures to shape (if only subtly) institutions and history. Although girls have often been doubly marginalized as both females and youth, historians of girlhood recognize girls as social agents. As Elliott West and Paula Petrik remind us in *Small Worlds: Children and Adolescents in America*, "common sense, not to mention experiences with our own offspring should tell us that . . . no child has ever been entirely 'programmed,' nor is socialization a one-way street."[3] Indeed, youth of both sexes influence the flow of a day, the choices made by parents, and the policies of governments, shaping society and culture through their needs and desires. The time is ripe to study girls' agency and experience on a global scale.

Scholars have now begun to address women's history globally. As Alice Kessler-Harris writes, "Gender has been one of the integrative devices that have enabled the practice of international and transnational history. . . . Once historians began to imagine gender as a cultural framing device, a set of expectations, and an ideology that moved individuals and groups to act in certain kinds of ways, questions emerged as to how that ideology was articulated differently in different places and we made efforts to examine its effects."[4] A significant contribution to the literature on women in the world is the Coordinating Council of Women Historians' three-volume *Women's History in Global Perspective* edited by Bonnie G. Smith. The first volume's thematic approach is complimented by the regional and time-specific approach of the second and third volumes, and it is this type of expansive history with its cross-national, cross-continental comparisons that our own volume seeks to promote. Although girls' experiences appear in *Women's History in Global Perspective*, the work's focus, like much of women's history research, only rarely considers the role of age or generation in gendered identities. Similarly, women's historians have explored the international context of women's reform and feminism, the movement of gendered ideas about science, reproduction, and health across borders, the effects of imperialism and militarization on women and their roles in producing colonial states, the formation of transnational identities among migratory populations, and the global aspects of labor and consumer markets.[5]

Also promising are the comparative approaches adopted by historians Louise Tilly, Peter Sterns, and Merry Wiesner-Hanks.[6] Still, as historians Margaret Strobel and Marjorie Bingham admit, an integrative approach to the history of women in the world "is still in process."[7] Regional approaches are still more common than histories that examine broad themes such as religion, economics, and nationalism from a cross-cultural perspective. Any synthesis of girls' history is similarly in the making. With the exception of the Modern Girl Research Group, historians have not looked at girlhood in a global context. This group's comparative research seeks to answer how the "modern girl," defined by her "provocative fashions," pursuit of romantic love, and "disregard [for] roles of dutiful daughter, wife, and mother," came to be a global phenomenon in the early twentieth century.[8]

Like the study of gender, the study of childhood is one particularly well suited to an international and transnational perspective. As Fass writes, "At birth, all children are members of a world community, still unmarked by most social, national and cultural boundaries. . . . Thus, children are by nature 'citizens' of the world. . . . Adopting a wider global perspective allows us to study [how children become attached to specific identities] by looking at how children become bounded by nations and cultures, and how they contribute to those formations through their mental and behavioral interactions."⁹ Moreover, childhood is a category defined by the complex interplay of biological development and the social and historical meanings that societies attribute to physical and mental changes over time. Thus, it is a field that brings into sharp relief the ways in which cultural productions of childhood differ across cultures even as they underscore the significance of similarities in youth experience.

Peter Stearns's *Childhood in World History*, for example, looks at how the major themes in world history, such as the contested question of modernization, agricultural and industrial revolutions, the spread of literacy, cultural contacts, and the development of world religions, have all affected children but in uneven ways. Ultimately, Stearns finds that when viewed through the lens of childhood, the typical periodization of these events shifts; children often felt their impacts on a slightly altered timetable. Other recent studies, such as those of historian E. Thomas Ewing, have examined education in an international and comparative context.¹⁰

The summer 2005 special issue of the *Journal of Social History* on the subject of children, youth, and globalization edited by Stearns was the first scholarly work that measured the degree to which globalization "builds on the complex evolution of previous stages of interregional interconnectedness" to produce a phenomenon that is substantially new in degree and quality. With this issue, Stearns sought to produce analyses of childhood that are "less regionally confined," arguing that that the development of "modern childhood," marked by schooling rather than labor, falling death and fertility rates, and a higher degree of parental investment within a child-centered family, began to take shape in western Europe and the United States with industrialization and was spread through imperialism and the choices of non-Western societies to incorporate elements of this model. In the twentieth century, the process of change accelerated and a cross-cultural concept of childhood and adolescence emerged, as evident through such venues as the human rights movement and consumer marketing.¹¹ Our present volume, *Girlhood: A Global History*, expands on the arguments first posited by Stearns by collecting local and international studies together in one volume and by further interrogating the concepts of modern childhood and globalization. This volume asks the degree to which a global concept of childhood is gendered and the ways different societies (and girls themselves) negotiate this process of change.

Although Stearns's work focuses on childhood, and women's historians generally do not examine age itself as a separate category of analysis, a few collections have addressed the history of girlhood in the United States and Europe. Jennifer Lee and Min Zhou's *Asian American Youth* and Sherrie Inness's *Delinquents and Debutantes* discuss the history of girls in American culture, while Mary Jo Maynes, Birgitte Søland, and Christina Benninghaus reconceptualize modern European girls' roles as workers, students, consumers, daughters, friends, and mothers, in *Secret Gardens, Satanic Mills*.

Claudia Nelson and Lynne Vallone's *The Girls' Own* compares British and American girlhoods.[12] Other scholars present microstudies of girlhood, or specific histories of girls in regional and temporal contexts. The pathbreaking work of Miriam Forman-Brunell, editor of *Girlhood in America: An Encyclopedia*, for example, and Joan Brumberg, author of *The Body Project*, examines how girls have disrupted and mediated socializing forces. There are similar projects researching girls' cultures in North America and in Europe. Fewer works examine girls in Africa, Asia, Latin America, and Australia separate from boys, but this body of research is also growing.[13]

The growing body of literature that examines the affects of globalization on today's girls also points to interest in girls' international roles. Claudia Mitchell and Jacqueline Reid-Walsh, for example, bring together essays that analyze the effort to market consumer goods to preadolescent girls, in *Seven Going on Seventeen: Tween Studies in the Culture of Girlhood*. Cultural anthropologist Lenie Brouwer has brought a comparative framework to her analysis of contemporary girl cultures in the Netherlands as she has studied migrant communities from Turkey and Morocco. Sociologist Marion H. G. den Uyl's "Dowry in India: Respected Tradition and Modern Monstrosity" examines shifts in local or cultural traditions. Similarly, Anita Harris's reader, *All about the Girl*, and Anoop Nayak's *Race, Place and Globalization* examine consumer culture, feminism, and a myriad of other themes in a global and globalizing context.[14] *Girlhood* extends this research in girls' studies by examining, through a historical and comparative lens, the history of girlhood in a global context.

Conclusions

Although the chapters in this volume are divided into four thematic sections, several concerns emerge throughout the volume: (1) cultures' struggles to make meaning out of girls' biology and development at different times and in different places; (2) girls' responses as agents to international and transnational developments—even in the most patriarchal societies, girls' voices matter; and (3) the correlation of girls' well-being with national and international choices regarding girls' education, health, and welfare. To unpack these concerns, this volume examines how international developments, such as migrations, wars, globalization, labor, economic markets, and international diplomacy, influenced girls' cultures and identities; how girls' have created communities and shaped cultures internationally, nationally, and locally; the extent to which girls have operated as global actors or agents of change; how and for what purposes girls have been imagined by governments, the media, consumer marketers, educators and reformers, and religious bodies; how girls' cultures have been constituted through their responses to cultural, institutional, and familial expectations; and how the well-being of girls correlates with their access to material culture, education, health, and legal rights. Transnational comparisons and categories such as race, class, ethnicity, sexuality, and religion further complicate the narrative of girls' history, yet add texture to that narrative, as girls encounter historical events as individuals with overlapping identities and loyalties. Each section in this book includes essays on girls from different parts of the world and at different historical periods. This framework lends itself to methodological and thematic comparisons, and through it we begin to see the commonalities in girls' experiences across time and place as well as the ways in which time, region, and political institutions created distinct histories.

Part 1, "Girls' Cultures and Identities," explores the various means used by girls to create their own cultures and identities by analyzing the intersections of gender, ethnicity, class, and youth with particular focus on how national identity coexists, challenges, and reflects the experiences of girls of various backgrounds. While casting identity formation as part of the story of international migrations, the four chapters in this section collectively suggest that girls form multifaceted identities when confronted with competing claims for their cultural allegiance. As part of the Jewish diaspora, the U.S. girls whom Melissa Klapper writes about contend with pressures from family, religion, and nation, yet they form a coherent "tripartite identity": Jewish, female, American. A similar struggle characterizes the attempts of the minority migrant girls in contemporary Amsterdam, who, according to Marion den Uyl and Lenie Brouwer, negotiate "street" and "decent" cultures in a "superdiverse" setting. Christa Jones also describes a struggle in her examination of writer and artist Assia Djebar, who, although not a migrant, must contend with a bicultural identity as a result of her Arab girlhood in colonized Algeria and French colonial schools. Unlike the vibrant girls' culture of Jewish peers that Klapper describes, those described by both den Uyl and Brouwer and Jones point to the divisions that punctuated girls' worlds: in the Amsterdam case as they were both drawn to and repelled by "street" culture, and in Djebar's case as education set her apart from her confined female peers and relatives. Fran Martin concludes this section by charting the formation of a different kind of identity, that of *nütongzhi*, or lesbian girl identity, in contemporary Taiwan. Martin finds that the new identity is produced as ideas about gay and women's rights cross borders, mix with local cultures, and create something that is both locally specific and an expression of global movements.

In part 2, "The Politics of Girlhood," the chapters look at girls' various relationships to the state by asking how girls were implicated in major national and international conflicts ranging from the rise of oppressive dictatorships to the emergence of world war. Of concern are representations of girls and the uses of those representations for institutional, legal, and political purposes. Different models of female citizenship have been deemed necessary across cultures and within societies at different time periods. Authors in this section understand girls as producers as well as recipients of cultural messages. As E. Thomas Ewing explains in his chapter, "Girls learned to negotiate among different demands while also creating spaces in which to enact their own identities." Thus, the self-preservation seen in the diary of a persecuted Soviet girl marks agency. Similarly, Jesse Hingson shows that in nineteenth-century Argentina, girls used their protected status to advantage by appealing to courts for restitution in the wake of the oppressive Rosas regime. While Ewing and Hingson show how girls enacted personal strategies of survival and resistance, Jan Voogd, in an essay on African American egg candlers, demonstrates how girls impacted international relations when their choice to seek employment in the industry threatened to undermine a Chicago union stronghold and the food supply to wartime England. Meanwhile, Lisa Ossian, Ann Kordas, and Jessamy Harvey add another dimension to our understanding of girls' effect on the international stage. All three of their chapters show how, in the different contexts of World War II, athletics, and religion, the symbolism of girlhood could be as powerful a mover of populations as were the girls' real actions. Harvey points out that the Spanish girl visionaries enacted a cultural model for female submission to a transcendent will, one that required submission but also opened avenues of authority. These symbolic roles, she argues, deserve attention as sites for agentic action if the girls themselves felt empowered by their role. Girls (both real and imagined), then, have played national and international political roles, and developed coping strategies in the hardest of times, and they have done so in gender-based locally and culturally specific ways.

Part 3, "The Education of Girls," brings together case studies of girls in socializing institutions. As with the chapters in "The Politics of Girlhood," issues of girls' relationship to the state are analyzed as girls come into contact with public and private youth organizations and schools, two institutions whose spread has been associated with modernization and the evolution of youth cultures. Education and youth organizations have prolonged adolescence for youth across the globe. Assessing the role of education in girls' lives and the means for which education was offered, our authors demonstrate how education served as an agent of the state and a tool of colonialism, yet at the same time empowered girls to shape their own worlds, identity, and destiny. As both Nancy Stockdale and Christine Cheater explain, schools in British Palestine and mid-twentieth-century Australia had colonizing aims. British missionaries sought to convert Palestinian girls (Jews and Muslims) to Christianity and to teach them British models of domesticity, while Australian state officials targeted mixed-blood girls for assimilation schools to train them for domestic service and to remove them as a potential sexual threat to society. In these cases, schooling aimed to erase local cultures and to Anglicize, but as both of these authors point out, girls resisted, spitting out food during Ramadan and running away. Although the girls at the Huguenot Seminary that served Dutch Afrikaner girls in South Africa did not face the same religious or racial oppression, S. E. Duff shows that still they combated a discourse on femininity that ushered them into maternal roles or careers as teachers to claim a transitional stage in which they could be recognized as *girls* entitled to fun and adventure. Corrie Decker argues that later, in mid-twentieth-century colonial Mombasa, Kenya, education signaled modernization and a new model of girlhood experience in which careers and exposure to "Western" ideas were embraced. Even though those schools often trumpeted distinct gender roles, the fact that fathers pushed for the education of their daughters meant that Mombasans' local, cultural response to the spread of Western education undermined a hegemonic discourse on schooling's gender ideals.

Youth organizations such as Iraq's al-Futuwwa and the United States' Camp Fire Girls provide examples of another educational institution. As we know, education for girls was not limited to schoolhouses. As Peter Stearns and many authors in this work attest, it is only with modernization that girls' education moves out of homes and into the public spaces of the schoolroom. Peter Wien and Jennifer Helgren find that, like schools, youth organizations sought to socialize youth as citizens of the state. In both cases, girls' roles as citizens were located within the family. Iraqi girls were the future mothers of warriors and therefore represented national strength. U.S. girls were to offer service beginning with their families and then reaching outward to spread democracy abroad. These chapters suggest parallels in the experiences of girls' education. Colonialism and imperialist policies, for example, shaped girls' socialization in many regions of the world (including colonies and super powers). Alternatively, education could be profoundly empowering. Educational institutions usually trained girls for their roles in the family. Whether they were the future mothers of warriors or, as Patricia Sloane-White argues in the next section, "sisters" to the nation, women were trained for citizenship roles that were defined in a family context. Native populations navigated educational institutions, at times embracing them as conducive to a progressive concept of womanhood or cosmopolitanism and at other times rejecting or chafing under their social control.

The final section in the volume, "Girls to Women, Work, Marriage, and Sexuality," confronts the concept of girlhood directly. Chapters in this section explore a variety of "coming of age" experiences around the world. They focus on challenges to girlhood and probe the definition of girlhood in light of the seemingly adult experiences of labor, sexual activity, rape, and marriage. As Colleen Vasconcellos, Liat Kozma, and Kathryn Sloan demonstrate, girls' roles in the work force (slave and wage), the sexual exploitation and choices of girls, and their marriage options and constraints suggest the difficulty of theorizing a universal biological category of girlhood. Girls in the world faced a variety of sexual experiences, from the oppressive sexual coercion met by Jamaican enslaved girls forced to "breed" to what Sloan characterizes as the empowering prospect of petitioning for "emancipation" from one's family and eloping with a boyfriend, and representations of young female sexuality. In many instances, girls' sexuality has been portrayed as threatening to the nation-state. This was true in 1990s Malaya, according to Patricia Sloane-White, whose chapter in this section examines Muslim Malay girls.

This theme of threatened or threatening sexuality emerges elsewhere in this volume as well. Boarding schools in Australia, Cheater argues, were designed to contain the sexual threat of mixed race Aboriginal girls; Jones explains that traditional girls in Algeria were expected to veil themselves; and "delinquents" in the United States and Britain during the Second World War were perceived as a threat to the nation's war effort, according to Ossian. The irony is that whereas the role of girl as sexually dangerous has provided reason for societies to sequester her, her role as sexually vulnerable has also led to the protections from the state that have benefited her. Thus, while girls learned to use their sexuality or their subordinate position within the family to their own ends, these efforts have more often than not led to only limited agency—a chance to write in a diary but not a chance to explode restrictive gender categories.[15]

The editors and contributors to this volume hope these essays will spark further dialogue and research into the international and transitional histories of girlhood. As Kirk, Mitchell, and Reid-Walsh assert in the pages immediately following this introduction, more work is needed to uncover the interdisciplinary intersections that may ameliorate conditions for girls worldwide and help them act as agents of change in their own lives. By bringing together local studies within a comparative framework alongside research on girls whose bodies, ideas, and representations cross national boundaries, we hope to begin moving toward an integrated field of girls' history. Ever mindful of the necessity of taking girls on their own terms and accepting girlhood itself as a cultural and historical construct, we believe that the time is especially critical for such studies because globalization brings people closer together, even as it magnifies the likelihood of conflict.

NOTES

1. Paula Fass, *Children of a New World: Society, Culture, and Globalization* (New York: New York University Press, 2006), 12.

2. See Mary Celeste Kearney, "Coalescing: The Development of Girls' Studies," *NWSA Journal* 21, no. 1 (Spring 2009): 1–28, for a discussion of girls' marginalization in youth studies and women's studies.

3. Elliot West and Paula Petrik, introduction to *Small Worlds: Children and Adolescents in America, 1850–1950*, ed. E. West and P. Petrik (Lawrence: University Press of Kansas, 1992), 6.

4. Alice Kessler-Harris, "A Rich and Adventurous Journey: The Transnational Journey of Gender History in the United States," *Journal of Women's History* 19, no. 1 (2007): 153–155.

5. Bonnie G. Smith, ed., *Women's History in Global Perspective*, 3 vols. (Urbana: University of Illinois Press, 2004, 2005, and 2005). On women's reform, see Ian Tyrrell, *Woman's World, Woman's Empire: The Women's Christian Temperance Union in International Perspective, 1880–1930* (Chapel Hill: University of North Carolina Press, 1991); Leila Rupp, *Worlds of Women: The Making of an International Women's Movement* (Princeton, NJ: Princeton University Press, 1997); Ellen

Carol DuBois, *Harriot Stanton Blatch and the Winning of Woman Suffrage* (New Haven: Yale University Press, 1999); Bonnie Anderson, *Joyous Greetings: The First International Women's Movement, 1830–1860* (New York: Oxford University Press, 2001); and Rumi Yasutake, *Transnational Women's Activism: The United States, Japan, and Japanese Immigrant Communities in California, 1859–1930* (New York: New York University Press, 2004). On the movement of scientific ideas about population control and birth control, see Laura Briggs, *Reproducing Empire: Race, Sex, Science and U.S. Imperialism in Puerto Rico* (Berkeley: University of California Press, 2002). On the women's health movement, see Kathy Davis, *The Making of "Our Bodies, Ourselves": How Feminism Travels across Borders* (Durham, NC: Duke University Press, 2007). For discussions of imperialism and militarization, see Anna Davin, "Imperialism and Motherhood," *History Workshop Journal* 5 (Spring 1978): 9–66; Ann Laura Stoler, ed. *Haunted by Empire: Geographies of Intimacy in North American History* (Durham, NC: Duke University Press, 2006); Cynthia Enloe, *Globalization and Militarism: Feminists Make the Link* (Lanham, MD: Rowman and Littlefield, 2007); Allison L. Sneider, *Suffragists in an Imperial Age: U.S. Expansion and the Woman Question, 1870–1929* (New York: Oxford University Press, 2008); and Mire Koikari, *Pedagogy of Democracy: Feminism and the Cold War in the U.S. Occupation of Japan* (Philadelphia: Temple University Press, 2008). For an exploration of imperialism that includes analysis of gender and generation, see Kristine Alexander, "The Girl Guide Movement and Imperial Internationalism during the 1920s and 1930s," *Journal of the History of Childhood and Youth* 2, no. 1 (winter 2009): 37–63. On migrations and labor markets, see Donna R. Gabaccia and Franca Iacovetta, eds., *Women, Gender, and Transnational Lives: Italian Workers of the World* (Toronto: University of Toronto Press, 2002); Catherine Ceniza Choy, *Empire of Care: Nursing and Migration in Filipino American History* (Durham, NC: Duke University Press, 2003); and Rhacel Salazar Parreñas, *The Force of Domesticity: Filipina Migrants and Globalization* (New York: New York University Press, 2008). On consumer culture, see Kristin L. Hoganson, *Consumers' Imperium: The Global Production of American Domesticity, 1865–1920* (Chapel Hill: University of North Carolina Press, 2007).

6. Louise A. Tilly, "Industrialization and Gender Inequality," in *Islamic and European Expansion: The Forging of a Global Order*, ed. Michael Adas (Philadelphia: Temple University Press, 1993); Peter N. Stearns, *Gender in World History* (New York: Routledge, 2006); Merry E. Wiesner-Hanks, *Gender in History* (Malden, MA: Blackwell, 2001).

7. Margaret Strobel and Marjorie Bingham, "The Theory and Practice of Women's History and Gender History in Global Perspective," in Smith, *Women's History in Global Perspective*, 1:23.

8. Tani Barlow, Madeleine Dong, Uta Poiger, Priti Ramamurthy, Lynn Thomas, and Alys Weinbaum, "The Modern Girl around the World: A Research Agenda and Preliminary Findings," *Gender and History* 17, no. 2 (Fall 2005): 245.

9. Fass, *Children of a New World*, 11.

10. Peter N. Stearns, *Childhood in World History* (New York: Routledge, 2006); E. Thomas Ewing, "Shaking the Foundations of Education: An Introduction to Revolution and Pedagogy in Transnational and Interdisciplinary Perspective," 1–18; and "Gender Equity as Revolutionary Strategy: Coeducation in Russian and Soviet Schools," 39–60; in *Revolution and Pedagogy*, ed. E. Thomas Ewing (New York: Palgrave Macmillan, 2005).

11. Peter N. Stearns, "Preface: Globalization and Childhood," *Journal of Social History* 38, no. 4 (Summer 2005): 845 (quotation).

12. Jennifer Lee and Min Zhou, eds., *Asian American Youth: Culture, Identity, and Ethnicity* (New York: Routledge, 2004); Sherrie A. Inness, ed., *Delinquents and Debutantes: Twentieth-Century American Girls' Cultures* (New York: New York University Press, 1998); Mary Jo Maynes, Birgitte Søland, and Christina Benninghaus, eds., *Secret Gardens, Satanic Mills: Placing Girls in European History, 1750–1960* (Bloomington: Indiana University Press, 2005); and Claudia Nelson and Lynne Vallone, eds., *The Girls' Own: Cultural Histories of the Anglo-American Girl, 1830–1915* (Athens: University of Georgia Press, 1994). On American childhood and youth, see N. Ray Hiner and Joseph M. Hawes, eds., *Growing Up in America: Children in Historical Perspective* (Urbana: University of Illinois Press, 1985); West and Petrik, introduction to *Small Worlds*; Caroline F. Levander and Carol J. Singley, eds., *American Child: A Cultural Studies Reader* (New Brunswick, NJ: Rutgers University

Press, 2003); Joe Austin and Michael Nevin Willard, eds. *Generations of Youth: Youth Cultures and History in Twentieth-Century America* (New York: New York University Press, 1998); Paula S. Fass and Mary Ann Mason, eds., *Childhood in America* (New York: New York University Press, 1999); Anya Jabour, ed., *Major Problems in the History of Families and Children* (Boston: Houghton Mifflin, 2004).

13. See Miriam Forman-Brunell, *Girlhood in America: An Encyclopedia* (Santa Barbara, CA: ABC-CLIO, 2001); Miriam Formanek-Brunell, *Made to Play House: Dolls and the Commercialization of American Girlhood, 1830–1930* (Baltimore: Johns Hopkins University Press, 1998); and Melissa Klapper, *Jewish Girls Coming of Age* (New York: New York University Press, 2005). On the United States, see also Joan Jacobs Brumberg, *The Body Project: An Intimate History of American Girls* (New York: Vintage Books, 1998); Kelly Schrum, *Some Wore Bobby Sox: The Emergence of Teenage Girls' Culture, 1920–1945* (New York: Palgrave Macmillan, 2006); Jane Hunter, *How Young Ladies Became Girls: The Victorian Origins of American Girlhood* (New Haven: Yale University Press, 2002); Mary Rothschild, "To Scout or to Guide? The Girl Scout–Boy Scout Controversy, 1912–1941," *Frontiers: A Journal of Women's Studies* 6, no. 3 (1981): 115–121; Ruth M. Alexander, *The Girl Problem: Female Sexual Delinquency in New York, 1900–1930* (Ithaca, NY: Cornell University Press, 1995); Wini Breines, *Young, White, and Miserable: Growing Up Female in the Fifties* (Boston: Beacon Press, 1992); Georganne Scheiner, *Signifying Female Adolescence: Film Representations and Fans, 1920–1950* (Westport, CT: Praeger, 2000); Vicki Ruiz, " 'Star Struck': Acculturation, Adolescence, and Mexican American Women, 1920–1950," in West and Petrik, *Small Worlds*, 61–80; and Valerie J. Matsumoto, "Nisei Daughters' Courtship and Romance in Los Angeles before World War II," in Lee and Zhou, *Asian American Youth*, 83–100. On girls in Europe, see Angela McRobbie and Jenny Garber, "Girls and Subcultures," in *Feminism and Youth Culture: From "Jackie" to "Just Seventeen,"* ed. Angela McRobbie (Boston: Unwin Hyman, 1991), 12–25; Sally Mitchell, *The New Girl: Girls' Culture in England, 1880–1915* (New York: Columbia University Press, 1995); Penny Tinkler, *Constructing Girlhood: Popular Magazines for Girls Growing Up in England, 1920–1950* (London: Taylor and Francis, 1995); Rebecca Rogers, *From the Salon to the Schoolroom: Educating Bourgeois Girls in Nineteenth-Century France* (University Park: Pennsylvania State University Press, 2005); and Meg Gomersall, *Working-Class Girls in Nineteenth-Century England: Life, Work and Schooling* (New York: St. Martin's Press, 1997). On girls in Asia, Africa, and Latin America, see Sita Anantha Raman, *Getting Girls to School: Social Reform in the Tamil Districts, 1870–1930* (Calcutta: Bhatkal Books International, 1996); Liat Kozma, "Negotiating Virginity: Narratives of Defloration from Late Nineteenth-Century Egypt," *Comparative Studies of South Asia, Africa and the Middle East* 24, no. 1 (2004): 57–67; Tobias Hecht, ed., *Minor Omissions: Children in Latin American History and Society* (Madison: University of Wisconsin Press, 2002).

14. Claudia Mitchell and Jacqueline Reid-Walsh, *Seven Going on Seventeen: Tween Studies in the Culture of Girlhood* (New York: Peter Lang, 2005); Lenie Brouwer, "Good Girls, Bad Girls: Moroccan and Turkish Runaway Girls in the Netherlands," in *Muslim European Youth: Reproducing Ethnicity, Religion, Culture,* ed. Steven Vertovec and Alisdair Rogers (Aldershot, UK: Ashgate, 1998), 145–167; Marion H. G. den Uyl, "Dowry in India: Respected Tradition and Modern Monstrosity," in *The Gender Question in Globalization: Changing Perspectives and Practices,* ed. Francien Van Driel and Tine Davids (Aldershot, UK: Ashgate, 2005), 143–159; Anita Harris, *All about the Girl: Culture, Power and Identity* (New York: Routledge, 2004); and Anoop Nayak, *Race, Place and Globalization: Youth Cultures in a Changing World* (New York: Berg Publishers, 2003).

15. There is a need for greater scholarly attention to the experiences of same-sex and transgender girlhoods around the world, for example, if we are to fully understand girlhood as a historical and social construct. In addition to Fran Martin, scholars working on girls and same-sex relationships include Catriona Rueda Esquibel, "Memories of Girlhood: Chicana Lesbian Fictions," *Signs: Journal of Women in Culture and Society* 23, no. 3 (Spring 1998): 644–681; and Lillian Faderman, *Odd Girls and Twilight Lovers: A History of Lesbian Life in Twentieth-Century America* (New York: Penguin, 1992).

Toward Political Agency for Girls

MAPPING THE DISCOURSES
OF GIRLHOOD GLOBALLY

JACKIE KIRK

CLAUDIA MITCHELL

JACQUELINE REID-WALSH

*"Mapping, by forcing us to think in terms of discrete
entities occupying specific spaces, makes us aware of the
spaces we inhabit and the positions we take relative to
others."*

—Nellie Stromquist, "Mapping Gendered Spaces
in Third World Educational Interventions"[1]

There is an increased interest around the globe in girls and girlhood.
Although a tendency to refer to "womenandgirls" still pervades, blurring
the specificity of girls' experiences, there is increased attention to girls as a
special group within the study of gender and gendered experiences.[2] This
interest has multiple dimensions and multiple implications, and can be
attributed to various, yet at least to some extent, interconnected tendencies.
These discourses cut across and intersect with the theoretical fields and bodies
of literature that address girls, girlhood, and girls' issues, including girls'
psychological development, girls in development contexts (particularly
girls' education), girls and popular culture, and historical and literary representations of girls. Although we are aware of the problematic nature of
terms such as "third world" and "developing country," especially when contrasted with "first world" and "developed countries," we use the term
"development context" to refer to particular locations in countries, regions,
and communities like the South of Africa, often referred to as developing,
majority, or third world. The relationships among the recurrent discourses as
well as project and program experience, particularly in the health and education sectors, indicate the scope and complexity of girlhood. Yet the tendency
is to divide girls' lives and experiences into sectoral or subject categories.
This partition results in an ignoring—or at least a marginalization—of girls'

agency and of the potential for creating a multidimensional, girl-focused platform for action and social change.

To move beyond this situation, to ensure that girls are located at the center of policy-making processes, and to stimulate approaches to working with and for girls' political agency, in 1998 we embarked upon an ongoing mapping project within girlhood studies. This project argues for the need to work across disciplinary borders and to interrogate our own work for its potential to speak across different fields, generations, and geographic spaces;[3] this stance is imperative if we are to understand girls and girlhood in transnational, international, and globalized contexts. We consider feminist mapping to be an approach that helps identify relationships, disconnects, power dynamics, similarities, and differences in a way that transcends a review of the literature. Drawing on the feminist mapping ideas developed by Nellie Stromquist, we did not claim to possess an objective worldview. On the contrary, we approach the idea of mapping the research on girls from the position of partial advocates. Nor do we presume a totalizing approach—our mappings leave great areas of research uncharted. Instead, our maps are done in the spirit of social cartography, which encourages the creation of smaller and contextualized narratives—essentially what might be described as a "boundary project" with fluid boundaries that may resist established power relations and promote nontotalizing epistemological values.[4]

Our purpose in mapping is to ascertain possible points of convergence among those studying girlhood and to discover what we can learn (and also what we may lose) when we cross disciplinary borders. In so doing, we argue for the need for a discourse community that does not "cut up" girls lives, but rather one that seeks to establish a framework for common understandings. Our aim ultimately is to establish an "imagined community" among scholars, practitioners, and activists;[5] such a community did not exist when we first began advocating for or, more concretely, initiating its formation. We want our mapping exercise to provide insights into why it did not exist, if it is a feasible project, and even whether a community can be realistically imagined. In our earlier work we sought to persuade the feminist community to contemplate such an aim by using maps and mapping as metaphors in order to tap into the rhetorical persuasiveness often attributed to maps.[6]

As highlighted in the introduction to this collection and as can be seen across many of the essays in this book, there are a variety of ways that different cultures at different times make meaning out of girls' bodies (especially their sexual and biological development), there are many different ways that girls have responded as agents to international and transnational developments (even in the most oppressive societies girls' voices matter), and there are many different ways that girls' well-being is correlated with national and international choices regarding girls' education, health, and welfare. Mapping these varying responses and approaches, we argue, is critical. In this chapter we go beyond using mapping as a rhetorical device that seeks to bring feminist researchers together. Here we extend the notion of mapping girlhood to include a wider range of categories about the study of girls and girls' lives and more explicitly apply the mapping methodology to the international, transnational, and globalized contexts in which we work with girls and on girlhood issues. We begin with our own brief history of mapping girlhood, where we explore the emerging field of feminist mapping and offer a sense of why we see this as an important girl-centric, agency-oriented project. We then look at three separate yet interrelated thematic areas of girlhood—pathologizing girlhood, consuming girlhood, and agency and girlhood—showing the ways in which a mapping project allows us to read across borders and boundaries of development studies, popular culture, and participatory process. We conclude the chapter by arguing that an ongoing mapping project can contribute strategically to girlhood studies as an emerging field and ultimately as a global project. We have three major aims: to develop strategic alliances between researchers and funding bodies, to develop new methods in the study of girls and girlhood, and to raise new questions in order to further our understanding of girls and girlhood.

Girl Mapping: A Brief History

Our work on girl mapping draws on feminist mapping and social cartography. Although we use "mapping" in a figurative sense, because it is important to remain cognizant of the patriarchal and colonial implications of the term, we also interrogate the limitations of our conceptual tools. We ask ourselves a number of interrelated questions: What can we learn when we cross disciplinary and geographical borders? How can work in one area inform work in the other areas? How can we avoid unnecessary duplication? Is there any practical value to working with the diverse bodies of literature mentioned earlier? This last question is particularly key when we think about the urgency for change in the lives of girls in developing countries. Many countries do not have the luxury of long periods of time to develop action plans. In the developed world, where there may be only limited funds for researching girls' lives, we need to be more strategic in the use of these funds. We need to look critically at the key messages—and the inherent challenges of different bodies of research and literature—to consider how each informs others, and overall what an emerging interdisciplinary field of girlhood studies can teach us.

Our goal in mapping girlhood has not been to reposition girlhood studies as a monolithic enterprise, but rather to see the term "girlhood" as one that can (and should) invoke strategic alliances within research communities so that our overarching questions point to the strength of interdisciplinarity. Starting with the superordinate question "Who cares about girls, anyway?" (a rephrasing in some cases of the question "Who funds research about girls?"), we have developed a series of questions that we regard as useful starting points for working across disciplines, across geographies, across time periods, and that acknowledge the significance of gender and generation.[7]

The questions that follow provide for a meta-analysis of research on girlhood, or what we call "girl method":

1. How is girlhood defined and why? Who is a girl?
2. What are the temporal spaces of girlhood? How has the idea of girlhood changed across time?
3. What are the cultural spaces of girlhood? How has the idea of girlhood changed across cultures and within cultures?
4. What are the geopolitical spaces in which research takes place?
5. Who is engaging in this kind of research?
6. What is the critical reception of this research? Who funds girlhood studies?
7. Who are beneficiaries of the research on girlhood?
8. What are the kinds of questions that are being taken up?
9. What is the history of this field? How has the focus of the work changed over time?
10. How does the research link the lives of girls and women?
11. To what extent does the research draw on gender relations?
12. What is the main agenda of the work? To what extent is it regulatory and protective? Advocacy and action oriented? Policy oriented?
13. What methodologies are being employed? How do girls and women participate? To what extent is the work girl-centered?

This list expands our initial questions,[8] for we realize that the mapping girlhood project is a generative and iterative one. This implies that the project, rather than beginning with a fixed set of questions, starts with an initial set that are modified over time since the findings of each stage of research guide the subsequent steps. For example, as we ourselves engaged in more method-related work, we realized that methodology is itself a critical feature of girlhood studies.[9] We therefore found ourselves adding new questions: What methodologies are being employed? How do girls and women participate? To what extent is the work girl-centered? What has become apparent is that girl-method invites its own mapping, with attention to such features as age disaggregation, participation, and intergenerationality.

Like many of the authors in this collection, we are interested in age itself as a definer of girlhood. (See, for example, the chapters by Christa Jones, Jessamy Harvey, Colleen Vasconcellos, Liat Kozma, and Kathryn Sloan.) In relation to girlhood and age, product and service marketers have already done a certain amount of age disaggregation in terms of the construction of "tween culture,"[10] but the significance of this work to policies and practices was less apparent. How do we acknowledge and build in the significance of age into studying girls and girlhood? How and when do we disaggregate girlhood according to age, and what do we lose when we do not? Can we talk across ages and experiences of girlhood? For instance, does it matter if the girl is of preschool age, or between the ages of ten and fourteen (a tween or a "very young adolescent" as defined by the 2006 Population Council),[11] eighteen and at the age of consent in many countries, or twenty-four and at the far edge of North American adolescence yet still within the category of "young" as defined by the UN? Furthermore, the category "girl" can refer to the baby girl who is sexually abused by a man who believes the myth that having sex with a baby can cure AIDS, the little girls whose imitations of adult social roles in Sally Mann's photography stir controversy, and the tween-age "whistleblower" girls that, psychologists Lyn Mikel Brown and Carol Gilligan write, challenge norms indirectly and with subtlety.[12] "Girl" can also be a category within youth studies—defined by UN agencies as being between the ages of fifteen and twenty-nine. As we point out in *Researching Children's Popular Culture: Cultural Spaces of Childhood*, at least five generations of women may classify themselves or be classified as girls, and relate as consumers to the term "girl." This trend may be seen with fifty-five-year-old women who are themselves Gap shoppers, shopping with their Baby Gap granddaughters. "Just a girl" might invoke girl rock bands (see Fran Martin, chap. 4, this volume), the antics of bad girl celebrities ranging from Monica Lewinsky's affair with former president Bill Clinton to Paris Hilton's continuing media coverage, or the commodification of girlhood nostalgia through American Girl dolls. In some cases, con- sumerism defines who a girl is (according to Gap, all females might be girls), but the media and policy makers also define girlhood. If, for example, a young female is married or is a mother herself, if she is orphaned and head- ing a household of younger brothers and sisters, as so many girls do in rural South Africa, is she still a girl? What services can she access because she is a girl or because she is a mother or because she is a head of household? Is the ten-year-old girl child in Rwanda still a "girl child" when she moves to Montreal as a refugee? When life expectancy for females is thirty-nine, as it now is in some countries in sub-Saharan Africa as a result of HIV and AIDS, what does it mean, in defining "girlhood," to know that more than half of your life is over by age twenty?

"Participation" is also a term used across a variety of disciplinary areas related to girlhood—frequently under the umbrella term of "girls' voices." Many researchers, activists working on girls and girlhood, and service and program providers for girls want to claim to hear the voices of the girls (of whatever age) with whom we work. The participation of those who are usually marginalized is a growing area of research in relation to the devel- opment of appropriate methodologies and to unpacking the complexities and fraughtness of issues such as ethics, levels of participation, tokenism, and privileging or romanticizing the voices of participants, adding additional interpretations onto the words of the participants. Questions must be asked about how to acknowledge the power differentials between adult researchers and child participants. How do we minimize the presence of the former and maximize the presence of the latter? And equally important, what specific issues that pertain to the participation of different girls and groups of girls do we need to take into account? We see the interrelatedness of these two questions, a good example of which is how the devaluing of women's culture is carried over into the devaluing of girls' culture. Women in a Western context are often in the position of apologizing for reading romances, magazines, and even novels. As Cinthia Gannett and many others point out, certain writing genres such as journal and diary writing, when they are associated with women, are also seen to have little value. Even the status of blogging by girls and other computer uses may be under scrutiny.[13] This situation means that to try to understand girls' play, and in particular the links between girls' play and other aspects of girls' identity, by relying on the so-called authentic voices of girls may be problematic. As David Buckingham and others have pointed out in their work with children's television viewing, children have usually figured out what they "should" say to adults.[14] As we argue elsewhere in our discussion of the political spaces of research with children, this prescriptive understanding may be reconfigured into self-censoring when speaking to adults.[15] Even worse, children may interpret the intrusiveness of the adult questioner to indicate that play activities must be engaged in secretly. For girls this may mean not admitting to having had, or to still playing with, Barbie dolls or My Little Ponies after the age of nine. The point is not that these political spaces cannot be negotiated (through child-to-child research, for example, or studying our own daughters or nieces), but only that the genuine participation of girls is devalued if the actual status of the texts is not explicitly discussed and if we do not take into account the relatively low status of texts when attempts are made to invoke the voices of girls. As we note elsewhere, even a savvy four-year-old will know enough to conceal a Barbie or other contraband on the way to day care. One alternative approach that we have developed is that of photovoice, in which girls and boys were invited to engage in their own self-representation by photographing their bedrooms with the idea that they would themselves represent their play and uses of popular culture.[16] Such an alternative approach and the use of arts-based methodologies may encourage the emergence of a different, "free" voice, and one that is less subject to self-censor.

These issues should not be separated from those that seem of a more dire "life and death" status. Here we are thinking of girls' sexuality, of the fact that, worldwide, girls are more likely to be sexually abused than boys, and of the gendering of HIV and AIDS, that is, the multiple ways in which risk, infection, response services, and family and community support are largely determined by gender. (For example, girls are often less able to protect themselves against infection, they may have less access to resources to help them if infected, and they are more likely to take on the care of infected relatives.) As researchers, how do we ensure the full participation of girls in talking about what has happened to them or about what might happen to them? In such situations, retrospective accounts are too late. In one study with twelve- and thirteen-year-old girls in a peri-urban school in Swaziland where the incidence of sexual abuse at school, in the community, and at home is high, we used photo-voice techniques in which we asked girls to photograph places at school that they regarded as "safe" and "not so safe."[17] We were struck by the numerous photographs they took of toilets (toilets, they said, were dangerous because they were too far from the rest of the school and you could be raped there, or they were in such a bad state that you had no privacy and could be attacked). But we were equally struck by the responses of some of the teachers: they were surprised that the girls had taken such pictures and said they had had no idea how the girls felt.[18] Critical, then, is finding ways to ensure that the voices of real girls become central to the project of mapping girlhood.

Expanding the Map: New Discursive Spaces

The previous section explores the multiple meanings of "girl" in a variety of contexts and briefly describes some of our ongoing projects. Here, we briefly investigate or map three discursive themes around girls' lives and the ways in which girls are now studied, described, and programmed for: pathologizing girls, consuming girls, and girls and agency. By using a thematic approach, we link together the various disciplinary approaches within these discursive approaches to identify commonalities across the lives of different groups of girls as well as the perspectives of those who work with them; we use a mapping approach in order to ascertain possible points of convergence, as well as tensions. Rather than further entrenching these perspectives, we unpack them, relate them to each other, and use this process to start to reconfigure the parameters for thinking about girls, for studying girls and girlhood, and for developing policies and programs for them.

Pathologizing Girlhood

The first theme is often associated with girls in developing countries, where they are objectified as victims and defined by what they often lack materially. Studies of girls in development contexts are scarce and rarely take account of the unique sociocultural issues facing these girls, such as sexual violence and transactional sex, biological and social vulnerability in the context of HIV and AIDS, the heading of families at an early age, and the cultural oppression experienced by girls through early marriage. Outside the body of so-called gray literature, such as donor reports, agency literature such as that produced by the United Nations, and commissioned studies on targeted development issues such as girls' education, little sustained and scholarly dialogue about girlhood in the developing world has occurred. Menstruation, for example, is a barrier to education where girls have no access to sanitary materials or to adequate toilets and water in or near the school building; girls have to stay home during menstruation rather than attend school and risk possible embarrassment. This barrier, however, may be overcome with practical fixes such as the provision of "comfort kits" to girls, which include reusable sanitary pads, underwear, and soap. Such interventions should be designed in response to more in-depth understandings of girls' experiences and perceptions, yet there has been little in-depth study of the diverse menstrual identities of girls in development and humanitarian contexts in which these are critical issues.[19]

There exists an established academic literature on gender and development, one that is concerned primarily with women rather than girls and with issues of empowerment, especially of those marginalized by poverty, class, geographic location, and ethnic and religious affiliation. This literature looks at the issue of gender equality and discusses strategies for creating long-term changes in gender roles, relations, and expectations in societies, suggesting that education is a key process for achieving this empowerment. And of course, it is the field of girls in development where the focus on limited access to schooling is most apparent. Girls are to a large extent portrayed as objects of gender-based exclusions that are exacerbated by other identity markers such as disability, ethnicity, or HIV and AIDS status. In the context of conflict and insecurity, especially, girls are in need of protection, most especially from sexual abuse and exploitation. Girls' education is a particularized case. Although the girl child has been at the center of national government and donor policies on education and other issues for a number of years, she herself tends to be a silent figure. She has been photographed for the cover of attractive donor agency publications, been the subject of a number of meetings and conferences, and has been written about in numerous reports and policy briefs. Strategies to promote her educational opportunities, improve her health, and protect her from abuse, early marriage, and genital mutilation have been developed and implemented by a large number of well-intentioned individuals and organizations. Yet in most of these instances, the girl child remains voiceless. She is seen as a passive object suffering a series of interlocking oppressions and discriminations taking place at the family, school, community, and state levels. She has to be protected by others. Children are often considered as future adults, rather than individuals and citizens with a full set of rights and expectations right now. This emphasis is especially true for girls, who are seen mainly in terms of their future roles as mothers and the nurturers and mainstays of families and communities.[20]

Although gender issues may be a stated educational priority for governments and multilateral agencies, education in development contexts per se is rarely subjected to deep gendered analysis or critical feminist investigation. Scholars such as Patti Lather highlight that gender issues may only be "tacked on" as a stated educational priority by governments, agencies, and others, with attention divided between many other cross-cutting development themes.[21] Other scholars problematize the way that gender, education, and development programs are developed and implemented, critiquing the way international agencies "espouse" and "attend" to gender issues but fail to understand the significance of gender ideology within educational institutions. Fiona Leach points out that although gender issues may be stated as an educational priority, education in development itself is rarely subjected to gendered analysis or to critical feminist investigation.[22]

Perhaps even more than in other development contexts, the vulnerability (and pathologizing) of girls is particularly noted in humanitarian, crisis-affected contexts, and in relation to educational access. Although educators may advocate for education as the fifth pillar of humanitarian aid,[23] at the same time there is increasing acknowledgment of the fact that in many contexts—not only in emergency situations—schools are not necessarily safe or protected places for children. Going to school can put children at significant physical risk—for example, of being abducted or forcefully recruited into fighting forces; schools are also attacked as targets. It can as well put them at psychosocial risk from brutal and demeaning treatment at the hands of teachers. Moreover, some teachers and education personnel abuse their positions of power and are guilty of sexual exploitation and abuse of students, especially girls. Furthermore, while we strive to support schools as sites in which open expression, creativity, questioning, and discussion can take place, the reality is that classrooms are often repressive and unimaginative, and schools can be places where intolerance is commonplace, where bias against certain ethnic, religious, and other groups is openly promoted, and where societal and community conflicts and divides are reinforced. The work of June Larkin and Carla Rice in North America on body-based harassment raises similar issues in relation to a pathologizing of girls' lives.[24]

Consuming Girlhood

In contrast to the first theme, which is often associated with girls in development contexts who are often objectified and defined by lack, girls as consumers are identified with the "first" world, where there is an abundance of commodity merchandise. Those of certain ages, such as preadolescent and young adolescent girls, are seen as occupying a marketing category called "tweens." Young girls (as opposed to female children or adolescent girls) suddenly have a currency all of their own, and there is now no shortage of public data on the dollar figure attached to the purchasing power of nine- to thirteen-year-old girls to consume clothing, hair products, CDs, rock concert tickets, and the like. Tween culture has been growing at a rapid pace, with new dolls, such as My Scene, Flava, and Bratz; clothing, such as Bratz clothes, Hilary Duff fashions, and thong underwear; and novels and films about and for young adolescent girls. To keep pace, some long-lived popular culture icons are reinventing themselves. Notably, there is a new series of Nancy Drew mysteries narrated in the first person by a "tween-age" Nancy herself. For our purposes, though, the media coverage around girls of this age has helped to draw attention to the specificity of preadolescent girls within the emerging area of girlhood studies, and to create a way to break down the amorphousness of the concept of girlhood. Taking a globalization perspective of the topic of consuming girlhood raises many more questions. We see Barbie dolls on sale in the national outfits of many different countries, a Barbie who herself is a jet-setting traveler, even a sometime air hostess. But is Barbie relevant to the lives of girls in Africa and South Asia? How does she appear to them—if in fact she ever does appear to the many millions of girls for whom a commercial toy is an unimaginable luxury?

Tween is not a neutral term by any means, for much of the discourse about tween commodity culture concerns contestations of sexuality as progressively younger girls seem to be sexualized though clothing, music, and popular culture. Ironically, much of the discourse of concern around teen culture in the 1950s and 1960s now seems eerily to be replaying in the ears of the baby boomers, who previously helped define the generation. Now, though, the formerly teenaged attributes have been "downshifted" or "downsized" to a younger group still categorized as children. In most commentary about tween girls there is the recognition and concern that the category is one constructed by marketers to exploit a vulnerable age group, rather than a "natural" or developmental category. Although, as we discuss, there are moves to claim and assert girlhood and girl power by different groups of girls, we also recognize the tendency for girls and girlhood to be constructed by others to contain, mark, and potentially control girls. This tendency is captured in recurring phrases such as "just girls," "the girl child," and "Daddy's girl."

Of course the ages of girls and ideas of girlhood, as in other constructions around youth, necessarily possess a biological or physiological dimension. For instance, although the teenager is understood as a post–World War II invention, the stage seems linked with physiological puberty and entering adolescence. Regarding tweens, mention is often made of an earlier onset of puberty occurring more commonly in girls.[25] This allusion may concern breast development, menarche, or stories about girls giving birth. In some cases concerns about the "death of childhood" and "hurried childhood" seem to be becoming true for some Western and Westernized girls; the irony is that with high rates of gender-based violence, teen pregnancy, school dropouts, and the transference of household chores and responsibilities from adults, the majority of girls in developing countries throughout the world fail to enjoy a full period of childhood.

Girls and Agency

For many years, women's movements have fought—and continue to fight—for widespread recognition of women's agency.[26] They have insisted that women's voices be heard and respected in decisions affecting them, that they have the right to participate in policy development at all levels, and that they have important contributions to make. In more recent years, young women activists, individuals, and organizations (such as the Young Women and Leadership Programme of the Association for Women's Rights in Development, and the Girls' Power Initiative based in Nigeria) have, in many different domains, called for girls' voices to be heard in public policy development processes. Critical as well is the recovery of girls' voices within the historical record, something that the essays in this volume also address. Explicit attention to girls' participation, however, is less common. In North American and European countries, although "girl power" may be a forceful concept to be reckoned with, it is more likely to be emblazoned on a T-shirt or another consumer product rather than used in a formal policy setting. Scholars such as Catherine Driscoll, Anita Harris, Angela McRobbie, and Valerie Walkerdine have questioned the co-optation of girls' culture and agency by fashion, media, and music industries and have suggested that "girl power" provides an ideal that is almost impossible for girls to attain.[27] Those working with girls, or making policy decisions that impact their lives, therefore must question how seriously girls and their opinions are being taken when their identities and participation are framed within these parameters.

Although there are changes in the formal education sector with the introduction of student representatives on governing boards in countries such as Canada and South Africa, many child and youth participation projects take place in the nonformal sector, at either the community or municipal level. It is less common to see notions of child participation expressed in the formal education sector, for example, within ministries of education. In Africa and elsewhere the formal education sector remains particularly bureaucratized and hierarchical, and slow to respond to trends outside of schools. Child-centered, girl-friendly approaches to teaching may be widely promoted in teacher-training programs, but rarely does this methodology involve consideration of what the children, or the girls themselves, would consider child or girl friendly. World Vision's report card for a girl-friendly school includes core components such as flexible hours and curriculum, "a hassle-free environment," gender sensitivity, and positive attitudes toward girls' education, but mentions only briefly, under the heading of "joint effort," that "girls, teachers, families, communities and government are involved."[28] The many projects that have had considerable impact in the past in development and nondevelopment contexts by actively involving young people in decision-making processes have tended to avoid much explicit attention to gender issues beyond a concern to have equal numbers of boys and girls participating.

Reading across Thematic Areas

What we want to emphasize here is that placing these three areas of research, activism, and practice "on the map" of girlhood helps us to raise questions that cut across geography, social locations, and time periods. Indeed, this book as a whole reads across these issues. It is important to consider, for example, questions related to how the work on pathologizing girlhood in development contexts crosses over into an understanding of work in the first world. How might this work help to deepen an understanding of power and patriarchy? The work on consuming girlhood often positions girls simultaneously as dupes (taken in by advertising, located within a "buy buy buy" culture) and, as Farah Malik points out, as agents who have their own mind and their own tastes.[29] To what extent does this work, then, feed in to the literature on pathologizing girlhood as well as to the literature on girls and agency? Indeed, agency, read across these three areas, may insert itself into the larger map of girlhood particularly when it comes to studying girls and policy.

What happens, for example, when we juxtapose notions of tweenhood and vulnerability in relation to the lives of girls growing up in poor households in cities and villages in South Asia, or in the refugee camps of West Africa? Can we even compare across types of vulnerability? Are there theoretical and methodological issues connected to gender/age power dynamics which relate to these different contexts? Does such questioning help to nuance apparently simplistic discourses of Western "girl power" and non-Western "girl powerlessness"? VACHA Women's Resource Center and Kirk, for example, examine the lives of *balkishori* girls in Mumbai, India, whose lives are impacted by the pervasive images of fashionable, beautiful, and thoroughly modern Bollywood film star women, but whose sex, age, and status in poor families mean that life possibilities are limited and very different from those of the women seen on the silver screen.[30] We have to find ways to elicit the girls' perceptions of their own positions and those of the women around them, and their feelings and expectations of the future in relation to the films' images. We can then interpret these data in light of the transnational, globalized contexts in which these girls live part of their lives, yet also in the light of the specific, narrowly localized worlds—and gender regimes—of the family in which the realities of the girls' current lives are lived out.

In terms of girls and agency, although we might like to think that this discursive space opens up possibilities for girls in different contexts—developed and developing, historical and contemporary, and of different ages—can we actually work to support the agency of a young girl in rural Uganda or Pakistan in the same way that we can a tween in North America or the United Kingdom? Or, as Jackie Kirk and Stephanie Garrow ask, are there some conceptual and methodological notions, such as "girls as knowers" and "girls in policy," that relate to different contexts but allow for interdisciplinary sharing? These concepts, emerging from the study of girls' participation in education policy development in Uganda, refer to approaches that recognize girls' unique positions as experts on their own experiences and as identifiers of realistic solutions to address the challenges they and their peers face.[31]

In the growing body of literature on girlhood, the notion of girlhood has become increasingly diverse as scholars in cultural studies have taken up issues of agency with respect to popular culture and race and class.[32] It is, however, rarer to see a sustained analysis of girls and agency in the context of the literature of development. What this burgeoning body of work invites, we posit, is its own mapping agenda in relation to constructions such as agency.

Strategies for Future Girlhoods

Through our mapping exercise we recognize that placing girls at the center of the policy-making process, where they move beyond simply taking part in international conferences and workshops in a token way toward shaping policies and programs, requires a great deal of thought, commitment, time, flexibility, and political will. This circumstance may be especially so in the formal education sector. Furthermore, we have to be prepared to engage with the complex, transitory, shifting, and contradictory nature of girlhood. In so doing we have to be prepared to create a new subset of mapping questions: Are girls involved in shaping the language and terms used in defining research priorities? At what point in the research processes are they invited to contribute? Have the problems already been defined? The adoption of a "girls in policy" approach clearly requires some radical shifts in organizational and individual attitudes, cultures, structures, and processes. NGOs and other implementing partners may be challenged to do so with limited human and financial resources. It is one thing for girls to be able to come into an office to work on their action plans, conduct research, and discuss their future projects, but it is quite another for their own perspectives and priorities to be integrated into the vision and direction of the organization itself. To what extent are the internal structures and processes being shaped by the girls with whom organizations are working? Are girls joining the boards of these groups? Are they attending the annual general meetings? Or do girls ultimately remain as beneficiaries for whom programs are developed?

Mapping girls in a global context is an ongoing task. There is a burgeoning body of literature on the whole area of girlhood, and on the three areas we have identified as pathologizing girlhoods, consumption and commodification, and girls and agency. These three themes are only part of a "map of girlhood," with great areas of research uncharted. Girlhood has the potential to draw together people and projects as the center of a constellation of research about girls and girlhood from many different disciplines, such as girls' psychological development, the study of historical girlhood in different countries, the representation of girls in literature or in popular culture, including old and new media, and girls writing and cultural production, in parallel to the study of juvenilia.

We have used the formerly colonizing metaphor of mapping to organize our argument for studying girls' lives and girlhood in a global framework, in a way that does not divide up girls by categorical distinctions of age, ethnicity and so on, and by programming location, sector, or funding body. Rather our purpose in using mapping has been to ascertain possible points of convergence and to discover what can be learned when we cross disciplinary borders. By sketching ideas for a map in the spirit of postmodern, social cartography, our project has fluid boundaries that we hope can resist established power relations and promote nontotalizing epistemological values. We thereby seek to undo the binary oppositions that hem in girls and researchers of girlhood studies and encourage critical perspectives that examine the interplay of age, cultural context, sex, and gender so that issues of the cultural construction of girlhoods are at the center of inquiry.

NOTES

1. Nellie Stromquist, "Mapping Gendered Spaces in Third World Educational Interventions," in *Social Cartography: Mapping Ways of Seeing Social and Educational Change*, ed. Rolland G. Paulston (New York: Garland, 1996), 233.

2. For example, there is growing awareness of the linkages between political violence and violence against women and girls, and of the extent of different forms of gender-based violence in conflict-affected communities. At the same time, there is less specific attention paid to the experiences of girls—and it may even be assumed that their experiences and the impacts of their experiences are the same as for older women. For more on this topic, see Jackie Kirk and Suzanne Taylor, *Gender, Peace and Security Agendas: Where Are Girls and Young Women?* (Ottawa: Gender and Peacebuilding Working Group of the Canadian Peacebuilding Coordinating Committee, 2004), http://action.web.ca/home/cpcc/en_resources.shtml?x=73620.

3. Claudia Mitchell, Jacqueline Reid-Walsh, M. Blaeser, and A. Smith, "Who Cares about Girls?" in *Centering on . . . the Margins: The Evaded Curriculum*, proceedings of the second biannual Canadian Association for the Study of Women and Education (CASWE) International Institute (Ottawa, 1998), 169–176.

4. Stromquist, "Mapping Gendered Spaces." Nikolas Huffman, "Charting the Other Map(s): Cartography and Visual Method in Feminist Research," in *Thresholds in Feminist Geography: Difference, Methodology, Representation*, ed. John Paul Jones, Heidi Nast, and Susan Roberts (Lanham, MD: Rowman and Littlefield, 1997), 255–283.

5. Benedict Anderson, *Imagined Communities* (London: Verso, 1983).

6. Geoff King, *Mapping Reality: An Exploration of Cultural Cartographies* (New York: St. Martin's Press, 1996).

7. Claudia Mitchell, "Mapping a South African Girlhood in the Age of AIDS," in *Gender Equity in South African Education*, ed. Linda Chisholm and Jean September (Cape Town: HSRC Press, 2005), 92–112; Mitchell et al., "Who Cares about Girls?"; and Claudia Mitchell and Jacqueline Reid-Walsh, *Researching Children's Popular Culture: Cultural Spaces of Childhood* (New York: Peter Lang, 2002).

8. Questions are adapted from a table in Mitchell et al., "Who Cares about Girls?"

9. Mitchell and Reid-Walsh, *Researching Children's Popular Culture.*

10. Claudia Mitchell and Jacqueline Reid-Walsh, eds., *Seven Going on Seventeen: Tween Studies in the Culture of Girlhood* (New York: Peter Lang, 2005).

11. United Nations Population Fund (UNFPA) and Population Council, *Investing When It Counts: Generating the Evidence Base for Policies and Programmes for Very Young Adolescents* (New York: UNFPA and Population Council, 2006).

12. See Anne Higonnet, *Pictures of Innocence: The History and Crisis of Ideal Childhood* (London: Thames and Hudson, 1998), Lyn Mikel Brown and Carol Gilligan, *Meeting at the Crossroads: Women's Psychology and Girls' Development* (Cambridge: Harvard University Press, 1992).

13. Janice Radway, *Reading the Romance: Women, Patriarchy, and Popular Literature* (Chapel Hill: University of North Carolina Press, 1991); Claudia Mitchell, "I Only Read Novels and That Sort of Thing: Exploring the Aesthetic Response," *English Quarterly* (Summer 1982): 67–77; Cinthia Gannett, *Gender and the Journal: Diaries and Academic Discourse* (New York: State University of New York Press, 1992); and Brandi Bell, "Girls and Blogging: Private Writing in Public Spaces?" paper presented at Childhoods Conference, Oslo, Norway, June 29–July 3, 2005.

14. David Buckingham, *Moving Images: Understanding Children's Emotional Responses to Television* (Manchester: Manchester University Press, 1996).

15. Mitchell and Reid-Walsh, *Researching Children's Popular Culture*.

16. Ibid.

17. Caroline Wang, "Photovoice: A Participatory Action Research Strategy Applied to Women's Health," *Journal of Women's Health* 8 (1999): 85–192; Claudia Mitchell, N. De Lange, Relebohile Moletsane, J. Stuart, and T. Buthelezi, "Giving a Face to HIV and AIDS: On the Uses of Photo-Voice by Teachers and Community Health Care Workers Working with Youth in Rural South Africa," *Qualitative Research in Psychology* 2 (2005): 257–270; and Claudia Mitchell and Iwani Mothobi-Tapela, *No Turning Back: Youth and Sexual Violence in and around Schools in Swaziland and Zimbabwe* (Nairobi: UNICEF ESARO, 2004).

18. Claudia Mitchell, Shannon Walsh, and Relebohile Moletsane, "Speaking for Ourselves: Visual Arts-Based and Participatory Methodologies for Working with Young People," in *Combating Gender Violence in and around Schools*, ed. Fiona Leach and Claudia Mitchell (Stoke on Kent: Trentham, 2006), 103–111.

19. Jackie Kirk and Marni Sommer, "Menstruation and Body Awareness: Linking Girls' Health with Girls' Education," Royal Tropical Institute (Amsterdam) Web site, Gender and Health / In Depth, http://docs.google.com (accessed July 28, 2009).

20. Jackie Kirk and Stephanie Garrow, "Girls in Policy: Challenges for the Education Sector," *Agenda* 56 (2003): 4–15.

21. Patti Lather, "Post Colonial Feminism in an International Frame: From Mapping the Researched to Interrogating Mapping," in *Social Cartography: Mapping Ways of Seeing Social and Educational Change*, ed. P. Rolland Paulston (London: Garland Publishing, 1996), 357–375.

22. Fiona Leach, "Gender Implications of Development Agency Policies on Education and Training," *International Journal of Educational Development* 20 (2000): 333–347.

23. Eldrid Middtrun, *Education in Emergencies and Transition Phases: Still a Right and More of a Need* (Oslo: Norwegian Refugee Council, 2000).

24. June Larkin and Carla Rice, "Beyond 'Healthy Eating' and 'Healthy Weights': Harassment and the Health Curriculum in Middle Schools," *Body Image* 2 (2005): 219.

25. Joan Jacobs Brumberg, *The Body Project: An Intimate History of American Girls* (New York: Random House, 1997).

26. Judith Butler, *Feminists Theorize the Political* (New York: Routledge, 1992); Marianne H. Marchand and Jane L. Papart, *Feminism, Postmodernism, and Development* (New York: Routledge, 1997); and Uma Narayan, *Dislocating Culture: Identities, Traditions, and Third World Feminism* (New York: Routledge, 1997).

27. Catherine Driscoll, *Girls: Feminine Adolescence in Popular Culture and Cultural Theory* (New York: Columbia University Press, 2002); Anita Harris, *Future Girl: Young Women in the Twenty-First Century* (New York: Routledge, 2004); Angela McRobbie, "Free Market Feminism,

New Labour, and the Cultural Meaning of the TV Blonde," in *Market Killing: What the Free Market Does and What Social Scientists Can Do about It*, ed. Greg Phil and David Miller (Essex, UK: Longman, 2000), 140–151; Valerie Walkerdine, Helen Lucey, and June Melody, *Growing Up Girl: Psychosocial Explorations of Gender and Class* (New York: New York University Press, 2001); and see Gerry Bloustien's work with aboriginal girls and video, *Girl-Making: A Cross-Cultural Ethnography on the Process of Growing Up Female* (New York: Berghahn Books, 2004).

28. World Vision, *Every Girl Counts: Development, Justice, and Gender* (Ontario: World Vision International, 2001).

29. Farah Malik, "Mediated Consumption and Fashionable Selves: Tween Girls, Fashion Magazines, and Shopping," in Mitchell and Reid-Walsh, *Seven Going on Seventeen*, 257–277.

30. VACHA Women's Resource Center and Jackie Kirk, "Reclaiming Girlhood: Understanding the Lives of Balkishori in Mumbai," in Mitchell and Reid-Walsh, *Seven Going on Seventeen*, 135–147.

31. Kirk and Garrow, "Girls in Policy."

32. See, for example, Penny Tinkler, *Constructing Girlhood: Popular Magazines for Girls Growing Up in England, 1920–1950* (Basingstoke, UK: Taylor and Francis, 1995); Ruth O. Saxton, ed., *The Girl: Constructions of the Girl in Contemporary Fiction by Women* (New York: St. Martin's Press, 1998); and Sherrie A. Inness, ed., *Millennium Girls: Today's Girls around the World* (Lanham, MD: Rowman and Littlefield, 1998); and Sherrie A. Inness, ed., *Delinquents and Debutants: Women Warriors and Wonder Women in Popular Culture* (New York: New York University Press, 1998). There are also a number of influential studies on girls and popular culture, notably, Valerie Walkerdine, *Schoolgirl Fictions* (London: Verso, 1990); Angela McRobbie, *Feminism and Youth Culture: From "Jackie" to "Just Seventeen"* (New York: Routledge, 1991); Sharon R. Mazzarella and Norma Odom Pecora, *Growing Up Girls: Popular Culture and the Construction of Identity* (New York: Peter Lang, 1999); Driscoll, *Girls*; Anita Harris, ed., *All about the Girl: Culture, Power, and Identity* (New York: Routledge, 2004); Mitchell and Reid-Walsh, *Seven Going on Seventeen*; and Lauren Greenfield's controversial photo essay, *Girl Culture* (San Francisco: Chronicle Books, 2002). Agency sits as a critical issue running across much of this literature. There has also been some interesting work on girls and agency with regard to issues of race and class, as we see in Yasmin Jiwani, Candis Steenbergen, and Claudia Mitchell, eds., *Girlhood: Redefining the Limits* (Montreal: Black Rose Books, 2006); and Daisy Hernández and Bushra Rehman, eds., *Colonize This! Young Women of Color on Today's Feminism* (New York: Seal Press, 2002).

PART I

GIRLS' CULTURES AND IDENTITIES

The chapters in this section analyze the intersections of gender, ethnicity, class, sexuality, and youth through a variety of female subcultures that have operated in relation to, but also separate from, dominant societal and adult values. Girls' cultures have been distinct both from boys' cultures and from the world of adults. Although girls are influenced by socializing institutions, they have also developed their own distinct values, activities, rituals, and understandings. Sometimes these coincide with adult expectations; other times they do not. The chapters in this section explore how national identity coexists, challenges, and reflects the experiences of girls from various backgrounds as well as how the movements of peoples, ideas, and products across borders can disrupt or offer tools for shaping youth culture.

This section casts identity formation as part of the story of international migrations. In the first chapter, Melissa Klapper argues that Jewish girls in twentieth-century United States formed "tripartite identities" that combined female, Jewish, and American traditions in ultimately affirming ways. Jewish identity provided girls with special rewards and satisfactions through spirituality, family closeness, and community involvement that shaped their experiences with both adolescence and modernity. Next, Christa Jones adopts a biographical approach to understand the life of Algerian writer and filmmaker Assia Djebar. As with the other works in this section, the reader sees a girl negotiating complex and often contradictory cultural messages to come to understand herself and her community. The third chapter in this section, by anthropologist Marion den Uyl and sociologist Lenie Brouwer, looks at contemporary girls' experiences in Amsterdam. Specifically, den Uyl and Brouwer use methods developed in studies on African American girls to understand the multicultural experiences of girls from minority migrant families in the Netherlands. Finally, Fran Martin examines non-Western ideas of girlhood through the lens of popular culture in late twentieth-century Taiwan. Through her examination of Taiwanese pop feminism, specifically the influence of independent folk-rock singer-songwriter and producer Sandee Chan on a generation of girls, Martin illustrates the complex interrelation between two contemporary feminine identity categories—girlhood and lesbianism—to show how girl power challenges masculine authority, but creates powerful new forms of intra-gender sociality and solidarity between women and girls.

Read together, these chapters suggest the hidden strength that margin-alized girls possess in defining their own identities. In each case, the authors demonstrate how girls struggle against institutions and dominant cultures that conflict with their familial backgrounds or generational desires, while negotiating these forces successfully. Their experiences show agency rather than a fragmented identity in shaping coherent concepts of themselves and their communities.

1   *American Jewish Girls and the Politics of Identity, 1860–1920*

MELISSA R. KLAPPER

On a typical day in New Orleans during the Civil War, sixteen-year-old Clara Solomon rose early to go to the Louisiana Normal School. She dawdled over breakfast and left the house reluctantly, complaining of poor health. She would have much preferred to stay home with her mother. After a school day spent learning lessons in deportment as well as geography, arithmetic, elocution, and literature, Clara walked slowly home with friends, their usual after-school gatherings curtailed by the exigencies of war. When she got home, she discussed her day with her mother, sewed, played the piano, and waited to see if her father would be able to return from his business travels that evening. She accompanied her mother to pay a call on their Jewish neighbors and went home in time for a meal meager by prewar standards. After supper she settled down to read and do some schoolwork, all the while waiting impatiently for her sister to come upstairs to their room and companionably "book it" with her in their diaries. As she wrote her diary entry for the day, she privately cursed the war and all despicable Yankees. She and her sister washed up, returned to their diaries for a few more lines scribbled before bed, blew out the candles, and went to sleep.[1]

Half a continent and half a century away, eighteen-year-old Emily Frankenstein hopped out of bed early to get started on her day in Chicago during World War I. She joined her father for breakfast and helped pack him up for the day at his medical office. After getting dressed and briefly practicing her piano exercises, she walked to school. Later she took the tram downtown with several of her Jewish neighborhood friends who did not attend the same exclusive private institution she did. Then she made an excuse to her friends and left to meet her beau, Jerry, home on leave from his post as a quartermaster in the U.S. Army. When they returned to Emily's house, they stayed outside and spooned on the porch swing until her father came out and suggested that it was time for Jerry to leave. With his departure went all thoughts of the war. Emily had not been home all day and stayed up for a while to read, do homework, and update her diary. Moving quietly around the room she shared with her sister, she prepared for bed in silence and fell asleep almost immediately.[2]

The girlhood experiences of Clara and Emily appear to differ in many respects. The Civil War affected Clara much more directly than World War I did Emily, especially in terms of the dislocations and straitened financial circumstances of the Solomon family. Clara spent much of her day at home with her family, while Emily spent most of her time with friends outside her house. Girls in New Orleans during the early 1860s spent a minimum of time walking around by themselves because of both social convention and physical danger in the tightly guarded city. Girls in Chicago during the late 1910s enjoyed more freedom to travel about the city. The schooling Clara received at the Louisiana Normal School in 1861 was considerably less rigorous than the education offered to Emily at her private girls' school in 1918. Clara sewed daily as part of the household economy, whereas if Emily found time to sew at all, she was most likely to knit something as a present for her father or her suitor.

Despite the significant gaps between their experiences, Clara and Emily also shared a great deal. Both were born in the United States. Both kept diaries as a matter of course. Both played the piano and read for pleasure on a daily basis. Both shared bedrooms with their sisters. Although they spent their time with friends differently, both held their friends in great esteem and enjoyed the activities that took place in peer environments. They both had close relationships with their families.

On the surface, little of Clara's or Emily's daily routine seemed much affected by the fact that they were Jewish. Neither prayed daily, observed the dietary laws of kashruth, or attended Jewish schools.[3] Both noted Christmas in their diaries. Yet in countless small but important ways, the fact of their Jewishness affected the very shape of their lives. Clara never attended school on Saturdays because it was the Sabbath. Her family went to great lengths to obtain matzoh for Passover, no easy feat in wartime New Orleans. Whenever finances allowed, Clara's family owned seats in both the men's and women's sections of their synagogue, Dispersed of Judah. Emily attended services at Chicago's Temple Sinai. Her extended family had elaborate Sabbath dinners at her maternal grandmother's house with some regularity. She decorated her bedroom with rugs produced by the Bezalel School of arts and crafts in Jerusalem.[4]

Most significantly of all, Clara's and Emily's social circles away from school were primarily Jewish. The neighbors Clara and her mother visited, the group of girls Emily spent time with after school, the eligible young men both thought about—whether in the abstract for Clara or in the flesh for Emily—all were Jewish. This detail was no coincidence. Nothing in their girlhood experiences forced them to socialize exclusively with other Jewish people. Both of them made non-Jewish friends at school. Yet the thorny problems of identity and integration for Jewish girls in America stretched across the decades from Clara to Emily and were to a great extent resolved by the American Jewish social world surrounding them. There were times

and places where they were in specifically American environments, such as
the public high schools most adolescent Jewish girls attended by 1900.
There were also times and places where they were in specifically Jewish
environments, such as synagogues. Much of the time they moved easily in
and out of a variety of turn-of-the-century settings. They were, however,
most often in the company of other American Jewish youth like them, who,
whether they thought about it or not, faced the same issues of integrating
youth culture and Jewish identity in America.

Although Jewish girls resembled other American girls in many ways, the
role that Jewish tradition and religious culture played in their lives set their
adolescence apart. Throughout this period of modernization, they continued to cling to some tradition. Jewish identity provided girls with special
rewards and satisfactions through spirituality, family closeness, and community involvement, which shaped their experiences with both adolescence and modernity. The tripartite identities of adolescent Jewish girls in
the United States—female, Jewish, American—had to be learned within the
context of a time period in which each of those identities was in flux. This
type of challenge was faced across the world by girls from minority groups.
Jewish girls did not necessarily feel deep conflict at all times, but the potential tension between American and Jewish identity found expression in
nearly all of their adolescent activities.

The increasing importance of peers as well as parents in dealing with
these issues arose from changes in ideas about adolescence. New space for
youth culture emerged during the second half of the nineteenth century
and continually widened at the beginning of the twentieth century. More
than ever before, adolescents interacted with peers as much as, if not more
than, with members of their families. In the United States, expanding educational opportunity and the growing trend toward a stage of life between
schooling and marriage left girls and boys with the time and, depending on
class, wherewithal to develop a culture of their own, centered on shared,
social, cultural, and even economic experiences. During this period, schools
around the world became critical settings for both explicit and implicit con-
siderations of girlhood and femininity, as S. E. Duff establishes in her analysis of a South African school for the daughters of the Dutch Afrikaner gentry
in this volume.

Gender was also an important factor in the development of youth culture. Assumptions about differences between men and women exerted considerable influence on the coming of age of boys and girls and resulted in the
creation of a separate girl culture within American youth culture. This girl
culture was significantly affected by changes in gender ideology. By the end
of the nineteenth century, the model American girl was defined by more
than earlier ideals of morality and domesticity. These qualities retained
cultural significance in most Western societies. The model American girl,
however, was also known for blooming health, independence of spirit, and

cultivated taste.[5] She was educated and active, and her freedom and autonomy increased as time went on.

Notwithstanding continuities in the impact of class, gender, and family
structure that contributed to fundamental consistencies throughout the
period, there never was a singular "American girlhood"; indeed, this concept changed in response to social metamorphosis during the decades from
1860 to 1920. Despite the growing viability of youth culture as the focus of
American adolescence, the effects of various distinguishing factors differentiated the experiences of white American youth. For example, although
growing numbers of American teenagers received some sort of secondary
schooling, boys were still far more likely to go to work before finishing, and
girls were more likely to graduate from high school. The social activities
that brought girls and boys together in environments and spaces other than
school exposed class divisions, because adolescent leisure was a marker of
some teenagers' freedom from family economic responsibility. Regardless
of class, some families were more reluctant than others to allow their
daughters to spend time with peers rather than parents and siblings.

Immigrants especially struggled with finding a balance, a problem not
unique to Jewish families. In settings ranging from early twentieth-century
America to current-day Holland, as Marion den Uyl and Lenie Brouwer
demonstrate in this volume in their chapter on contemporary immigrant
girls in Amsterdam, immigrant parents have understood that their children's
interactions with peers would provide a path toward acculturation. They
have remained torn between wanting their children to integrate and wanting them to stay close to family and tradition. If immigrant and working-
class Jewish girls wished to become American, they did so at the risk of
distancing themselves from their families in ways that middle-class girls did
not need to worry about as much. They found idealized American girlhood
more difficult to realize but generally held themselves to the standard
nonetheless. By adapting their dress, directing their reading, and adopting
some of the manners of the model American girl, immigrant Jewish girls
could not only become part of a significant social trend but also elevate their
families' status by achieving social integration.

Adolescent Jewish girls of all backgrounds thus found that their relationship to American girl culture reinforced their feelings of being American. By
sharing the activities and experiences of other girls their age, they could
identify with American girlhood on every level. Jewish girls participated in
the evolution of American girl culture in a number of ways. If able to attend
high school, they joined their classmates in school activities and class
events. Whenever circumstance allowed, they acquired skills like piano
playing and dancing as external manifestations of internal cultivation. They
exercised their bodies as well as their minds in pursuit of the good health
associated with American girlhood. They read the same books as other
American girls, which helped develop shared literary idioms and ideas

about the narratives of their own lives. They joined clubs and societies of peers with similar interests. They participated in evolving systems of dating that provided common experiences for adolescents all over the country while still encompassing a variety of ethnic and religious traditions of courtship. Without abandoning their religiously defined roles as keepers of tradition, they mediated their families' integration into American society by pursuing cultural and social experiences that would link them to their peers and allow them to help construct the meaning of American girlhood.

Social Lives: Schools, Music, Literary Pursuits, and Courtship

At the turn of the century, adolescent Jewish girls had to add their religious and ethnic affiliation to the mix of peer identification and school culture. It was not always easy. In 1900 Edna Ferber was an enthusiastic member of the debating society at her beloved high school in Appleton, Wisconsin, but she and her friend Esther were torn every week between their participation in the synagogue choir and the high school debating society. As Ferber recalled, "Friday night's service held an agony of suspense for Esther and me. . . . Would Dr. Gerechter have a sermon or would he not? A sermon meant being hideously late. . . . There was the final hymn to be sung. . . . Having galloped through the hymn we clapped the books shut, bowed our impatient heads for the benediction. . . . We turned and fled down the temple steps with a clatter of heels and sped toward the Ryan High School, temple of learning."[6] Edna found it difficult to balance her commitments as a member of both her Jewish and school communities. For her the challenge was all the greater because her family was not ritually observant but still maintained strong Jewish affiliations. Her parents had no objections to Edna spending Saturdays at the high school instead of observing the Sabbath more traditionally, but they did expect her to attend synagogue on Friday nights. Still, as her experience made clear, Jewish identity remained visible in America despite the expansion of peer socialization.

One reward of the hustle and bustle of Jewish girls' academic and social calendars was their integration into the larger community. School graduations gave Jewish girls further opportunities to display this integration publicly. Emily Frankenstein's 1918 graduation from Kenwood-Loring, a private high school in Chicago, reflected both school spirit and the heightened patriotism engendered by World War I. The student body sang the school song, and the whole audience joined in "Keep the Home Fires Burning" and "My Country 'Tis of Thee." Although she was pleased her family attended in recognition of her accomplishments, Emily chose to spend the rest of her graduation evening at a school dance with her boyfriend Jerry, away from her family. Graduation was not only a mark of educational attainment for her but also a sign of her enlarged freedom to choose where to go and what to do. In the course of that one graduation day, Emily affirmed her position as an educated American Jewish young woman.

Dressed in pink organdy as an American girl, surrounded by Jewish friends from similar backgrounds, and accompanied by a young Jewish man on leave from the U.S. Army, Emily danced the night away in a contented fusion of cultures and sensibilities.[7]

Certain feminine accomplishments as well as school and social events facilitated Jewish girls' experiences with American girlhood. Acquiring particular skills, such as proficiency in music or dancing, helped Jewish girls become or at least appear more like other American girls. Playing the piano demonstrated the kind of cultural achievement Jewish families often aspired to. Knowing how to dance was a prerequisite for one of the most important social interactions young men and women could share.

Learning to play the piano was a pursuit common to middle-class American girls of all backgrounds, and Jewish girls were no exception. Many Jewish girls took piano lessons for granted. They were as natural a part of their routine as homework. Most middle-class Jewish girls who lived from the 1860s through the 1910s and beyond wrote regularly in their diaries about playing the piano. Helen Arnstein's mother insisted that both her daughters conform to the expectations of their turn-of-the-century San Francisco Jewish community and learn to play. The girls had little say in the matter. Helen Arnstein and her sister practiced "for hours and hours" but were not "especially talented or eager."[8]

The class status associated with girls' musical endeavors made piano playing a presence in the lives of immigrant Jewish girls as well. Whenever they could, working-class families were willing to make sacrifices to support the personal and family benefits that might accrue from their daughters' feminine accomplishments. Although Rose Cohn's Colorado music teacher "would rap my knuckles with a ruler from time to time when I made mistakes, which was often," Rose's immigrant mother was committed to the idea that playing the piano would help make her daughters American girls.[9] Immigrant girls who played the piano were aware that their music lessons were a bridge to American girlhood. When Louise Berliawsky took piano lessons in Rockland, Maine, she was "very self-conscious and aware of the difference in environments" between her own home and the home of her "fancy teacher."[10] Her weekly trip to the piano teacher's house was a journey in social and cultural space as well as physical distance. By joining thousands of other American girls learning to play the piano, she also helped set her family on the road to social integration.

Piano lessons led naturally to another favorite pastime of Jewish girls, dancing. From New York to Chicago to San Francisco, Jewish girls learned dancing and the social graces that supposedly accompanied it. Hilda Satt, who arrived in the United States in 1892 at the age of ten, learned to dance at Hull House, an important settlement house in Chicago. Jewish communal institutions often offered dancing instruction as a supervised form of recreation for working-class and immigrant youth. The Educational Alliance, a community center in New York with a largely Jewish population at the turn of the century, sponsored large dances intended to ensure that dancing took place among well-matched adolescents in a suitable environment rather than in a more heterogeneous, less-supervised, neighborhood dance hall.[11]

Dancing became an important point of departure into social interaction with peers, especially Jewish male peers. While visiting a Catskills resort on what amounted to a husband-hunting trip in 1877, Amelia and Fannie Allen attended dances especially to look for eligible Jewish bachelors.[12] They used their well-rehearsed feminine graces to demonstrate their desirability as American wives while also restricting themselves to a pool of Jewish men. As far as Fannie and Amelia were concerned, any potential husband must be able to match their own combination of American experiences and strong Jewish identity. Ann Green, whose crowded college social life in early 1920s Maine included frequent dances, made a point of mentioning in her diary that she and her date were often the only Jewish couple in attendance.[13] Even when finding a marriage partner was not the immediate motivation for attending a dance, girls like Ann still tended to prefer Jewish escorts.

Cultural standards for American girlhood could also be expressed in more private ways than social dancing. Reading was a critical, if usually less public, step along Jewish girls' path toward becoming American. Sharing books and literature with their non-Jewish counterparts helped them develop a literary idiom that affected and was affected by girls' common pleasures and hopes for the future. From learning to read in English, a first step for immigrant girls, to learning about literature, an important step for girls who explicitly set out to acquire cultivated taste, reading was a critical component of American girl culture. Girls were already used to the idea that the people around them identified themselves with larger groups by choosing to read about them or read the same material as they did. The turn-of-the-century American Jewish press offered passports into various segments of the Jewish community in America. Subscribing to a periodical published in German for liberal Jews made one kind of statement about identity, subscribing to a Yiddish newspaper for socialist Jews another, and subscribing to an English weekly for immigrants intent on rapid acculturation still another. Making decisions about the kinds of things they read placed Jewish girls in the position of choosing their own communities: American readers, American girls, Jewish adolescents, supporters of Western culture.

Lucy Fox, for instance, was first exposed to radical ideology through reading. After arriving in the United States at age nine, she immediately went to work in a cigar factory in Chicago, eventually taking English and citizenship classes at Hull House at night. She read perennial classics like *Little Women* and Shakespeare. Her radical friends at work also encouraged her to read Edward Bellamy's *Looking Backward* and William Morris's

News from Nowhere. She studied these texts "as my grandfathers Reb Chaim and Avrom Boruch had studied the Bible," and she became a committed anarchist by the time she turned fifteen in 1899.[14] Lucy, like other adolescents, internalized what she read. The cumulative effect of reading the same books as their non-Jewish counterparts was the construction of a shared culture and idiom. Through a kind of literary osmosis, reading served as a basis for American girlhood that was as accessible to Jewish girls as to any other readers.

If a Jewish girl like Lucy could be drawn to the Christian moralizing in *Little Women* or the radicalism of *News from Nowhere,* then her religious identity was clearly not restricting her engagement with literature far from her own tradition. Jewishness expanded rather than limited Jewish girls' reading practices. It seems likely that Lucy was first inspired to read anarchist literature by her mostly Jewish coworkers. More to the point, Jewish girls read books on religious subjects that their non-Jewish contemporaries were probably not encountering. Sophie Ruskay considered nineteenth-century author Grace Aguilar's Jewish-themed writings among her favorite works of literature. During the 1870s and 1880s, Sophie read and reread Aguilar's novel *The Vale of Cedars,* crying every time over the persecution of the Jews depicted in the book.[15] Despite her affection for George Eliot's other novels, Helen Jacobus was less satisfied with Eliot's *Daniel Deronda,* which she felt "gave an untrue picture of Jewish life."[16] Adolescent Jewish girls' reading practices reflected the ways in which they synthesized American and Jewish culture. They read the same things as their American peers but also read literature tied to their religious and ethnic identities.

Adolescent Jewish girls parlayed their reading interests into participation in activities of other kinds, joining literary societies, forming reading clubs, and publishing anthologies or newspapers. Like other young women, they consciously set out to enhance the cultural levels of their communities—often, in their case, the American cultural levels of their Jewish communities. It was not that Jewish girls never joined literary societies or clubs outside their Jewish communities. Eighteen-year-old Hannah Greenebaum was only too pleased to become the first Jewish member of the prestigious Chicago Women's Club in 1876. Hannah, however, was acceptable to the Chicago Women's Club not only on her own merits but also on those of her family, which was wealthy and widely perceived to be thoroughly American and integrated into the Chicago elite.[17] Genteel and often unacknowledged exclusion combined with attachment to Jewish community to steer most Jewish girls in the direction of Jewish clubs and societies, even when they also belonged to non-Jewish social organizations. During World War I, for example, Emily Frankenstein belonged to the club that middle-class Jewish girls in Chicago were expected to join, despite facing far fewer social barriers than Hannah Greenebaum had two generations earlier. Still Emily opted for a community of peers from similar Jewish backgrounds.[18]

Throughout the period between the 1860s and 1910s, much of Jewish girls' peer socialization took place in a Jewish environment.

Adolescent literary activities were a critical part of adaptation to American society and participation in girl culture. In 1909, a group of girls living at the Jewish Foster Home in Philadelphia started a Girls' Literary Society. Even if their families could not provide stable American Jewish homes, they wanted to be sure they could behave as their peers did. At a typical meeting, the program opened with a song sung by all the members and then continued with readings, recitations, and songs by individual girls, followed by a group session of riddles and jokes. Mindful of their home at a Jewish institution, they consistently incorporated Jewish themes into the program. In December 1909, for instance, Lena Berkowitz presented an essay on Chanukah as her contribution.[19] A program combining self-conscious exploration of literature with a discussion of Jewish holiday origins and observances was a typical example of the synthesis that resulted from Jewish girls' participation in youth culture.

The immigrant and working-class girls at the Jewish Foster Home used literary societies in the ways that American-born and middle-class Jewish girls had long known they could be used, as organizations that both preserved Jewish identity and promoted American identity. At the time Jennie Franklin went to high school in Chicago during the late 1880s and early 1890s, there were several Jewish literary groups in the city. Jennie preferred the Hebrew Literary Society, which met every Friday night for debate and reviews. Members of the Hebrew Literary Society did not shy away from controversial topics, debating, for instance, the question of whether "the intellect and faculties of the darker races [are] essentially inferior to those of white."[20] After graduating from high school, Jennie continued to bring together her Jewish social world with her American cultural interests by joining the Philomathians, a new Chicago Jewish literary society composed of fifteen women above the age of eighteen and fifteen men above the age of twenty-one. Aiming "to promote mental development," the literary society met every other Sunday morning for good conversation. When the Philomathians disbanded in 1895, its unstated purpose had also been fulfilled: several of the original Jewish Philomathians were married to each other.[21] Mutual interests in literary activities and American culture brought young Jewish men and women together in the most suitable of environments, a triumph for the acculturating American Jewish community of Chicago.

For the most part, girls in urban areas with large Jewish populations had little trouble developing a Jewish social life. In San Francisco during the 1890s, Amy Steinhart took for granted the entirely Jewish social circles she moved in. "We had a pretty well separated social life. We went to parties given by Jewish people with very few exceptions. . . . We just took it for granted. And I think there was a little bit of feeling about people who broke away from Jewish friendships."[22] Even Helen Arnstein's parents, who identified as Jewish but practiced no religion, joined the Jewish social club in San Francisco to make sure their daughters would meet—and eventually marry—young Jewish men.[23] In addition to literary societies and clubs, communities sponsored picnics, lectures, dances, and other social events as a means of bringing Jewish couples together. Everyone involved understood that a fifteen-year-old girl might not marry the seventeen-year-old boy with whom she shared a dance or two at a Purim ball, but the event allowed her to spend time with a Jewish peer group that would function as a de facto marriage pool for her within a few years. The presence of adults as well as adolescents at many of these functions underlined the Jewish social life that girls could expect to continue as adults.

There was a mix of tradition and modernization present in Jewish girls' social encounters. The all-Jewish cast of characters was traditional, but within the framework of Jewish community, the courtship and dating practices of Jewish girls and boys changed dramatically during the latter part of the nineteenth century and early twentieth century. As for other American youth, nineteenth-century patterns of supervised courtship in a family setting gradually shifted to public group activities, mixed peer group interactions, and ultimately to dating.

Still, although in general Jewish girls participated fully in contemporary youth culture, their experiences with courtship and dating revealed the limits of their social integration. Adolescent Jewish girls had non-Jewish classmates, coworkers, and friends, but they almost never dated them, let alone married them. The intermarriage rate was lower than 2 percent in 1910 and did not reach 3 percent until the 1940s.[24] Dating was one of the only ways in which Jewish girls were at all restricted by religious tradition. Few considered this restriction a negative one, given their typically solid sense of Jewish identity.

Even though by 1920 it was widely accepted that adolescent dating did not lead directly to marriage as courtship once had, marriage was still very much on Jewish girls' minds. If that had not been the case, they might have been more likely to spend time with non-Jewish young men, but since they virtually all were committed to the idea of marrying only Jewish men, they also dated only Jewish men. With endogamy as a given, there were, of course, other factors involved in Jewish girls' decisions about whom to date and ultimately to marry. Some of these factors were also connected to Jewish identity. Mary Upsico, a seventeen-year-old eastern European immigrant living in Des Moines in 1886, was so committed to living a Jewish family and community life that, caught "between faith and love," she broke her engagement to a Jewish man who refused to leave Deadwood, South Dakota, for a town with a Jewish community. Marriage, for her, was also about family life, and she believed that both needed to be infused with the kind of Jewishness only a sizable community would provide.[25]

Other factors were not necessarily connected to Jewish identity per se, although they did have to do with the conflict between tradition and modernity. Jewish girls wanted a say in what their marriages would be like, regardless of tradition. Once Rosa Wachtel and Martin Marks became engaged in 1890 and began to plan their wedding, they corresponded about everything from living arrangements to the balance of power between spouses. Martin assured Rosa that he disagreed with her father's old-fashioned opinion that wives must obey their husbands. He explained, "I don't believe that way—I believe that a wife is every way the equal of her husband and for complete happiness there must be complete equality between husband and wife. I don't believe in a submissive wife—when you become my wife I want you to become my partner—not a silent partner but an equal partner with all that implies."[26] American-born Rosa and Martin imagined themselves as pioneers of the coming century, in which marriage would become a match of equals. Although Rosa did tend their home and children after they married, Martin never failed to discuss all his business concerns with her in order to make the best decisions for their family. The emerging model of modern marriage enveloped Martin and Rosa's life together as an American Jewish couple committed to both tradition and modernization in their lives and love.

There were additional hurdles for Jewish couples. Class, ethnicity, and religious observance mattered too. During the 1880s, Clara Lowenburg faced sustained opposition to her adolescent sweetheart, Hymie Jacobs, who came from one of the first eastern European immigrant families to settle in Mississippi. The expulsion of Jews from Russia was a community concern for the American Jews in Natchez, not a question of family inclusion. The Lowenburgs joined the rest of the community in collecting money for the immigrants who came to live among them but maintained a social distance whenever possible. Hymie and his brother Aaron ran a small country store, another mark against them in a milieu where educated Jewish girls were expected to marry professionals or big businessmen. Clara cared about Hymie, who "thought I ought to promise to wait for him until he had made enough money to marry me." Her father, however, "didn't approve of him and thought it an impossible match for me, who had had every advantage of education and he had scarcely been educated at all." The economic and educational obstacles were not the only ones; another problem was the fact that "the Jacobs were Polish and were looked down upon by the German Jews." Clara eventually chose to marry a man whose background she and her family deemed a more suitable match for her own.[27]

Clara was more candid than Emily Frankenstein was years later about the prejudices she shared with her family. Emily's parents' concern about Jerry's background and their disdain for his poor education continued a long-standing pattern of social divides among the various segments of American Jewry that was as much in evidence in Chicago after World War I as it had been in Natchez during the 1880s. Emily's beau Jerry was from a very different background than hers, which deeply disturbed her parents and came to trouble Emily as well. Her parents criticized Jerry's spotty education and lack of definite plans for the future, but their major objection was his eastern European origin. For an upper-middle-class Jewish family of German descent, the possibility of a daughter marrying an immigrant, no matter how charismatic, was deeply disturbing. During Jerry's period of military service, the Frankensteins confined themselves largely to silent, if obvious, displeasure. In March 1919, however, Emily was forbidden to see Jerry again and was taken to Baltimore, Annapolis, and Washington, D.C., on an extended round of family visits. Upon returning to Chicago, Emily continued to meet Jerry clandestinely. They made plans for their shared future, and Emily began to wear his ring on a chain around her neck. Eventually, however, the combination of her parents' certain disapproval and the persistence of Albert Chapsky, her would-be suitor and the son of a middle-class German Jewish family in Minneapolis, took its toll. After Albert proposed to Emily over Thanksgiving, she began to grow disaffected with Jerry's lack of ambition and education. Following months of soul searching, she broke off her engagement with Jerry and ultimately accepted Albert's proposal, resolving to start a new diary to write about their married life together.[28]

The new life Emily envisioned for herself and Albert would not be so different from her old one. Far from rejecting tradition or her parents' lives, she ultimately chose to embrace them. She was not even willing to marry within her faith but outside her social circle, especially a religious doubter like Jerry who posed a double threat to her class status and her Jewish values. Her Jewishness, shaped by her class, education, and family background, played a critical role in her life decisions, even though Emily did not think of herself as particularly religious. For Emily, as for other American Jewish girls, Jewish identity mattered. For Emily, as for other American Jewish girls and ultimately for the American Jewish community in all its variety, it was not only possible but positive to combine elements of Jewish tradition with elements of American modernization.

It is telling that everyone involved in both Clara's and Emily's choice of a husband was Jewish. Participation in the modernization of courtship, dating, and sexuality was no threat to the American Jewish community as long as young Jewish people remained true to tradition in their choice of partners. Although Clara's and Emily's decisions about their futures were heavily influenced by the expectations of their families and the conventions of their communities, the two girls still took for granted their power to make these decisions. Their freedom to choose beaus and husbands was largely a product of acculturation into an increasingly individualist American society, although Jewish law had always required the consent of both parties to a marriage. Most Jewish girls freely chose to seek out Jewish men with backgrounds and sensibilities similar to their own as the basis for establishing integrated American Jewish homes.

The Significance of Jewish Girls' Participation in U.S. Girls' Culture

Jewish girls joined their non-Jewish counterparts in a process of peer socialization and by so doing placed themselves in relation to changing American standards of gender, youth, and coming of age. At the same time, the fundamental continuities of girl culture over a long period as well as the similarities between ideas about American and Jewish girlhood made it easy for them to adopt these standards without wreaking havoc on religiously informed cultural continuities within American Judaism. Their successful construction of an identity as American girls that would not require the abandonment of all Jewish religious culture reflected the struggle of their families and communities for integration into American society. Consistent with their dual roles as keepers of tradition and agents of acculturation, adolescent Jewish girls made a smooth transition into contemporary youth culture by transforming it into something that moved them toward acculturation without requiring the relinquishment of religious sensibilities.

The fluid boundaries of "Americanness," which expanded at the turn of the century—however slowly—in reaction to mass immigration and increased urbanization, allowed Jews in America to retain religious distinction as part of their conceptions of self. Most Jewish girls accepted their Jewishness, and many took great pride in it, but few chose to be defined solely by it. By virtue of their age, they were part of a group just beginning to be recognized as a distinct social category. In some cases, their primary allegiance was to youth culture rather than religious culture, but rarely did they have to make such a stark choice. It was not only possible but also desirable for Jewish girls to participate in the American youth culture of the moment without ever turning away from their Jewish identities.

NOTES

This chapter is an abridged version of Melissa R. Klapper, "'Such a World of Pleasure': Adolescent Jewish Girls and American Youth Culture," in *Jewish Girls Coming of Age in America, 1860–1920* (New York: New York University Press, 2005) and is included here with gracious permission of New York University Press.

1. The narrative is drawn from *The Civil War Diary of Clara Solomon: Growing Up in New Orleans, 1861–1862*, ed. and with an introduction by Elliott Ashkenazi (Baton Rouge: Louisiana State University Press, 1995). Clara Solomon Lilienthal Lawrence (1844–1907) was the daughter of Solomon P. and Emma S. Solomon. She grew up in New Orleans and was a student at the Louisiana Normal School during the Civil War and the Yankee occupation of New Orleans. In 1865 she married Julius Lilienthal, who died two years later, and in 1872 she married her deceased husband's doctor, George Lawrence.

2. The narrative is drawn from the Emily Frankenstein diary, Emily Frankenstein Papers, Chicago Historical Society (CHS hereafter). Emily Louise Frankenstein (b. 1899) was the daughter of American-born Jews of German descent. Her father, Victor Frankenstein, was a doctor and prominent member of the established Jewish community in Chicago. She grew up

in Chicago and took classes at the University of Chicago after graduating from the Kenwood-Loring School in 1918.

3. Jewish law prohibits certain foods altogether, such as pork and shellfish, and also bans the mixing of meat and dairy products. Kosher meat and poultry must be slaughtered and prepared in the prescribed ritual manner. Not only raw ingredients but also cooking, serving, and eating utensils must be kosher.

4. See *Civil War Diary of Clara Solomon*, 4, 412 (June 19, 1862), 295 (March 20, 1862), and 326 (April 12, 1862); and Emily Frankenstein diary, January 19, 1919, April 30, 1918, and December 25, 1918.

5. See Frances B. Cogan, *All-American Girl: The Ideal of Real Womanhood in Mid-Nineteenth-Century America* (Athens: University of Georgia Press, 1989). Cogan suggests that the "real womanhood" of educated, healthy, independent American women was available throughout the nineteenth century as an alternative to the "true womanhood" of piety, purity, domesticity, and submissiveness outlined by Barbara Welter in *Dimity Convictions: The American Woman in the Nineteenth Century* (Columbus: Ohio University Press, 1976) and had superseded it by the turn of the century.

6. Edna Ferber, *A Peculiar Treasure* (New York: Doubleday, Doran, 1939), 75–76. Edna Ferber (1885–1968), daughter of Jacob and Julia Neumann Ferber, was born in Kalamazoo, Michigan, and lived with her family in small, often anti-Semitic towns throughout the Midwest. As a child she wanted to be an actor but at seventeen went to work as a journalist instead to help support her family. She slowly made a name for herself as a writer, and after moving to New York in 1912, she became part of the Algonquin Round Table. She became one of the most popular novelists and screenwriters in America, winning a Pulitzer Prize in 1925 for *So Big*.

7. Emily Frankenstein diary, June 7, 1918.

8. Helen Arnstein Salz, "Sketches of an Improbable Ninety Years," transcript of interview conducted by Suzanne Riess for the Regional Oral History Office of the Bancroft Library, University of California, Berkeley, 5, 1975, SC-10726, American Jewish Archives (AJA). Helen Arnstein Salz (b. 1883) was the daughter of Ludwig and Mercedes Mandelbaum Arnstein. She grew up in San Francisco's heavily acculturated Jewish community during the 1880s and 1890s. Her wealthy parents gave their children an eclectic education but also encouraged their individual talents, including Helen's gift for poetry and other writing. She married Ansley Salz in 1911.

9. Rose Cohn Brown, "The Story of the Years in Colorado from 1890–1903," 25, 1971, SC-1435, AJA. Rose Lenore Cohn grew up in Carbondale, Colorado, and later married Abraham L. Brown.

10. Louise Nevelson, *Dawns + Dusks: Taped Conversations with Diana MacKown* (New York: Scribner's, 1976), 18. Louise Berliawsky Nevelson (1900–1988) was born in Russia to Isaac and Minna Ziesel Smolerank Berliawsky. She was four years old when her family came to the United States and settled in Maine. As traditionally observant Jews who spoke Yiddish at home, the Berliawsky family was fairly isolated in rural New England, but Louise was certain from a young age that she was an artist. She married Charles Nevelson and moved to New York, where she had a son and spent the 1920s studying at the Art Students League and with private teachers. She gradually built a reputation, primarily as a sculptor, and her worldwide travels greatly influenced her work. By the time of her death, she was a member of the American Academy and Institute of Arts and Letters and an influential artist.

11. Hilda Satt Polacheck, *I Came a Stranger: The Story of a Hull House Girl*, ed. Dena J. Polacheck (Urbana-Champaign: University of Illinois Press, 1989), 76–77. Allan Davis, "The Work of the Educational Alliance," September 16, 1910, box 2, Educational Alliance Papers, MS-JCC.E28, American Jewish Historical Society (AJHS hereafter). Hilda Satt Polacheck (1882–1967) came to the United States as a young child when her parents Louis and Dena Satt immigrated from eastern Europe. She and her siblings attended Chicago's Jewish Training School. Although Hilda went to work in a knitting factory at age thirteen, she was drawn into the social service networks of Hull House and developed a relationship with Jane Addams, who encouraged her to write and even helped arrange a semester of study at the University of Chicago.

12. Amelia Allen diary, July 25, 1877, ACC 1603, Philadelphia Jewish Archives Center (PJAC hereafter). Amelia (b. 1856) and Fannie (1855–1937) Allen were the daughters of Lewis Marks and Miriam Arnold Allen, both from Philadelphia families associated for decades with Congregation Mikveh Israel. Amelia taught in the Philadelphia public schools and became active in the Hebrew Sunday School Association founded by Rebecca Gratz. She was among the founders of the Young Women's Union and took charge of its kindergarten and Household School in 1886. Fannie was less involved in the Philadelphia Jewish community but, at the urging of her future husband Moses de Ford, she went to medical school. She both graduated and married in 1887. She and her husband campaigned for improved public health in Philadelphia, and Fannie also supported women's suffrage. She had three children.

13. Ann Green diary, May 12, 1922, Robison Family Papers, P-678, AJHS. Ann Eleanor Green Robison (1904–1995) was born in Russia but immigrated with her family to Maine as a young child. She graduated from the University of Maine and spent decades as a journalist, educator, and philanthropist. She married Adolph Robison in 1927.

14. Lucy Robins Lang, *Tomorrow Is Beautiful* (New York: Macmillan, 1948), 29. Lucy Fox Robins Lang (1884–1962) was the daughter of Moshe and Surtze Broche Fox. She was born in Kiev, Russia, and her family immigrated to Chicago when she was ten. She went to work immediately and took classes at Hull House at night. She married fellow anarchist Bob Robins in 1904 and moved to New York, where Lucy worked as a political activist and coordinated campaigns for Emma Goldman, Tom Mooney, and other radicals. In 1918 she met Samuel Gompers and later became his unpaid assistant. After a divorce in the mid-1920s, she married Henry Lang, who stimulated her interest in Zionism.

15. Sophie Ruskay, *Horsecars and Cobblestones* (New York: A. S. Barnes, 1948), 66. Sophie was one of the earliest Jewish girls to attend what later became Hunter College, a popular institution of higher learning among Jewish girls in New York.

16. Helen Jacobus Apte, *Heart of a Wife: The Diary of a Southern Jewish Woman*, ed. Marcus D. Rosenbaum (Wilmington: Scholarly Resources, 1998), 198 (December 12, 1901). Helen Jacobus Apte (1886–1946) was the daughter of Joseph and Alice Selig Jacobus, German immigrants. She grew up in Richmond and Atlanta. Due to poor health, she never finished high school. She married Day Apte in 1909 and had one daughter.

17. Hannah Greenebaum Solomon, *The Fabric of My Life: The Autobiography of Hannah Greenebaum Solomon* (New York: Bloch, 1946). Hannah Greenebaum Solomon (1858–1942) was the daughter of Michael and Sarah Spiegel Greenebaum, prominent members of Chicago's Jewish community. She was a serious student of music as a girl. She married Henry Solomon in 1879 and had three children. Hannah chaired the Jewish Women's Committee at the 1893 Chicago World's Fair, a role that ultimately led to her position as the first president of the National Council of Jewish Women. She frequently spoke in public about a variety of reform activities and became a strong supporter of women's suffrage in addition to her work for Jewish women.

18. *The Chicago Jewish Community Blue Book* (Chicago: Sentinel Publishing, 1917), 202.

19. Minutes of the Girls' Literary Society, December 4, 1909, Jewish Foster Home and Orphan Asylum Papers, series 1, Association for Jewish Children Records, MS 5, PJAC.

20. Jennie Franklin diary, February 2, May 9, and February 14, 1890, MS 502, AJA. Jennie Franklin Purvin was the daughter of Henry B. and Hannah Mayer Franklin. She was born and educated in Chicago. She married Moses L. Purvin in 1899 and had two daughters. She became active in a variety of Chicago civic causes, including a successful campaign to clean up the city's beaches. She was also active in the National Council of Women and the early Jewish camping movement.

21. Philomathian record journal, box 2278L, folder "Literary Activities—Philomathians," Jennie Franklin Purvin Papers, MS 502, AJA.

22. Amy Steinhart Braden, as quoted in "San Francisco's Jewish Women: Assorted Models, 1890s," in *The American Jewish Woman: A Documentary History*, ed. Jacob Rader Marcus (New York: Ktav Publishing House and American Jewish Archives, 1981), 361. Amy Steinhart Braden

(1879–1978) grew up in San Francisco. She went to Sabbath school and attended Madame Ziska's school for girls. She graduated from the University of California, Berkeley, in 1900 and became a social worker, marrying H. Robert Braden in 1924.

23. Salz, "Sketches of an Improbable Ninety Years," 14.

24. Gerald Sorin, *Tradition Transformed: The Jewish Experience in America* (Baltimore: Johns Hopkins University Press, 1997), 168.

25. Mary Upsico Davidson autobiography, 11–12, 1969, SC-2667, AJA.

26. Martin Marks, Manchester, Ohio, to Rosa Wachtel, Cincinnati, June 12, 1890, Wachtel-Marks Papers, SC-12643, AJA.

27. Clara Lowenburg Moses, "My Memories," 68–69, 1939, SC-8499, AJA. Clara Lowenburg Moses (1865–1951) was the daughter of Isaac and Ophelia Mayer Lowenburg, German immigrants to the United States. She grew up in Natchez, Mississippi, where there was a small, tightly knit Jewish community. She attended school in both Natchez and Germany. In 1890 she married Adolph Moses, who committed suicide in 1899; in later life she became a Christian Scientist.

28. Emily Frankenstein diary, undated entry describing the spring of 1919, CHS.

2 Growing Up in Colonial Algeria

THE CASE OF ASSIA DJEBAR

CHRISTA JONES

The work of French francophone novelist and Algerian national Assia Djebar was recognized most recently when she was welcomed into the prestigious Académie française on June 22, 2006, filling the vacant seat of the late Georges Vedel. An accomplished novelist as well as playwright, poet, essayist, journalist, professor of French and francophone literature, literary critic, filmmaker, and university-trained historian, Assia Djebar was born Fatma Zohra Imalayène in the Algerian coastal town of Cherchell on June 30, 1936.[1] Her narratives focus on her native Algeria and its complex colonial and war-ridden history, and in particular on the lives of girls and women in Algeria, both in the past and at present.[2]

In this chapter I examine Djebar's girlhood, as depicted in her autobiographical novels *L'amour, la fantasia* and *Vaste est la prison*, two volumes of her so-called Algerian quartet, which also includes *Ombre sultane* and *Nulle part dans la maison de mon père*.[3] Both *Fantasia* and *Vast* reflect Djebar's training as a historian and a consummate novelist as well as her bilingual upbringing in Arabic and French. *Fantasia* is a fictional historiography of French colonization, decolonization, the Algerian War of Liberation (1954–1962), and postwar Algeria, written from a predominantly female point of view.[4] As numerous critics have noted, *Fantasia* intermingles family history with colonial history and fiction by juxtaposing and alternating fragments taken from the author's personal life and family history with accounts of the 1830 French conquest of Algiers, episodes from the Algerian War of Liberation, and postwar Algeria.[5] These key historic episodes are revisited, recounted, and to a certain extent freshly staged and reinvented from an indigenous and female point of view that calls into question and undermines the "official" historiography, which is a legacy of the French colonizer. In this novel, the author identifies with an anonymous female narrator who takes the reader on a journey beginning with the siege of Algiers in 1830, through 132 years of French colonization, to the national War of Liberation and postwar independence. In *Fantasia*, Djebar creates a polyphonic composition of female voices, both imaginary and real, which allows her to bridge geographical, temporal, cultural, and spatial boundaries.[6] *Fantasia*, Djebar tells Mildred

Mortimer in an interview, is a "preparation to an autobiography."[7] Years later, Djebar writes that *Fantasia* is "openly autobiographic."[8] Djebar has referred to *Vast* as her most overtly autobiographic novel.[9]

Djebar's girlhood and coming of age in colonial and wartime Algeria were instrumental in shaping her awareness of different and conflicting cultures, languages, and religions, a perception that paved the way for her future professional career. Through her bilingual upbringing, Djebar developed what W.E.B. Du Bois termed a "double consciousness."[10] Undoubtedly, this double consciousness—the ability to look at one's self through the eyes of others—informs her writing and shapes her as an intellectual whose career spans the Atlantic. As she writes in *So Vast the Prison*, she was welcomed to the world by the midwife who delivered her in an isolated village, as daughter of the mountain, in a hurry, and destined to travel far: "Hail to thee, daughter of the mountain. You were born in haste, you emerge thirsty for the light of day: you will be a traveler, a nomad whose journey started at this mountain to go far, and then farther still! (247). This prediction did indeed come true in that the Djebar family spent many years living in France as well as in the United States. Throughout her girlhood, Djebar managed to fashion a complex, bicultural identity and worldview that empowered her to liberate herself from some of the constraints of a highly traditional patriarchal Muslim society, allowing her to assert her independence as a writer, a woman, an educator, and an intellectual, without, however, sacrificing her cultural heritage.[11] As a result of her acute double consciousness and her dual knowledge, she was able to step out of accepted patterns of societal behavior imposed on Arab women in a male-dominated society and look at her own society from a different perspective. She achieves this viewpoint by looking at the condition of third world women through the lens of a third world woman who has joined the first world but remains deeply committed to and anchored in the culture, traditions, religion, and Arabic and Berber languages of the third world. This clash of opposing worldviews, or dual perspective, informs her work and makes it unique, valuable, and intellectually challenging.

As Djebar shows by the constant juxtaposition and alternating of historical and autobiographical chapters—both in *Fantasia* and *Vast*—as well as by the narrator's omnipresence, collective history and personal story are inseparable. As literary critic Hafid Gafaïti pertinently states, the female narrative voice in these texts is in search of her "self" within a patriarchal society that is based on the subjugation of all girls and women. Therefore, the narrator links her personal struggle to the resistance of the girls and women of her tribe, as well as that of Arab girls and women in general.[12] From this we can deduce that the narrative "I" stands not only for a personal self and life story but signifies the collective identities of many Arab girls and women. In keeping with postcolonial narrative, the narrator in *Fantasia* gives a voice to the voiceless, in particular to Algerian freedom fighters, so-called *maquisardes* who actively supported their brothers in the fight against the French by working as nurses, cooks, seamstresses, and inform-ants.[13] Thanks to the narrator their accounts of torture, killing, burnt houses, and rapes reach the outside world. For instance, a chapter titled "Voice" is an anonymous first-person account by an Algerian girl who works as a nurse for the freedom fighters until she is captured by French troops, held prisoner, and tortured (130–140). Many of the girls portrayed in the book come from underprivileged backgrounds; because they are illiter-ate and so cannot tell their stories to the outside world, it is the narrator's job to testify and make their voices heard.[14]

Although Djebar has revealed that both novels contain autobiographical elements, she does not use her own name in either novel. The narrator in *Fantasia* is an anonymous female; in *Vast*, she is called Isma. Because of Djebar's reticence to speak in the first person, a subject I address later in the chapter, I refer to the authorial voice as the narrator.

Schooling and Writing as Means of Liberation and Emancipation

As a teenager, thanks to her predominantly French schooling, Djebar escaped the fate of female enclosure and went on to study history at the uni-versity. Her freedom, however, came at the price of being excluded from the female community. Again, solitary reading and higher education rein-forced her future exclusion from the communal sphere of her female peers. As Mildred Mortimer states, "Liberated from the female enclosure of her Algerian sisters, she reached maturity haunted by the weight of exile."[15] At age fourteen, she started keeping a journal. Daily writing occupied an increasingly important part of her life. Self-determination, she decided, would shape her life: "*I want to obey, I wrote, my own rule of life, the one I choose for myself today, at the age of fourteen, and I promise to do so*" (*Vast*, 301). Yet her dilemma as a writer, throughout her teens, twenties, and thirties, was that she could speak out in the affirmative "I" only by veiling herself in anonymity for reasons of respect and propriety deeply entrenched in her Muslim upbringing.

While writing *La soif* (1957) and *Les impatients* (1958), her first and second novels, Djebar felt she did not dare use the "I" widely employed in Western novels.[16] Certainly she could not affirm and disclose her identity by writing in the autobiographical mode. Quite the contrary, the authorial voice must efface itself beyond recognition. Her desire to remain unidentified and "safe" is encapsulated in her wish to communicate without being identified: "I speak, I speak, I speak, I do not want them to see me" (*Vast*, 305). According to the late literary critic Jean Déjeux, this anonymity is desired because auto-biographical writing, a genre widely practiced in the Western world, cannot be practiced in deeply religious Muslim societies in which holism takes prece-dence over expressing one's individuality.[17] To speak as "I" is not possible unless one has attained a high age: "How could a woman speak aloud, even in Arabic, unless on the threshold of extreme age? How could she say 'I,' since that would be to scorn the blanket-formulae which ensure that each individual journeys through life in a collective resignation?" (*Fantasia*, 156).

At all costs Djebar would avoid use of the first-person singular in her writing.[18] In an interview, Djebar stressed that she was brought up never to talk about herself using the affirmative "I" and, should the word be unavoidable, to speak in an anonymous fashion. When she was still a young girl, Djebar strongly objected to autobiographical writing, a genre that is, by definition, the writing of and about the self, the intimate or hidden, an act of unveiling and confession. She distanced herself from any form of autobiographic disclosure and instead wrote fiction. At that point, she defined writing as veiling herself and placing herself as far as possible from what she describes as a complacent confessionary mode.[19] In essence, writing meant hiding and protecting herself, her family, her privacy, and her authorial voice. Not surprisingly, when penning *La soif* she deliberately avoided the use of her maiden name, Fatma Zohra Imalayène, to claim authorship and instead used a pseudonym.[20]

Fantasia marks a turning point in Assia Djebar's writing and her attitude toward autobiographical writing. As her girlhood came to a close, her concept of writing dramatically changed: writing no longer signified hiding but showing, excavating as well as, paradoxically, not showing what should not be unveiled. Writing became a vehicle that allowed the narrator to travel through time and geographical spheres; it became an act of both love and transgression (*Fantasia*, 62–63). Interestingly, all of Djebar's published works are written in French—the language of the colonizer or the enemy, which she refers to as *langue adverse*, the enemy language—rather than in Arabic, a fact that has been widely discussed by critics as well as by the author herself. One reason for her choice of French, she regretfully confessed in an interview, is that she lacked the expertise to write in classical Arabic (*Vast*, 206).

Writing an autobiography in French, however, the language of the former colonizer, a language drenched in blood, is an inherently violent act. The French language evokes memories of a history of brutal colonial oppression and a bloody war of liberation.[21] *Fantasia* contains numerous graphic episodes of violent encounters between the French and the indigenous population, for instance, the asphyxiation of the Ouled Riah tribe in 1845, carried out under the orders of General Pélissier, when some six hundred men, women, and children huddling in a Dahra mountain cave were cruelly asphyxiated—an entire tribe wiped out forever.[22]

For the narrator, writing in French entailed unveiling herself and cutting herself off from her Arab sisters, exiling herself from her childhood. At the same time, writing an autobiography in French was a painful, visceral enterprise that reveals the narrator's innermost, never-before-voiced thoughts and sentiments: "Speaking of oneself in a language other than that of the elders is indeed to unveil oneself, not only to emerge from childhood but to

leave it, never to return. Such incidental unveiling is tantamount to strip-
ping oneself naked, as the demotic Arabic dialect emphasizes" (*Fantasia*,
156–157). Writing in French was painful because the French language continued to resonate with colonial brutality and massacres. It also served as a
catalyst of physical and sexual liberation, a process also inherently violent as
it necessitates a break with tradition. Interestingly, the "emancipation" of
the writer's voice went hand in hand with a desire for sexual liberation and
independence, as suggested by her platonic affair and midlife divorce,
related in the first part of *Vast*.

In both *Vast* and *Fantasia*, girlhood is mediated, as it is seen and analyzed
in retrospect, through the eyes of an adult narrator. This mediation suggests that in 1940s Algeria, the vast majority of indigenous Arab girls, including the narrator in both narratives, did not have a voice. They could not
speak out publicly and politically, through words or action. In *Vast*, for
instance, the adult narrator recalls her girlhood in a country torn apart by a
war fought against the French colonizer. She recalls that as a fifteen-year-
old, during the Algerian War of Liberation, she would have liked to join the
freedom fighters in the mountains to help fight for Algerian independence.
Her family, however, would not let her do so. At that time, Arabic and
French were two idioms at war. While French was still the language of governmental power, Arabic was the language of fire and subversion—that of
the freedom fighters, of people willing to die for their country's independence. Although she might secretly have wished to join her younger brother,
who in 1959 was a political prisoner incarcerated in a prison in Metz, France,
in the freedom fight against the French, she did not have the opportunity to
voice this desire, much less to join the freedom fighters, because she had
grown up in a sheltered and protective upper middle-class home. Although
she was a fervent patriot, proud to be a Muslim and to speak Arabic in a
country then still colonized by the French, the narrator also felt a close
affinity to the French language and culture.

In this chapter, I focus on the autobiographical aspects of *Vast* and *Fantasia*, in particular those parts relating to the narrator's girlhood and coming of
age in colonial, war-ridden, and postcolonial Algeria. I show that as a result of
her upbringing in French colonial Algeria, the narrator is the "product" of a
dual French and Muslim education, which enables her to operate within two
cultures and to form a dual identity, both French and Muslim. She attended
Koranic school as a child, but her subsequent French colonial schooling, combined with the influence of her Muslim parents, who imparted modern values to her, eventually isolated her from the girls and women in her
immediate family circle, particularly as she reached adolescence.

In *Fantasia*, Djebar writes, history functions as a quest for identity on the
part of the individual as well as the whole country.[23] In other words, for the
narrator, as an individual and as an Arab and Muslim girl and woman, a
fruitful and insightful quest for identity can only take place through an

in-depth investigation into her native country's history, and into the personal histories and tragedies of largely occulted Arab girls and women. The narrator needs to find out what it means for a girl to grow up in a colonized country steeped in a history of colonial violence, subjugation, and assimilation. As an adult writer, she uncovers some of the implications of growing up as a Muslim girl and speaker of both French and Arabic at odds with the French culture and language, in a country that is fighting for its political and economic independence. In the same vein, Djebar, in her novels, sheds light on the roles of girls and young women in precolonial, colonial, and postcolonial Algeria. As readers, we are prompted to wonder if girls' lives change over time. In *Fantasia* and *Vast*, Djebar addresses these questions by placing the female autobiographic narrator in a historical framework and by establishing a complex web of links between this narrator and her family genealogy. Both novels are part of her project to resurrect and reconstruct national history and to position girls and women from all walks of life within a precise cultural and historical context.[24]

In both narratives, we learn that the narrator was born and raised in French colonial Algeria in an Arabic-speaking household with Berber ancestors. *Fantasia* opens with an account of a crucial event in the narrator's life, namely, the day in the 1940s when she embarks on her first journey to foreign ground. Indeed, her admission to French colonial school, which she attended from ages five to ten, turns out to be a decisive factor for her subsequent literary and academic career. The famous opening paragraphs of *Fantasia* map out the girl's future, which is rooted in tradition, genealogical awareness, and pride, yet also marked by an increasingly nontraditional and Westernized, nomadic lifestyle: "A little Arab girl going to school for the first time, one autumn morning, walking hand in hand with her father. A tall erect figure in a fez and a European suit, carrying a bag of school books. He is a teacher at the French primary school. A little Arab girl in a village in the Algerian Sahel" (3). As suggested by the description of the Western suit and the fez, the girl's father is both a modern and tradition-minded man, convinced that girls should receive the benefits of education but also respect their origins. By permitting his daughter to attend school, he sets her free and saves her from future enclosure and a life revolving around childbearing and domestic confinement in what was then a highly patriarchal society.

A Happy, Carefree Childhood in French Colonial Algeria

Preschool girlhood appears to have been a happy, carefree time for the narrator; essentially, her life paralleled the lives of other little Muslim girls in her village. Her early childhood was a period of joyous laughter, daily discoveries, and hours of play in a picturesque setting. Early girlhood was a time of "relative" freedom of movement. In the courtyard of the apartment building, the girl played with other little girls. Their games included ball playing, counting rhymes, hopscotch, and swinging. Her father, however, who prohibited her from wandering off into the street or the village, firmly set spatial boundaries from early childhood on. The little girl was only allowed to play in the front garden and in the courtyard.

Although she was allowed to play with Maurice, a little French boy, segregation by sex was enforced from an early age. For instance, boys and girls attended separate primary schools. Even then, however, Djebar's father broke a societal taboo by routinely taking his little girl to his classroom, where she was allowed to sit in the back row and watch him teach. She never talked to any of the boys but sat quietly, waiting for her father to finish his lesson. The class consisted of some forty boys aged seven to ten, sons of workers, people who had been dispossessed in what the narrator describes as a village in the Sahel surrounded by the richest farms of colonial Algeria. On one occasion, in 1940, the father placed his little girl in the middle of his class for a school photograph. Even though she was only four or five years old, she sensed that her father's unusual move constituted a transgression that singled her out as a special little girl: "I see them all from the back. I do not remember any one in particular. I never speak to them of course, neither before nor after. Not one word: they are boys. Despite being so very young I must sense what is forbidden. . . . For them I must signify some privileged image of 'the teacher's daughter.' Their sisters, obviously, do not go to the French school" (*Fantasia*, 273–274). Interestingly, already this young, pre-school-age girl appeared to be aware of separation by sex and sensed that she was in a privileged position and that, as the teacher's daughter, she deserved respect. Until reaching puberty, the narrator and her Arab girlfriends enjoyed relative physical freedom, as suggested in *Fantasia*. The narrator recalls that when she was ten years old, her friend, the youngest of the three sisters, was still in primary school and had not yet been cloistered. That summer, the two little girls carried out errands, going to the bakery and delivering messages to the policeman's wife.

This freedom of movement was about to change, at least for her little friend, with the onset of puberty. As the narrator in *Fantasia* notes, thanks to her father's singular choice to send her to a French school, this little girl grew up to be a free and independent woman: "My father's preference will decide for me: light rather than darkness. I do not realize that an irrevocable choice is being made: the outdoors and the risk, instead of the prison of my peers" (184). Again, girlhood signifies a certain lack of power and a limited choice of possibilities. The little girl could not make and embrace her own choices. Decisions were made on her behalf, and it is only in retrospect that the adult could analyze her own girlhood and judge the validity of the decisions made on her behalf.

Djebar's "Westernized" French Education

As we learn in *Fantasia*, attending elementary school from age five reinforced the narrator's immersion in the French language, although at that time Arabic remained the only language used at home. In fact, her Muslim education was by no means neglected, as she was also one of only four or five girls attending Koranic school, where she studied the Sacred book from age five until around age ten. Shortly before reaching puberty, she was no longer allowed to attend Koranic school. She then started attending a French boarding school in a town nearby, where she would spend ten months out of the year. Consequently, she became increasingly mobile and independent at a time when her cousins had to don a full-body veil and live indoors, waiting to be married off to suitable young men most likely chosen by their parents. As she approached her early teens, she realized that her upbringing and education were dramatically different from those of her cousins, who were shut inside a traditional harem. At an age where she might have been veiled already, she could still move around freely. Every Monday she took the village bus to the neighboring town, returning to her parents' home only on Saturdays. Because she continued her schooling beyond the elementary-school level, her Arab girlfriends perceived her to be a French girl, somehow different from them. The narrator recalls one particular humiliating episode that occurred when she was around six or seven. While she was playing with her girlfriends, they forcefully held her down to see what kind of under-clothes she was wearing. To their satisfaction, they found she was wearing European underwear, in this instance a Spanish embroidered satin slip chosen by her mother. Thus even her clothes singled her out as different since her friends had never seen such a piece of lingerie before. Later on, as a teenager, she continued to dress like a French woman, wearing skirts required by the French school rather than the traditional *seroual*, the loose trousers her cousins wore. This custom, however, made her feel awkward at family gatherings, where she found it difficult to sit cross-legged, as was customary, and hide her legs. Even though she dressed like a European girl, she was at the same time very shy and prudish as a result of her Muslim education and by no means willing to parade her body.

With the onset of puberty, she started secondary school while her peers were being incarcerated. As her friends and cousins were starting to cover and hide their developing bodies from the male gaze, the narrator, like her French schoolmates, was allowed to wear shorts, to play basketball, and to participate in track and field competitions. Slowly, her body became irrevocably accustomed to physical freedom: "I had passed the age of puberty without being buried in the harem like my girl cousins; I had spent my dreaming adolescence on its fringes, neither totally outside, nor in its heart; so I spoke and studied French, and my body, during this formative period, became Westernized in its way" (*Fantasia*, 127).

During the school week, she and her half-Italian friend devoured works of French and Arabic mysticism as well as French literature, including the correspondence of Alain Fournier and Jacques Rivière, and books by André Gide, Paul Claudel, Jean Giraudoux, and Blaise Pascal.

The narrator's mother, Bahia supported her daughters' emancipated lifestyle. In *Vast*, for instance, we learn that Bahia sent her fourteen-year-old daughter—in this instance the narrator's younger sister—to a summer camp for adolescent girls in southern France (193). On numerous occasions, Bahia found herself criticized for allowing her eldest daughter to move about unveiled, an accusation to which she stiffly replied that her daughter was acquiring an education. Clearly, French education was used as an excuse for her daughter's ostentatiously faulty physical appearance and perceived lack of prudishness. Because the teenager attended French boarding school, she was allowed to dress just like any other pied-noir French girl. She was to pay a high price for freedom, however, as she would find herself increasingly left out of the camaraderie, solidarity, and intimacy shared by the girls and women in her family. Gradually, she felt cut off from the oral tradition that marked her childhood, and it was only years later, in the process of writing *Fantasia*, that she was able to reach those women who never had the power to tell stories because they were illiterate.

In contrast to her cousins, whose segregated lives were firmly anchored in a predominantly feminine and oral culture of singing, dancing, and storytelling, the narrator found herself in a world centered on the written word. Later, her sense of "linguistic" and emotional exile from her peers translated into a real, geographical exile in France, Tunisia, and the United States.[25]

Similarly, in *Vast*, the narrator highlights the deep divide between tradition—which demands that girls be kept in confinement to preserve their virginity up to the day when they are safely married off—and modernity. In the narrative, modernity is symbolized by a Westernized lifestyle, which appears to border on debauchery. This modern lifestyle was introduced by the French pieds-noirs—French settlers who allowed their daughters to grow into free, professional women and to become active members of the workforce. The narrator herself frowns on the European lifestyle of French women, recalling her own prudishness, especially in matters of love. For instance, she recalls being amused and shocked to witness Marie-Louise, a young French girl, kiss her fiancé Paul, a young officer, in front of her father, a Frenchman, even calling him "Darling Pilou," a nickname for Paul. Although parts of the Arab population allowed their daughters to get jobs, flirting and premarital relations were clearly off limits. Djebar writes, "I had seen those young girls in their temporary confinement, who one day were going to work as doctors. . . . Virgins, no doubt, twenty-five or twenty-six at the oldest. Pale, faces, diaphanous beauties, as if they were leaving their youth behind, and at the same time still awaiting it" (*Vast*, 46). This passage illustrates the paradox resulting from two conflicting cultures: although evidently Westernized and emancipated, given their professions and economic independence, these young girls remained virgins, perhaps failing to find a husband. By embracing a modern lifestyle, they simultaneously sacrificed a more traditional lifestyle.

French colonial education opened doors for a few lucky girls, as it did in the case of Djebar. Still, girls could not take higher education for granted. As Algerian francophone novelist Malika Mokeddem points out, no more than a dozen Algerian girls attended French colonial school in her desert hometown of Kénadsa in the 1950s.[26] While making a documentary about Algerian country life in the 1990s, Assia Djebar expressed her dismay upon meeting a little girl called Aichoucha, an "illiterate shepherdess, eight years old, scandalous in today's Algeria—and this was only seventy kilometers from Algiers" (*Vast*, 257). In the 1940s, limited schooling and physical confinement were still a reality for girls, as they were in Djebar's extended family. Although Djebar never wore a veil, her girl cousins lived in prisonlike conditions, cloistered inside a harem and draped in veils, seldom leaving the house and never venturing outside unaccompanied. Djebar, the documentary maker, describes the image of the Arab women of her childhood. In this community of women, women's bodies were fully hidden, draped with white cloth concealing the face and leaving a hole solely for the eyes. While these women looked like ghosts, their bodies were even more desirable, precisely because they were hidden. Even for a veiled woman, venturing outside, be it to the hospital or the workplace, was a trying experience: "You hurry; you try to make yourself invisible. You know that they have learned to make out your hips or your shoulders through the cloth, that they are judging your ankles, that in case the wind lifts your veil, they hope to see your hair, your neck, your leg. You cannot exist outside: the street is theirs, the world is theirs. Theoretically you have the right to equality, but shut up 'inside,' confined. Incarcerated" (*Vast*, 178–180).

Again, it is only in retrospect, as an adult, that the narrator fully comprehends and analyzes the implications of the veiled woman, this all too familiar and "normal" image of her childhood. Looking back, the narrator is acutely aware of the prisonlike lives of her cousins. During her girlhood, she herself lived an enclosed life during the long summer months and school breaks. At the time, she considered this condition normal. Although she felt like a prisoner during the summer months, she felt no need to rebel. Confinement, she knew, was temporary and soon the school year would start again and set her free. Her girl cousins, who were confined throughout the year, coped as best they could. Singing and dancing provided some emotional release, as did the many weddings and family celebrations, which served as opportunities for girls, young women, and old women to gather in solidarity. On these special occasions, which the narrator attended from age sixteen to her midthirties, she liked to highlight her individuality by asserting her own style of dancing and refusing to conform to tradition, according to which each woman dances in the manner traditional to her hometown. The women of her community perceived her solitary, improvised dancing style as modern—an ostensive and stubborn betrayal of tradition, which removed her further from her sisters.

Interestingly, on one occasion the narrator captured the attention of a middle-aged woman, who said she would instantly ask her in marriage for her son, if only the girl could be forced to wear a veil. The narrator's mother firmly rejected the offer. In fact, she was offended by it, because it came from a family whose bourgeois social standing was inferior to her own centuries-old lineage. Furthermore, she considered the offer indecent and unacceptable because the woman said she would describe the girl's physical attractiveness to her son. More important, however, she was adamant that her daughter must complete her education: "In any case, the father will let his daughter complete her studies. Tell that lady to look somewhere else for a daughter-in-law" (*Fantasia*, 287). Again, the narrator found allies in her parents, who promoted a Westernized, French education and instilled in her a need for freedom and intellectual independence.

Girlhood Games and Pastimes

The narrator was not the only young girl eager to break free from traditional constraints and in particular from the demand for segregation by sex. During the spring and summer holidays, for instance, she frequently visited her three girlfriends, the eldest of whom was Bahia's only friend. These young teenagers lived an essentially indoor life, scrupulously sheltered from the male gaze and the public sphere, in what could be termed circumstances reminiscent of a traditional "harem," a word Djebar uses frequently throughout the text. The youngest girl, we learn, was cloistered after completing elementary school, awaiting some future suitor. For these girls, swinging in the garden was one way to vent their pent up frustration. Swinging—uninhibited movement as opposed to a static squatting or cross-legged position, the one usually adopted at girls' and women's gatherings—allowed the girls to develop a sense of selfhood and individuality concomitant with a sense of release and physical freedom.

Swinging as high as they possibly could, they tried to break through the high walls surrounding their father's estate to catch a glimpse of the outside, forbidden world. This episode underlines the dichotomy of space: the outside world was forbidden for young girls who were considered fit for marriage. In *Vast*, the outside is portrayed as a bright, unpredictable, uncontrollable, boisterous, loud, dangerous, and risky environment, and hence the prerogative of boys and men, whereas the inside space is domestic, shady, and dominated by soft whispers, dancing, and storytelling, a quintessentially feminine space. In 1940s Algeria, spatial segregation went hand in hand with segregation by sex, which was so deeply entrenched that even within a marriage, a man and woman were never to call each other by their names, a rule Bahia breached when she referred to her husband by his first name, Tahar.

For the narrator's girlfriends, intellectual freedom, and in particular secret letter writing, became another vital act of transgression. Perusing popular women's magazines for ads from young men wishing to exchange letters with young, romantic Arab girls, they started to correspond with young men from all over the Arab world: "These girls, though confined to their house, were writing; were writing letters; letters to men; to men in the four corners of the world; of the Arab world, naturally. And letters came back from far and wide: letters from Iraq, Syria, Lebanon, Libya, Tunisia, from Arab students in Paris or London. Letters sent by pen-pals chosen from advertisements appearing in women's magazines with a wide circulation at the time in the harems" (*Fantasia*, 11). The narrator was shocked when she found out about her friends' secret correspondence. She was aware that this subversive channel of communication with the outside and male world constituted an act of transgression and, if discovered, was punishable. As Hafid Gafaïti points out, women in the Maghreb, and in the Arab world in general, are aware that writing is an essential source of power.[27] Consequently, he argues, education has always been one of the most important resources in combating patriarchy. In this instance, writing personal letters to the opposite sex can be seen as an act of empowerment and an assertion of selfhood: the girls do, in fact, have a voice.

Much like swinging, writing became a necessity for these teenage girls, as vital as breathing oxygen. Writing and communicating with the opposite sex allowed them to build a world of romance and daydreaming, and to temporarily escape from their real, physical imprisonment. More important, writing allowed them to indulge in imaginary romantic love affairs without actually compromising their virginity. During the long and stifling summer months, the narrator started writing love letters to alleviate her sense of confinement as she awaited the beginning of the new school year: "First love-letters, written in my teens. The journal of my cloistered day-dreams. . . . Soon the new school year will begin and lessons will bring the promise of quasi-freedom. Meanwhile, my epistles written in French fly far away in an attempt to widen the boundaries of my confinement" (*Fantasia*, 58).

Writing secret love letters was clearly a breach of paternal obedience and an act of transgression on the narrator's part. These letters were potential bombshells, for if they were discovered, they would bring shame to the whole family in a society in which a girl's innocence and virginity were quintessential tenets of a family's honor and standing.

By ensuring his daughter's early French schooling and literacy—at a time when few Algerian girls attended French colonial schools—and by promoting a French, Westernized education, the narrator's father instilled in his daughter an acute sense of duality, a sense of pride and individuality, as well as a growing need for freedom of thought and movement. He was not prepared to entirely let go of tradition, however; he insisted on arranging her marriage and even signing the wedding documents on behalf of his daughter, who then was already in Paris with her fiancé. Although it seems that the couple married for love, the narrator does not indicate whether this was indeed a thoroughly traditional, arranged marriage or if she chose her groom. It appears that despite her Westernized upbringing, the young girl found herself semi-emancipated—highly educated yet still unable to shake off centuries-old traditions and etiquette.

In 1940s French colonial Algeria, the gendered dichotomy of space went hand in hand with a linguistic dichotomy. As the narrator in *Vast* puts it, Arabic is the language of the inside, and the home, whereas French is the language of the outside, essentially the colonial sphere. Similarly, in *Fantasia*, the narrator explains that even though she attended French colonial school, she did not experience family life in a typically French household: "Throughout my childhood, just before the war which was to bring us independence, I never crossed a single French threshold, I never entered the home of a single French schoolfellow" (23). Although Arabic and French were initially strictly separate, the foreign French element slowly seeped into the Arabic/Berber household. The gradual intrusion of French language and culture manifested itself early in the narrator's life. As an adult thinking about her childhood, the narrator in *Vast* recalls a night of heavy bombing during World War II when she was age three and the family was living in a village in the Sahel. That night, her parents' French neighbors, a lone woman and her infant son, appeared in the middle of the night, frightened out of their wits, pleading to spend the night at her parents' home. When she woke up in the morning, the little girl saw a foreigner, a plump, blond French woman and her son Maurice, in her parents' marital bed, a scene that made a lasting impression on her. Looking back years later, she concluded that from that moment, the foreign element seemed no longer utterly foreign to her. That morning, as she awoke to the French language, the outside, foreign element became familiar, and French would remain part and parcel of her mental makeup and cultural and linguistic baggage for the rest of her life. In this crucial moment, she consciously became aware of the French language and culture, which would become her language of rational thought and writing, whereas Arabic would remain an oral language, the language of singing and dancing as well as the langue of emotions and love.

Another key event occurred when, as a thirteen-year-old teenager, she attended a cousin's wedding with her mother, who shockingly allowed her to wear a dress that exposed her back, arms, and shoulders. Not only did she wear what her relatives considered an indecent dress, but she also went unveiled at a time when most of her cousins were about to be cloistered permanently and married off. The young girl's unconventional physical appearance and her joyful and seemingly carefree dancing further underlined her individuality and her progressive drift away from her culture's traditions and morals, and foreshadowed her future separation from her cousins. Watching her dance, the older women predicted that her peers would shun her: "She goes out, she reads, she goes to the cities like that, naked, her father, bizarre, lets her. . . . She goes into the homes of those other people there and walks around like that in the enemies' world, well, in fact, the free world, but far away, far away! She makes her way around in it—her poor parents when they find out that she will never come back" (*Fantasia*, 285–286). In this passage, her body had already become accustomed to freedom; she was thus not only destined to be spared from confinement but she also found herself irrevocably separated from her sisters' warmth and company. Even though the narrator in *Vast* stresses that her upbringing was firmly anchored in Arabic and Berber tradition, as illustrated by the importance attributed to family genealogy, be it through storytelling, singing, religious ceremonies, or dancing, French cultural elements are not entirely absent within the parental home. For instance, we learn that Bahia also broke with tradition as a young girl by wearing a European-style white dress to her wedding, in compliance with the wishes of her fiancé, a future French elementary school teacher, the narrator's father, and the very man who walked the narrator in *Fantasia* to her first day in French colonial primary school.

In both *Fantasia* and *Vast*, Djebar primarily aims to reimagine and reconstruct the largely forgotten or undocumented lives of Arab girls and women. This intent is particularly evident in *Fantasia*, in which several chapters give voice to voiceless, brave, strong, courageous Arab girls and women. The narrator's upbringing can be characterized as unconventional. She received a traditional Muslim education, as, for instance, illustrated by her Koranic schooling, as well as a French education. Given her country's violent colonial history, she feels ambivalent toward the French language, but as a writer she does not shy away from using it.

Although the Westernized lifestyle plays a prominent role in Djebar's life, given that she spent several decades of her adult life in France and that her narratives are written in French, tradition and family genealogy are important aspects in the narrator's life, and to a large extent her narratives revolve around family traditions. The narrator in *Fantasia* focuses not solely on her own family history but also sketches the individual histories of girls and women in Algeria. Colonization and French schooling contributed to the emancipation of *some* lucky girls, as illustrated by the narrator, who embraced the French language, culture, and civilization without, by any means, compromising her Muslim education and beliefs.

NOTES

1. Among numerous other literary honors, Assia Djebar was awarded the German Peace Prize at the Frankfurt Book Fair in 2000 and the Neutstadt International Prize for Literature in 1996. Today, her influence and recognition, both as a scholar and internationally acclaimed writer who considers herself a francophone voice, span both sides of the Atlantic, where her works are widely read, discussed, and critiqued. Assia Djebar headed the Center for French and Francophone Studies at Louisiana State University in Baton Rouge from 1995 until 2001 before moving to New York University, where she was appointed Silver Chair and Professor for French and Francophone Literature in 2002.

2. See Mildred Mortimer, *Assia Djebar* (Philadelphia: Celfan Éditions Monographs, 1988), for a concise overview of her early novels. See Mireille Calle-Gruber, *Assia Djebar* (Paris: ADPF, 2006); and Mireille Calle-Gruber, ed., *Assia Djebar, nomade entre les murs* (Paris: Maisonneuve et la Rose, 2005), for critical essays on her more recent works.

3. Assia Djebar, *L'amour, la fantasia* (Paris: J.-C. Lattès, 1985); translated into English by Dorothy S. Blair under the title *Fantasia: An Algerian Cavalcade* (London: Quartet Books, 1985); *Vaste est la prison* (Paris: Michel Albin, 1995); translated into English by Betsy Wing under the title *So Vast the Prison* (New York: Seven Stories Press, 1999); *Ombre sultane* (Paris: J.-C. Lattès, 1987); translated into English by Dorothy S. Blair under the title *A Sister to Scheherazade* (Portsmouth, NH: Heinemann, 1987); and *Nulle part dans la maison de mon père* (Paris: Éditions Fayard 2007). Quotations in English of *L'amour, la fantasia* and *Vaste est la prison* are from the published English translations; hereafter they are cited in the text in parentheses. All other English translations are mine. Djebar's latest novel, *Nulle part dans la maison de mon père*, appeared after this chapter was written and so is not considered here.

4. See Anne Donadey, *Recasting Postcolonialism: Women Writing between Worlds* (Portsmouth, NH: Heinemann, 2001); and Debra Kelly, *Autobiography and Independence: Selfhood and Creativity in North African Postcolonial Writing in French* (Liverpool: Liverpool University Press, 2005), for insightful analyses of the links between historiography and autobiography in Assia Djebar's novels.

5. As Donadey points out, *Fantasia* puts women's testimonies "in relation, in dialogue, with the French colonial archives that she uses in the historical chapters of the first two parts of the book. The personal story and the collective history intersect again, since the women she interviews are relatives of hers" (*Recasting Postcolonialism*, 44).

6. See Anna Rocca, *Assia Djebar, le corps invisible: Voir sans être vue* (Paris: Éditions L'Harmattan, 2004), for the use of polyphony in both *Fantasia* and *Vast*.

7. Mildred Mortimer, "Entretien avec Assia Djebar, écrivain algérien," *Research in African Literatures* 19, no. 2 (summer 1988): 203.

8. Assia Djebar, *Ces voix qui m'assiègent* (Paris: Albin Michel, 1999), 51.

9. "'A fugitive and unaware of it,' is how I defined myself in my novel *So Vast the Prison*, undoubtedly the most autobiographic one" (ibid., 207).

10. W. E. B. Du Bois, *The Souls of Black Folk* (New York: Penguin, 1989).

11. Alison Rice, *Time Signature: Contextualizing Contemporary Autobiographical Writing from the Maghreb* (Oxford: Lexington Books, 2008), points out that Djebar remains prudish: "despite her interest in the 'liberated' customs of the Western world, Djebar is restrained from complete action in her personal life. Alone in an elevator with a younger man with whom she is smitten, she is unable to speak or move," a paralysis, Rice continues, caused by her husband, who was responsible for her cultural complex, which kept her in the position of an Oriental rather than a Westernized Algerian (121).

12. Hafid Gafaïti, *La diasporisation de la littérature postcoloniale: Assia Djebar, Rachid Mimouni* (Paris: Éditions L'Harmattan, 2005), 160–161.

13. See Franz Fanon, *Sociologie d'une révolution* (Paris: François Maspéro, 1968), for a detailed analysis of wartime functions carried out by the female freedom fighters.

14. *Vast* includes the example of the narrator's paternal grandmother, who is presented as a modest, silent, introverted, and loving person. At a young age she finds herself a widow and mother of two. She then marries an older retiree, who in turn soon dies, leaving her with a house and two more children—one of whom is the narrator's father.

15. Mildred Mortimer, "Assia Djebar's *Algerian Quartet*: A Study in Fragmented Autobiography," *Research in African Literatures* 2, no. 2 (Summer 1997): 102.

16. Assia Djebar, *La soif* (Paris: Julliard, 1957); and Djebar, *Les impatients* (Paris: Julliard, 1958).

17. Jean Déjeux, "Au Maghreb, la langue française 'langue natale du je,'" in *Littératures autobiographiques de la francophonie*, ed. Martine Mathieu (Paris: Éditions L'Harmattan, 1996), 182.

18. Clarisse Zimra, "Das Gedächtnis einer Frau umspannt Jahrhunderte: Interview mit Assia Djebar," in *Durst*, trans. Rudolf Kimmig (Zurich: Unionsverlag, 2002), 144.

19. Clarisse Zimra, "Ecrire comme on se voile: La première venue à l'écriture d'Assia Djebar," in *Assia Djebar*, ed. Ernstpeter Ruhe (Würzburg: Königshausen & Neumann, 2001), 80.

20. For the circumstances and motivations that led Djebar to adopt a pseudonym, see Alison Rice, "The Improper Name: Ownership and Authorship in the Literary Production of Assia Djebar," in Ruhe, *Assia Djebar*, 49–77.

21. Éveno writes that estimates of the number of deaths among the French military, Algerian freedom fighters, and civilians of both sides vary considerably. The National Liberation Front said in 1964 that over one million "martyrs" died in the war. The official number released by the Algerian government is that of one and a half million Algerians killed. The French army claims to have killed 141,000 rebels, whereas General Charles de Gaulle spoke of 145,000 victims in 1959 and of 200,000 in November 1960. The French military said 27,500 French soldiers were killed in the war and one million disappeared. The losses among the Muslim Algerian population are difficult to evaluate as sources vary considerably. See Patrick Éveno, "Premier Bilan," in *La guerre d'Algérie (1954–1962)*, ed. Yves Marc Ajchenbaum (Paris: Le Monde and E.J.L., 2003), 109–110.

22. In *Fantasia* Djebar pays tribute to the victims of this massacre in a chapter titled "Women, Children, Oxen Dying in Caves" (64–79).

23. Mortimer, "Entretien avec Assia Djebar," 201.

24. For instance, the narrator interviews girls and women about their wartime experiences and delves into colonial archives and travelogues—written by men—to probe, reconstruct, and reinvent her country's colonial and postcolonial history and tell her illiterate ancestors' stories. Thus history blends into fiction in a text that clearly privileges female voices, those of girls and women alike, voices that by and large were ignored by the colonizers and largely omitted from official historiography. For an analysis of the role of epitaphs used in the text, including those of Ibn Khaldun and St. Augustine, as well as an in-depth analysis of its palimpsestic structure and the use of historical sources in postcolonial contexts, see Kelly, *Autobiography and Independence*. For a detailed analysis of the complex structure of *Fantasia*, see Donadey, *Recasting Postcolonialism*.

25. For the links between history, exile, and identity in *Vast* and in *Fantasia*, see Valérie Orlando, *Nomadic Voices of Exile: Feminine Identity in Francophone Literature of the Maghreb* (Athens: Ohio University Press, 1999).

26. Malika Mokeddem, *La transe des insoumis* (Paris: Bernard Grasset, 2003), 56.

27. Gafaïti, *Diasporisation de la littérature postcoloniale*, 156.

3 Immigrant Girls in Multicultural Amsterdam

JUGGLING AMBIVALENT CULTURAL MESSAGES

MARION DEN UYL

LENIE BROUWER

At school, they tell me I need to work on my verbal and non-verbal presentation and expression. Well, then you try. And then you're with your classmates. In the classroom. And then my teacher says in front of the whole class something like, like that is not verbally expressive, or something like that. And at that moment I think: what the hell is this? I'm trying, I'm doing my best. I don't like it when people try to change me. Take me as I am, or don't take me at all. *I am who I am.* And then it just came out. I said: "Fuck the whole verbal and nonverbal shit, just fuck it!"

These are the words of Davinya, a teenage girl from the Bijlmer, a disadvantaged, culturally diverse neighborhood in the district of Amsterdam South-East. At the time of the interview, Davinya was seventeen and living with her Surinamese mother; her Antillean father had moved back to the Caribbean and started a new family there. Davinya continued, "When one of my friends calls, I say: 'Bitch! Whore! Cunt! Cow!' When my mother hears that, she really stares at me, disapprovingly, but I say to her that it's just the way we say hallo to each other, we're not calling each other names."

Davinya was far from shy, timid, or soft; she spoke loudly and, often, crudely. She said that she enjoys the cultural codes she shares with her friends and that she wants to be respected for who she is. Her native Dutch teacher tries to polish and soften her behavior and language, and her Surinamese Dutch mother frowns at the rude communication codes of Davinya and her friends. The cultural messages that her teacher and her mother try to instill in her can be interpreted as "decent," that is, these messages represent a set of values associated with various aspects of middle-class culture.

The teenage girls in our research area are growing up in a district with other immigrants from more than one hundred different countries of origin. The girls therefore have to deal with the different cultural messages, or desired behavior, that their parents and teachers transmit to them. These messages, however, have to compete with less decent messages—with "street" messages of desired behavior—offered by the girls' peers, the media, and street role models. These various messages can be incongruent or even conflicting.[1]

The population of the Bijlmer is composed mainly of immigrants from a variety of non-Western countries such as Surinam, Dutch Antilles, several African countries, in particular Ghana, and some Asian countries. During our anthropological study, which we carried out during several periods between 2004 and 2007, we interviewed teenage girls, mothers and fathers, youth workers, social workers, teachers, and district officials. We also attended discussion meetings and observed at various locations such as schools, churches, and community centers.

During our research, we studied the girls' dreams and desires, the tensions and conflicting cultural messages they are confronted with, and the ways they negotiate, as active or competent agents, these different cultural messages.[2] The importance of girls' own voices and their articulation of their needs and wants must be a centerpiece of girls' studies. We argue, in line with Sherry Ortner, who advocates that we look for agency and for significant intentionalities, that girls perform as active agents in dealing with the different messages they receive from parents, school, peers, and the media. In Ortner's words, agency is "defined minimally as a sense that the self is an authorized social being."[3]

In this chapter, we first discuss the dynamics of the different cultural messages by using the conceptual framework of Janis Lynn Goodman, who studied identity formation among African American schoolgirls in inner-city Philadelphia.[4] We use her framework to analyze the different cultural scripts of female identity and behavior in our research area. Next, we elaborate on the social context of the district, in particular its "superdiversity," which refers to the local multitude of ethnicities, religious convictions, and histories of migration.[5]

Our analysis pays special attention to the important role of mothers in a neighborhood where the majority of children grow up in single-parent households. We then focus on the core role played by sexual codes and sexual behavior in differentiating and negotiating "decent" and "street" cultural messages. Finally, we look at the ways in which the girls handle the different messages they receive from parents and peers, school and neighborhood, and we look at their ethnic background in relation to mainstream Dutch society.

The Dynamics of Different Cultural Messages

Research among schoolgirls in disadvantaged neighborhoods shows that street culture and decent culture present adolescents with what are often conflicting messages. Goodman found that black girls at a Catholic school in

Philadelphia experience differences between decent culture and street culture. She found that the school (and most of the girls' parents) supports decent values, which include going to school regularly, doing homework, dressing modestly, not wearing makeup, not showing an interest in boys, not hanging out on the street, and not taking drugs. Street culture, however—a culture with which the girls are familiar because they live in a disadvantaged neighborhood—encourages showing interest in boys, wearing sexy dresses and makeup, having a good time, and taking drugs. Moreover, street culture discourages doing homework and showing an interest in school. These different cultural messages result in conflicting cultural scripts of female identity and behavior.

Goodman emphasizes that decent culture cannot simply be equated with the dominant white culture, nor can street culture simply be equated with the black peer group culture: the relation between decent culture and street culture is complex. A central and strongly respected value of the girls in Goodman's research is "acting who you are"; for black girls in the inner city, this notion means that "expressing blackness," by dress, speech, and behavior, is valued positively, whereas "acting white" is valued negatively. Acting white is thus stigmatized in the girls' world, whereas expressing one's blackness is esteemed and connected with the criterion of self-respect. Respecting oneself means acting and being who you are.[6]

The black girls' mothers, who are central figures in their lives, give girls the message that decent culture is important, but that the desired behavior and the desired norms should not be an exact copy of the dominant, white decent culture. The girls' dress, speech, and behavior should express the local black cultural script of decent culture.

In our research, we applied the cultural scripts of street culture and decent culture that Goodman used in her analysis of African American girls in Philadelphia to girls in multicultural Amsterdam. Although in some ways our research area is similar to that of Goodman, in some ways it is different. The African American population, and hence the culture she depicts, is relatively homogenous, whereas the Bijlmer population consists of a great number of different groups originating from different African, Latin American, and Asian countries. Although the Caribbean culture is influential in the Bijlmer, other cultures such the Dutch and Ghanaian are important too. As a result, it is possible that the cultural messages in the Bijlmer are more complex, mixed, or diffused. In addition, the street culture as portrayed by Goodman seems more violent and aggressive than does the street culture in the Bijlmer. Although the latter is a disadvantaged area in which many people depend on welfare, it is not as violent or isolated as an American inner-city ghetto. As a result, we expected to find a less crude and violent variation of street culture in the Bijlmer, and consequently less distance between street culture and decent culture.

Between 1996 and 2002, the American anthropologist Bowen Paulle worked as a teacher in two deeply troubled schools, one in the Bronx (New York) and the other in the Bijlmer. The latter school, where he taught for three years, provides pre-vocational education to children aged twelve to sixteen. Paulle shows that in both schools, numerous pupils from different ethnic backgrounds are vulnerable and easily disturbed. There are frequent emotional outbursts, and it is hard to teach in this disruptive and unstable school climate. With regard to our research, it is interesting that he notices different roles among the pupils, for example, "ghetto-related behavior, dominant pupils and nerds." In the Bijlmer, he found the most disruptive "street" and "hard" students almost exclusively among African Surinamese and African Antillean youth, although there were also large percentages of soft-spoken and mild-mannered youth. Hindustani Surinamese youth, for example, were often labeled "soft" or "nerdy."[7]

In terms of decent culture and street culture, it might be assumed that there are different role models at school and among peers. Paulle states that gang and street culture, which often includes drugs and violence, must be considered a negative influence, whereas family and the nonstreet neighborhood person as positive influences. Notwithstanding his vivid descriptions of the chaotic educational climate, he concludes that most pupils end up on a positive path and that only a minority drop out.[8]

Our findings are based on the qualitative research we conducted in the Bijlmer with the assistance of several groups of anthropology students.[9] We applied a wide range of data collection methods, such as conducting taped interviews with thirty adolescent girls of Surinamese, Antillean, African, Dutch, and mixed descent; running several focus group sessions; and debating the topics of love and sexuality at a local community center. We also went to school evenings, church events, and the local shopping center, and attended several gatherings in the neighborhood, including a discussion of teenage sexuality held by the district council. During these visits, we had the opportunity to speak with key informants such as youth workers and teachers. The girls who took part in the taped interviews were approached at different locations, such as school, church, youth meetings, community centers, or on the street.[10] The aspect of coping with sexual messages was complemented by a survey carried out in the shopping center among thirty teenagers who were out shopping.

The Bijlmer: A "Superdiverse" Immigrant Area

Some ethnic minority groups in the Bijlmer are relatively large, whereas others are composed of only several hundred people, or even fewer. The population of the Bijlmer is gradually changing in that the number of immigrants from non-Western countries is increasing, while the native Dutch residents are leaving the area.

In 2007, the Bijlmer had slightly more than 43,000 residents. The first stream of immigrants came to the Bijlmer from the former Dutch colony of Suriname, which became independent in 1975. The background of the Surinamese population in the Bijlmer is diverse in both an ethnic and a religious sense: there are Christian Creoles, Hindustanis (both Muslim and Hindu), and people of Chinese and Javanese descent. Nowadays Surinamese people make up 37 percent of the population.

The more recent immigrants come from a variety of countries throughout the world. Some of these people arrived as labor immigrants; others are refugees or asylum seekers. The largest group among the new immigrants consists of Christians and Muslims from Ghana.[11] Together, immigrants from non-Western countries make up 74 percent of the population. Immigrants from Western countries form 7 percent of the population, whereas the native Dutch account for 19 percent.[12]

Amsterdam's South-East district, to which the Bijlmer belongs, is working hard to improve its negative image. In the past, it was plagued by criminality, unemployment, and row upon row of empty apartments. The district council decided that a thorough rebuilding program was needed to revitalize the area. Despite the spatial and social renewal programs, however, the area is still one of the poorest neighborhoods in Amsterdam. In the South-East district, more than 40 percent of those under eighteen grow up in households from the lowest income category.[13] Crime, particularly drug-related crime, continues to be a problem, and youth crime rates are among the highest in the Netherlands. Youth crime is gender sensitive in that boys in particular are engaged in street robbery, theft, public violence, and vandalism.[14]

Steven Vertovec recently introduced the term "superdiversity" to describe the changing setting of anthropological research in modern urban environments. His discussion of the concept refers to current changes in Britain. Superdiversity is "a notion intended to underline a level and kind of complexity surpassing anything the country has previously experienced. Such a condition is distinguished by a dynamic interplay of variables among an increased number of new, small and scattered, multiple-origin, transnationally connected, socio-economically differentiated and legally stratified immigrants who have arrived over the last decade."[15] The term can certainly be applied to the Bijlmer. Vertovec further discusses the new patterns of segregation, the new experiences of space and contact, and the new forms of cosmopolitanism and creolization, or the creation of new cultural forms, that accompany increasing superdiversity. With respect to the appearance of Creole languages and the practices of crossing or code-switching (recent and actual experiences that are developed and activated in the context of superdiversity), he refers in particular to young people, who invent these practices in the first place.

The ethnic background of the girls in our study reflects the diversity of the Bijlmer population. For instance, they have their roots in Ghana, the Antilles, or Suriname.[16] Although the Bijlmer girls come from diverse backgrounds, they have a lot in common—after all, they have played in the same playgrounds and attended the same primary schools. Youths living in the Bijlmer are generally positive about the neighborhood. One of our respondents remarked that in this area, people live more outdoors, which she likes a lot. The girls said they regret the negative image of their neighborhood, explaining that "You'd better not say you're from the Bijlmer when you're applying for a job." One Ghanaian girl, seventeen-year-old Ashandan, said she likes the multicultural character of the neighborhood: "Yesterday Ghana won a match during the world football championships. After the match, many people went outside, all kinds of people, Surinamese, Hindustani. Dutch people, too. Celebrating. Playing bongos. Well, I don't think you'll find something like that in any other neighborhood!"

All the girls feel attached, although in different ways, to their neighborhood. During a panel discussion the district council organized to investigate the hopes and wants of the local youth, the boys and girls were asked to write down statements about their neighborhood. The participants came up with statements such as "Breathing Bijlmer!"; "South-East, many parts become one!"; "Bijlmer: Rootboy Gangsta town!"; "A neighborhood for all cultures that want to live together without moaning and groaning!"; and "Bijlmer: Gangsta Paradize!"[17]

Mother-Centered Messages

The majority of the children in the Bijlmer grow up in single-parent households, and the number of these households is increasing.[18] There are twice as many households with one parent as with two parents, and these households are among the poorest in the Netherlands.[19] Single-parent households are especially prominent among Surinamese, Antillean, other Latin American, and various African groups. The growing number of these households is rooted in different histories of migration and kinship structure. The matrifocal kinship structure of the Caribbean is well documented.[20] Matrifocality refers, in this context, not only to the central role of women as mothers and income earners (and to the concomitant weak marital bonds), but also to a relatively strong female gender identity and a form of masculinity expressed in the roles of men as sons and lovers rather than as husbands and fathers. The relatively fragile marriage structure and the dominant gender identities among these matrifocal groups—phenomena that accompany single parenthood—are rooted in histories of slavery and poverty.

The largest African immigrant group in the Bijlmer originates from Ghana and consists mainly of Twi-speaking matrilineal descent groups. The process of migration, together with the relatively open sexual and marriage structure of many matrilineal groups, contributes to the high incidence of single parenthood. Adjusting to new marriage codes, which is an ongoing process in the country of origin, is reinforced in the process of migration because traditional bonds are weakened and Western values come to the fore in the new social setting.[21]

As a result of these different migration histories, there is a growing concentration of mother-centered kinship structures in the Bijlmer.[22] A mother often functions as head of the household, as income earner, and as the main bearer of responsibility for bringing up the children. One of our findings concerns the importance of mothers as role models for girls: nearly all the girls mentioned their mothers as the most central figure in their lives.[23] The girls mentioned different reasons for admiring their mothers. For example, when asked about the most important figure in her life, Gloria, a seventeen-year-old girl from a Surinamese background who was living with her mother, her sister, and her mother's new boyfriend, replied, "My mother. She is organized. Everything with her fits. The household is organized. Everything is clean. I don't like things to be dirty, and with her everything is clean. She works really hard. Yes, I want to be like her, later. Sometimes my mother yells at me. When I quarrel with my sister. Then I get angry. I shout and yell. Then I have to go to my room. Count to ten. I have to think, yes, she's my mother. Later, we talk; always we talk. And then it's: sorry, I am sorry." The girls gave different reasons for the great respect or esteem they show their mothers. Mary, a churchgoing fifteen-year-old, was born in Ghana but was now living with her parents and her brother in the Bijlmer. She said about her mother, "She's good, my mother. A good woman is someone who is sweet. Someone who is not lazy. When you come home from school, she should ask you how your day was and whether you did your homework."

Other girls did not refer to their mothers' sweetness or housekeeping qualities but to their power. Patricia, seventeen, was born in the Bijlmer and has an African Surinamese background. Although she reported quarrelling with her mother, she said that when it comes down to it, her mother is the person she admires the most: "Most important? That is my mother. Yes. Because my mother is a single mother after all. A single mother with three children, and there's my little niece too. You must be strong, really, really strong, to manage that all, at least that's what I think."

Mothers are clearly important to the girls in our research. They represent such personal qualities as being organized, being in control, taking responsibility, and providing care. The bond between mother and daughter is often intense and close, but this relationship does not exclude fierce quarrelling. Although many of the girls, particularly the African Surinamese and the African Caribbean girls, reported having heated arguments with their mothers, they also said that they can talk with their mothers and that they trust and respect them.

Although the role of fathers varies within different ethnic groups, fathers tend to be absent. Many girls of African Caribbean or African Surinamese descent who are growing up in single-parent households expressed negative feelings about and even contempt for their fathers. Patricia commented, "He doesn't understand anything, nothing, he simply sees me as a little girl." Seventeen-year-old Davinya, whose father left and went back to the Antilles, said, "I don't miss him at all. And, anyway, he used to fight with my mother." Other girls expressed more positive feelings about their fathers. The Ghanaian girls in our research, even those who were not living with their fathers, were less negative than most of the African Surinamese and African Antillean girls. Some of the Asian and Hindustani Surinamese girls mentioned their fathers as important and beloved figures in their lives.

A comparison of our findings with Goodman's reveals a remarkable similarity between the African American girls in her research and the African Caribbean girls in ours. In Goodman's research, 66 percent of the girls were growing up in female-headed households, roughly the same percentage as in the Bijlmer. As in Goodman's research, the importance of mothers is stressed: almost 90 percent of her respondents named their mothers as the most important and the most admired person. Goodman states that women, in their role as mothers, are related to decent culture, whereas men turn to street life and fail to provide a positive role model as fathers: "The girls lived in a world, then, in which decent women characteristically held things together, while men characteristically pursued the life of the street. Mothers worked to support children, while fathers were irresponsible, undependable, or simply absent."[24]

A clear and repeated message that many girls in the Bijlmer receive from their mothers is that men, although they may be great lovers, are unreliable. "Your diploma is your man" is a well-known Surinamese saying, one that indicates that school, work, and income are more reliable than marriage.[25] This stress on the importance of education can also be found elsewhere in this volume, in Christa Jones's chapter on girls in the Arab world, where literacy, especially the ability to express oneself in letters, is seen as a source of empowerment.

Decent and Street Messages about Sexuality

The Bijlmer has a negative image because the neighborhood is associated with unemployment, antisocial behavior, and criminality.[26] With respect to the Bijlmer youth, outsiders associate boys with criminal and sometimes violent behavior, and teenage girls with promiscuity and prostitution.[27] The newspapers present an image of the Bijlmer as a place where teenage girls are involved in prostitution, and where teenage motherhood and sexuality, loose morals, and loose manners predominate. It is, however, repeatedly stressed (by, for example, the district council) that this promiscuous behavior involves only a small minority of Bijlmer girls and that the majority have more decent sexual norms and values.[28]

Sexual behavior was important for our study because sexual codes form a significant marker of the differences between decent and street culture.[29] Moreover, we found that even if only a few of the girls actively participated in the street culture, almost all of them knew that *banga* (whores), group sex, rape, and violence exist; nearly all of them had heard of cases of youth prostitution or gang rape. This awareness means that street culture offers its own script of female behavior and identity.

The existence of street culture, and its expression in sexual codes, was outlined by eighteen-year-old Mercedes. The parents of this tall, strong, Antilles-born girl had died a year earlier, and since then she had been living alone in a rented room. She reported that "There's a lot of teenage prostitution in the Bijlmer. Not as much as they say in the papers, but it happens more and more. I think today's youth are a bit obsessed with sex. Everything is about sex. Skirts as short as possible. Dancing as close as possible. Touching with bums. Everything now is about sex." Mercedes continued her general story of street sexual codes in the Bijlmer by talking about the relationship she had had with a boy: "I broke up with my boyfriend, after we'd dated for three years. When we'd just broken up, I went to a lot of parties, to have fun, but now I've started to miss him. I miss someone when I come home, to hug, to talk to. But anyway, it's not that important. I can be on my own. Yes. You know it's important that you love and respect yourself. You don't need to take the first man, just because you . . . well, because you want to be loved." Mercedes, who was studying to be a social worker, knows the street scene but had decided that it is more important to respect herself than to be involved in the party scene. She also said that she longs for tenderness and understanding, "someone to hug, to talk to," and that this longing might easily be translated into sexual feelings. For a while, she had gone to parties "to have fun"; in Goodman's terms, she had turned to street culture, but now she had reverted to a more decent code of dress and sexual behavior.

Adolescent girls in the Bijlmer are interested in boys, as are most girls of their age. Moreover, having a boyfriend may give some status to a girl in the eyes of her girlfriends. Young girls regularly go to the shopping center, where they stroll the streets and are the target of comments from boys and men of many different nationalities.[30] Behavior toward boys and men is pre-eminently a contested field between the prescribed modesty of decent culture and the sexual encounters of street culture. The girls in the Bijlmer have to negotiate between the different messages they receive and to position themselves in these contested fields. The girls' appearance, clothes, and behavior give multiple signals. While some girls wear sexy clothes and use lots of makeup, others wear sweaters and jeans and disdain makeup.

During our research we organized several focus group discussions on falling in love and the pleasures and dangers of sexuality. It became clear that the girls had been warned by their mothers, sisters, and grandmothers to watch out for men. Seventeen-year-old Gabriella—who has a Surinamese background and at the time was studying hotel management and living with her mother and little brother—reported that "You're a girl, you're a woman; you have to respect your body. If a boy goes with sixteen girls, he's cool and a player, but if a girl goes with sixteen boys, she's a slut and a whore. That difference you need to know. You know how boys are. They're like tigers; they can play with you, but then suddenly their animal instinct comes up and they'll eat you!" The messages about sexuality from many of the African Surinamese and African Antillean mothers in the Bijlmer are ambivalent. Men are compared with animals, tigers, or wolves, which indicates that they are dangerous but also wild and attractive. Moreover, although jokes and loud, playful, or aggressive verbal exchanges between the sexes are common, many of the girls are aware of their mothers' feelings of distrust, pain, and confusion, feelings that are described as common characteristics of African Surinamese and African Caribbean male–female relationships.[31] Sex itself is not considered a topic of discussion: several girls reported that they do not talk with their mothers about menstruation or the use of condoms. Some mothers who were present at one of the discussion evenings, however, said that sex education was improving because *their* mothers had never told them anything. One of the mothers commented, "When I started bleeding, I didn't even know I had a little hole down there."

The message of the Bijlmer's religious institutions—the churches, the mosque, and the Hindu temple—is that one must not have sex before marriage. It is preached in the popular Pentecostal church that sex must be holy and that only married couples can practice holy sex. "You shall not eat from another plate," exhorted the priest every Sunday. Although the converted girls from the Pentecostal church have accepted this message, they sometimes find it difficult to put it into practice. For example, eighteen-year-old Gracy—a young woman of mixed Antillean and Ghanaian descent, whose boyfriend attends the same church—explained her dilemma: "Everything must happen in good time—in God's good time, not ours. Christians have strict rules, but it's not easy to ignore seduction, not to make mistakes. The two of us do not stay alone together, because that can lead you astray. Nothing's happened yet, but we're humans, who can slip up."

We carried out a survey among thirty teenagers in order to supplement the data obtained from the interviews and focus group discussions. The respondents were aged thirteen to nineteen and had Surinamese, Antillean, Ghanaian, mixed, Dutch, and Moroccan backgrounds. One of the questions asked was whether the girls considered themselves sexually active. It appears that age is an important factor in this field. None of the twelve respondents who were younger than fifteen said that they were sexually active, whereas all the respondents above the age of eighteen said that they were. Those aged fifteen to eighteen presented a mixed picture.[32]

Almost all the girls who participated in the survey saw differences in the ways girls and boys experience love and sexuality: "The difference is that boys want it right away, and then girls do it, because they think the boy will stay with them" (Antillean girl, fourteen); "At the moment I just don't want love or sex: men are animals!" (Surinamese Egyptian girl, fourteen); "Girls take it more seriously than boys" (Ghanaian girl, nineteen).

The survey indicates that girlfriends are important when it comes to talking about love and sex. Nearly all the girls mentioned girlfriends as the persons with whom they were able to discuss love and sex, whereas nearly 50 percent mentioned their mothers.[33] Only one Antillean girl, aged fourteen, said that she talked about sex with her boyfriend: "We talk. We've been together for eight months. I'm happy that we're not yet sexually active."

With respect to love and sexuality, girls in the Bijlmer have to negotiate between different, often ambiguous messages. Although many mothers tell their daughters not to trust men, boys are made attractive and important by media youth culture, especially in MTV and TMF clips, and they are a popular subject to talk about among girlfriends. The message some mothers give their daughters is ambivalent: although the mothers warn their daughters not to trust men, the mothers try again (and again) to live with a lover, after they have been disappointed and divorced. This situation means there is often a contradiction between the direct (spoken) and the indirect (lived) messages the girls receive.

Messages of Peers

Almost all of the girls said that school is important. Although not all of them liked school, most girls agreed that "without education you can't do anything." We found that the importance attached to school was prevalent among the pupils, regardless of whether they had chosen the higher or lower educational path.[34]

Willem, who teaches science and mathematics at a comprehensive school in the Bijlmer, said that the school had not changed much during the fifteen years he had been there. He made it clear that the school presents decent cultural messages, such as the importance of doing homework, showing respect for teachers, and not disturbing fellow pupils. At the same time, he is confronted with behavior, especially among pupils on the lower pre-vocational path, that can be characterized as street culture: talking and joking during classes, fighting, disturbing other pupils, and so on.

Bijlmer youth culture is well known outside Amsterdam, and even outside the Netherlands, for its music and street language: Bijlmer hip-hop groups and brass bands play at many youth festivals. The street language practiced in the Bijlmer has borrowed numerous words from Sranang Tongo (Surinamese), Papiemento (Antillean), and English. The Dutch linguist René Appel found that the Bijlmer youth language influences other youth languages and other youth cultures. He concludes that street language is considered "cool." It is a way to distinguish oneself from the grown-up world, from teachers and parents. Not a static language, street language is fluid, with its speakers continuously adding their own words. Appel emphasizes that the use of street language should not be seen as a lack of sufficient knowledge of Dutch, as it is also spoken by youngsters who are fluent in Dutch but use street language to express their solidarity with their cohorts.[35]

Sixteen-year-old Erna is one of the girls who expressed herself in the street language of hip-hop. Erna is from an Antillean background and was living with her mother and grandmother. She said she likes to entertain as a hip-hopper: "Actually, hip-hop brings people together." She reported that this notion of bringing people together is the message she wants to transmit to her audience. The Bijlmer is a source of inspiration, albeit an ambiguous one, for her songs: "Shit, if I walk through the Bijlmer I'm afraid I'll be shot. I will not say this, because this will not happen, you know, we are not in America, you know. We must keep it real. Everybody wants to look nice on the street and you want to buy dope clothes for your matties [mates]."

Erna said that she could not afford to buy expensive clothes because she has to "struggle" to make ends meet. She emphasized that race is no longer important, and that rap music surpasses differences and unites youths with various backgrounds. Most of her friends are involved in music: "They must be creative, ambitious, you know, that gives you power. If I hear a mattie of mine rap, then I think, shit, I must do it better. It becomes a sort of competition; it stimulates you to improve yourself. The best rapper is white, Eminem; besides, the best golf player is black. Skin color doesn't make any difference any more. I am always hip-hop. When I take a shower, I rap, you see; when I go to bed, I finally have a break. Actually, it is a reload for the next day to be hip-hop again." Erna's loose, baggy clothes showed that she is part of the hip-hop scene. In terms of different cultural messages, it appears that Erna is capable of dealing with the practices of crossing or code-switching. As an entertainer she can be easily seduced by the codes of the street culture, but this selection seems not to be the final choice she wants to make.

Friends and peer groups are important to nearly all the girls. "You can discuss everything with friends," said eighteen-year-old Sharon, who is of Javanese Surinamese descent. She was living with her mother (her father lives elsewhere in Amsterdam) and studying to be a social worker. She said that she likes going out on weekends:

I have three best friends. One is from Poland, one from the Antilles, and one from Suriname. We are just a crazy bunch of girls. We tell each other everything. About boys, about how awful they are. We try to protect each other. Take care. Watch out. We go always out together. We dance, we drink, we get a bit drunk. When it is too much, you must stop. But when I'm drunk, I'm very cosy. I stop when it is too much. And we do not take drugs. Never. I think that people who never go out, never go dancing or drinking, do not know how to enjoy life. They are boring.

Sharon and her girlfriends go out together; they enjoy dancing to reggae and Latin house music. Together they balance between street and decent culture, between going out and "protecting each other," and between getting drunk but not too drunk. They dress up and meet boys but at the same time tell each other "how awful boys are." The impact of decent culture has become part of their discourse; these girls are serious students who want to succeed in school. This ambition, however, does not stop them from going out dancing, getting drunk, or getting involved with boys on weekends.

A group of girls who regularly attend a local Pentecostal church reported that their girlfriends are all from the same church. They consider them family: "Over the years, we've become closer: we're now one big gospel family." They attend regular church activities, such as singing in the choir, to keep themselves on the straight and narrow. "If I didn't do that," one girl said, "I'd associate with people who do drugs, since the temptation is very strong." Hannah, an eighteen-year-old with an Antillean background who had recently converted to Pentecostalism, said that she no longer wants to dance, flirt, or use drugs, as she used to do: "You can still go out with your friends: you don't *have* to drink or smoke."

These girls continuously negotiate between decent and street codes of cultural behavior and adhere to them in a dynamic and flexible way. Some of them behave decently during the week, when they study and attend school, but on weekends they dress up, drink alcohol, and have fun. Other girls have gone through a period in their lives when they neglected school and homework and focused on boys and sexual relationships, but after undergoing a religious conversion they now dress modestly, refrain from alcohol and drugs, and take their homework and school seriously.

Juggling Multiple Cultural Messages

The Bijlmer girls are positioned in fields of messages that are often conflicting. Growing up in such a superdiverse area means that they receive multiple cultural messages—not only decent and street culture messages, but also different messages from school, home, and peers. They come into contact with "white" values, especially at school, while at home they receive cultural messages often related to their ethnic background.

Many of the girls are capable of handling these various messages and choose their own position. Usha, a fourteen-year-old Hindustani Surinamese girl who was in pre-vocational education, said that when she is at school, she prefers to listen to her teachers. She turns her back on her noisy fellow pupils but not on her close friends: "I don't need much contact with other pupils. They're noisy and loud. They shout. They don't listen to the teachers. They throw tables and chairs, that kind of thing. I don't social-ize with them very much. I don't share their taste in music. I love art, I love books, I like those kinds of things. You know, when I was very young I started to listen to heavy metal music and punk. You know, when I grew up, I made friends, and with these friends we developed together, and that's why I became a bit different." Usha's story brings to mind Paulle's descrip-tion of the chaotic educational environment he experienced at the Bijlmer pre-vocational school. He notes that many pupils who were eager to learn were disturbed by the noisy minority. Usha was open to the message that school is important; she said that one day she wants to work in a laboratory. She secluded herself from her noisy fellow pupils. At the same time, she indicated that her friends, her peers, whom she meets outside school, are important to her, explaining that "We developed together." She likes heavy metal music, which she had discovered all by herself. She has not only made her own choices from among the messages of her parents, her school, the Hindu temple, and her peers, but she has also found room for individual choice.

Growing up in a superdiverse neighborhood means learning to juggle different cultural messages. Seventeen-year-old Ashandan was living with her mother in a renovated apartment in one of the Bijlmer high-rises; her older sister lives in Ghana, her older brother in England. She regularly attends one of the local churches frequented mainly by Ghanaians. She said that she likes to chat on the Internet, that her school marks are very good, and that she likes mathematics and wants to become an accountant. She also reported that she has to do a lot of domestic work. All this is because "as a Ghanaian girl, you have to do the housework," and also because her mother is not well. She socializes easily. She has friends, boys as well as girls, from different cultures. She explained:

> With my mother at home I speak Twi, our language. Because my mother could not go to school in her village, she never learned English well. But with other people from Ghana I sometimes talk in English, and we speak English in the church, too. With my friends I speak a mixture of Dutch, English and Twi, and also street language, youth language, you know. My best friend comes from Ghana, but I also socialize with a Dutch girl, and with a Chinese boy and a Moroccan boy. At school most of the pupils are Dutch; I'm the only one from Ghana in my class. I like school, but they sometimes tell me off because I'm noisy. I simply like laughing a lot!

Ashandan's story is an excellent example of how girls integrate different cultural aspects (language, clothes, networks) with their personal identities. She is a master of crossing or code-switching, although sometimes messages get lost in translation: "My mother values obedience. And respect; yes, that too. In the Ghanaian culture, we have to show respect for all older people. You address everyone who is older than you are, who are old enough to be your mother or aunt, even if they are not your blood relative, in a respectful form of language. So, when I'm in Ghana, I get scolded because I address people in a rude way. But I don't mean to insult them, I'm simply translating from Dutch into Twi." Ashandan was playing different roles: at school, she was a bright pupil who did her homework and planned to go to university, while at home she was a respectful, churchgoing Ghanaian girl who helped her mother every day. Finally, besides being from Ghana and from Holland, she also identifies herself as a girl from the Bijlmer, as someone who knows how to use the special local street language among her peers. She is aware of the messages of decent and street culture, of school and home, the Netherlands and Ghana, and chooses her own repertoire from these cultural alternatives.[36]

We found that many girls in the Bijlmer seem able to switch from one cultural code or language to another and from one social role to the next, and to do so in a surprisingly fluent way. They participate in a new, dynamic, and continuously changing youth language. They present themselves differently in different contexts; they are who they are, or, in the words of Davinya, "I am who I am."

Conclusion

Girls in the Bijlmer grow up in a neighborhood that can be characterized as superdiverse. It is an area with many recent immigrants who have introduced a variety of languages, religious beliefs, and cultural practices. To analyze the different messages the girls receive as well as their responses to them, we used Goodman's schema of different cultural scripts of female identity and behavior. It turned out to be possible to analyze the choices of the teenage girls in the Bijlmer by using Goodman's schema, even though the Bijlmer differs from inner-city Philadelphia. Furthermore, we used Ortner's concept of agency, which stresses the position of research subjects as autonomous actors and decision makers.

We found that the Bijlmer girls are, in different ways, attached to their neighborhood and value it positively, although they are aware of its negative image and bad reputation. They particularly value the multicultural character of the neighborhood. The local youth culture—as characterized by, for example, street language, fashionable clothes, and hip-hop and rap music—influences youth groups also outside the Bijlmer. Youth culture connects them with youth outside the Netherlands, and outside Europe, across boundaries. In their creative use of street language, and in the fluid way in which they change from one cultural code to the next, the girls are continually involved in processes of crossing or code-switching. We advocate applying these new fields of crossing and code-switching not only to linguistic analysis, as Vertovec proposes, but also to social and cultural fields, to the superdiverse context of choices between various social and cultural repertoires.

The authority and influence of the mothers in our research area were striking. The mothers' presence in the daily lives of girls, with whom they often have strong emotional bonds, gives their messages a central value. The messages from some mothers are ambivalent, however, in particular with respect to men and sexuality. We found that, most of the time, the majority of the girls turn to a more or less decent script of female identity and behavior. Yet the decent and the street codes are not fixed; they are flexible and change over time. Some girls express themselves in different cultural scripts during the week and on the weekend, whereas others change their behavior and appearance after undergoing a religious conversion.

The Bijlmer girls are aware of the decent messages from parents and teachers, as well as of the messages from the street, which are embedded in youth culture. We found that girls switch between roles, depending on the context and time. Most of the girls speak two, three, or even four languages, and they switch between these languages during the day or the week. They are involved in local networks as well as in a globalizing youth culture and in international family networks overseas. Home, church, school, and friends, embedded in a superdiverse setting, offer different contexts with ambivalent cultural codes. Immigrant girls juggle these multiple cultural messages and play them according to their own tune.

NOTES

1. See Janis Lynn Goodman, "Identity Formation within a Multicultural Context: A Field Study of Early Adolescent African American Girls Set in an Inner-City Community in North Philadelphia (Pennsylvania)" (Ph.D. diss., University of Pennsylvania, 2005).

2. See, for example, Gill Valentine, Tracey Skelton, and Deborah Chambers, "Cool Places: An Introduction to Youth and Youth Cultures," in *Cool Places: Geographies of Youth Cultures*, ed. Tracey Skelton and Gill Valentine (New York: Routledge, 1998), 1–35. See also Helena Wulff, "Introducing Youth Culture in Its Own Right: The State of Art and Possibilities," in *Youth Cultures: A Cross-Cultural Perspective*, ed. Vered Amit-Talai and Helena Wulff (New York: Routledge, 2005), 1–19.

3. Sherry Ortner, *Making Gender: The Politics and Erotics of Gender and Sexuality* (Boston: Beacon Press, 1996), 10.

4. Goodman, "Identity Formation."

5. Steven Vertovec, "The Emergence of Super-diversity in Britain," Working Paper 25 (Oxford: Centre on Migration, Policy and Society [COMPAS], 2006).

6. Goodman, "Identity Formation," 111.

7. Bowen Paulle, *Anxiety and Intimidation in the Bronx and the Bijlmer: An Ethnographic Comparison of Two Schools* (Amsterdam: Dutch University Press, 2005), 117.

8. Ibid., 185.

9. We thank the participants in the various student groups (especially the groups on hip-hop and gospel, sexuality, respect and aggression, immigrant churches, the weekend school, and "Tha Spot") that took part in the Amsterdam Global Village project. They made valuable contributions to our research.

10. Although some interviews lasted only thirty minutes, others took several hours.

11. There are smaller groups in the Bijlmer composed of between several hundred and a thousand persons from African countries (for example, Nigeria, Cameroon, Somalia, and South Africa), Latin American countries (for example, the Dominican Republic and Colombia), and Asian countries (for example, Indonesia, Pakistan, China, the Philippines, and Sri Lanka).

12. Figures are from Dienst Onderzoek en Statistiek Amsterdam 2007, http://www .os.amsterdam.nl (accessed June 15, 2007). Antilleans account for 7 percent of the population, whereas the largest African group (Ghanaians) accounts for around 10 percent. Other groups are from other African countries, and from Asia and Latin America. There are also smaller groups of Turkish and Moroccan immigrants (3 percent), who form large immigrant groups in Amsterdam but not in the Bijlmer.

13. See Armoede Fact Sheet Zuidoost, Dienst Onderzoek en Statistiek Amsterdam, 2004, http://www.os.amsterdam.nl (accessed December 17, 2005).

14. *De Bijlmer monitor* 2005 (Amsterdam: DSP-Groep, 2006), 70–71.

15. Vertovec, "Emergence of Super-diversity in Britain," 1.

16. Besides girls from Suriname, our respondents included immigrant girls from Ghana, Nigeria, Columbia, Pakistan and Turkey. Some native Dutch girls were also included, as were girls with a mixed background (for example, Ghanaian/Antillean, Surinamese/Egyptian, Bangladeshi/Dutch, Surinamese/Dutch). Nearly all the girls had been born and raised in the Bijlmer; the remainder had arrived in the Bijlmer at a young age.

17. Stadsdeel Zuidoost, *"Zuidoost open huis" Ontwerp-Structuurvisie Zuidoost* 2020 (Amsterdam: Stadsdeel Zuidoost, 2005), 88.

18. *De Bijlmer monitor* 2005, 122.

19. Armoede Fact Sheet Zuidoost.

20. The study of matrifocality in the Caribbean began in the 1950s. Raymond T. Smith, *The Negro Family in British Guiana: Family Structure and Social Status in the Villages* (University College of the West Indies, Jamaica: Routledge and Paul, in association with the Institute of Social and Economic Research, 1956). Matrifocality in Surinam and the Netherlands has been analyzed by several Dutch authors. See, for example, Aspha Bijnaar, *Kasmoni: Een spaartraditie in Suriname en Nederland* (Amsterdam: Bert Bakker, 2002); and Gloria Wekker, *Ik ben een gouden munt: Ik ga door vele handen, maar ik verlies mijn waarde niet* (Amsterdam: Vita, 1994).

21. Marloes Kraan, *Blijven of teruggaan? Een sociologische analyse van potenties en problemen van Ghanezen in Amsterdam Zuidoost* (Amsterdam: Wetenschapswinkel Vrije Universiteit, 2001).

22. See also Ypeij Annelou and Gerdien Steenbeek, "Poor Single Mothers and the Cultural Meanings of Social Support," in *Focaal: European Journal of Anthropology* 38 (2001): 71–82.

23. The girls also referred to their grandmothers, aunts, or cousins as the most important figures in their lives. One of the girls cited the Lord, while another said that her newborn baby came first. Several girls who had been brought up by both parents declared that both their parents were central figures.

24. Goodman, "Identity Formation," 97, 105–106 (quotation).

25. An interesting study of the crucial role of mothers in neighborhoods that are dominated by black, single-parent households was performed by Sharlene Hesse-Biber and her fellow researchers among African American teenage girls. These researchers argue that black mothers act as mediators between black culture and the dominant culture. It is their role to instill in children the coping mechanisms needed to survive in the larger world. As a result of this mediation, African American adolescent females are selective when it comes to internalizing

messages related to beauty, while giving priority to the messages of significant others, particularly their mothers. They internalize only "their notions of beauty, not those of larger society, even though such a society may be dominant and invasive in their lives." As a result, the girls can develop a positive image of themselves without being forced to strive for white standards, which are unattainable. See S. Hesse-Biber, S. A. Howling, P. Leavy, and M. Lovejoy, "Racial Identity and the Development of Body Image Issues among African American Adolescent Girls," *Qualitative Report* 9, no. 1 (2004): 49–79, 64.

26. *De Bijlmer monitor* 2003 (Amsterdam: DSP-Groep 2004).

27. Several reports discuss teenagers having sex in exchange for a Breezer (an alco-pop), a Big Mac, or a cell phone top-up card, and report that girls as young as twelve or thirteen seek sexual contacts in the streets or participate in sex parties. See D. J. Korf, E. van Vliet, J. Knotter, and M. Wouters, *Tippelen na de Zone: Straatprostitutie en verborgen prostitutie in Amsterdam* (Amsterdam: Rozenberg Publishers, 2005); and Z. van Dijk, *Seksueel gedrag in een subcultuur van tieners in Amsterdam Zuidoost: Rapportage van een quick scan* (Amsterdam: GGD, 2006).

28. "Belliot: Vooral in Zuidoost is het ernstig," *Het Parool*, June 6, 2005; and "Stadsdeelvoorzitter Sweet: Het ging slechts om enkele gevallen, maar in de media werd het breed uitgemeten," *Het Parool*, July 22, 2005. See also Dorien Pels, "Ik wist niet dat hij dat bedoelde: Jongeren en seks," *Trouw, De Verdieping*, June 24, 2006.

29. Our respondents included one teenage mother and two girls who have a violent history of prostitution. The stories of rape and incest, however, are not representative of the majority of the stories of the girls who participated in the research (such stories were told by about 10 percent of our respondents). Nevertheless, these stories are a part of the lives of nearly all the girls, because they have all heard them.

30. In her research, Goodman distinguishes several factors that contribute to African American girls' interest in boys: "The biological burgeoning of adolescence; the developmentally grounded desire to experience and experiment, particularly with forbidden fruit; and the behavioural requisites of their peer arena" ("Identity Formation," 121).

31. See Wekker, *Ik ben een gouden munt*.

32. With respect to being sexually active, ethnic background did not seem to play a major role. All three age categories included girls from different ethnic backgrounds.

33. The girls gave multiple answers to the question about the person with whom they were able to discuss love and sex: 24 of the girls mentioned their girlfriends, 12 their mother, 5 their sister, 5 their cousin, and 2 their father.

34. In the Dutch educational system, secondary school starts at the age of twelve, after eight years of primary education. In the Amsterdam South-East district, in which the Bijlmer lies, 43 percent of students follow the higher path of secondary education. A relatively large percentage (almost the same as in Amsterdam as a whole) of the Bijlmer youth succeed in gaining admission to higher education, which eventually allows access to university education. See M. Babeliowsky and R. de Boer, *Voortgezet onderwijs in beeld* (Amsterdam: DMO, 2007), 57–58.

35. See René Appel, "Straattaal: De mengtaal van jongeren in Amsterdam," *Toegepaste Taalwetenschap in Artikelen* 62, no. 2 (1999): 39–56.

36. In her chapter, in this volume, about the political identity of American Jewish girls, Klapper describes how adolescent Jewish girls maneuver between their religious background and American youth culture. Although all the girls in her study took pride in their Jewishness, in some cases their primary allegiance was to youth culture rather than religious culture; this allegiance was made possible by the fluid boundaries of "Americanness," which came up as a reaction to mass migration and increased urbanization. As a result, girls were able to construct their own cultural repertoire based on different cultural messages.

4 Feminist Girls, Lesbian Comrades

PERFORMANCES OF CRITICAL GIRLHOOD IN TAIWAN POP MUSIC

FRAN MARTIN

During the 1990s, the popular concept of the girl—as in girl power, girl bands, girl rock, the Spice Girls, Riot Grrrl, cybergirls, and others—became increasingly prominent not only in Euro-American commercial music cultures but also outside the West. How does the category of girlhood function in non-Western contexts, and in languages other than English? Through which channels were 1990s commercial and popular movements such as the "girl power" of the Spice Girls translated into local contexts outside the West, and what effects did they produce there for local girls and women? In this chapter I tackle these questions by analyzing a non-Western manifestation of globally mobile configurations of girl culture in an example with which I became familiar after extended periods living and researching in Taiwan during the mid- to late 1990s: independent folk-rock singer-songwriter and producer Sandee Chan. Through this case study I consider how we can conceptualize the complex cultural interchanges between globalizing musical girl cultures and their local instances in Taiwan.

Although the analysis that follows focuses on a real young woman musician and her female fans, this chapter is principally interested in girlhood understood as a discursive category rather than as a concrete group of persons defined by their inhabitation of a specific gender and age bracket. There exist several modern Mandarin terms approximating the English word "girl" in current colloquial use in Taiwan. The term *nüsheng* comes closest to and is most commonly rendered as a translation of "girl" in pop-cultural and pop-feminist usages. Other terms include the Japanese-derived *shaonü*, literally, "female youth," which is commonly used to refer in a fairly literal sense to adolescent girls (young women between about twelve and twenty).[1] Another term for girl is *nühai* (or *nühaizi*), literally "female child"; today this term is used loosely in colloquial speech, somewhat similar to *nüsheng*, but arguably with a more infantilizing overtone. Etymologically derived from the longer term "female student" (*nüxuesheng*) and in vernacular use since around the late nineteenth century, *nüsheng* does not really function in contemporary Taiwan to specify a particular group of individuals delimited by literal girlhood age: women of any age under about forty could be referred to as *nüsheng* if the circumstances were right. Instead, the category *nüsheng* works as a pop-cultural signifier of a particular conceptualization of feminine gender in the contemporary world: a conceptualization, I argue, that references a certain attitude connected with globalizing formations of both pop feminism and female-targeted entertainment cultures.

In addition to *nüsheng*, I look at another current category of feminine identity as well: *nütongzhi*, one of several available terms to refer to female same-sex desires, cultures, and identities. By focusing on responses to critical, pop-feminist performances of girlhood by Sandee Chan, as gathered from a group of her local lesbian-identified fans, I consider *nütongzhi* as a parallel and related category to *nüsheng*, one that has arisen more recently. A key question concerns how exactly *nütongzhi* as a relatively new (post-1990) identity category in Taiwan relates to the broader category of girlhood (*nüsheng*). Through the example of Sandee and her lesbian fans, I demonstrate how the categories *nüsheng* and *nütongzhi* are related, first, through shared connotative associations with varieties of popular feminism.[2] I then move on to suggest a further conceptual linkage between the category "girl" and the topic of same-sex love by highlighting the prevalence of a universalizing discourse on same-sex relations between girls and young women that coexists in Taiwan alongside the minoritizing discourse on *nütongzhi* identity. To begin to approach a non-Euro-American sexual identity category like *nütongzhi*, however, I must first consider the broader question of how to theorize sexuality in a transnational frame.

Theorizing Sexuality Transnationally

As Foucauldian scholarship on the history of sexuality has taught us, sexual identities like lesbian, gay, bisexual, and heterosexual—indeed, even sexuality itself, understood as a discrete and inherent property of individuals—are concepts that were first invented in, and hence are historically specific to, the modern period.[3] As David Halperin succinctly puts it, "Sexuality . . . does have a history—though . . . not a very long one."[4] Historical studies of the emergence of contemporary minority sexual identities such as "lesbian" and "gay" have illustrated how these identities emerge as a result of particular social, economic, cultural, and spatial transformations in the West over the course of the twentieth century—transformations connected with increasing urbanization and changes to older family structures as a result of the deepening entrenchment of capitalist modes of production.[5] If sexuality, sexual categories, and sexual identities are historically specific, they are also *geographically* marked: the ways in which subjects understand and experience sexualities vary across space as well as across time. Over recent years, a key question for scholars working in sexuality studies has been how best to approach the globalization of Euro-American formations of minority sexual identities, styles, and subcultures—a phenomenon that has been called "global queering."[6] Recent work across the humanities and social sciences that has effected what Elizabeth A. Povinelli and George Chauncey call the "'transnational turn' in lesbian and gay studies" assumes the syncretic character of contemporary sexual knowledges, emphasizing translocal flows and "glocalization."[7] Criticizing the tendency of the Euro-American academic center to presume the universal relevance of its sexual and gender categories and histories, scholars have highlighted the need for the elaboration of diverse histor*ies* of sexuality.[8] Summarizing these developments, one might say that in general, a classical-anthropological model of discrete sexual "cultures" bounded by easily defined geopolitical or linguistic borders has given way to a model of sexual cultures closer to James Clifford's theorization of cultures as "traveling" rather than "dwelling."[9] At the same time, the Eurocentric arrogance that would claim, on the one hand, that "gay identity" is a universal, transhistorical given, or, on the other hand, that "Western gayness" has the power to obliterate all other forms of intragender eroticism and identification, has largely made way for the recognition that the specificities of cultural location continue to matter for the practice and conceptualization of diverse sexualities, even in a world more than ever transnationally connected. This conceptual background provides a useful theoretical context for considering the appearance of *nütongzhi* as a sexual identity category in contemporary Taiwan. In what follows, I offer a brief account of the local social and historical contexts against which the category emerged in the early 1990s.

Taiwan Feminism and the Emergence of the Category *Nütongzhi*

The 1990s in Taiwan was a decade of rapid social change, as illustrated by the rise of a series of activist movements after the lifting of martial law in 1987; these included the feminist movement and, marginally later, the lesbian and gay movement, among a host of others.[10] One of the oldest and most influential feminist organizations, the Women's Awakening Foundation (Funü Xinzhi Jijinhui), was founded in the early 1980s and expanded rapidly to become Taiwan's largest women's activist organization by 1988.[11] Among its many achievements, Women's Awakening has published a regular newsletter and journal since the 1990s; established Taipei's feminist bookstore, Fembooks (Nüshudian), in 1994; and worked with the legislative Yuan (Taiwan's lawmaking body) to negotiate far-reaching reforms to the highly patriarchal family law code. Yet the cultural effect of Women's Awakening and other feminist NGOs cannot easily be quantified by reference to such concrete projects, vital though these are.

Since the late 1980s a basic shift has taken place in relation to the question of gender in Taiwanese society: that is, gender and gendered power relations have become a salient question referenced regularly at different levels of Taiwan's public culture, from the rarefied realms of legal reform;

to discussions in popular media of gender "issues" such as the status of career women, sexual harassment, sex education, and feminism itself; to the emergence of questions about gender and feminism in popular cultural forms such as music, women's magazines, talk radio, and local free-to-air television. The popularization of debates about patriarchy, sexism, women's status, and feminism over the past twenty-odd years provides the crucial, enabling background against which oppositional forms of feminist popular culture, such as the feminist music cultures discussed in this chapter, were able to emerge. In an important sense, the rise of institutional and popular feminisms in Taiwan provided the space of possibility for girls and women—particularly those most exposed to feminist discourses, that is, young, educated, middle-class women—to begin imagining and practicing alternative forms of feminine subjectivity: new ways of being a girl.[12]

The emergence of the identity category *nütongzhi* (lesbian) in Taiwan during the 1990s can be interpreted as an example of sexual glocalization: the local take-up, indigenization, and active adaptation of a globally mobile term and category outside the West, where the globalizing meanings of the term interact with local context to produce a culturally syncretic category and identity. During the 1990s, available models for representing homosexuality (*tongxinglian*) in Taiwan underwent an unprecedented transformation. Existing same-sex bar and cruising subcultures were joined by a public gay (*tongzhi*) political movement, the consolidation of a tongzhi commercial culture (in new bars, clubs, and lifestyle magazines), and waves of tongzhi literature, tongzhi film, tongzhi art, and tongzhi studies.[13] The term *tongzhi* literally means "comrade" in modern Mandarin, and has been appropriated to translate "gay" partly as a result of its inclusion of a character (*tong*, "same") that is also found in the word "homosexuality" (*tongzhi*, "same will"; *tongxinglian*, "same-sex love"). *Nütongzhi*, then, literally translates as "female comrade," but in current usage it approximates the English term "lesbian" in that it indicates a woman's same-sex sexual preference consolidated as a substantive identity. Further, in distinction to the range of other available terms designating women's same-sex sexual preference, the term *nütongzhi* often carries connotations of a feminist cultural politics.[14] As Jenpeng Liu and Naifei Ding have persuasively demonstrated, in distinction to older forms of working-class female same-sex culture organized around secondary gender (*T/po*, comparable to butch/femme), when *nütongzhi* first appeared around 1990 it was closely associated with the local appropriation of lesbian feminist ideology by largely young, middle-class, and intellectual women on university campuses and within emergent social and activist groups in metropolitan, Mandarin-speaking northern Taiwan.[15] During the 1990s, *nütongzhi* thus arose as an alternative female sexual identity associated with a younger generation of urban, middle-class, educated, feminist women. In the following section I explore how the categories *nüsheng* and *nütongzhi*, both freshly salient in the 1990s, became articulated with performances of critical girlhood in local music cultures.

Globalizing Girl Rock

Since the mid- to late 1990s, "girl rock" (*nü yaogun*) has arisen in Taiwan as both a musical phenomenon and a topic of public discussion. This expression could be interpreted, in part, as a localized manifestation of a globalizing tendency identified by Gayle Wald in Euro-American rock whereby "the performance of girlhood . . . can now be said to constitute a new cultural dominant within the musical practice of women in rock."[16] The rise to popularity of musical "girl cultures" in Euro-American contexts in the 1990s has been analyzed in detail by feminist scholars of popular and music cultures. Particular attention has been paid to Riot Grrrl, a musical and subcultural movement in underground women's rock that grew out of the punk moment and originated in the northwestern United States in the early 1990s.[17] Bands generally taken to be representative of the Riot Grrrl movement include Bikini Kill, Hole, L7, Bratmobile, and 7 Year Bitch. As many of these band names and the term Riot Grrrl itself suggest, as a youth culture and music style Riot Grrrl was characterized by its angrily oppositional gender politics. Riot Grrrls expressed their critique of hegemonic femininity and resistance to masculinist "boy rock" culture through their own independently produced post–punk rock music. As both Catherine Driscoll and Joanne Gottlieb and Gayle Wald demonstrate, the Riot Grrrl culture often relied on the ideological opposition of the "mainstream" to the "underground," privileging the latter and devaluing the former.

Driscoll's work raises some particularly pertinent questions for my discussion here. Resisting the common position that denigrates the populist "girl power" of the British band the Spice Girls to champion the "radical" character of Riot Grrrl, Driscoll addresses a major question raised by the Spice Girls' popularity: "Can feminism be a mass-produced, globally distributed product, and can merchandised relations to girls be authentic?" Driscoll does not venture definitive answers to these questions, but she does argue persuasively that the Spice Girl phenomenon and the associated populist discourse of "girl power" warrant serious attention from feminist researchers. Significantly for my discussion in what follows, Driscoll also makes the point that the rise of music-based girl cultures of fandom and consumption—as seen in relation to both the Spice Girls and Riot Grrrl—tends to militate against the usefulness of maintaining a conceptual division between the "mainstream" and the "alternative."[18] In what follows, by discussing the example of Sandee Chan, I further explore how the globalizing pop-feminist phenomenon instructively complicates any clear-cut division between oppositional and dominant forms both of music and of gender politics, and indeed confounds the persistent presumptive distinction between the commercial and the political in the field of popular music cultures.

Sandee Chan, Pop Feminism, and Globalizing Girl Power

Of Shanghainese descent, Sandee Chan lives and works in Taiwan. She has, to date, produced nine albums as well as a book of prose, numerous works of poetry, and several musical scores for theater.[19] She has collaborated in arranging scores for recent Hong Kong films, including Wong Kar-wai's *In the Mood for Love* (2000) and Tsui Hark's *Time and Tide* (2000), and in recent years has become well known through writing and producing music for other Mandarin singers. In 2005, she won the Golden Melody Award for Best Mandarin Pop Album, as well as Best Producer, with her latest album, *When We All Wept in Silence* (2005). Sandee's early CDs were dominated by an acoustic, folk-rock sound with simple instrumentation; strong, rich vocals (then as now purely in Mandarin); unpredictable but catchy melodies; and a thematic preoccupation with both young women's everyday experience and feminist cultural politics. The cheerful "Café Inn" ("Kafeiyin") for example, on her 1994 *Four Seasons* album, features Sandee's voice accompanied by a single acoustic guitar. On the same album, "Recycling" ("Dao lese"), a slow, dark, minor-key environmentalist ballad, is dominated by the brooding bass, whereas "Speed" ("Chaosu"), with its fast beat and insistent guitar, is more self-consciously grungy. Sandee's later albums tend at times toward a more straightforward pop style; the song "Perfect" from *Perfect Moan* (2000), for example, is a highly polished electronic number far removed from the acoustic folk sound Sandee cultivates elsewhere. And the ten tracks on her 2005 album with Hong Kong singer Veronica Lee, *Material Girls* (*Bai jin xiaojie*, literally "Gold-worshipping misses"), are again for the most part highly produced electronic pop-style numbers, although diverse in style and musically still somewhat left of center.

Sandee has been instrumental since the mid-1990s in both the popularization of feminist topics in pop songs and the increasing public discussion of women in the music industry. Her public statements frequently foreground a feminist cultural politics: she has spoken out against the pressure on female singers to conform to oppressive social standards of feminine bodily perfection and denounced the music industry's exploitation of women singers' bodies for commercial gain.[20] Sandee chooses Taipei's Witches' Pub (Nüwudian) as a venue for her live performances, a bar housed on the ground floor of the Fembooks building—a choice that signals her deliberate alignment with Taiwan's local feminist movement. She has also collaborated with contemporary feminist poet Hsia Yu, setting some of her poems to music.[21]

Sandee's lyrics, too, frequently highlight issues around feminism and gendered power relations. The song "Surveillance/Violating Vision" (a pun on homophonic Mandarin terms *jianshi/jianshi*), for example, uses the scenario of a woman in an elevator being observed by a security camera as the basis for a meditation on the objectification of women's bodies in patriarchal culture:

> You look at my eyes: what color are they, anyway?
> You ardently love my body, yet can move no closer to me.
> . . .
> I am cruelly sliced open, the blood that flows is not free to have its own
>   color.
> You do what you love to do, with your eye.
> In your eye I am as simple as black and white,
> My head so big you can look right through it,
> My body so small it can't run fast enough.
> Everything depends on your love.[22]

The abstract, allusive quality of these lyrics, together with their mixing of ruminations on everyday urban life with a feminist commentary on contemporary society and gendered power relations, makes them typical of much of Sandee's work. Particularly characteristic is the paralleling of the personal—the address to someone who seems to be a lover in the lines "you ardently love my body" and "everything depends upon your love"—and the more broadly social, in the metaphor of patriarchal culture as a visual surveillance technology that objectifies, reduces, attacks, and renders powerless women's bodies. The final line, in particular, exemplifies this suggestive ambiguity. At once a fairly conventional pop lyric lamenting the woman singer's masochistic attachment to a heartless lover, and an ironic critique of the masochism required of feminine subjects by a patriarchal culture that both denigrates them and demands their devotion, the lyric exemplifies Sandee's proficiency in integrating incisive feminist critique into the pop-song form.

As Sandee's use of the globally recognizable star persona of "feminist singer-songwriter" illustrates, local specificity and cultural particularity form only one part of the picture in these Taiwanese interpretations of girlhood. How might we think more explicitly and critically about the workings of cultural globalization in these musical girl cultures in Taiwan? In 2001, Yang Jiu-ying's book *Grrrl Rock* (*Nü Yaogun*) was published with a foreword by Sandee in which she reviews her experiences attending live performances by Patti Smith, Laurie Anderson, Kristin Hersh, Ani Difranco, Kim Gordon, and others. Sandee ends with the sassy, girl power–style challenge: "We girls aren't going to simply don pretty bathing suits and appear for a single summer—we're going to keep on stirring things up, and we're going to do it in a very girl way [*yong yizhong hen nüshengde fangshi*]."[23] The following year, Yang published a translation of Andrea Juno's *Angry Women in Rock* (*Yaogun Nunü*), at whose launch Sandee also spoke.[24] Both of these books explore the history of women in rock and the music industry in Europe and the United States from the 1960s to the 1990s. The publication in Taiwan of these books tracing genealogies of women in Western rock shows that the rise of girl rock in Taiwan is inherently linked to transnational cultural flows and the globalization of musical girl cultures. One particularly interesting way in which this happens is in the local reworking of globalizing discourses of pop feminism and "girl power."

In May 2000, Friendly Dogs released a collaborative Mandarin double album titled *Girls Going Forward (Nüsheng Xiang Qian Zou)* by a diverse group of local women musicians, including Sandee. The pop-ish, upbeat title track, cowritten and coperformed by Huang Yun-ling, Lin Shao-pei, Tang Na, Sandee Chan, Meng Ting-wei, Ding Xiao-qin, Huang Xiao-zhen, Hong Yun-hui, Wang Song-en, and Wu Pei-wen, was organized around a refrain written by Sandee urging solidarity among girls (*nüsheng*):

> Girls going forward: if girls want to go forward, go together
> Girls going forward: if someone has to criticize, let it be boys
> Girls, don't criticize each other, don't be jealous, and cut each other some
>   slack once in a while.
> [Repeat]
> Girls shouldn't put other girls down: appreciate their good points and
>   every day you'll be free.[25]

In a 2000 interview at music543.com, Sandee gives a telling response to a pointed question about "Girls Going Forward" e-mailed in by a fan:

> FAN: Recently the collaborative work "Girls Going Forward" has been criticized because it is felt that in itself, the idea that "girls shouldn't criticize girls" is not necessarily terribly "forward looking." What does Sandee think about such criticism? In future will she intentionally try to include more feminist ideology in her songs, and become a more active spokesperson for girl-power rock [*nüli yaogun*]?
>
> SANDEE: . . . I know a lot of people criticized [this song], but I still feel it's quite forward looking, and I don't really understand the criticism. Look [at the question]: "will she intentionally try to include more feminist ideology in her songs?" [The fan] has a set idea of what she wants—of what feminist ideology should be like; [and feels] that it's not as simple [as the song implies]. But the most difficult things to put into practice are often the simplest ones. . . . Of course it isn't necessarily such a great song, but criticisms like that are too superficial. . . .
>
>   . . . In the past few years I've realized very clearly—especially in the last two years—that I have a great liking for popular things [*tongsude dongxi*]. . . . But many people have a very bad impression of the popular, and feel that populism is always a negative thing. This opinion influences their musical taste, and I think that's a really serious problem.

> Many people use this as a means of evaluation. For example with "Girls
> Going Forward" I wanted to make it popular, although in reality it's not
> as popular as all that. Yet there are some who feel it's still too popular,
> and they end up making really weird demands of [such a song].[26]

Sandee's response indicates a self-conscious engagement in the project of
creating a locally situated, avowedly populist, pop-music feminism. Her
conceptualization of her own pop-feminist project in *Girls Going Forward* is
explicitly differentiated from what she characterizes, later in the same interview, as the views of those who "go on so earnestly about feminism and
whatever" yet fail to understand the potential of "too-simple" popular cultural forms like pop songs effectively to disseminate feminist meanings.
Sandee's linkage of her feminist politics to the popular proposes that the
ideological challenge of feminism can—and should—be encoded effectively
in commercial pop music; in Driscoll's words, Sandee argues precisely for
"girl culture as a form of feminism as popular culture."[27]

The appearance of the Taiwan Mandopop album *Girls Going Forward*—
and especially Sandee's defense of it in these terms—perhaps indicates the
global reach of what Driscoll identifies as "a shift in the dominant paradigms
of cultural production directed to girls which . . . is . . . newly inflected by
an embracing of popular rather than avant-garde cultural production."[28]
Lending weight to this idea of a globalizing pop-musical feminism is the use
of an intriguing neologism by the fan who e-mailed the question to Sandee
about the efficacy of her populist strategy. In asking whether Sandee plans
to become a spokesperson for "girl power rock," the fan uses the phrase *nüli
yaogun*, the first two characters of which—*nüli*—stand out as at once lin-
guistically awkward and weirdly familiar. This pair of simple characters
would in fact be recognizable to audiences around the world as none other
than the tattoo on Sporty Spice Mel C's right shoulder—her own freeform
Japanese translation of "girl power." Appearing now in Taiwan Mandarin,
the term has come full circle: invented on an orientalist whim by Mel C or
her tattooist out of Japanese kanji meaning "female" and "strength," the
sign inscribed on the Spice Girl's skin makes the return journey from the
United Kingdom to East Asia via countless mediatized images of the pop
singer's body, and in the wake of Spice Girl fever across the East Asian
region, Sporty Spice's invented Japanese word is now read in Mandarin by
audiences in Taiwan as *nüli*. A clumsy Japanese term invented by a British
pop star reemerges as a Mandarin neologism: the whole process exemplifies
the integrative effects of the transnational circulation of musical girl culture. But perhaps more interestingly, it demonstrates the unpredictable
"feedback effect" these circuits can also precipitate, whereby decreasing distance between a transmitted signal's source and its projection leads to the
emission of strange and unanticipated new sounds—in this case, a global
pop star's exoticist appropriation of kanji is reappropriated as feminist

vernacular among young Taiwanese fans of a local musician, illustrating the potential productiveness of populist feminism in facilitating gender-critical discussion throughout the global body politic. If *Girls Going Forward* thus demonstrates a strong linkage between the category "girl" (*nüsheng*) and transnational musical pop-feminism, how can we account for Sandee's popularity among self-identifying lesbians (*nütongzhi*)? How can we map the triangulation between "girl," "lesbian," and pop feminism, in this example? In the next section I address these questions.

Sandee's Lesbian Reading

In 2000–2001, as part of a research project investigating my observation of the remarkable popularity of (married, straight) Sandee among young, urban Taiwanese lesbians, I posted calls at a number of Chinese-language lesbian Internet and Bulletin Board System (BBS) sites for volunteer Sandee fans to fill out questionnaires on their fandom.[29] As a result of these calls, I received responses from eighteen nütongzhi fans and fully completed questionnaires from ten of those. All ten of the fully completed questionnaires came from Taiwan. While this sample is far too small to draw quantitative conclusions about the nature of Sandee's nütongzhi fan base, the aim of my project is to make a qualitative study of the responses of Sandee's nütongzhi fans. Certain limits regarding the sample of respondents must be noted. Most important, because the calls for respondents were posted on the Internet, largely at BBS sites on university servers, it must be assumed that, on the basis of larger-scale surveys of Internet use by lesbians in Taiwan, the majority of respondents to my questionnaire are either students or young (twenty-something) white-collar workers with the knowledge, leisure, and resources to spend time socializing in these nütongzhi cyberspaces.[30] Despite the limitations, my research illuminates a branch of the available discourses through which lesbian fans interpret Sandee's significance, especially in relation to feminism and lesbianism.

Fan responses to the question of why they like Sandee indicate that much of the singer's attraction for these young, lesbian-identified women lies in their perception of her self-assurance and uncompromising adherence to her own opinions, including the feminist social critique that fans read in her songs and public statements:

> Now she's a famous musician, but in her music and her thinking she still holds to her own opinions. Maybe that's the reason I liked her as soon as I heard her music. Many of her lyrics are concerned with social critique and feminism, and they give you lots of different points of view to consider. . . . I think she does have a connection with feminism, because what the opinions expressed in her lyrics criticize is masculinist power.

> My favorite is her album that's a best-of plus live recordings, because on that album the musical expression is the most spirited, and the lyrics

contain the most social criticism. I like the way her music shakes you up, plus the directness of her lyrics.

I like her true boldness in writing her own feelings into her lyrics—it's very real, just great. I like her languorous voice that nevertheless shows she has her own opinions and beliefs. I like so much, so much [about her].

As this final response in particular suggests, these fans' perception of Sandee's independent-mindedness articulates to strong affective responses as much as—perhaps inextricable from—the fans' intellectual commitment to a shared feminist politics. Perhaps these fans' construction of Sandee as a boldly self-defining woman artist activates such powerful affective responses due partly to the parallel relation one can infer with the fans' own activity of identification. We might even ask whether Sandee's star image speaks so forcefully to these young feminist women precisely because her public performance as a self-assured young feminist expressing "her own opinions," "her own beliefs," and "her own feelings" offers a model and a mirror of the same self-fashioning processes in which the young fans engage through their fandom.

The attraction of Sandee's fans to her star image's signification of female independence echoes statements made by fans of Hong Kong–based Cantonese-/Mandarin-/Japanese-/English-singing pop superstar Faye Wong, as analyzed by Anthony Fung and Michael Curtin.[31] Through a discussion of Faye's constantly metamorphosing star persona, Fung and Curtin demonstrate the new profitability in regional Chinese markets of female star images associated with nonconformity and challenges to conservative gender ideologies.[32] The authors show that Faye's superstardom is, paradoxically, centrally reliant on the idea of her "alternativeness," in a twist that complicates the dialectics of the "mainstream" versus the "alternative" as well as the presumptive opposition between the "politics" of feminism and the "commercialism" of the music industry.[33] Sandee's music is far less commercially successful than Faye's, and her challenge to conservative gender ideologies is significantly more overt—particularly insofar as Sandee openly avows a feminist position. Nevertheless, both of these star phenomena attest to the increasing salience, and indeed remarkable salability, of a critical politics of "girlhood" in Chinese popular music since the mid-1990s.

In addition to her overtly stated feminist politics, Sandee's music for some of her nütongzhi fans also encodes a certain, much less clearly stated lesbian significance. One female Taiwanese student living in the United States gave a compelling account of how Sandee's nütongzhi significance has resonated in her own life: "One reason [why I think there's a link between Sandee and the topic of nütongzhi] is that my first—and only—partner's voice sounded a lot like Sandee's. When speaking on the phone with her I discovered her voice was very pleasant, just like Sandee's, and it was then that my desire to love women was aroused." In this response, the particularly "pleasant-sounding" (*haoting*) quality of Sandee's singing voice appears to act as a catalyst for both the desire between the respondent and her distant partner, on the other end of the phone, and the respondent's recognition of her own queer longing. Such a response demonstrates that the absorption by a particular star of nütongzhi significance for particular listeners is a highly unpredictable process, based on the idiosyncrasies of individual association, memory, and desire as much as on the ostensible content of a star's image and musical output. The same fan continues: "Another reason [why I think there's a link between Sandee and the topic of nütongzhi] is that I think Sandee is a singer with a female consciousness. Her personal life, her public statements, her essays and song lyrics, her whole image, all have quite a different feel than [those of] a mainstream, heterosexual woman. I think this image has a great capacity to draw my identification."

Sandee speculates that her image as freethinking and independent may be one reason for her popularity with a young lesbian audience: "maybe because originally, homosexuals felt they were a minority within society, and at that stage in Taiwan my music was fairly alternative, also a minority thing, they were naturally attracted to it."[34] As another fan put it, "you might say that her bold, unique, marginal style (in contrast with the mainstream market) has attracted many lesbian fans, who are similarly positioned outside of mainstream society." What attracts these particular fans is, in part, the idea of difference or alternativeness that adheres to Sandee's image—even while the ambiguous appearance of the lesbian topic in popular music like Sandee's is in fact enabled by the new interiority of this subject to public discourse.[35]

Same-Sex Love and the Ordinary Girl

In my analysis I suggest that the appeal of Sandee's music to women who identify with the category nütongzhi can be partly explained through the shared investment of Sandee and this group of women in a feminist critique of hegemonic, patriarchal social relations, and relatedly through the fans' identification with Sandee's star image as a confident, independent, and unconventional woman. I also think, however, that Sandee's music is itself particularly amenable to lesbian interpretation, and indeed, many of the respondents told me that they particularly enjoy Sandee's incisive lyrics.

The song that most closely references the subject of lesbianism is her 1999 song "Beautiful Girl" ("Meilide nüsheng"). The lyrics of this upbeat pop song are as follows:

Falling in love with a beautiful girl
Pretty wig
Falling in love with a beautiful girl
Opium scent

Falling in love with a beautiful girl
Artistic nails
Falling in love with a beautiful girl
Nylon stockings.

I want to fall in love with a beautiful girl
No matter what she looks like.
I want to fall in love with a beautiful girl
At this moment.

Falling in love with a beautiful girl
Split skirt
Falling in love with a beautiful girl
Wonder Bra
Falling in love with a beautiful girl
Elegant heels
Falling in love with a beautiful girl
Shhh! Don't speak.

(Refrain)

My love is too much
The elevator won't close
If I turn my eyes I'll lose control
My heart falls nervous of its own accord.

I want the beautiful girl
To live downstairs.
I want the beautiful girl
To move into my place.
I want the beautiful girl
To look at me.
I want the beautiful girl
to take me home.[36]

Sung by a woman known for her support of gay politics and for her lesbian
fan base, these lyrics seem to encode a fairly obvious invocation of lesbian
identity and desire. Interestingly, however, when asked to interpret the
degree of lesbian signification encoded in the lyrics of this song, Sandee's
nütongzhi fans gave a mixed response. In answer to the question "Do you
think 'Beautiful Girl' is a nütongzhi song?" fans provided the following
array of answers:

> I don't really think so, but I don't really *not* think so, either. . . . I think girls
> who aren't nütongzhi are also able to appreciate other girls, so I don't think
> there's anything strange about it.

> I don't think so!

Yes, it is. [Sandee] said so herself. It's very obvious from the lyrics.

[Sandee] said she wrote "Beautiful Girl" from the point of view of a boy looking at a girl.

No. Ordinary heterosexual girls can gasp in admiration of a beautiful girl, too!

It could be applied to nütongzhi; I guess it all depends on how the individual interprets it. I think if a woman sings . . . this song, it can be used to express the feelings between two nütongzhi. But if it was sung by a boy, then it's no different from normal heterosexual feeling!

It seems to be the projection of a masculine desire for a woman. Perhaps because I've always heard Sandee's lyrics from a very female, slightly ironic perspective, I haven't interpreted them in a nütongzhi way.

Yes, I think it is! But some people tell me it's just her satirizing the state of contemporary society.

Yes! But I think you could also say no. Because I guess everyone loves a beautiful girl: boys and girls are all attracted by a beautiful girl's loveliness.

Rather than simply claiming the song as a straightforward expression of nütongzhi as a minority sexual identity, these fans give voice to the insight that the song is not exactly a nütongzhi song, but not precisely *not* one either.[37] There are at least two possible interpretations of the fans' collective ambivalence. In an earlier analysis of these mixed responses, I proposed that because the song lyrics allowed for both queer and straight readings, they echoed the broader conditions of presence of the lesbian topic in 1990s public culture in Taiwan. That is, they positioned *nütongxinglian* (female homosexuality) in continual oscillation between reticence and audibility, between silence and speech—not exactly a presence but not exactly an absence in the culture at large. Arguably, that interpretation implicitly understands sexual desire between women on a minoritizing model: it tends to presume that female homosexuality is only truly (as opposed to ambiguously) present if linked with a substantive individual identity—by implication, an identity proper to a defined minority group of women who identify through the category nütongzhi. Hence, my earlier analysis proposed that "according to these fans' responses, 'Beautiful girl' dramatizes the precipitous moment when 'an ordinary girl's appreciation of another girl' threatens . . . to become a desire explicitly linked with the relatively new sexual and political identity nütongzhi." Even though the point being made was about precisely the blurriness of the line dividing these two terms, nonetheless, in that sentence "an ordinary girl's appreciation of another girl" remains conceptually distinct from "the relatively new sexual and political identity nütongzhi." For the two to become equivalent, the former, implicitly "heterosexual," situation would need to change to become a "homosexual" one, as in the latter case. And indeed, the minoritizing, identitarian associations of the term *nütongzhi* itself support such a reading: in a strong sense, in self-identifying as a nütongzhi, a girl ceases to be "ordinary" insofar as in dominant understandings, an "ordinary girl," as the fan quoted earlier suggests, is defined by her potential for heterosexual attachment.[38]

I now complicate my previous analysis by coming at the issue from another angle—one that privileges not the specific minority identity-category *nütongzhi* and its presence or absence in popular culture but rather the idea of the "ordinary girl's" potential love for another girl—a potential that may exist in conceptual parallel with, rather than simple contradiction of, a concurrent potential for heterosexual love. In other words, instead of understanding Sandee's song as being about a heterosexual norm tipping over into a nonnormative lesbian identity and desire, we may interpret it as presenting a universalizing model of same-sex love among girls.[39] Rather than indexing a crossing from a purely straight femininity to a purely lesbian identity, the song could be seen as suggesting that the potential for same-sex love may be internal to the category "girl" (*nüsheng*) itself—and hence can be avowed without the necessity to claim a minority sexual identity like nütongzhi. This interpretation sits well with the fans' responses, which, taken as a group, seem wary of too straightforward a link between the song's lyrics and the minority sexual identity nütongzhi referenced in my question to them.

Such an interpretation is also consonant with an influential discourse in representations of girls' and young women's same-sex love seen throughout modern and contemporary Chinese-language media and literary cultures. That discourse, which I analyze in detail elsewhere, constructs female same-sex love (*nütongxinglian*) on a universalizing rather than a minoritizing model, as an experience that might be had by *any* woman or girl, rather than only by a minority of specific women demarcated by their embrace of a nütongzhi identity. Interestingly for the current analysis vis-à-vis the category of girlhood, this universalizing discourse on female same-sex love frequently constructs it as an experience proper to girls and young women—an experience that will in time, albeit often regretfully, be superseded by the demands of marital heterosexuality.[40] A classic and economical illustration of this pervasive discourse on same-sex love as a quasi-universal experience of feminine girlhood is found, for example, in female author Chu T'ien-hsin's story "Waves Scour the Sands" ("Lang tao sha"). First published in 1976, when Chu herself was still a schoolgirl, "Waves" is a coming-of-age narrative centering on the adolescent girl Little Qi.[41] Qi is depicted quasi-satirically, yet also empathetically, as embodying an amalgam of characteristics conventionally associated with girlishness in 1970s Taiwan. She is dreamy and shy; favors pleated skirts, pinafores, ankle socks, and fabrics printed with tiny flowers, puppies, and kittens; affects a flirtatious, childlike demeanor; writes using different colored pens in her diary each night while gazing at the moon; is subject to fits of romantic melancholy similar to those of heroines in popular romance novels; and falls passionately in love with two successive tomboy best friends before ultimately, regretfully, giving in to the romantic attentions of a local boy.[42] According to the discourse of girlish same-sex love that Chu's story both reflects and reproduces, female homosexuality is conceptually delimited by a particular period in a woman's life rather than by a particular category of persons; it is defined according to a temporal rather than a minority-identitarian logic.[43] As some of Sandee's fan responses imply, any girl, not only a nütongzhi , may fall in love with a beautiful girl. In that construction as, arguably, in Sandee's song, we see a culturally specific popular definition of both normative girlhood and female homoerotic desire, with the latter figured relatively openly as internal, rather than exterior or other, to the former.

Conclusion

In the first part of this chapter I illustrated the complex interrelation between two contemporary feminine identity categories in Taiwan, girlhood (nüsheng) and lesbianism (nütongzhi), by exploring how each term is articulated with varieties of popular feminist discourse, from "girl power" and "girl rock" in music cultures to lesbian feminism as a key influence on nütongzhi identities and politics. That linkage via feminist rhetoric, I argued, accounts in some measure for the popularity of a feminist singer-songwriter like Sandee Chan with a self-identifying nütongzhi public. As that analysis shows, the category nütongzhi enables novel conceptualizations and practices of critical girlhood in Taiwan; it produces ways of "being a girl" that not only openly challenge masculinist cultural authority but also precipitate powerful new forms of intragender sociality and solidarity between girls and between women. The final section of this analysis, however, begins to point toward some of the gaps and occlusions in nütongzhi conceived, as it usually is, as an identity. Liu and Ding have shown how the emergence of middle-class, intellectual formations of lesbian-feminist nütongzhi culture and identity in the early 1990s marginalized and demonized earlier, working-class female same-sex subcultural formations such as those found in T/po (comparable to butch/femme) bar cultures. Nütongzhi leaves out other forms of women's same-sex love as well. These include formations of feminine homoeroticism conceived on a universalizing rather than a minoritizing model and not attached to a concretely distinct sexual identity, as I have shown in the final section on the pervasive cultural understanding of the "ordinary girl's" (temporary) capacity for same-sex love. Other formations of same-sex sociality, sex, and romance among young women that are not fully encompassed by the nütongzhi identity include identifications as lala and lazi—terms that have risen to popularity in the Chinese-language cyberspaces spanning Taiwan, Hong Kong, China, and the worldwide Chinese diaspora and are arguably more associated with the playfulness, ephemerality, anonymity, and disembodiment of computer-mediated communication than with the clearer-cut identity and body politics of the term *nütongzhi*. Although undeniably representing a form of critical femininity in Taiwan today, *nütongzhi* should not be reified as a locus of essential "resistance," "transgression," or "subversion" of hegemonic forces. Like the category "girl" itself, *nütongzhi* is a taxonomic device that enables certain positive identifications even as it disables and excludes other forms of subjectivity; it is marginalized by hegemonic formations in one area only to become itself hegemonic in relation to even more marginal formations somewhere else. Like any cultural category, it is also situated in both history and geography; it is formed and destined ultimately to be unformed by the emergence of new social forces that make and remake gendered and sexual selves in ever-shifting configurations.

NOTES

Parts of this chapter appeared in Fran Martin, "Women on This Planet: Globalisation and Girl Rock in Taiwan," *Perfect Beat* 7, no. 4 (2006): 5–31; and in Martin, "The Perfect Lie: Sandee Chan and Lesbian Respectability in Mandarin Pop Music," *Inter-Asia Cultural Studies* 4, no. 2 (August 2003): 264–280. They are included here with gracious permission of *Perfect Beat* and of Taylor and Francis Journals. Some material is paraphrased from the introduction to my book *Situating Sexualities: Queer Representation in Taiwanese Fiction, Film and Public Culture* (Hong Kong: Honk Kong University Press, 2003).

1. On transforming categories of feminine gender in early twentieth-century China, see, for example, Sarah E. Stevens, "Figuring Modernity: The New Woman and the Modern Girl in Republican China," *NWSA Journal* 15, no. 3 (Fall 2003): 82–103.

2. The industrial background on Mandarin pop production in 1990s Taiwan can be found in my essay "Women on This Planet: Globalisation and Girl Rock in Taiwan," *Perfect Beat* 7, no. 4 (January 2006).

3. See, for example, Michel Foucault, *History of Sexuality*, vol. 1, trans. Robert Hurley (London: Penguin, 1990); David Halperin, "Is There a History of Sexuality?" in *The Lesbian and Gay Studies Reader*, ed. Henry Abelove, Michele Aina Barale, and David M. Halperin (New York: Routledge, 1993), 416–431; John D'Emilio, "Capitalism and Gay Identity," in *Powers of Desire: The Politics of Sexuality*, ed. Ann Snitow, Christine Stansell, and Sharon Thompson (New York: Monthly Review Press, 1983), 100–113; Jeffrey Weeks, *Against Nature: Essays on History, Sexuality, and Identity* (Concord, MA: Paul and Co., 1991).

4. Halperin, "Is There a History of Sexuality?" 416.

5. D'Emilio, "Capitalism and Gay Identity."

6. For an Australian-published conversation on "global queering," see Dennis Altman, "The New World of 'Gay Asia,'" in *Asian and Pacific Inscriptions: Identities, Ethnicities, Nationalities*, ed. Suvendrini Perera (Melbourne: Meridian, 1995), 121–138; Altman, "On Global Queering," *Australian Humanities Review* 2 (July–September 1996), http://www.lib.latrobe.edu.au/AHR/home.html (accessed September 10, 1996); and Altman, "Rupture or Continuity? The Internationalization of Gay Identities," *Social Text* 48 (1996): 77–94; Donald Morton, "Global (Sexual) Politics, Class Struggle, and the Queer Left," *Critical InQueeries* 1, no. 3 (May 1997): 1–30; Peter Jackson, "The Persistence of Gender: From Ancient Indian *Pandakas* to Modern Thai *Gay-Quings*," *Meanjin* 55, no. 1 (1996): 110–120; and Fran Martin and Chris Berry, "Queer 'n' Asian on

the Net: Syncretic Sexualities in Taiwan and Korean Cyberspace," *Critical InQueeries* 2, no. 1 (June 1998): 67–93.

7. Elizabeth A. Povinelli and George Chauncey, "Thinking Sexuality Transnationally: An Introduction," *GLQ* 5, no. 4 (1999): 439. See also the entire special issue, E. Povinelli and G. Chauncey, eds., "Thinking Sexuality Transnationally," *GLQ* 5, no. 4 (1999); Phillip Brian Harper, Anne McClintock, José Esteban Muñoz, and Trish Rosen, eds., "Queer Transexions of Race, Nation, and Gender," special issue, *Social Text*, nos. 52–53 (Fall–Winter 1997); Cindy Patton and Benigno Sánchez-Eppler, eds., *Queer Diasporas* (Durham, NC: Duke University Press, 2000); and Chris Berry, Fran Martin, and Audrey Yue, eds., *Mobile Cultures: New Media and Queer Asia* (Durham, NC: Duke University Press, 2003).

8. Inderpal Grewal and Caren Kaplan, "Global Identities: Theorizing Transnational Studies of Sexuality," *GLQ* 7, no. 4 (2001): 663–679, 667; Peter Jackson, "An Explosion of Thai Identities: Global Queering and Re-imagining Queer Theory," *Culture, Health and Sexuality* 2, no. 4 (2000): 405–424; Lawrence Cohenm, "Holi in Banaras and the Mahaland of Modernity," *GLQ* 2, no. 4 (1995): 399–424, 401.

9. James Clifford, "Traveling Cultures," in *Cultural Studies*, ed. Laurence Grossberg, Cary Nelson, and Paula Treichler (New York: Routledge, 1992), 96–117.

10. Other social movements include the trade union movement, the environmental protection movement, the indigenous people's movement, and consumer rights groups.

11. Lee Yuen-chen, "How the Feminist Movement Won Media Space in Taiwan: Observations by a Feminist Activist," in *Spaces of Their Own: Women's Public Sphere in Transnational China*, ed. Mayfair Mei-hui Yang (Minneapolis: University of Minnesota Press, 1999).

12. Mayfair Mei-hui Yang, introduction to *Spaces of Their Own*.

13. See Fran Martin, "Taiwan's Literature of Transgressive Sexuality," in *Angelwings: Contemporary Queer Fiction from Taiwan*, ed. and trans. Fran Martin (Honolulu: University of Hawai'i Press, 2003), 1–28, for a more complete account of these cultural movements.

14. These include *T* (tomboy/butch), *po* (wife/femme), *lala*, *lazi* (associated with queer Internet cultures), and *nütongxinglian* (female homosexual). Some of these alternative terms are discussed again at the conclusion of this chapter. See also Tze-lan D. Sang, *The Emerging Lesbian: Female Same-Sex Desire in Modern China* (Chicago: University of Chicago Press, 2003), esp. 225–254.

15. Liu and Ding argue that the new, middle-class, feminist-inflected category *nütongzhi* arose in explicit contestation of older, gender-based same-sex identities as found in working-class *T/po* (comparable to butch/femme) bar cultures. Ding Naifei and Jenpeng Liu, "Crocodile Skin, Lesbian Stuffing: Half-Man Half-Horse Qiu Miaojin" (in Chinese), in *Penumbrae Query Shadow: Queer Reading Tactics* (Chungli: Zhongyang Daxue Xingbie Yanjiu Shi, 2007), 67–105; and Fran Martin, "Stigmatic Bodies: The Corporeal Qiu Miaojin," in *Embodied Modernities: Corporeality, Representation and Chinese Cultures*, ed. Fran Martin and Larissa Heinrich (Honolulu: University of Hawai'i Press, 2006), 177–194.

16. Gayle Wald, "Just a Girl? Rock Music, Feminism, and the Cultural Construction of Female Youth," *Signs* 23, no. 3 (1998); reprinted in *Rock over the Edge: Transformations in Popular Music Culture*, ed. Roger Beebe, Denise Fulbrook, and Ben Saunders (Durham, NC: Duke University Press, 2002), 587–588.

17. Mavis Bayton, "Punks, Feminists, Lesbians, and Riot Grrrls," in *Frock Rock: Women Performing Popular Music* (New York: Oxford University Press, 1998); Catherine Driscoll, "Girl Culture, Revenge and Global Capitalism: Cybergirls, Riot Grrrls, Spice Girls," *Australian Feminist Studies* 14, no. 29 (1999); and Driscoll, *Girls: Feminine Adolescence in Popular Culture and Cultural Theory* (New York: Columbia University Press, 2002); Joanne Gottlieb and Gayle Wald, "Smells Like Teen Spirit: Riot Grrrls, Revolution, and Women in Independent Rock," in *Microphone Fiends*, ed. Andrew Ross and Tricia Rose (New York: Routledge, 1994); Mary Celeste Kearney, "The Missing Links: Riot Grrrl—Feminism— Lesbian Culture," and Marion Leonard, " 'Rebel Girl, You Are the Queen of My World': Feminism, 'Subculture' and Grrrl Power," in *Sexing the Groove: Popular Music and Gender*, ed. Sheila Whitely (New York: Routledge, 1997); and Leonard,

"Paper Planes: Travelling the New Grrrl Geographies," in *CoolPlaces: Geographies of Youth Cultures*, ed. Tracey Skelton and Gill Valentine (New York: Routledge, 1998); Neil Nehring, "The Riot Grrrls and Carnival," in *Popular Music, Gender, and Postmodernism: Anger Is an Energy* (Thousand Oaks, CA: Sage, 1997); and Simon Reynolds and Joy Press, "There's a Riot Going On: Grrrls against Boy-Rock," in *The Sex Revolts: Gender, Rebellion and Rock 'n' Roll* (London: Serpent's Tail, 1995).

18. Driscoll, *Girls*, 272, 275–276.

19. Sandee Chan, *Hai hao: Chen Shanni de shu* (Taipei: Shangzhou Chuban, 2000).

20. Sandee Chan, interview by Ma Shi-fang, November 9, 2000 (my translation), http://music543.com/feature/activities/sandee04.htm (accessed October 3, 2002); Angry Women in Rock Web site, http://music543.com/feature/AngryWomenSW.htm (accessed October 3, 2002).

21. For a selection of Hsia Yü's poetry in English, see Hsia Yü, *Fusion Kitsch: Poems from the Chinese of Hsia Yü*, trans. Steve Bradbury (Brookline, MA: Zephyr Press, 2001).

22. Sandee Chan, "Surveillance/Violating Vision," from *Humor?* 1999 (my translation).

23. Chan, as quoted at Grrrl Rock Web site, http://music543.com/community/read.doml?now=GrrrlRock&file=M.986437627.A (accessed August 23, 2001).

24. Angry Women in Rock Web site.

25. Various artists, "Girls Going Forward," on *Girls Going Forward* (*Nüsheng Xiang Qian Zou*), May 2000 (my translation).

26. Chan, interview by Ma Shi-fang.

27. Driscoll, "Girl Culture," 173–74.

28. Ibid., 186.

29. I am indebted to Josette Thong for her generous assistance in refining my translation of the questionnaire and posting it at local Taiwan BBS sites. Many, many thanks, too, to all the questionnaire respondents.

30. See Fran Martin, "That Global Feeling: Sexual Subjectivities and Imagined Geographies in Chinese-Language Lesbian Cyberspaces," in *Internationalizing Internet Studies*, ed. Mark McLelland and Gerard Goggin (New York: Routledge, 2008); see also the 2001 Fourth Taiwanese lesbian Internet census, *Di si jie wanglu lazi renkou pucha*, http://98.to/lalasurvey/ (accessed February 14, 2007).

31. Anthony Fung and Michael Curtin, "The Anomalies of Being Faye (Wong): Gender Politics in Chinese Popular Music," *International Journal of Cultural Studies* 5, no. 3 (September 2002): 186.

32. See also J. Lawrence Witzleben, "Cantopop and Mandapop in Pre-Postcolonial Hong Kong: Identity Negotiation in the Performances of Anita Mui Yim-Fong," *Popular Music* 18, no. 2 (1999).

33. Fung and Curtin, "Anomalies of Being Faye," 274.

34. Chan, as quoted by Angry Women in Rock Web site (my translation).

35. Again, the limited character of the audience demographic reached with this survey must be emphasized here. Although particular fans, and Sandee herself, construct Sandee's lesbian fandom as based on a shared significance of "outsiderness," it is by no means the case that all Taiwanese lesbians become attracted to Sandee's music as a result of suffering outsider status. In fact, many T bar DJs favor mainstream Mandarin and Minnan pop music over the singer-songwriter sound of artists like Sandee, and it is evident that many factors other than sexuality—including region, first language and family history, class affiliation, level of education, generation, and the like—play important roles in influencing any individual's taste in music.

36. Sandee Chan, "Beautiful Girl" ("Meilide nüsheng"), 1999 (my translation).

37. One fan, however, cites "Beautiful Girl" as one of her favorite songs "because I think about beautiful girls, too."

38. Fran Martin, "The Perfect Lie: Sandee Chan and Lesbian Respectability in Mandarin Pop Music," *Inter-Asia Cultural Studies* 4, no. 2 (August 2003): 264–280.

39. On universalizing versus minoritizing conceptualizations of sexualities, see Eve Kosofsky Sedgwick, *Epistemology of the Closet* (Berkeley: University of California Press, 1990), chap. 1.

40. Fran Martin, *Backward Glances: Chinese Popular Cultures and the Female Homoerotic Imaginary* (Durham, NC: Duke University Press, 2010).

41. Little Qi is referred to most frequently in Chu's story as a *nühai*; the term's infantilizing overtones sit appropriately with her character.

42. Chu T'ien-hsin, "Waves Scour the Sands," trans. and with a critical introduction by Fran Martin, *Renditions* 63 (Spring 2005): 7–32; see also my analysis in *Backward Glances*.

43. However, the universalizing, temporal discourse on the girlhood same-sex love of the feminine "everywoman" coexists with a parallel gender-minoritizing discourse on the T (tomboy), or masculine same-sex loving woman, as a specific category of person. The relation between the T discourse and the universalizing one is complex and is explored at length in *Backward Glances*.

PART II

THE POLITICS OF GIRLHOOD

The chapters in this section explore how girls have responded to global developments such as war and political unrest, as well as how girls operate as global actors and agents. How has girlhood been imagined within the context of the nation-state and international politics? Do girls have unique roles to play as citizens of their nation and of the world? The authors in this section seek to answer these questions, revealing how institutions reflect ideologies of the state and how girls react in various ways to those messages.

Both Jesse Hingson and E. Thomas Ewing examine girls in autocratic political systems. Hingson compares the discourse of patriarchal protection of family and children in nineteenth-century Argentina with the forced confiscation and exile of one girl and her family during the Rosas regime. Moving beyond a narrative of victimization, Hingson finds the agency of the young girl as she presses a law suit for restitution over a decade later. Similarly Ewing examines the broad institutional shape of a dictatorship through the experience of one girl. His research focuses on 1930s Soviet Russia and the suspicion that befell a particular family, but in the process he shows how a girl, even in a repressive political climate, claimed a space for herself and sought to construct her own identity through her diary writings. Ironically, the diary was used by the state as evidence to impose exile on her and her family.

Jan Voogd and Lisa Ossian examine British and American girlhood through the lens of world war. Voogd argues that the participation of African American girls in nonunion labor threatened to disrupt not only Chicago's labor movement but allied cooperation during World War I, as unions sought to halt the shipment of non-union-produced supplies to Great Britain. Ossian contends that British and American girls during World War II were defined as vulnerable victims of wartime upheaval but also tapped to encourage morale and militarism. Similarly, Ann Kordas examines representations of girls and their connection to national identity and international politics. Looking specifically at images of girl gymnasts from the United States, the Soviet Union, and Romania during the Cold War, Kordas demonstrates how girlhood symbolized and served as an outlet for the anxieties and competitive national identities of this era, especially for the press.

Last, Jessamy Harvey examines the Marian visions of four adolescent girls in Garabandal, Spain, between 1961 and 1965, arguing that the actions and words of these girls left traces—written, visual, and material—that have been preserved because they were endowed by adults with symbolic significance. The girls' visions sparked a global counterrevolutionary Catholic movement that repudiates the Second Vatican reforms. What is of interest is how national and international believers have interpreted the girls' actions by forming and maintaining an international religious movement.

A comparison of girls' experiences in different contexts illustrates that girls were not only affected by forces beyond their control but they were also engaged, even in repressive systems, in actively shaping their worlds. These authors show how girls were not only victims of political developments, but also how they resisted or participated as agents of the state. Taken together, these chapters show how girlhood struggles to survive in even the most disruptive of times.

5 Girlhood Memories and the Politics of Justice in Post-Rosas Argentina

THE RESTITUTION SUIT OF OLALLA ALVAREZ

JESSE HINGSON

In 1853, a young woman named Olalla Alvarez returned to the province of Córdoba, Argentina, after a twelve-year forced exile in Chile, demanding to see a judge. She sought to initiate a lawsuit against Pedro Sueldo, who was a provincial judge during the reign of Juan Manuel de Rosas, the Federalist dictator who had ruled most of Argentina between 1829 and 1852. In an affidavit, Olalla recalled what happened to her and her family. One night in October 1841, when she was only twelve years old, she awoke to the sounds of horses and wagons riding up the path to her home, a modest-sized farm with a variety of livestock. Several men, including the local magistrate, Sueldo, and a large number of tough-looking gauchos, dismounted from their horses and gathered in front of the farmhouse. Sueldo shouted forcefully into the house for Jesús Pérez, Olalla's stepfather, to come outside. After not receiving a response, the exasperated judge then announced that Jesús had been publicly denounced as a deserter, a "savage," and a Unitarian, that is, a member of the political party opposing Rosas's rule. With the full authority of the governor, moreover, Sueldo declared that the house and all "moveable property" would be confiscated. At that moment, Olalla's mother, Teresa, ran out of the house and pleaded with the judge that her husband was innocent of these charges and that she and her only daughter should be spared. Unflinching, Sueldo promptly ordered his men to strip the entire estate of its livestock and tools.[1]

In her 1853 lawsuit, Olalla argued that because she was no longer legally a "girl" but a "woman," she had the "right" to accuse Sueldo of abusing his authority when he was employed as a *rosista* official and of profiting personally from the confiscation of her family's property.[2] In seeking justice, Olalla wanted Sueldo jailed for "abusing his authority" and "using and enjoying" her family's property "like he was the legitimate owner of it" and for her family's property to be promptly returned to her.[3] Indeed, she chose a favorable moment to initiate such a request, as Argentina was making a transition from one regime to another. Rosas and his provincial allies had been toppled in the year prior to her suit, and dozens of individuals and families within and beyond Argentina were claiming that they had been wrongfully attacked by the regime. Olalla, however, insisted that the provincial judge make time to hear her complaint. She had traveled a long way to make her claims and believed that political events were now in her favor.

Although the authorities of the new regime were sympathetic to her plight, Olalla would endure a difficult process, both emotionally and legally. Within the context of mid-nineteenth-century Argentina, she had few rights and privileges. As a young unmarried woman in exile for political reasons, Olalla was expected to be compliant in her role—appreciative to the judge and the provincial state for hearing her case. She also had little evidence to prove her claims. She was only twelve years old when this traumatic event happened, and she had been forced into exile for more than a decade. By the time she returned to Córdoba, both parents had passed away, and only overgrown fields and a decrepit house remained of her family's property. In her escape from Argentina during the early 1840s, she and her mother had barely enough time to leave, much less gather documents such as wills, titles, deeds, and letters to be used at a later, indeterminate date. She never knew if she would ever return. To make matters worse, many potential witnesses such as friends and neighbors were not available because they, and hundreds of others living in the province, had either died or moved away. Moreover, the political instability, civil wars, and state violence that characterized the Rosas era forced thousands throughout Argentina out of their homes. The absence of eyewitness testimony meant that Olalla would have to shoulder more responsibility in keeping her lawsuit alive. How could she possibly overcome these odds?

In this chapter I narrate the story of Olalla Alvarez, who, as an adolescent girl, survived the political purges of the Rosas era and who, as a young woman, sought restitution after the regime met its end in 1852. I tell her story by interpreting a single lawsuit that she filed with provincial authorities in the early nineteenth century. Interwoven in these rare legal narratives are the recollections of a young woman who experienced loss, death, exile, and return in just a few short years.[4] As she approached womanhood, Olalla had lost her parents, heritage, lands, and possible livelihood. Even at an early age, she found the wherewithal to initiate court proceedings and fight for her family's property rights. In this way, she demonstrated that local justice and politics were not abstract principles. Both as an adolescent girl and someone on the verge of womanhood, Olalla forced authorities to pay more attention to questions of justice and restitution.

This analysis of Olalla's memories through her restitution suit against Pedro Sueldo makes several important contributions to the history of girls and girlhood. First, it confirms the theoretical proposition that girls throughout world history have been capable of using a variety of strategies to survive dangerous political, economic, and social circumstances.[5] Forcibly uprooted and exiled from her home with little to no assistance, Olalla relied primarily on her mother as they eked out an existence and slowly made their way out of Córdoba. Yet, even at what seems like a young age by today's standards, Olalla contributed a great deal to the family's welfare and made sure to get a firm grasp of the legal proceedings that her family had initiated. Second, Olalla's story puts into stark relief the unique experiences of a girl in nineteenth-century Argentina. Historians of Latin America have made tremendous strides during the last two decades in advancing the history of children, a growing yet complex subfield of history.[6] These studies have greatly added to our understanding of the relationships between children and parents in maintaining wealth within difficult political and economic contexts and the efforts by leaders of emerging nation-states in Latin America to control delinquency and create formal educational institutions that would socialize boys and girls as "citizens."[7] Yet, on a conceptual level, these scholars in Latin American history often conflate the history of girls and girlhood with the field of the history of children in general. As a result, few studies in Latin American history have focused exclusively on girls as historical actors.[8] This telling of Olalla's story is one of the few attempts to emphasize girls' experiences within a context of civil war and nation building in Latin America.

Evidence of Olalla's traumatic story is located primarily in the provincial archives of Córdoba, Argentina's second largest province. Her restitution petition represents one among many cases that date back to the 1840s, when hundreds of families were suspected of political subversion and stripped of their rights, until the 1850s, when the new regime allowed claims for the return of their rights and property. To look at how these cases were resolved after 1852, I cross-referenced notarial accounts with previous accounts; lawsuits by other former exiles seeking restitution also filled in important gaps. Ultimately, Olalla's traumatic memories of her childhood and the laws that gave girls specific rights in marriage, inheritance, and education were the most important bases of her claims.

Reconstruction of the events that led up to Olalla's restitution, through reliance on legal proceedings and recollections, must be done with great care. Memory is fleeting as time passes, and people (either consciously or unconsciously) may want to block out traumatic events in their lives. In his recent study of war veterans and laborers in Argentina during the Rosas era, historian Ricardo Salvatore discovered evidence that hundreds of war veterans could only selectively remember the names of officers in their units, characteristics of enemy soldiers and officers, and battles and raids in which they had participated.[9] Young girls like Olalla, although not participants on the front lines of these battles, had experiences that were no less traumatic to them, as recent scholarship on the impact of full-scale war and military conflict on children's memories confirms.[10] Olalla's life was fragmented and unstable, and the details that provide the evidentiary basis of her life story are too. What is known about her (and her family) may be gleaned from legal documents produced first by Córdoba's local law enforcement officials. We know much more about her as the child of an accused political criminal and then through provincial judicial institutions as a plaintiff in a lawsuit. Olalla's demands, wishes, and more importantly, memories are filtered through the transcriptions of adults, primarily men, in official positions, such as the judges, scribes, and lawyers who took on her case.

Olalla's World: Girlhood, Local Justice, and Loss

During the early nineteenth century, new nation-states throughout Spanish America experienced the rise of brutally repressive regimes ruled by regional strongmen, or caudillos, in response to the disorder left over from the independence movements.[11] During a moment of political crisis in 1829, Juan Manuel de Rosas assumed power in Buenos Aires, Argentina's wealthiest and most populous province. As an ideology, rosismo required unwavering belief in Rosas as the embodiment of Federalism and support for his control of import revenues in and out of the port city.[12] His main enemy, the Unitarians, imagined a liberal nation that promoted European-style "progress" and "civilization" and rejected the "barbarism" of Rosas's Federalist supporters, including Argentina's poorer gaucho population and their caudillo leaders. Like Rosas, Unitarians sought to concentrate economic and political power in Buenos Aires, but they favored the liberalization of domestic and foreign trade and policies that encouraged European immigration. As Rosas and other Federalist propagandists told it, Unitarians embodied everything that was nefarious, defiant, cunning, sophisticated, unscrupulous, wealthy, anti-Catholic, xenophilic, and evil.[13] The Rosas regime and its allies within the interior sanctioned confiscation, execution, torture, and forced exile as ways of punishing Unitarian suspects.

Controlling Córdoba became an essential element of Rosas's overall strategy to subjugate the interior and eliminate political opponents. With a population of more than 76,000, the province was second largest only to its neighboring province, Buenos Aires.[14] Córdoba also served as an important trade conduit between the interior of Argentina and the bustling port city of Buenos Aires, approximately 420 miles away. Rosas eventually assumed leadership over Córdoba in late 1835 by engineering the election of its governor, Manuel López. Both men defended the large landed and commercial families of the region by launching a series of violent reprisals against those who threatened these interests. These purges lasted until both the López and Rosas regimes fell in 1852.

In October 1840, a severe drought in Córdoba's northern regions sparked a large-scale insurrection.[15] These conditions exposed the entire province to violent insurgent attacks, as Unitarian armies took advantage of the chaos, swept down from the north, and temporarily took the capital. Fighting, however, continued in rural areas as Federalist forces regrouped.

Both Unitarian and Federalist armies rolled through the province, confiscating animals, burning farms, and stealing tools and other implements useful for maintaining their armies.[16] It took several weeks for Federalist leaders to regain full control. After doing so, Manuel López passed an emergency law that gave the provincial state the right to "classify," or identify political suspects in the vernacular of the day, and punish them through imprisonment, capital punishment, and confiscation of property. He ordered local judges to gather information on all of those who were sympathetic to the insurrection and to confiscate their lands and property as punishment.

It is within this context of civil war and violence that Olalla Alvarez's life changed forever. The harsh treatment that Olalla and her mother received at the hands of Pedro Sueldo in October 1841 undoubtedly shaped her worldview, yet well before that fateful night she knew a great deal already about the contours of local legal authority and political culture. Olalla understood, even as an adolescent, that Sueldo was a "judge" and an "authority" who "kept the peace," although she probably could not articulate the complexities of the provincial judicial system. In early nineteenth-century Argentina, peasants and landowners, men and women, young and old, and rich and poor all came to understand judges as stewards and protectors of rural communities. This portrayal meant that local jurists would provide assistance during periods of hardship or aid in the settlement of debts and local disputes.[17] Requests for money, supplies, and animals poured into the offices of local judges, who were more often the only proximate means of recourse. Local judges were especially keen on listening to these cases if the petitioners could provide a concrete example of a male family member who served as a soldier, officer, judge, or any other servant of the Rosas state. Female supplicants would invoke their "service" as mothers, wives, and daughters.[18] These legal demands served to connect society's most affected groups, such as the poor, widows, and laborers, with the state.[19]

During this period, patriarchal authority within the household seemed in decline, in part the result of the absence of male family members due to war, political purges, and the like. Women and girls were able to gain limited independence within the household, and adolescent girls—in particular, in Córdoba, and throughout Argentina—likely were familiar with the practice of crafting petitions to local judges. According to laws in existence within Córdoba and Buenos Aires during the early nineteenth century, twelve-year-old dependent girls had the legal right to hold property on their own if their parents wished it.[20] Even at the height of the Rosas era, girls often sued their parents for property, dowry rights, and the right to marry.[21] In these types of proceedings, girls presented evidence, witnesses, and testimony, which helped them gain experience in front of judges.[22] So although Olalla likely could not demonstrate a sophisticated knowledge of local or national politics, she probably understood that law and politics in her world began and ended with Sueldo as local arbiter and "protector."

Olalla personally knew Sueldo before she was forced out of her home. She had heard friends, neighbors, and her own mother talk about him as the "truest Federalist" but also as a cruel dispenser of justice against Unitarian suspects. Indeed, according to provincial records, he had purged ten families, the highest number among all provincial judges.[23] Confiscation of property was the most common method and also a key component in the war against Unitarians.[24] Gossip quickly spread that Sueldo regularly appropriated furniture, clothes, and money from the "savage Unitarians" for his personal use.[25] According to census records, between 1839 and 1845 Sueldo increased his net worth by more than two thousand pesos, which made him an elite member of society.[26] Manuel López, the provincial governor, favored Sueldo because he hardly ever missed a payment of livestock and materials to the provincial state or the military when it was required.

When Sueldo issued the arrest warrant against Jesús Pérez and confiscated the house and all of the family's property, Olalla experienced a sense of trauma and loss as never before. Rather than arrest the frightened girl and her mother, Sueldo forced them to "abandon" their home with only a "few provisions of food and water" and the clothes on their backs. Although he kept control of Pérez's house, he never intended to live there. Furniture from the house, tools, implements, and farm animals taken during the raid went to a variety of destinations. After being forced out of the house, Olalla recalled wondering about why it was happening to her and why otherwise "good men" would come and take what was "rightfully" hers. She did not mention that she knew about her stepfather's activities or that he had violated political customs or rules. All she knew from Sueldo on that October night in 1841 was that her stepfather had left the province without permission. From her perspective, her stepfather was justified in leaving because he, like many others, needed to find work in financially "desperate times." She did not mention and probably would not have known that her stepfather's absence violated laws that strictly regulated the movement of people within the province during times of political emergency. After all, he had been away on "business" on many occasions and never before had had problems with local authorities. The circumstances in the early 1840s, however, had changed dramatically.[27]

Although her stepfather was away for long stretches, Olalla's testimony reveals a particular closeness with him. For Olalla, Jesús Pérez was a "caring" father who loved her and her mother after her own father had died, for reasons she never shared with the court. Olalla also never indicated whether she knew her stepfather's political tendencies, but she certainly took her "mother's word" later that he was "wrongly accused" of being a "savage Unitarian." Olalla's worldview was thus rooted in the hatred for those responsible for her family's breakup, material loss, and humiliation. Because matters of justice were intensely local, moreover, she consistently maintained from an early age that Sueldo (and not necessarily Rosas or López) was first and foremost culpable for these "crimes."[28]

In late 1841, tapping into the practice of petitioning, Olalla's mother sent quick petitions to Sueldo and then to Governor Manuel López in the hopes that they would see that her husband was wrongly accused. She requested that her property (or at least the property she brought with her as a dowry) be returned to her. These types of requests were not unheard of. Women invoked a variety of legal devices to protect themselves and their property from confiscation for political reasons. They used dowry, divorce, and inheritance to argue that their property was separate from that of their politically accused husbands. Indeed, authorities in postindependence Argentina recognized and protected dowries, which represented the most successful method for women to preserve their property.[29] Women, however, did not have the right to dispose of their property as they wished. In early republican Argentina, women had to surrender their lands and dowries to their husbands after marriage.[30] In addition, women were at a distinct disadvantage as landowners. Land laws were complicated and confusing, especially for those who could not read well. Yet women without husbands had rights, and conflict-ridden Argentina added the novelty that a husband could be physically *or* civilly dead for a wife to separate her dowry.[31] As in the cases of dozens of women in Córdoba during the Rosas era, that brought by Olalla's mother claimed her dowry as a "public instrument" to be respected, even as her husband was labeled a subversive.[32]

Olalla proved crucial in these legal proceedings. In the first place, the beleaguered mother sought to inspire sympathy among authorities by having her daughter present throughout the entire legal process. Citing Olalla's inability to live without her guidance and support, Teresa revealed to Sueldo that she was in a "desperate" situation in that she was unable to "provide" for her only daughter.[33] Indeed, women from politically accused families invoked certain rhetorical devices in hopes of inspiring compassion and pity among officials.[34] This appeal, however, was more than an emotional one. Provincial laws provided limited financial assistance and legal protection for children who could not afford to live on their own. This argument was risky, however, because the state could have taken Olalla away from Teresa. In Argentina during the Rosas period, the state took great interest in placing girls in particular with "good families" more capable of providing a better life and education than poorer ones. Judges often instructed parents not to allow daughters into the street, a site of loose morals.[35] This is probably why Olalla and her mother emphasized legal arguments.

In addition, Olalla took particular advantage of a legal instrument available to adolescent girls: she attached her own supporting petition in which she argued that the family's property would eventually be given to her to be used for her dowry.[36] This *donación* (or literally, "donation") made it possible for property to be transferred to an indigent or poverty-stricken recipient.[37] After transfer, the property became Olalla's, whereupon it was unlawful for any judge to confiscate it unless authorities provided evidence that she committed a political crime.

Invoking this rule touched on the ambiguous nature of girls' legal standing during this period. Argentine jurisprudence during the nineteenth century operated under the legal concept of *patria potestad*, whereby power relations within the household flowed through the male, giving him legal sanction over female subordinates.[38] This rule meant that parents, fathers in particular, would have, in theory at least, absolute authority over their daughters' life decisions, particularly those concerning when and whom they would marry. By law, girls could marry and hold a dowry as early as twelve years of age, but they had to wait until they were twenty-three before they could marry without first seeking permission from their parents.[39] Thus, age became an important benchmark in the legal distinction between "girl" and "woman" and how a female could interact with the Argentine state.

Beyond these legal struggles, however, these experiences must have greatly helped girls, like Olalla, in nineteenth-century Argentina develop not only a sense of family obligation and responsibility but also a sense of rights and entitlement. In fact, dozens of petitions attest to the fact that girls and young women in Argentina frequently turned to the courts and the Catholic Church in seeking greater independence from their parents, especially in matters related to marriage choice.[40] Particularly in Córdoba, the political crises during the Rosas era and the rise of republicanism and individualism in the nineteenth century loosened the power that fathers, as patriarchs, held over their wives and daughters. Indeed, Jesús Pérez's tenuous political status and absence only made his family's situation more untenable and was representative of the declining power of patriarchs by the mid-nineteenth century.[41] As a result, provincial officials had to adopt legal practices that allowed women and girls to be entrusted with property and land tenure decisions. When human and material resources were stretched to the utmost, local authorities were forced to come to terms with the fact that many women and children were left behind as hundreds of male heads of household were imprisoned, fled the province, or took extended leaves for business or seasonal labor. This situation meant that Olalla, like many girls in Europe and the United States during the nineteenth century, had to take on more responsibilities both within and outside of the household when circumstances forced them to do so.

Unfortunately for Olalla and her family, their hopes for a favorable outcome were dashed when Sueldo and then López rejected their legal arguments. Adding to their troubles was the news that Pérez, after being captured, had died in prison. Even though at the time of the confiscation she did not yet know her husband's fate, Olalla's mother certainly understood that they were in danger as long as they continued to live in the province. Within this violent context, Teresa, like hundreds of other political refugees, headed for Chile with Olalla in tow. In her 1853 testimony, Olalla never mentioned the journey itself, but their vulnerability to cruelty and exile had to have been psychologically devastating.

Finding a way out of the province was the most ominous barrier to escape. Local judges, especially those in departments or districts bordering other provinces, were always on the lookout for individuals or groups attempting to flee. Provinces experienced acute labor shortages, and authorities sought to maintain strict controls over the supply of laborers. In the confusion of escape, families were often forced to split up, but Olalla and her mother were able to stay together. Making the journey beyond the local community into often unknown territory was a risky enterprise for even the most skilled frontier survivalist. Many families opted for exile in Bolivia, Chile, Paraguay, or Uruguay, but as correspondence among authorities indicates, Chile and Uruguay received the most political refugees.[42] Olalla and her mother chose Chile because they had distant family members there. The trek westward through San Luís and Cuyo provinces seemed much less dangerous than heading toward Buenos Aires, the heart of *rosismo*. Mendoza, western Argentina's largest town, provided an acceptable hiding place because it provided numerous safe houses that had become launching points to Santiago, Chile's capital. Olalla and her mother crossed the Andes into Chile sometime in December, during the summer season. Traveling more than three hundred miles first from Córdoba to Chile's border was difficult, but continuing the journey across these treacherous mountains was daunting even when the weather cooperated. Yet Olalla and her mother considered it worth the risk because of their family connections in Chile.[43]

Almost nothing is known about Olalla's life growing up in exile. She mentioned only briefly during her 1853 restitution suit that she and her mother often found themselves in the precarious position of having to rely solely on others for care and guidance. Both survived the journey to Chile, but her mother died a few years after their arrival. Before her mother passed away, Olalla must have learned a great deal from her. In rural areas of Argentina and other parts of the world, parental instruction constituted a much more common method for educating girls; indeed, Olalla would have learned a variety of skills, such as weaving, sewing, horticulture, animal care, and domestic service.[44] Additionally, the conflicts of the period demanded the mobilization of girls for civilian support services such as nursing, textile and clothing production, munitions, slave and land management, and even agriculture.[45] Considering the evidence gleaned from her 1853 lawsuit, we see that Olalla had gained an appreciation for her family's history, local legal and property rights, regional and national identity, and the political situation.

This worldview was primarily shaped by her mother in relative isolation from the Argentine state's efforts to socialize children politically into national and civic life. In the city of Buenos Aires, for example, leaders attempted to create a rational schooling program. Girls, in particular, were allowed to attend Catholic school, and private donations funded a number of girls-only scholarships. Historians have shown that these institutions served to educate an entire generation of "submissive" citizens, which meant that boys *and* girls would have been taught respect for state authority, republican hierarchy, and patriotic values.[46] This curriculum did not mean that girls living in cities had an absolute advantage over rural girls in what they learned. Reformers throughout Latin American during the late nineteenth century often complained that girls received an inferior education from the Church.[47] Indeed, Olalla, as a young girl living through Argentina's civil wars, received a much different education based on local knowledge, survival skills, domestic service, and local justice.

Invoking Girlhood Memories: Olalla's Restitution Case

In 1852, political events favored Olalla and hundreds of other Argentine exiles seeking to return to their homes. Justo José de Urquiza, another powerful caudillo from the province of Entre Ríos, defeated Juan Manuel de Rosas at the battle of Caseros. After repeatedly warning Rosas to remove all trade restrictions, Urquiza, in 1851, declared himself an enemy of Buenos Aires and, in the following year, raised an army and defeated Rosas's army at Caseros, just outside the port city. As he entered triumphantly into Buenos Aires, Urquiza promised its inhabitants a new brand of Federalism, arguing, like Rosas before him, that provincial autonomy and property rights would be respected. As his armies were ransacking the homes of loyal Rosas supporters, Urquiza declared an immediate end to all political purges and confiscations.[48]

In the wake of Urquiza's triumph, his chief ally, Alejo Guzmán, in Córdoba likewise defeated Manuel López. Now in control, Guzmán immediately issued a decree renouncing all confiscation policies of the Rosas regime, arguing that Rosas loyalists were excessive and that they had strayed from "true" Federalism.[49] Echoing many of the calls from Buenos Aires for full compensation to victims of the Rosas regime, Guzmán implemented a new law in May 1852 that directly impacted Olalla and other children of "classified" families. In the "spirit of restoration," he decreed, legal rights and property would be returned to those who had been "classified" during Rosas's tenure.[50] This law also allowed families to bring civil suits against officials of the previous regime. Ever mindful of local corruption, however, Guzmán emphasized to judges trying these cases that "you must be fair and pay attention to the claims that have been made by various individuals of these Departments against people who served in the judicial system prior [to 1852]."[51] This process required witnesses to come forward, documents to be presented, and questions to be asked. Guzmán's decree offered at least a glimmer of hope to those "classified" families who believed that they had yet to realize a modicum of restitution, justice, and perhaps, revenge.

Olalla was one of the first to cite this new law in her suit against Pedro Sueldo. In recalling the events of her childhood, she began her restitution petition with the following words: "It is public and notorious, Sir, the wrongs that I have received from Mr. Sueldo." In a courtroom, twelve years after her first traumatic meeting with him, she explicitly named Sueldo as her family's assailant and accused him of treating them brutally, stealing her family's property, and acting "without honor." By the time she brought this case, however, both her parents had passed away—her mother in exile and her stepfather in prison—and it was up to her to secure the family's "honor" and "reputation."[52]

Olalla based her restitution petition on two key arguments that were central to her legal status as a girl. First, according to her, this "criminal" had violated a sacred trust between communities and local provincial officials. What Olalla found particularly "revolting" was that he had failed then to offer "protection" in making legal devices available to her and her family. These practices, she argued, were deeply ingrained norms in rural Argentina during the nineteenth century. Olalla cast Sueldo as an "abusive representative" of the Rosas state, preying on families, profiting from their plight, and casting them out of their homes with no recourse, either financial or political.[53] Sueldo had not merely confiscated her family's property, but he had enriched himself in the process. This corruption added to the emotional trauma that came with her displacement and lack of protection. Moreover, she argued, as a local jurist, Sueldo had shirked his responsibilities in not recognizing her original legal status as a girl with certain rights.

Olalla's second argument in her petition for restitution pointed out the huge problems involved in correctly identifying Unitarian suspects. In her suit, she recalled: "How could my [step]father be a Unitarian when his only crime was not being at home at the time of the classification?" And, in an argument that echoed the sentiments of numerous others claiming restitution, she stated that Sueldo's "lack of honor" in dealing with families in his jurisdiction gave him little "credibility" in correctly being able to "know" the difference between a Federalist and Unitarian.[54] In arguing this position, she articulated a commonly held assumption among her neighbors during her childhood: all local officials could be enticed by the bounty of confiscated property to overlook mistaken classifications. In this sense, the personal became political, and ideological loyalty was intricately tied to self-enrichment.

Although these arguments resonated among the post-Rosas generation of judges, Olalla still faced substantial obstacles as she wended her way through the bureaucratic morass of the provincial legal system. She provided lists of property, including furniture, animals, and titles to land, attesting to what and how much her family owned, and she interviewed Sueldo's former business associates, employees, and neighbors. She remembered many of these witnesses from her childhood. Most agreed to testify that they had seen the brand marks of other ranchers, including those of Olalla's family, burned into the hides of Sueldo's herds. Despite Olalla's corroborating testimony, however, most of the witnesses, given the confusion of the times, could not remember important details, including whether they saw Sueldo personally take possession of Jesús Pérez's land and animals. It is most likely that many of these witnesses had benefited from Sueldo's confiscations.[55] In fact, Sueldo cited this complicity as evidence that the witnesses brought forward by Olalla and others were tainted and that any testimony against him was only motivated by rancor and vindictiveness.[56]

Sueldo mounted a steadfast legal defense against Olalla. He claimed that Olalla was not entitled to anything because she was unmarried and still too young to bring a lawsuit. This argument centered on the legal definition of when a girl became a woman. An astute legal mind in his own right, Sueldo noted that Olalla had no parental permission to interact with the state on her own. According to the laws still in effect after the 1852 regime change, an unmarried woman had to be twenty-three years old to represent herself in court. She could do so as early as twelve years old, but she had to have permission from her parents or an older family member, an impossible proposition at this point for Olalla. Although she could not immediately produce a birth certificate or any proof of her age, the judge dismissed Sueldo's motion. The court considered Olalla a legal adult woman capable of bringing a suit, but Sueldo's argument is still significant in that it illuminates the ambiguous nature of defining the legal boundaries of girlhood and womanhood.

Sueldo responded by arguing that Rosas-allied leaders empowered him with the authority to take "all necessary extraordinary measures," such as confiscation, against Unitarian suspects. More specifically, this "public authority" meant that the provincial governor himself "authorized and legalized these acts" to battle those elements "against the government as a representative of society." According to Sueldo, Olalla's stepfather represented a real threat at the time because he was actively assisting Unitarian armies. Olalla, however, retorted that Sueldo could not have known of her stepfather's whereabouts because he reported Pérez missing rather than engaging in treasonous acts. Most of the court's rulings were in Olalla's favor, and her specific memories seemed to win out over Sueldo's vague recollections. Sueldo continued to deny culpability: "I have already washed my hands of the matter by presenting documents that prove [that] what I was doing was under orders from the governor."[57] He testified that he was an honorable "true Federalist" and had every "right" at the time to take what he wanted and noted that his service and sacrifice as a judge gave him additional justification to take liberties, especially against "savage Unitarians."[58] Finally, he presented documents from the 1830s and 1840s confirming that the legislature had authorized him to take more than a thousand pesos as compensation for his losses and his expenses during the Unitarian invasions.

After some deliberation and a few delay tactics by Sueldo and his lawyer, the judge rendered his decision: Olalla's request for full restitution would be granted. This ruling was based in part on the fact that Sueldo was unable to impeach the various detractors who had come forward to testify against him. In addition, the judges did not accept his main argument, which was that he was vested "under the orders of the provincial governor" with emergency powers. This concept of establishing law and order clashed directly with a local judge's duty to protect families and communities, a "higher" Federalist principle that trumped all others. On the basis of this "failure," Sueldo would have to compensate Olalla for all of the property her family had lost. Yet his defense against Olalla foreshadowed one of the thorniest problems facing Córdoba's judiciary in its handling of restitution cases: How would compensation be determined considering that more than eleven years had passed? Jurists, victims, and classifiers had no answer. Olalla, for example, would never see any of the animals that had been taken. While in Sueldo's possession, her family's livestock had either been used up or sold. Those animals, such as horses and goats, that did survive were too old to be useful,.[59]

The favorable resolution of Olalla's case led, in turn, to other families achieving victory in their cases against Sueldo.[60] Believing the ex-jurist to be a flight risk, the governor revoked his passport and prohibited him from leaving the province until the lawsuits against him were resolved. Despite the order, however, Sueldo fled the jurisdiction. For Olalla and others who had filed complaints against him, his flight was sure evidence of his guilt. A panel of judges declared him a "notorious outlaw." He never again returned to Córdoba, nor did he resolve his disputes with Olalla and the other families who sought restitution. In January 1854, provincial authorities seized Sueldo's remaining property and assets to be distributed among the families, including Olalla, who could now start a new life as a single and independent young woman.[61]

Conclusion

These girlhood experiences of one woman are an important yet untold story of the struggle for justice, redemption, and restitution in post-Rosas Argentina. Olalla's testimony and petitions represent some of the most complete accounts, among those of hundreds who actively pursued claims against officials for past injustices and abuses. These claimants included small farmers, large landholders, merchants, women, artisans, the physically and mentally ill, slaves, soldiers, and judges, and they offered a wide range of responses to their conditions. This observation challenges a long-held assumption that the civil wars between Federalists and Unitarians during the Rosas era primarily involved elite actors.[62] Families fighting for their honor and the protection of their daughters, and those daughters themselves, were an integral part of this struggle.

What general conclusions about girlhood may we draw from Olalla's story? In the first place, Olalla's restitution suit provides us with a rare glimpse into early nineteenth-century perspectives on girlhood within the context of the decline of patriarchal authority. Life was difficult for girls who lived on the Argentine frontier during the early nineteenth century. Just like girls in Europe and North America, Olalla took on great responsibilities both within and outside of the household. At the same time, she depended greatly on her family for her education, sustenance, and socialization within the context of authoritarianism and civil war. Whether actively engaged with the legal system or not, girls were also important actors in the transfer of property from one generation to the next, especially in wealthier families. Olalla's parents were not wealthy within the context of the times, yet hiding land through a legal mechanism that only a girl could invoke was critical for their survival.

Second, the tale confirms scholars' findings that girls were savvy legal and political actors who were able to operate within the context of a patriarchal political and social order. Olalla had learned at an early age about the local legal and political contexts in which she lived and the range of survival strategies available to her. In traditional Platine culture, members of local communities, regardless of socioeconomic status, gender, or age, looked to judges as stewards to settle disputes, provide financial assistance, and uphold the laws. When judges like Pedro Sueldo failed in their obligations, girls like Olalla pointed out their errors through petitions and lawsuits and exercised legal protections, such as dowry rights and inheritance. In many ways, this story confirms the observation by both Christa Jones and E. Thomas Ewing, in chapters in this volume, that girls could often wield writing itself as a powerful instrument. The fact that the legal arguments offered by Olalla and her mother did not work initially does not diminish the significance of these legal instruments. In other contexts within Córdoba during the Rosas era, numerous restitution claims were granted. The corrupt nature of political institutions at the local level hurt Olalla's chances at restitution, yet she was able to survive the trauma of political purge through family members' support and her own willingness to seek some kind of restitution. Her mother, in particular, was crucial in her daughter's legal and political education. This knowledge would later serve Olalla well in her and her family's quest for restitution and justice. She spoke her mind to those in power as she participated actively in the everyday politics of restitution and justice.

This case was not an easy one to win. Continuing the suit many years after her and her mother's forced exile, Olalla had to file another restitution petition, invoke legal instruments and norms, challenge evidence, and hold local authorities to certain obligations. In doing so, she used the legal knowledge that she gained from her experiences as a girl in order to counter her adversary's tactics. By sharing her childhood experiences and citing the cultural traditions that authorities knew well, she argued that local authorities had violated their roles as protectors, caretakers, and stewards of local communities, crucial aspects of dispensing justice and maintaining stable state-society relations at the local level. As a result, Olalla was able not only to survive but, like so many other girls, also challenge dominant standards of political identity, patriarchy, and justice.

NOTES

1. Archivo Histórico de la Provincia de Córdoba (cited hereafter as AHPC)-Escribanías, registro 4, 1852, legajo 99, expediente 43.

2. The term *rosista* denotes any follower of Juan Manuel de Rosas, who dominated Argentine politics between 1829 and 1852. Rosas became the embodiment of Federalism, a broad, elite-based political movement that promoted, in theory, a decentralized political structure, revenue sharing, and economic nationalism. In practice, Rosas adopted policies that concentrated power and wealth in Buenos Aires Province at the expense of the rest of Argentina's interior. Federalists' mortal enemies were the Unitarians (Liberals), who looked to Europe for political and cultural inspiration and sought economic policies that favored free trade, foreign (particularly European) investment, and pro-European immigration policies.

3. AHPC-Escribanías, registro 4, 1852, legajo 99, expediente 43.

4. As many authors in this volume may attest, biography in particular serves as an important tool for understanding the history of girls and girlhood. See the chapters by E. Thomas Ewing and Christa Jones in this volume.

5. See Mary Jo Maynes, Birgitte Søland, and Christina Benninghaus, eds., *Secret Gardens, Satanic Mills: Placing Girls in European History, 1750–1960* (Bloomington: Indiana University Press, 2005).

6. See Tobias Hecht, ed., *Minor Omissions: Children in Latin American History and Society* (Madison: University of Wisconsin Press, 2002); Bianca Premo, *Children of the Father King: Youth, Authority, and Legal Minority in Colonial Lima* (Chapel Hill: University of North Carolina Press, 2006); Ondina E. González and Bianca Premo, eds., *Raising an Empire: Children in Early Modern Iberia and Colonial Latin America* (Albuquerque: University of New Mexico Press, 2007); Mark D. Szuchman, "A Challenge to the Patriarchs: Love among the Youth in Nineteenth-Century Argentina," in *The Middle Period in Latin America: Values and Attitudes in the Seventeenth–Nineteenth Centuries*, ed. Mark D. Szuchman (Boulder, CO: Lynne Rienner Publishers, 1989), 141–165; Mark D. Szuchman, "Childhood Education and Politics in Nineteenth-Century Argentina: The Case of Buenos Aires," *Hispanic American Historical Review* 70, no. 1 (February 1990): 109–138.

7. In comparison to the number of studies on girlhood in English-language Latin American scholarship, there seems to be much more attention paid to the subject within the United States and Europe. In addition to Maynes, Søland, and Benninghaus, *Secret Gardens, Satanic Mills*, see Jane Hunter, *How Young Ladies Became Girls: The Victorian Origins of American Girlhood* (New Haven: Yale University Press, 2003); Miriam Forman-Brunell, *Made to Play House: Dolls and the Commercialization of American Girlhood, 1830–1840* (New Haven: Yale University Press, 1993); Mary E. Odom, *Delinquent Daughters: Protecting and Policing Adolescent Female Sexuality in the United States, 1885–1920* (Chapel Hill: University of North Carolina Press, 1995); Sherrie A. Inness, ed., *Delinquents and Debutantes: Twentieth-Century American Girls' Culture* (New York: New York University Press, 1998); for a brief literature review on the growing history of girlhood, see Leslie Paris, "The Adventures of Peanut and Bo: Summer Camps and Early Twentieth Century American Girlhood," *Journal of Women's History* 12, no. 4 (Winter 2001): 47–76.

8. As Raymond Grew has observed, "the meaning of childhood is deeply embedded, in a family, a particular culture, and the social conditions of a specific time and place. These multiple vectors of meaning make childhood both a telling social indicator and a peculiarly complex topic." See Grew, "On Seeking Global History's Inner Child," *Journal of Social History* 38, no. 4 (Summer 2005): 849–850.

9. Ricardo D. Salvatore, *Wandering Paysanos: State Order and Subaltern Experience in Buenos Aires during the Rosas Era* (Durham, NC: Duke University Press, 2003), 326.

10. For example, Elizabeth McKee Williams and Bruce C. Scates have written articles on childhood memories of war and violence during the American Revolution and World War I, respectively. See James Marten, ed., *Children and War: A Historical Anthology* (New York: New York University Press, 2002).

11. For an effective overview of the rise of caudillos in Spanish America during the early nineteenth century, see, for example, David Bushnell and Neill Macaulay, *The Emergence of Latin America in the Nineteenth Century* (New York: Oxford University Press, 1994).

12. John Lynch, *Argentine Dictator: Juan Manuel de Rosas, 1829–1852* (Oxford: Oxford University Press, 1982).

13. See Jorge Myers, *Orden y virtud: El discurso republicano en el régimen rosista* (Buenos Aires: Universidad Nacional de Quilmes, 1995).

14. David Bushnell, *Reform and Reaction in the Platine Provinces, 1810–1852* (Gainesville: University Presses of Florida, 1983), 89.

15. Jonathan C. Brown, *A Socioeconomic History of Argentina* (Cambridge: Cambridge University Press, 1979), 126–128.

16. Richard W. Slatta and Karla Robinson, "Continuities in Crime and Punishment: Buenos Aires, 1820–1850," in *The Problem of Order in Changing Societies: Essays on Crime and Policing in Argentina and Uruguay, 1750–1940*, ed. Lyman L. Johnson (Albuquerque: University of New Mexico Press, 1990), 22–25.

17. The inconsistent flow of goods into the market was also thanks in large part to the French and British blockades of Buenos Aires during the 1840s. See Silvia O. Romano, "Finanzas públicas de la provincia de Córdoba, 1830–1855," *Boletín del Instituto de Historia Argentina y Americana "Dr. Emilio Ravignani"* 6 (1992): 109.

18. Seth Meisel, "War, Economy, and Society in Post-Independence Córdoba, Argentina" (PhD diss., Stanford University, 1998), 135–140.

19. Roberto I. Peña, "Los jueces pedáneos en la provincia de Córdoba: 1810–1856, algunos aspectos de sus atribuciones," *Revista de Historia del Derecho* 2 (1974 [1975]): 137.

20. See María Isabel Seoane, *Historia de la dote en el derecho argentino* (Buenos Aires: Instituto de Investigaciones de Historia del Derecho, 1982).

21. See Szuchman, "Challenge to the Patriarchs."

22. Francie Chassen-López confirms that the "Spanish legal system permitted women in colonial Mexico to buy, sell, rent, inherit, administer, and bequeath property . . . her husband could do anything he wished with her property short of selling it. . . . Property acquired during marriage was jointly owned, and only *bienes parafernales* (clothes, jewels, or property received during the marriage through inheritance or donation) were under the wife's sole control." See Chassen-López, "Cheaper Than Machines: Women in Agriculture in Porfirian Oaxaca," in *Creating Spaces, Shaping Transitions: Women of the Mexican Countryside, 1850–1990*, ed. Mary Kay Vaughan and Heather Fowler Salamini (Tucson: University of Arizona Press, 1994), 29.

23. AHPC-Gobierno, tomo 157, folios 412, 414–427; AHPC-Gobierno, tomo 158, folio 498.

24. Juan Carlos Garavaglia and Jorge D. Gelman, "Rural History of the Río de la Plata, 1600–1850: Results of a Historiographical Renaissance," *Latin American Research Review* 30, no. 3 (1995): 91; Andres M. Carretero, *La propiedad de la tierra en la época de Rosas* (Buenos Aires: Editorial El Coloquio, 1972), 31.

25. AHPC-Gobierno, "Copiador de comunicaciones dirigidas al Exmo Sr Gobierno Propietario por su delegado," folio 24.

26. Emiliano S. Endrek, "Los dueños de Córdoba en la época de Rosas: Datos para un estudio de la oligarquía criolla cordobesa (1839–1845)," *Revista de la Junta Provincial de Historia de Córdoba*, no. 8 (1978): 84.

27. AHPC-Escribanías, registro 4, 1852, legajo 99, expediente 43.

28. Ibid.

29. In a survey of 77 restitution petitions crafted between 1840 and 1846 (at the height of political purges), the vast majority (66 of 77) were approved. See Jesse Hingson, " 'Savages' into Supplicants: Subversive Women and Restitution Petitions in Córdoba, Argentina during the Rosas Era," *Americas* 64, no. 1 (July 2007): 59–85; Seoane, *Historia de la dote*, 162–163.

30. Donna J. Guy, "Lower-Class Families, Women, and the Law in Nineteenth-Century Argentina," *Journal of Family History* 10 (Fall 1985): 322–324; in comparison, Victoria Bynum, in her discussion of the legal status of women in the southern United States during the early nineteenth century, concludes that these women "obviously lived in a patriarchal society that merged the legal identities of wife and husband into one. . . . The legal submersion of a woman's identity upon marriage affected more than just her right to own and control property. The law granted husbands control over the family purse strings, full custody of children, and the right and responsibility of governing wives' behavior, by physical force if necessary." See Bynum, *Unruly Women: The Politics of Social and Sexual Control in the Old South* (Chapel Hill: University of North Carolina Press, 1992), 60–61.

31. Rosalind Z. Rock, in her study of colonial New Mexico, has also found that it was possible for women to attain some degree of control over their property. According to colonial law, she notes, "a woman could not exercise control over the entire estate unless her husband specifically gave her permission to do so. In case of death, absence, or incapacitation a court official could grant her that permission." See Rock, " '*Pido y suplico*': Women and the Law in Spanish New Mexico, 1697–1763," *New Mexico Historical Review* 65, no. 2 (April 1990): 150.

32. Hingson, "Savages into Supplicants," 61; AHPC-Gobierno, legajo 181, expediente 13; AHPC-Escribanías, legajo 103, escribanía 3, cuadernos 1, 2, and 4; AHPC-Gobierno, tomo 177, folios 323 and 330.

33. AHPC-Gobierno, tomo 177, folios 323 and 330.

34. Hingson, "Savages into Supplicants," 75–79.

35. Jeffrey M. Shumway, *The Case of the Ugly Suitor and Other Histories of Love, Gender, and Nation in Buenos Aires, 1776–1870* (Lincoln: University of Nebraska Press, 2005), 64–65.

36. Transferring property to children was possible within the context of Western jurisprudence. In her study of early Anglo-American legal norms, Holly Brewer notes that parents often gave wealth or property to their children but were still able to control and manipulate it. See Holly Brewer, *By Birth or Consent: Children, Law, and the Anglo-American Revolution in Authority* (Chapel Hill: University of North Carolina Press, 2005).

37. To complete this transaction, all that was needed was testimony from a priest, notary, or judge regarding the status of the recipient and the transfer of the property. See, for example, AHPC-Escribanías, registro 3, 1859, legajo 122, expediente 16; only after the López regime fell in 1852 did many families admit that it was "very common to hide property under the veil of a donation or [any] other type of capital [investment] that one has." See AHPC-Gobierno, tomo 138, folio 189; Archivo de la Legislatura de la Provincia de Córdoba, tomo 11, folio 136; AHPC-Escribanías, legajo 103, escribanía 3, cuaderno 4; endrek 84; AHPC-Escribanías, registro 3, 1859, legajo 122, expediente 16.

38. As Guy has argued, the Argentine state during the nineteenth century became more involved in family matters and subsequently took over traditionally male roles. This switch occurred especially in the regulation of labor whereby the state "took over the patria potestad of the working-class family, in some cases sending women and children to work outside the

home as domestic servants and in others employing females in state-controlled activities" ("Lower-Class Families," 322).

39. As the basis of Spanish colonial social policy and legal codes within newly formed Spanish American nation-states, the *Siete partidas* made clear that girls could marry as early as twelve, whereas boys could do so at fourteen. The age at which a person could marry was not seriously reexamined until Liberal reformers raised the issue in the latter part of the nineteenth century. See Shumway, *Case of the Ugly Suitor,* 60, 75.

40. As historian Mark D. Szuchman notes, by the time the 1860s approached, the Catholic Church and the Argentine state were "putting up diminished resistance to the youth who wished to run the risk of moral disapproval by their own families and communities" See Szuchman, "Challenge to the Patriarchs," 150–155. According to Jeffrey Shumway, when girls were not given permission by their parents to marry, they often eloped (*Case of the Ugly Suitor,* 86).

41. According to Jonathan C. Brown, "Women, backbone of the rural family, were present everywhere on the pampa. Many women were married, others were common wives, and a few were foreigners. Males outnumbered females, but households headed by widows with children were not unusual. Rural censuses even listed a few estancias and chacras in women's names" (*Socioeconomic History of Argentina,* 157).

42. AHPC-Escribanías, legajo 103, escribanía 3, cuaderno 2.

43. Ibid., cuaderno 4.

44. Donna J. Guy, "Women, Peonage, and Industrialization: Argentina, 1810–1914," *Latin American Research Review* 16, no. 3 (1981): 70–72; for example, Olalla's education compares favorably to girls' experiences in the U.S. South in that the basis of a southern middle-class girl's education tended to be drawn from her experiences on the frontier and, interestingly, the relationship that she developed with her mother. See Anna Jaybour, " 'Grown Girls, Highly Cultivated': Female Education in an Antebellum Southern Family," *Journal of South History* 64, no. 1 (February 1998): 23–64.

45. John Charles Chasteen, "Trouble between Men and Women: Machismo of Nineteenth-Century *Estancias,*" in *The Middle Period in Latin America: Values and Attitudes in the Seventeenth–Nineteenth Centuries,* ed. Mark D. Szuchman (Boulder, CO: Lynne Rienner Publishers, 1989), 125–126.

46. Szuchman, "Childhood Education and Politics in Nineteenth-Century Argentina," 112–113; Shumway, *Case of the Ugly Suitor,* 61.

47. Steven Palmer and Gladys Rojas Chaves, "Educating Señorita: Teacher Training, Social Mobility, and the Birth of Costa Rican Feminism, 1885–1925," *Hispanic American Historical Review* 78, no. 1 (February 1998): 48.

48. Nicolas Shumway, *The Invention of Argentina* (Berkeley: University of California Press, 1991), 171.

49. Instituto de Estudios Americanistas de la Facultad de Filosofía y Humanidades de la Universidad Nacional de Córdoba, no. 12636.

50. Diana Balmori and Robert Oppenheimer, "Family Clusters: Generational Nucleation in Nineteenth-Century Argentina and Chile," *Comparative Studies in Society and History* 21 (April 1979): 250.

51. AHPC-Gobierno, Copiador de Notas, 1852, tomo 5, folios 233–234.

52. AHPC-Escribanías, registro 4, 1852, legajo 99, expediente 43.

53. Ibid.

54. Ibid.

55. Ibid.

56. In fact, in another case, he accused one witness, Pilar Gudiño, of seeking revenge because of a whipping she had received from him for stealing sometime in the late 1830s. See AHPC-Escribanías, registro 3, 1854, legajo 114, expediente 22.

57. AHPC-Escribanías, registro 4, 1853, legajo 100, expediente 15.

58. AHPC-Gobierno, tomo 157, folios 412, 414–427.

59. Antonio Dellepiane, *Los embargos en la época de Rosas* (Buenos Aires: Academia Nacional de Ciencias, 1968), 22–23.

60. AHPC-Escribanías, registro 3, 1853, legajo 113, expediente 11.

61. AHPC-Escribanías, registro 3, 1854, legajo 114, expediente 22.

62. See Mark D. Szuchman, "Disorder and Social Control in Buenos Aires, 1810–1860," *Journal of Interdisciplinary Studies* 15, no. 1 (Summer 1984): 83–110.

6   *"A Case of Peculiar and Unusual Interest"*

THE EGG INSPECTORS UNION,
THE AFL, AND THE BRITISH MINISTRY
OF FOOD CONFRONT "NEGRO GIRL"
EGG CANDLERS

JAN VOOGD

In autumn of 1918, because of the food shortages brought on by the First World War, the British Food Ministry contracted with the Davies Company, an American company in Chicago, to supply shipments of eggs for hospitals in France. This agreement led to what the U.S. Department of Labor's annual report eventually referred to as "a case of peculiar and unusual interest." The Egg Inspectors Union, affiliated with the American Federation of Labor (AFL), objected to the Davies Company using nonunion egg candlers, most of whom were "Negro girls" who were paid wages at "decidedly less than union scale."[1] Representatives from the AFL, and its local Chicago Federation of Labor (CFL), protested vehemently, threatening to stop all union work being done for the British government. The story of this peculiar and unusual case is illuminating in many ways in that the employment of underpaid black girls threatened to upset a delicate balance not only in Chicago's internecine labor network but in international relations as well.[2] Officials of the governments involved could not allow the interference of organized labor to delay the delivery of the desperately needed food. These young nonunion egg candlers were actors in a political drama being played out on a global stage, in the limelight of war and postwar rebuilding.

Surrounded by high stacks of egg cases, egg candlers worked in thick, stench-laden air. A small metallic oil lamp, attached by a wooden fixture to the end of the middle of three open egg cases, was the only light in the room, the "candle" by which the work got its name. As a Chicago newspaper described the task in 1882, the "candler walked up to the bench [and] plunged both hands into the middle box," lifting out four eggs. "With the thumb and forefinger of each hand the uppermost eggs were caught up and held for an instant only in front of the flame. There was a convulsive movement of the hands, and, with all the dexterity of a sleight-of-hand performer, the uppermost eggs had given place to the other two, and were being more carefully examined before the light." A "vividly rosy light showing through" indicated a fresh egg. If the light showed spots, the egg was potentially stale and would have to be sold and used quickly. A broken yolk made it a baker's egg rather than a household egg. "The term *candler* however, is a misnomer for workmen in this industry today," the article asserted, as the ancient candle flame "has been superseded by the more effective and penetrating electric light."[3]

By the time the First World War was over, technology had advanced such that egg candlers were using an electric light rather than a candle, but in many ways, not much else had changed. The industry was dominated by the male Jewish immigrants who had brought egg-candling expertise with them from the old country.[4] A multifaceted confluence of factors, then, brought the black girl workers into the vortex of union machinations and international relations. Opportunities increased the need for black workers, but working conditions remained poor. Despite the few alternatives, black female workers came to rely on their earnings and cherish their independence. Egg candling offered relatively good wages with safe and quiet, if not entirely pleasant, working conditions. After considering the factors that led the girls to work as egg candlers, I place the occupation of egg candling in the context of Chicago's unionism and corruption, and the world's food needs. By weighing the union's objection to the Davies Company policy, the situation of the Jewish unionists, and the resolution of the conflict, I illuminate the crucial role played by the black girl workers in this labor drama. To do so requires the piecing together of clues from negative space because the labor history of nonwhite, nonmale, and nonadult workers is well hidden in this country. The clues live buried in government records and deep within newspaper articles, and often require extrapolation through the stories of others.

The Factors Leading the Girls to Work as Egg Candlers

The Great War brought many changes to society worldwide. Nancy Stockdale, in her chapter in this book, describes the increase in varied work opportunities for women and girls in Palestine after the war. In the United States, the war had increased the demand for goods and labor but at the same time brought to a halt the waves of immigration supplying the workers. Concurrently, the war required many men to fill the battlefield trenches, lowering still further the number of available workers. Along with white women, black workers filled the void, and southern black men, women, and families migrated to Chicago in record numbers.[5]

Wartime labor shortages induced Chicago hotels, restaurants, laundries, and factories, particularly those in the packing industry, to hire black women for the first time. The Chicago Commission on Race Relations (CCRR) reported that all the firms employing large numbers of black women and girls gave the labor shortage as the reason. "Before the war Negro women were popularly thought of as a class of servants unfitted by nature for work calling for higher qualifications. It is difficult to say how long this popular misconception might have survived had it not been for the labor shortage which forced employers to experiment."[6] By 1920, black women and girls worked as clothing folders, drapers, or finishers, map mounters, bookbinders, box makers, twine weavers, silk shade makers, food packers, paper sorters, riveters, laundry workers, and machine operators.[7] Melissa Klapper points out in her chapter in this book that girls in Chicago at this time enjoyed more freedom to move independently about the city. Many of these girls would take advantage of this new mobility to obtain gainful employment. With the various opportunities available, it is worth considering what may have motivated these girls to fight the union for egg-candling work. In the following section, I explore the working conditions, pay rates, and legitimacy of the other choices available to them.

Working conditions in establishments employing black women were often deficient. A federal government investigation, conducted at that time by the Women's Bureau of the U.S. Department of Labor, found that in many cases, black women were working in old factory buildings "which managers considered beyond the hope of cleaning," while white women worked in new factory buildings constructed especially for them. Many factories employing black women and girls had only makeshift seats, if any, such as stools or wooden boxes, with no back supports. The government report stated that having no provision for sitting was common and that ten of the managers interviewed "said the women would go to sleep if they provided them with seats, but there was no evidence that this happened in the places where seats were provided." Management neglected ventilation, cleanliness, and sanitation, as well. "One woman remarked, 'It just makes you sick to work in this filth.'"[8]

Even the lighting in the factories posed problems. Thick dust on the workroom windows in some factories obscured what little light might have shone in, whereas in other plants, workers resorted to curtains of clothing, burlap bags, and aprons to shade the sunlight that would have otherwise glared into their eyes. The federal investigation reported on one manufacturer of fiber-wood envelopes who employed "forty young Negro girls [in a] dark, damp cellar. Electric bulbs, the sole source of light, hung so nearly on a line with their eyes as to be almost blinding."[9]

Companies applied many rationalizations to excuse the poor working conditions. In the case of the well-paying lampshade industry, the investigation reported, managers explained the bad working conditions there "by saying that the product was a fad which might pass out of favor at any time, and so they were reluctant to improve their plants." Lampshade manufacturing was one of the few industries employing "skilled, well-trained Negro girls"; the production of silk shades for electric lamps involved "not only knowledge of drawing and drafting, which was done by the Negro forewomen, but skill in the use of the needle." Some of the lampshades were hand painted by the women as well, making this a highly desirable occupation despite the working conditions, because of the artistry required and status earned.[10]

The federal investigation found that Chicago's stockyards offered black female workers easily available opportunities, but even here the women "were barred from the more desirable work of canning and wrapping meat and its by-products. The work of Negro women was usually in the wet, slippery part of the establishment where unpleasant odors filled the air and where marked variations in temperature and humidity made the surroundings hazardous to health. . . . Negro women trimmed, sorted, graded, and stamped different portions of the carcasses, separated and cleaned the viscera, and prepared the meat for curing and canning."[11] With the noisy and hazardous work of the stockyards as their most available option for employment, it is no wonder that the gentle, quiet occupation of egg candling appealed to the girls.

The general disparity in pay structures between blacks and whites may have been a factor in the girls' choice of egg candling for work. The widely held belief that white workers were paid more than black workers was occasionally verified. According to the CCRR, in one case an employment manager, "in mistaking a colored girl for a white one," inadvertently revealed the fact that "the white girls employed by the same company received a higher wage than that paid the colored girls."[12] Because egg candling was not an occupation in which white women worked, however, there was one less layer of salary discrepancy. Black girls earned less than white men, but by only one step rather than the usual two.

Despite the unpleasant working conditions in factories, black female workers, if they had the opportunity, chose factory work over better-paying domestic work because free time was more important than money. The CCRR found a significant shortage of domestic help from 1918 to 1920. "Colored girls and women deserted this grade of work for the factories, where shorter hours and free Sundays were secured." The commission report described T.S., twenty-two years old, whose mother had died when she was about seventeen. T.S. had worked as a cook for a large family in Lexington, Georgia, for about three years and then moved to Chicago, where she worked as a waitress and then in a box factory. The report quoted her as saying, "I'll never work in nobody's kitchen but my own any more. No, indeed! That's the one thing that makes me stick to this job. You do have some time to call your own, but when you're working in anybody's kitchen, well, you're out of luck. You almost have to eat on the run, you never get any time off, and you have to work half the night, usually."[13]

Domestic work, low-paying retail jobs, and dangerous or uncomfortable factory positions aside, another major arena of gainful employment for girls was that of the illicit occupations. Opportunities abounded in Chicago to make a lot of money in prostitution. If a girl did not have an agent, or "cadet," to pay off, the money was much better than any legitimate job could offer. The Juvenile Protective Association (JPA) surveyed the various recreations centered around theaters, dance halls, cabarets, and amusement parks and was alarmed by the increasing popularity of cabarets and the fine line separating legitimate and illegitimate work found there. Louise de Koven Bowen, who worked for many years with the JPA, later wrote that there were "a vast number of young girls who find this occupation a new opportunity for earning money . . . [and] thus make their first acquaintance not only with public drinking, but with disreputable characters and become familiar with that sinister evil which apparently has a never-ending capacity for masquerading as recreation."[14]

The First World War ushered in an era in which girls struggled with new moral parameters, and not only in the United States. An Illinois Senate vice committee, with the power to subpoena witnesses, documents, and records, and to administer oaths, officially found that "poverty is the principal cause of prostitution" and that "thousands of girls are driven into prostitution because of the sheer inability to keep body and soul together on the low wages received by them."[15]

Roy Jones, one of the leaders of Chicago's vice trust, ran an infamous café and restaurant at Twenty-first and Wabash. A cabaret performed there regularly, with ten black entertainers—two men and eight women—who would sing popular songs, play the piano, and dance. Concerned citizens disagreed on what should be considered appropriate dancing. Some people found the cabaret dancing to be outrageously lewd. One of the few black women interviewed by the commission gave only her stage name, Natalie. At twenty years old, she had been a cabaret dancer since she was fifteen. She is on record as testifying that her version of the tango and the turkey trot were as acceptable as anyone else's, just perhaps "better."[16]

A series of girls working in the vice industry were brought in to testify before the senate committee. Their names were withheld to protect their privacy, so there is no way of knowing if any were among the egg candlers, but their words and stories capture the tenor of the life choices available to girls, and the time and the spirit in which they made their choices. Relating a story that was all too typical, fifteen-year-old E.T. testified that a man named Eugene Nani escorted her into "leading a life of shame" when she was fourteen by promising to marry her and then taking her away from home to Chicago. He installed her in an apartment at 1230 Wabash Avenue, at Twelfth Street, where he forced her to give any money she earned to him. If she refused to "hustle for him," he would withhold food from her. If she made no money, he would beat her, as he also would if she hesitated to give him the money earned.[17] Such stories contrast sharply with those of the Mexican "defiant daughters" of Kathryn Sloan's chapter in this book.

Sloan's girls asserted their independence by leaving their families of origin in an autonomous declaration of allegiance to a worthy suitor, whereas the Chicago girls interviewed by the vice committee, although believing they were making a similar choice, were actually being duped by pimps.

Georgia Hall testified that she had been keeping a house of prostitution, a sporting house, with three girls at 221 North G Street and had been in the business for twenty-two years. When asked by the commission to say why girls turn to this type of work, she stated her views plainly: "My opinion is that it is low wages, and girls are thrown out on the world without a home. They haven't any companionship, and they naturally fall into prostitution for the sake of company and companionship. . . . They haven't money enough to eat, half of them, when they try to get along and pay their own expenses on the wages they get in stores, factories, and offices."[18]

In their interview with G.B, previously a laundry worker, the vice committee voiced skepticism about the sporting life. G.B. did not hesitate to explain:

> Well, I am not infatuated with the life, I will say that. However, it does give you a chance to live and take care of yourself. It gives you food fit to eat, and hours for sleep and rest. . . . You get three nourishing meals a day and a good substantially comfortable room. You have a warm room, and a bath . . . there is companionship, too. In a rooming house you have no companionship. . . . We don't go into that life with the motive that we like the life for itself. We go into it because there is a better living to be earned in it.[19]

These girls in Chicago were making choices but operating from a place of inadequate information and experience. Some chose the sporting life because they were tired of drudgery, or tired of being "kicked around as a servant," or were like Rosie, a dressmaker who discovered the sporting life was easy money and better than "ruining her eyes sewing." Girls working in low-paying department stores were sitting ducks for the glamorous madams and handsome cadets, who would befriend them as customers at the counter or approach them in the restrooms to entice them into the world of prostitution with gifts, meals, finery, drinks, and fast-flowing cash.[20]

Writing in the *Survey*, Bowen in her work with the JPA found that "young colored girls . . . often become desperately discouraged in their efforts to find employment other than domestic or personal service." Even in the context of the war-related labor shortages, these girls "will find nothing open to them in department stores, office buildings, or manufacturing establishments, save a few positions as maids placed in the women's waiting rooms." Instead, the jobs available to them are those "as domestics in low class hotels and disreputable houses."[21] It was all too easy for discouraged or financially desperate girls to see vice-related occupations as a viable, even appealing, option. As Lisa Ossian suggests in her chapter in this book, these conditions endured during the Second World War as well.

Some of the black female workers were adults who still lived with their families of origin; some were child workers living at home. Many of the adult women and older girls were single and living alone, in commercial or organizational boardinghouses, or in company-owned housing. Older girls would likely have lived in the boardinghouses run by organizations in part because they were more affordable than commercial rooming houses. The Phyllis Wheatley Home,[22] one of the most well-known organizational boardinghouses, offered protection from the temptations of the vice-filled city surrounding these women and girls by providing a safe and homelike environment. Girls arrived at the Phyllis Wheatley Home having been referred by Travelers' Aid, the juvenile court, or the Court of Domestic Relations. Some were students at the University of Chicago. In 1915, the home moved to 5128 South Michigan Avenue, with accommodations for "22 girls in a home-like atmosphere with cooking privileges." In addition to the Phyllis Wheatley Home, the Melissa Ann Elam Club Home for Girls, and other organized boardinghouses in Chicago housed 2,000 black women and girls in 1914, and more than 4,000 in 1926.[23] In contrast to the wholesome environment the organizational homes attempted to provide, the more anonymous rooming houses, without parental authorities, offered instead an independent living situation for young people. Their residents, often runaways who had escaped highly constricted or unsafe home situations, appreciated the freedom of the rooming house.[24]

Although direct evidence is in short supply, some of the "Negro girl" egg candlers may have been from local families; others may have been "good" girls far from home who were staying in organizational houses such as the Phyllis Wheatley Home and hoping to find gainful employment. And some may have been runaways or orphans, living in rooming houses, and struggling to find any kind of legitimate work to ward off the "sporting life." Egg candling offered the independence of factory work without the loud, hazardous conditions of Chicago's stockyards. Although candling would not have paid as well as prostitution, it certainly presented no moral dilemma and was likely to be safer, although, like the girls in Egypt described by Liat Kozma in this volume, girls in Chicago were vulnerable to violation in the workplace. In any case, what the girls may not have realized was that, in venturing into the seemingly harmless world of egg inspection, their locally made choice of employment was going to have a transnational impact.

The General State of Egg Candling in the Context of Unionism and Corruption

Chicago has long served as a main stage for the enactment of labor union struggles, activity, and posturing, and in 1915, union corruption was already so rife that it was the subject of an investigation by the U.S. Commission on Industrial Relations. Although not all unions or trades were infected with corruption, egg candling, as part of the poultry industry, shows evidence of being so. Harold Seidman found that by 1911, "poultry dealers and the unions joined together to 'organize' the industry and set up a monopoly. Since that time, through the judicious use of bombings, arson, and murder, the industry has remained organized." Bernard Baff, a partner in an independent poultry supplier, was murdered in 1914 for refusing to join the association. Baff was only the first of many.[25] Even if by 1918 the association was no longer taking violent action, its history of doing so would likely have intimidated anyone attempting to negotiate with the organized poultry industry or its affiliates. The girl egg candlers, by virtue of their youth and inexperience, may have been unaware of the poultry racketeers' power. More likely they had an inkling of the danger but chose to minimize or ignore it out of optimism or financial desperation.

The power to call a strike was in the hands of a business agent, or "walking delegate." The business agent, as sociologist C. Wright Mills describes him, served as "an intermediary who could represent labor and who was not dependent upon the employers for his job. . . . He was a salaried man usually appointed by a local or a citywide federation." The full-time business agent could amass a great deal of power, calling strikes without a formal vote. The job attracted and rewarded "businessmen full of personal initiative."[26]

In Seidman's analysis, a business agent might be simply corrupt or might be attempting "to perpetuate himself in office." In either case, taking advantage of "innocent employers," he could successfully make "unwarranted and unreasonable demands" against them. In 1921, the Illinois legislature's Dailey Commission investigated corruption in the building industry, eventually indicting 218 labor leaders and "union sluggers."[27] Historian Andrew Cohen points out that the walking delegate was perceived to be a "notorious character much like a ward boss or precinct captain. . . . In short, business agents were the figures centrally responsible for maintaining private economic governance and market control."[28]

Historian Leon Fink finds that, particularly in Illinois, AFL affiliates "were advancing more state-oriented strategies of protection" by using the successful approach established by the British trade unions, which was to change any legislation that would have made their activities illegal. The Egg Inspectors Union, led by business agent P. F. Donlan, proved adept at this maneuver and made "secure their social function with the help of an egg inspection law in 1919." Donlan had represented the Egg Inspectors Union, along with its president, O. E. Thursie, and secretary-treasurer I. Unkerholz, in a conference with the health commissioner John Dill Robertson, convincing him, according to a Chicago newspaper, that the law was necessary "to safeguard Chicagoans against bad eggs which pass through cold storage."[29]

Donlan used the standard practice of the walking delegate in his work as the business agent for the Egg Inspectors Union. Moving through union work locations to check for violations of trade agreements and association rules, the walking delegate watched for the presence of nonunion workers, materials made by an unapproved vendor, or wage payment below the agreed scale. If any violations were discovered, the delegate contacted the employer or worker and began a negotiation. If the initial talks regarding an agreement or rules violation were fruitless, the delegate would meet with his organization and discuss the appropriate action: a fine, a strike, a boycott, or all of the above. Donlan followed this course exactly when he set in motion the action against the Davies Company. According to Labor Department records, the Donlan-driven egg candler dispute directly affected four hundred workers.[30]

Thousands of cases of eggs, packed by the dozen, arrived in the Chicago market daily. Each egg was to be inspected before being sold or put in cold storage. The work was done mostly in dark basements in the big storage houses of South Water Street and vicinity. By 1900, the egg candlers of Chicago had organized into a union. Of the roughly two hundred men inspecting eggs, three-fourths of them were members of the first egg candlers' union.[31] By 1906, the number of unionized egg candlers had increased to three hundred, and by 1916 there were five hundred members of the Egg Inspectors Union, which represented 90 percent of Chicago's egg candlers.[32]

In 1904, the *New York Times* profiled the "craft of the egg testers," calling it an "ancient guild." The Egg Inspectors Union, which joined the Central Federated Union that year, as well as the AFL, decreed that "candlers must have unusually good eyesight and a steady hand, . . . sobriety is rigidly enforced, [and] few people are competent after they are forty years of age." The average egg tester could inspect nine hundred dozen eggs in a nine-hour day, and "some experts could 'candle' 1000 dozen in that time."[33]

Because so many of the egg candlers were Jewish, the Egg Inspectors Union was considered a Jewish trade union and by the 1930s was affiliated with the Federation of Jewish Trade Unions.[34] Although many immigrants changed their work in the new country because opportunities were so different, egg candlers, along with tailors, were some of the few tradespeople who tended to persevere in their Old Country occupations.[35] Occupations invested with the baggage of tradition can be particularly difficult for new workers to break into. This power of tradition may have influenced the particular objection the unionized egg candlers had to "Negro girls" joining the trade. As Bryant Simon suggests, when previously clear gender roles become clouded, men whose self-worth is linked to their work fall prey to "an almost universal crisis of male identity."[36] The unionized egg inspectors themselves, in veneration of the traditional nature of their trade, may have been unable to accept the new candlers not only because they were female, but perhaps because they were black, and young as well. Adding race and age to the mix made for a powerful brew.

Chicago's Jewish community demonstrated no fear of strong and dissenting opinion within, hosting activism in both its radical and its conservative elements. The food industry, involving trade in kosher bread, meat, and poultry, offered Jewish residents a platform for such activism. As Cohen has asserted, "the persistence of religious laws regulating the production of certain foods illustrated the stubbornness of traditional identities. By eating kosher meat, a Jewish consumer demonstrated not only obedience to God's law, but also a dedication to Old World culture and a reluctance to assimilate." The kosher food industry in Chicago developed slowly through the early twentieth century because of the plethora of unions and associations. "Kosher bakers enforced standard prices. . . . Kosher butchers regulated their trade even more closely. Associations pressured retailers into joining and adopting standard prices." At the same time, dissent arose in the community, as not all businesses wanted to go along with the associations. Jacob Weller and David Trabish were butchers on Chicago's near southwest side. When they refused to join the Chicago Hebrew Master Butchers Beneficial Association, the business agent of Local 598, the Amalgamated Meat Cutters, called their bluff. He called Weller and Trabish's employees out on strike and "hired a 'gang of sluggers' to brandish revolvers, throw stink bombs, break windows, intimidate drivers." In a gesture of high theater, the "sluggers" were even enlisted to come into the shop and swear in front of customers.[37]

Such control of the market by these associations ensured high prices and a limited selection for consumers. Not to be ignored, in 1912 and 1917, Jewish women of the southwest side organized boycotts of kosher butchers who were members of the association. Cohen has argued that the "development of mass culture thus divided immigrants. A radical Jewish public defended their right to consume. . . . Craftsmen regulated consumer options, prices, routes, distributors, and wages in many service and retail trades, including milk, laundry, barbering, shoe shining, ice delivery, building maintenance, and advertising."[38] It was in this climate of conflict that the Davies Company took its stand against the Chicago Egg Inspectors Union by hiring black girls as candlers and paying them significantly less for their nonunion work.

The Union's Objection

After the business agent P. F. Donlan reported to the CFL, the union's president John Fitzpatrick contacted the British Food Ministry. He received in reply a letter written on October 18, 1918, from the office of the ministry encouraging him to make an appointment with the head of the department, Mr. Horrocks.[39]

The U.S. Department of Labor also became involved in the dispute in October 1918. They summed up the situation as follows: "A case of peculiar and unusual interest arose at Chicago affecting the supply of food under contract for the British Government. It appears that a contract had been given for the candling and shipping of eggs to the Davies company, of Chicago. This company was alleged by the Chicago Egg Inspectors Union to be employers of nonunion labor, mostly Negro girls. The union threatened to suspend all work being done for the British Government unless the Davies company were compelled to employ union help." Labor Department officials conferred with the official British representatives and found that a delay of any kind would be serious. The Davies Company "had sublet their contract to an egg broker who had had trouble with the union in the past; that he had employed Negro girls at wages decidedly less than the union scale; and that he had advertised his intention of teaching these girls the egg-candling business for the purpose of breaking up the Egg Inspectors Union. Such announcement had aroused the union and caused them to threaten strike."[40]

As yet, no explicit evidence has come to light that proves the Egg Inspectors Union prohibited black workers or women workers from joining, but even unions that officially allowed either, or both, often in actuality were completely closed to such members. It was not uncommon in Chicago for black workers to be set in opposition to one union or another. "The seeds of discord between white and Negro job competitors in the Chicago labor market had been planted in the stockyards in 1894," according to historian William Tuttle, "when masses of packing and slaughterhouse workers had conducted a sympathetic strike with Eugene V. Debs' American Railway Union. Violence marked this strike; and, in the midst of it, Negro strikebreakers were hired for the first time in the history of the meat packing industry." Firms were known to advertise in the national black publication the *Defender* during labor disputes, looking to hire black workers as strikebreakers. Anne Meis Knupfer asserts that because settlement houses were funded by white philanthropists and businessmen, many of the workers who found employment through referral bureaus were sent to jobs as strikebreakers amid labor disputes. The C. B. Shane Company, a maker of raincoats, was one company at which "colored girls were employed to replace striking white union workers."[41]

Many unions denied workers, particularly African Americans and women, the opportunity to join, leaving strikebreaking as the only employment option. Black women suffered double jeopardy in this situation. As Cohen states, "Though the AFL expressly forbade its constituent internationals from formally restricting the race of their members, many craft unions managed to retain an entirely white membership. Some overtly barred female members, alleging they possessed insufficient skill to warrant membership."[42]

The CCRR had found this practice to be true in its investigations. Its report stated emphatically that although the AFL always had a policy of no racial discrimination, the policy was not carried out in practice by the locals, because the AFL had "no power to compel its constituent national and international unions to follow this policy." The CCRR found that although, during the war, manufacturers "worked in harmony with the unions because they had to," once the war ended, many manufacturers opened shops on the South Side and set about "employing only non-union colored girls." In fact, with many of the strikes at that time, "the strike breakers have been Negro girls secured for the employers through a Negro minister acting as a labor agent or solicitor."[43]

Being seen as a strikebreaker could endanger a person's safety. In a 1904 strike, according to Tuttle, a "mob of 500 mauled a black laborer and his 10-year-old son. . . . Other black people were hauled off streetcars. . . 2000 angry strikers hurled brickbats and other missiles at 200 Negro strikebreakers and their police escorts." One action during a 1905 strike in Chicago demonstrates how even young white children regarded race and labor disputes. Hundreds of grade-school students protested "the delivery of coal at school buildings by black strikebreakers employed by the Peabody Coal Company." The students threw bricks, stones, and pieces of wood at the drivers and at classmates who refused to join them. "Many parents supported the strike [and] sanctioned violence. One father, for example, told a judge that his son was 'amply justified' in flinging coal at Negro drivers because these men were 'black' and 'nonunion.' "[44]

James Grossman has delineated the divergent opinions in Chicago's black community regarding unionism. "A few black ministers were pro-union, allowing organizers to speak on Sunday, permitting their churches to be used for meetings . . . : [others, including] pastors at most of Chicago's large black churches tended to agree with AME Bishop Archibald J. Carey, that 'the interest of my people lies with the wealth of the nation and with the class of white people who control it.'" Grossman argues that "substantial contributions" to the churches from "the industrialists" influenced this view. Black newspapers, another voice of community leadership, also diverged in their political thought. Grossman has found that only "two newspapers unequivocally and consistently opposed unions or encouraged strikebreaking . . . Parker's *Negro Advocate* . . . and the *Broad Ax*. . . . The *Defender* . . . was the most influential newspaper in black Chicago . . . [and it] reflected the ambivalence many black leaders felt toward unions."[45]

Labor activist and journalist Bertha Wallerstein, writing in the *Nation* in 1923, said, "Labor is waking up to the fact that, when the Negro is a strikebreaker, it is usually the white man's fault. . . . The New York Waist and Dress Makers first encountered the colored problem in the big 1919 strike, when the strikers' places were filled by Negro girls. Instead of denouncing them as 'scabs' and letting it end there, the union went to work to organize them, until nearly all came out with the white workers and helped to win the strike and share the fruits of victory. They have been faithful members ever since."[46] Apparently the Egg Inspectors Union did not subscribe to this view, and they did not avail themselves of a similar opportunity to welcome new members.

The hesitancy on the part of the Egg Inspectors Union would not have been the result of a CFL stance against women union members. The CFL had accepted the affiliation of the predominantly female Chicago Teachers' Federation (CTF) as early as 1902. According to her biographer Robert Reid, Margaret Haley, the leader of the CTF, was great friends with John Fitzpatrick, and she deflected criticism that the CFL was part of the "unruly and turbulent class represented by the labor movement." Haley and Fitzpatrick's friendship endured throughout Haley's life, so perhaps Fitzpatrick was broadminded enough to suggest to the Egg Inspectors Union that the girl candlers be allowed to join the union.[47] If he did, the union does not appear to have taken his suggestion. An opportunity missed, for as W.E.B. Du Bois wrote, if black workers "had been received into the unions and trained into the philosophy of the labor cause . . . they would have made as staunch union men as any. They are not working for low wages because they prefer to but because they have to."[48]

In protesting the employment of nonunion candlers, the CFL and AFL threatened to strike against the British government in any area of involvement. This threat could have been interpreted broadly. Concurrent with the egg issue, Fitzpatrick and the CFL were negotiating with great promise the organization of packinghouse workers, the small retail butcher shops, and the steel industry. In addition to those groups, other trades doing work for the British, and therefore part of the power being leveraged with the British government, likely were the longshore and trucking industries. "Early in the city's history," as Barbara Warne Newell has pointed out, "labor learned the power it could attain over the mobility of men and materials."[49]

The British Ministry of Food encompassed the Ministry of Food in New York and was related to the Allied Provisions Export Commission (APEC).[50] Britain was getting eggs from a variety of places, primarily Denmark, but also Russia, the Netherlands, China, and the United States. Eggs were not supplied locally within Britain because grain shortages and governmental directives to farmers not to use their grain rations to feed poultry had driven down poultry production.[51] A British government official, assessing the situation years later, determined that the world war had forced Britain to rely more on the United States for food imports because the North Atlantic trade route was "the shortest and most defensible" of the remaining open sea routes. Other sources were increasingly cut off, "partly through the German blockade of Britain and partly through the British blockade of Germany." Shipping from the United States was efficient, and supplies were plentiful, but the British had nothing of interest to export to the United States, which meant that Britain had to simply pay for imported food. Because money was in short supply, the British Food Ministry was motivated to make a deal with the Davies Company for the price of eggs.[52]

Resolution

Up to the end of November 1918, Britain had purchased more than six thousand tons of eggs from the United States. Correspondence between British and U.S. officials shows agreement that the prices of food had to be regulated to avoid profiteering if the ministry was going to be able to secure supplies. British officials held that to effectively control prices, "all buying of food in the US for Europe should be coordinated. Even the separate governments of the Allies must avoid competing with one another as buyers, lest prices be unduly inflated both against them and against an American public."[53] This policy determined, then, the interwoven fates of the various governments, unions, workers, and citizens of the various nations, with the nonunion egg candlers at the vortex of the controversy.

In reports from the secretary to the Special Food Mission to the United States, William Piercy described in vague terms the organization's dealings with the United States. In late August 1918, before the labor conflict surfaced, Piercy noted that because of the inferior quality of the eggs, the British agency required any eggs they bought to be recandled and repacked. "Another difficulty we are at the moment experiencing is the shortage of labor of experienced candlers." Two months later, in October, "finding it impossible to induce the merchants to recandle and repack for export certain quantities of eggs, we decided to establish egg candling and repacking stations to do this work for us, and so enable us to buy eggs as they now stand in storage." This arrangement then developed into "labor trouble, etc., etc., because we found that it is impossible to get reputable exporters to take this work in hand." In November, Piercy reported that the agency's attention shifted to stock from Canada, despite "delay [due to] want of candlers owing to the influenza epidemic." By this point, Herbert Hoover, as administrator in charge of the U.S. Food Administration, had stopped the British government from buying any more eggs, but the British were still recandling and repackaging already purchased eggs that had been in cold storage. Egg shipments were delayed in transport, as reported by Beveridge on November 19, 1918.[54]

Piercy's weekly reports are colorful yet vague descriptions of the process, and they generate more questions than answers. Why did the agency procrastinate in the actual purchase of the eggs for weeks, with various excuses? Did Hoover restrict the British from buying eggs in the United States because of the labor trouble? Was Piercy completely forthright in his reports or was Horrocks, the British representative on site in Chicago, withholding information from Piercy? Was Horrocks being pressured, or corrupted, by Donlan, the business agent of the Egg Inspectors Union? There is scant evidence to supply answers, but the papers, nonetheless, reveal that egg candler issues strained relations between the United States and England. Moreover, a handwritten note in the papers of John Fitzpatrick, dated October 23, 1918, describes the eventual agreement between the union and the British Food Ministry:

Article of Agreement . . . for the purpose to conduct the labor of candling eggs for the Minister of Food of Great Britain and Allied Commission of

Food. . . . Members of committee are John J. Fitzpatrick the President of the CFL, Pat Donlan business agent of the Egg Inspectors Union, Leopold Oxhandler member of committee, Ed Henry member of committee and F. Cavanaugh member of committee. . . . The English Minister of Food and Allied Food Commission Party of the first part agrees none but union egg candlers should candle eggs for the first party to the amount of six cars per day, between now and the first of the year 1919. . . . It is the mutual agreement between both parties to assist one another in good faith in a patriotic obligation to our country the United States of America and to our allies to conduct our obligations faithfully and honestly to the best that human endeavor to be right and just that we are all striving for.[55]

The agreement illustrates historian Leon Fink's assertion that the "AFL disengaged from the tradition of labor republicanism that had identified workers' interests with the rights and welfare of American citizens in general."[56] It was hardly the union's "patriotic obligation to our country" to deprive the girl egg candlers of their jobs. It was hardly "right and just" to negotiate seven dollars a day, with time and half for overtime for the union, when the girls had likely been making far less.

The memorandum delineated that the Egg Inspectors Union agreed to supply, within ten days, up to fifty egg inspectors for work at the Chicago Cold Storage and Warehouse Company, as well as an additional number of inspectors to do "the work now being done at the Davies Company's warehouse, which is approximately two and one-half to three cars a day—500 cases per car packed for export."[57] This agreement effectively ended the employment of approximately fifty nonunion egg candlers, including the Negro girls.[58]

Despite the international implications, there was but a quiet announcement when the situation was resolved. A tiny article appeared in the Chicago daily newspaper under the headline "Egg Candlers' Strike on British Purchases Settled." The article included the summary that a "difficulty between the British food purchasing mission here and the egg inspectors' union of Chicago has been settled . . . by agreement to employ only union men."[59] This resolution put the nonunion Negro girl egg candlers out of work, leaving them to face once again a narrow range of options. Perhaps some were fortunate and landed good-paying work in a hat or lampshade factory or relatively comfortable work as clerks, but chances are that most had to settle for low-paying, unpleasant jobs in Chicago's stockyards or in other factories, or for demanding, low-status positions as housekeepers or nannies. The ubiquitous temptation of the sporting life's money and dangerous glamour lurked behind all of these options.

So the CFL union machinery, with Donlan driving, mowed down everything standing in its path: the Davies Company, the British government, and the nonunion egg candlers. The CFL sacrificed the livelihoods of the black girl egg candlers, putting at risk the lives of the French hospital patients by potentially depriving them of much needed supplies, all for the sake of exerting a broad-sweeping show of union force and mettle. At the same time, these young black girls, facing discrimination because of gender, race, and age, had weighed their options and took their stand, and for a while in the autumn of 1918 they had the full attention of the world's most powerful men, machinery, and governments. Despite their crucial role in a situation of international import, the girls' story lay hidden, obscured by the lack of information, records, and sources, ignored by the record keepers and the press, and waiting to be pieced together out of negative space. This essay is a beginning, but only that, because like the dozens of eggs packed in a crate, for every story uncovered, there are dozens more that must be held up to the light.

NOTES

1. Department of Labor, *Annual Report of the Secretary of Labor, 1919* (Washington, DC: GPO, 1919), 50–51.

2. The actual age of a person called a "girl" can vary. On the one hand, in 1918, just as now, many people used the word "girl" to refer to an adult female, particularly if she were young and single. On the other hand, government researcher Janet Hooks demonstrated that the U.S. Bureau of the Census has done the opposite, referring to female workers fourteen years old and over as "women." In 1920, there were about 7.5 million such women working, of which more than six million were single. If we define girls as females under eighteen, about 17 percent, or at least one million of those six million workers, were girls. For black "women," again, fourteen years old and over, in 1920, nearly half were gainfully employed. In much the same way that women's history had to be freed from its cloak of invisibility, girls' history must be unveiled as well. Janet M. Hooks, *Women's Occupations through Seven Decades*, Women's Bureau Bulletin, no. 218 (Washington, DC: GPO, 1947), 38–39; Mary Jo Maynes, Birgitte Søland, and Christina Benninghaus, eds., *Secret Gardens, Satanic Mills: Placing Girls in European History, 1750–1960* (Bloomington: Indiana University Press, 2005), define "girls" as "unmarried young women who were seen as no longer children but not yet fully adult" (1).

3. "Egg-Candlers: A Trade Which Will Be New and Strange to the General Reader," *Chicago Daily Tribune*, October 8, 1882. "Egg Testers Form a Union," *Chicago Daily Tribune*, October 28, 1900.

4. Charles S. Bernheimer, "The Jewish Immigrant as an Industrial Worker," *Annals of the American Academy of Political and Social Science* 33, no. 2 (March 1909): 175–182.

5. Chicago Commission on Race Relations, *The Negro in Chicago: A Study of Race Relations and a Race Riot* (Chicago: University of Chicago Press, 1922), 357–358.

6. Ibid., 380, 385.

7. James R. Grossman, *Land of Hope: Chicago, Black Southerners, and the Great Migration* (Chicago: University of Chicago Press, 1989), 186. Chicago Commission, *Negro in Chicago*, 367.

8. Women's Bureau of the U.S. Department of Labor, *Negro Women in Industry* (Washington, DC: GPO, 1922), 27–28.

9. Ibid., 29.

10. Ibid., 39.

11. Ibid., 34.

12. Chicago Commission, *Negro in Chicago*, 369.

13. Ibid., 371, 387.

14. Louise de Koven Bowen, *The Road to Destruction Made Easy in Chicago* (Chicago: Juvenile Protective Association, 1916), 15.

15. *Report of the Senate Vice Committee: Created under the Authority of the Senate of the Forty-ninth General Assembly as a Continuation of the Committee Created under the Authority of the Senate of the Forty-eighth General Assembly, State of Illinois* (1916), 127–128.

16. Ibid., 474–477.

17. Ibid., 139–142.

18. Ibid., 327–328.

19. Ibid., 338–339.

20. Vice Commission of Chicago, *The Social Evil in Chicago: A Study of Existing Conditions* (Chicago: Gunthorp-Warren Printing, 1911), 172, 188, 207–210.

21. Louise de Koven Bowen, "The Colored People of Chicago," *Survey* (November 1, 1913): 117–120.

22. Named in honor of the poet Phillis Wheatley, the organization used a variant spelling in its name.

23. "The Phyllis Wheatley Home for Girls" brochure, Phyllis Wheatley Association, 1966, Phyllis Wheatley Association Papers, box 1, folder 3, University of Illinois Chicago, Daley Library Special Collections; Ann Elizabeth Trotter, *Housing of Non-Family Women in Chicago* (Chicago: Chicago Community Trust, 1921); Edith M. Hadley, "The Housing Problem as It Affects Girls," *Survey* (April 19, 1913): 94. Anne Meis Knupfer, *Toward a Tenderer Humanity and a Nobler Womanhood: African American Women's Clubs in Turn-of-the-Century Chicago* (New York: New York University Press, 1996), 81, 83; Joanne J. Meyerowitz, *Women Adrift: Independent Wage Earners in Chicago, 1880–1930* (Chicago: University of Chicago Press, 1988), 171n58; Allan H. Spear, *Black Chicago: The Making of a Negro Ghetto, 1890–1920* (Chicago: University of Chicago Press, 1967), 102.

24. Meyerowitz, *Women Adrift*, 112.

25. Harold Seidman, *A History of Labor Racketeering* (New York: Liveright Publishing, 1938), 187, 198; John Landesco; *Organized Crime in Chicago: Part III of the Illinois Crime Survey 1929* (Chicago: University of Chicago Press, 1968).

26. C. Wright Mills, *The New Men of Power: America's Labor Leaders* (New York: Harcourt, Brace, 1948), 123–125.

27. Seidman, *History of Labor Racketeering*, 55, 103.

28. Andrew Cohen, *The Racketeer's Progress: Chicago and the Struggle for the Modern American Economy, 1900–1940* (New York: Cambridge University Press, 2004), 71–73.

29. Leon Fink, *In Search of the Working Class: Essays in American Labor History and Political Culture* (Urbana Champaign: University of Illinois Press, 1994), 153, 157–159. "Urge Licenses for Candlers in Bad Egg War," *Chicago Daily Tribune*, December 1, 1916.

30. Preliminary Report of Commissioner of Conciliation, October 24, 1918, 33/2602 (FMCS) Case Files, Dispute Case Files, box 79, RG 280, National Archives.

31. "Egg Testers Form a Union," *Chicago Daily Tribune*, October 28, 1900.

32. "Urge Licenses for Candlers"; "Egg Testers Form a Union"; "Egg Candlers to Strike," *Chicago Daily Tribune*, June 5, 1906.

33. "The Professional 'Egg-Tester' Must Be Born to His Art," *New York Times*, October 9, 1904.

34. Irving Cutler, *The Jews of Chicago: From Shtetl to Suburb* (Urbana Champaign: University of Illinois Press, 1996), 190.

35. Charles S. Bernheimer, "The Jewish Immigrant as an Industrial Worker," *Annals of the American Academy of Political and Social Science* 33, no. 2 (March 1909): 175–182.

36. Bryant Simon, *Fabric of Defeat: the Politics of South Carolina Millhands, 1910–1948* (Chapel Hill: University of North Carolina Press, 1998), 15.

37. Cohen, *Racketeer's Progress*, 198–200.

38. Ibid., 201–202.

39. Letter from WAC, British Ministry of Food in U.S.A., Meat and Provisions Sections, to John Fitzpatrick, October 18, 1918, box 7, folder 50, Chicago Federation of Labor Papers, Archives and Manuscripts Department, Chicago Historical Society.

40. Department of Labor, *Annual Report,* 50–51. Oscar F. Nelson to H. L. Kerwin, November 3, 1918, 33/2602 (FMCS) Case Files, Dispute Case Files, box 79, RG 280, National Archives.

41. William M. Tuttle, Jr., "Labor Conflict and Racial Violence: The Black Worker in Chicago, 1894–1919," *Labor History* 10 (1969): 86–111; Grossman, *Land of Hope,* 185; Knupfer, *Tenderer Humanity and Nobler Womanhood,* 106; and Chicago Commission, *Negro in Chicago,* 367.

42. Cohen, *Racketeer's Progress,* 105.

43. Chicago Commission, *Negro in Chicago,* 405–406, 414.

44. Tuttle, "Labor Conflict and Racial Violence," 86–111.

45. Grossman, *Land of Hope,* 230–231.

46. Bertha Wallerstein, "The New Emancipation of the Negro," *Nation* 117 (September 12, 1923): 30–36.

47. Robert Reid, ed., *Battleground: The Autobiography of Margaret A. Haley* (Urbana Champaign: University of Illinois Press, 1982), xii.

48. W.E.B. Du Bois, in *American Labor Yearbook, 1917–1918,* ed. Alexander Trachtenberg (New York: Rand School, 1919), 182.

49. Barbara Warne Newell, *Chicago and the Labor Movement: Metropolitan Unionism in the 1930s* (Urbana Champaign: University of Illinois Press, 1961), 119, 155–156.

50. William H. Beveridge, *British Food Control* (London: Oxford University Press, 1928), 119.

51. Report of the APEC and British Ministry of Food in the USA, MAF 60/529 Ministry of Food and Board of Trade Food Departments Papers, British National Archives, Kew; Eggs and Poultry, MAF 60/137 Ministry of Food and Board of Trade Food Departments Papers, British National Archives, Kew.

52. Beveridge, *British Food Control,* 134.

53. Food Appendices, 8/37–38, D134I, and Food Memorandum, D134Ia, William Piercy Papers, London School of Economics Archives; and Beveridge, *British Food Control,* 117–119.

54. Diary of William H. Beveridge, MAF 60/307, Ministry of Food and Board of Trade Food Departments Papers, British National Archives, Kew. Weekly reports, 2/21 British Ministry of Food in the United States, Provision Section, William Piercy Papers, London School of Economics Archives.

55. Handwritten "Article of Agreement" between British Ministry of Food in the United States and the Egg Inspectors Union of Chicago, October 23, 1918, box 7, folder 50, Chicago Federation of Labor Papers, Archives and Manuscripts Department, Chicago Historical Society.

56. Fink, *In Search of the Working Class,* 153.

57. Memorandum of Understanding reached in conference between the committee representing the Egg Inspectors Union, Mr. Horrocks, British Ministry of Food in the United States, and Oscar R. Nelson, U.S. Commissioner of Conciliation, October 25, 1918, 33/2602 (FMCS) Case Files, Dispute Case Files, box 79, RG 280, National Archives.

58. Using the figures quoted in Louis Dwight Harvell Weld, *The Marketing of Farm Products* (New York: Macmillan, 1916), 156–157, we find that with thirty dozen eggs per case, and up to three cars of five hundred cases, there were 45,000 dozen eggs being shipped out daily by the nonunion girl egg candlers. If they were candling at the standard 900 dozen eggs per day, fifty candlers would have been needed. If they were not quite as fast as the average experienced candler, more than fifty would have been needed.

59. "Egg Candlers' Strike on British Purchases Settled," *Chicago Daily Tribune,* October 27, 1918.

7

"Life Is a Succession of Disappointments"

A SOVIET GIRL CONTENDS WITH
THE STALINIST DICTATORSHIP

E. THOMAS EWING

In the spring of 1934, a Soviet teenager, Nina Lugovskaya, recorded the following entry in her diary:

> The last few days I've sometimes wanted so much to tell someone everything, to open up completely, to shout: "I want to live! Why do you torment me, force me to go to school, teach me manners? I don't need anything! I want to live, laugh, sing, and be happy. I'm only fifteen years old, you know, that's the best time of life. I want to live! Teach me to live!" But I won't tell anyone this truth. They wouldn't understand, they'd only make fun of me. I don't even need them to understand, all I'm asking is that they take my thoughts seriously. The other day when I told Papa I was bored, he just laughed at me and said: "I hate people who always say, 'I'm bored, I'm bored.'" "Well you can be sure I'll never say that to you again!" I shot back. The same thing happened with Mama.[1]

At first glance, this entry appears representative of a developmental stage in the lives of adolescent girls: the challenge to conventional rules and restrictions as represented by the school and the family; the escapist desire to sing, dance, and be happy; and the conflict with parents whose guidance is both sought and rejected. Lugovskaya's sentiments match many of the psychological traits assumed to be characteristic of adolescence, including rapid emotional shifts, alienation from parents, and a desire for individual autonomy.[2]

Such presumptions of the universality of girls' lives need to be situated in specific historical circumstances, however. At the time of this diary entry, Lugovskaya's father, who so contemptuously rejected her feelings of boredom, was the target of political repression, having been exiled from the city of Moscow, and was subject at any time to arrest, imprisonment, and even death. The family home had already been searched by the security police, and Lugovskaya's own diary was a source of political vulnerability, as she admitted in numerous entries. The "manners" that she was being taught included not just how to behave in the family, school, and society, but also how to conform to the emerging Stalinist dictatorship.[3] The desire to live, which is repeated throughout the diary, acquires specific meaning in a context in which the threat of death hangs over citizens, particularly those, like Lugovskaya's family, who had already been targeted for political repression. The desire to live may have been an expression of teenage rebellion against boring routine, but in this context, this desire was also a challenge to the dictatorship that had appropriated the power to determine life and death.

Born one year after the establishment of communism in Russia, Lugovskaya was a child of a revolutionary generation in that her entire life was shaped by the expanding power of the Soviet system. Her first ten years during the 1920s were spent in the relative stability of the New Economic Policy, but she experienced adolescence in the 1930s—a time of growing fear, suspicion, surveillance, and punishment. Lugovskaya used her diary as a means to understand, and also to document the experience of living in these extraordinary times. Her sentiment that "Life is a succession of disappointments"[4] clearly illustrates the traumatic effects of constantly negotiating her own sense of reality with that imposed by the communist regime. Educated by a government that promised to build communism for the future, Lugovskaya was a victim of the same system that she conformed to, even as she struggled, internally and through her diary, to define her identity in opposition to the regime's repressive power.

A close reading of this diary also demonstrates that the political context was only one, and not always the dominant, influence on the girl's experiences, identity, and practices. Her sense of acute disappointment, which is quoted in the title of this chapter, was a response not to political repression but to her own family:

> Life is a succession of disappointments. Ever since I can remember I've been disappointed. First came my disappointment in people, and then my bitter and painful disappointment in life. I remember a time when the world seemed wonderful to me. I hadn't yet considered the whole terrible injustice of life, I didn't know how mean people were, I saw only life's beautiful façade and didn't look behind the scenes. That was such a happy time!

After reflecting on *"childhood with its short-lived joys and sorrows,"* Lugovskaya continued to express her sense of being *"disappointed in absolutely everything"*:

> In Mama, in Papa, in my sisters . . . I can now see everything as it really is. And I'm coming to the bitter conclusion that there is nothing wonderful in this world. The one thing I'm not yet disappointed in is myself. Ha-ha! Isn't that strange? I still believe in myself, I believe in the possibility of my own happiness. But I'm afraid the day will come when this last hope will melt away and the worst disappointment will set in, disappointment in myself.[5]

As this excerpt indicates, Lugovskaya's emerging sense of identity was profoundly shaped by relations within her family. In particular, the sense of always being disappointed seems to reflect a three-way relationship between her parents, the surrounding political environment, and Lugovskaya's own sense of herself as a person. While proclaiming her disappointment in her family, however, this adolescent girl also looked at herself both introspectively, as she was at the time, and predictively, as she might become in the future. Because it provides these multiple perspectives—on self and society, on past, present, and future experiences, and on the emotional component of historical experiences—this excerpt demonstrates the great possibilities of using Lugovskaya's diary to understand the lives of Soviet girls in the context of the Stalinist dictatorship. Although a diary is by definition a personal document, it also provides a perspective on broader processes, such as changes in identity associated with age as well as political outlook, and contexts, particularly the position of women in the Soviet dictatorship. These contexts are especially revealing of the ways that gender and generation shaped the identities of Soviet girls during this crucial decade.[6]

The fact that these sentences are underlined in the published version dramatically confirms the political dimension of the diary.[7] After Lugovskaya's apartment was searched in January 1937, agents from the People's Commissariat for Internal Affairs (NKVD) confiscated Lugovskaya's diary. During a subsequent investigation, an agent underlined sections deemed "incriminating." Two months later, in March 1937, Lugovskaya was arrested, as were her mother and two sisters, thus following her father, whose repeated arrests and exiles in the preceding years were a constant reminder of political repression. In June 1937, this diary was included along with other materials as "documentary corroboration of the counter-revolutionary views toward Soviet power of all of the accused members of the Lugovskaya family." Lugovskaya was sentenced to five years of hard labor followed by seven years of exile for "terrorist attempt on the life of comrade Stalin, and also on other leaders of the Party and government."[8] Although there was clearly a sense of political danger in other passages that expressed strong opposition to the Soviet regime and Stalin personally, as discussed later, this chapter also asks what was so threatening to the authorities about the statement that *Life is a succession of disappointments*"? The fact that these sentiments, articulated in response to personal and familial circumstances, were marked as politically dangerous provide further evidence of both the power of the Stalinist dictatorship and the significance of individual responses to this system.

Studying the History of Girls and Stalinism

For Soviet authorities, the slogan that youth is the future provided an important rationalization for the difficulties of the immediate context.

Communist youth organizations, the ideological values associated with education, and the promise of a better future were all evidence of the central place assigned to youth within the Stalinist system. Yet this same system was built on essential contradictions: state child care was never sufficient for the demand created by the mass mobilization of working mothers, the educational system was ideologically constrained with limited resources, and, most significantly, children as young as twelve were subject to the same severe sanctions for state crimes as adults. As with so many other social groups, the promises made to youth were never fully realized, as systemic shortages, political repression, and ideological contradictions undermined the promised utopia of communism.[9]

Yet the history of childhood, and particularly of girls, offers unique perspectives on the meanings of Stalinism in the 1930s.[10] As a generation whose lives were concurrent with Soviet power, young people experienced a collective biography similar to the revolution itself: the promise of the first decade of revolution coincided with their early childhood, whereas the repression but also the achievements of the Stalinist era evoked the impressions of a troubled "adolescence."[11] Although certainly not immune from repression, as this diary vividly illustrates, youth provided an especially valuable vantage point for understanding what the terror meant to those along the spectrum of responses between active support and helpless victimization. Finally, this perspective calls attention both to the lived experience of youth, and girls in particular, and to the rhetorical construction of childhood as a social, discursive, ideological, and rhetorical category.[12] As Lugovskaya clearly recognized, she lived the contradiction between what she was "supposed" to be, whether this normative definition was associated with state power or her own parents, and her own experiences, which revolved around personal relations, daily crisis, long-term ambitions, and constant adjustments to circumstances.[13] Focusing on a girl's diary thus makes it possible to understand the Soviet construction of childhood as perceived by the girl herself, while also exploring the daily experiences, perceptions, and practices that responded to, and thus transformed, her emerging identity.

In this chapter I draw on recent studies of girls in contemporary and historical contexts to explore the ways that adolescents made sense of the relationship among individual identity, familial relations, and more powerful forces seemingly beyond the adolescents' control. According to psychologist Mary Pipher, American girls are forced to conform to expectations that are complex and contradictory, yet extremely powerful: "The rules for girls are confusing and the deck is stacked against them, but they soon learn that this is the only game in town."[14] Rather than presuming that girls must conform to these rules, however, Pipher recognizes where and how girls can assert their own identity and agency: "Once girls understand the effects of the culture on their lives, they can fight back. They learn that they have conscious choices to make and ultimate responsibility for those choices."[15] Exploring similar dynamics in the context of nineteenth-century French boarding schools, historian Rebecca Rogers argues that girls were "learning to perform within a universe whose constraints they also learned to negoti- ate and circumvent."[16] In a related way, historian Christina Benninghaus concludes that "neither structural conditions nor cultural discourses trans- late directly into peoples' lived experiences." Understanding the latter thus calls attention to the relationship between these "external" structures and discourses, on the one hand, and "the experiences, self-perceptions, and expectations of girls," on the other.[17] Although the "structural conditions" of Stalinism ensured that the "rules" and "constraints" were inevitably political, this approach calls attention to the ways girls learned to negotiate among different demands while also creating spaces in which to enact their own identities. Thus even in this context of repressive dictatorship, individ- ual identity and collective behaviors shaped the lives of Soviet girls, who sought ways to exercise "a limited form of power."[18]

Lugovskaya lived in the shadow of the Stalinist dictatorship, but the meaning of her life was not imposed by the dictatorship.[19] For an earlier generation of Western scholars, the 1930s were most easily explained in terms of Stalin's personal dictatorship, Communist Party officials, victim- ized opponents, and apolitical masses.[20] Yet scholarly research for the past thirty years has questioned these simplified categories, and now historians seek to understand how individuals lived their lives in the context of a pow- erful but not omnipotent dictatorship and a destabilized but not atomized society. In this chapter I draw on an emerging body of scholarship con- cerned with the ways that "ordinary" Soviet people responded to "extraor- dinary" conditions in the 1930s.[21]

Although Lugovskaya's diary offers a uniquely personal perspective of what it meant to grow up in the time of Stalin, this source has significant limits. Lugovskaya lived in Moscow, in a far different context than did the peasant majority of the population or even the girls living in towns and cities across the Soviet Union. This location in the Soviet capital placed her in direct contact with key elements of the dictatorship, making her encoun- ters with Stalinism particularly intense. Having a father who was subjected to increasing political repression and then being arrested herself made Lugovskaya an exception in terms of the whole population, yet these were increasingly common experiences in the later 1930s. Although not representa- tive of the experiences of all Soviet girls, these aspects of Lugovskaya's expe- rience, and more importantly her self-reflection on these experiences through her diary, offer unique insights into those of Soviet girls in the Stalinist context. For this reason, understanding Stalinism through this diary offers insights not otherwise easily or reliably available with existing resources.[22]

This history of girls in the Stalinist era draws on and contributes to comparative and transnational approaches. Most obviously, Lugovskaya's contemporaries, Jewish girls who lived in Europe during the Holocaust, described similar perceptions of vulnerability, pursued their own survival strategies, and responded to the destructive consequences of state power. For these girls, the experience of living in a dictatorship demanded a constant recalculation of the meaning of loyalty, of attitudes toward the security apparatus, and of personal relationships in a time of acute vulnerability. Although sharing certain similarities with Anne Frank's diary, the most famous girl's account of the Holocaust, Lugovskaya's diary is most different in revealing how she saw herself as part of the Soviet system, even as her family was destroyed by that system's paradoxical patterns of repression.[23] These similarities, but also the differences, are suggestive of new ways to understand girls living in contexts determined by oppressive and dictatorial systems.[24]

This chapter also draws on interdisciplinary studies of adolescent girls that suggest frameworks for considering the emergence of female identity across the stages of personal development.[25] Diaries have proven to be an especially useful source for historical analysis. As argued by historian Jane Hunter, girls' diaries served a "mediating function," as they became a "protected space" within which nineteenth-century American girls could "entertain imaginative freedom while preserving the networks of affiliation at the center of their lives."[26] According to historian Joan Jacobs Brumberg, girls' diaries "recapture the familiar cadences of adolescent emotional life, and they provide authentic testimony to what girls in the past considered noteworthy, amusing, and sad, and what they could or would not talk about."[27] Finally, the ways that the diaries of specific girls—most recently, Zlata Filipovic's diary of the war in the former Yugoslavia—have influenced global perspectives of key historical events provide further evidence of how this kind of historical source can shape the formation of collective memory and interpretations.[28]

As Lugovskaya recognized, she lived in a deeply gendered social environment, despite the Soviet regime's promise of equality for women. In a context in which official rhetoric proclaimed that girls would receive equitable educations, could aspire to any professional role, and should expect full equality before the law, Lugovskaya confronted her father's traditional attitudes toward daughters, observed the tensions embedded in her mother's balancing of work and family, and experienced the contradictory standards of female sexuality. Although studies of Stalinism have devoted increasing attention to gender, these same accounts rarely consider the intersection of age and gender in shaping the experience of this repressive system.[29] By making a girl into the central subject of analysis, this chapter focuses on what it meant to be young and female in a time of social transformation, political repression, and generational change.

To explore these issues, I focus on Lugovskaya's relations with her family, especially her mother and father, and her response to the political situation, starting with the first search of the apartment and ending with the arrest of her entire family.[30] By using the experience of a girl to understand Stalinism, I provide a basis to consider the comparative history of girls in contexts of political repression, personal vulnerability, and social tension. As argued by a recent study of Stalinism, during "this cruel time, when they found themselves face to face with calamity, children matured with astonishing speed and learned what was by no means juvenile wisdom and responsibility."[31] Exploring "this cruel time"—or what Lugovskaya described as "a succession of disappointments"—through the lens of one girl's diary provides insights not only into her character, but into the world she inhabited and attempted to understand, shape, and even escape, but with limited effectiveness, until her own arrest ended the diary entries.

Family Relations

Lugovskaya's life was shaped directly by her position as the youngest daughter in a family in which both parents were educated professionals under increasing pressure from an authoritarian regime. In this respect, understanding Lugovskaya's relationship with each of her immediate family members is crucial to understanding what her diary reveals about the lived experience of Stalinism in the 1930s.[32] Lugovskaya's father, Sergei Rybin-Lugovskoi, was born into a peasant family and, as a young man, became active in the Socialist Revolutionary Party, an agrarian populist movement. His first arrest and exile were at the hands of the czarist authorities; later, after 1917, he worked briefly in the new revolutionary government. He was again arrested and exiled, this time by the Soviet government, in 1919. It was during this brief period between the revolution and exile that his daughter Nina Lugovskaya was born in December 1918. After three years, and following the introduction of the New Economic Policy, which allowed for a measure of private enterprise, Rybin-Lugovskoi returned to Moscow, where he started a cooperative bakery. This successful business expanded to employ four hundred people. With the introduction of the Five-Year Plan in 1928, however, Communist authorities closed employee cooperatives as part of the shift to state enterprises. Rybin-Lugovskoi was arrested and exiled to a small town north of Moscow, where he was living when his daughter began the diary in late 1932.

Nina's mother, Lyubov Lugovskaya, was the daughter of a village teacher and attended a Moscow girls' gymnasium before the revolution. While teaching in a rural school, she met and married her husband and then gave birth to twin daughters in 1915. In the 1920s, she worked in the baking cooperative but lost her position when her husband was arrested. During the 1930s, she worked as a school administrator. Older sisters Evgenia (also called Zhenya) and Olga (also called Olya) attended an arts institute during the years of the diary. This family constituted the most immediate context for Lugovskaya's emerging personality; they also shared with her the status of victims of dictatorship in that all five of them were eventually arrested and sentenced to exile. Serving as neither a buffer nor a transmission belt, Lugovskaya's family became part of her subjectivity, as they provided both resources upon which to draw and forces that directly shaped her emotional, mental, and physical well-being.

Judging by the diary, Lugovskaya did not live in a particularly happy family.[33] In one of her first entries, at the age of fourteen, she described these responses to her mother's request that the two older sisters go to the store: "They got into an argument, as usual, with all three of them screaming at each other while I sat in my room, praying they wouldn't ask me. Zhenya and Olya are still yelling at each other. Oh God! It is really funny and pathetic to look at them and think how badly we all get along."[34] This entry sets up three key themes for the rest of the diary: first, the often contentious nature of relations among family members; second, the importance that Lugovskaya attached to her perceptions of these relations; and third, her own status as both participant in and influence on these family relations. As the youngest of three girls, she was always involved, yet the diary also reflected her attempts to define (and control) the meanings of these interactions.

From the beginning of the diary, Lugovskaya's relations with her father are a point of contention. She frequently referred to her father in negative terms: he "scorns us, grumbles constantly, tells us every day that we're silly and practically calls us fools"; he pontificates and then cuts her off when she tries to speak; and he calls his youngest daughter "narrow-minded."[35] At one point, after waiting for her father to come home, she admitted that *"in my heart of hearts I didn't want him to come,"* which then prompted further reflections on her outlook: "How mean, how wrong of me! I can't understand why I should feel that way. I was sitting calmly at the table, reading a book, and I knew that if Papa came I would be deprived of that calm. I'd have to put my book away and force myself to smile and, worse still, talk about myself."[36] In subsequent entries, Lugovskaya offers an even more painful account of this relationship: *"Sometimes I just can't bear him and often I hate him. It's rather unpleasant when he suddenly starts nagging me. Yesterday we quarreled about something: he called me a fool and made all sorts of rude remarks."*[37] Later that spring, when Lugovskaya was sixteen years old, the deteriorating relationship provoked even more intense frustration: *"I just can't bear him these days; every word he says makes me angry. I'm rude and sarcastic back. No matter how much I promise myself to reform, nothing comes of it."*[38]

Although these entries express a high level of alienation, disappointment, and hostility, other entries that describe specific experiences, dialogues, and exchanges reflect a more positive impression of Lugovskaya's relationship with her father. In the spring of 1933, for example, she complained because her father wanted the family to come visit him in exile: "but . . . what about my plans for the summer? Can it really be that I won't be able to realize my dreams?"[39] Once she is in the country, however, she has a wonderful time. After spending time on the river, in the woods, and engaged in other activities, she was openly affectionate to her father: "We left about nine o'clock and I kissed Papa especially warmly since I felt a little ashamed that I wasn't staying on."[40]

A key theme that emerges from these experiences, and which Lugovskaya acknowledges, is that she and her father are very much alike. While complaining that she got along "horribly" with her family, in part because she could not stand "to be criticized or lectured," she pointed to the tense relationship with her father as a particular source of concern: "Why? I have no idea. He and I are more or less alike and that must have everything to do with it." As this comment suggests, Lugovskaya's relations with her father were refracted through her own emerging and changing personality as well as new facets of her father's behavior, emotions, and interactions. Although Lugovskaya's changing perceptions can be readily explained by the developmental stages of an adolescent, this relationship was certainly also affected by the father's increasing—and increasingly obvious—hostility to the Soviet regime. As this same entry continues, the impact of political circumstances was evident to Lugovskaya, and was noted by the security police, who marked the entire passage in the confiscated diary: "This doesn't keep me from respecting him, however, and respecting him greatly. If there is an opinion I value, it's Papa's. His opinions mean everything to me (his opinions about politics and science, that is). I accept his words of anger and sarcasm as the truth, and the harsher they are the better. I really admire Papa: from a simple peasant he became an educated, intelligent, and astonishingly sophisticated person. That's not easy, and we, of course, are no match for him." But the personal relationship described by Lugovskaya is also connected to her father's differentiated perspective on the opportunities and abilities of his daughters. Lugovskaya complained that the three daughters have "a low opinion of ourselves, but Papa has an even lower one." According to Lugovskaya, her father "rails at all Soviet young people, but to him we are the stupidest and most limited," which she then interpreted as a result of chauvinist gender prejudice: "Plus we're women and all women are worthless, not just to him but to most men. It's good we don't have a brother: the difference between Papa's treatment of him and his treatment of us would have been colossal."[41]

Embedded in this entry are a whole series of emerging perspectives: a father's changing relation with his daughter, the father as representative of a revolutionary generation transformed by work and education, the tension between patriarchal views of women and Soviet rhetoric of equality, and the conflict between Lugovskaya's desire to be heard and her reluctance to speak out. By complaining about her father's low opinion of women, by generalizing this perspective to "most men," and by speculating about how her father could have responded differently if she had a brother, Lugovskaya revealed specific ways in which her experiences and perceptions within the family were "gendered" by her position as a girl. At the same time, by exposing the inconsistency between her father's low opinion of girls and the Soviet regime's official ideology of women's equality, Lugovskaya also provided further evidence of his political deviation—which may explain the interrogator's marks on this particular passage.

The reality of political repression was a constant, if mostly unspoken, factor in this relationship between father and daughter. On March 29, 1933, Lugovskaya began her entry with a single word: "Konets," which translates simply as "The end." This sense of finality reflected her response to the fact that her father had been denied his Moscow residency permit and would have to leave his family, which led to these reflections: *"Papa's gone. He left this morning. Where has he gone? I'm afraid to write it down: the walls will see and inform. But he's no longer with us. What difference does it make where he went?"* Later that evening, Lugovskaya continued her entry with further reflections on how this relationship was shaped by an evolving perception of her father: *"In the last few days I've come to love him so. Before I didn't feel much for him, but now that they've refused him a residence permit, ordered him to get out of Moscow within ten days, it's entirely different. I love him when he's a revolutionary. I love him as a man of ideas, a man of action, a man who sticks steadfastly to his views and won't trade them for anything in the world."*[42] Two days later, while her father awaited news of his sentence, Lugovskaya reaffirmed this new appreciation of her father: *"If Papa has hope, that means a lot. I really do love him and I like the feeling of that love since once I doubted it and those doubts tormented me."*[43]

In early 1936, Lugovskaya visited her father in a Moscow prison, not long before he was exiled to Kazakhstan with a three-year sentence. Her diary entry combined her emotional responses to terrible prison conditions, where "sobs, cries, and hysterics" were "like a dream," with a promise to follow her father into exile, and then ended with this simple statement: *"I love him now."*[44] One of the last entries mentioning her father comes just one week later, as Lugovskaya recorded that the family had not received any letters from him: *"That's strange. I expect one every day. What could have happened to him? No, no, nothing terrible. So why do I keep having all sorts of ridiculous thoughts?"*[45] While illustrating a growing sense of maturity, as manifested by the determination to control "ridiculous thoughts," these entries also reflect an increasing awareness of political vulnerability, as her father, like hundreds of thousands of other Soviet citizens, was being made to disappear. Lugovskaya's perception of the political situation was directly shaped by her father's experiences, as well as by the threat of repression, which increased at the same time that her personal identity evolved.

Lugovskaya's relations with her mother were different yet also reflected the power of underlying structures. In one entry, Lugovskaya contrasts her own desire for meaningful activities with her mother's apparent submission to her fate: "Mama just cannot understand me. She demands that I help with the housekeeping, cleaning, and cooking. That's easy for her to say since she has nothing else to do. Isn't it all the same to Mama whether she goes to work or does the housekeeping? She loses time either way." By contrast, Lugovskaya describes her approach as one in which "every minute is precious": "I'm always looking for something new and useful. In school and at home my one thought is to experience. And suddenly I have to peel the potatoes and wash the dishes which means I'm falling into a stupor for an hour or even two while saying to myself over and over: 'Time is going by and you're losing it, this golden time.'" This passage illustrates how Lugovskaya's emerging sense of personal identity was defined at least partially by avoiding or negating the identity attributed to her mother. As this passage continues, moreover, Lugovskaya generalized this perception into a broader statement of gender and generational identity:

> I often wonder if I should give up all physical work, devote myself to my studies and stop listening to Mama when she reproaches me for sitting and reading while she, tired and aged, cooks lunch. Or, on the contrary, help Mama with everything, be a dutiful daughter and woman, and so remain a silly mediocrity forever. No, not for anything! I must prove that a woman is as smart as a man; that she is a person, too; and that she can work and create. I know what men think, what a high opinion they have of themselves and how it wounds them when a woman beats them at something. I want to prove that we can beat them, that we have more on our minds than boys and clothes.[46]

Echoing early Soviet rhetoric about the numbing effects of housework, this statement illustrates how gender creates the conditions in which girls and women shape their activities and identities. As the latter paragraph indicates, Lugovskaya feared the choice between two seemingly irreconcilable fates: to be a "silly mediocrity" who does the housework and is submissive, with the implication that her mother chose this identity, or to be "smart" and "beat" the men, thus rejecting the path taken by her mother.

This sense of needing to choose between opposites echoed a previous entry that, at an earlier age, articulated—and resisted—her mother's decisions. Lugovskaya began with complaints about having to do the washing and ironing, followed by more introspection: "Two different people are struggling inside me: one is the woman who is always setting the house to rights, straightening and cleaning; the other is the person who wants to devote her life to something greater." Conceding this "painful struggle" between these two alternative identities of women, Lugovskaya declared that she could not "conquer the woman in me" even as a sense of "fairness with respect to Mama" forced her to surrender to these expectations.[47] By implicitly comparing the life lived by her mother with the life she hoped to live in the future, Lugovskaya acknowledged the tension embedded in the situation of young Soviet women, who were promised equality and emancipation even as they continued to fulfill more "traditional" domestic and maternal roles. This passage personalizes this conflict, as in the desire to "conquer the woman in me" and the admission that a "sense of fairness with respect to Mama often forces me to surrender." Her diary thus appears to serve as a kind of "transitional object," as Lugovskaya defines her goals in opposition to the actions and identity of her mother, yet her diary also affirms, however reluctantly and bitterly, an allegiance to and affiliation with not only her mother but more generally to the role of women in the family and household.[48]

By early 1936, however, Lugovskaya's perceptions of her mother had changed in significantly more positive and empathetic directions:

> Poor Mama. I feel so badly for her and I so want to help her sometimes. Any minute, it seems, something unexpected will happen and everything will change, but nothing happens. She has become old, sick and apathetic toward everything, even toward us and Papa. She's like an exhausted workhorse that keeps on going in its stiff harness out of inertia, keeps pulling heavy loads even though it hasn't the strength, and meekly endures the beatings. Mama knows her duty and she will do it as long as she possibly can, until she drops dead.

As this passage continues, Lugovskaya provides an extended reflection that begins, "Mama is the ideal mother" in that she had "given her whole life to us," because "having children was the most important thing in life to her because having children means losing oneself, renouncing oneself, and living only for them." While admitting that "I didn't know that people could work that nightmarishly much, from morning till night, without respite and without pleasures," Lugovskaya also recognized that these efforts reflected her mother's fear that "every hour of rest deprives us of badly needed money."[49]

In contrast to this idealized description of her mother, in which elements of self-sacrifice, denial, and suffering acquire almost religious connotations, the rest of this entry presents a self-critical assessment of her mother's three daughters: "But her daughters, to whom she is devoted and for whom she has ruined her life, go around with noses in the air and refuse to see anything beyond their own petty lives. They imagine (the youngest one, especially) that they were created for a higher purpose, that they have extraordinary talents and that therefore it is a sin to waste time on things like cleaning the apartment." Chastising her sisters and herself for not making any effort to improve and live up to her mother's expectations for their appearance, attitudes, or behavior, Lugovskaya mocked the self-righteousness of the "lofty ideas, glorious thoughts and plans" that filled the heads of girls in her generation as they lay in bed "dreaming of their futures."[50]

Two important factors explain the contrasting descriptions of her mother. First, Lugovskaya was undergoing significant changes as she matured. In fact, in an earlier entry, she had diagnosed her previous behavior, including her acute frustration with her mother as expressed in the diary, as "the sickness that some have in adolescence. I seem to have come out of it the victor, though with great losses."[51] The other entries in late 1936 reflect this change in personality, as Lugovskaya became more tolerant and generous in her opinions of others, including her mother. Second, conditions had changed, as the constant threat of repression made life extremely difficult for her family. Yet this entry also suggests that in many ways life changed relatively little for the sisters, who "go around with noses in the air and refuse to see anything beyond their own petty lives." This sentiment suggests both the power of adolescents to focus on their own lives and the successful efforts made by Lugovskaya's mother to protect her family from the effects of both political repression and the demands of caring for the family. Even as she appreciated her mother's commitment to protect her family, Lugovskaya distanced herself from this maternal role "because having children means losing oneself, renouncing oneself, and living only for them." In other words, the self-absorption that Lugovskaya denounced in her sisters and herself very much shaped her assessment of how her mother lost her own sense of identity by devoting herself to her children. For Lugovskaya, whose entries were increasingly focused on availability and desirability of different options, "renouncing herself" was always a path to be avoided.

As the underlined sections of this entry suggest, the repressive forces of the regime assigned political meanings to Lugovskaya's perceptions of her family relations. The interrogator marked references to the father's arrest, his criticism of the regime, or his absence from the family, but also a daughter's statements of dislike for her father, questions about her mother's choices, and doubts about women's emancipation. In other words, the interrogator assigned political meaning to statements that suggested non-conformity, disobedience, or independent thinking on the part of an adolescent girl. Although it is difficult to speculate on the meaning of these notations, considering how the diary was read by the forces of repression indicates the extent to which political structures shaped girls' lives in the Stalinist era.[52] Lugovskaya's experiences were clearly different from the happy childhood promised by Stalinist propaganda. Instead, the realities of Soviet life shaped her childhood: family members either absent or intimidated, the double-burden of paid employment and housework that sapped women's time and energy, and a constant tension between the direct experience of these events and the meanings imposed by the regime. Lugovskaya may have been unusually critical of the regime, and certainly unusual in recording her heretical thoughts, but her lived experience was shared by many Soviet girls, as they too dealt with the multiple pressures of family, gender, and experience.

Yet Lugovskaya also responded to the opportunities promised by the Soviet system of the 1930s.[53] She was frustrated with both parents, for example, partly because their expectations, attitudes, and behavior contradicted the message of women's equality and emancipation absorbed from the Soviet environment. The sentiment of wanting to live was not just resistance to Stalinist repression or alienation from parental authority, but was also a desire to participate in building a new society in which young women could transcend the limits of traditional roles, familial duties, and household obligations to pursue "a higher purpose" in life. This desire for new roles in a changing society, even as she remained highly skeptical of the propaganda claims, bitterly hostile to Stalin, and oppositional in her political views, suggests that Lugovskaya had more in common with the Soviet regime than she wanted to admit—even as the forces of repression denied her the possibility of achieving these desired objectives.

Conclusion

Although the diary begins with an account of the security police searching the family's apartment, in the years that follow Lugovskaya actually portrays a decreasing sense of vulnerability. Even as her father is banished farther from the family—first he is barred from Moscow, then imprisoned, and finally sentenced to many years of exile in a distant region—Lugovskaya's diary entries, which are increasingly infrequent and brief, overwhelmingly concentrate on her classmates, changing relationships with boys, her educational opportunities, and the position of women.[54] Lugovskaya does not mention her father, nor does she express the intense political alienation of earlier years. In fact, the final entry of the diary offers a measure of optimism, as Lugovskaya reflects back on the year that had seen, among other events, the exile of her father to distant Central Asia: "Another year of my life has flown past—another small, insignificant year that I don't need anymore. I don't want to remember it or think about it. Why should I? I'm looking ahead and only ahead. All my past failures are making me reform. But I won't torment myself because we learn from our mistakes. That's a sort of preface to the New Year."[55]

Two days later, the NKVD searched the home and confiscated the diary as evidence of "terrorist" views. Lugovskaya was arrested on March 20, 1937; there is no record of her activities between the search and the arrest. During her interrogation, she was confronted with entries "proving" her "extremely hostile attitude toward the leaders of the Bolshevik Party and primarily toward Stalin," and in particular her "terrorist designs on Stalin." Interrogators using threats of execution forced Lugovskaya to confess her intention to assassinate Stalin. On June 20, 1937, Lugovskaya, her mother, and two sisters were sentenced to forced labor for their "anti-Soviet" views. After living in the shadow of repression for so many years, Lugovskaya and her family now entered the even more terrifying world of the Gulag, an acronym that defined the emerging network of prisons, camps, and settlements across the USSR.

As I have argued in this chapter, Lugovskaya's diary offers powerful insights into Stalinism and thus demonstrates how research on girls can contribute to new historical understandings. In particular, studying the history of girls illustrates the interpenetration of personal and political spheres at the level of daily practice. Lugovskaya's diary entries about her parents and political conditions reflect processes of negotiating personal needs, interests, and emotions within more powerful structures, processes, and systems. Just as Lugovskaya's relations with her parents shifted, evolved, and developed, so too did her relationship with Stalinist political structures. The patterns and especially the costs were quite different, yet mutually influential, for as the political repression escalated, Lugovskaya drew closer to her parents. In regard to both relationships, however, this diary reveals the efforts of a girl determined to make sense of conditions, to shape her own interests and identity, and to act in ways that allowed some agency in response to these conditions. In this way the perspective of a girl reveals both the tremendous power of the Stalinist system and the importance of individual agency, action, and intentions in determining the meanings of this system.

Comparative and global perspectives reveal that Lugovskaya's diary also offers insights into girls' lives in a dictatorship as well as during other times of intense political conflict. The obvious similarities with Anne Frank's diary are proof of the former comparison. Both girls describe the effects of living under the threat of repression, their own development as adolescents in these destructive contexts, and the ways individuals made sense of these mortal threats. Both diaries thus provide unique insights into the processes through which individual girls made sense of the ways in which they, along with their families and literally millions of others, were made victims of repression. Whereas Frank and her family understood the danger posed by an avowedly hostile Nazi occupation of Holland, Lugovskaya and her family never really understood the danger they faced because the regime itself operated on the basis of constantly evolving, expanding, and even self-consuming definitions of "enemies." Because of the nature of the threat she faced, Lugovskaya's diary is perhaps more revealing of the more widespread experiences of girls living in times of intense political conflict, including military occupation, civil war, ethnic conflict, or revolutionary transformations. In these cases, categories such as age and gender intersect in complex and contradictory ways with shifting, evolving, and ambiguous patterns of violence, opportunity, repression, liberation, and development. For girls in these situations, as for Lugovskaya, the challenge of survival demanded insights into the forces that threatened their lives, even as they coped with the stresses and opportunities associated "in normal times" with adolescence. This diary also offers insights into girls in more "stable" circumstances, when the turmoil of adolescence, as expressed in personal writings, may seem at odds with the apparent prosperity and peace of the historical context.[56] By revealing how Lugovskaya was forced to live through an extremely difficult and unstable time while also dealing with a range of family issues, this diary illustrates the importance of studying girls' history at the point of intersection between the personal and the political.

Lugovskaya, her sisters, and her mother worked in a concentration camp in the far northeastern region of Kolyma for the next five years. On June 17, 1942, one year after the German invasion, they were released from the labor camp but confined to this remote region as so-called civilian workers. Lugovskaya's mother died in the Magadan region on December 7, 1949; her father was released in 1947 and returned to Moscow, where he died in the late 1950s. Her sisters, now married, sought "rehabilitation" in the decade that followed Stalin's death in 1953. Evgenia was the first to have her sentence overturned, in 1957, for lack of evidence; their father was rehabilitated posthumously in 1959 and their mother in 1961; Olga was rehabilitated in 1962. Authorities, however, rejected each request for the rehabilitation of Nina Lugovskaya. Finally, in 1963, she sent a letter to Soviet leader Nikita Khrushchev in which she declared that the arrest of her father "painfully traumatized a child's soul, and left bitterness for many years, which provoked in the diary the bitter lines against the cruelties of Stalin." Apparently this appeal worked: on May 27, 1963, Lugovskaya's conviction was overturned on the basis of "unproven accusations."[57]

Lugovskaya spent the fifty years after her release in 1942 from the concentration camp working in a variety of artistic and theatrical occupations. After she was allowed to leave the Far East in 1953, Lugovskaya moved with her husband, Viktor Templin, also a former political prisoner, to the Siberian city of Perm, and then to Vladimir, located to the east of Moscow. She worked as an artist for a regional theater company and then became a painter. In 1977, she held a one-woman show in Vladimir, and her paintings were displayed in many buildings, including the public library. Lugovskaya died on December 27, 1993, at the age of seventy-five.[58] Her views and actions from six decades earlier—her fear that "life is a succession of disappointments" and her determination to make choices that would lead to a better life—are now contributing to a deeper understanding of Stalinism and the history of girls.

NOTES

1. Nina Lugovskaya, *The Diary of a Soviet Schoolgirl, 1932–1937*, trans. Joanne Turnbull (Moscow: Glas, 2003), March 21, 1934, 84–85. Nina Lugovskaya began her diary in 1932 and wrote the final entry in January 1937, shortly before she was arrested and the Soviet regime sent her, along with her sisters, father, and mother, into exile. Her diary, discovered in secret police archives by Irina Osipova, was published first in Russian and then in English translation. Nina Lugovskaya, *Khochu zhit': Iz dnevnika shkol'nitsy, 1932–1937: Po materialam sledstvennogo dela sem'i Logovskikh* (Moscow: Formika-S, 2003). A new English translation was published in 2006, with a title matching the Russian version, *I Want to Live: The Diary of a Young Girl in Stalin's Russia* (London: Doubleday, 2006). Lugovskaya's diary has been reviewed by historians but has not

been the subject of scholarly analysis. The most thorough review is by the preeminent Soviet historian Sheila Fitzpatrick, "Pessimism and Boys," *London Review of Books* 26, no. 9 (May 6, 2004), www.lrb.co.uk. See also Donald Morrison, "In the People's Paradise: Boys, Pranks and Police Raids—A Teen Diary Gives Rare Insight into Everyday Life under Stalin," *Time Europe Online*, July 23, 2006, www.time.com/time/europe/magazine/ (accessed September 6, 2006); Donald Rayfield, "A Russian Anne Frank," *Literary Review*, July 2006, www.literaryreview .co.uk (accessed October 17, 2006); Gaby Wood, "I Was a Teenage Anarchist . . . Nearly," *Observer*, August 6, 2006, http://books.guardian.co.uk/reviews/ (accessed September 6, 2006); and the review by Alison Rowley in *Canadian Slavonic Papers*, September–December 2004, www.findarticles.com (accessed October 17, 2006). Quotations in this chapter are from the Turnbull translation cited earlier, with clarifications from the Russian version as necessary. The original diary is preserved in the State Archive of the Russian Federation in a KGB file (file 10035). Access to these materials is restricted to relatives and those with special permission; this chapter thus relies on the published versions of the diary and related materials.

2. For historical studies of girls' adolescence, see Irene Hardach-Pinke, "Managing Girls' Sexuality among the German Upper Classes," 101–114; Rebecca Rogers, "Porous Walls and Prying Eyes: Control, Discipline, and Morality in Boarding Schools for Girls in Mid-Nineteenth Century France," 115–130; Celine Grasser, "Good Girls versus Blooming Maidens: The Building of Female Middle- and Upper-Class Identities in the Graden, England and France, 1820–1870," 131–146; Kathleen Alaimo, "The Authority of Experts: The Crisis of Female Adolescence in France and England, 1880–1920," 149–163; Christina Benninghaus, "In Their Own Words: Girls' Representations of Growing Up in Germany in the 1920s," 178–191; Pamela Cox, "Girls in Trouble: Defining Female Delinquency, Britain, 1900–1950," 195–205; Elizabeth Bright Jones, "Girls in Court: Mägde versus Their Employers in Saxony, 1880–1914," 224–238; and Tammy M. Proctor, "'Something for the Girls': Organized Leisure in Europe, 1890–1939," 239–253, all in *Secret Gardens, Satanic Mills: Placing Girls in European History, 1750–1960*, ed. Mary Jo Maynes, Birgitte Søland, and Christina Benninghaus (Bloomington: Indiana University Press, 2005); Jane Hunter, *How Young Ladies Became Girls: The Victorian Origins of American Girlhood* (New Haven: Yale University Press, 2002); Linda W. Rosenzweig, *The Anchor of My Life: Middle Class American Mothers and Daughters, 1880–1920* (New York: New York University Press, 1993), 70–90.

3. Although "manners" is a sufficient translation, the Russian phrase *prilichie* can also mean "decency," "propriety," or "decorum," suggesting a more formal category of behaviors deemed proper in a particular context. Lugovskaya, *Khochu zhit'*, 109.

4. Lugovskaya, *Diary*, August 28, 1933, 61.

5. Ibid. The underlined sections of the diary found in the Russian state archive are re-created in published and translated versions of the diary; they are italicized in this chapter.

6. For more discussion of the diary as a source for understanding Soviet identities in the Stalinist context, see Jochen Hellbeck, *Revolution on My Mind: Writing a Diary under Stalin* (Cambridge: Harvard University Press, 2006); Hellbeck, "The Diary between Literature and History: A Historian's Critical Response," *Russian Review* 63 (October 2004): 621–629; Hellbeck, "Working, Struggling, Becoming: Stalin-Era Autobiographical Texts," *Russian Review* 60 (July 2001): 340–359; Hellbeck, "Self-Realization in the Stalinist System: Two Soviet Diaries of the 1930s," in *Russian Modernity: Politics, Knowledge, Practices*, ed. David Hoffmann and Yanni Kotsonis, 221–242 (New York: Palgrave Macmillan, 2000); Hellbeck, "Speaking Out: Languages of Affirmation and Dissent in Stalinist Russia," *Kritika: Explorations in Russian and Eurasian History* 1, no. 1 (2000): 71–96; E. Thomas Ewing, "Revolution in My Relationships: A Soviet Girl Writes a Diary in the Stalinist Era," manuscript, 2008.

7. This information, derived from the archival files for the Lugovskaya family, is provided in Lugovskaya, *Diary*, 213–215; Lugovskaya, "Zakliuchenie," in *Khochu zhit'*, 272–278.

8. Lugovskaya, "Zakliuchenie," in *Khochu zhit'*, 275.

9. For Soviet childhood and generational identities within the context of preschool and school institutions, see Larry Holmes, *Stalin's School: Moscow's Model School No. 25* (Pittsburgh: University of Pittsburgh Press, 1999); Lisa Kirschenbaum, *Small Comrades: Revolutionizing*

Childhood in Soviet Russia, 1917–1932 (New York: Routledge Falmer, 2001). See also the interpretation of how family relations were affected by escalating political repression in Robert W. Thurston, "The Family during the Great Terror," *Soviet Studies* 43, no. 3 (1991): 553–574.

10. See also the chapters by Jesse Hingson and Corrie Decker in this volume for similar interpretations of political transformations through the perspectives of adolescent girls.

11. See the discussion of youth experience and identity in Lewis Siegelbaum and Andrei Sokolov, *Stalinism as a Way of Life: A Narrative in Documents* (New Haven: Yale University Press, 2000), 357–420.

12. For discussion of how the generation of Kenyan girls who lived through the first decades of independence saw themselves as "historical actors," see Decker, in this volume.

13. This approach is suggested by Pamela Cox in her discussion of the "different turn" that was presumed for girls' route "to status, selfhood, and womanhood," because the important relationships were "played out in very different spaces: the family, the domestic, the home." Experts declared that girls' proper development depended not on their public performance of roles, but "upon their private performance as daughters, partners, and parents" ("Girls in Trouble," 199).

14. Mary Pipher, *Reviving Ophelia: Saving the Selves of Adolescent Girls* (New York: Putnam, 1994), 39.

15. Ibid., 44. Making a similar point in a different historical context, a recent study that focuses on leisure organizations of the interwar period concludes that European girls "were fed a mixed message," with recurring tensions resulting from society's demand for respectability, the family lessons of household management, girls' desire for fun, and the shaping of an identity of individuality, self-sufficiency, and independence. Proctor, "Something for the Girls," 240.

16. Rogers, "Porous Walls," 127.

17. Benninghaus, "In Their Own Words," 179. See also the call for understanding children's agency, "the extent that children can participate in determining the frameworks within which they live," in Peter N. Stearns, "Preface: Globalization and Childhood," *Journal of Social History* 38, no. 4 (Summer 2005): 846. Lugovskaya's relationship to Stalinism may be productively compared to the relationship between girls and globalization, which is defined as "not an irresistible juggernaut that rolls in only one direction but rather a piecemeal series of reinterpretations and responses expressed through concrete activities rooted in specific needs, cultures, and choices." Raymond Grew, "On Seeking Global History's Inner Child," *Journal of Social History* 38, no. 4 (Summer 2005): 854.

18. See the analysis of girls' exercise of "a limited form of power" in Mary Jo Maynes, "In Search of Arachne's Daughters: European Girls, Economic Development, and the Textile Trade, 1750–1880," in Maynes, Søland, and Benninghaus, *Secret Gardens, Satanic Mills*; and Benninghaus, "In Their Own Words," 50. In this volume, see Nancy Stockdale's analysis of how Palestinian schoolgirls used "the small amount of power" available to them in their relations with English missionary teachers.

19. The formulation "in the shadow of Stalinism" is suggested by the title of the edited collection by Sheila Fitzpatrick and Yuri Slezkine, eds., *In the Shadow of Revolution: Life Stories of Russian Women from 1917 to the Second World War* (Princeton, NJ: Princeton University Press, 2000).

20. Robert Conquest, *The Great Terror: A Reassessment* (New York: Oxford University Press, 1990); Merle Fainsod, *How Russia Is Ruled* (Cambridge: Harvard University Press, 1963).

21. Sheila Fitzpatrick, *Stalin's Peasants: Resistance and Survival in the Russian Village after Collectivization* (New York: Oxford University Press, 1994); Fitzpatrick, *Everyday Stalinism: Ordinary Life in Extraordinary Times: Soviet Russia in the 1930s* (New York: Oxford University Press, 1999); Stephen Kotkin, *Magnetic Mountain: Stalinism as a Civilization* (Berkeley: University of California Press, 1995); Sarah Davies, *Popular Opinion in Stalin's Russia: Terror, Propaganda, and Dissent, 1934–1941* (New York: Cambridge University Press, 1997); Lynne Viola, *Peasant Rebels under Stalin: Collectivization and the Culture of Peasant Resistance* (New York: Oxford University Press,

1996); E. Thomas Ewing, *The Teachers of Stalinism: Policy, Practice, and Power in Soviet Schools of the 1930s* (New York: Peter Lang Publishing, 2002); Holmes, *Stalin's School*. See the range of narratives, as well as the critical analysis, in Fitzpatrick and Slezkine, *Shadow of Revolution*.

22. See a similar study based on a single schoolgirl's diary: Rebecca Rogers, "Schools, Discipline, and Community: Diary-Writing and School Girl Culture in Late Nineteenth-Century France," *Women's History Review* 4, no. 4 (1995): 525–555. The study of Stalinism has been significantly influenced by research in diaries kept during the 1930s, including some, like Lugovskaya's diary, that have been unavailable in the decades since they were written. For the use of diaries to understand the formation of Stalinist subjects, see Veronique Garros, Natalia Korenevskaia, and Thomas Lahusen, eds., *Intimacy and Terror: Soviet Diaries of the 1930s* (New York: Free Press, 1995); Natalia Kozlova, "The Diary as Initiation and Rebirth: Reading Everyday Documents of the Early Soviet Era," in *Everyday Life in Early Soviet Russia*, ed. Christina Kiaer and Eric Naiman (Bloomington: Indiana University Press, 2006), 284–285; Hellbeck, *Revolution on My Mind*; Ewing, "Revolution in My Relationships."

23. Anne Frank, *The Diary of a Young Girl: The Definitive Edition* (New York: Bantam Books, 1996). See also the essays in Hyman Aaron Enzer and Sandra Solotaroff-Enzer, eds., *Anne Frank: Reflections on Her Life and Legacy* (Urbana Champaign: University of Illinois Press, 2000). The similarities to Frank's diary have been noted in recent reviews of the English translations of Lugovskaya's diary. See Wood, "I Was a Teenage Anarchist"; Rayfield, "Russian Anne Frank"; and the back cover of the 2003 English translation.

24. For a vivid memoir by a Jewish girl in Poland, which offers a strikingly different account than that of Frank, see Alicia Appleman-Jurman, *Alicia: My Story* (New York: Bantam, 1988).

25. Influential recent studies include Joan Jacobs Brumberg, *The Body Project: An Intimate History of American Girls* (New York: Vintage Books, 1998); Judy Mann, *The Difference: Discovering the Hidden Ways We Silence Girls: Finding Alternatives That Can Give Them a Voice* (New York: Time Warner, 1994); Peggy Orenstein, *SchoolGirls: Young Women, Self-Esteem, and the Confidence Gap* (New York: Anchor Books, 1994); and Pipher, *Reviving Ophelia*.

26. Hunter, *How Young Ladies Became Girls*, 47. See also Hunter's statement from an earlier article: "As both discipline and technique, diary-keeping contributed to the process by which late Victorian girls amassed fragments of experience into identity." Jane Hunter, "Inscribing the Self in the Heart of the Family: Diaries and Girlhood in Late-Victorian America," *American Quarterly* 44, no. 1 (March 1992): 52.

27. Brumberg, *Body Project*, xxvii.

28. Zlata Filipovic, *Zlata's Diary* (New York: Viking, 1994).

29. Important studies of Soviet women during the 1930s include Melanie Ilič, ed., *Women in the Stalin Era* (London: Palgrave, 2001), 49–68; Wendy Z. Goldman, *Women, the State, and Revolution: Soviet Family Policy and Social Life, 1917–1936* (Cambridge: Cambridge University Press, 1993); Goldman, *Women at the Gates: Gender and Industry in Stalin's Russia* (Cambridge: Cambridge University Press, 2002); Rebecca Balmas Neary, "Mothering Socialist Society: The Wife-Activists' Movement and the Soviet Culture of Daily Life, 1934–41," *Russian Review* 58 (July 1999): 396–412; David L. Hoffmann, "Mothers in the Motherland: Stalinist Pronatalism in its Pan-European Context," *Journal of Social History* 34, no. 1 (2000): 35–54; Thomas G. Schrand, "Soviet 'Civic-Minded' Women in the 1930s: Gender, Class, and Industrialization in a Socialist Society," *Journal of Women's History* 11, no. 3 (1999): 126–150; Amy E. Randall, "Revolutionary Bolshevik Work: Stakhanovism in Retail Trade," *Russian Review* 59, no. 3 (July 2000): 425–441; Randall, "Legitimizing Soviet Trade: Gender and the Feminization of the Retail Workforce in the Soviet 1930s," *Journal of Social History* 27, no. 4 (2004): 965–990.

30. Other important aspects of Lugovskaya's life, including her relations with girlfriends, increasing interest in boys, school activities, and perceptions of her role in society, are the subjects of other publications of mine in progress: "The Exercise of Power in an Authoritarian School" (manuscript, 2008), which uses firsthand accounts by Soviet girls to explore gender identities and social relations in schools of the 1930s; and "Revolution in My Relationships,"

which contrasts Lugovskaya's diary with recent historiographical debates on the formation of Soviet subjectivities.

31. Siegelbaum and Sokolov, *Stalinism,* 414.

32. The background information on the family is provided by the editors of the Russian- and English-language versions of the diary. Lugovskaya, foreword to *Diary,* 5–8; Lugovskaya, "Vstuplenie," in *Khochu zhit',* 5–14.

33. This formulation draws upon Leo Tolstoy's famous opening line from *Anna Karenina:* "All happy families are alike but an unhappy family is unhappy after its own fashion." Leo Tolstoy, *Anna Karenina* (New York: Penguin, 1984), 13.

34. Lugovskaya, *Diary,* October 17, 1932, 13.

35. Ibid., January 18, 1933, 33; December 20, 1933, 73; February 10, 1934, 82.

36. Ibid., May 24, 1933, 49–50.

37. Ibid., April 18, 1934, 92.

38. Ibid., May 18, 1934, 94.

39. Ibid., May 24, 1933, 50.

40. Ibid., June 4, 1933, 54.

41. Ibid., December 26, 1933, 75 (all quotations in the paragraph).

42. Ibid., March 29, 1933, 41–42, 42–43.

43. Ibid., March 31, 1933, 44.

44. Ibid., March 16, 1936, 202–203.

45. Ibid., March 23, 1936, 203.

46. Ibid., November 17, 1935, 191–192 (all quotations in the paragraph).

47. Ibid., October 1, 1934, 112.

48. Hunter argues that girls' diaries both "moderated parental dictates" and "mediated parental identifications" and thus served as "transitional objects" that facilitated processes of adolescent separation. Through their diaries, "Victorian girls embarked on imaginative journeys which did not threaten to take them too far from home" (Hunter, "Inscribing the Self," 65).

49. Lugovskaya, *Diary,* January 17, 1936, 201.

50. Ibid.

51. Ibid., October 5, 1936, 206–207. For "scientific discourse" surrounding girls' adolescence in early twentieth-century Europe (but with no discussion of the Russian or Soviet context), see Alaimo, "Authority of Experts," 149–163.

52. One reviewer noted the "uncanny" effect of reading the underlined passages: "Though there is only one narrator, the diary comes to us with two built-in points of view: we read her words through their eyes. There is a sense of reading over someone's shoulder." Wood, "I Was a Teenage Anarchist."

53. For an interpretation of how political instability could create new opportunities for young women, even as they created new dangers, see the chapter in this volume by Hingson.

54. These views, which were of course political as well as personal, are discussed more fully in my unpublished papers "Exercise of Power" and "Revolution in My Relationships."

55. Lugovskaya, *Diary,* January 2, 1937, 212.

56. See discussion in Brumberg, *Body Project,* 134–135; Pipher, *Reviving Ophelia,* 12–28.

57. This additional information comes from the afterword to the English translation (213–215) and the "Zakliuchenie" to the Russian text (272–278).

58. Photographs of Lugovskaya during this era are included in the published diaries; the Russian version also contains self-portraits and other reproductions of her artwork. *Khochu zhit',* 192–193.

8   *Fragilities and Failures,*
Promises and Patriotism

ELEMENTS OF SECOND WORLD WAR
ENGLISH AND AMERICAN GIRLHOOD,
1939–1945

LISA L. OSSIAN

*"Into the sunlit gardens of childhood come the fury and
storm of war."*   —*Time*, March 8, 1943

"How you expect to get married and keep house is beyond me, Alicia," the cartoon-character mother began her lecture, "you can't cook and you wouldn't know the first thing to do about an incendiary bomb on the roof!" In another wartime illustration, a little girl in a pinafore played tea party with a doll dressed smartly in a military uniform. In England and the United States, girls received an interesting and mixed set of messages during World War II: dolls and bombs, tea parties and battles, dresses and uniforms, domesticity and tenacity, femininity and bravery.

Trying to be a good little soldier, Margaret Shelton explained to reporters in 1941 that she could "leave her British home but not her doll, Pat." As an evacuated child, Margaret wanted her doll to share this expected happiness in America. Another little Margaret, a four-year-old refugee, clutched a very different memory of her homeland: her most cherished possession was now a two-pound magnesium incendiary bomb. The small but deadly cylinder fell from the skies into her London garden but had not detonated. As *Life* magazine surmised, "Reared in a war-torn city, Margaret could not cry."[1]

Elements of a Second World War girlhood combined politics, sentiment, danger, and action. Girls became a needed faction to fight this war, contributing to the home front in both a military and domestic fashion, yet these children's necessary contributions remained marginalized even though these stressful war years emerged as terribly significant in the emotional and physical development of girls growing up on both sides of the Atlantic Ocean.[2] English and American girls faced severe wartime challenges during the era of the Second World War. Caught between, girls occupied liminal spaces—a threshold both physiologically as well as psychologically between childhood and womanhood. Changing concepts of girlhood as well as increasing traumas of home front social spaces propelled girls in both England and the United States into new roles and responsibilities, where they often felt both fragile yet brave within their new circumstances. Wartime girls faced failures and optimism within their new social roles, believed authoritative promises about protection and change, embraced increasing waves of patriotism and propaganda, and challenged society's juvenile labels and gendered biases. The elements of a Second World War English and American girlhood would, at times, offer girls greater agency—movement and independence—but the era also restricted girls' time and options as a result of the unquestioning demands and dangers of wartime production. Girls in both countries necessarily spent more time within the adult spaces of employment and homemaking rather than in childhood's creative and imaginative places of play. War, as an ultimate stress on society, compressed the stage of girlhood, offering little time to enjoy girlish gardens when, realistically, food and freedom were at a premium. The result would be competing girlhood narratives of both wartime strength and fear, promise and failure.[3]

Danger and disruption were elements of girlhood in both England and the United States during the Second World War. Government strategies for coping sent mixed messages about girls' vulnerabilities and strengths. After refusing defeat in 1940, England battled alone against Hitler's Nazi forces. "Whenever the sirens went," Christine Powell recalled of her London childhood, "I was yanked out of bed, put into my pink siren suit to keep warm, and together we would sit huddled under the stairs till the 'All Clear' was sounded." Teenager Nina Masel also remembered her first air raid alert. She was playing the piano when her dad yelled out, "All get your gas masks. . . . Steady, no panicking! . . . Every man for himself. . . . Keep in the passage!" Nina's eleven-year-old sister could only sob during their first ordeal: "Will it be all right?"[4]

In preparation for possibly deadly bombings, the British distributed bomb shelters on a mass scale. Called Anderson shelters, the structures were shaped of corrugated steel sheeting and sat buried four-feet deep in family gardens, with fifteen inches of soil on top. Sheila Garrigue recalled "the dank air" of her family's shelter and "the flat, chill smell of mildew and moss and mouldering underground things." Victoria Massey remembered watching construction as metal sheets, joined with a wrench, formed their "igloo-like shelter." Victoria and her brother found sliding on the slippery metal roof great fun until workers covered it with dirt, and it became "a jerry-fooling bank of flowers." Most British grew vegetable gardens on their Anderson shelter covers, and for children, these bomb shelters became one of the "small spaces," albeit somewhat frightening places, of childhood play.[5]

To ensure the physical safety of children from bombing and possible invasion, the British government proposed massive evacuation; officials began planning this Government Evacuation Scheme two years before war began. To transport two million urban children in four days at the cost of half a billion dollars equaled "the greatest rearrangement of population in modern times." The ministers' unanimous decision remained grim but determined: "The children, England's future, came first."[6]

M Day meant the declared movement of children. At 5:30 A.M. on September 1, 1939, the first day of the massive government scheme, almost 30,000 special trains transported 700,000 children. Seventy-two subway stations were closed to the public to accommodate evacuees, and nine main London roads were turned into "one way evacuation arteries." Parents attached labels to children's coats and packed knapsacks according to government instructions. Each child carried a gas mask in its cardboard box and a postcard to be mailed home to the parents upon arrival at a final destination. Children remained billeted with mandated rural families in "safe areas" and attended schools in "double shifts." As *Time* magazine announced, "This was War and [the children] were in it."[7]

Still, over 100,000 children remained in London, a city now without public schools or other places for children's education and safety. The evacuation scheme remained voluntary; many parents seemed unconvinced of war's immediate dangers and so preferred to keep their children close despite tragic risks. Children were soon "running wild" in Manchester, Birmingham, and Liverpool because the government refused to reopen the urban schools. Other evacuations followed, both planned and spontaneous, especially during severe bombing. "By the time war ended in 1945," wrote Carlton Jackson in *Who Will Take Our Children?* "the British had evacuated over four million vulnerable people—mostly children—from the larger cities to the countryside, and to various places overseas."[8]

Evacuation experiences varied. From the safe distance of America, *Life* published romanticized images of England's urban children: "Youngsters, untouched by war and excited at the idea of going to the country, press their noses to the train window and grin as they leave London." Actual events never seemed as carefree. "All the mothers stood on their doorsteps crying as we walked to the station," Irene Weller began her "vac" story, "and I said to my brothers as we walked past our house, 'don't look round whatever you do,' because I knew my mum would be there waving. So we just looked straight ahead and when we got past I looked at my brothers and they were still looking straight ahead like I'd told them to but tears were just pouring down all our faces."[9]

Most British children remained stoic, seemingly determined not to exhibit any swirling emotions as they ventured on. War meant movement. "A trail of mothers and children with bags and gas masks slung over shoulders, and with packages under arms, labels flapping in buttonholes," elaborated Victoria Massey, "made their way along the dock road towards the village school, to be swallowed by the gate in the wall, and like the Pied Piper's children, perhaps never to return." Victoria described the perplexing picture: "We must have looked a sorry sight with pixie-hoods drooping, and our identity labels flapping sharply into our faces, the string of our gas mask boxes cutting into shoulders and our arms aching from the weight of haversacks. Our faces were thin and white after long nights spent in shelters and it was perhaps no wonder that the people who awaited our arrival thought they had got what they feared—a bunch of kids from the city slums." Her father's final comment remained locked in Victoria's memory: "Chin up!"[10]

Although many memories remain poignant but proud for these girls, a certain amount of anger and remorse surrounds the British government's evacuation scheme. One evacuee later emphasized this policy as "a monstrous thing to do." "Even the despised Nazis thought no children under ten should be evacuated without their parents," wrote H. V. Nicholson at the beginning of her personal investigation. "The British Government of 1939 is the only one in the history of the world which carried out such a policy on such a scale." Traumatic—many children recalled.[11]

"How could air raids, sleepless nights, and shelter life lead to a more stable personality than fresh air, uninterrupted studies, and a steady home?" asked Sir Geoffrey Shakespeare, director of Children's Overseas Reception Board (CORB), who estimated that more than 10,000 children might be evacuated to Canada and America. Plans abounded. Before the United States entered the war, organizations such as the American Red Cross, League of Mercy, and Society of Friends announced joint efforts to evacuate British children. "Once they were at sea," wrote the author of *Who Will Take Our Children?* "the evacuees did what children all over the world have done: they improvised and organized, and simply got down to the business of living."[12]

The journey proved too treacherous when the passenger ship *Lancastria*, carrying three hundred "little refugees" to American, sank after being struck by a German torpedo. The children, with coats quickly slung over pajamas, boarded lifeboats without panic as childish voices sang "Roll Out the Barrel" and "There'll Always Be an England." When they finally reached a safe British port, Geoffrey Shakespeare greeted the rescued children.

After transporting thousands of children safely, CORB experienced its first tragedy in mid-September 1940 when a German U-boat sunk the transport ship *City of Benares* one night in "tempestuous weather." Despite "gallant rescue efforts," eighty-three children and seven volunteer escorts drowned. Soon after, another transport was torpedoed, and the Germans refused to guarantee safe passage for English children, so the overseas evacuation efforts ceased.[13]

War came to America the first Sunday in December 1941. On that morning of December 7, Patricia and Eleanor, fourteen and eleven, found their mother shaking them and rushing everyone downstairs for protection. The

Bellingers lived in officers' quarters, part of an old fort on Oahu, and the sisters ran to the shelter still in pajamas, although Patricia managed to snatch her lipstick. Other startled women and children began finding their way to this cellar. "They were white-faced," Mrs. Bellinger remembered. "I kept thinking, what if this caves in and we're covered up. Will I be able to stand it?"[14]

Other girls, aptly named Noel, Merrily, and Gerta, ran to their neighbor's house for safety during the bombing just weeks before Christmas. Their mother believed the younger girls did not seem too worried throughout the attack, although two-year-old Noel continuously hugged her doll. In Honolulu, children ran up the streets, seeking any type of shelter. Near Alewa Heights, a father clutched his daughter like a tragic rag doll. Blake Clarke described the citizens' chaos: "The family of five had been standing on the doorstep when the bomb fell. A piece of shrapnel had flown straight to the girl's heart. The man looked helplessly about him for a moment, then ran up the steps of his home and disappeared into the house with his dead daughter."[15]

Pearl Harbor's victims numbered not only military men but also island residents. The day after the attack, the *Honolulu Star-Tribune* reported forty-nine civilians dead, including four girls. The injured totaled eighty-three, including several girls who suffered bullet wounds, ragged cuts, compound fractures, and internal injuries.[16] The Hawaiian garden paradise suddenly was shattered with torpedoes, bombs and bullets.

In the continental United States, news of Pearl Harbor shook all Americans, regardless of age. One fourteen-year-old believed that "the Victory girl grew up in a hurry." "What I feel most about the war," this now-grown woman told Studs Terkel for his oral memoir *The Good War*, is that "it disrupted my family. That really chokes me up, makes me feel very sad that I lost that. On December 6, 1941, I was playing with paper dolls: Deanna Durbin, Sonja Henie. I had a Shirley Temple doll that I cherished. After Pearl Harbor, I never played with dolls again." Vesta Lou Hubbard, age fifteen that fateful day, remembered asking her father about the attack, "What does it mean?" Her father replied with simply one word: "War."[17]

War also meant movement for many American children, although they usually moved with parents as part of the defense migration northward and westward into inadequately prepared "war boom" communities fraught with hazards for unwary children. Michigan's Ypsilanti, known as Bomber City, boomed with bomber construction in Henry Ford's largest factory ever. The first housing units for families, however, were not built until months after the factory began production. "Most workers and their families lived in cramped and often squalid quarters," writes historian Richard Overy, "half of them in shacks, tents, and trailers, often miles from the nearest shops, without laundry facilities or even running water. School construction lagged as well, so most of their children were in badly overcrowded classrooms or else on half-day schedules." Many industrial cities appeared to be so unprepared to meet children's basic needs that a 1943 congressional committee, led by Senator Claude Pepper, began an investigation.[18]

On the West Coast, the involuntary internment of over 110,000 Japanese Americans, including whole families, dramatically affected the children involved, as these nisei, second-generation Japanese and full American citizens, were subjected to loss of their Fourteenth Amendment rights. Parents and camp teachers were determined that, within the camps, their children would experience as normal and active—and American—a childhood as possible, with a regular school curriculum, recreational activities such as swimming and hiking, organized clubs such as scouting, voluntary war bond drives, and holiday celebrations. Christmas arrived complete with Santa Claus and presents. During one war bond drive, Aiko Kakimonto of Intermediate Troop 11, at Heart Mountain camp, won first prize of $3.50 by selling $90.25 worth of war bonds. Helen Kato sold $75.50, receiving second prize of $1.50. Families remained interned until 1945.[19]

Economies of Girlhood in Wartime

In addition to physical dangers and disruption, girls confronted wartime shortages. As a priority group, British children under six received a green government book for half the adult meat ration and no tea allowance, but they qualified for extra eggs and milk when available. Older children, five to sixteen, received a blue book. Ann Stalcup realized the importance immediately, "I'll never forget the number on my ration book: ODIJ2293." She remembered "clutching it and hoping that, magically, enough coupons would appear in it so I could get some new shoes."[20]

A special childhood moment for Ann involved her mother's rationing creativity. "Even though food was in short supply," Ann recalled, "Mum somehow managed to gather enough extra food for me to have a birthday party." One girl sat with hands in her lap and ate nothing throughout the party—waiting for the cake to be served. When Ann's Mum finally explained that the cake was a fake bakery prop (a solution due to severe sugar rationing), the girl burst into tears. Another evacuee remembered some celebrations during the war but mostly constant pangs of hunger at her severely food-rationed school: "As the months went by we all became increasingly obsessed with food, and most of us would have lied, cheated or stolen for a morsel of bread." On a lighter note, a Bradford teenager remembered worrying about a shortage in cosmetics. Describing herself as "a hoarder," she wrote that "I once counted thirty-one boxes of face powder I had stored away in an old gramophone."[21]

Rationing was also part of the American home front, although it was never as drastic as in England, and it was in force only for the duration, whereas in England rationing continued until the early 1950s. Each American child received a government-issued booklet containing coupons for sugar, meat, and canned fruits and vegetables, in amounts similar to those of adults, although children received no coffee stamp. Hot school lunches and penny milk supplemented many children's diets. Although American children usually enjoyed more material comforts than European or Asian children did, they suffered from a loss of care and attention while their parents labored at military or defense positions. Wartime conditions took their toll on the most vulnerable of citizens, explains historian Robert Kirk in *Earning Their Stripes: The Mobilization of American Children in the Second World War*: "Like sugar, coffee, and gasoline, sufficient time for children was severely rationed."[22]

Children on both sides of the Atlantic worked in volunteer and paid capacities, usually surpassing extraordinary expectations. Scrap drives were a volunteer undertaking desperately needed for wartime production, and children everywhere led as "scrappin'" soldiers. "Like lots of other British children," Ann Stalcup explained, "I worked to collect reusable scrap metals. We would go from house to house, asking for things like old saucepans that could be melted down and used to make plane or tank parts.... Kitchen waste was collected and fed to pigs. Everything was recycled in those days, including paper." In September 1942, the U.S. Treasury Department and Office of Education launched the Schools at War Program with the children's motto "Save, Serve, Conserve." The motto proved accurate. During the first half of 1943 alone, American elementary school children collected thirteen million tons for the school's program Salvage for Victory.[23]

Much of the war work demanded of children meant factories and farms, and by March 1943, English boys and girls born between September 1926 and March 1927 registered at juvenile employment bureaus. Writer Nancy Fyson describes other dynamics of the wartime work world: "In 1943 there was strong pressure to keep working hours down for young people, to 48 hours for those over sixteen and 44 for those under sixteen. But the demands of war production made this difficult."[24]

War work also escalated for America's children. Teenagers filled a desperate wartime labor need. Although the concept of middle-aged women doing their "bit" for the war effort as Rosie the Riveter certainly contributed to the remarkable home-front war production effort, the ones who solved the war's "manpower" shortage were mostly teenage boys and girls. According to historian William O'Neill in *A Democracy at War*, child labor in the United States escalated during World War II, reversing what had been a downward trend. In 1940, the number of employed teenagers between the ages of fourteen and seventeen was 1.7 million, but by 1944, that number had increased to 4.61 million. The National Labor Committee also found that the illegal employment of minors rose during the war years.[25]

Although teenagers sought employment for adult reasons—a paycheck and patriotic contribution—some educators worried about lost opportunities. In thirty-four states children were able to quit school and work at age fourteen, and high school enrollments decreased 8.3 percent for boys and

4.2 percent for girls from 1942 to 1943. In 1943, the Department of Labor created various work-school programs. As *Education for Victory* commented, "Since Pearl Harbor, many students have been leaving the classroom, sacrificing their education to take part in the war effort." The Los Angeles school system proposed the 4–4 Plan: four hours in school and four hours at work. Still, this trend was met with alarm by some. As New York City's school superintendent commented, "When hostilities have ceased, we shall probably have a larger number of college-trained people available for employment than at any other time in our history [as a result of the G.I. Bill], and it is not difficult to see how unfortunate will be the position of the young man or woman who has not even completed high school."[26]

The Work Study Plan as proposed by the War Manpower Commission arose from educational concerns as states relaxed and even abandoned child labor standards. Farm work carried few regulations regarding hours or safety, yet the desire to contribute as a dutiful soldier on the farm front remained strong. An Iowa farm girl recounted a typical story of milking cows by hand and dutifully tending ever-increasing flocks of chickens for the war effort. "I graduated from high school last spring," she began, "and am staying on the farm to help my folks. I also have a brother in the army. There have been more days I've put in sixteen hours than days I haven't during the summer and fall."[27]

Employment of girls escalated during World War II not only because of the country's severe labor needs but also because of girls' "yearning to be somebody," according to surveys completed by thousands of girls in 1942 for *Calling All Girls* magazine. "I have four cousins and two uncles in the Services of our nation" wrote one fourteen-year-old. "The other night I had a dream that they were killed in action. Now of course that was a silly dream, but it could so easily happen and it got me thinking that I wasn't doing very much for the war effort. Of course I buy war stamps regularly and this summer I am helping harvest the crops (such as berries, beans, etc.) . . . I think that many girls think the same as I do."[28]

For girls, war work also meant an increase in domestic responsibilities. "Oh, I cook a little at home," eleven-year-old Mary Frenna commented after winning the Children's Aid Society's Economy Meal Contest. "Sometimes I burn things though. I never expected my things would be best today." The *New York Times* recognized these "pigtailers" as making a necessary domestic contribution to the war effort's kitchen front. *Ladies' Home Journal* recognized its aspiring young readers as "sub-debs"—again demonstrating how girls occupied the liminal space between a child's playfulness and a mature woman's responsibilities.[29]

Sexuality and Innocence during Wartime

Emotions, moods, and hormones, a troublesome site of fragility for young females during the best of times, accelerated during World War II. In a romantic Coca-Cola advertisement of the era, a confident and caring American serviceman offers a Coke to a demure Irish girl. In reality, relationships between military men and local girls were fraught with complications, severely challenging such traditional depictions. Groups of young military men traveling to new training centers proved to be both a sexual temptation and a physical danger to local girls. Particularly during the intensity of wartime, girlhood occupied another liminal space between innocence and sexuality.[30]

"Wartime London reeked of sex," according to George, who was a little boy at the time. "We got our first sex lessons from watching the American GIs in the public underground shelters." George then enthusiastically described his "lessons": "The number of girls who lost their virtue for a pair of nylons was nobody's business! A friend of mine would tell us what his sister had done with a Yank to get her nylons, and when we didn't know whether to believe him or not he'd hide us in the shelter so that we could watch them. That's how we got our sex education, and learned about condoms, the lot." George's story reflected the culture at large: "Of course, what got the British serviceman's back up was that the Americans had four times as much pay: you've heard the old joke, 'overpaid, oversexed, and over here.'"[31]

Experiences certainly varied "over here." A Southampton woman in England retained innocent girlhood memories of wartime encounters with young people attending evening church services and gathering in halls for "sing-songs," and tea and biscuits. "How we enjoyed those days!" she wrote. "Later at night teams of young people from the church would visit air raid shelters for the public and hold services there. Then we would walk home through what seemed like showers of shrapnel."[32]

Other British girls perceived an atmosphere clouded with confusion and daring. Victoria Massey remembered her younger brother Pat trying to protect her from a GI's advances. The siblings had simply approached the soldier, wanting gum or chocolates. Instead Victoria received an unwanted fondling, but her little brother Pat insistently interrupted any potentially dangerous advances. As Victoria made her escape, "I felt a swift depression, and stumbled away between the rows of vehicles, the stars and stripes, and the trodden gorse, after Pat. I felt suddenly ashamed, but still annoyed that Pat should have spoiled my chances of adventure and chocolate, though I knew him to have been the sensible one."[33]

Other girls played the sexual games as best they could. "I didn't want the GIs to know that I was only twelve and a half," explained Connie Stanton. "I wanted them to think that I was sixteen." She avoided having soldiers see her on the afternoon playground but would later catch "the liberty bus" (or passion wagon) as it lumbered to the American Red Cross in Bedford. "Collections of all the local girls for the base dances were determined to hear Glenn Miller playing one night," Connie confided. So she decided to sneak out. "Whenever I hear 'Moonlight Serenade' now," she recalled, "I still remember that evening. . . . It was wonderful."[34]

Some girls celebrated the new opportunities, but adults reacted with appropriate concern when adolescents' drinking in public houses increased along with venereal diseases. Some authority figures envisioned wartime girls through the lens of "a moral panic." In England, health authorities estimated a 70 percent increase in venereal disease, and in 1943 the minister of health began a public message titled "Ten Plain Facts about VD" by warning that 70,000 new cases among civilians developed annually. New sulfa drugs could now cure gonorrhea patients within a week, and syphilis patients could be cured in six weeks compared to the older, less successful treatment of seventy injections over eighteen months. Perhaps modern medicine made sex seem a little less scary to young girls, but with few dependable birth control options and the ever-present double standard, pregnancy could still scare and deter. Illegitimate babies became somewhat accepted during wartime with its heightened tensions, especially in the United Kingdom with the presence of foreign troops, but a baby still remained a dangerous prospect for an unmarried girl and for her family's reputation during the 1940s.[35]

Wartime brought dangers to girls' emerging sexual lives, but the era also unintentionally brought new freedoms. "For me the war years were happy," said one Sheffield woman looking back. "We had more freedom than we would have done had the men been at home. We were allowed to roam in the woodlands, and on the golf course without supervision. Parents didn't fear lurking prowlers in lonely places, as they assumed all the men who might do us harm were busily occupied." War's conditions heightened "the agentic capacity of girls" through enlarged spaces and opportunities. Margaret Butler remembered her parents' stern warnings regarding American troops stationed nearby, although one day her friends described an upcoming dance. "Do you want to come?" her friends asked. "And I said, 'Yes, but please don't tell my mum.' So I went and when we got to the camp this American said, 'Well, look, sneak around the back.' And that was the night that Glenn Miller came and played."[36]

Girls who might resort to sneaking out were sometimes formally transported to the military bases when spatial boundaries for girls came into flux with the new social arrangements of wartime. With several thousand soldiers on furlough near San Antonio, busloads of Liberty Belles (girls seventeen to twenty-five) traveled, with some chaperones, for supervised visits; they were to encourage soldiers' morale with these instructions: "Be sympathetic to troubles but careful with phone numbers." City officials organized the prettiest Liberty Belle contest, but winner Agnes MacTaggert relinquished the questionable honor because she was only sixteen.[37]

Farther north along the Nebraska rail line in North Platte, townspeople established a daily reception hall with homemade refreshments to greet every troop train that passed through. "I wasn't old enough to work in the Canteen, even as a platform girl," said Doris Dotson, who was twelve at the war's start. Doris and her girlfriends jitterbugged to the jukebox, encouraging soldiers to have some fun during their brief stop for the trains to refuel. "You know that expression, 'I'd rather dance than eat'?" she explained. "The boys would pass up the food tables to come down and dance with my friends and me." Although this young girl spent a lot of time dancing with military men at this small town depot, her mother never worried about consequences. "As far as I was concerned," Doris concluded, "I was being very patriotic."[38]

Sometimes behavior might be deemed patriotic, but when girls initiated questionable contact, the label quickly reverted to "delinquent." In the United States, authorities continuously lamented the problem of juvenile delinquency among teenage girls. Girls with tight sweaters and bright lipstick received such insulting labels as Victory Girls, uniform chasers, khaki wackies, cuddle bunnies, round heels, patriotic amateurs, chippies, or goodtime Charlottes. "The Victory Girl is Menace No. 1" the military poster warned, blaming girls rather than soldiers for misbehavior and unintended consequences. Juvenile crimes with which girls were charged included running away, truancy, and petty thievery, but increasingly "crimes against common decency," such as vagrancy, drunkenness, disorderly conduct, and prostitution, were added to the list of offenses. In the first nine months of 1943, the number of American girls arrested on such charges increased 69.6 percent from the previous year.[39]

"The teen-age girl, with a pretty but empty head," *Life* editorialized, "and an uncontrolled impulse to share somehow in the excitement of the war, has become a national problem child." This "distorted patriotism" meant that Indianapolis girls of fifteen frequented the bus depots to pick up servicemen on liberty, and problem areas flared in Portland, Norfolk, and San Antonio. War has always created unintended victims, but adult authorities usually critiqued and rarely sympathized with these young girls, who were rapidly developing in a rapidly changing world. Girls felt forced to grow up too quickly as a result of external conditions of war and internal battles. Girlhood became situated, as sociologists Marion de Ras and Mieke Lunenberg describe, as "a conflicting and uneasy intersection between a presumed childhood innocence and eroticized femininity." Or as cultural historian Ilana Nash has noted regarding society's excessive blaming, "the exaggeration reflects the extent to which such girls challenged normative notions of femininity." Labeled promiscuous, Victory Girls endured name-calling, blame, and stigmatization resulting from the resilience of the sexual double standard.[40]

The United States experienced increased birth rates and sexually transmitted diseases because of wartime stresses and exhilarations. The birth rate dramatically increased in 1941 and 1942, as the average age of mothers dropped into the teen years; the maternity clothing industry tagged these younger pregnant women "junior mothers." The defense boom had exploded with a baby boom: every minute during 1941, more than four babies were born.[41]

Illegitimacy, black markets, and illegal abortions increased during the war years. The United States Children's Bureau acknowledged that fewer than half of the forty-eight states possessed laws adequate to prosecute baby brokers, who openly advertised payments as high as $2,000 plus hospital expenses for babies. Maud Morlock, a Children's Bureau consultant, believed it was common practice for unwed mothers to sign away their babies before birth. For example, of the 3,259 adoptions recorded in Illinois in 1943, only 885 were known to child welfare agencies or the Department of Public Welfare. Illegitimate births had increased 20 percent in Chicago in 1943.[42]

The freedom of the times, however, offered American girls moments they might not have experienced otherwise, an agentic capacity within this liminal space. More than ever during this world war, girlhood emerged as a social construction rather than a simple biological stage. Later in the war, *Life* published an essay titled "Teen Age Girls": "Some 6,000,000 U.S. teen-age girls live in a world all their own—a lovely, gay, enthusiastic, funny and blissful society almost untouched by the war. It is a world of sweaters and skirts and bobby sox and loafers, of hair worn long, of eye-glass rims painted red with nail polish, of high-school boys not yet gone to war." For "good girls," a tight sweater formed "the worst breach of etiquette," and "necking" in the movies remained "absolutely out." Still, a seriousness permeated the era, and many girls refused to submit to the media's labels. When the March of Time released a stereotypic newsreel titled "Teen Age Girls," hundreds of girls wrote to the youth magazine *Scholastic* in protest. One young teenager, according to Nash, spoke for many: "What about our brothers, fathers, and close friends who went away to war? Many of them will never return and those who come back may be changed. I speak for many girls when I say that we think a great deal about the deeper and more important things in life: religion, economic and social problems. Perhaps we haven't solved any of them, but we're trying. Isn't that something?"[43]

As the war finally ended, the long-awaited Victory in Europe Day meant street parties, bonfires, firecrackers, and midnight celebrations. "We children sat on the window ledge and smiled," Victoria Massey recalled, "just as though it was Christmas, and as though we expected lollipops to fall from the sky." *Newsweek* labeled V-E Day the "Biggest Holiday in the World": "The war-weary people of Britain clogged the streets, the churches, and the pubs. The London sky was reddened by the flames of victory bonfires. Up and down the streets in the center of town GI's, Tommies, women in long dresses, and bare-legged girls sang and shouted. Many of them wore pink paper caps and swung rattlers. London's pent-up emotions boiled over."[44]

Other girls remembered the postwar years as "an anticlimax" compared to the war. A young Battersea girl, eleven when the war began, felt that "everything seemed dull and flat after the excitement and friendliness." Or as Ann Stalcup recalled, "In looking back on that period of my childhood, I have many memories of how the war changed the reserved British people. They helped and supported each other. They shared what little they had. They comforted those who received tragic news. They fought bravely and didn't give up. They treated their prisoners kindly. They laughed and cried together. And I was a part of it all."[45]

The war years certainly brought challenges and complications, but memories of the experiences remained difficult to decipher because the postwar emphasis remained on the soldier; civilian participants on the various home fronts received scant, if any, attention. The dangers for civilians during this world war, however, had escalated. Civilian deaths in Great Britain by May 8, 1945, had reached 26,920 men, 25,392 women, and 7,736 children killed, and those injured totaled 86,175, including more than 7,000 children. In the aftermath, English girls whose homes had been bombed and destroyed or whose families had been evacuated and dismantled realized, from war's proximity, that they had experienced history—perhaps traumatic but certainly life changing. Some of these girls, understanding their wartime girlhood experiences as autonomous and important, later wrote memoirs, whereas American girls seldom viewed their youthful war years with drama or significance and therefore only rarely formally recorded their personal experiences.[46]

Although life during the war years had not been as dramatic in the United States, the more than 400,000 American military deaths left thousands of grieving war orphans. Approximately 183,000 home front children lost their fathers during the course of this world war. Adding to these emotional complications, well-meaning adults often thrust girls into the public spotlight to receive their fathers' posthumous war medals in official ceremonies.[47]

Conclusion

War is often represented solely as an adult male experience. The Second World War, however, developed into a total war against civilians, which meant men, women, boys, and girls continuously faced real risks. Although girls could never volunteer or be drafted into the military because of their age and gender, they experienced many dangers and endured many responsibilities on the home front. In England girls died in Blitz bombings or left home for years on end as a result of evacuation schemes, and in both countries girls labored long hours in factories and farms, contributed to the household duties for extended hours, sacrificed schooling and other traditional opportunities, encouraged or endured military men's attention and advances, faced condemnation from society for delinquency and illegitimacy, and suffered in silent grief, all with an encouraging and dutiful smile, as they contributed their time, energy, money, talent, and even youth to the cause of world war. A prosperous postwar future depended on this consistent war work of English and American girls. Fragilities of youth and failures of governments certainly emerged during the war years, and promises of peace and patriotism also intensified, factors that represented the various elements of British and American girlhood during the Second World War.

The ideal garden of girlhood withered during World War II. This supposed sunlit spot for little girls with its hopeful rays of optimistic sunshine, elaborate tea parties, and dressed-up dolls suddenly transformed during the war years to a frighteningly realistic landscape that grew dark with Anderson shelters, incendiary bombs, military uniforms, and memories of absent fathers. The garden of youth during this world war now meant planting needed victory gardens of rationed vegetables, searching neighborhood alleyways and mothers' kitchens for available scrap contributions, and marking hours at less pay in war's booming factories and farms. Throughout the war years, British and American girls proved themselves, over and over, to be very good soldiers indeed.

British girls' courage during wartime was sometimes rewarded. In September 1940, Charity Bick became the youngest person to be awarded the George Medal for her "outstanding valour on the Home Front," even though she had lied about her age, raising it from fourteen to sixteen, in order to serve on the Air Raid Precaution Services Dispatch Riders team. Most girls, however, rarely received recognition. In an unusual example, a war poster that appeared a year after the Pearl Harbor attack was captioned: "Avenge December 7th! Make sure he grows up a free man!" The poster's photograph, however, mistakenly depicted a young girl, Linda Peterson. Linda received an apologetic $50 war bond for the error, but no public recognition for her actual war efforts ever materialized.[48]

In London, signs of new life began emerging as evacuees returned. "There is play, there are smiles and laughter," an American visitor commented. "The prams are reappearing on the streets and some of the children have returned to what was once almost a city without youth." Recovery from the Blitz also seemed symbolized by a thriving vegetable garden growing in a bomb scar left by a Nazi plane.[49] Plants, with their urge toward biological growth, seemed far easier to transplant—they recovered and thrived—whereas children needed to grow psychologically as well.

After almost three years of exile, British children who had been evacuated to America began to make plans for their return. They had developed bonds with their American foster families but still displayed strong loyalties to their English backgrounds. As the *New York Times* commented, "Transplanting 4,000 children after the experience of the Blitz to a strange environment an ocean away may have been a bold experiment but its success was assured from the first children themselves. Our young guests have shown that the tender plant of childhood contains a tough fiber of courage. England will be proud of them."[50] The "war waifs" had survived and would continue to grow if not thrive, despite the world's complications.

On V-J Day in August 1945, Dorinda Makanaonalani watched the wild celebrations near Pearl Harbor, where the war had begun for the United States. Now a ten-year-old, Dorinda was filled with joy and gratitude. "We could see the fireworks from the harbor, and hear the air raid sirens wailing and whistles from the ships," she said. "The sky over the harbor was flashing brightly with flares, each one adding its notes in a symphony of light. . . . The war was over."[51]

NOTES

1. *Des Moines Register*, August 11, 1940, 2; and *Life*, December 8, 1941, 83.

2. *Los Angeles Times*, April 14, 1942, 14; and *Los Angeles Times Home Magazine*, August 22, 1942, cover.

3. Claudia Mitchell and Jacqueline Reid-Walsh, eds., *Seven Going on Seventeen: Tween Studies in the Culture of Girlhood* (New York: Peter Lang, 2005), 6; Claudia Mitchell and Jacqueline Reid-Walsh, *Researching Children's Popular Culture: The Cultural Spaces of Childhood* (London: Routledge, 2002), 7; Pamela J. Bettis and Natalie G. Adams, eds., *Geographies of Girlhood: Identities In-between* (Mahwah, NJ: Lawrence Erlbaum Associates, 2005), 6; and Yasmin Jiwania, Candis Steenbergen, and Claudia Mitchell, eds., *Girlhood: Redefining the Limits* (Montreal: Black Rose Books, 2006), xiii. I thank sociologist Stephen Svenson for introducing me to the concept of liminal spaces.

4. Grace Horseman, ed., *Growing Up in the Forties* (London: Constable and Company Limited, 1997), 20 and 21; and Juliet Gardiner, *The Children's War: The Second World War through the Eyes of the Children of Britain* (London: Portrait, 2005), 35.

5. Nance Lui Fyson, *Growing Up in the Second World War* (London: Batsford Academic and Educational Limited, 1981), 7; Sheila Garrigue, *All the Children Were Sent Away* (Scarsdale, NY: Bradbury Press, 1976), 8; Victoria Massey, *One Child's War* (Whitstable, UK: Whitstable Litho Ltd., 1978), 25; and Mitchell and Reid-Walsh, *Researching Children's Popular Culture*, 8.

6. *Life*, October 16, 1939, 58.

7. Ibid., 59, 60, 62; and *Time*, September 11, 1939, 61.

8. *Newsweek*, December 22, 1941, 62–63; *Life*, January 1, 1940, 40; and October 16, 1939, 57; Gardiner, *Children's War*, 20, 24; and Carlton Jackson, *Who Will Take Our Children? The Story of the Evacuation in Britain, 1939–1945* (London: Methuen London Ltd., 1985), xiv.

9. *Life*, October 16, 1939, 57; and Gardiner, *Children's War*, 20.

10. Massey, *One Child's War*, 37–38.

11. H. V. Nicholson, *Prisoners of War: True Stories of Evacuees/Their Lost Childhood* (London: Gordon Publishing, 2000), 1.

12. Jackson, *Who Will Take Our Children?* 71, 95; and *Atlanta Constitution*, January 16, 1942, 22.

13. *London Times*, January 1, 1941, ii; and September 23, 1940, 4; and *Newsweek*, August 12, 1940, 16; September 2, 1940, 16; and September 9, 1940, 23.

14. Gordon W. Prange with Donald M. Goldstein and Katherine V. Dillon, *December 7, 1941: The Day the Japanese Attacked Pearl Harbor* (New York: McGraw-Hill, 1988), 164.

15. *Des Moines Register*, January 1, 1942, 1; Blake Clark, *Remember Pearl Harbor!* (New York: Modern Age Books, 1942), 17, 18.

16. *Honolulu Star Tribune*, December 8, 1941, 1, 2.

17. Studs Terkel, *"The Good War": An Oral History of World War II* (New York: New Press, 1984), 8; and K. D. Richardson, *Reflections of Pearl Harbor: An Oral History of December 7, 1941* (Westport, CT: Praeger, 2005), 80.

18. David M. Kennedy, *Freedom from Fear: The American People in Depression and War, 1929–1945* (New York: Oxford University Press, 1999), 747–748; Richard Overy, "The Success of American Mobilization," in *Major Problems in the History of World War II*, ed. Mark A. Stoler and Melanie S. Gustafson (Boston: Houghton Mifflin, 2003), 71; and William M. Tuttle Jr., *"Daddy's Gone to War": The Second World War in the Lives of America's Children* (New York: Oxford University Press, 1993), 64, 65.

19. *Heart Mountain Sentinel*, November 14, 1942; April 24, 1943; and August 7, 1943; from the American Heritage Center, box 2, University of Wyoming, Laramie.

20. Gardiner, *Children's War*, 120, 123; and Ann Stalcup, *On the Home Front: Growing Up in Wartime England* (North Haven, CT: Linnet Book, 1998), 15, 16.

21. Stalcup, *On the Home Front*, 16; Eva Fige, *Little Eden: A Child at War* (New York: Persea Books, 1988), 68; and Norman Longmate, *How We Lived Then: A History of Everyday Life during the Second World War* (London: Pimlico, 2002), 277.

22. Robert William Kirk, *Earning Their Stripes: The Mobilization of American Children in the Second World War* (New York: Peter Lang, 1994), 28.

23. Stalcup, *On the Home Front*, 43; and Tuttle, *"Daddy's Gone to War,"* 121–123.

24. *London Times*, March 11, 1943, 2; and Fyson, *Growing Up in the Second World War*, 35–36.

25. William L. O'Neill, *A Democracy at War: America's Fight at Home and Abroad in World War II* (Cambridge: Harvard University Press, 1993), 249.

26. *New York Times*, March 3, 1943, 14; *Life*, May 17, 1943, 45; *Education for Victory*, September 1, 1943, 1; February 3, 1944, 1; and December 15, 1943, 13.

27. *Wallaces' Farmer*, December 26, 1942, 8.

28. Ilana Nash, *American Sweethearts: Teenage Girls in Twentieth-Century Popular Culture* (Bloomington: Indiana University Press, 2006), 158, 159.

29. *New York Times*, January 22, 1943, 23L; *New York Times Magazine*, March 7, 1943, 19; *Washington Post*, November 1, 1941, 15; *Good Housekeeping*, May 1942, 73; and Nash, *American Sweethearts*, 12, 23.

30. *Life*, January 10, 1944, back cover; and Bettis and Adams, *Geographies of Girlhood*, 6.

31. Sally Alderson, comp., *War All over the World: Childhood Memories of WWII from 23 Countries* (Troinex, Switzerland: Salenca Press, 2003), 215.

32. Longmate, *How We Lived Then*, 390.

33. Massey, *One Child's War*, 120.

34. Gardiner, *Children's War*, 169.

35. Mitchell and Reid-Walsh, *Seven Going on Seventeen*, 1; *London Times*, February 23, 1943, 5; Horseman, *Growing Up in the Forties*, 123, 124; *Newsweek*, August 30, 1943, 88; and *London Times*, February 19, 1943, 2.

36. Longmate, *How We Lived Then*, 200, 201; Jiwani, Steenbergen, and Mitchell, *Girlhood*, xiii; and Phil Robins, *Under Fire: Children of the Second World War Tell Their Stories* (London: Scholastic Children's Books, 2004), 227.

37. Bettis and Adams, *Geographies of Girlhood*, 11; and *Time*, October 30, 1941, 38.

38. Bob Greene, *Once upon a Town: The Miracle of the North Platte Canteen* (New York: Perennial, 2003), 94, 95.

39. Kenneth Paul O'Brien and Lynn Hudson Parsons, *The Home-Front War: World War II and American Society*, Contributions in American History, no. 161 (Westport, CT: Greenwood Press, 1995), 122; *Life*, December 20, 1943, 102; and O'Neill, *Democracy at War*, 264, 265.

40. Marion de Ras and Mieke Lunenberg, eds., *Girls, Girlhood, and Girls' Studies in Transition* (Amsterdam: Het Spinhuis, 1993), 3; Nash, *American Sweethearts,* 137; *Life,* December 20, 1943, 96, 97, and 102; and *Time,* March 29, 1943, 46.

41. *Life,* August 31, 1942, 41; and *Time,* December 8, 1941, 36.

42. *Newsweek,* January 22, 1944, 38.

43. Sinikka Aapola, Marnina Gonick, and Anita Harris, eds., *Young Femininity: Girlhood, Power, and Social Change* (New York: Palgrave Macmillan, 2005), 1; *Life,* December 11, 1944, 91, 92, 95, 96, 98; and Nash, *American Sweethearts,* 137, 143.

44. Massey, *One Child's War,* 123; and *Newsweek,* May 14, 1945, 33.

45. Longmate, *How We Lived Then,* 506; and Stalcup, *On the Home Front,* 81.

46. Martin Gilbert, *The Day the War Ended: May 8, 1945—Victory in Europe* (New York: Henry Holt, 1995, 2004), 123; and de Ras and Lunenberg, *Girls, Girlhood, and Girls' Studies,* 61.

47. Tuttle, *"Daddy's Gone to War,"* 44. 123; and *New York Times,* August 11, 1943, 13.

48. Gardiner, *Children's War,* 107; and *Los Angeles Times,* December 10, 1942, B.

49. *New York Times,* May 16, 1943, 41.

50. Ibid., 23.

51. Emmy E. Wener, *Through the Eyes of Innocents: Children Witness World War II* (Boulder, CO: Westview Press, 2000), 77.

9 Holy Girl Power Locally and Globally

THE MARIAN VISIONS
OF GARABANDAL, SPAIN

JESSAMY HARVEY

In a journalistic article on the importance of the 1917 Marian apparitions in Fatima (Portugal) for understanding the history of the Cold War, Joseph Bottum recasts the part of the cold warrior. Bottum speculates that the real shaper of the Cold War is not, in fact, an adult political leader but a young peasant girl:

> Here's a curious thought. Maybe the single most important person in the 20th century's long struggle against communism wasn't Ronald Reagan. Maybe it wasn't Karol Wojtyla or Margaret Thatcher, Lech Walesa or Vaclav Havel, Aleksandr Solzhenitsyn or Mikhail Gorbachev. Maybe it wasn't anyone whose name might leap to a cold warrior's mind—for the most important figure in that long, dark struggle might have been a 10-year-old girl named Lucia dos Santos.[1]

Bottum makes the intriguing proposition that Lucia, a Portuguese Catholic peasant girl visionary, played a significant role in international politics. Individual girls, as well as the category of girlhood itself, can be understood to serve as a vehicle for the expression of any number of identities, values, and histories. As Ann Kordas notes elsewhere in this section, girls were endowed with great symbolic value during the Cold War, but whereas she examines the ideological use of images of American and Soviet gymnasts, I focus on the symbolic value of four Catholic girls from rural Spain to a transnational religious community.

On June 18, 1961, María Concepción [Conchita] González (b. 1949) and three other girls of similar age, Mari Cruz González, Jacinta González, and María Dolores [Loli] Mazón, from San Sebastian de Garabandal (Spain), an isolated mountain community in the northern region of Cantabria, claimed to have a religious vision, the first of many.[2] The experiences of these four girls, based on their account of seeing and communicating with Saint Michael the Archangel, the Virgin Mary, and the infant Jesus between 1961 and 1965, were rapidly transformed into socially constructed events that have become part of what Paolo Apolito calls "Catholic visionary culture,"[3] a transnational religious culture with a long tradition. As William A. Christian notes, "Visions of the divine are as old as humanity. They have continued in the postindustrial age."[4] In visionary culture, the participants share, to use Manuel Vásquez and Marie Marquardt's phrase, "generalised apparition scripts" that shape and make sense of their personal experiences.[5]

In this chapter, I do not address the question essential to many believers: did these girls really see and speak with divine beings? Here I contend that these girls established their participation in culture and society through the experience of visions, and the believers and promoters who recognized and validated this experience then found ways of defining and articulating their beliefs, values, and hopes through the girls. These girls came to see themselves, over time, as significant not only in relation to their own lives but also in relation to a broader moral order. Although as grown women these girls are no longer primary actors in a global religious community, for the duration of the apparitions they took on a distinctive role, that of holy messengers who not only reversed everyday structures of authority at the time but also can be seen, in the longer term, to have shaped the local landscape as well as contributed to manifestations of global devotional culture. Although the impact of the visionaries on the national stage was inhibited, to a certain extent, through coercive measures by both the Diocese of Santander and the National-Catholic dictatorial regime led by General Franco (1939–1975), the cult spread internationally through European and American promoters.[6] Today not only are there Garabandal centers in Europe, the United States, South Africa, and Australia, but the Internet is a powerful tool in the dissemination of the movement's information and beliefs.[7] Both still and moving images of the girls, individual and collective memories, and prescriptive messages of salvation continue to circulate in contemporary culture in a wide variety of formats thanks to the efforts of the Workers of Garabandal and other devotees. In this chapter I do not ponder the veracity of the girls' visions; instead, by working within a culture-centered girlhood studies approach, I consider to what extent, and in which ways, the girls were able to achieve a form of social self-definition within a devotional subculture that, as visionaries, they were instrumental in generating.

Because these girls are the foundational figures of the Garabandal movement, their actions and words have left traces—oral, written, visual, and material—that have been preserved because they were endowed by adults with symbolic significance. The traces grant the opportunity to study girlhood historically, specifically the tradition of peasant Holy Children, to which these girls belonged. Holy Children have, at various points in history, found openings and accepted an unparalleled gift of authority first in their villages and later on in the world. Interpreting how the visionaries of Garabandal constructed themselves, as well as how they have been constructed by others within this shared tradition of visionary culture or apparition scripts, gives us insights into the conceptualization of the girl in popular Catholic culture. Girlhood is a relative concept, and it is important to attend to the ways in which the girl is differently constructed and variously recognized depending on her context, yet it is also crucial to attend to the continuities, to that which makes female childhood appear familiar, immutable, and fixed. Indeed, the longevity of the peasant Holy Girl cultural model facilitates the study of the tensions between continuity and change in the construction of girlhood.

The events of Garabandal have been studied by academics previously, mainly by Christian, Sandra Zimdars-Swartz, and Apolito.[8] Christian uses an ethnographic and historical approach, aiming to locate the Marian visions in the context of geographically specific social and cultural forces, whereas both Zimdars-Swartz and Apolito include the Garabandal events within a global overview of Marian apparitions, the latter specifically on Marianism and the World Wide Web. My project on Garabandal, while seeing their work as a vital part of the foundations, updates and further develops the study of Garabandal by examining the play among the local, the national, and the global and by researching not only the apparitions themselves but also the Marian movement that emerged from it. My intervention in this topic for this volume discusses how existing models of Holy Girls in Catholic culture create narrative structures that inform how real girls come to see themselves and are seen by others. I argue that the adherence of girls to a religion that pursues practices and ideals embedded within a tradition and history that accords them a subordinate status can, nevertheless, be understood as enabling them to become active participants in culture and society.

Holy Girls in Catholic Culture

Catherine Driscoll points out that "if I want to think about girls, I am impelled to look at representations, images, or figures of girls as crucial benchmarks for what will be recognized as girlhood."[9] Girls themselves, of course, also seek to recognize what might define girlhood, for they are not simply learning how to do "woman" but how to do "girl." Representations, images, figures, or models of girls matter, and furthermore, to borrow a phrase coined by Jane M. Ussher, "representations have real effects."[10] Slightly over a decade ago, Sherrie A. Inness, upon reviewing scholarly literature on girlhood and after admiring the breadth of research, made the following striking observation: "The books tend to favor studying representations of girls, not actual girls' lives; thus 'real' girls seem curiously absent from most of these texts."[11] Inness noticed that scholars in the emerging field of girlhood studies tended to focus on conduct literature and other print culture that could be found on a girl's bookshelf. In fact the studies favored what one might call paper girls. Since then, real girls' lives have

been explored by Inness herself and by others.[12] Although these investigations are an important corrective to the field of girlhood studies, in the
move toward including real girls we must not forget that representations
are of central importance in the construction of girls' subjectivities. After
all, what is a "real" girl? And can an "actual" girl's life be told without
recourse to the abundant cultural representations of girls? Does the "real"
girl stand alone, unmoored, free-floating, unaffected by the representations
of girls that cast shadows across the social world she inhabits? In this
chapter I do not seek to understand the real flesh-and-blood girls from
Garabandal—whoever they were in everyday life—but to understand how
their words and actions were interpreted by themselves and others as part
of an established tradition of Holy Girlhood, which meant they were
endowed by others with symbolic significance that raised them above other
girls and made them the object of collective emotional investment.

Holy people in all times, places, and religions are the product of historically specific environments in which certain models of behavior, out of a
much larger repertoire available in their cultural tradition, are presented for
imitation. The repertoire of Holy Girlhood in Catholic culture, from which
all girls affiliated with the faith can draw, includes at least four important
models: the Virgin Mary, the martyr of chastity (a closely related model of
virginity), the victim soul, and the mystic, a category to which the peasant
girl as visionary belongs.[13] Ruth Harris notes the longevity of such a peasant
model of holiness in her study of the apparitions of Lourdes (France): "All
over the Pyrenees, between the thirteenth and seventeenth centuries, shep-
herds and shepherdesses had direct contact with the Virgin, either though
visions or the miraculous discovery of images."[14] William A. Christian's
research focuses on legends of similar apparitions that occurred in Spain in
both the early and the modern periods.[15] Some of the main European protagonists of this tradition in the modern period are the fourteen-year-old
visionary Melanie Matthieu (1831–1904) and the eleven-year-old Maximin
Giraud (1835–1875) of La Salette (France); the fourteen-year-old visionary
Bernadette Soubirous (1844–1879) of Lourdes (France); and the ten-year-old
visionary Lucia dos Santos (1907–2005) and her eight-year-old cousin Jacinta
de Jesus Marto (1910–1920), as well as Jacinta's ten-year-old brother
Francisco Marto (1908–1919), of Fatima (Portugal).[16]

To read accounts of the early lives of Melanie, Bernadette, or Lucia is to
encounter narratives of girlhood that were similar to those of girls from
preindustrial European society. Deborah Simonton explains that this girlhood was experienced as a period of preparation: "From the time they
could walk, girls expected to assist mothers by performing simple tasks at
home. As they grew older, more able, and more experienced, tasks became
more complex. They were virtually apprentices, learning domestic, agricultural or technical skills as well as roles and attitudes required to manage
their own future households."[17] At the time of their religious experiences,

Melanie Matthieu was "a seasoned shepherdess at 14," and Bernadette "had only recently returned to her family after spending some time working as a shepherdess in a neighbouring village to spare her desperately poor parents the cost of her upbringing."[18] Bernadette, through the gathering of "wood, scrap iron, and bones" and the sale of this debris, "helped support her family."[19] The memoirs of Lucia (written in adulthood, for she, like Melanie and Bernadette, was an illiterate and unschooled child) are full of picturesque details that reveal a girlhood experienced as a series of steps. At age six, Lucia cared for the neighbors' younger children, often teaching them how to prepare the yarn for weaving, as their household had a loom. Then Lucia was entrusted at the young age of seven with the household's flock of sheep, for her mother maintained that her elder sister was already of an age to take on a more complex task: "Carolina is already twelve years old. That means she can now begin to work in the fields, or else learn to be a weaver or a seamstress, whichever she prefers."[20] The girlhood trajectories of these three young visionaries should have prepared them to manage their own households and, in all likelihood, to follow society's expectations of marriage and motherhood. This trajectory was interrupted, however, because becoming accepted as a Holy Girl—for as Harris and Christian note, not all who take up the position of visionary are accepted by the community[21]—altered each girl's life course to the extent that she exited the framework of a household-centered economy and took on another role, that of mediator between the divine and the human, within an alternative economy: the sacred. Therefore, through mystical experience, a girl was sometimes able to escape the limitations of an ordinary female existence. But how do we interpret this form of action, if, indeed, it can be understood as a form of action?

At the risk of simplifying decades of debate, discussions of female mysticism tend to portray this form of experience within the spectrum of resistance/subordination.[22] Mysticism can be understood, on the one hand, as a form of resistance, because popular manifestations of religion are sometimes championed as transgressing the practices and ideals embedded within an institution such as the Catholic Church that has historically accorded women and girls not only a subordinate status but granted them no role within the hierarchical structure. Mysticism, however, can also be interpreted as the most extreme form of subordination in that it is valued precisely because "the aim of mysticism is the loss of the self."[23] The female mystic can negate herself so fully that the self is lost and becomes that place in and through which only the divine speaks, but she does not. The paradox is that the Holy Girl as visionary and mystic attains authority in her very act of self-denial. Recently, Saba Mahmood has sought to reformulate the resistance/subordination debate in the field of gender studies and religion by questioning the tendency in feminist scholarship to understand agency "as the capacity to realize one's own interests against the weight of custom, tradition, transcendental will, or other obstacles (whether individual or collective)." In her study of a grassroots women's piety movement in contemporary Egypt, Mahmood makes it clear that she had to overcome her own "repugnance," a feeling that emerged from working with women who uphold, and are structured by, "a discursive tradition that regards subordination to a transcendent will (and thus, in many instances, to male authority) as its coveted goal." Mahmood insists, however, that "the meaning of agency must be explored within the grammar of concepts within which it resides."[24] My aim is not to unpack Mahmood's compelling study here but to open the debate to an appreciation of how forms of religious culture, however we might personally interpret them as oppressive, can be productive or generative for those who are living through a historically and culturally specific moment.

In and Out of Modernity: Girlhood in Garabandal

Although the Garabandal visions took place in the second half of the twentieth century, the village was both isolated and unmodernized: no tarmac road, no train station, no telephone.[25] As Gisela Kaplan states, "The Franco years froze the countryside in time and space," which meant that in areas with no electricity, "the entire burden of raising children, washing by hand, looking after the men and a rural household not cluttered by a range of appliances, fell exclusively on the women."[26] William A. Christian, when researching the belief systems of the Nansa valley in 1968, where the village is located, found a scrap of paper written by a schoolchild that outlined the preindustrial division of labor within the family:

> The father: Go to the cows. Work to give us food. Sell the animals to give us
> food. Plough the earth.
> The mother: Give us food. Wash clothes. Iron clothes. Buy clothes to dress
> us so we won't be cold.
> The children: Go to school. Bring water for those who are old. Do the errands
> that older people order. Go and hunt firewood.[27]

Still, the everyday lives of the Garabandal visionaries differed from the girlhoods of nineteenth-century visionaries like Melanie and Bernadette in one crucial aspect: schooling. As Peter N. Stearns remarks, "Modernity generated a crucial new version of childhood," one in which "schooling replaced work as the child's primary social obligation, a radical departure from the norms that had predominated, for most families, in agricultural economies."[28] As I outlined earlier, even little Lucia's girlhood in early twentieth-century rural Portugal is still clearly recognizable as typical of a preindustrial or agricultural girlhood, but the Garabandal visionaries experienced a rural childhood transformed by modernity as their identity was reformulated from household apprentice to schoolgirl.

By schoolgirl, in this instance, I mean a girl who attends an institution, the school, to receive a formal education designed, controlled, and implemented by a range of agents and experts on behalf of the state, and more specifically the girl who attends school because it has become compulsory for her to be there, rather than at home, in the fields, or in the factories.[29] Stearns, building on Philippe Ariès's proposal in *Centuries of Childhood* that childhood has not always been the same, presents the modern model of the child as the school pupil. Ariès and Stearns, in their own ways, focus on the impact of the obligation of schooling on the definition of childhood, as well as on the economics and emotional dynamics of the family unit. Given the centrality of schooling as a marker for childhood, however, as Ariès noted, the first "modern" child was gendered as a boy, because historically girls did not partake of this unique experience until a much later date: "Boys were the first specialized children" because "they began going to school in large numbers as far back as the late sixteenth century," whereas education for girls developed much later. Ariès believed that, in the eighteenth century, "childhood separated girls from adult life less so than it did boys" and that "without a proper educational system, the girls were confused with the women at an early age just as the boys had formerly been confused with the men."[30] Sally Mitchell, however, suggests that "schools were responsible for creating girlhood" in that schools separated girls from boys and later girls from women.[31] Stearns is more interested in painting a broader picture, so he does not dwell on the implications of gender in his discussion of the globalization of schooling and its transformation of childhood, but maintains that schooling, "through the ordering of classrooms, increasing age grading, and broadly similar curricula, simply add[s] to the shared process of change." Stearns observes that the modernity model of childhood, although common, is not homogenous across the globe, because "local adaptations and constraints may apply." Moreover, he points out that the distinctions between as well as within, particularly in relation to rural and urban experience, complicate the modern model of childhood.[32] Nevertheless, the model Stearns describes radically departs from previous definitions of childhood at local levels. Although the content of the education of Garabandal visionaries was not progressive, in fact, quite the opposite, it is still compatible with the modernity model that Stearns proposes and, therefore, presents a degree of departure in the Holy Girl model.

During the regime of General Franco, the nation-state had devised a highly normative program for Spanish boys and girls "founded on two simple principles: the 're-Spanishification' and 're-Catholicization' of society."[33] Whereas in many other European countries it was possible to openly express secular, left-wing, or anticlerical thought, that was not the case in National-Catholic Spain.[34] The impact on children was that a complex fusion of religious and patriotic content permeated the classroom, coeducation was banned, and girls were taught a different curriculum, one that was based on the traditional notions of womanhood. It was common for school-books to teach girls, as *Enciclopedia Hernando: Niñas* (1954) did, that their future role was to be religious, moral, lovers of their homes, and vigilant mothers to their children.[35] In the Garabandal classroom in the 1960s, the education girls received would have been profoundly marked by Catholicism. And, as Christian's research reveals, this belief system was reinforced within village life and the home, encouraging a localized fear of purgatory and a gendered sense of sin.[36] Even in the late 1970s, after the death of the dictator, Spanish feminists considered the education of rural girls seriously compromised. Margarita Escanciano demanded that the curriculum for girls in the countryside needed, among other changes, to be reformed so as to break down the dominant theme of religious fatalism, because rural girls tended to believe that they were not in charge of their own destinies.[37] This example enables us to understand the Catholic worldview of Conchita, Mari Cruz, Loli, and Jacinta, all exposed to the National-Catholic curriculum and immersed in the rural Nansa valley belief systems, which could be interpreted as reducing girls' future field of action beyond the classroom to the domestic sphere and placing them as subjects of a transcendental will. But to perceive them as victims fails to recognize the validation these rural girls would have received when they took on the role of Holy Girls.

Importantly, these girls were on the periphery of the rapidly modernizing flow of a Spanish society that was shifting dramatically as a result of mass migration, industrial development, and exposure to other ways of living through the growth of tourism, emigration, and the—albeit regulated—importation of foreign mass culture such as Hollywood films. The devotional literature on the girls' visions, nonetheless, maintains that the girls only encountered the "outside" world and modern artifacts because of the apparitions, which brought believers and curiosity seekers, who were equipped with newfangled things such as movie cameras and tape recorders, up to the remote village in cars.[38] Although such an idyllic rural preindustrial image of Garabandal may be a picturesque touch to enhance the village's appeal as an ideal apparition site in the contemporary godless era, the visionaries' girlhoods had already been inserted into modernity through their schooling.[39] These girls, unlike their Holy Girl predecessors, could read and write. One visionary in particular, Conchita, left a diary of her experiences. Unlike the memoirs of Lucia dos Santos, the peasant girl visionary at Fatima, Conchita's diary was not written retrospectively by an adult, but at a time that was fairly close to the events and while Conchita was still a young girl.[40]

The term "diary" has to be qualified because this document is actually a reconstruction of events written when Conchita was thirteen years old during the second year of the sequence of visions. The apparition sequence itself had a relatively long duration (1961 to 1965), and, in fact, the visions continued after Conchita stopped writing her diary. The complexity of the apparitions themselves is not my focus, as both Christian and Zimdars-Swartz analyze and reconstruct the events in detail;[41] instead, I examine Conchita's "diary" to interpret the way in which these girls established their participation in culture and society through the experience of visions and to examine the extent to which adults mediate girls' participation. I consult the Spanish-language edition, *Diario de Conchita de Garabandal*, and the English-language translation by Father Joseph A. Pelletier, *Our Lady Comes to Garabandal (Including Conchita's Diary)*, both published by organizations linked to the Garabandal network of devotees based in America.[42]

Although there were four visionaries, and the photographs of the visions taken in the early 1960s show all the girls as equally involved, over time the movement has tended to privilege Conchita as the main Holy Girl. This is partly because she took a central role in the visions over a longer period, actively spread the messages of the Virgin in her writings and in interviews with the Catholic press, and maintained ties with some of the most influential international promoters, such as Italo-American Joey Lomangino. Also, many of the chroniclers of the events found her the most charismatic of the girls; the prologue to the Spanish edition of Conchita's diary eulogizes her presence at the age of fifteen in terms of power and authority:

> Una castellana de la montaña. Alta, sólida, regia. Tiene una mirada noble, fresca, limpia, a veces meditativa, que penetra y llega hasta lo intimo. (*Diario*, 8)
>
> [A Castilian from the mountains. Tall, strong, queenly. She has a noble gaze, fresh, clean, sometimes thoughtful, that penetrates and reaches the most intimate space.]

Such is the devotion she herself inspires that her childhood home has been converted into a museum.[43] Similarly, although less active, Loli also continued to play a supporting role in the movement that emerged once the girls ceased to have visions, forging links with another international promoter, Maria Saraco. Mari Cruz, however, stopped having visions in the autumn of 1962, which, as she explained, impacted the way the community judged her: "The people do not like me because I see the Blessed Virgin less often" (*Our Lady*, 196n1). Jacinta did not become as involved in the active promotion of the messages by the emerging Garabandal movement during or after the vision sequence ceased. Although this topic is as yet unexplored, it is possible that Conchita and Loli forged these links because their families had more social status in the village; for example, Loli's family owned the only bar and restaurant in Garabandal, and one of the main sacred sites, a pine forest behind the village, was planted by Conchita's grandfather.

Conchita's Diary

The diary was written between 1962 and the middle of 1963, and Conchita intended it to be a "faithful" account of the events in Garabandal between

1961 up to the time of completing the writing. Conchita narrates the events surrounding the apparitions, including the content of the dialogues with the Blessed Virgin, and records in her own words the way the events were interpreted by others: with initial skepticism by her mother, hostility by the Diocese of Santander, and favorably by a growing number of believers. There are glimpses of her personal spiritual journey to be had toward the end of the document: "Oh, what happiness when I have the Blessed Virgin in me!" (*Our Lady*, 120). It is possible to derive a sense of Conchita's everyday life in the rural village from her diary, a life that was structured around attending school in both the morning and afternoon during term time, helping stack the hay during harvest time, running errands such as buying milk, and generally helping around the house (22, 38). There was still time for games such as marbles and hide and seek, though. Moreover, there is a sense that the girls inhabited a world with its own geography and its own special places beyond the village square, such as the alleys and the hills above the village. The diary begins with a highly biblical account of the girls stealing apples and feeling a deep sense of remorse; then, as Conchita describes, "Suddenly, there appeared to me a very beautiful figure that shone brilliantly but did not hurt my eyes at all": an angel (16). It is the irruption of the sacred into the everyday which grants her, and her fellow visionaries, a special status. Initially, they gained a sense of importance and protagonism at a local level: "The girls who were with us at school [the next day] were filled with wonder at what we said" (21). Over time, however, they attracted the attention not only of their peers, but also of their schoolteacher, the local pastor, the police, and nearby villagers: "The people of the village continued to be more and more impressed, and those from other villages were also much impressed" (30). As the news of these visions spread, the girls attracted the attention of adults beyond the local environs: many doctors, such as child psychology expert Dr. Celestino Ortiz Pérez; men of the cloth, such as Canon Francisco Odriozola and the Jesuit priest Luis María Andréu;[44] American Catholics who became highly active promoters of the messages of Garabandal around the world, like Joey Lomangino and Maria Saraco; and photographers, journalists, and camera teams for national and international media.

The girls themselves took an active part in promoting the visions, for both Loli and Conchita wrote letters to announce forthcoming events. The diary records one particular instance: "When the day arrived on which I was supposed to announce the date [the miracle of the visible host], I told it to the people of the village and I also wrote some letters" (103), despite being advised by the men in her village not to. Although it is not made clear who she was writing to at that point, Conchita had found a new role as religious campaigner and had begun to master the process of letter writing as a form of communication and activism. The prologue to the Spanish edition states:

Recibe una voluminosa correspondencia a la que no puede contestar. En estas montañas de cartas, escritas en todos los idiomas, se encuentran

mezcladas cartas con torpe mano que denotan un origen humilde. Pero
también hay cartas que emanan de personas de gobierno e incluso esposas
de jefes de Estado. (8)

[She receives a voluminous correspondence to which she cannot reply.
In this mountain of letters, written in all languages, there are letters written
with a clumsy hand which denote a humble origin. But there are also letters
that have been sent by government officials and even wives of political
leaders.]

This passage is misleading in that it is particularly evident in materials about
the apparition that Conchita did indeed maintain her correspondence with
a wide range of people: the workers of the Blessed Virgin (American adher-
ents to the Garabandal movement) and Joey Lomangino (*Our Lady*, 222–223,
226–227); and Father P. Alba (Barcelona), Father Gustavo Morelos (Mexico),
and Vicente Puchol, bishop of Santander (*Diario*, 87–88, 91, 114–115).

As Mary Celeste Kearney asserts, "Writing has a liberating effect on many
girls" mainly "because it allows female youth to transcend at least temporarily, their familial roles, spaces, and responsibilities."[45] Conchita's literacy enabled her to engage with the outside world through correspondence,
as well as to document the events at Garabandal in her words. Another
scholar, however, Carolyn Steedman, who has focused on the meaning of
writing by girls, does not highlight this issue of the emancipatory potential
but instead raises the thorny issue of adults' involvement in the publication
and dissemination of children's writing.[46] We must be wary of interpreting
this document as giving us—adults—privileged access to Conchita's inner
world, because in the text she documents her social and religious life while
conscious of the potential audience, rather than using the writing for private exploration or a means to self-discovery. Furthermore, two acts of
mediation take place in this diary. First, Conchita acts as a Holy Messenger,
privileging communications from the Virgin over expressing her own personal opinions or emotions. Second, adult figures, such as Father Pelletier
in the English translation, take on the role of editor and intermediary, constantly interrupting the narrative with annotations and commentary.[47] The
Spanish edition is, perhaps, a little less intrusive, and uses footnotes instead,
although they are so lengthy that they are hardly unobtrusive.

Steedman demonstrates how girls' published writings can be perceived
as binding matter, the link that connects the past and the future and maintains stability. I argue that it is not only the four girls' visions that perform
this function but Conchita's writings as well. Conchita's diary was taken up
by a Catholic collective at a time of crisis, when a fissure in the symbolic
order was perceived by those who, until that moment, felt in full control.
Those who felt threatened held on to what they regarded as symbols of
hope and the continuity of traditional values. The devotion of Garabandal
can be interpreted as the negative reaction of a community—at both a local
and a global level—to the Catholic Church's liberal reforms during and after

the Second Vatican Council (1961).[48] As Rupert Shortt comments, "Most striking for laypeople, perhaps, was the reform of eucharistic and other rites set in train by *Sacrosanctum Concilium* (the main document on liturgy)."[49] Some of the changes perceived as disturbing to the faithful were the priest speaking the Mass in vernacular, not Latin; the removal of saints, such as the popular Saint Christopher, from the liturgical calendar; the denial of the reality of miracles; and the appearance of a new type of priest that erased the need for divine intermediaries and questioned the traditional forms of prayer and devotion.[50] Conchita emphasizes throughout her diary that one of the principle functions the Virgin performed was educational: "She recited it [the rosary] with us in order to show us how to say it well" (38), and during another vision, to say it slowly (87). The movement that emerged during and after the Garabandal apparitions resembles the majority of other Marian movements in that it represents a powerful force of traditionalism, because Garabandal devotees are antimodernist and reactionary in their vision of the Church. Conchita's diary was published and remains in circulation not because she gives us insights into a rural girlhood in a rapidly modernizing world, or because the diary describes the transformation of an ordinary girlhood into an extraordinary one, but because her words are held by a particular community as offering internal evidence to a series of Marian apparitions.

Conclusion: The Legacy of Holy Girl Power

In this chapter I have considered how a historical model of girlhood can have a real effect on girls' lives, not only because it is projected onto girls by society and culture, but also because girls find it opens up a series of new possibilities and experiences hitherto unavailable to them. The historical model of girlhood, though, may constrain the girl to a particular script that does not have an emancipatory project at its core, and yet it nevertheless may enable her to become influential locally, nationally, and indeed, globally. The religious experience of girls has a symbolic value that can—if accepted by a community—leave a lasting legacy.

In Garabandal, the apparitions filled in the empty slot on the landscape, resignifying the village and the natural habitat that surrounds it as sacred within the Catholic tradition. For example, an uphill path strewn with jagged rocks, once a cattle route, is now used by pilgrims. Its hazards are symbolic of suffering, and ceramic plaques are embedded in the landscape to illustrate the Calvary. At the end of the path is a group of pine trees central to the apparitions, at which pilgrims gather to pray and leave flowers, photographs of loved ones, written requests, and other objects. Pilgrims need not leave Garabandal empty-handed, because one of the village houses is now a religious gift shop where a wide range of devotional material and souvenirs can be purchased. The apparitions not only altered the landscape but also transformed the economy of the village from an agricultural one to an important destination on the many Marian tours of Europe designed for Catholic tourists. As has been mentioned, Garabandal is not simply restricted to the local; the name of the village is also the name of the devotional movement. Today, the Garabandal devotees have organized around centers where they meet for prayer and from which they spread their devotion in cities and towns in South Africa, India, Australia, and, recently, in England. Not only is this movement established as a social and organizational force, but it also employs modern communication methods and fields. There are almost as many official Garabandal movement Web sites as there are centers dedicated to spread devotion. In 1999 these Web sites organized a federation devoted to digitally preserving the memory of the movement and allowing free access to devotional materials. In fact, a wealth of still and moving images and sound recordings is digitally recycled online. You weren't there? Don't worry, you can be.

NOTES

This chapter has emerged from an ongoing research project provisionally titled "Holy Girls and Sacred Spaces," which has received financial support from the Faculty of Arts, Birkbeck, University of London.

1. Joseph Bottum, "What Happened at Fatima: John Paul II, Lucia dos Santos, and the End of Communism," *Weekly Standard* 10, no. 23 (2005), http://www.weeklystandard.com/Content/Public/Articles/000/000/005/284douan.asp (accessed February 2007).

2. None of these girls are related, despite sharing a common surname. Mazón died in April 2009.

3. Paolo Apolito, *Apparitions of the Madonna* (University Park: Pennsylvania State University Press, 1998), 15.

4. William A. Christian, *Visionaries* (Berkeley: University of California Press, 1996), 1.

5. Manuel Vásquez and Marie F. Marquardt, "Globalizing the Rainbow Madonna: Old Time Religion in the Present Age," *Theory, Culture and Society* 17, no. 4 (2000): 126.

6. A survey of the local and national press published between 1961 and 1967 clearly demonstrates that reports on the apparitions were initially suppressed. At the time, the theologian Saiz wrote a four-part column on the need for the Church and the faithful to exercise caution regarding religious apparitions and messages, but he failed to mention the events at Garabandal directly. Jose Maria Saiz, "Apariciones y revelaciones privadas," *Alerta*, July 13–16, 1961. This column was also published in other newspapers, such as *El Diario Montañés*. Many accounts, however, refer to the presence of Spaniards from neighboring villages and distant cities such as Barcelona, so evidently information about the apparitions was spreading through other channels. In 1967, a national newspaper published a report that the bishop of Santander officially condemned the apparitions as an innocent children's game that had grown out of proportion. "La Iglesia en el mundo de hoy," *ABC*, March 16, 1967.

7. I do not, however, wish to exaggerate the cultural importance of the devotion to the Garabandal apparitions on the current world stage. Given that the visions have not been approved by the Catholic Church, the movement may not survive the lifespan of the first generation of devotees.

8. William A. Christian, *Person and God in a Spanish Valley*, rev. ed. (Princeton, NJ: Princeton University Press, 1989); and Christian, "Holy People in Peasant Europe," *Comparative Studies in Society and History* 15, no. 1 (1973): 106–114; Sandra Zimdars-Swartz, *Encountering Mary: From La Salette to Medjugorge* (Princeton, NJ: Princeton University Press, 1991); Paolo Apolito, *The Internet and the Madonna: Religious Visionary Experience on the Web* (Chicago: University of Chicago, 2005).

9. Catherine Driscoll, *Girls: Feminine Adolescence in Popular Culture* (New York: Columbia University Press, 2002), 142.

10. Jane M. Ussher, *Fantasies of Femininity: Reframing the Boundaries of Sex* (New Brunswick, NJ: Rutgers University Press, 1997), 3.

11. See, for example, Penny Tinkler, *Constructing Girlhood: Popular Magazines for Girls Growing Up in England* (London: Taylor and Francis, 1995); Lynne Vallone, *Disciplines of Virtue: Girls' Culture in the Eighteenth and Nineteenth Centuries* (New Haven: Yale University Press, 1995); Carolyn Stewart Dyer and Nancy Tillman Romalov, *Rediscovering Nancy Drew* (Iowa City: University of Iowa Press, 1995); Shirley Foster and Judy Simons, *What Katy Read: Feminist Re-Readings of Classic Stories for Girls, 1850–1920* (Iowa City: University of Iowa Press, 1995); Sherrie A. Inness, "Review Essay: Girl's Culture," *Contemporary Women's Issues Database* 8 (1996): 151.

12. See, for example, Sherrie A. Inness, *Millennium Girls: Today's Girls around the World* (Lanham, MD: Rowman and Littlefield, 1998); Sinikka Aapola, Marnina Gonick, and Anita Harris, *Young Femininity: Girlhood, Power, and Social Change* (New York: Palgrave Macmillan, 2005); Yasmin Jiwani, Candis Steenbergen, and Claudia Mitchell, *Girlhood: Redefining the Limits* (Montreal: Black Rose Books, 2006).

13. There is a vast body of literature that focuses on Mary of the Christian scriptures, but a couple of titles that are relevant to understanding the potential impact of this impossible role model on girlhood are Marina Warner, *Alone of All Her Sex: The Myth and Cult of the Virgin Mary* (London: Weidenfeld and Nicolson, 1976); Elizabeth N. Evasdaughter, *Catholic Girlhood Narratives: The Church and Self-Denial* (Boston: Northeastern University Press, 1996); and Jeana DelRosso, *Writing Catholic Women: Contemporary International Catholic Girlhood Narratives* (New York: Palgrave Macmillan, 2005). The martyr of chastity model has a long history, but the figure most presented to Catholic girls to admire as a heroine of resistance in the twentieth century was the murdered twelve-year-old girl Saint Maria Goretti (1890–1902). See Kathleen Norris, "Maria Goretti—Cipher or Saint?" in *Martyrs: Contemporary Writers on Modern Lives of Faith*, ed. Susan Bergman (San Francisco: HarperCollins, 1996), 299–309. I have previously explored how a Spanish girl's life and death have been, and continue to be, interpreted as a personal and heroic spiritual response to the suffering of the Spanish Civil War, in Jessamy Harvey, "Good Girls Go to Heaven: The Venerable Mari Carmen González Valerio y Sáenz de Heredia (1930–1939)," in *Constructing Identity in Twentieth-Century Spain: Theoretical Debates and Cultural Practice*, ed. Jo Labanyi (Oxford: Oxford University Press, 2002), 113–127. For an account of an American icon of suffering girlhood, see Paula M. Kane, "'She Offered Herself Up': The Victim Soul and Victim Spirituality in Catholicism," *Church History: Studies in Christianity and Culture* 71 (2002): 80–119.

14. Ruth Harris, *Lourdes: Body and Spirit in the Secular Age* (London: Penguin Press, 1999), 36.

15. William A. Christian, *Apparitions in Late Medieval and Renaissance Spain* (Princeton, NJ: Princeton University Press, 1981); see also Christian, *Visionaries*.

16. Interestingly, Harris makes the point that the representation of the holy peasant as accompanied by sheep is "an iconographic device that simplified the reality—they herded donkeys, cows, sheep, or any other animal—in favor of an evocation of biblical imagery" (*Lourdes*, 38).

17. Deborah Simonton, "Earning and Learning: Girlhood in Pre-Industrial Europe," *Women's History Review* 13, no. 3 (2004): 368. See also Mary Jo Maynes, Birgitte Søland, and Christina Benninghaus, eds., *Secret Gardens, Satanic Mills: Placing Girls in European History, 1750–1960* (Bloomington: Indiana University Press, 1995).

18. Zimdars-Swartz, *Encountering Mary*, 27; Harris, *Lourdes*, 3.

19. Zimdars-Swartz, *Encountering Mary*, 44.

20. Lucia dos Santos, *Fatima, in Lucia's Own Words*, ed. Fr. Louis Kondor, with an introduction by Dr. Joaquin M. Alonso, and trans. Dominican Nuns of Perpetual Rosary (Fatima: Postulation Centre, 1963), 58.

21. Harris, *Lourdes*, 83–109; Christian, *Visionaries*, 26.

22. Donn Cupitt, *Mysticism after Modernity* (Oxford: Blackwell Publishers, 1997); Karen Armstrong, *The Gospel according to Woman* (London: HarperCollins, 1986).

23. Armstrong, *Gospel according to Woman*, 215.

24. Saba Mahmood, *Politics of Piety: The Islamic Revival and the Feminist Subject* (Princeton, NJ: Princeton University Press, 2006), 8, 38, 2–3, 34.

25. "Prologo," in *Diario de Conchita de Garabandal* (New York: Nuestra Señora del Carmen de Garabandal, n.d.), 7.

26. Gisella Kaplan, *Contemporary Western European Feminism* (New York: New York University Press, 1992), 204.

27. Christian, *Person and God in a Spanish Valley*, 33.

28. Peter N. Stearns, "Conclusion: Change, Globalization, and Childhood," *Journal of Social History* 38, no. 4 (2005): 1041–1043.

29. Although something resembling Anglo-American girlhood studies has yet to emerge in the field of Spanish studies as an object of scholarly attention, the overwhelmingly visible girl figure is that of the schoolgirl and the way she has been, and is, located in the social world by her curriculum. See, for example, Inmaculada Pastor, *La educación femenina de la postguerra (1939–1945): El caso de Mallorca* (Madrid: Instituto de la Mujer, 1984); Alicia Alted Vigil, "Education and Political Control," in *Spanish Cultural Studies: An Introduction—The Struggle for Modernity*, ed. Helen Graham and Jo Labanyi (Oxford: Oxford University Press, 1995); María Luisa Sagalaz Sánchez, *La educación física femenina en España* (Jaén: Universidad de Jaén, 1998); Catherine Jagoe, "La enseñanza femenina en la España decimonónica," in *La mujer en los discursos de género: Textos y contextos en el siglo XIX*, ed. Catherine Jagoe, Alda Blanco, and Christina Enriquez de Salamanca (Barcelona: Icaria, 1998), 105–145; Aurora Morcillo Gómez, "Shaping True Catholic Womanhood: Francoist Educational Discourse on Women," in *Constructing Spanish Womanhood: Female Identity in Modern Spain*, ed. Victoria Loree Enders and Paula Radcliff (New York: SUNY Press, 1999), 51–69; Agustín Escolano Benito, *El pensil de las niñas: La educación de la mujer: Invención de una tradición* (Madrid: EDAF, 2001); Pilar Ballarín Domingo, *La educación de las mujeres en la España contemporánea (siglos XIX–XX)* (Madrid: Sintesis, 2001).

30. Philippe Ariès, *Centuries of Childhood*, trans. Robert Baldick (London: Pimlico 1996), 56 (quotations).

31. Mitchell, *Girlhood*, 74.

32. Stearns, "Change, Globalization, and Childhood," 1043, 1045.

33. Alted Vigil, "Education and Political Control," 197.

34. The feminist Lidia Falcón, in her memoir of growing up in a left-wing family during the Franco regime, demonstrates how, for survival, it was necessary to keep up appearances and remain silent by conforming to the dominant ideology. Unlike the majority, but common to many sons and daughters of those on the losing side of the civil war, her childhood was marked not only by the official rhetoric but also by the ideals and memory of a defeated democratic Spain. Lidia Falcón, *Los hijos de los vencidos: (1939–1949)* (Madrid: Vindicación Feminista, 1989).

35. A. J. Onieva and F. Torres, *Enciclopedia Hernando: Niñas (período de perfeccionamiento)* (Madrid: Librería y Casa Editorial Hernando, 1954), 336.

36. Christian, *Person and God in a Spanish Valley*, xv. He also notes that "just as the man is the family head in practical matters, the woman has a certain responsibility and authority in spiritual matters," particularly in relation to "the masses for the dead, the children's prayers, the husband's annual communion, and the regulations with the important divine figures" (134).

37. Margarita Escanciano, "Campesina que huyes del campo te guarde Dios," *Vindicación Feminista* 20 (1978): 51.

38. The apparitions in Garabandal were, as is characteristic of other twentieth-century apparitions, technological: devotees and others who attended the apparitions made full use of sensory media such as photography, film, and sound recording to capture the phenomenon. In fact, one of the prime "miracles" or "wonders" is the appearance of the Host on Conchita's tongue. The captured image attests to the veracity of the event, as Apolito has noted: "the camera becomes the auctoritas that decides the first sign of the world's prodigiousness" (*Apparitions*, 213).

39. As one Web site proclaims, "Where and what is Garabandal? It is an isolated hamlet of some 300 people nestled in the Cantabrian Mountains of Northwestern Spain. Like Fatima and Lourdes, Garabandal is a place of unearthly serenity and beauty. A fiction writer's imagination could not create a more appropriate setting for a religious event of great significance." See http: // www.garabandal.us/garabandal.html (accessed February 2007).

40. A poignant passage in Lucia's memoirs hints at her frustration at being unable to read, let alone write, as a girl: "I kept silence, not wishing to put the blame on my mother, who at that time had not yet allowed me to go to school. At home, they said it was out of vanity that I wanted to learn to read. Until then, hardly any girls learned to read. The school was just for boys. It was only later that a school was opened in Fatima for girls" (dos Santos, *Fatima*, 178).

41. Christian, "Holy People in Peasant Europe"; Zimdars-Swartz, *Encountering Mary*.

42. *Diario de Conchita de Garabandal* (New York: Nuestra Señora del Carmen de Garabandal, n.d.); Joseph A. Pelletier, *Our Lady Comes to Garabandal (Including Conchita's Diary)* (Worcester, MA: Assumption Publication, 1971). Hereafter, citations of these two volumes are give in the text in parentheses. The translations of *Diario* that are given in brackets are mine. All other translations come from the English edition *Our Lady*.

43. See http: // www.garabandal.us/conchita_house1.html.

44. Luis María Andréu, it is maintained, had a Marian vision within the village in the summer of 1961.

45. Mary Celeste Kearney, *Girls Make Media* (New York: Routledge, 2006), 30–32.

46. Caroline Steedman, *The Tidy House: Little Girls Writing* (London: Virago, 1982), 61–84.

47. A further process of mediation takes place in the act of translating.

48. Although the topic is outside the scope of this chapter, it is vital to note that between 1960 and 1962, as a quick glance through the local newspapers confirm, the nearby port of Santander was receiving hundreds of nuns and priests who had been expelled, or were emigrating under duress, from Cuba after the Revolutionary victory of 1959. This influx helps explain the anti-communist and pro-clerical aspect of the visions and the reason that many perceive Garabandal as a continuation of the events in Fatima.

49. Rupert Shortt, *Benedict XVI: Commander of the Faith* (London: Hodder and Stoughton, 2006), 33.

50. Ibid., 33; Kenneth L. Woodward, *Making Saints inside the Vatican: Who Become Saints, Who Do Not, and Why* (London: Chatto and Windus, 1991), 104; Christian, *Person and God in a Spanish Valley*, xv.

10 Rebels, Robots, and All-American Girls

THE IDEOLOGICAL USE OF IMAGES OF GIRL GYMNASTS DURING THE COLD WAR

ANN KORDAS

Gymnastics, a sport that cultivates and rewards agility, grace, and elegance in young women, would, on the face of it, seem unlikely to generate controversy in the international arena. Women's gymnastics, however, has long had a political dimension to it. Although women's gymnastics has been an Olympic sport since 1928, its political import first became apparent at the 1952 Helsinki Games, when the young female gymnasts from the Soviet Union dominated the competition, garnering hundreds of points for the USSR and enraging the American media.

The newly politically charged nature of gymnastics, and of the gymnasts themselves, was the result of the Cold War. During the period ranging from the late 1960s to the 1990s, changes in the presentation of girl gymnasts in the American media accompanied changes in the Cold War relationship between the United States and the Soviet Union. In this chapter I explore the ways in which the American media employed images of both U.S. and Eastern-bloc girl gymnasts to convince American citizens, and presumably citizens of the unaligned nations of the world as well, of the benevolence and superiority of the United States and the evil nature of the Soviet Union and its Eastern-bloc allies.

Cold War Gymnastics: Girls' Bodies as Sites of National Reproduction

Following the end of World War II, the United States and the Soviet Union entered into a fifty-year battle for world dominance. Beginning with Stalin's demands for control of eastern Europe at Yalta in 1945 and ending with the dismantling of the Soviet Union in 1991, the two superpowers confronted one another in many arenas: political, economic, military, social, and athletic. During this period, girls around the world found themselves drawn into the international arena as both agents and pawns in the new realignment of world power as both the United States and the Soviet Union used images of girls, especially girl gymnasts, to serve the ideological purposes of their respective regimes.

Since its founding, the Soviet Union had recognized, as E. Thomas Ewing discusses in his chapter in this volume, the importance of youth to the reproduction of the political order. In the post–World War II era, the United States also made great use of images of young girls, especially girl gymnasts, to tout the superiority of the U.S. political and economic system. During the Cold War, teenage girls became objects of great interest in the United States, and many organizations assumed the task of preparing them for the roles they would one day play as citizens of both the United States and the world. Although organizations that sought to prepare girls for adult roles, such as those Melissa Klapper mentions in her chapter on Jewish girl-hood in turn-of-the-century America, had existed in the United States for many years, during the Cold War such groups assumed a new political dimension. For example, the Camp Fire Girls, as Jennifer Helgren discusses in her chapter, sought to prepare young girls for world citizenship by teach-ing them to respect the cultures of other nations and urging them to work for world peace, while simultaneously conveying the message that peace and unity could best be achieved if other countries adopted American cul-ture and values.

During this period, girl gymnasts gained prominence as defenders and reproducers of American values. There are many reasons why girls, espe-cially girl gymnasts, were readily co-opted as objects of nationalistic propa-ganda during the Cold War. Lauren Berlant argues that, as innocent beings needing protection, children become the subjects of state action. Unable to care for themselves, children exert "ethical claims on the adult political agents who write laws, make culture, administer resources, control things." In caring for children, states display "the nation's value."[1] Girls, who occupy the vulnerable position of being both female and children, are thus ideal subjects of state action and perfect vehicles for conveying nationalistic prop-aganda.

If girls in general are the natural subjects of propaganda, girl gymnasts are even better at serving such nationalistic needs. As Ann Chisholm, build-ing on Berlant's theory of "infantile citizenship," argues, Americans have long displayed concern for girls because their bodies serve as sites of both physical and cultural reproduction. According to Chisholm, girls who have trained their bodies to be strong, healthy, graceful, and disciplined through the practice of gymnastics are perceived as best prepared for their future roles as wives, mothers, and guardians of cultural values.[2] Girls, especially girl gymnasts, are accordingly an embodiment of the nation's strength as well as a reflection of the benevolence of its government. The use of images of girl gymnasts during the Cold War to represent conflicting political ide-ologies can, as a result, easily be understood.

The Battle for Helsinki: "Girl Soldiers" Win Olympic Honors

The first shot in this proxy war fought by female gymnasts was fired at the 1952 Helsinki Olympics. During the Cold War, both the United States and the Soviet Union regarded the Olympics as the perfect venue for advertising the superiority of their respective ways of life. The 1952 Olympics, the first Olympics in which the Soviet Union competed, provided the opportunity for yet another showdown between the United States and the USSR in the international arena. Before 1952, tallying the number of medals won by the athletes of individual nations had been of relatively little importance. When the Soviet Union made its first appearance in Olympic competition in Helsinki, however, all of this changed. Both the Soviet Union and the United States became obsessed with keeping "medal counts" and point tallies—records of how many gold, silver, and bronze medals, as well as fourth- through sixth-place finishes, had been won by each of the participating countries.[3]

Adding to Americans' concern regarding the point count after 1952 was the Soviets' dominance of a sport in which Americans could not possibly hope to win a medal, a sport in which the Soviet Union could easily amass a large number of medals as well as fourth-, fifth-, and sixth-place finishes: women's gymnastics.[4] With three medals to be won in each of six events,[5] a total of eighteen medals were at stake in the women's gymnastics competition. As many as sixteen medals could, theoretically, be won by the gymnasts of one nation—fifteen medals in each of the five individual competitions plus one medal in the team competition.[6]

In the 1950s, gymnastics was a little practiced sport in the United States. In the Soviet Union, however, gymnastics was studied by all children as part of the elementary school curriculum, and special sports schools existed to provide advanced training for the most talented young athletes.[7] In Helsinki, the performance of the Soviet women's gymnastics team added 602 points to the overall Soviet "score"; the United States won no points in gymnastics.[8]

Many Americans were greatly disturbed by the addition of so many points to the Soviet total as the result of the women's gymnastics performances. Even U.S. State Department officials reportedly worried about what such scores would do to the international image of the United States.[9] From this point forward, women's gymnastics, a sport soon to be dominated by teenaged and prepubescent girls, became a Cold War battleground, and female Soviet gymnasts were denounced in the American press as enemies of the West. Repeated mention was made in American newspapers of the "fact" that Soviet athletes, including teenaged gymnasts, were members of the Soviet army and often trained at military sports facilities.[10] Even the tiny, teenaged gymnast Olga Korbut, who stood less than five feet tall, wore her hair in pigtails, and carried a stuffed hedgehog to competitions as a good luck charm, was identified in a *New York Times* article as an "84-Pound Soviet 'Soldier.'" The article warned Americans that although they might see in Olga only a charming adolescent girl, Soviet fans "cheer[ed] Olya as a fine young athlete defending the colors of the Soviet Army."[11]

Cold War, Warm Olga: The Americanization of Olga Korbut

Ironically, if any one Soviet citizen was responsible for convincing Americans that not all Soviets posed a threat to the American way of life, it was the eighty-four-pound "soldier" Olga Korbut. Although identified in the press as a member the Soviet army, most Americans saw in Olga only a tiny, impish teenaged girl. Television coverage of the 1972 Munich Olympics helped to transform Olga from a member of the fearsome Soviet team to an ordinary girl and endeared her to the hearts of millions. When Olga made an error in her performance on the uneven parallel bars and earned a shockingly low score, she burst into tears. Television cameras immediately focused on her, beaming the image of the weeping seventeen-year-old to millions of spectators around the world and earning her sympathetic fans on all continents.[12] Cameras also recorded her daring moves on the uneven parallel bars and the balance beam and showed her jubilant smile when she mounted the winner's platform.[13] Olga Korbut had arrived at the 1972 Munich Olympics as a gymnast largely unknown in the West; she left as a newly minted celebrity and the world's darling.

Olga's transformation from a soldier in the war against freedom to America's sweetheart was not simply a response to her performance in Munich. It reflected, and was perhaps aided by, changes in the relationship between the Soviet Union and the United States in the early 1970s. If girl gymnasts could be used as symbols of East–West competition and Communist aggression, they could also be used as agents of détente. As Olga was perfecting her gymnastics skills in the late 1960s and early 1970s, U.S. president Richard Nixon and Soviet premier Leonid Brezhnev attempted to relieve tensions between the two countries by jointly seeking a solution to the nuclear arms race. On May 22, 1972, shortly before Olga Korbut competed at the Munich Olympics, Nixon, hoping to come to an agreement with Brezhnev regarding the proliferation of nuclear weapons, became the first U.S. president to enter the Kremlin.

A series of scientific and cultural exchanges accompanied the political and military aspects of détente. Soviet cosmonauts and American astronauts worked together on the exploration of space. Soviet athletes toured the United States demonstrating their skills and occasionally competing against Americans. Olga Korbut, who already displayed a predilection for Western culture, was an ideal cultural liaison. According to Gwen Evans, the author of a children's book on the gymnast, when Korbut performed in post-Olympic gymnastics exhibitions in the United States, she was, in effect, "on a diplomatic mission for the Union of Soviet Socialist Republics."[14]

Olga's age, sex, and diminutive appearance in many ways made her the perfect go-between in the relationship between the United States and the Soviet Union. Olga was charming and nonthreatening in appearance.[15] Her position as a gymnast carried no overt political connotations. As Evans states, "At a time of political tensions between nations, she offered something everyone could share: the joy and drama of sports." Indeed, Olga's Olympic triumph had made her "a citizen of the world."[16] She could charm Western leaders with her personality and interact with them in ways that adult, male Soviet politicians and diplomats could not. Olga Korbut could openly meet with Western politicians without arousing debates in the press over whether establishing closer relations with the Soviet Union was a wise or desirable move.

Such meetings between Olga, the "Soviet Pixie," and Western politicians were common and became a regular part of the exhibition tours of Western nations that the Soviet gymnastics team took following their triumph at Munich.[17] Photographs showed Olga departing from 10 Downing Street after a meeting with the British prime minister.[18] Mayors John Lindsay of New York and Richard Daley of Chicago met with Olga when she toured the United States. Mayor Lindsay presented the Soviet gymnasts with the key to the city and expressed his wish that Olga be "nice" to the mayor of her hometown.[19] Mayor Daley grandly proclaimed March 26, 1977, to be Olga Korbut Day.[20] Olga and her Soviet teammates also visited Richard Nixon at the White House. Nixon commented on how tiny Olga was; Olga commented on how big Nixon was. Polite laughter ensued as photos were snapped, and Nixon congratulated Olga on her "ability to land on [her] feet."[21] Although meetings between Olga Korbut and world leaders were not necessarily regarded as serious events in the United States, they nevertheless symbolized the willingness of the USSR to establish closer relations with the West. Olga gave a human face to the Soviet Union and convinced Americans that friendship between East and West was possible.

Western politicians were not the only ones who found Korbut charming. Millions of American girls also became fans of Olga. The adulation by American girls of a Soviet gymnast, however, posed a potential problem. In the minds of cold warriors not willing to accept or believe in the possibility of friendlier relations with the Soviet Union, American admiration of Olga Korbut might potentially lead to admiration of the USSR and the Soviet way of life. A solution to this perceived dilemma needed to be found. Thus, before a young "Communist" gymnast such as Olga could be presented as a heroine and an appropriate role model for American girls, she had to be "Americanized." That is, the American media needed to depict her as possessing interests and personality traits that were approved of and valued by Americans. The media also needed to separate Olga as much as possible from the nation she represented and the government that sponsored her training.

The American media accomplished this feat in various ways. One way was to emphasize how enamored Olga Korbut was of Western culture. Another means of Americanizing Olga was to stress the characteristics that made her seem more American than Soviet, to present her as closer in thought, feeling, and personal style to American girls than to young women from her own country. Korbut proved amenable to the process. She was indeed fascinated by American culture and consumer goods. When Olga toured the United States with the Soviet gymnastics team, photographs appeared in the American press showing her, dressed in the latest styles of the 1970s, shopping her way through American stores such as J. C. Penney.[22] Frequent mention was made of Olga's predilection for Western fashions and pop culture. In interviews given to American reporters, Olga made clear her love of "modern dances, modern songs."[23] She expressed a desire to dine at McDonald's.[24] While on tour of the United States in December 1976, Olga danced at a disco, saw the movie *Carrie*, and visited Disney World.[25]

Tellingly, American love for Olga Korbut did not always extend to all members of the Soviet women's gymnastics team. Olga's fame and the relative obscurity of her teammates were not the result of her superior gymnastic abilities. Olga's coaches never considered her the best gymnast on the Soviet team. As one of the many books about Olga Korbut written for American children explained, however, Olga was charming. She seemed always to be smiling. In this she differed from the American stereotype of Soviets as stern and dour. Unlike other Soviet athletes, who, "it seemed, preferred not to show much emotion," Olga had a "broad, bright smile." While her teammates "display[ed] a serious, almost mechanical manner," Olga, in contrast, was "a bundle of bubbly energy."[26] Olga's emotional nature and boundless enthusiasm were reportedly what attracted the attention of future Olympic gymnast Mary Lou Retton. According to Retton, "Russians were supposed to be stone-faced, but not Olga. She showed emotion. She laughed when she won and she cried when she fell. I liked that. That's like me. I show emotion."[27] Korbut, at least in her emotional style, was more American than Soviet. Americans liked Olga because Olga was like Americans.

Olga's vivacious personality and extroverted nature sometimes proved problematic, however. If Olga was oppressed and discontented with life in her native land, as the American media insisted all Soviet citizens were, why did she always seem so joyful? Presenting Olga as happy and content with her life behind the Iron Curtain was not acceptable, for it might give Americans, especially the impressionable young, the notion that life in the Soviet Union was not as awful as they had been told it was. Olga Korbut's seeming acceptance of life in the USSR needed to be explained in a way that assured Americans that Soviet life was indeed harsh and that Olga's happiness was not occasioned by a love of Communism but was instead the result of her remarkable ability to triumph over adversity, a trait highly valued by Americans.

Stories about Olga intended for an American audience thus focused on those personal qualities that apparently allowed her to overcome hardship and made her seem like a freedom-loving American. In keeping with this approach, books, newspaper and magazine articles, and anecdotes about Olga Korbut frequently stressed her independence and sense of individualism, "American" traits that even the oppressive Soviet regime could not destroy. Indeed, Olga's ability to accept life in her "not . . . exciting" hometown of Grodno, a small industrial city near the Polish border, was attributed by author Justin Beecham to an inner freedom, a freedom of the heart. Seemingly unsuited to the drab and boring environment of Grodno, where buildings were "concrete and uniform" and the large squares so beloved of Soviet urban planners were "scantily landscaped," Olga, the "woodsprite," nevertheless managed to survive through her ability to "escape" periodically into "the Belovezh, the largest surviving primeval [read pre-Soviet] forest in Europe," where dwelt "animals threatened with extinction." Here "Olga [took] her . . . longed-for walks" alongside the other free-roaming but dwindling creatures of an earlier, pre-Soviet era.[28]

Olga Korbut was also frequently depicted as something of a rebel. Americans, whose own country had been born of revolution, prized rebelliousness, provided that it was not capitalism or the U.S. government against which one was rebelling. During the Cold War, Americans particularly cherished the image of the "good" rebel. A refusal to conform to externally imposed restrictions and the sometimes unreasonable expectations of society, a frequent theme in American novels, movies, and songs of the Cold War era, supposedly protected the United States from conquest by the Soviet Union; a nation of freedom-loving individualists would never be duped by Communist propaganda that stressed conformity and collectivism. As Leerom Medovoi argues, American psychologists and psychoanalysts of the postwar period, such as Robert Lindner, regarded the desire of American youth to establish their own independent identities as a form of "positive" rebellion that would prevent the United States from ever becoming a totalitarian state. Lindner even encouraged the readers of *McCall's* magazine to "Raise Your Child to Be a Rebel." In the postwar period, Americans reveled in the popular literary and cinematic depictions of disruptive but inherently moral and virtuous "good bad boys" (in the words of literary critic Leslie Fiedler), such as Marlon Brando's character Johnny in the 1953 film *The Wild One*. Depicting Olga Korbut as a "positive" rebel, someone who, in Linder's words, had "a sense of [her] own individuality, [her] uniqueness as a human being, [her] assets and potentialities as a person," thus made her appealing to Americans while also calming fears that the joyful Olga might actually be a willing member of a totalitarian society.[29]

Olga Korbut's rebelliousness was emphasized in a variety of ways. Numerous books about her noted that "she could be very headstrong," a trait "that caused her early trainers concern." The very fact that Olga had

been attracted to gymnastics as a child was seen as an indication of her indi-
vidualistic nature. Her biographer Justin Beecham claimed that unlike her
childhood friends, Olga Korbut would not have been content as a factory
worker, the occupation of most adults in Grodno: "Olga, by her very nature,
wanted something different." This was why she had chosen to pursue the
creative sport of gymnastics. Clearly, Olga was not one to follow the path of
conformity like other Soviet citizens. Indeed, Beecham even attributed
Olga's love for the woods to "a part of her spirit that seems unwilling to
accept the constraints of a postwar Soviet industrial urban environment."[30]

The most often repeated story about Olga's famed rebelliousness
involved the floor exercise that her coach and the gymnastics team's chore-
ographers had designed for her to perform at the Munich Games. Five days
before the Soviet team was scheduled to arrive at the Olympics, Korbut
informed her coach that she would not perform the routine in competition.
The exercise had been designed to evoke the spirit of the bumblebee, and
Korbut declared that she would not imitate the movements of a hideous bee.
Although one might expect Soviet gymnastics trainers to insist that she obey
them and perform the exercise as planned, Olga's trainers, realizing that she
would not give in to their demands, hastily chose a new piece of music and
designed a new program for her.[31] Olga's rebellion had succeeded.

Cold War, Cold Nadia: The "Abuse" of
Girl Gymnasts by Eastern-Bloc Countries

Although extroverted, freedom-loving, rebellious Olga Korbut quickly
became America's darling, other Eastern-bloc gymnasts were not as easy to
Americanize. Romanian gymnast Nadia Comaneci proved particularly
problematic. Nadia, at the time she became a superstar at the 1976 Montreal
Olympics, did not possess the vivacious, ebullient nature of the charismatic
Olga. Nadia seemed introverted and unemotional. She displayed no fasci-
nation with American consumer goods. The possibility of her possessing a
rebellious nature seemed belied by the perfection of her performance.
There seemed to be little in Nadia's life or personality that would cause
Americans to perceive in her a freedom-loving imp who, through some per-
verse quirk of fate, had been born and raised in a totalitarian society.

The media, however, needed to make Nadia presentable to Americans
by reassuring them that their latest idol could never be used to argue for the
superiority of Communism, despite her unparalleled gymnastic abilities and
her spectacular success at the Montreal Games. Because Nadia could not
easily be "Americanized," the American media chose instead to emphasize
her distance from the system that had created her by insisting that she was
the victim of her own government. The media also used this tactic in their
depiction of other girl gymnasts from Communist nations to illustrate the
cruel and oppressive nature of the systems that had produced them. Despite
the period of détente that led the American media to humanize selected

Eastern-bloc athletes during the early 1970s, tensions between East and West continued to exist and were reflected in the media's depiction of Eastern-bloc athletes. Negative depictions of the ways in which Eastern-bloc nations trained and treated their athletes, especially gymnasts, were common in the late 1970s, a time marked by the presidency of Jimmy Carter, whose concern for human rights abuses on the part of the Soviet government led him to call for a U.S. boycott of the 1980 Moscow Olympics.

Criticisms of the way in which gymnasts were treated in Communist countries often focused on the specialized sports schools that such nations provided for their youth. Commenting on the importance of these schools in the training of young Soviet athletes, author Justin Beecham noted that such training facilities offered instruction in both athletics and political ideology; Olga Korbut, as a little girl first embarking on her gymnastics career, was taught that gymnastic success depended on "an appreciation of the sport within the framework of Soviet goals." The presence of sports in the Soviet school curriculum, Beecham argued, was the result of the Soviet belief "that every child should be encouraged to gain proficiency in at least one sport, not for its own sake, but for the sake of the improvement of society."[32]

Other writers on the subject of sports agreed with him. Mimi Murray, the author of a manual for gymnastics coaches, a book one would not expect to be ideological in tone, stated that the training received by gymnasts "often reflects the political structure of their homeland." Although Murray conceded that at times the United States did "use athletics as an instrument of foreign policy," she insisted that Eastern European gymnasts like Olga Korbut and Nadia Comaneci trained not for love of the sport, as American gymnasts supposedly did, but solely to become "the perfect gymnast for the express purpose of political propaganda."[33]

So Eastern European sports schools were portrayed in the West as bastions of Communist ideology in which young girls "were reared by state instructors for the purpose of winning gold medals," and the life of girls studying gymnastics at such schools was depicted as unbearably harsh. The children of Eastern Europe, author Guy Odom insisted, were removed from their homes and packed off to state boarding schools, where, with single-minded determination and without "parental intervention," coaches molded their minds and bodies to make them perfect competitors and Olympic-caliber athletes.[34] Indeed, Nadia Comaneci's perfect routines, "performed . . . with a joyless expression," were attributed to her devoting her life entirely to gymnastics, giving up such girlish pleasures as riding her bicycle and swimming in favor of "rigorous three to four hour daily practice routines after school."[35]

According to the American media, such harsh physical training was paired with the denial of food, leaving the young gymnasts malnourished and starving. An article on Olga Korbut in *Seventeen* magazine revealed that Olga's coach, Renald Knysh, kept her on a diet that was nutritious yet "sparse."[36] Accusations of deliberate underfeeding also appeared in articles about Romanian gymnast Nadia Comaneci. Articles on Comaneci referred to "[her] strict diet of fruit, milk, cheese and protein (forget sugar and bread)." At parties given in Montreal in honor of the victorious Romanian gymnasts, New York Times sports editor Neil Amdur noted, Nadia ate "only salads."[37] In a 1977 New York Times article, written when the Romanian gymnastics team was touring the United States together with the U.S. Junior team, an American male gymnast reported what he interpreted as abuse of the Romanian girls: When the American gymnasts attempted to share some of their high-calorie treats with the Romanian girls, they learned that the Romanian team "[couldn't] have chocolates, no soda, no sweet rolls."[38]

The restricted diet of Eastern European gymnasts was portrayed in the American media in two ways. The spartan diets of Romanian and Soviet gymnasts were commonly presented as evidence of the cruel and repressive nature of totalitarian Communist regimes. The Romanian prohibition on sweets, which the American team readily violated by giving candy and soda to the Romanian girls, was interpreted by the American athletes as a form of deliberate deprivation, not a dietary restriction intended to prevent the gymnasts from gaining weight—a concern of gymnasts and their coaches in all countries.[39]

Limited diets were also interpreted as evidence of the failure of Communist societies to meet the most basic needs of their citizens. Perhaps the reason that Eastern European gymnasts were denied food, the American media suggested, was that the Communist regimes of Eastern Europe did not have sufficient food to give them. Seventeen magazine, for example, reported that although Olga Korbut and her teammates were allowed to eat fruit, they rarely did so because fruit "isn't always available to them." Indeed, the editors of Seventeen noted, the Soviets seemed to be so deprived that they were "delighted [at the very sight of] the limes we had set aside for a beauty demonstration."[40] The message was clear: Soviet girls were forced to do without basic foods, while American girls, living in a capitalist society, were so well provided for that they not only had enough food to eat but enough to waste on beauty applications.

Just as the American teens had gamely come to the rescue of the sugar-deprived Romanians, Americans readily remedied the hunger of the Soviets. Olga's love of ketchup, "an unusual treat that has no equivalent in the Soviet Union," was provided for when the generous staff of Seventeen gave her a ketchup recipe so that she could make the delicacy for herself at home.[41]

Just as horrifying to Americans as the inability of Eastern European gymnasts to eat the foods they loved was the inability of Soviet and Romanian girls, once again as the result of the supposed economic deficiencies of Communism, to properly groom themselves. A description of Nadia Comaneci at a gymnastics exhibition in the United States indicated that her hair was dirty and "in need of a shampoo."[42] According to Seventeen, Olga Korbut and her teammates were unable to maintain American standards of cleanliness and beauty despite their apparent desire to do so. They washed their hair with ordinary soap instead of shampoo. They lacked hair conditioner. They did not wear cosmetics. The Soviet girls even "bathe[d] less often."[43]

Once again, however, generous Americans stood ready to present the Soviets with items that, while rare in the USSR, were common in capitalist America. The charitable staff of *Seventeen* provided the Soviet girls with "a hair-trimming and face-care session." The gymnasts were reportedly delighted. Sixteen-year-old Nina Dronova was seemingly entranced by electric rollers. Olga Korbut was delighted by the gift of an eyelash curler.[44]

Not only were food and physical comforts presented as lacking in the lives of young Eastern-bloc gymnasts, but affection and sympathy were also supposedly nonexistent. The American media claimed that, deprived of the loving embrace of their parents, girls were entirely dependent on their coaches for emotional support. Such support, it was reported, was denied them, however. American reporters commented that Eastern European coaches rarely comforted or congratulated gymnasts after their Olympic performances. Nadia Comaneci completed perfect routines only to return to the sidelines without "a gesture of congratulation from her coach, Bella [*sic*] Karoly."[45] The same American boy who revealed the stark no-chocolate-or-soda diet of the Romanian gymnasts also reported that Nadia's coach often yelled at her, reducing her to tears.[46]

Béla Karolyi often received a drubbing in the American press. He was routinely depicted as manipulative and uncaring. On a 1979 trip to Déva, the small town in the hinterlands of Romania where Karolyi trained his gymnasts, *Sports Illustrated* reporter Bob Ottom described Béla Karolyi as an "unshaven and grumpy" man who "emit[ed] an occasional growl" as he watched his gymnasts practice.[47]

If Nadia's coach Béla Karolyi was depicted in the American media as cold and uncaring, Soviet coaches were portrayed as nothing short of nightmarish. For example, Renald Knysh, Olga Korbut's coach, was reported to have said that the tears of his gymnasts did not move him.[48] According to American gymnastics coach Muriel Grossfeld, "[she] would never consider [herself] . . . as mean or tough as Olga Korbut's coach."[49]

Eastern European gymnastics trainers were also often accused by Americans of manipulating the emotions, the demeanor, and the very personality of young female gymnasts. Nadia Comaneci's coaches were particularly liable to such accusations. Americans readily interpreted Comaneci's typically dour expression as proof of the misery of living in a Communist country where her every thought and move were controlled by her coaches. Ironically, when she did smile, American reporters likewise interpreted this display as a result of manipulation by Béla and Marta Karolyi. Remarked one reporter, "Her coaches knew that a smile would warm that chill [that Nadia radiated]. Now she smiles." Even her youth was depicted as somehow the result of duplicitous maneuvering by the Karolyis. Commenting on the pubescent Nadia's doll-like appearance and her childish hairstyle, the same reporter who accused the Karolyis of forcing Nadia to seem joyful likewise berated them for having "carefully choreographed [fourteen-year-old Nadia] to project that child image."[50]

At times, the American media even implied that life under Communism had completely robbed certain gymnasts, especially Nadia Comaneci, of their humanity. Nadia was frequently depicted in the American press as robotic, more mechanical than human. In journalistic coverage of a pre–Montreal Olympics international competition, Nadia was described as "The Bionic Woman" and "a marvel of exactitude."[51] In response to a *New York Times* article in which Nadia was described as "Fearless and Tireless," Adam C. Redfield, a New York City resident, wrote to the sports editor of the *Times* maintaining that fear and the ability to feel fatigue were not "the only human qualities she lacks. As a matter of fact, she seems to lack all of them." The problem with Nadia, Redfield declared, was that her routines lacked "love" and "soul."[52] Another letter to the editor, this one written by City College of New York philosophy professor Michael E. Levin, commented on Nadia's apparent lack of human feeling and attributed it to her life in Romania. Levin warned that before Americans congratulated the Eastern Europeans for the success of their gymnasts and considered Nadia's perfection "a triumph of the Communist way of doing things . . . some facts should be remembered. Only a totalitarian regime could produce such . . . androids as Nadia Comaneci."[53]

Baseball, Apple Pie, and Mary Lou: American Gymnasts Take the Stage

At the same time that Soviet and Romanian gymnasts were either Americanized or depicted as victims of totalitarian governments in order to make the adoration of them by U.S. audiences more acceptable, American gymnasts were portrayed in the media as wholesome, feminine, family-oriented, and patriotic. In their lives and in their performances, they were presented as demonstrating the superiority of the American way of life. This was particularly true in the case of popular American gymnasts Cathy Rigby, who competed in both the 1968 and 1972 Olympics, and Mary Lou Retton, the star of the 1984 Los Angeles Olympics.

Pretty and perky Cathy Rigby, the diametric opposite of the sober, robotic Soviet gymnasts, was the first American gymnast to win a medal in international competition.[54] She was also the first American gymnast to become a celebrity. Rigby's popularity, however, was not so much the result of her gymnastic talents; she failed to medal at either the Mexico City or Munich Olympics. Rather, Cathy Rigby's popularity can largely be attributed to her wholesome, all-American nature. Cathy Rigby was routinely presented in the media as the perfect American girl. The blonde-haired, blue-eyed, diminutive Rigby projected an aura of sweetness and innocence. The media described her as looking more like a "team mascot" than an athlete.[55] Articles about Rigby referred to her as a "pretty kid," and her parents were reported to have sent her schoolbooks to her while she trained for competition.[56] She was described as America's "tiniest Olympian," picture-perfect with her "photogenic" looks and "dainty dark eyelashes."[57] She even "spit delicately."[58] According to her male coach, should she ever lose her modest manner and start to act like a star, he intended to spank her.[59]

The comment by Rigby's coach that he intended to spank her also carried problematic sexual connotations. It was important for the American media to portray Cathy Rigby as attractive and feminine, for female Soviet athletes were often depicted as mannish and unattractive, but this picture had to be drawn in a way that did not make Rigby appear overly sexual and thus impure and unwholesome. As a result, sometimes it was necessary to give carefully worded clarifications of some of the statements made by Rigby's coaches. For example, although coach Ginny Coco described Rigby as having "curves . . . in all the right places," she was quick to note that Rigby was not inappropriately sexual in appearance; Rigby's curves, Coco assured *New York Times* readers, were "not at the level Hugh Hefner might want."[60] Besides being appropriately sexual, Cathy Rigby, the media informed Americans, was also a homebody, as all-American girls were supposed to be. Cathy enjoyed cooking dinner for her family.[61] When she was away training or competing, journalist Neil Amdur noted, her brothers washed the dinner dishes, implying that this was normally Rigby's job.[62] To round out the picture, the "feminine and well-mannered" athlete also loved animals and had a pet snake and a pet monkey, the latter a gift from her parents after she made the 1968 Olympic team.[63]

Although Cathy Rigby was popular and remained so after her gymnastics career had ended, the most popular American gymnast by far was Mary Lou Retton, the first American to win a gold medal in women's gymnastics in an Olympic competition. Retton won gold by finishing first in the all-around competition in Los Angeles in 1984. The 1984 Olympics, however, were boycotted by the Soviet Union and most of the other nations of Eastern Europe. The absence of the Soviet and Eastern European teams meant that Retton won her medals (one gold, two silver, and two bronze) in a competition from which most of the world's best gymnasts were absent.[64] This fact was largely ignored, however, and continues to be, mainly because Mary Lou Retton was a perfect representative of U.S. strengths and ideals at a time when tensions between the United States and the Soviet Union were extremely high.[65]

In the summer of 1984, as Mary Lou Retton was competing in Los Angeles, President Ronald Reagan was running for reelection. Reagan, a dedicated cold warrior, had won the presidency in 1980 by promising to restore pride to a battered America reeling from the blows of economic recession.

Reagan also openly proclaimed his enmity toward the Soviet Union and called for increases in America's nuclear arsenal. As Ronald Reagan threatened the "evil empire" of the USSR, Mary Lou Retton's success in a sport traditionally dominated by the Soviet Union provided demonstrable "proof" of American strength, determination, and superiority. She also perfectly conveyed the image of a wholesome, happy American "girl-next-door," the opposite of the stern, robotic Soviet girls who had not competed in Los Angeles and the sad, beleaguered Romanian girls who had.[66]

The sixteen-year-old Mary Lou was the perfect representative of the "average" American. Born in West Virginia, the great-granddaughter and granddaughter of coal miners, Mary Lou grew up in a "working-class town" where most of the residents depended on the local mines to earn a living. Mary Lou's fellow townsmen were "resilient, resourceful, and scrappy"—in other words, real Americans. The father of this all-American girl had been a minor league baseball player, and her parents had been married in "a baseball wedding." An honor guard of ball players created "a double row of bats" for the happy couple to walk beneath, and "mom cut the cake at home plate." The Rettons owned a collie and vacationed at Sea World. As a young gymnast, Mary Lou was funded by a "booster group" led by the owner of several McDonald's franchises.[67] No one could possibly have been more American.

Mary Lou also had an effervescent personality, unlike many Eastern-bloc gymnasts. Author Seale Ballenger described Mary Lou as combining a "warm, sunny, down-home disposition" with a "spunky spirit."[68] Others described her personality as "almost madly extroverted."[69] Mary Lou was also portrayed as an independent young woman who made her own decisions, unlike Eastern European gymnasts, who were depicted as unwilling pawns of ruthless totalitarian regimes. Ironically, many of Retton's decisions led her to do willingly many of the same things that Soviet and Romanian gymnasts were "forced" to do. For example, just as many young Romanian girls left home to train with Béla Karolyi, the fifteen-year-old Retton moved to Texas to train with Karolyi after his defection to the United States in 1981.[70]

Not only was Mary Lou driven, determined, and hardworking, but she was also unquestionably patriotic, and Retton's triumph at Los Angeles had a political dimension, just as the triumphs of Eastern European gymnasts had always had. Although Romanian gymnasts such as Nadia Comaneci might be exploited by their government and Russian gymnasts like Olga Korbut might bravely resist the oppressive nature of the Soviet regime, Mary Lou wholeheartedly celebrated the nation that had produced her. After winning a gold medal in the Olympic women's gymnastics all-around competition, Mary Lou Retton became an American heroine. President Ronald Reagan traveled to Los Angeles to congratulate America's Olympians in person. According to a presidential radio address delivered a few days after the Olympics ended, as Reagan embraced Mary Lou, he wondered, "How can anyone not believe in the dream of America?" Celebrating American athletes like Mary Lou, Reagan proclaimed, was "a celebration of the new patriotism."[71] Retton later visited the White House and presented Reagan with an official U.S. Olympic team blazer. New York City awarded her "its first ticker-tape parade since the hostages returned from Iran." (Mary Lou also received the more dubious honor of being enshrined in a "Doonesbury" cartoon as a quintessential American icon much like "Old Glory and nuclear superiority.")[72]

With her victory in Los Angeles, Mary Lou seemingly had restored the blemished reputation of the United States brought about by the Iranian hostage crisis. Indeed, author John Powers, with whom Retton coauthored the story of her life, credited Mary Lou with erasing the bitter memories of all the humiliations of America's recent past, including, apparently, Watergate and America's ignominious exit from Vietnam. Mary Lou had not only restored America's reputation in the eyes of the world, but she had also restored America's faith in itself. In the words of Powers, Americans lived in "a country of dreamers and gamblers, brought up to believe that anything was possible. If the seventies had made them doubt that, one of their own teenagers had just restored their faith." Overnight she had become "a symbol of American optimism and toughness and exuberance, and America loved her for that. In a society that urged you to Go For It, to roll the dice and dare to dream, Mary Lou had made it happen."[73]

As adoring fans stole pieces of her family's lawn, like medieval clergy vying for the relics of a beloved saint, Mary Lou was transformed not only into a symbol of American spunk and determination but also into a cheerleader for American capitalism. She bought a Corvette and a condominium. Her face appeared on Wheaties boxes, and she endorsed athletic gear, hair care products, and McDonald's hamburgers.[74]

By winning a gold medal in Los Angeles, Mary Lou had become a symbol of American political and economic strength in the international arena. She had achieved the defeat of Communism in the sports arena just as America's superior nuclear stockpile would, or so Ronald Reagan believed, force the Soviet Union to relinquish its quest for world domination. She freely bought and sold consumer products, demonstrating the abundance of capitalism and the strength of a thriving American economy at the same time that the Soviet Union found itself unable to keep store shelves stocked with basic necessities for its citizens. Mary Lou had brought home the gold in more ways than one.

America Triumphant: The 1996 Olympics and the New World Order

Even though Mary Lou Retton had apparently restored America to its rightful place in the eyes of the world through her defeat of the absent Soviets in 1984, and the Soviet Union itself had collapsed in 1991, the American media continued to resort to Cold War imagery in its depiction of Russian, Romanian, and American gymnasts throughout the 1990s. Indeed, the American–Soviet Cold War in the world of gymnastics lasted until the American women's gymnastics' team defeated the Russian team at the 1996 Atlanta Games to win the team gold medal for the first time in Olympic history.

In typical Cold War fashion, the young Americans who won this victory were depicted as proud exemplars of the American way of life. Numerous books portrayed the gymnasts as family-oriented and religious. In the team biography *The Magnificent Seven*, all of the gymnasts were shown posed with parents, siblings, cousins, and pets.[75] Shannon Miller and Dominique Dawes mentioned their dependence on God for their "strength."[76] In another book, Kerri Strug's remarkable vault, which won the team gold medal for the United States, was presented as an example of "Christian . . . fortitude."[77]

The triumph of the Magnificent Seven in Atlanta marked the end of a long ideological battle fought between the Soviet Union and the United States using girl gymnasts as weapons. Equating the strength of a nation with the success of its athletes in international competition, both the United States and the Soviet Union looked to girl gymnasts for validation of the nation's political ideologies. Embarrassed by the inability of the United States to compete against the Soviet Union in women's gymnastics, the American media looked for another way to prove the superiority of the American system. The means chosen by the American media was to trumpet the American way of life by constructing images of American gymnasts as happy young patriots, while simultaneously depicting gymnasts from Eastern-bloc countries as either the oppressed, robotic products of Communist dictatorships or as rebels against totalitarianism. In the end, victory for the American gymnastics team at Atlanta was equated with victory for the American way of life.[78] Kerri Strug, the heroine of the Atlanta Games, succinctly described the new world order in her account of the competition: "[It was] like a big national meet with some foreigners involved."[79]

NOTES

1. Lauren Berlant, *The Queen of America Goes to Washington City: Essays on Sex and Citizenship* (Durham, NC: Duke University Press, 1997), 6.

2. Ann Chisholm, "Defending the Nation: National Bodies, U.S. Borders, and the 1996 U.S. Olympic Women's Gymnastics Team," *Journal of Sport and Social Issues* 23 (May 1999): 130, 131.

3. Alfred E. Senn, *Power, Politics, and the Olympic Games* (Champaign, IL: Human Kinetics, 1999), 102.

4. Ibid.

5. The six events were floor exercise, balance beam, vault, uneven parallel bars, the best all-around competition, and the team competition.

6. Justin Beecham, *Olga* (New York: Paddington Press, 1974), 39.

7. Ibid., 30; Allen Guttmann, *Women's Sports: A History* (New York: Columbia University Press, 1991), 175.

8. Senn, *Power, Politics, and the Olympic Games*, 103, table 7.1. All point totals given are based on the number of points awarded to first- through sixth-place finishers according to the Soviet system. If the American system (which awarded ten points for first-place finishers) were used, the number of points amassed by the Soviet women gymnasts would be even greater.

9. Ibid., 102.

10. John Nelson Washburn, "84-Pound Soviet 'Soldier,'" *New York Times*, November 5, 1972; Washburn, "Blowing the Whistle," *New York Times*, April 22, 1973. To some extent, the media's statements were true. In the Soviet system, all athletes belonged to sports clubs attached to a workplace; the workplace might be a factory, or it might be a military installation. Because great prestige was attached to having winning athletes as part of one's club, the more prominent clubs, such as those belonging to the army and the secret police, commonly recruited elite athletes from a variety of sports disciplines. Athletes recruited by sports clubs belonging to the military and the secret police trained at the facilities these groups provided. See Senn, *Power, Politics, and the Olympic Games*, 89; Guttmann, *Women's Sports*, 174.

11. Washburn, "84-Pound Soviet 'Soldier.'" Olya, the affectionate, diminutive form of the name Olga, was the name often given to Korbut by the Soviet press. In the 1970s, Washburn brought a case before the U.S. Olympic Committee urging them to restore Jim Thorpe's Olympic medals. He argued that Thorpe should not have lost his medals for playing semiprofessional baseball for a meager sum when Olga Korbut, a member of the Soviet army who received financial support from the state, was allowed to keep hers. See *City Paper Online*, October 31, 2006, 10, http://www.nashvillecitypaper.com/index (accessed November 5, 2006).

12. Beecham, *Olga*, 99; Gwen Evans, *Eastern Superstar: Olga Korbut* (Milwaukee: Raintree Editions, 1976), 8.

13. Beecham, *Olga*, 98.

14. Evans, *Eastern Superstar*, 6. Wendy Varney also mentions the use by the Soviet Union of female gymnasts as agents of international diplomacy. See Wendy Varney, "A Labour of Patriotism: Soviet Female Gymnasts' Physical and Ideological Work, 1952–1991," *Genders Online Journal* 39 (2004): 57, http://www.genders.org (accessed July 25, 2006).

15. In her article, Ann Chisholm also notes the nonthreatening appearance of girl gymnasts and remarks that their seeming fragility assuages fears of both the transgression of gender roles associated with their ability to perform fantastic feats of athleticism and the transgression of sexual boundaries evoked by their often androgynous appearance. Chisholm, "Defending the Nation," 134.

16. Evans, *Eastern Superstar*, 12, 13.

17. Neil Amdur, "A Soviet Pixie Invades the United States," *New York Times*, March 8, 1973.

18. Beecham, *Olga*, 34.

19. Gerald Eskenazi, "Even Her Quotes Are Guarded," *New York Times*, March 23, 1977.

20. Guttmann, *Women's Sports*, 20; Beecham, *Olga*, 121.

21. Lawrence van Gelder, "Gymnasts See Nixon," *New York Times*, March 22, 1973.

22. Tony Kornheiser, "Olga Korbut, Still the One They Like to Watch," *New York Times*, December 17, 1976.

23. Evans, *Eastern Superstar*, 34.

24. "On Tour with Olga: A Super Gymnast's Story," *Seventeen*, February 1975, 72.

25. Kornheiser, "Olga Korbut."

26. Wayne Coffey, *Olga Korbut* (Woodbridge, CT: Blackbirch Press, 1992), 6, 7.

27. Mary Lou Retton, as quoted in Ken Rappoport, Barrie Wilner, and Billie Jean King, *Girls Rule!* (N.p.: Andrews McMeel Universal, 2000), 73.

28. Beecham, *Olga*, 24.

29. Leerom Medovoi, *Rebels: Youth and the Cold War Origins of Identity* (Durham, NC: Duke University Press, 2005), 32, 33, 42, 33.

30. Beecham, *Olga*, 66, 26.

31. Ibid., 94.

32. Ibid., 30.

33. Mimi Murray, *Women's Gymnastics: Coach, Participant, Spectator* (Boston: Allyn and Bacon, 1979), 3.

34. Guy R. Odom, *Mothers, Leadership, and Success* (Houston: Polybius Press, 1990), 329.

35. Neil Amdur, "All-Round Gold to Rumanian Star, 14," *New York Times*, July 22, 1976; Robin Herman, "Gymnast Posts Perfect Mark," *New York Times*, March 28, 1976; Neil Amdur, "The Measure of Greatness: Nadia Comaneci: Fearless and Tireless," *New York Times*, July 25, 1976. Depictions in the American media of young gymnasts being taken forcibly from their homes without parental consent and imprisoned in state schools far beyond the reach of their families were common during the Cold War. (The same stories are often repeated today whenever the Chinese gymnastics program is mentioned.) Such depictions, however, had little basis in reality. Parents willingly enrolled their children in sports schools, often at the children's insistence. Many children continued to live at home. Children who left home to attend sports schools often enjoyed living at the schools. Neither Nadia Comaneci nor Olga Korbut has ever claimed to have been abused. In her book, *Nadia Comaneci: Letters to a Young Gymnast*, written after moving to the United States, Comaneci expresses gratitude to the Romanian government for making it possible for her to become a gymnast. See Nadia Comaneci, *Nadia Comaneci: Letters to a Young Gymnast* (New York: Basic Books, 2004), 16–21, 42.

36. "On Tour with Olga," 72.

37. Amdur, "Measure of Greatness."

38. Robin Herman, "A New-Look Miss Comaneci at the Garden," *New York Times*, October 10, 1977.

39. Ibid.

40. "On Tour with Olga," 72.

41. Ibid.

42. Herman, "New-Look Comaneci."

43. "On Tour with Olga," 73.

44. Ibid.

45. Herman, "Gymnast Posts Perfect Mark."

46. Herman, "New-Look Comaneci."

47. Bob Ottom, "The Search for Nadia," *Sports Illustrated*, November 19, 1979, 92, 94.

48. Michael Suponev, *Olga: A Biographical Portrait* (Moscow: Novosti Press Agency Publishing House, n.d.; New York: Warner Books, 1976), 56.

49. Cheryl Bentsen, "A Dream for Gymnastics," *New York Times*, November 12, 1978.

50. Dave Anderson, "Nadia Comaneci Takes Gymnast Title on 4th and 5th Perfect Scores," *New York Times*, July 22, 1976.

51. Robin Herman, "U.S. High School Gymnast Tops World Stars," *New York Times*, March 29, 1976; Herman, "Gymnast Posts Perfect Mark."

52. Adam W. Redfield, "No Love, No Soul, and No Graciousness from Nadia," Sports' Editor's Mailbox, *New York Times*, August 15, 1976.

53. "American Way Means Winning Isn't Everything," letter to the editor, *New York Times*, August 1, 1976.

54. Rigby won a silver medal in the balance beam competition at the 1970 World Championships.

55. Neil Amdur, "U.S. Girl Is Unusual Olympian," *New York Times*, October 10, 1968.

56. "A 90-Pound Blonde May Lead U.S. at Munich," *New York Times*, April 2, 1972; photo caption, *New York Times*, April 20, 1969; Amdur, "U.S. Girl Is Unusual Olympian."

57. Amdur, "U.S. Girl Is Unusual Olympian"; "90-Pound Blonde."

58. Steve Cady, "Gymnasts Display Grace, Skill, Strength and Courage in U.S.-Japan Meet," *New York Times*, January 30, 1972.

59. "90-Pound Blonde."

60. Cady, "Gymnasts Display Grace."

61. Neil Amdur, "Race Relations Crisis Poses Serious Threat to Olympic Games," *New York Times*, August 20, 1971; "90-Pound Blonde."

62. Amdur, "U.S. Girl Is Unusual Olympian."

63. "90-Pound Blonde"; Amdur, "U.S. Girl Is Unusual Olympian." After retiring from gymnastics at the age of twenty, Rigby began to work as a commentator for televised gymnastics events. It was perhaps as a commentator that Cathy Rigby was at her most American. While covering the 1976 Montreal Olympics for ABC, Rigby blamed the American gymnasts' low scores on Eastern-bloc manipulation, implying that it was difficult to win if "you're from the United States and don't have that hammer and sickle." As quoted in John J. O'Connor, "Olympics Are Bettered by Commercialism," *New York Times*, July 20, 1976. In the 1980s, Rigby actively campaigned for Ronald Reagan as part of the group Athletes for Reagan-Bush. See Thomas Rogers, "Scouting," *New York Times*, May 23, 1984.

64. Romania was the only Eastern-bloc country to participate in the 1984 Olympics.

65. Mary Lou Retton's official Web site makes no mention of the Soviet boycott in describing her achievements in Los Angeles in 1984; http://www.marylouretton.com/new_site_biography.htm (accessed August 16, 2006).

66. Mary Lou Retton and Béla Karolyi, with John Powers, *Mary Lou: Creating an Olympic Champion* (New York: McGraw-Hill, 1986), inside cover.

67. Ibid., xvi, 4, 2, 5, 18.

68. Seale Ballenger, *Hell's Belles: A Tribute to the Spitfires, Bad Seeds, and Steel Magnolias of the New and Old South* (San Francisco: Conari Press, 1997), 161.

69. Guttmann, *Women's Sports*, 248.

70. Ballenger, *Hell's Belles*, 161.

71. Ronald Reagan, presidential radio address, August 18, 1984.

72. Retton and Karolyi, with Powers, *Mary Lou*, 164, 166.

73. Ibid., 159, 165.

74. Ibid., 164, 167, 165.

75. Nancy M. Kleinbaum, *The Magnificent Seven: The Authorized Story of American Gold* (New York: Bantam Books, n.d.), 2, 3, 10, 16, 17, 18, 22, 30, 36, 44, 48, 49, 58, 61, 62, 76, 78, 83, 86, 89, 90.

76. Ibid., n.p.

77. Janie Gustafson, *Building Catholic Character: Developing Christian Life Skills*, student ed. (Notre Dame, IN: Ave Maria Press, 1998), 120.

78. See also Andaluna Borcila, "Nationalizing the Olympics around and away from the 'Vulnerable' Bodies of Women: The NBC Coverage of the 1996 Olympics and Some Moments After," *Journal of Sport and Social Issues* 24 (2000): 135, 137–138.

79. "They Said It . . . Really," *International Gymnast*, October 1996, 53.

PART III

THE EDUCATION OF GIRLS

"The Education of Girls" brings together six case studies that assess the role of education in girls' lives and the reasons why education was offered. The authors in this section demonstrate how education can be an agent of the state or a tool of colonialism, while at the same time a way of empowering girls to shape their own worlds, identity, and destiny. Together, these chapters suggest that girls are educated (at home, in school, and in other institutions) for aims that not only further nationalism and empire but also promote family and individual status. Girls have found education empowering when it gives them tools to succeed and survive, and confining when it erases culture and identity.

First, Nancy Stockdale reviews the work of British missionary women who established educational institutions in Palestine in the mid-nineteenth century as part of a larger effort by European imperial powers to wrest control of the "Holy Land" from the Turks and claim political and spiritual authority over this contested region. By examining the interaction of missionaries and girls and discussing how representations of Palestinian girls labeled them as victims of cruel patriarchy, Stockdale looks at counternarratives that more accurately depict the complexity of the cross-cultural interactions and the impact of missionary activity on the spiritual and family life of these girls. Next, S. E. Duff considers the position of the Huguenot Seminary and College in relation to the construction of the feminine identities available to bourgeois Dutch Afrikaner girls in the Cape Colony between 1895 and 1910. Duff argues that three conflicting discourses on femininity emerged, each justifying education for girls and limiting the definition of what a girl could be. Huguenot's senior staff proposed that education prepared girls to be more efficient and competent wives, mothers, and matriarchs for their community. This discourse was challenged by the thinking of a younger generation of teachers, familiar with the concept of the New Woman, who had not entered the profession because of a religious calling but because they wanted a career, and by young women themselves who felt entitled to a transitional stage of relative irresponsibility.

Carrying the theme of education to colonial Australia, Christine Cheater explores what it meant to grow up as an Aboriginal girl under Australia's assimilation policies. During the nineteenth century, Aboriginal girls were constructed as future mothers, and as such they could be either a civilizing force in their communities or a potential danger to the future of "white" Australia. To encourage the former, government officials removed

Aboriginal girls from their communities for education. Cheater construes this endeavor as an attempt to breed out Australia's indigenous population or to civilize Aboriginal communities through the education of the mothers. Corrie Decker discusses colonial Mombassa, Kenya, in the 1930s, 1940s, and 1950s. There, British administrators relied on missionaries and colonialism to spread education to girls and women, although the predominance of Islam meant limited success for mission schools. Gradual government commitments to girls' education in Mombasa came only in response to persistent demands from prominent men for the education of their daughters.

Two chapters address education through the lens of youth organizations. Peter Wien finds that although the Iraqi al-Futuwwa was traditionally a masculine institution, and despite the fact that male leaders of the movement wanted to restrict the role of women in society to household duties, the organization did contain a girls' section. Wien shows that in the 1930s and 1940s, female Futuwwa members challenged Islamic notions of femininity to claim a position for themselves as the actual providers of strength in the society in that it was they who took care of and raised future warriors. Jennifer Helgren continues the examination of girls' citizenship roles through an assessment of the Camp Fire Girls, a U.S. organization designed to promote traditionally feminine attributes among American girls and teens. She argues that the organization's leaders envisioned girls who reached out through pen pal letters as peacemakers and citizens of the world during the post–World War II era. The practice of sharing American culture abroad, however, ultimately reaffirmed these girls' sense of patriotism and limited the degree to which they were able to connect meaningfully with girls in other nations.

These stories of girls' education and socialization in various local contexts provide an understanding of the spread of modern education within the colonial or nationalist context. Importantly, although such education is often associated with the expansion of nationalistic or "Western" values, in each case intervening factors, such as religion, local sentiment, teachers, or the girls themselves, provided a counter to the socializing influence of schools. Schools had the power to undermine local cultures, but they also had the power to offer girls and women opportunities for authority within and beyond their communities.

11 Palestinian Girls and the British Missionary Enterprise, 1847–1948

NANCY L. STOCKDALE

In the nineteenth century, imperial-minded Britons became increasingly fascinated with the fate of Palestinians, the residents of the "Holy Land," who came to figure prominently in Orientalist imaginations. Alternately viewed as living examples of biblical characters, decadent "Orientals" who did not deserve to reside in the sacred space of Christianity's origin, and pitiful Others oppressed by Islam and Ottoman despotism, Palestinians were targeted by British missionaries for religious and cultural conversion. Children figured large in missionary plans because they were viewed as pliable and more easily swayed than adults. Missionaries hoped to bring children under their religious and cultural influence, converting children in an effort to convert society. As a result of Palestinian society's segregation of the sexes as well as British assumptions about the importance of educating girls for future roles as wives and mothers, British women missionaries in Palestine during the late Ottoman and the British Mandate periods targeted local girls for outreach. In the schools and orphanages that they established or managed, these women missionaries attempted to disconnect Palestinian girls from their indigenous cultures and families and convert them to Protestant faith and British cultural values. They hoped to create new generations that would embrace British faith, manners, and imperial authority among the diverse population of the Holy Land. In this way British missionaries attempted to lay claim to Palestine, the Holy Land of Jews, Christians, and Muslims, by co-opting the youngest members of its society. Moreover, missionaries' representations of the lives of Palestinian girls and their families reinforced strong Orientalist stereotypes about supposed moral decay in the Ottoman Empire, and glorified both British values and the actions of British missionaries striving to permanently alter Palestinian girls' lives. In this chapter I provide an introduction to the history of British women missionaries' work among girls in Palestine during the late Ottoman and British Mandate eras, detail their methods of education as directed toward Palestinian girls from several ethnic and confessional communities, and explore reactions of Palestinian girls to these potent cross-cultural encounters. By examining the contentious and sometimes violent impact of British women missionaries on the lives of Palestinian girls, we may better understand the significance of Orientalist and imperialist attitudes on individuals' lives during their formative years.

The Landscape of Late Ottoman Palestine and the British Missionary Endeavor

Like many societies of the Middle East during the Ottoman period, that of Palestine was composed of people from diverse ethnic and religious backgrounds; the majority of the population were Arab Muslims, but there were Arab Christians, Jews, Greeks, and Armenians as well. The majority of girls in nineteenth-century Palestine lived in villages or larger towns and were integral members of their families, assisting their mothers with household needs, working in agricultural or craft production, and preparing for lives as mothers and wives. Schooling was a luxury that most families could not consider for their daughters; local religious schools were populated almost exclusively by boys, although educational reform was being debated throughout the Ottoman Empire. For Palestinian girls, however, be they Muslim, Christian, or Jewish, education was defined as oral tradition and working side by side with the women of the family in preparation for their own adult lives.

For middle-class British missionaries, however, such traditional education was unacceptable. They viewed Palestine's girls as desperately deprived and in need of formal literacy training. More important, however, they were appalled by the lack of Protestant reach in the country and by Palestinian society's "Oriental" approaches to religion, social customs, and government. This sentiment was enhanced by Palestine's position as the "Holy Land," and the promise of British control over the Land of the Bible was increasingly popular as imperialism, Orientalism, and mass culture collided with Evangelicalism in Victorian Britain. In 1841, the first Protestant church of Jerusalem opened its doors, and from that point, a small but steady stream of British missionaries came to the country, hoping to sway Palestinians to abandon their own faiths and cultural traditions and embrace British forms of Protestantism, social values, and customs. For many British women missionaries, establishing small schools seemed the logical way to indoctrinate Palestinian girls, who they hoped would carry a newfound faith in British values to their families and into the lives of subsequent generations.

The earliest missionary schools employing British women in Palestine, such as the Diocesan Schools for Girls in Jerusalem (founded in 1847) and the Church Missionary Society/Society for the Promotion of Female Education in the East school in Nazareth (founded in 1859), were devoted to teaching basic literacy skills using the Bible as the primary text, as well as domestic talents such as needlework and housekeeping. As competition mounted, however, between an increasing number of political and religious concerns interested in educating the girls of Palestine (including the

Ottoman government, Islamic endowments, and other European traditions, such as the Roman Catholics and the Kaiserwerth Deaconesses),
British schools became more rigorous in their curricula. By the dawn of the
Mandate era in 1922, several schools (such as the English High Schools for
Girls in Jerusalem and Haifa) provided comprehensive programs of study
that prepared girls for British university entrance exams. A comparison of
the subjects taught in various schools illustrates the dynamism of British
education over the course of time. As late as 1901, attendees of the girls'
school run by the London Society for Promoting Christianity amongst the
Jews (otherwise known as the London Jews' Society, or LJS) in Safed—in
the tradition of the nineteenth-century mission schools—spent most of their
days studying religion. That year, head teacher Miss Gisella Friedmann
reported that the sixty-one girls in her institution studied English, Hebrew,
Arabic, Scripture, needlework, and singing. The Scripture classes were
conducted in "English, Arabic, and Jargon [i.e., Yiddish], as we have both
Sephardim and Ashkenazim."[1]

In the aftermath of World War I, the Ottoman Empire was dismantled
by the victorious powers and Palestine was handed over to British imperial
rule by the League of Nations. The imperialist government, called the
Mandate government, was charged with "training" Palestinians to rule
themselves; only when the British determined they were "ready" for independence would freedom from foreign rule be granted. With these dramatic changes in Palestinian society, school syllabi changed markedly. The
1931 prospectus for the Jerusalem and the East Mission's English High
School for Girls in Haifa declared the aim of the school "to give, under the
direction of a well educated and cultured Christian Staff, a preparation for
home life and for the professions which are now open to trained and educated girls." Younger girls in the first six years studied in Arabic, whereas
older students conducted their last five years of lessons in English. The curriculum consisted of "Scripture, English language and literature, Arabic,
French, General History, Geography, Science and Nature Study, Mathematics, Drawing, Needlework and Domestic Science, Class Music, [and]
Gymnastics and games," and after-school activities included Girl Guide,
Ranger, and Brownie meetings, gardening, debating teams, and a variety of
basic-level sports (such as netball). Girls who excelled in their studies were
encouraged to take the School and Lower Certificate Examinations of the
Oxford and Cambridge Joint Board, and each girl who completed the appropriate units was able to skip the Mandate government's Palestine Matriculation Exam and receive her diploma.[2]

Despite the evolution of mission schools for girls from basic literacy
projects aimed at teaching pupils to read the Bible to competitive matriculation institutions that sought to prepare girls for life in a world with more
public opportunities for women—a dramatic difference that cannot be
underestimated—the missionaries' primary goal was to teach Protestant

Christian religion to the girls. The religious targets of such instruction would vary according to the community, the mission organization, and the political situation,[3] but the hope that girls would come to confess belief in Protestant Christianity remained constant. This objective was coupled with an intense desire to educate girls in British domestic values, such as housekeeping, hygiene, and needlework. Teachers wished that girls would embrace Christianity and the rules of domesticity, and then impart them to other members of society, particularly their own families. Once the girls were converted, missionaries hoped that they would spread Protestant values to their mothers and, later in life, that they would raise their own children along British domestic models. Lessons in British domesticity, moreover, were considered de facto lessons in Christianity. Such an attitude was eloquently expressed in 1854 by the Society for the Promotion of Female Education in the East (otherwise known as the Female Education Society, or FES) missionary Mrs. Krusé, who wrote that she had established a small girls' school in Jaffa because "I found these girls untrained, and having all the vices of lying and bad conduct that we so painfully find in the East; it is my aim, with the blessing of God, not merely to teach them to read, but by degrees to instill in their minds habits of order, cleanliness, good behaviour, and, above all, to train them to the first great duty of making every thing subservient to the love of God."[4]

In the period before the Mandate, missionaries presented this training in the context of a dichotomy that contrasted the ways of a sensible and logical advanced nation to those of a backward and degenerate one. This comparison often came at the expense of congenial relationships between the families of the girls in the schools and the missionaries who taught them. Reports from the teachers of British mission schools continually promoted two specific themes: the notion that their students clamored to embrace the Christian gospel, and that the girls' families—in their ignorance of the redeeming features of Christianity—desperately tried to prevent that. Conversion narratives of schoolgirls were common in missionary correspondence and stressed the importance of scriptural instruction as the foundation of the schools' curriculums. For instance, Miss Gisella Friedmann, missionary and head teacher in the LJS school for girls in Safed, wrote in 1907 of the balancing act Jewish girls attending her school had to carry out between their supposed burgeoning Christian faith promoted at school and their parents' resistance at home. Friedmann's account glorifies her mission's work in unsubtle terms and was typical of the sort of reports sent back to England about the work done in mission schools:

> The love for the Bible has been so great that if any lesson has had to be omitted the children would it was any but the Scripture. One child said, "I believe in Jesus, but what can I do! . . . if I told my father he would kill me.". . . The children repeat their lessons in their homes, and their parents

know that what they learn is in the Bible, and so they also hear about the Lord Jesus. Many speak quite openly about Him, some more to their mothers, others more to their fathers. The influence also spreads. A young man, who lives in Peking, married one of our girls, and his cousin told me he is quite a Christian. He comes to Safed often, and whilst here speaks quite openly to his relatives.[5]

In her comprehensive account, Friedmann assured her society's leadership and contributors that the Gospel was being taught to willing young scholars and, indeed, that they brought the message of Jesus to their families. At the same time, her letter contained a potent indictment of Palestinian parenting, alluding to a parent's threat to murder a child who embraced Protestantism openly. Regardless of the influence of parents who may not accept Jesus as the Jewish messiah, the girls leaving her school, according to Friedmann, were capable and willing to influence even their husbands and their families in later years. She assured her readers that progress, however slow, was being made.

Mission teachers commonly expressed the hope that childhood lessons would be remembered after girls left their schools and that their lessons of faith and social practice would remain with their students and wards throughout their lives. For instance, Miss Elizabeth Carey Fitzjohn of the LJS girls' school in Jerusalem wrote in 1895, "We parted with great regret with some of our elder girls, feeling how hard it would be for them to obey their Heavenly Master while living with those who hate and despise Him. They have been the subject of many prayers, and we have received tokens that they have been heard." Fitzjohn tempered this fear, however, with positive news: "We have also been cheered by good news from some other girls who had left before. Two are supporting themselves respectably by giving lessons. One has been in a situation for nearly seven years, and is about to be married to a Christian. Four are happily married to Christians in Jerusalem, and sometimes bring their children to visit us."[6]

Missionaries such as Fitzjohn were aware that their students who became active Christians needed to garner an ability to support themselves, lest their relatives decide to abandon them upon conversion. As late as 1930, Ruth Clark, an LJS missionary in Jerusalem, wrote about the need she saw for job training in case of such circumstances:

In Class VI, there are five girls who are all very loath to leave school—and we do not want them to go until they are better able to earn their own living. To this end we are hoping to start a seventh class, which would be a kind of commercial class, where the girls could go on with their education and at the same time prepare themselves to earn a living. . . . Our Jewish girls are so entirely dependent on their parents. If they are ever to attain to liberty of thought in spiritual things, they must be able to "stand on their own feet," in material things.[7]

Even girls who might not need to work outside the home to support them-selves benefited from mission education, according to lady missionary "W.D." of the Jerusalem and the East Mission. She wrote in 1913 that "the hours spent at school are probably the happiest to these children who come from poor and unhealthy quarters of the town, for here they have a brief respite from the troubles and discomforts of their homes, while at the same time they learn lessons of tidiness and cleanliness which will help them later on in life when they too have homes of their own to keep."[8] Whether girls remained in their homes of origin or left to establish their own homes, mis-sionaries hoped that girls educated in mission schools would assimilate les-sons of British religious and domestic principles and implement them in their daily lives.

Girls' homes were seen as dangerous places, where the influence of their non-Christian parents could undo all of the Christian training of the school. Miss Martin of the LJS Safed school wrote, "Day Scholars are very apt to have the religious impressions which they have received while at School, driven from their memories by the influence of a home formed by members of another faith, and in this way the work of the day is constantly being retarded. 'The rain does not make me wet here,' is their oft repeated remark."[9] Often, British missionary teachers considered Palestinian society detrimental to their pupils, especially when local religious leaders made public announcements against the missions. Miss Friedmann wrote in 1904 of dissent within the Jewish community of Safed against the LJS school and the impact the dissent had on her students:

> The Jews persuaded our elder girls to leave us by making them pupil teach-ers in their own schools;[10] they also went from house to house promising all sorts of help, and even money, for each girl withdrawn from us. They sent people to watch, and even a servant to take our children by force. The chil-dren tried always not to be seen. Sister[s] would come in separately, and one child hid herself for two days with some friends. Once, when they had left after school, one came back crying, "Oh! Jews, Jews!" I asked her what had happened, and she said the Jews were at both roads watching for them, so I went a little way with them to see them safe. One day I heard a little girl say to the other, "I shall know that GOD can still do miracles if we meet no Jews on the way."[11]

In this letter, Friedmann portrayed her Jewish students as coming to fear and despise the elders of their own community, going so far as to pray that they will "meet no Jews on the way" to their lessons. Education in the LJS mission school drove a wedge between the girls and their community; Friedmann portrayed Jewish leaders as incapable of affecting progress in Safed without the use of bribes and physical intimidation. In missionary fantasies, however, the girls remained devoted to their Christian school, despite such threats, and their missionary teacher became a sort of surrogate parent protecting them from their irrational families of origin.

For teachers, a solution to the negative influences of home and society was to infuse the children so thoroughly with Protestant values that the children would carry them into their homes, transforming the lives of family members and their attitudes toward the missionaries, and ultimately converting all of them to Protestant Christianity. This central—and essential—element of their missions in Palestine brought the teachers in line with the general spirit of European missionary work and the "civilizing mission" of empire. For instance, Miss Jane Walker Arnott, the headmistress of the Scottish Mission School in Jaffa,[12] reported to the FES in 1880 that one of her students was actively altering her home environment as a result of her mission education: "The youngest of the Jewesses is a sweet, engaging little girl of five. She picks up everything very quickly, and her mother remarked to me one day, 'My child repeats to us everything she learns in School, and it is so sweet to hear the name of Jesus from her lips.' . . . May we not hope that the lispings of little ones may be the means of leading that mother's heart to the Saviour!"[13] Arnott's hopes for her mission went far beyond the children she interacted with every day; she wanted those children to act as ambassadors of Jesus to their families, so that all would come under the sphere of the mission's influence. Similarly, Miss Friedmann in Safed wrote that a mother told rabbis opposing the LJS school that "I have learned from my children that cursing, lying, and swearing are sins. How can that teaching be bad?"[14]

It was, however, Miss Emma Carolina Fitzjohn of Jerusalem, the sister and coworker of Elizabeth Fitzjohn, who provided her sponsors in England with one of the most encouraging reports of missionary success when it came to schoolgirls influencing their families. She wrote:

> The children's services are a great boon, to which we owe much of the improvement in some of the girls. Many of them realize the power of prayer and feel that God is very near to all that call upon Him. One of our girls said one day, "I used to be very frightened at night, but I prayed about it, and it seemed as if Jesus came and stood beside my bed, and I do not feel afraid any more." After her baptism she said, "I am so glad and happy, because God has heard and answered my prayers. I have been praying so long, every night and morning, that my father would allow me to be baptized, and himself become a Christian, and now all our family are baptized."[15]

Whereas Arnott's, Friedmann's, and Coral's students had begun to influence their families by repeating their lessons to their parents, Fitzjohn believed that her student—through the power of prayer—was able to effect a radical transformation in her family: their conversion from Judaism and baptism into the Protestant faith. None of these changes, according to the teachers, could have been possible without the missions and their agents, who presented themselves as struggling against an often hostile local society in an effort to better Palestinian lives through education and, more importantly, afterlives through conversion.

The Power of the Deathbed and the Difficulties of Creating "Protestant Wives and Mothers"

Another dramatic and common way that mission teachers wrote about the transformation of their students was in the context of deathbed conversion narratives. These were potent accounts—at times even hagiographic in nature—and usually presented the dead girl as a saintly figure who had embraced Christianity in her final days, in the process softening the hearts of her often stubborn parents and serving as a role model for other school-girls. Miss Fitzjohn wrote of one such girl from Jerusalem: "One dear little one has gone to the Heavenly Home. She caught diphtheria at her home during the long holidays and died in our hospital, notwithstanding the care of the doctors and nurses. She was a gentle, good child, and during the four years she was in school never required punishment for rudeness or disobedience. Her only trouble was her inability to learn her lessons, but lately she had found that when she prayed about them she received help and got on much better."[16] Similarly, the last words of one of Miss Friedmann's students were related to her religious lessons: "One of our dear girls died from fever, and almost the last thing she said to her mother was, 'Who will read my books and my new Bible?' "[17] Both of these girls showed model behavior in their diligence to learn and their faith that God could help them succeed, and were used by their teachers as examples of why the missions in the Holy Land needed to be supported by Christians back in Britain.

Perhaps the most dramatic deathbed narrative published in missionary literature from Palestine was an article written by Miss Arnott, titled "Zakeeji of Jaffa," and printed in the FES's *Female Missionary Intelligencer* in 1871. In this account, Arnott told the story of one of her students, a thirteen-year-old Muslim girl named Zakeeji, who "was a very fair and lovely girl, not the least like an Arab; and but for her Oriental dress, might have passed for a European child." According to Arnott, Zakeeji was betrothed and was thus prevented by her parents from coming to school in November 1870, "it being considered a shame for Moslem girls of that age to be going to school." The teacher, however, persuaded the girl to come back to the school when she "promised if she would come out of her window to my housetop, I would let her come down on my ladder, and so avoid the street." The girl came via the street rather than the ladder and attended classes for ten days, a move her teacher later interpreted as Providential: "It seems as if the Lord had just brought her back those few days to hear more of His word, and that we might not be left without hope in her death." Arnott reported that Zakeeji's final days in the school were characterized by an endless barrage of questions by the girl about various theological issues.

For instance, she asked, " 'Was it really our sins that crucified Him, and did His blood still flow for our sins?'. . . 'If our sins are as scarlet, they shall be as white as wool; how is that? then, if they are red like crimson they shall be as wool? but snow is whiter than wool.' " Moreover, the girl asserted a budding love for Jesus several times, proclaiming, for example, "that every night she and her sister prayed together, 'Jesus, tender Shepherd, hear me,' etc. . . . and the Lord's prayer, and repeated some of their texts." Arnott and her local assistant Regina thus wondered if all of this was "the Spirit of God touching her heart, making her feel her need, and showing her how all her need was met in Jesus?"[18]

Suddenly the girl became ill, and on March 15, 1871, she was dead. Arnott wrote, "The children all loved her, and that afternoon no one could attend to work. It was very touching to see Christians and Jewesses shed tears together for their Mohammedan companion, and repeating to each other little pleasant remembrances of her." Two days later Arnott and Regina visited Zakeeji's grave, and Regina inquired of her relatives "if Zakeeji, whilst she was ill, had alluded to anything she had learned in the school." One of her aunts clandestinely whispered that the girl exclaimed "shortly before she died . . . 'My Saviour, Jesus, save me.' " For Arnott, this was an enormous victory, despite the pain caused by the girl's death. She wrote, "Perhaps the Lord took her away because He had better things in store for her. I think with comfort of those words, 'He shall not quench the smoking flax' (in Arabic, 'the glimmering wick'). If it were but a little spark of *His* kindling, He would never let it go out."[19] This remarkable story includes several of the themes common in missionary conversion narratives, coupled with a compelling sentimentality that exceeds most reports. According to Arnott, Zakeeji seemed to sense that her death was imminent and made an effort to understand finer points of theology in order to accept Jesus as her savior in her last days. She was such a charismatic girl that, in her death, she was able to unite Jews, Christians, and Muslims, who all mourned her openly. Moreover, she gave hope that the Christian message promoted by teachers was being heard by their students; Zakeeji did not just return to school for the love of school itself but to continue her religious learning. Such stories were not only inspirational for missionaries such as Arnott, but, when published in journals like the *Female Missionary Intelligencer*, served to pique the British public's interest and to help raise funds for the schools.

Such funds were also used to support orphanages for Palestinian girls, who were either genuine orphans or children whose parents were too indigent to take care of them properly. Widowed mothers in particular occasionally gave their children to orphanages run by British missionaries, hoping that their girls would receive an education and that they would be better fed and clothed by the foreigners than the mothers could provide in their penury. British missions, however, insisted that girls relinquished to orphanages could only be redeemed by their families if the parents paid an indemnity; this requirement, and various stories of abuse that surfaced from time to time, resulted in the orphanages acquiring a dubious reputation among Palestinians.[20]

Although education was a hallmark of these institutions, physical labor was an even greater element of a girl's daily life. This model found its prototype in British orphanages of the period;[21] in the context of the imperial project, however, missionaries presented their orphanages in Palestine as primarily educational facilities that would give girls practical domestic skills as well as advanced literacy, and of course, "Christian education." This education placed a prominent value on girls' work as a virtue, as well as girls' work as an economic savings. Examinations of missionary accounts reveal that Palestinian girls in British orphanages indeed provided large amounts of labor in the context of their education. The FES orphanage in Nazareth, established in 1867 and operating under that organization's guidance until 1899, presents a fine case for realizing the extreme amount of physical labor required of Palestinian girls by their missionary guardians.

Work was linked to the privileged education the orphanage was giving the girls not only in Protestant religion and values and secular scholastic topics, but also in domestic science, which was essential knowledge for running a "respectable" home. It was also a way for the mission to cut costs. For example, the supervisor of the orphanage in 1884, Mrs. Norgate, wrote that "the girls of this Orphanage are all made useful and active, doing all the work, and washing, with only a little help. It is like a beehive, the girls running about with their bare brown feet; they wear no boots, except when any of them are sent to town, and stockings are never worn by them. This is a saving, of course, and they are used to it."[22] Mrs. Norgate also mentioned that the girls ground and sifted the wheat for their bread before it was sent to the mill, a point corroborated by orphanage agent Miss Baker in 1885. Besides sifting grain, Baker reported that the girls were responsible for the all of the institution's housekeeping. She wrote, "Each girl possesses her pail, scrubber, flannel, sweeping-brush, and duster. I am glad to be able to tell you I see a decided improvement in their cleanliness and industry." Moreover, Miss Baker's girls were also responsible for making their own beds, doing their own washing, and baking bread. They also had serious kitchen duties; when it was their turn to be "table girls," they prepared the meals and cleaned up afterward.[23] The large amount of work performed by Nazarene girls in the orphanage served, in the eyes of missionaries, as a way to train them for future housekeeping duties as (hopefully Protestant) wives and mothers, or at least as domestic servants; to teach them discipline and submission to authority, in this case, to the authority of the missionary mistresses of the orphanage; and to save the FES money in maintaining the facility.

Costs were also cut with the building of a new FES orphanage in Nazareth in the mid-1870s; a large portion of the huge two-story institution was built by Palestinian girls. Along with an unknown number of men from the town, twenty local girls were employed on the building site; they carried mortar and "toil[ed] from five in the morning till eight in the evening." Miss Dickson, the headmistress, wrote to her mission's main offices in London that the girls worked on the site in order to be rewarded with beds in it once the building was completed. She had to explain to them, however, that a position at the orphanage may not be the result of their labor: "They look a little puzzled on being told that if so it must be as a thank offering to God for His having heard and answered prayers on their behalf" and not as a result of the FES taking pity on their unfortunate lot in life.[24]

FES missionary Miss Baker reported that in addition to housework, food preparation, and other labor, her girls also made their own clothing,[25] and it was in the realm of sewing that the girls of the Nazareth orphanage worked the longest hours. The reports of how much sewing the girls did are astonishing. For instance, the *Female Missionary Intelligencer* reported, "A little fancy needlework is taught [at the orphanage]. Much time and attention is given to plain needlework; all the clothes worn by the girls are cut out, made, and mended in School, as well as all other needlework for the house. From October 1st, 1886, to July 31st, 1887, 6,887 articles passed through the School in this way."[26] A more elaborate breakdown of this staggering number was given over a year later, by FES secretary Miss Gage Brown: "I asked to have another look at the sewing record; and I find that last year 6,887 articles passed through the hands of the sewers; 3,967 articles were mended, 1,157 marked, 550 altered, 182 pinafores were made, also 400 undergarments, 130 dresses, and 168 collars were crocheted, caps and pockets made up the number, with a few aprons for the bigger girls."[27] Although many of these pieces were used by the orphanage itself, some were also sold in a shop run by the orphanage,[28] and still others found their way back to Britain. The most famous example of such an article was a presentation of silk lace made by orphanage girls to Queen Victoria "as a humble offering on the occasion of Her Majesty's Jubilee" in 1897.[29]

Indeed, mastery of needlework was considered as crucial to the future success of a girl upon leaving the orphanage as accomplishments in academic subjects. Training in sewing gave each girl a marketable skill and a potential source of livelihood as well as the ability to make and mend clothing for herself and her future family. The irony in the orphanage's great stress upon sewing lay in the fact that Palestinian Arabs were famous for their elaborate traditional embroideries and other forms of needlework. Regardless of the traditional forms of needlework already popular in Palestinian culture, the FES agents who ran the orphanage made certain that girls in the institution were capable seamstresses on an English model, or else they would fail their annual exams, which devoted a great deal of attention to sewing skills. The program for the 1885 examinations demonstrated how integral this form of labor was to the orphanage's overall philosophy of education. Along with several recitations from memory of biblical scripture, the singing of hymns, and exams on reading, writing, and arithmetic, girls were ardently examined on their sewing and needlework skills. The program shows that skills such as patching, stitching, darning, hemming, and buttonhole making were tested, along with girls' abilities in making seams and fells.[30] The inclusion of needlework as a distinct subject among the ranks of biblical and scholastic topics shows that the FES believed that rigorous training in such a precise domestic handicraft provided girls not only with a useful skill, but also with the discipline and attention to detail necessary for success in the domestic realm as wives and mothers.

Like Palestinian Arab and Jewish society, British society considered wifedom and motherhood the paramount professions for women; Palestinian girls under British missionary influence, therefore, were in training for the same position to which they had been trained by their own society. Missionaries, however, denigrated the traditional values and mores of what they considered "Oriental" Palestinian society in favor of their own "enlightened" British Protestant culture and values. Not all Palestinian girls accepted this cultural hierarchy, however, and resistance to teachings that undermined their faith and families started at a young age in mission schools. For instance, the LJS girls' school in Jerusalem was the scene of direct resistance by school girls in 1908. British missionary Miss E. Perry wrote of resistance to her preaching by Jewish school girls who were tired of studying Christian scripture: "Many of the girls are very prejudiced and bigoted Jewesses who, when they first come, will not say the Name of Jesus Christ in prayer, and some have erased the Name from the Hebrew-Spanish Testaments we use in the class, and even spit on the floor when His Name has been mentioned."[31] Such strong opposition to Christian teaching was an affront to their work in the eyes of English missionaries, but to Palestinian Jews the denial of their religion and the forced study of Christianity, with its negative historical relationship with Judaism, must have seemed threatening. The girls who defaced Perry's textbooks and openly challenged participation in Christian ritual must have felt that such actions were crucial for maintaining their own beliefs in the face of adults who preached allegiance to a faith doctrinally at odds with their own.

Muslim Arab schoolgirls confronted with similar affronts to their religion by English teachers were equally adamant in their resistance. For example, Mrs. Joyce Nasir, a graduate of the Jerusalem Girls' College during the Mandate period and an Arab Christian, remembered in a later interview that during Ramadan, English teachers refused to allow Muslim girls to fast and forced them to eat in front of all the students. She says that at times girls would spit the food pushed into their mouths back into the faces of their English teachers, an act of defiance for which they would be severely punished.[32] In cases such as these, Palestinian girls used the small amount of power they had to make clear their political and religious beliefs and assert themselves as viable actors against privileged adults who were overtly attempting to sever them from their own society, families, and religious beliefs.

Just as nationalism and communal concerns influenced Palestinian schoolgirls in their rejection of British demands on their identities, so too did nationalism motivate many British women in their work educating Palestinian girls. An excellent example of such purpose is found in Frances E. Newton's autobiography, *Fifty Years in Palestine*. A missionary for the Church Missionary Society (CMS) in Jaffa and Galilee from 1889 until 1914 and a philanthropist and government advisor in Palestine from 1919 until 1938, Newton was ardently committed to using mission education to elevate the social position of Arab girls and to promote British values among them. She believed that missionaries were stellar role models not only of piety and ethics, but also of civic and career opportunities. Moreover, the transition from Ottoman to British rule was, in the mind of Newton, a landmark moment of opportunity for Palestine's girls and women. Newton, reflecting on the beginning of the Mandate, wrote:

> The British flag flying on Government buildings was a token of a new orientation in the life of the people who would now find fuller opportunity for progress in every direction. Women and girls, in particular, could now find scope for the expression of their own special contribution in service to the community in both private and public life. It was a source of real joy to me to feel that an awakening to a sense of the part women could take in social activities and responsibilities was due in great measure to the work of mission schools in the past.

Reflecting on the crisis between Arabs and Jews in the decisive year of 1948, Newton continued:

> It is no exaggeration to say that the influence of [British] boarding schools, and the many mission day schools throughout the length and breadth of the country, has been the chief contribution to Arab progress. It has also created among the younger generation an appreciation of the British character and moral standards which has made of these former pupils some of the best friends of Britain to-day.[33]

It is obvious that as a missionary, Newton approached her work as a British ambassador as well as a Protestant Christian. She hoped to infuse her students with British notions of young women's independence as well as foster loyalty to the British Empire, which she believed was founded on high "character and moral standards." The glorification of such self-described altruism was common among missionaries, whether they were working with children or adults. It is in the work with children, however, that the intentions of British missionaries reveal themselves most clearly.

Missionaries viewed girls as pliant and easily swayed, and they often bragged in their correspondence about their "successes"—girls who gave up their local customs and even family ties and embraced British social values and religious faith. The vast majority of Palestinian girls who entered missionary establishments, however, did not convert to Protestantism, and some, such as the Muslim girls who spit food in the faces of their teachers or the Jewish girls who refused to accept Christianity despite their teachers' desires, illustrated their individual and collective abilities to resist the missionaries' assaults on their families and traditions.

Girls as Imperial Prizes

Girls could even become battlegrounds on which resistance among missionaries, government officials, and the girls' relatives was played out. Families repeatedly challenged the indemnity that the FES, the LJS, and the CMS charged those who wished to remove their young relations from English institutions. Incidents of parents "kidnapping" their children were not uncommon.[34] Sometimes the disagreements became so grave that Ottoman and British governmental officials were forced to intervene. During the pre-Mandate period, such interventions could escalate into serious challenges to Ottoman authority, as correspondence between John Dickson, the British consul in Jerusalem during 1890–1906, and Edmund Fane at the Foreign Office in London demonstrates. In a letter dated August 5, 1891, Dickson wrote Fane asking for guidance concerning a custody struggle between the LJS girls' school in Jerusalem, run by Miss Elizabeth Carey Fitzjohn, and the mother of a child who wanted to remove her from the institution. Dickson explained to Fane that the LJS "has been in the habit of receiving girls into the school on condition that the parents give a guarantee that the pupils will remain in the school until the age of sixteen. This condition appears to be necessary, otherwise a number of indigent Jews would avail themselves of the School in question in order to put their children in it, where they would be well clothed and fed, gratis, and then take them away again as it suited them." Dickson, however, knew from the outset that there could be a problem with demanding an indemnity as a condition for return of children; he warned Fane that "it is doubtful whether it is binding according to Ottoman law."[35]

Regardless of this crucial point, Dickson hesitated to demand that the school return a child to her mother, even at the request of the Ottoman governor of Jerusalem, because "the mother is a divorced woman . . . and is stated to be the keeper of a house of ill fame in Port Said, and from what I have seen of her, she would seem to bear out this report." Despite repeated requests from the governor for assistance in removing the girl from the LJS school (which refused to surrender her), Dickson was concerned that returning the girl was immoral: "In principle His Excellency would seem to be in the right in demanding the girl, who is an Ottoman Subject, although not a Mohamedan, but for reasons of morality it is doubtful whether the Rev. A. H. Kelk [head of the LJS mission in Jerusalem] is not justified in refusing to comply with His Excellency's demand."[36] Dickson told Fane that he would do what the Foreign Office requested regarding the case, but made it clear by his report of the situation that he believed it was the moral duty of both the mission and his consulate to keep the girl away from the corrupting influence of her mother and her original Jewish community.

This case is but one example of a continuing trend toward flagrant disregard of Ottoman authority and law by missionary bodies in Palestine—a disregard supported by British government officials—and shows how deep moral assumptions about "the East," shared by both missionaries and politicians at the height of British imperial authority around the world, ran in terms of policy as well as missionary outreach. That the British consul was willing to risk diplomatic relations with the Ottomans in the Holy City of Jerusalem over the fate of one girl scholar in a missionary school speaks volumes about the connection between transmission of English values among the population of Palestine in Protestant church institutions and larger desires for influence by the British political authorities in the region. The assault on the mother's sexuality and character, the disregard for Ottoman law, and the slanderous words about the Palestinian Jewish community, spewed out in the context of "saving" one girl from her family and culture, reinforces clearly the precarious position Palestinian girls, like other girls throughout the world, found themselves in during this dynamic period of empire and European expansionism.

The missionary work of British women in Palestine, both in the late Ottoman era and the Mandate period, targeted girls of all local faiths—Christian, Muslim, and Jewish—for spiritual and social conversion. Through their educational and charitable organizations, these missionary women bombarded girls with messages of religious conversion in an effort to convince them to abandon their beliefs and the beliefs of their families in exchange for British forms of Protestantism. In tandem with efforts to change the girls' religious beliefs and disassociate them from their families spiritually, British missionary women struggled to convince Palestinian girls to adopt European modes of domestic life and attitudes toward gender, as part of the larger imperialist "civilizing mission" and assertion of British hegemony over the Holy Land and its populace. These activities were similar to those in other areas of the globe where British missionaries were deeply entrenched, such as India, Australia, and the Caribbean.[37] As in other parts of the world targeted by European empire in the late nineteenth and early twentieth centuries, Palestine was the site of a contest over the future of cultural and political authority, and controlling the futures of the country's girls was perceived as an ultimate prize for missionaries who hoped to bring all Palestinians under their spiritual, moral, and national sway.

NOTES

1. "Safed," in *The Ninety-third Report of the London Society for Promoting Christianity amongst the Jews* (London: London Jews' Society, 1901), 104.

2. *Prospectus of the English High School for Girls, Haifa, 1831–1932* (Haifa: Printing Press Haifa, 1931), 4, 5. Mabel C. Warburton, the longtime headmistress of the Mandate-era Jerusalem and the East Mission's Jerusalem Girls' College, wrote in 1923 that education for Christian and Muslim Palestinian girls was important not only for providing opportunities outside the home but for promoting the future of the family as well. See Mabel C. Warburton, "Women's Part in the Future of Palestine," *Bible Lands: Quarterly Paper of the Jerusalem and the East Mission* 6, no. 95 (January 1923): 304. For an insightful history of the Jerusalem and the East Mission's educational system in Palestine, see Inger Marie Okkenhaug, *The Quality of Heroic Living, of High Endeavour and Adventure: Anglican Mission, Women and Education in Palestine, 1888–1948* (Leiden: Brill, 2002).

3. The Society for Promoting Christianity amongst the Jews, as its title suggests, saw its mission primarily among the Jewish population, although Arabs could also be found in its schools. The Society for Promoting Female Education in the East did not focus on any specific population, but the location of its missions in Palestine dictated that most of its students were Arabs (both Muslim and Christian). The Church Missionary Society made it a policy to focus attention on Eastern Christians, but people of all faiths came under its sway as well.

4. "Jaffa: Extract of a Letter from Mrs. Krusé," *Female Missionary Intelligencer* 2 (1855): 22.

5. "Safed Mission School," *Jewish Missionary Intelligence* 23, no. 269 (May 1907): 67.

6. "Jerusalem," in *The Eighty-seventh Report of the London Society for Promoting Christianity amongst the Jews* (London: London Jews' Society, 1895), 116, 116–117.

7. Ruth L. P. Clark, "In the Girls' Day School, Jerusalem," *Jewish Missionary Intelligence* 20, no. 3 (March 1930): 39.

8. W. D., "A Visit to the Girls' Day School, Jerusalem," *Bible Lands: Quarterly Paper of the Jerusalem and the East Mission* 4, no. 55 (January 1913): 97–98.

9. "Mission School, Safed," in *The Eighty-ninth Report of the London Society for Promoting Christianity amongst the Jews* (London: London Jews' Society, 1897), 91.

10. Friedmann is probably referring to the Alliance Israelite school in Safed.

11. "Safed," in *The Ninety-sixth Report of the London Society for Promoting Christianity amongst the Jews* (London: London Jews' Society, 1904), 66.

12. This school was opened under the auspices of the Church of Scotland in 1862 but received substantial funding from the English FES throughout the reign of Miss Arnott and beyond. The school is still functioning today. For a comprehensive history of Scottish missions in Palestine, see Michael Marten, *Attempting to Bring the Gospel Home: Scottish Missions to Palestine, 1839–1917* (London: I. B. Taurus, 2005).

13. "Annual Report No. 46, 1881 [re 1880]," in *Female Education Society 1873–1882 Annual Reports*, 29, Female Education Society Papers, Church Missionary Society Papers, FES/Z1, University of Birmingham Library, Special Collections, Birmingham, England.

14. "The Safed Mission," *Jewish Missionary Intelligence* 19 (n.s.), no. 1 (January 1903): 10.

15. "The Girls' School, Jerusalem," *Jewish Missionary Intelligence* 13 (n.s.), no. 4 (April 1897): 53.

16. "Jerusalem," in *The Ninety-first Report of the London Society for Promoting Christianity amongst the Jews* (London: London Jews' Society, 1899), 89.

17. "Safed," in *The One Hundredth Report of the London Society for Promoting Christianity amongst the Jews* (London: London Jews' Society, 1908), 55.

18. Miss [Jane Walker] Arnott, "Zakeeji of Jaffa," *Female Missionary Intelligencer* 14, no. 10 (October 1871): 169–170.

19. Ibid., 171–172.

20. For a dramatic and heart-wrenching case of abuse in the FES orphanage in Nazareth, see Nancy L. Stockdale, "An Imperialist Failure: English Missionary Women and Palestinian

Orphan Girls in Nazareth, 1864–1899," in *Christian Witness between Continuity and New Beginnings: Modern Historical Missions in the Middle East,* ed. Michael Marten, 213–231 (Münster: LIT-Verlag, 2006).

21. For a fascinating study of the position of the orphan in Victorian culture, see Lydia Murdoch, *Imagined Orphans: Poor Families, Child Welfare, and Contested Citizenship in London* (New Brunswick, NJ: Rutgers University Press, 2006).

22. "Annual Report No. 50, 1885 [re 1884]," in *Female Education Society 1883–1899 Annual Reports,* 43–44.

23. "Letters from the Nazareth Orphanage," *Female Missionary Intelligencer* 6 (n.s.), no. 3 (March 1886): 40–42.

24. "The Orphanage at Nazareth. By Miss Dickson," *Female Missionary Intelligencer* 18, no. 1 (January 1876): 8.

25. "Letters from the Nazareth Orphanage," 43.

26. "Protestant Orphanage, Nazareth. Miss Newey's Report." *Female Missionary Intelligencer* 8, no. 1 (January 1888): 12.

27. "A Peep into the Schoolroom of the Protestant Orphanage, Nazareth, in Sewing Time," *Female Missionary Intelligencer* 9 (n.s. 5), no. 3 (March 1889): 47.

28. The FES hoped all of its institutions would be self-sufficient, but none of their Palestine missions were. From the 1870s, the Nazareth orphanage relied on sponsorships from Britain that ranged from seven to ten pounds per girl per annum.

29. "Annual Report No. 63, 1898 [re 1897]," in *Female Education Society 1883–1899 Annual Reports,* 21.

30. "The Nazareth Orphanage—Letter from Miss Newey," *Female Missionary Intelligencer* 5 (n.s.), no. 11 (November 1885): 158–159.

31. *One Hundredth Report of the London Society for Promoting Christianity amongst the Jews,* 63.

32. Mrs. Joyce Nasir, interview by the author, East Jerusalem, November 9, 1998.

33. Frances E. Newton, *Fifty Years in Palestine* (London: Coldharbour Press, 1948), 161, 162.

34. See, for example, "Jerusalem," in *The Sixty-eighth Report for the London Society for Promoting Christianity amongst the Jews* (London: London Jews' Society, 1876), 90–93; Miss Creasy to Miss Sterry, Jerusalem, May 12, 1858, Finn Papers, MSS Finn File D, Yad Ben Zvi Library, Jerusalem, Israel; "Jerusalem," in *The Eighty-fourth Report for the London Society for Promoting Christianity amongst the Jews* (London: London Jews' Society, 1892), 118; "Jerusalem," in *The Ninety-second Report for the London Society for Promoting Christianity amongst the Jews* (London: London Jews' Society, 1900), 100–101.

35. John Dickson to Edmund Fane, Foreign Office 195/1727 (no. 30), reprinted in Albert M. Hyamson, ed. *The British Consulate in Jerusalem in Relation to the Jews of Palestine 1838–1914,* 2 vols. (London: Edward Goldstein, 1939), 2:466.

36. Ibid., 467.

37. See, for example, Anna Johnston, *Missionary Writing and Empire, 1800–1860* (Cambridge: Cambridge University Press, 2007); David Savage, "Missionaries and the Development of a Colonial Ideology of Female Education in India," *Gender and History* 9, no. 2 (August 1997): 201–211; Delia Davin, "British Women Missionaries in Nineteenth-Century China," *Women's History Review* 1, no. 2 (1992): 257–271; Patricia T. Rooke, " 'Ordinary Events of Nature and Providence': Reconstructing Female Missionary Experience in the British West Indies, 1800–1845," *Journal of Religious History* 19, no. 2 (December 1995): 204–226.

12   *"The Right Kind of Ambition"*

DISCOURSES OF FEMININITY AT
THE HUGUENOT SEMINARY AND
COLLEGE, 1895–1910

S. E. DUFF

The period 1895 to 1910 is a particularly useful window through which to analyze the production of white femininities in the Cape Colony.[1] The late nineteenth and early twentieth centuries represent a major turning point in South African history, as the country shifted from being a collection of British colonies and Boer republics to becoming a unified and semi-independent state in 1910. This process entailed major social upheaval as people defined themselves in relation to the massive changes under way. Whites were more sharply differentiated between English- and Afrikaans-speaking groups, whereas both communities distanced themselves from the waves of immigrants arriving in the country, who were drawn, predominantly, by hopes of benefiting from the South African mineral revolution.[2] The conclusion of the South African War (1899–1902) and the consequent peace negotiations had the effect of politicizing minority groups, and although the movement was never as much of a powerful social and political force as it was in Britain, the first signs of interest in women's suffrage appeared.[3] In Cape Town, for example, the Women's Christian Temperance Union (WCTU) developed a political wing, the Women's Enfranchisement League (WEL), in 1907.[4] The National Council of Women emerged in 1909 to act as an umbrella body to foster women's interests, demonstrating the extent to which women's organizations had proliferated.[5]

Much of this activity was also connected to the rising levels of education among white, middle-class South African women, the growing numbers of professional middle-class women, as well as an awareness of the global interest in women's franchise and rights during the period.[6] Elaine Showalter has written about the fin de siècle as a significant watershed in the formation of gendered identities and relations for the twentieth century. As a period of profound global social, economic, and political transformation, much of the anxiety arising out of this change resulted from a heightened awareness of the fluidity of the "proper" places for middle-class men and women, and was directed toward those young people being prepared for these roles. Questions about the degree of education a middle-class girl should receive, the preparation of girls for marriage, and the extent to which the appeal of the New Woman began to challenge traditional modes of domesticity preoccupied writers, journalists, moralizers, and educators.[7] Such questions received much consideration at the Huguenot Seminary and College.

Andrew Murray, the moderator of the (Calvinist) Dutch Reformed Church, founded the Huguenot Seminary and College (HSC) in Wellington, a rural town about fifty miles from Cape Town, in 1874. The HSC was the school of choice for the daughters of the Cape Colony's Dutch Afrikaner gentry until the mid-twentieth century. The term "Dutch Afrikaner" refers to the Cape's middle-class Dutch population as it negotiated an identity that was no longer exclusively European, yet distinct from the English-speaking and indigenous inhabitants of the colony during the latter half of the nineteenth century. As leader of the Dutch Reformed Church's evangelical wing, Murray believed that education could be used to convert adults and children to Protestant Christianity. It was partly for this reason that he applied to the Mount Holyoke Seminary in South Hadley, Massachusetts, a school established in 1837 originally to train female teachers and missionaries, for teachers to found a similar institution in his parish.[8] The first of nearly thirty American teachers from Mount Holyoke arrived at the Cape at the end of 1873. Abbie Park Ferguson (1837–1919) and Anna E. Bliss (1843–1925), Huguenot's first, joint, principals, brought to Wellington the curriculum, rules, roster, traditions, even the architectural plans, of the South Hadley school and met with resounding success. From its first year, the Huguenot Seminary, which offered a secondary school education and teacher training to girls between the ages of fifteen and twenty, was constantly in need of extra room to house its overflow of pupils, and the girls ranked near the top on the colony's teaching examinations from 1875 onward.

Although the seminary's original purpose was to train teachers and missionaries, its popularity was such that by the 1890s it was a prominent and respected feature of the Cape's educational landscape, providing girls between the ages of five and twenty with a rigorous academic education. Indeed, the closely affiliated Huguenot College (established in 1898) was one of the first institutions in South Africa where girls could study for university degrees. In 1908, it was estimated that around four thousand girls had attended the institution since 1874, and many of them had taken up prominent positions in public life.[9]

The HSC's teachers were acutely aware of the school's unique influence over a sizable proportion of the daughters of the Dutch Afrikaner elite. Being a boarding school, it was responsible not only for the education but also for the upbringing and socialization of the girls who would become the wives of the next generation of South African leaders. The teachers and pupils of the HSC were conscious of the difficulties of reconciling the institution's overtly academic training with the expectations of the girls' parents and community regarding correct feminine behavior. In this way, the HSC became a site where girls were exposed to a remarkable variety of arguments surrounding "ideal" femininity.

In this chapter I consider the position of the HSC in relation to the construction of the feminine identities available to bourgeois Dutch Afrikaner girls in the Cape between 1895 and 1910. I draw information from the school's annuals, which the girls edited themselves. These annuals provide insight into the girls' experiences of, and perspectives on, the education provided to them at Huguenot. A number of both conflicting and complimentary discourses on femininity emerge in the annuals, each of them attempting to explain and justify the importance, place, and role of the educated middle-class woman at the turn of the century. These discourses can be labeled "hegemonic," "professionalist," and "College Girl." The first seeks to demonstrate that education does not prevent girls from becoming successful wives and mothers and, indeed, causes them to fulfill these roles more successfully than if they had not been properly educated. The second discourse belongs to a younger generation of teachers who believed that they were entitled to a tertiary education as part of their training to become professional educationalists. Finally, the discourse of the College Girl accepted the relative normality of university education for girls but conceptualized female students as girlish and fun loving, thus undermining commonly held views that education would render girls masculine or socially deficient.

Through these discourses, the annuals attach subtly differing meanings to the terms "girl" and "young woman." Although the teachers at the HSC referred to their pupils as girls, students hoped to become accomplished young women upon completing their education. The discourses on femininity within the annuals both conform to and gently subvert this supposed division between youth and maturity.

Discipline or Punish? Self-Reporting at Huguenot

In this chapter I argue that one way of examining the HSC's response to these debates on the position of the educated woman is to understand its insistence on maintaining a self-reporting system of discipline. As at Mount Holyoke, the HSC's disciplinary system was based on the principle of self-reporting. Each pupil was provided with a booklet in which she was to record whenever she, or her friends, broke a rule.[10] The booklets were handed in once a week, and then all would gather for the "Reporting," during which the headmistress would read aloud misdemeanors and mete out suitable punishments.[11] The most minor infractions (such as speaking Dutch in an English-medium school) were punished by confining pupils to "punishment seats" at the front of the classroom for a week, whereas those guilty of serious infringements (such as meeting boys without permission) could be suspended for up to six months.[12] This practice was an attempt to instill in the pupils a strong sense of self-discipline that, it was felt, they would need when working as teachers or missionaries. In South Africa, the system worked in fits and starts. All would proceed well when girls would forget to record their (and their friends') transgressions. Ferguson would then call them together and would speak earnestly about the necessity of being truthful. After this presentation, pupils would troop into her office, frequently in tears, to apologize. In presenting the rationale for the system to the girls, Ferguson invoked religious imagery, asking them to model their behavior more closely on Christ's.

Between 1874 and 1885, when the school's small size encouraged the development of a family-like community, the girls strove to earn their teachers' affection by being obedient, learning their lessons, and noting their rule breaking. A desire to please—both teachers (who were often perceived, and saw themselves, as surrogate mothers) and God—motivated the girls.[13] As the school grew and maintaining a close family of teachers and pupils proved difficult, this impetus for self-monitoring and submission fell away. Indeed, as the teachers' letters demonstrate, the "naughty" girls received the greatest attention; the particularly submissive received less notice.

Self-reporting was a highly contradictory form of control. Although the HSC's teachers felt that self-reporting fostered the self-discipline required by future teachers and missionaries, the complete submission required by the HSC's rules prevented girls from controlling the decisions that determined the order, nature, and outcomes of the day's activities. They had the option only to obey or disobey the rules. During the 1880s, girls began to undermine this system because its religious underpinnings were no longer as relevant to the majority of girls as they had been ten years earlier. Whereas in the 1870s the school attracted pupils who sympathized with its religious aims, by the 1880s and 1890s the HSC was one of many good girls' schools available to parents who sought a high standard of teaching and not necessarily a Christian environment for their daughters' schooling. Nevertheless, Christianity remained of central importance to the lives of the senior teachers and founder of the school throughout the period. It is not surprising, then, that Ferguson, Bliss, and Murray, who attached a religious significance to self-reporting, chose to implement the system even when it did not seem effective. I propose that the persistence of the self-reporting system was a manifestation of the school's belief in the vital importance of inculcating self-discipline in its pupils. In the remainder of the chapter, I demonstrate the extent to which self-discipline was of pivotal importance to the three main discourses on femininity that appeared in the annuals.

Hegemonic Narratives of Middle-Class Femininity

Of the multitude of gendered identities available to a society, one, usually because of its association with social, economic, or political power, is considered to be dominant and is thus held up as an ideal worthy of emulation. This supremacy is maintained in opposition to other, subordinate gendered identities and is reproduced within social institutions—one of the most potent of which is the school.[14] R. W. Connell argues that in schools, children and adolescents encounter a variety of gendered identities around which they define themselves. Although the ethos of the institution tends to promote a hegemonic masculinity or femininity, other gendered identities are also open to the pupils and are accepted or rejected by the school's staff, parents, and alumni.[15]

Hegemonic femininity differs in its construction and maintenance from hegemonic masculinity. Whereas the latter is associated with the exercise of power and the subjugation of other gendered identities, hegemonic femininity is described, typically, as passive and domesticated. It is possible to identify such a form of hegemonic femininity in the late nineteenth-century Cape Colony. In the 1897 and 1898 annuals for the Good Hope Seminary, known as the "highpriced, fashionable school of Cape Town," marriages of past pupils are listed before the institution's (relatively limited) academic achievements.[16] Training in feminine "accomplishments" is given greater prominence than academic study, and an article on college education for women concludes, "Though the privilege of adding B.A. to one's name is envied by most, yet the exertion of reaching this is a severe strain on the whole of a girl's nature, and it is questionable whether this giddy height should be aspired to by her."[17]

The hegemonic femininity promoted by the teachers at the HSC differed from the anti-intellectualism at Good Hope, but consistently understood women's "proper place" to be the home. Teachers, alumnae, and winners of essay competitions authored the articles that most vigorously expounded this understanding of femininity, demonstrating the extent to which this view was the HSC's "official" feminine discourse. They propose that educated women had a wider, spiritual duty toward their communities and demonstrate that a young woman had to be properly self-disciplined in order to perform work that was frequently arduous and poorly remunerated. In the 1898 annual, Bliss queried, "Do you ask me whether this education is fitting our young people for their homes and for a wider and better influence over others?" She described the choice of an ex-pupil whose academic success at the HSC qualified her to look for relatively well-paid work, but who instead chose to work in a small school in a rural area "and then married a farmer in the neighborhood." Bliss queried her readers: "Was her education thrown away?" The answer was no: "It seemed strange in that out-of-the-way place, in an ignorant community, on a Dutch farm, to see volumes of Longfellow, Tennyson, Browning, and Ruskin lying on the table, evidently used. . . . She is raising the intellectual and moral tone of the whole community."[18]

Despite her academic achievements, the subject of Bliss's parable eschews worldly success so that she may put her skills to good work in a rural area; it is easy to confuse her teaching activities with those of a missionary. Yet it is after her marriage, which is implied to be an act of heroic surrender, that she does the most good for the community. By making works of "culture" available, she is able to raise the "intellectual and moral tone" of the area. In this way, her education acquires a spiritual and moral function that obliges her to assist in the uplift of the "waste places of Africa." It also allows her to perform her work successfully in that she has been trained to be self-denying and focused. The education of women, therefore, is justified by pointing to the broader good that it will do for the (white) population of South Africa.

The HSC argued for its own importance by showing how an "academic" education could be applicable to the responsibilities of a wife and mother. Writing with her tongue in her cheek, one pupil argued that "cooking or dusting" become "fascinating . . . if studied with the same ardor as botany, and astonishing how much time is saved in these and other domesticities when dealt with by a mind trained by a course of mathematics to reject all arguments which can only lead *ad absurdum*." Her point was that "housekeeping is in itself a wonderful school for mental culture." Yet she admitted that "many women, of whom the number is rapidly increasing, shine also outside the home."[19] This statement hints at the reality that many girls leaving the HSC would not marry and would, besides running households for friends and relatives, work as teachers or, less frequently, missionaries. Of the 1,222 of the pupils who left the HSC between 1874 and 1897, only 565, or slightly more than 40 percent, married.[20] How did the HMC reconcile its feminine discourse to the existence of these women?

In another article, Bliss described the fortunes of an ex-pupil who "had given up a position, where she loved the work, to take another that was then not so pleasant, because no one was ready to take it and the work must be done for Christ's sake." Although she had been "rewarded" with a post as a "head of a very large school with several assistants," she continued to do "much outside work, beside caring for a helpless sister."[21] This woman evinced a disciplined, self-denying dedication to the welfare of others, which entailed a great deal of willing self-sacrifice. Her independence and self-discipline allowed her to work as a missionary teacher, and her suffering lent her both nobility and a kind of quasi-sanctity. The account, however, did not allude to her agency; it suggested that she was simply led by God to her work. This mastery of self, which is, in many ways, a renunciation of self, allowed her a form of freedom, but, ironically, this independence was described as an absolute submission to a higher power.

These articles demonstrate how this "official" discourse was molded to adapt to the variety of futures awaiting the HSC's pupils. The authors attempted to prove that the education of girls actually prepared them to be effective wives and mothers, but that, equally, it allowed them to work, independently, as unmarried teachers and missionaries. In this way, girlhood was defined in relation to womanhood. It was a preparation for a life of noble hard work and, frequently, suffering. Girls needed, then, to be educated in order to become effective women. It is significant that girls themselves contributed to this discourse, which suggests that they too understood girlhood as a transitory period of "training" for full-fledged womanhood.

While they were pupils at the HSC, the girls had as their role models the institution's teachers, most of whom had been in a position to choose to teach and were not forced to do so for economic reasons. This group of women was not a homogenous entity; although Ferguson and Bliss may have promoted a discourse of Christian self-denial and self-sacrifice, their example was not followed among the younger teachers at the HSC. The American teachers who worked at Huguenot during the 1870s and 1880s were qualified by having graduated from schools that offered teacher training. Ferguson and Bliss did not possess formal degrees or teaching certificates. Yet as the college established itself at the end of the 1890s, it began to attract greater numbers of women holding degrees from single-sex and coeducational universities. How, then, did this hegemonic discourse accommodate this younger generation of teachers?

Educated Women as Professionals:
The Emergence of a Professionalist Discourse

From his appointment in 1892, Thomas Muir, the Cape's superintendent for education, made it increasingly difficult for unqualified teachers to hold positions of authority in the Colony's schools.[22] As a government-funded school, the HSC was obliged to comply with Muir's regulations, and by the 1910s, the majority of staff listed in the HSC's prospectuses possessed degrees from a variety of universities in America and Europe. At the seminary, of the ten teachers listed in the prospectus, five had tertiary qualifications.[23] It is difficult to gauge the degree of tension on a personal level between these two generations of teachers, one trained to become missionary-teachers, the other professional women, but it is clear that as the college expanded, the whole Huguenot institution changed from a religious, mission-based school for girls to a modern college. In 1899, Ferguson commented that the younger teachers "want more time for study, which seems to us [Ferguson, Bliss, and Murray] to mean less time for quiet time and prayer."[24] Ferguson was not inflexible. She acknowledged that the HSC had to hire staff on the basis of their qualifications and not their piety, and she admitted that "perhaps it is good that we should be shaken out of our traditions, and old ways of doing things, but it is hard all the same."[25] That the shift in principles did occur is clear. By 1917, Mount Holyoke–trained lecturer Sue Leiter wrote, "The girls . . . are like college girls the world over. It is not a missionary institution."[26] A good articulation of this more professional attitude toward the higher education of women is Elizabeth Clark's

"Abstract of a Paper on the Higher Education of Women in South Africa" (1905). Clark was a member of the staff at the HSC and had studied at Bryn Mawr College and the universities of Leipzig and Zurich.[27] She argued for the extension of secondary and tertiary education to young women in South Africa, not once justifying her stance through recourse to religion. She viewed the university as existing solely to provide an academic, not a spiritual or moral, education to both men and women. A belief that it is no more unusual for a woman to enter college than it is for a man underpinned her argument.[28]

It would be misleading to suggest that Ferguson and Bliss's understanding of women's education disappeared completely after the 1890s. In the annuals, their justification for the training of girls as teachers forms a basis for the HSC's hegemonic femininity. Running parallel to the hegemonic discourse in the annuals, however, was an increasingly strident discourse of professionalism, written by both younger teachers and girls studying to become teachers. It is particularly evident in a series of articles that describe student life at tertiary institutions in Britain and the United States. These pieces depict young women enjoying themselves at university or college. They are challenged by their academic work and have full and active social lives. A number of articles describing life and the "rounded" education of the young women in Wellington draw a similar picture. A prizewinning essay on the daily life of the HSC describes how classes in the morning are balanced by the half-hour's compulsory exercise in the afternoon and how homework in the evening is brought to a close by girls visiting and taking tea with one another before bedtime.[29] The HSC also functioned as a kind of "academic finishing school" where girls, in their friendships, social activities, and participation in organized sport, were prepared to take their place in the community. The annuals attended to parents' worry that girls would emerge from the college determined bookworms with little or no social ability, or "physically fit for nothing."[30]

The belief that education would transform girls into tomboys or "manly women" was by no means unique to some of the parents of the HSC students—it was an argument that had accompanied the extension of higher education to women since its inception in Europe and North America. With nineteenth-century notions of "true" middle-class womanhood revolving around women's ability to reproduce, educated women who did not marry, who chose to delay pregnancy, or who did not have children at all were clearly not fulfilling their "natural" roles. It seemed logical, then, to assume that their schooling had encouraged them to think and behave like men.[31]

Within the hegemonic discourse of femininity at work in the Huguenot College, there was little difficulty in reconciling the life of the female schoolteacher with that of the caring, self-sacrificing maternal ideal. For female teachers who subscribed to a professionalist understanding of teaching, the charge that they were "manly women" was more difficult to disprove.

As a result, in many schools and colleges students were required to behave and dress as "young ladies": they would dress for dinner, wear fashionable clothing, avoid romping on the sports' fields, and assiduously avoid contact with men deemed to be "unsuitable" by their teachers.[32] Still, although girls at the HSC were not permitted to meet boys during school hours or without the permission of their teachers, they did not lead an entirely cloistered existence. Older girls were allowed to correspond with young men, and from time to time the students from the neighboring Mission Institute would be invited to picnics.[33] The resistance to male company was not based on a dislike of men in general, but rather on a desire that the girls should mix with the "right sort" of boys.

In addition, the HSC rebutted critics of girls' education who— commenting on the HSC's emphasis on girls' physical activity—said that education made women susceptible to illness. Nearly every issue of the annual had at least one article on the HSC's athletic achievements or on the importance of girls taking regular exercise. These pieces demonstrate that with the proper attention to exercise, a girl at the HSC would emerge with both a bachelor's degree and perfect health. Compulsory exercise, in the form of tennis, basketball, and hockey, was imbued with the function of assisting pupils to perform better academically. Playing games would also teach girls to be more disciplined physically and allow them to learn to work in teams for a common goal. One article from 1897 went so far as to suggest that the advancement of the "modern" woman can be measured in terms of her physical betterment: "While the girl of yesterday fainted at the sight of a snake, the girl of to-day catches it by the tail and bottles it for exhibition and examination."[34]

By demonstrating that women could remain both feminine and healthy as professionals dedicated to a life of teaching, this professionalist discourse provided an alternate means of understanding the position of the educated woman that did not rely on religion or on the ideal of the "angel of the house." The suggestion that a woman could enjoy her independence upset notions of a woman needing to master herself in order to justify her autonomy. For the professional teacher, the acquisition of self-discipline was still useful in that it allowed her to study and work more efficiently. Girls need to be trained, but this secular mastery is expressed in terms of having a well-disciplined body, an ability to think rationally and logically, and a desire to succeed academically to secure a future career.

The differences between the hegemonic and professionalist discourses should not be exaggerated, however. Both required that the teacher remain single during her working life and that she devote herself entirely to her household should she marry. Teachers of the younger generation also had to submit to popular notions of what it meant to be feminine. Moreover, both discourses understood the girl's time at college as simply a phase in her development. A girl's need to study for a degree was defended in terms of what she would learn that would assist her in future life. Although neither group discounted the importance of a girl's enjoyment of her tertiary education, enjoyment alone did not justify it. The professionalist discourse defined girlhood as an important time of preparation for independent, adult womanhood. Despite emphasizing the ways in which girls at the HSC socialized with one another and behaved in typically "feminine" ways, this understanding of girlhood did not make allowances for less serious, more "adolescent" behavior. Indeed, both the hegemonic and professionalist discourses expected girls to be "young women," or younger versions of the women they were to become, rather than less serious adolescents more interested in enjoying themselves than in preparing for their future.

Yet a third, and possibly even more subtle, discourse is at work in the annuals—that of the College Girl, which was a celebration of a young woman's life at her university or women's college. It was a discourse that, although an American import, seems to have found some favor among the HSC's students.[35]

College Girls and New Women

The professionalist discourse was connected to the phenomenon of the New Woman that arose in Britain, Europe, and America during the closing decades of the nineteenth century. Only one article in the HSC annuals engages directly with the idea of the New Woman, and, interestingly, it was written by Maggie Ferguson, Abbie Ferguson's niece. Ferguson aligned herself with the values underpinning New Womanhood—she rejected the "very beautiful ideal of womanhood, which was to represent the hidden purity of the heart and home" on the grounds that it "ignored one factor, that woman was endowed with a mind to *think*, as well as to *feel*." Ferguson argued that women should participate actively in life and not vicariously through husbands and fathers: "The spirit of the age has produced women who begin to think, crudely no doubt, on many questions, for she is still handicapped by her long submission; but above all has made woman no longer willing to be a mere consumer, she must also be a producer." As a result, women needed to learn how to reason, and she felt that the female teacher had a duty to encourage the creative thought and individuality wherever she went. Nevertheless, Maggie's definition of the New Woman, "the woman who thinks and who recognizes her responsibilities as a human being," was more conservative than that in Europe or America.[36]

This ambivalence about the position of educated women pervades the annuals; the few references to women's suffrage and bluestockings (a derogatory description of educated and intellectual women) at the HSC are at once mildly supportive and faintly dismissive. One way of understanding this mixed response is to consider the extent to which the students at the HSC identified with the construct of the College Girl. The College Girl, at once a manifestation of and reaction against the New Woman in

America, appeared in a range of popular novels and magazine articles about college life. The concept arose from the illustrator Charles Dana Gibson's understanding of the "modern woman" (or the Gibson Girl as she rapidly became known). His drawings depicted her "as tall, long-legged and graceful, with upswept hair, faintly pink cheeks, a provocative eye, and a cool detached air . . . unencumbered by bustles or convention." The College Girl retained these qualities, but added to them a liveliness and playful impudence that were intended to render her even more charming. The College Girl and the Gibson Girl were conservative responses to the New Woman: what defined these "girls," as opposed to "women," were their physical attractiveness and their simultaneously coy and arch attitude toward men. The image of the College Girl calmed worries that education "spoiled" women for marriage in that it emphasized the lack of impact that the college had on the Gibson Girl: she attended classes and wrote examinations but otherwise retained her fun-loving demeanor.[37]

It would be an exaggeration to state that the girls at the HSC identified wholeheartedly with this College Girl understanding of female behavior, but it is striking how many of the leisure activities of the students mentioned in the annuals coincided exactly with those ascribed to College Girls: they held fudge, cocoa, and tea parties; possessed tea sets and cooking utensils; indulged in schoolgirl pranks and "larks"; went on picnics and shopping expeditions; and preferred basketball to study. Moreover, their gossip columns are packed with references to boys and tart remarks about classroom antics.[38] Although much of this conduct might be dismissed as typical of a group of girls confined to a strict timetable and living in close proximity to one another over a relatively long period of time, in a large proportion of these articles the students referred to themselves as College Girls and embraced a college culture that was more American than it was British.[39] It is likely that the HSC students would have come into contact with representations of College Girls. They would certainly have read about the Gibson Girl in the range of popular magazines and periodicals, such as the *Illustrated London News*, that were exported to South Africa. The young American teachers at the college would have been familiar with the College Girl, even if they did not approve of the idea; as E. M. Clark remarked, "In the States . . . girls go to college for the sake of the social life."[40] This is not an "official" discourse in the annuals in that it is expressed in pieces written by members of staff or the editorial board of the magazine, but it appears in the poetry, humorous articles, gossip pages, and student doggerel that provided light relief between the arguments about girls' education or reports on achievements in the missionary field.

For example, in "The Day's Journal," a satire on similar articles in the British political periodical the *Spectator*, the author provides a brief description of a typical Wednesday during which she "tried a new hair effect" and noted that she "look[s] best in mauve," "donned [a] frill" and "gazed at the effect in the glass," stole sweets from the pantry, met with "Mr. X" who "made an appearance with violets," and then "tried to solve the problem of the Intermediate examination in the bunch of violets" during evening study.[41] Attending classes seems, in this article, merely an excuse to have fun during free time.

Small parties of all kinds were popular in the evenings. As in America, the girls held "fudge parties" or simply offered cocoa and tea to one another.[42] Who was and was not invited to these little gatherings was a matter of some interest. Even though the gossip columns are frequently incomprehensible as a result of the students' slang or the opacity of their allusions, what emerges from them is an idea of the intricacy of the social life in the college. They are not preparing themselves for a higher cause or a successful professional career connected to notions of womanhood. They define themselves as College Girls and take pleasure in the experience itself, stressing their difference from their parents, families, and friends outside of the HSC by describing their unconventional behavior, providing glimpses into their apparently byzantine social network, and providing relatively detailed accounts of a lifestyle entirely unique to a student at a tertiary institution. This glimpse has the effect of celebrating the life of the student, and of validating it as an important phase in the life of a girl. Going to college was presented as an entirely normal activity for a girl that did not require elaborate justification. Moreover, students' "girlish" behavior suggested the relative harmlessness of the well-educated girl. Perhaps the best demonstration of this "domestication" of the woman with a B.A. is in a poem, written from a man's perspective, by one of the female college students:

My College Girl
She is skilled in mathematics,
And knows more of hydrostatics
Than I learned in all my plodding years at school.
She performs experiments
With divers elements,
That would make her little brother's blood turn cool.

She can Dutch and German speak,
And she writes in ancient Greek,
Getting all the various accents quite correct.
Though she deals hard blows at Russians
In historical discussions,
Not a flaw in all her logic I detect.

She, although 'tis not her habit,
Can dissect a good-sized rabbit,
Giving you the name of each and every bone;
And she knows each plant and tree

On the land or in the sea,
Slighting not meanwhile the all important stone.

Like a statue she can pose,
And interpret learned prose
In a way that makes my pulses wildly beat.
She has studied poetry lyric,
Epic also, and satiric,
Till her diction and her style are quite complete.

More than all, the little sinner,
She can cook as good a dinner
As a hungry man would ever wish to spy.
And I challenge the world over
If two folks they can discover
Quite so happy as my college girl and I.[43]

The poem expresses admiration for the female student's ability to acquire what was a kind of alternate set of "accomplishments" while at the HSC. The accomplishments have not rendered her "mannish" or in any way unattractive but instead have made her even more fascinating. This Renaissance woman, however, is brought to earth in the final stanza, where the speaker makes the point that "his" College Girl has not forgotten how to perform more traditionally "feminine" tasks. By referring to her as a "little sinner," the speaker belittles his girlfriend and her achievements, albeit in a way that suggests his affection for her. The poem can be read as an expression of how the girls at the HSC saw themselves, or as a wistful description of how these girls wished men would respond to them. They were not threatening, "unsexed" creatures forever spoiled by their education, but rather intelligent and also feminine girls who had the self-discipline to balance both academic and domestic interests with fun.

The College Girl did not have to master herself in the sense that she had to learn self-discipline; indeed, it was her lack of discipline that made her so charming. Instead, she had to cultivate behavior demonstrating that her position at a tertiary institution would not cause her to challenge commonly held assumptions about the "correct" mode of feminine behavior after graduation. Her time as a College Girl gave her license to indulge in relatively childish activities, to be irresponsible, and to become totally involved in the minutiae of her community. Still, at Wellington, either because the College Girl discourse was muted or because marriage was not described as students' ultimate goal, this College Girl was not as antifeminist as those in America: the South African College Girl attempted to reconcile the intellectual with the domestic, and as a consequence of the pervasive self-ridicule in many of the annuals' articles, the "silliness" of the

HSC students was not presented as a desired mode of behavior for these girls after graduation. The pupils' embrace of the idea of the College Girl would remain limited to their time at the HSC. After graduation, they were expected to become mature, responsible "women" who would not replicate their irresponsible, schoolgirlish behavior as they ran households or worked in schools and mission stations. Like the hegemonic and professionalist discourses, the discourse surrounding the idea of the College Girl firmly associated girlhood with schooling and education.

Conclusion

A single discourse of femininity does not dominate the HSC annuals. The hegemonic femininity to which the older generation of teachers subscribed served as the institution's "official" discourse. Key to this understanding of femininity was its emphasis on women's self-monitoring to ensure that the needs and wants of others were always uppermost in their minds; their willing self-sacrifice is what especially validated the existence of unmarried working women. Yet even though the professionalist discourse of the younger generation of teachers was not underpinned by evangelical Christianity, it shared with the hegemonic discourse the fundamental belief that girls had to be prepared for life after graduation. While it emphasized that the lot of the professional teacher did not render her masculine or physically deficient, it also showed the need for girls to acquire a mastery over their thinking, behavior, and bodies to allow them to perform better as teachers.

It appears, then, as if the relatively unconventional and frivolous activities of the imported discourse of the College Girl undermined this need for self-control; the College Girl's lack of discipline rendered her both charming and childlike, however, and in this way diminished whatever worry there may have been that educated women were willful and uncontrollable. Yet she needed to master herself in that she had to be self-consciously feminine and fully conscious of when she was expected to conduct herself more decorously. The greatest contribution of the College Girl discourse to the annuals was a validation of the life of the female student as an important period in itself, and as "normal" as it was for her brothers.

That these three discourses were able to coexist harmoniously points to the underlying similarity of their equal emphasis on self-discipline, but also to the HSC's willingness to tolerate a collection of discourses within its school and college. A variety of feminine identities was available to the young women at the HSC, and significantly both teachers and girls, old and young women alike, actively participated in defining, maintaining, espousing, and subverting these discourses. In this way, these girls can be seen as active agents of change rather than passive victims of social pressure.

NOTES

Portions of this chapter have been published in "From New Women to College Girls at the Huguenot Seminary and College, 1895–1910," *Historia* 51, no. 1 (May 2006): 1–27. They reappear here with the kind permission of the editors of *Historia*. Grateful thanks to Albert Grundlingh, Sandra Swart, and the editors for sources and advice.

1. The quotation in the title is from Frieda Riebeseel, "Junior Aspirations," in *Huguenot Seminary Annual* (1901), 40.

2. A. M. Grundlingh, "Prelude to the Anglo-Boer War, 1881–1899," in *An Illustrated History of South Africa*, ed. Trewhella Cameron and S. B. Spies (Johannesburg: Jonathan Ball, 1986), 191–192; Vivian Bickford-Smith, Elizabeth van Heyningen, and Nigel Worden, *Cape Town in the Twentieth Century* (Cape Town: David Philip, 1999), 24–25.

3. S. B. Spies, "Reconstruction and Unification, 1902–1910," in *Illustrated History of South Africa*, 219–222; Cherryl Walker, "The Women's Suffrage Movement: The Politics of Gender, Race and Class," in *Women and Gender in Southern Africa to 1945*, ed. Cherryl Walker (Cape Town: David Philip, 1990), 321–322.

4. Cherryl Walker, *The Women's Suffrage Movement in South Africa* (Cape Town: Centre for African Studies, 1979), 21–25.

5. Bickford-Smith, van Heyningen, and Worden, *Cape Town in the Twentieth Century*, 32.

6. Walker, *Women's Suffrage Movement in South Africa*, 19–21.

7. Elaine Showalter, *Sexual Anarchy* (London: Bloomsbury, 1991), 3–5.

8. Andrew Murray to the Principal of the Mount Holyoke Seminary, December 2, 1872, Wellington, K-Div 1103, private collection of Dr. Andrew Murray, Dutch Reformed Church Archive, Stellenbosch.

9. A. P. Ferguson, "First Impressions," *Huguenot* (1908): 7.

10. Petronella van Heerden, *Kerssnuitsels* (Cape Town: Tafelberg, 1963), 117.

11. Sophie le Roux, "Why Should Girls Go to College?" *Huguenot* (1905): 37.

12. P. J. Pienaar, *Ella Neethling*, 2d ed. (Paarl: Paarl Drukpers Maatskappy, [1927] 1928), 20; and Abbie Ferguson to Maggie Allen, Wellington, May 6 and June 29, 1884, K-Div 616, Huguenot Seminary Collection, Dutch Reformed Church Archive, Stellenbosch (hereafter HSC, DRCA).

13. Bronwyn Davies, Suzy Dormer, Sue Gannon, Cath Laws, Sharn Rocco, Hillevi Lenz Taguchi, and Helen McCann, "Becoming Schoolgirls," *Gender and Education* 13, no. 2 (2001): 170–174.

14. R. W. Connell, *Masculinities* (Cambridge: Polity Press, 1995), 76–78, 82–83.

15. R. W. Connell, *Gender and Power* (Stanford: Stanford University Press, 1987), 177–178; Connell, *Masculinities*, 238–239.

16. Anna Bliss to E. L. Bliss, Wellington, August 15, 1875, K-Div 606, HSC, DRCA. Good Hope Guild, *Annual Report* (Cape Town: Van de Sandt de Villiers, 1897), 11–13, 18; Good Hope Guild, *Annual Report* (Cape Town: Van de Sandt de Villiers, 1898), 5–7.

17. Good Hope Guild, *Annual Report* (1897), 1–6, 13. "College Life," in Good Hope Guild, *Annual Report* (1898), 11.

18. Anna Bliss, "Educational Growth," in *Huguenot Seminary Annual* (1898), 20–21.

19. M. Emma Macintosh, "Puddings, Politics, and Poetry," in *Huguenot Seminary Annual* (1898), 54, 53.

20. "Catalogue of the Boarders of the Huguenot Seminary, Wellington," in *Huguenot Seminary Annual* (1898), 59–89.

21. Anna Bliss, "Growth," in *Huguenot Annual* (1902), 7.

22. Geo. P. Ferguson, *The Builders of Huguenot* (Cape Town: Maskew Miller, 1927), 106–107; Ernst G. Malherbe, *Education in South Africa (1652–1922)* (Cape Town: Juta, 1925), 139–147;

James C. Albisetti, "The Feminisation of Teaching in the Nineteenth Century," *History of Education* 22, no. 3 (1993): 256–257.

23. *Calendar of the Huguenot College and Seminary, 1904–1905*, 47, 85.

24. Abbie Ferguson to Maggie Allen, Wellington, March 21, 1899, K-Div 615, HSC, DRCA.

25. A. P. Ferguson, "Address Given on Founder's Day, April 30, 1904," in *Huguenot Annual* (1904), 6. Abbie Ferguson to Maggie Allen, Wellington, April 18, 1899, K-Div 615, HSC, DRCA.

26. Sue Leiter, as quoted in Dana L. Robert, "Mount Holyoke Women and the Dutch Reformed Missionary Movement, 1874–1904," *Missionalia* 21, no. 2 (August 1993): 122.

27. *Calendar of the Huguenot College and Seminary, 1904–1905*, 47.

28. E. M. Clark, "Abstract of a Paper on the Higher Education of Women in South Africa," in *Papers on Cape Education*, ed. W.E.C. Clarke (Cape Town: Juta, 1905), 18–29.

29. K. Joubert, "Student Life at Wellington," in *Huguenot Seminary Annual* (1901), 18–20.

30. Jessie Deas, "Expectations," in *Huguenot Annual* (1904), 3.

31. Carroll Smith-Rosenberg, *Disorderly Conduct* (New York: Oxford University Press, 1985), 182–184; and Lynn D. Gordon, "The Gibson Girl Goes to College," *American Quarterly* 37, no. 2 (1987): 213–215.

32. Sara Delamont, "The Contradictions in Ladies' Education," in *The Nineteenth-Century Woman*, ed. Sara Delamont and Lorna Duffin (London: Croom Helm, 1978), 144–151; Elizabeth Edwards, "Educational Institutions or Extended Families?" in *Equality and Inequality in Education Policy*, ed. Liz Dawtrey, Janet Holland, and Merril Hammer (Clevedon, UK: Multilingual Matters, 1995), 94–98.

33. Abbie Ferguson to Maggie Allen, Wellington, February 13 1874, and November 11, 1884, K-Div 615, HSC, DRCA.

34. Florence Lawton, "Our Seminary Athletics," in *Huguenot Seminary Annual* (1897), 26–27.

35. Grateful thanks to Sarah Carter for drawing my attention to the phenomenon of the College Girl.

36. M. E. Ferguson, "Our Place as Teachers," in *Huguenot Seminary Annual* (1895), 30–31.

37. Gordon, "Gibson Girl Goes to College," 211, 215.

38. Ibid., 215–219.

39. Clark, "Abstract of a Paper," 20; Delamont, "Contradictions in Ladies' Education," 156–160; Edwards, "Educational Institutions," 94–97; and Helen Lefkowitz Horowitz, *Campus Life* (New York: Alfred A. Knopf, 1987), 4–11.

40. Clark, "Abstract of a Paper," 20.

41. "The Day's Journal," in *The Huguenot* (1909), 13.

42. Mattie Muller and Maria Anderson, "A Little Nonsense Now and Then," in *The Huguenot* (1906), 53; J. Retief, "College Home Life," in *Huguenot Annual* (1902), 34–35; and Ethel Doidge, ed., "Phases of Student Life," in *Huguenot Annual* (1904), 21–22.

43. A.W.K. "My College Girl," in *Huguenot Seminary Annual* (1896), 5.

13 Stolen Girlhood

AUSTRALIA'S ASSIMILATION POLICIES AND ABORIGINAL GIRLS

CHRISTINE CHEATER

In Darlene Johnson's short film *Two Bob Mermaid*,[1] an Australian Aboriginal mother peers through a wire fence watching her daughter, the two-bob mermaid, as she swims in the whites-only pool in Moree in northern New South Wales. The two-bob mermaid is pale skinned: she can pass as a white girl. As she leaves the pool with her white friends, a group of Aboriginal girls call out "Tidda" (or sister), a reminder of her hidden identity.[2] Like most of the creative works produced by Australia's Aboriginal people, *Two Bob Mermaid* is semiautobiographical. The Aboriginal mother is Darlene Johnson's grandmother, and the girl who passes for white is her mother. The film is a statement about the impact of racism on the lives of the women in her family. Swimming in the whites-only pool was an act of defiance, a brief chance to experience the privileges of a white girl that ended when the New South Wales Aboriginal Protection Board removed Johnson's mother from her family and sent her to live in a girls' home. Johnson suffered a similar fate, as did many Aboriginal girls. Some families suffered through three or four generations of child removal by the various Australian states.

This treatment resulted from the girls' standing as young members of a colonized people. From the first years of British colonization, Aboriginal Australians were viewed as an impediment to the successful settlement of the country and, after 1901, as a stain on Australia's projected image as a white nation.[3] According to historian Russell McGregor, solutions to what was termed the "Aboriginal problem" ranged from violence, to protection, to assimilation.[4] Aboriginal children became the focus of Australia's assimilation policies, because British officials thought that the way to break Australian Aboriginal culture was to break the link between parent and child. As other authors in this volume, especially Nancy Stockdale and Corrie Decker, have shown, this attitude influenced the treatment of indigenous children in many British dominions and became the guiding principal of assimilation policies in all the Australian states until the 1960s.[5] State governments defined Aboriginality according to physical appearance and lifestyle. Any person who looked Aboriginal, who lived in an Aboriginal community, or who socialized with other Aboriginal people required assimilation into mainstream society. Authorities thought that the fastest way to achieve this end was to remove children, especially female children of mixed descent, from their families.

Across Australia, authorities singled out children like Darlene Johnson and her mother because they could pass for white but continued to identify and socialize with other members of Moree's Aboriginal community. By removing these children from their families, authorities hoped to break their links with Aboriginal communities and thereby facilitate their absorption into white society. Similar practices occurred in other settler states, such as the Native boarding systems in North America, but in Australian states they were taken to extremes. In one of the first studies of the impact of assimilation policies on Aboriginal families, historian Peter Read called children who were removed from their families and placed in institutional or foster care "the stolen generations."[6] He found that even children who were not taken lived with the constant threat of permanent separation from their parents or of losing a sibling.

Since Read's study, the impact of child removal has become a dominant theme both in Australian Aboriginal studies and in the history of Australian childhood. In 1994, a nationwide judicial inquiry on "the stolen generations" estimated that around 20 percent of Australia's Aboriginal children were removed from their families and recommended the gathering of oral histories from the people involved.[7] The result was an oral history collection of 340 interviews conducted with removed children, their families, welfare workers, and policy makers.[8] These interviews reveal that although each Australian state developed separate assimilation policies, these policies and their impact on the lives of Aboriginal children followed similar trajectories.[9]

In this chapter I draw on these oral histories, along with the memoirs of four Aboriginal women, to reveal the experiences of girls trapped by the assimilation process. According to historian Heather Goodall, the majority of Aboriginal children removed from their families before the 1950s were girls.[10] Although Goodall based her observations on data from New South Wales, similar trends occurred in the other Australia states. To explain why girls bore the brunt of the assimilation polices, I first analyze the historical context in which these policies were developed between 1890 and 1950, and argue that anxiety about the girls' sexual behavior and demands for cheap domestic servants caused authorities to remove girls in higher numbers than boys. Second, I examine policy implementation and its impact on the lives of Aboriginal girls. Although removal disrupted girls' childhoods and their emotional well-being, they found ways to resist, forming bonds with one another and taking advantage of opportunities to be themselves.

Australian Protection and Assimilation Policies

The Australian states developed separate Aboriginal welfare policies, but they copied each other's legislation and were imbued with similar ideologies. The philosophical underpinning of their policies was inherited from their British founders, who thought that civilizing or Christianizing Australia's Aboriginal people would lift them from their savage state, teach them the virtue and advantages of good work habits, and eventually turn them into useful members of colonial society. The training of children featured strongly in their thinking in that both Christian and enlightenment philosophies viewed children as more malleable than adults and therefore more easily civilized. Settlers countered these views by observing that Aboriginal children who had been taken in by white families threw off their clothes and reverted to savagery when they rejoined their communities. High mortality rates among Aboriginal communities in contact with white society further fueled the settlers' belief that that the Aborigines were members of a primitive race heading toward extinction and that attempts to assimilate them were futile.[11]

Australian state governments aligned Aboriginal communities with other groups of people who required constant supervision, such as criminals, the diseased, the disabled, and the insane. They appointed Aboriginal Protection Officers who acted in loco parentis for Aboriginal people and had the power to remove any Aboriginal child deemed in physical or "moral" danger, the blanket excuse used when taking children from their families.[12] Under the guise of protecting Aboriginal people from the vices of white society and their own inadequacies, protection officers confined Aboriginal people to camps on the edges of country towns or placed them on church- or state-run reserves. Most of these areas were controlled by a superintendent, who drew up arbitrary rules of behavior, enforced standards of cleanliness, issued rations, decided when medical help was needed, and regulated movement in and out of the missions.[13]

In the 1890s, anthropologists noted that although the numbers of so-called full-blood Aborigines were declining, the numbers of "half-castes" were increasing.[14] At the same time, state governments became concerned that the birth rate was declining among white middle-class women, leading to white fears that Australia was in danger of becoming a nation of the "feebleminded." Included among the feebleminded were the rising numbers of "half-caste," "quadroon," "octoroon," or "yellow" children in rural areas. Supposedly the small number of white women in remote rural towns, the large number of lonely men, and sexually promiscuous Aboriginal women caused this problem.[15] In response, authorities designed policies to curtail miscegenation by controlling the movement of Aboriginal women. Women who found work in white communities needed papers to leave the mission and had to ask permission if they wanted to return to visit their families. Aboriginal women who remained on the mission lived under the constant threat of family dislocation, a threat that was used to control dissent.[16] The ultimate threat was the removal of children, who were then either placed in the mission's dormitory or sent to children's institutions or foster homes.

Initially authorities modeled the institutionalization of Aboriginal children on North American and Canadian Native American assimilation schools, but over time the permanent separation of children from their families became common practice. To make escape difficult, children were sent to homes on the other side of the state. Their names were changed, they were told their parents did not want them, and they were punished if they talked about their homes or spoke their native tongue. Siblings were separated according to age and gender, or according to the discretion of protection officers. Parents' attempts to trace their children were thwarted, and those who persisted were branded as troublemakers and subject to separation from their spouses, imprisonment, or exile to another mission.

Authorities justified these actions on the grounds that Aboriginal parents were unable to provide a moral upbringing for the children or to care for them financially, but in truth they were concerned about solving the "half-caste" problem. In addition to controlling miscegenation, authorities wanted to ensure that "half-castes" did not become a drain on state finances. Therefore, "half-caste" children had to be trained to be productive members of society, and the easiest way to achieve this goal was to place children in institutions where they could learn a trade. Most commentators agreed that it would be easy to assimilate children of mixed descent into the lower levels of white society. Because history had shown that Aboriginal children reverted to traditional behaviors if returned to their parents, removal would be permanent.

A two-tiered welfare system emerged—one level promoted the protection of "full-bloods," and the other level controlled the assimilation of "half-castes." Such distinctions, however, were arbitrary, based on perceived levels of acculturation as defined by white authorities. Aboriginal people who lived in remote northern communities and had little contact with white people were "full-bloods" in need of protection, whereas Aboriginal people who lived in southern regions, near towns, or who had regular contact with white people were "half-castes" in need of assimilation.

Protecting Aboriginal Girls

Child removal policies targeted girls in higher numbers than boys for various interrelated reasons, namely, the girls' sexual vulnerability, the authorities' desire to whiten the Aboriginal population through appropriate marriages, and an ongoing demand for cheap domestic servants. Generally girls were perceived to be in greater moral danger than boys. Until the early twentieth century, white men outnumbered white women in Australia's frontier settlements by as many as ten to one, and white men in these settlements often kidnapped or formed liaisons with Aboriginal girls.[17] Because many white men were of the opinion that Aboriginal women peaked, in looks and sexual maturity, around the age of eighteen, girls seized for this purpose were often between twelve and eighteen years of age, with some as young as nine. Attempts to ban cross-racial liaisons proved ineffectual. Often stockmen disguised the girls in men's clothing and passed them off as "drover's boys," making it easy for authorities to ignore the situation. In remote areas, police officers were usually single men who frequently used their position to coerce sexual favors. If a situation did gain public attention, district magistrates only reluctantly prosecuted offenders. In response, official inquiries into the problem urged the removal of young Aboriginal women and girls from the communities.[18]

Taking on the role of the girls' protectors, the states removed girls to remote mission stations or institutions where they could be protected while learning a useful trade. In his 1899 annual report, Walter Roth, protector of Aborigines in north Queensland, noted that girls were "tampered with by unscrupulous whites" and thus needed to be "protected by the missionaries, and, through them, by the State. [Otherwise] they are sent back to their camps as bad girls and left there to ultimate disease and ruin."[19] In 1902, Roth reinforced his views, stating that half-caste girls living in native camps on cattle stations should be removed to mission stations or reformatories, and on no account should girls be sent to male-only residences because such placements offered no protection from white bosses.[20]

Although government officials promoted the notion that girls needed to be protected from the corrupting influence of unscrupulous white men, the settlers claimed that girls welcomed their attention. One cattleman complained that the girls' presence made it impossible to hire young white men, as the girls soon "dragged them down to their level."[21] White women echoed these concerns. According to historian Ann McGrath, "White women were shocked by the black woman's more open approach to sex and felt threatened by white men's interests."[22] They perceived adolescent girls as acting in a flirtatious and overtly sexual manner and blamed the girls' parents for encouraging them. Such feelings were particularly evident among the white women who moved onto remote pastoral stations and faced the possibility that their husbands had formed relationships with adolescent girls and that some of the children on the station might be his.

As a result, settlers demanded that Aboriginal girls be removed to institutions where they could be socialized and taught virtuous behavior. Meanwhile authorities, worried that sexual promiscuity would increase the number of half-castes in rural regions, supported policies that explicitly aimed to control the sexual activity of fertile Aboriginal women by removing the girls from their families before they reached puberty. Goodall estimates that between 1912 and 1921, 81 percent of child removals in New South Wales were girls removed for this reason.[23] These girls were placed in single-sex institutions where they were cut off from all contact with parents and communities while being trained to work as domestic servants. Through these means, authorities hoped to socialize the girls into becoming chaste, pliable women who conformed to Christian ideals of womanhood and who would pass these values on to the next generation.

The less-populated northern states expressed similar concerns. From the 1930s, assimilation policies in Queensland, the Northern Territory, and Western Australia revolved around the removal of half-caste children (mainly girls) from their families. Through an ironic twist of reasoning and one that reveals their eugenic ambitions, authorities here encouraged institutionalized girls to marry either light-skinned half-caste men or lower-class white men. Marriage to lower-class white men alleviated the shortage of single white women in rural areas and provided a morally sanctioned outlet for the men's natural urges. Marriage to light-skinned half-castes, if continued across a number of generations, would gradually whiten the Aboriginal population and "breed out the colour."[24]

Historian Russell McGregor has labeled these tactics "Civilisation by Blood."[25] They were designed to transform Australia into a white nation through the gradual bleaching of the Aboriginal population.[26] The control of Aboriginal women and girls was central to this process. Beginning in the 1930s, no Aboriginal women could marry without the permission of Aboriginal protectors or mission superintendents who vetted their choice of husband. Although whites had blamed Aboriginal women for the rise in the number of half-castes, they also believed that young girls could be trained to control their sexuality and develop the habits of respectable women if they were isolated from the corrupting influences of their families.

In a debate on the issue in 1936, a Western Australia member of Parliament summed up popular opinion on the treatment of half-caste children and the reasons why it was necessary to remove girls from their families:

> We contaminated their blood and there is an obligation on us to see that the half-castes, at least, have an opportunity to earn a living, I refer particularly to the girls. . . . I understand that up to the age of eight, nine or ten, half-caste-children are capable of learning well at school. From then on to the age of puberty—and that is the dangerous time—they need to be taught other things, most important matters being . . . sex questions and cleanliness. They should be given a reasonable education and trained to take their place as domestics in the homes of white people.

Their removal to foster homes or institutions was necessary because "the native girl is a child of nature, and her character is not sufficiently strong to withstand the urge of nature."[27]

The idea that half-caste girls should be trained as domestic servants was another underlying reason why girls were removed in larger numbers than boys. As Australia industrialized, white working-class women moved out of low paid domestic service and into the factories, leaving white middle-class women struggling to find suitable domestic servants. Women living on pastoral stations in rural areas felt the shortages most. They not only were responsible for running the household but also were expected to help manage the property. Moreover, medical experts warned that in the heat of the tropics, too much heavy work would undermine a white woman's health and fertility. In these regions, middle-class white women took in Aboriginal girls to help with domestic or farm chores, accepting that it was their duty to train the girls to be good housekeepers and to control their sexual behavior. Their motivations were also self-serving. They needed domestic servants and feared that, if left unsupervised, the Aboriginal girls, with their supposed loose morals, would attract the men of the household.

In southern regions, Aboriginal Protection Boards used the shortage of domestic servants to secure employment for Aboriginal girls in controlled, low-paid positions. The boards viewed domestic service as good training in housekeeping and as an efficient means of injecting white values into Aboriginal communities. For instance, the New South Wales Protection Board expressed the hope that "having been removed from the environment of camp life at a fairly early age, trained and placed in first class private homes, the result must be that the standards of life of this younger generation will be superior to those of their parents, thus paving the way for the general absorption of these people into the general population."[28] Consequently the boards placed institutionalized girls in domestic service during their adolescent years.

Girls bound into this form of indentured labor were usually between fourteen and twenty-one years old. Authorities viewed adolescent Aboriginal girls as semi-mature adults. They were sexually mature and capable of adult work, but because of their perceived childlike attributes they had to be guided into suitable work. Domestic service, under the supervision of good housewives, seemed an ideal solution. It trained the girls in skills suited to their level of intelligence while alleviating the ongoing shortage of white women willing to work as domestic servants.[29] The Protection Boards relied on the housewives to protect the girls, but in many instances the boards were returning the girls to the same "moral dangers" used to justify their removal from their communities.

The boards did little to protect the girls from the unwanted attentions of male members of the household. Instead, board members asserted that respectable middle-class white men would not be attracted to Aboriginal girls without provocation. If the girls complained, they were called liars and moved to another position. The boards attributed any pregnancy to the low moral character of the girl. Thus pregnant girls, some as young as fourteen, were returned to an institution or placed in a reformatory. When their babies reached the age of two or three, the girls were sent to another position while the babies remained in the institution, thereby perpetuating the next generation of child removal.

Assimilating Aboriginal Girls

Once caught in the assimilation system, a girl suffered psychological distress and disruption of her childhood. Particularly onerous were the numerous separations that the assimilation system inflicted. The first separation occurred when a girl was taken from her parents and placed in an institutional home or in the mission dormitory. She next faced a series of separations as she matured and progressed through age-segregated dormitories until she was old enough to be placed in domestic service. Once in service she could be moved from position to position until she reached the age of twenty-one. At twenty-one, training ended and authorities expected the woman to remain in domestic service until she married. After marriage, a woman could either move onto a mission to raise her children or apply for an exemption on the grounds that she and her husband were capable of earning a living in white society.

Within institutions and missions, girls suffered the continual turn over of staff. Sue Gordon, who in the 1940s, at the age of four, was placed in Sister Kate's Home for Nearly White Children in Perth, remembers how caregivers "flowed in and out of our lives . . . the kids . . . watched house mothers leave on a regular basis, and we were the permanent fixtures."[30] According to Margaret Tucker, who in the 1910s was removed to Cootamundra Aboriginal Girls Home in central New South Wales at the age of thirteen, the girls' ability to cope with the lack of permanent ties and affection depended on their character, but mostly, she recalled, "we got used to accepting our fate."[31] The fatalism of this comment underscores the emotional and psychological distress the system inflicted on these girls.

Under usual conditions, Aboriginal girls learned from their mothers, grandmothers, and aunts. They played with sisters and cousins, and throughout their lives networks of women and girls of all ages supported them. The constant separations, however, limited the girls' abilities to form emotional attachments and denied them the normal friendships and learning activities of girlhood. When asked to recall their lives in the institutions, many women talked about loss of family and girlhood. Many commented that they had no mothers or normal girlhood memories. They felt they had been taught how to work but not how to live. They could clean a house but not raise a child. Most knew nothing about boys or sex until they left the mission. They had not been given the chance to make personal choices about what to wear, what to eat, or how to spend their time. They missed the endless social interactions that informed these mundane decisions and lacked skills that girls naturally developed through socialization with their mothers, other women, older girls, and their peers.

Because she was in her teens when she was taken from her family, Margaret Tucker remembered her Aboriginal name (Lilardia), her people (Wirrardjerie), her country, and her life before she was taken.[32] Her father was an itinerant sheep shearer who was away for long periods of time. Her mother worked as a domestic servant. Because work was scarce, the family moved regularly between Aboriginal settlements, and occasionally Margaret and her three sisters were left in the care of members of their extended family while their mother worked in a nearby town or on a farm. They lived in tin shacks with dirt floors in camps comprising four or five families who supplemented their meager wages by hunting and gathering. In these camps, women taught their children how to live off the land, how to fish, which roots and leaves to gather, where to find duck eggs and honey, how to cook directly on an open fire, and which berries could be used as medicine.

Margaret's grandparents told her stories about aunts, uncles, and cousins as well as stories from the Dreamtime, a term referring to the myths and traditional stories of Australia's Aboriginal people. She felt that "in spite of our walkabout existences, and often hard times, those days were the happiest of my life."[33] Her semi-traditional upbringing was typical of that of Aboriginal girls, who learned by watching and doing and whose maturation into womanhood was gradual and based on physical development. Other girls who were removed after the age of five also remembered living in tin shacks; having lots of aunts, uncles, and cousins; gathering bush tucker; hearing stories told by their grandparents; singing around the campfire; and enjoying a wonderful sense of freedom.

Even as girls enjoyed traditional childhoods, the threat of removal clouded their existence. Margaret's family was wary of the police, and the girls were taught to make themselves scare if any were seen near the camp. As arbitrary child removals became more common, Aboriginal communities organized signaling systems that warned of the approach of police or welfare officers. Children were taught to hide if they saw a black car, their usual means of transport, and in the north, where light-skinned children were routinely removed, mothers darkened the children's skin with charcoal. Some parents tried to turn these stratagems into games, but the children soon realized the consequences of being caught. Older girls matured quickly and took on the responsibility of organizing lookouts and hiding younger children from police or welfare officers. These girls spent their childhood in a state of constant vigilance, their play tempered by a wariness of strangers, responsibility for the safety of younger playmates, and constant fear that they or their siblings would be taken.

When Margaret and her sisters turned five, their parents sent them to the closest mission school. They were soon taken. The girls were given no warning and only got to say good-bye because of the delaying tactics of their teacher, who sent a message to their mother that the police had arrived to take her girls to Cootamundra Aboriginal Girls Home. Margaret recalled that her mother followed them to the police station "thinking she could beg once more for us. . . . My last memory of her for many years was her waving pathetically, as we waved back and called out good-bye to her."[34] Margaret considered herself lucky. Usually children had no opportunity to say good-bye to their parents.

Welfare officers preferred to take the children from schools or during their walk home, and their parents only later learned their fate. Some officers acted out of callous indifference to the feelings of Aboriginal families, but some found the act of removing children distressing. They wanted to avoid scenes of wailing women and children or confrontations like the one witnessed by Isobel Edwards when a welfare inspector came to take her from her home: "Donaldson came to our home and he asked mum if she had the children ready, and she said 'No, and you're not taking them.' Then dad stepped out from the bedroom door with a double-barrelled shotgun he had and he said 'You lay your hands on my kids Donaldson and you'll get this.' . . . when old dad stepped towards him old Donaldson went for his life."[35] Isobel was allowed to stay with her family, but usually parents accepted the inevitable, and the girls were told that they were going on a holiday. Oral histories taken as a result of the 1994 national inquiry revealed that parents acquiesced for a number of reasons. Some parents wanted to spare their children the trauma of their grief and humiliation. Some hoped to control where the children were sent and to maintain contact with them. Some bargained with welfare officers, offering older or light-skinned children in the hope of keeping one or two children at home.

After they were in the system, children were separated from their siblings according to gender and age.[36] This practice was carried out to suit the needs of the institutions, which received inadequate funding from the government. Most institutions grew their own food, and all relied on the children to clean the buildings. The children were grouped and housed according to the tasks they could perform. An increased workload accompanied each graduated move through the dormitories. The little girls were expected to strip and make their beds, clean the dormitory, scrub floors, feed the chickens, and help with the cooking and washing. Older girls carried wood and water for washing, bathed the younger girls, served the food, mended clothes, and worked in the laundry, dairy, or gardens after school. Most girls did not mind these tasks because they relieved the boredom of the strict routine: rise, wash, strip and make beds, eat breakfast, wash up, walk to school, sit for lessons, walk back, work, bathe, eat dinner, do homework, say prayers, and go to bed.

Weekends broke the monotony. Because the missions and institutions were chronically understaffed, caregivers used the weekends to visit friends and relatives or to pursue personal interests. After supervising Sunday services and assigning a few chores, the staff let the girls pursue their own interests. The weekends became prized times when the girls recaptured their girlhood and played in the bush as they had at home. They spent these precious days walking, climbing trees, or swimming. Girls who remembered traditional food-gathering skills taught the others how to eat bush tucker.

Weekends became the time when the girls forged friendships. During the week, daily routines and barracks-like accommodations limited their ability to form or maintain personal attachments. Ruth Hegarty was placed in a dormitory after her parents were forced to move to Queensland's Cherbourg mission during the Great Depression. Because Ruth was under five, she and her mother were separated from her father and brothers and placed in the nursery. She stayed with her mother until she started school and then moved into the little girls' dormitory, which was separated from the nursery by a lattice. Ruth was only allowed to talk to her mother with permission, and opportunities to see her mother were limited. Ruth had her own routines, and her mother was expected to work, first in the sewing room and later as a domestic outside the mission. Her mother's wages paid for Ruth's upkeep. Ruth found that as she grew up, she grew away from her mother and became "more dependent upon those girls I shared my life with in the dormitory."[37]

Even though girls were subject to continuous separations as they aged, many found themselves moving through the system with a core group of friends who became surrogate sisters. On cold nights they piled into the same bed to keep each other warm, they told each other stories, looked after new girls in the dormitory, played together, formed gangs, squabbled, and teased one another. As Ruth stated, "Our lives were governed by the same polices and what happened to one, happened to all of us. No one was treated as special or given privileges. We were treated identically, dressed identically, our hair cut identically. Our clothes and bald head were a give away. We were dormitory girls."[38] Dormitory friendships were particularly important for girls who were placed in institutions as babies or at an early age. They became sisters in a system in which family relationships were ignored. Even after they had left the institution, the girls attempted to maintain these friendships. Dormitory sisters often formed support networks that operated like extended families. These networks were particularly important for the girls who could not reestablish traditional family ties.

For Glenyse Ward, who as an infant was placed in a Catholic mission in Western Australia in the 1950s, her dormitory friends were her only family. At the age of five she moved from an infants' home in the city to a rural mission. On arrival she was given over to the care of a big girl who "soaked my dress with tears and squeezed me nearly to death. Then the big girl knelt down with me so that the smaller girl who had been pushing and shoving . . . could give me a big slopping kiss on the cheek. Little did I know that the big girl who was crying and the little girl who kissed me were my natural sisters. They were Nita and Sally." Two years later Nita, then fourteen, became a working girl and was sent to work for a white family. Sally, who was closer to Glenyse's age, remained in the same dormitory for a number of years, becoming a close friend, but no closer than five other girls who moved through the system with them. By the time she was ten, Glenyse thought of the mission as home and the caregivers as her parents. When a group of girls ran away, she decided to stay because "I felt that I was in my home already." When told by one of the other girls that the mission was not her home and asked where her mother was, Glenyse replied that the caregiver, who "wakes me up every morning," was her mother.[39]

Friendships developed away from the watchful eyes of the caregivers. On the weekends and after lights out, the girls were free to be children. They could joke, tell stories, and speak their own language. All institutions had a ghost that older girls invented to frighten younger girls and became the topic of many stories. In addition, each group of friends had a secret garden, a special place where they acted out their fantasies. For Ruth and her friends it was the duck pond, where the girls played at being movie stars and smoked cigarettes of rolled leaves or butts filched from the garbage bins.[40] For girls at Cootamundra Aboriginal Girls Home it was a grass field where the girls played at being hairdressers. They pretended that the little hillocks of grass were heads of hair and plaited the tufts into ponytails and decorated them with twigs.[41]

Because staff did not let the girls keep personal possessions, including toys, the girls collected buttons, pins, and bits of broken china and buried them in secret locations around the missions.[42] Girls showed these little collections, known as "secrets," to friends and told stories about how each piece was found. Collections could be built up through gambling with cards made from pages torn out of exercise books. Ruth's friend Pearl had a collection of safety and bobby pins that had been won from the other girls in card games and hopscotch. The extent to which the girls were able to develop friendships or play in this fashion depended on the culture of the institution. At Sister Kate's, for instance, girls were not allowed to sit next to friends or relatives at meal times, and they were punished if they talked or laughed during the meal.

Not being allowed to talk during meals was a common form of discipline and was enforced by most institutions as a means of controlling the girls' behavior. Another method of control was regimentation. Girls who did not finish their tasks satisfactorily or who missed the bell for the start of the next activity were punished. Punishments were varied, arbitrary, and ranged from the withdrawal of privileges to life-threatening beatings. The intensity and type of punishment depended on the personality of the caregiver. A priest at Glenyse's mission struck girls on the head if they failed to complete tasks to his satisfaction. The matron at Ruth's mission withheld privileges and had the girls perform extra duties to win them back. The cook at Margaret's mission flogged the girls with a wooden spoon if they failed to remember her instructions.

Over time, forms of punishment became institutionalized. Oral histories taken for the 1994 national inquiry spoke of ongoing incidents of physical, psychological, and sexual abuse. Interviewees accused some institutions of perpetrating all forms of child abuse. Sandra Hill, who was placed in Sister Kate's Home for Nearly White Children in the 1950s, described the discipline in that institution as "never-ending" abuse. A routine punishment for bed wetters was to stand the offender on a milk crate with the wet sheet draped over her head while the rest of the children filed past on their way to church. Children who refused to eat were force fed, and beatings were common. Sandra recalled, "One day Barbara [my older sister] happened to touch [my little sister] and she screamed and she lifted up her top and she had welts all the way across her back where she had been beaten."[43] Aboriginal Protection Boards made no attempt to control these abuses, but the girls organized small rebellions against the regimentation and abuses suffered.

Mostly these rebellions revolved around stealing food, for the girls were always hungry. They stole eggs from the hen house, fruit from the orchard, and anything they could lay their hands on from the kitchen. More adventurous girls raided nearby farms. The food was either eaten on the spot or hidden in the bush and eaten on the weekends. Sneaking baths after lights out and playing tricks on staff were other forms of rebellion. Staff whose actions were seen to be unjust might find their washing in the dirt or all the fruit in their garden stolen. If the girls were homesick or felt they had been unjustly punished too often, they ran away. Most girls made at least one attempt to escape.

When girls decided to run away it was usually in small groups from the same dormitory, and their destination was often one of the girls' homes. Even if they managed to escape for two or three days, the runaways rarely reached their destination because hunger eventually forced them to beg for food. Farmers who lived near institutions watched for runaways and reported their location to the police. Luckier girls were given a good feed while waiting to be sent back. One successful escape involved an epic 1,600-kilometer journey on foot by three girls—Molly (14), Gracie (11), and Daisy (8)—who absconded from Moore River Mission in 1931. Because they were light-skinned, they had been sent south from their home in the Pilbara region in far north Western Australia. From the start Molly resented being locked in the dormitory at night and was determined to go home.[44]

Unlike other runaways, Molly knew where she was going. Her father had worked on the rabbit-proof fence that ran the length of the state, and Molly planned to head northeast until she found the fence to follow home. She also knew how to live off the land, hide their tracks, and misdirect any white people they met who might report them to the police. Molly and Daisy made it back to their home at Jigalong after nine weeks, but Gracie, who was told her mother was working on a station farther south, was caught and shipped to an institution in Perth. The press reported on the girls' trek, embarrassing the Aboriginal Protection Board. When a local police officer spied Molly living with her relatives, he offered to pick her up, but the chief protector of Aborigines declared that he "did not desire any further action re: half-caste Molly because she has been a costly woman to the Department. Very heavy expenditure was incurred in securing her and when she decamped a lot of undesirable publicity took place."[45]

Although Molly's bid for freedom succeeded, most girls' attempts failed because they simply did not know enough about life outside the institution. The schools that were attached to each institution taught only elementary subjects, namely, reading, writing, and simple arithmetic. Teachers did not teach the girls anything about their own culture, nor did they impart any practical information on how to survive in white society. None of the girls were given the opportunity to extend their education past the age of fourteen. According to Ruth, "We were trained simply to be a source of cheap labour."[46] This training ensured that the girls knew nothing of the world outside the mission.

By the age of fourteen, the age when they were expected to start earning their keep, some girls living in institutions had never visited the nearest town, handled money, or interacted with adults other than their teachers and caregivers. Little wonder they experienced difficulties on being placed in domestic service. There the girls had to overcome not only ignorance but also loneliness and the sheer hard labor of domestic service. They were expected to clean, cook, wash, iron, garden, and chop and carry firewood. If the family had young children, the girls were expected to look after them, and in rural areas many took on extra duties as farm laborers. The amount of work and treatment varied. Although some families treated the girls fairly, others garnished their wages, and all viewed them as cheap labor. Their bedrooms were in out buildings, garden sheds, or above garages, and they were not allowed to eat with the family or use indoor bathrooms. When visitors called, the girls were expected to keep out of sight, or mistresses paraded them as incompetent maids in training.[47]

This kind of treatment shocked many girls, for the institutions had sheltered them from blatant racism.[48] Nor had the institutions taught them how to stand up for themselves. Shy girls harangued for not completing their tasks or for performing unsatisfactorily did not know how to react. They were isolated from the support networks they had developed in the institutions and were forced to cope as best they could. Margaret Tucker's first employer hid her mother's letters and rationed her food to the point where she was starving. She became depressed and attempted suicide by eating rat poison, after which the board moved her to another position. Ruth Hegarty learned to manipulate the system by accumulating numerous complaints about her "bad" attitude and thus spent her teen years being moved from position to position. Glenyse Ward began "playing a dummies life" and took revenge on her employer's uncompromising demands by raiding the refrigerator, using her employer's shower and perfume, and playing the piano when they were out.[49] After two years with the same employer Glenyse ran away and found employment in a country hospital.

Still, most girls stayed with their employers because they had nowhere to go and did not realize that their skills enabled them to earn a living. Margaret also ran away but went back because she felt vulnerable living on her own. Furthermore, her only way of finding her family was through the New South Wales Aboriginal Protection Board. This dependence on the Protection Boards and the girls' ignorance kept them tied to the institutions and helped perpetuate multigenerational child removals. Ruth claimed that although girls had been trained as good domestics, when it came to more serious matters, such as sex education, they had to learn by trial and error. She became a single mother at the age of eighteen: "I was painfully aware that our lives were beginning to mirror those of our mothers. We were still dormitory girls and so were our babies, and it looked as if it was continuing on through our children. The enormous irony for me was that, instead of ever reaching a point in life where I could escape from this system, the cycle had begun again."[50] Determined not to let this happen, Ruth turned to a married friend for help in raising her baby. Although girls like Ruth suffered separation from their families, more resilient girls were able to establish new support networks and, through their friendships, reestablish contact with Aboriginal communities.

Conclusion

The desire of white Australians to build a new Britannia in the Southern Hemisphere inspired Australia's assimilation polices before the 1950s. To achieve the desired end, authorities aimed to replace Aboriginal culture with white Australian working-class culture by breaking the links between generations. In a pattern that was repeated in places such as Palestine and Mombasa, girls became a focus of these policies because of their gender. Authorities believed that the girls, destined to become mothers, could become the conduits through which white values would enter indigenous communities. Girls, moreover, were supposedly easier to train, and half-caste girls in particular offered a medium for "breeding out the colour." Aboriginal girls removed from their families routinely faced control over their sexual knowledge and activities, experiences similar to girls in other modernizing cultures, or countries intent on building a modern nation-state. Welfare officers removed girls from corrupting influences, namely, Aboriginal communities, and placed them in institutions where they were trained as domestic servants, skills that would also make them good home-makers and by extension good citizens.

Consequently, Aboriginal girls lost their childhood and adolescent years in a haze of hard work. Their education was abridged, their contact with friends and family was limited, and the girls were isolated in a hostile environment where few cared about their emotional needs. The girls survived this system through small acts of resistance and the creation of spaces where they could be themselves. Most important, they survived by banding together and remaking families and their culture. Older girls looked after younger girls and taught them remembered traditions. Girls living in the same dormitory became a substitute family. They were sisters. Although many bore the scars of years spent in an uncaring environment, many became community leaders intent on rebuilding the family ties that Australia's assimilation polices were designed to break.

NOTES

1. *Two Bob Mermaid*, video recording, written and directed by Darlene Johnson (Sydney: Australian Film Institute, 1996).

2. I recognize that "aborigine" is a generic description, but capitalized it is a term that is "owned" by Australia's Aboriginal people, and in this chapter I use it to refer to them. I also employ the term "white," which is commonly used to designate Australians of European descent.

3. Upon the federation of Australian states in 1901, Australia's Aboriginal people were excluded from census counts and denied the right to vote.

4. Views on the status and fate of the Australian Aboriginal race varied throughout the eighteenth and nineteenth centuries, but a dominant theme was the need either to protect Aboriginal people from the vices of white society or to assimilate them. See Russell McGregor, *Imagined Destinies: Aboriginal Australians and the Doomed Race Theory, 1880–1936* (Melbourne: Melbourne University Press, 1997).

5. Australian states began abandoning their assimilation policies in the 1960s but continued to remove children in fewer numbers until the 1980s.

6. Peter Read, *The Stolen Generations: The Removal of Aboriginal Children in New South Wales, 1883–1969* (Sydney: Ministry of Aboriginal Affairs, 1983).

7. The report was published as *Bringing Them Home: Report of the National Inquiry into the Separation of Aboriginal and Torres Straight Islander Children from Their Families* (Sydney: Human Rights and Equal Opportunity Commission, 1997).

8. The collection is housed in the National Library of Australia. Excerpts were published in Doreen Mellor and Anna Haebich, eds., *Many Voices: Reflections on Experiences of Indigenous Child Separation* (Canberra: National Library of Australia, 2002).

9. For a comprehensive overview of the various state policies, see Anna Haebich, *Broken Circles: Fragmenting Indigenous Families, 1800–2000* (Fremantle: Fremantle Arts Centre Press, 2000).

10. Heather Goodall, "Saving the Children: Gender and Colonization of Aboriginal Children in New South Wales, 1788–1990," *Aboriginal Law Bulletin* 44 (June 1990): 6–9.

11. It has been estimated that within two to three years of contact with settlers, nearby Aboriginal populations declined by up to 80 percent.

12. Although some removals were triggered by child abuse or starvation, most removals were arbitrary and depended on the whim of missionaries, protection officers, or the police.

13. In New South Wales, the Aboriginal Protection Board appointed the superintendents. In the other states, church mission boards appointed the superintendents, who ran them under the auspices of Aboriginal Protection Boards.

14. Between 1880 and 1900, the percentage of the Aboriginal population known to be of mixed descent rose from 27 percent to 55 percent.

15. The ratio of white men to white women varied over time and from place to place. Generally a ratio of around five to one applied to most regions before the 1890s. In frontier settlements, however, especially mining towns and in tropical regions, this ratio could rise to over ten men for every woman.

16. The methods used to control the movement of Aboriginal people, their living conditions, and their ability to resist white authorities varied over time and from state to state and in some cases from mission to mission.

17. Liaisons ranged from prostitution to long-term de facto relationships.

18. For example, the 1905 Western Australian Royal on the Condition of the Natives and the 1913 South Australian Royal Commission on the Aborigines commented on the vulnerability of Aboriginal girls, the problems of protecting them from sexual exploitation, and their consequent need for institutionalized care.

19. Walter E. Roth, *Northern Protector of Aborigines Annual Report, 1899*, Queensland State Archives, ID 7328, 10.

20. Walter E. Roth, *Northern Protector of Aborigines Annual Report, 1902*, Queensland State Archives, ID 7328.

21. T.G.H. Strelow, Central Australian Field Diary (unpublished), October 26, 1935, South Australian Museum, AA316.

22. Ann McGrath, *Born in the Cattle* (Sydney: Allen and Unwin, 1987), 73.

23. Heather Goodall, "Assimilation Begins in the Home: The State and Aboriginal Women's Work as Mothers in New South Wales, 1900s to 1960s," in "Aboriginal Workers," special issue, *Labour History* 69 (November 1995): 81.

24. Breeding out the color was a policy proposed by Western Australia's chief protector of Aborigines, A. O. Neville, in *Australia's Coloured Minority: Its Place in the Community* (Sydney: Currawong Publishing, 1947).

25. McGregor, *Imagined Destinies*, 142.

26. From the nation's inception, politicians and settlers clung to the notion that only whites should populate Australia. Politicians passed laws, commonly called the White Australia Policy, to prevent Asian immigration, and Aboriginal people did not receive full citizenship until 1967.

27. *Western Australia Parliamentary Debates* (1936), 822, as quoted in Haebich, *Broken Circles*, 278.

28. As quoted in Goodall, "Assimilation Begins in the Home," 83.

29. Studies of domestic labor in Australia have noted that an ongoing concern of middle-class women before the widespread use of domestic appliances was the shortage of suitable maids. Cf. Beverley Kingston, *My Wife, My Daughter, and Poor Maryann* (Melbourne: Nelson, 1975), 29–55.

30. Mellor and Haebich, *Many Voices*, 201.

31. Margaret Tucker, *If Everyone Cared: Autobiography of Margaret Tucker* (Melbourne: Grosvenor Books, 1986), 101.

32. Australian Aboriginal people call tribal areas "country." Margaret's family moved around campsites in Wirrardjerie country, namely, land along the Murray, Murrumbidgee, and Lachlan rivers. This region was one of the few where superintendents did not control the campsites.

33. Tucker, *If Everyone Cared*, 61.

34. Ibid., 93–94.

35. As quoted in Peter Read, *A Rape of the Soul so Profound: The Return of the Stolen Generations* (Sydney: Allen and Unwin, 1999), 32.

36. It was standard practice on mission stations and in institutions to segregate children according to gender and age. See Haebich, *Broken Circles*, 342–348; and Mellor and Haebich, *Many Voices*, 166–207.

37. Ruth Hegarty, *Is That You Ruthie?* (St. Lucia: Queensland University Press, 1999), 51.

38. Ibid., 4.

39. Glenyse Ward, *Unna You Fullas* (Broome: Magabala Books, 1991), 2, 72, 70.

40. Hegarty, *Is That You Ruthie?* 63.

41. Mellor and Haebich, *Many Voices*, 81.

42. Only a few homes provided balls, books, and board games, which were kept under lock and key. Many of the oral histories related how children made their toys from bits of rubbish or natural materials and hid them from the staff. Cf. Mellor and Haebich, *Many Voices*, 172, 187.

43. Ibid., 201, 202.

44. This escape was popularized in *Rabbit Proof Fence*, video recording, directed by Phillip Noyce (Canberra: Ronin Films, 2002).

45. Commissioner of Aboriginal Affairs, as quoted in Doris Pilkington, *Follow the Rabbit Proof Fence* (St. Lucia: Queensland University Press, 2002), 125.

46. Hegarty, *Is That You Ruthie?* 75.

47. Many of the girls' oral histories and memoirs mention feeling isolated and lonely while working as domestic servants, being overwhelmed by the number of duties they were expected to perform, and being ostracized or mistreated by their mistresses. An overview of the problems they faced can be found in Jennifer Sabironi, "I Hate Working for White People," *Hecate* 19, no. 2 (1993): 7–29.

48. Some interviewees claimed that they were so isolated from the realities of life in the outside world that they did not think of themselves as black and were unprepared for the racism they encountered when sent into service. Cf. Mellor and Haebich, *Many Voices*, 181–185.

49. Glenyse Ward, *Wandering Girl* (Broome: Magabala Books, 1987), 131.

50. Hegarty, *Is That You Ruthie?* 126.

14

Fathers, Daughters, and Institutions

COMING OF AGE IN MOMBASA'S COLONIAL SCHOOLS

CORRIE DECKER

> We had a problem in our community . . . Islamic girls were not sent to school.[1]

> Mothers don't have time to check on education. They have time for weddings, but not for helping their children with school.[2]

The two women quoted here, both of whom attended primary school in Mombasa, Kenya, during the British colonial period (1895–1963), criticize mothers for not promoting the education of their daughters. They see marriage as an interruption of the complete education they believe all girls should receive. When they attended school in the 1940s and 1950s, their own mothers and grandmothers argued that schooling got in the way of initiation and marriage, traditional markers of entry into womanhood in Mombasa. Indigenous education was gender-specific; girls learned from older women about womanhood, marriage, and motherhood, while boys learned the work of their fathers. Colonial education was also gender-specific; girls received domestic as well as academic instruction, while boys were taught trades and vocations appropriate for "colonial development." As families were inducted into the Western education system, however, a peculiar gender crossover occurred. In the early colonial period, government and mission schools offered instruction almost exclusively to boys. A generation later (starting in the 1920s), these boys grew into men who demanded schools for their daughters. Fathers and daughters found themselves politically allied in their demands for girls' schools, a movement that ultimately redefined gendered and generational relationships in Mombasa. Amid a culture that expected girls to follow in the domestic footsteps of mothers and grandmothers and against a colonial power reluctant to see the value of educating girls, the combined efforts of fathers and daughters brought about profound changes not only in the culture and structure of childhood, but also in common understandings of the contribution of girls' education to development.

As is evident in Nancy Stockdale's contribution to this volume, discon-nections between the intentions of educators and the goals of parents expose the unsteady ground schoolgirls must navigate. Schoolgirls, as devoted daughters and participants in a foreign cultural system unevenly received by the community, created a space for themselves out of which emerged a new adolescence culture that redefined the transition between girlhood and womanhood. This new culture, related to the "modern girl" trend in 1930s and 1940s East Africa, reflects, in part, changes that Western education brought to the structure of female childhood, mainly an increase in the period between puberty and marriage.[3] The new girl culture was thus based as much on the experience of schooling and career ambitions as it was on sexuality and marriage, and impacted future generations of girls and women. Increased funding for women's teacher-training and nursing after World War II underscores the mounting importance of girls' education to Kenyan colonial policies. The stories of schoolgirls told here reflect these significant moments in the history of girls' education that led to the wide-spread influence of Western education in the postcolonial period.

Colonial Mombasa was a city in transition. The population of coastal Kenya reflected the area's long history of Arab settlement and rule, gradual widespread adoption of Islam, and nineteenth- and twentieth-century arrival of South Asian merchants and laborers and European Christian mis-sionaries and settlers. During the colonial period, an increasing number of Africans from the inland areas flocked to Mombasa in search of wage labor necessary for survival in the new cash economy. In the meantime, wealthy families, most of whom claimed Arab or Indian ancestry, struggled to hold onto their dominance over others of lower economic standing in and around Old Town, Mombasa's ancient trading center. Those looking to move up the social ladder saw colonial schools as an opportunity to get ahead in the post-emancipation colonial economy. Old merchants looked to the schools to reinforce their families' elite position in a time of drastic social, economic, and political change. Although Mombasans of various backgrounds saw Western schools for boys as the means for economic advancement, many worried that sending their daughters to school would unravel the social fabric of their community.[4] On the contrary, however, sending girls to school ultimately reinforced familial relationships, but under new gender configurations.

Colonial schoolgirls went to school at a time when their attendance was still a novelty in Mombasa. Their and their fathers' efforts to enter and keep them in school resulted in shifting ideals around gender and child-hood. Built into the structure and ideology of the Western school was a system of incremental grades, or stages of "progress."[5] The act of learning itself was experienced as a "progressive" act. The passing of each grade theoretically represented both the maturation of the individual and, by default, the new generation of society. According to anthropologist

Kathryn Anderson-Levitt, the period of the 1930s, 1940s, and 1950s—when many Mombasan fathers began sending their daughters to the Western schools—was on the cusp of an important phase in the global diffusion of Western education, when "mass education systems accelerated rapidly" around the world.[6] The first generation of girls to attend school in Mombasa witnessed during their lifetime the gradual acceptance of Western schools in their community. When the girls started school, many parents and elders refused to send their children to the Western institutions, but by the time they had become mothers and grandmothers themselves, Western education was in popular demand.

Education in Africa today, however, is not guaranteed; nor is it always free. As Anderson-Levitt explains, the schoolyard gate in the global North (Europe and America) is designed to keep children *in* school, whereas the schoolyard gate in Africa is meant to keep children *out*. She argues that children in Africa crave education, where it is seen as an attractive but not always available alternative to an economically difficult life, whereas children in the North resent being forced to attend school. As the first generation of Western schoolgirls in Mombasa, women who attended school during the colonial period see themselves as being ahead of the curve.[7] Former schoolgirls such as Fatma, Rose, Lucie, Eunice, Asmah, and others whose stories appear in this chapter considered themselves "modern girls" whose exposure to Western ideals resulted in their induction in an international culture of girlhood and whose education symbolized economic and social progress for Mombasa. With their advancement to each grade, they read their individual maturity as a sign of Mombasa's modernity in a complex colonial world.

Unlike in other parts of colonial Africa, Western education in East Africa did not always uphold patriarchal norms. With regard to the Belgian Congo, women studies professor Gertrude Mianda argues that "the colonial system of education . . . consolidated social-sexual roles on the basis of existing sexual discrimination, by offering women a feeble instruction which confined them to the household and fostered activities presumed to correspond to feminine nature."[8] Although *évolués*, educated elite men, were "modern" in that they encouraged girls to attend Western schools, this education ultimately reinforced overlapping "traditions" of both African and colonial forms of patriarchy.[9] In Kenya, Western education also placed more weight on domestic science than any other aspect of girls' education in order to instill such Western gender norms as a division between the male public sphere and female private sphere, and the creation of the nuclear family. I argue, however, that fathers and daughters in Mombasa did not reify these forms of patriarchy in the same way as those of the évolué families in the Belgian Congo did. Math and geography were Lucie's favorite subjects. Rose had high hopes of going on to nursing school after high school. Fatma, Lucie, Eunice, and Asmah all became schoolteachers with the encouragement of their fathers and uncles.[10] Educated girls in Mombasa worked *with* their male elders in making both career and personal decisions in the face of complex colonial racial politics and community gender ideals. This is not to say that the educated girls completely overturned these gender ideals. The ethics of motherhood and wifehood were central to both colonial schools and traditional systems of socialization. In the case of Mombasa, though, girls' experience of attending Western schools introduced a new path from girlhood to womanhood. Like their female ancestors, schoolgirls in Mombasa grew up to become wives and mothers, but as educational and work opportunities arose before them, the point at which these "girls" became "women" extended into a period of transition no longer defined exclusively by initiation and marriage. Graduation, training, and work added new dimensions to this rite of passage.

Education Policy in Colonial Mombasa

Mombasa had been an important trading port along the East African coast for centuries. Trade in ivory and slaves between the interior and the coast increased dramatically during the nineteenth century. Arab and Swahili merchants were valuable allies to the British in their conquest of the African interior during the period before Britain established the East African Protectorate over the region in 1895. The British abolished slavery in 1907. Former slave owners and traders began to demand that the administration reinforce their economic standing through education and employment. Meanwhile, many newly freed slaves and their descendents either became destitute or remained dependent on their former masters. By this time, Britain had established headquarters for the Kenya colony inland in Nairobi. The Nairobi administration also governed the Coast Protectorate, but the region was less valuable to it than were the upcountry highlands where a number of European farmers had settled.[11] The coast was economically, politically, and religiously marginal to the colonial administration.

Colonial government investments in education were uneven, reflecting both economic constraints and colonial ideologies of race. From its inception in 1911, the Education Department in Kenya was organized along racial lines into European, Indian, Arab, and African divisions, although Arab and African education was sometimes lumped together administratively or fiscally. The department disproportionately invested in European and Indian education than it did in Arab and African education.[12] Although many Arab and African children in the predominantly Muslim Mombasa attended private Qur'an schools, mission schools offered instruction to freed slaves and Christian converts.[13] Some Muslims rejected mission schools, because they feared conversion of their children, and government schools, because the schools directed students and income away from local Qur'an teachers. Others saw the limited opportunities at government schools as the only way to get ahead under the colonial system. According to Sarah Mirza and

Margaret Strobel in *Three Swahili Women: Life Histories from Mombasa, Kenya*, the colonial state in Kenya functioned on a "racial hierarchy" that placed Europeans above Indians, Indians above Arabs, and Arabs above Africans.[14] These identities were constantly in flux during the colonial period, reflecting both the complex history of ethnicity along the coast and the politics of shifting legal delineations between Africans and non-Africans, natives and nonnatives.[15]

In the early 1920s, the Phelps-Stokes Fund, an American organization concerned with education of African Americans and Native Americans, urged colonial educators in Africa to adopt its "adapted" education scheme. "Adapted" education rested on instruction adapted to the student's cultural, moral, and economic environment. Working from the assumption that all Africans were rural villagers, the Phelps-Stokes Commission recommended "simple manual training" in woodworking, shoe mending, tailoring, furniture repair, and other vocational skills for African boys, and, for girls, instruction in cooking, sewing, housekeeping, and other domestic skills. The commissioners strongly encouraged cooperation between missionaries and government.[16] These recommendations provided direction for officials in dealing with African populations at a time of increasing racialization of colonial policy.[17] As a result, the government opened schools for Africans only in the villages. In Mombasa Town, the colonial education department built public schools for Indian and Arab communities, leaving urban African education in the hands of missionaries. Overall, education was a low fiscal priority, and girls' education was even lower on the list.

Government Involvement in Girls' Education

By 1928, the director of education, an advocate of girls' education, assumed that objections from influential Islamic leaders meant that a Western girls' school was only a "remote possibility."[18] Select Mombasans lobbied against such a scheme after a government girls' school opened in Zanzibar in 1927.[19] Among other objections, they opposed teaching girls how to write, fearing this would lead them to write letters to boys.[20] As a result, with the exception of the Government Indian Girls' School and grants for missionary girls' schools, administrators saw little purpose in proceeding with the plan. Throughout the colonial period, a number of men in Mombasa actively pursued Western education for their daughters in spite of protests from family members and procrastination from officials. These fathers and the daughters they educated transformed the way both officials and Mombasan residents viewed female education.

Contrary to colonial belief, coastal communities did not deny women an education. Indigenous educational institutions marking the transition from girlhood to womanhood included domestic training in the home, instruction as part of initiation, and for Muslim girls, Qur'anic education at home or in the *chuo*, or Qur'an school. African education expert Sorobea

Nyachieo Bogonko explains that precolonial forms of African education were designed to teach children about their culture, prepare them for their work as adults, and inculcate a sense of community. Girls also learned domestic tasks by helping their mothers and aunts in the home.[21] Although few girls attended Qur'an schools with boys, many received religious instruction in the home or at private schools.[22] By the end of the nineteenth century, many former slaves and others influenced by Christianity began sending their children to mission schools. The Church Missionary Society's (CMS) Buxton School in Mombasa Town, for example, accepted Muslim and Christian children but instructed few girls before 1940.[23] Many girls also received sexual instruction by a female teacher known as a *somo* or *kungwi* in preparation for marriage.[24] The spread of Western schools in the twentieth century interrupted this direct transition from girlhood to marriage and displaced or altered the other existing forms of girls' education.

Government commitments to girls' education were sporadic and limited during the colonial period. As a result of the Indian community's ability to "agitate," according to Mbarak Ali Hinawy, a government school for Indian girls was established comparatively early, in 1925.[25] Colonial commitments to Arab girls' education came in 1938 when the administration took possession of the Ghazali Muslim School and formed the Arab Girls' School.[26] The Ghazali Muslim School was part of an Islamic modernist movement that promoted the education of girls. As such, it was a sign to government that Arabs were "ready" for the implementation of girls' schools. The Arab Girls' School initially welcomed "Twelve Tribes, Arabs, Swahilis, Bajuni and Asian girls," in part to encourage all Mombasans to educate their daughters.[27] As attendance at the Arab Girls' School increased, however, it became more racially exclusive, increasingly denying "Africans" a place at the school in the 1940s and 1950s.[28]

Even though Africans made up the majority of the population, no government school specifically for African girls existed in Mombasa Town during the colonial period. In 1935, a total of thirty-eight African girls attended government schools in all of Kenya, but none of these were in Mombasa. Mission schools were not much better.[29] Missionaries viewed Islam as an obstacle to their work, so the CMS taught female students primarily at the Freretown school on the mainland. The main school for Africans in Mombasa, the Buxton High School, which opened in 1897, became drastically overcrowded by the 1940s.[30] While CMS schools catered to both Christian and Muslim girls, the few African girls who attended the Star of the Sea school for girls, a Roman Catholic mission school established in 1909, were Christian.[31] The Mvita Primary School, a coeducational, "interdenominational" school which "cater[ed] to Muslim children," was established by a mission in 1953.[32] The missionary dominance of education for Africans, in spite of the reluctance of most Muslims to send their children to Christian schools, continued to characterize government approaches to girls' education throughout the colonial period. Muslim parents who did send their girls to mission schools clearly wanted them to learn something other than what they learned at Qur'an schools and from private instruction. Modernity movements resting on the overlap of Islam, Christianity, and colonialism served as the backdrop against which these decisions were made.[33]

In 1939, the Colonial Office's Advisory Committee for Education in the Colonies (ACEC) took on the issue of women's and girls' education in Africa. With pressure from the ACEC, Kenyan education officials followed suit by the late 1940s. The two main aspects of the ACEC recommendations were emphasis on domestic science instruction and reliance on missionaries to carry out the educational program.[34] In spite of increasing discourse on girls' education, actual plans for Mombasa were slow to emerge. Finally, in 1960, the provincial education officer for the coast urged the director of education to build a government school for African girls in Mombasa. "In view of the fact that there are Girls Schools specifically for Europeans, Asians and Arabs," the officer reasoned, "an African Girls Primary School is long overdue for the Mombasa Area." The biggest problem, according to the officer, was "an extreme shortage of qualified female teachers suitable for employment in Mombasa schools."[35] Meanwhile, from the late 1940s, in the areas just inland of Mombasa, like Wusi and Ribe, mission schools had developed teacher-training programs for young African women.[36] Many of these women eventually migrated to Mombasa to teach. After Kenya gained independence in 1963, the new government embarked on a campaign to train women teachers, including African women.[37]

Stories of Fathers and Daughters

Fathers interested in sending their girls to school faced a number of difficulties, including the racial character of colonial schools, the government's unwillingness to make girls' education a top priority, and in many cases, the disapproval of family and friends. Between the 1920s and the 1960s, both officials and coastal residents became more open to the idea of educating girls regardless of ethnicity or religion. This is not to say that everyone supported this idea by the time of Kenya's independence in 1963, or even today, but that the efforts of fathers and daughters in carving out a new place for girls redesigned female adolescence in East Africa.

One of the first stories of a father's attempt to educate his daughter in Mombasa comes from the life history of Shamsa Muhamad Muhashamy, an Arab woman from Old Town, as recorded by Sarah Mirza and Margaret Strobel. In the late 1920s, Shamsa was among the first girls to attend a Western school in Mombasa. She recalls how her nickname, European Girl, conveyed her unconventional upbringing. Her father sent her to the CMS's Buxton School because the European and Indian schools refused to accept Arabs and Africans, but Shamsa did not stay long at the school. She explains one of the problems: "The teacher at that time was Miss Lloyds [an English lady], but no English was taught. . . . My father was not pleased because even he himself could teach me Swahili at home. After two years he withdrew me from that school. . . . When my father spoke to them and asked them to teach me just a little [English] at a time, they said, 'No, the government doesn't give me permission to teach girls.'" The ability to speak English was an employable skill for boys and the quintessential marker of modernity for both boys and girls in colonial Mombasa. By objecting to English instruction in mission schools, the government maintained the racialized class order and made it harder for Africans to climb the social ladder. In addition to disagreements with the mission staff, Shamsa's father faced opposition from his wife's relatives, who worried that Shamsa would "go and sin, [and] . . . change her religion." Her "father's persistence" was ultimately no match for her grandparents' "hassling." Mirza and Strobel explain that Shamsa had, "by virtue of her class background, education, and experience, a sense of herself and her family as historical actors." As such, she "saw her family's history in terms of progress." Shamsa begins her story by relaying how her father had studied in Egypt for four years, long enough to help her and her "four other brothers progress."[38] Shamsa's memories shed light on a moment in Mombasa's history when colonial subjects co-opted diverse forms of modernity as part of the struggle against colonial subjugation.

Shifting attitudes toward education often surfaced where Islamic modernism and Western modernization overlapped. Many Muslims in Mombasa looked to Egypt and India for models of progress. Islamic modernism, which emerged out of Egypt and India in the latter half of the nineteenth century and spread to East Africa by the 1890s, offered a bridge between Islamic and Western education and a place for girls' schools.[39] Sheikh al-Amin b. Ali Mazrui (1890–1947), a prominent Islamic teacher and scholar from Mombasa, "felt that it was necessary for Muslims to become skilled in Western science and technology in order to progress."[40] He and other Mombasan scholars, influenced by Egyptian modernists such as Qasim Amin, the "pioneer" of Islamic feminism, began to reevaluate the position of women in Islamic society.[41] According to anthropologist Mary Ann Porter, "many Swahili people" were opposed to the education of girls "until the agitation in the 1930s by Sheikh al-Amin who pointed out repeatedly that the Koran indicates that both men and women should be educated." Sheikh al-Amin's encouragement was one of the forces driving Sheik Ghazali to establish the Ghazali Private Muslim School in 1933, which the government took over in 1938. "Although this indigenous attempt at providing a modern education in an Islamic setting lasted only five years," Porter argues, "the Ghazali Muslim school left a very important legacy: all contemporary oral accounts of the beginning of the modern education of Swahili girls . . . begin with Ghazali's *madarasa*."[42] Shamsa's account of her father, like the story of the Ghazali School, pivots on the points of intersection between Islamic modernism and Western modernity. Her father's education in Egypt and his life in early colonial Mombasa allowed him to pass on to his daughter these two ideologies of progress as one.

In 1943, Mahmoud Fadil Albakry, a father in Lamu, about 300 kilometers north of Mombasa, searched for a school for his daughter Fatma. At the age of seven, Fatma went with her brother to Mombasa, where she was to attend the Catholic Star of the Sea School. No girls' school existed in Lamu at that time. In fact, as a result of local opposition from the Qur'an teachers, the only boys' school that had not been shut down operated at night.[43] Fatma enjoyed studying and wanted to stay in Mombasa, but her father withdrew her after the annual holiday, most likely so she could go to Zanzibar to study.[44] Fatma and her two sisters were to begin at the Zanzibar Government Girls' School, where they could stay at the attached Girls' Hostel. Their father readied them, even providing them with new dresses, but when the boat from Zanzibar arrived, it brought with it a note of apology saying the Zanzibar school could not accept the girls. Apparently the problem was the lack of accommodation during school holidays. Fatma's father remained determined in spite of these setbacks. In 1946, he sent his two eldest daughters along with a few of their female cousins and friends—less than ten girls altogether—"without permission" to the boys' night school in Lamu. Fatma claimed that "no one opposed" initially.[45] A few years later, however, when Fatma's younger sister, Jahi, and her niece, Sauda, attended the school, "once a group of Madrassa boys followed them on their way to school, teasing them and it is alleged, throwing stones at them. Next day the girls were escorted by a policeman and there was no more repetition of the problem. The elders were furious and *madras* teachers and managers were warned; so nothing happened to the girls after that."[46] When Fatma began at the school, she immediately advanced to Standard III (third grade) because of her home schooling, and continued through Standard VII (seventh grade) there, the only girl in her cohort.[47] Mahmoud Fadil Albakry continued his campaign in the community. He and fourteen other men wrote to the liwali of Lamu in 1951 requesting that the government set up a school for girls in Lamu.[48] One of the main obstacles was the lack of suitable female teachers. Fatma and her sister would later be chosen to take on that responsibility themselves.

Rose Ali Noormohamed, daughter of an Omani father and Baluchi (Pakistani) mother, also attended the Catholic Star of the Sea School amid much conflict.[49] Just as Shamsa's father faced opposition from his in-laws, Rose's father's main opponent was her maternal grandmother. Rose explains:

> First I started school at Star of the Sea. It was a very good school. I really liked it. But my grandmother started saying "No, it's not a good school." You know, our parents were primitive. They didn't go to school. They didn't understand anything. So they said, "No, that school is not good. Our kids go outside. There is Maria carrying the cross, and this girl is a Muslim

girl. It's not fair." And she started to pump my father, "See, no, that is not a proper school. This and that." And then my father got a headache. He said, "Look, I want my kids to go to school. . . . They have to be educated. . . . See [how] this life is changing now. We are going to [the] '60s and so forth. . . ." And then we went to the Indian school. Mbeheni was an Indian school. They were mixed, Hindus and Muslim girls. So it was better for us to go to school instead of staying home.[50]

Rose's father's determination likely derived from his own education at a mission school in Uganda, where his father took him after leaving Oman. Neither Rose's mother nor her mother's mother received formal education, however. Rose's opinion that this lack of Western education made her female elders "primitive" in comparison with her mission-schooled father is striking in that it suggests Rose had a stronger connection with her father than with family members of her own sex. Ultimately the grandmother's objections subsided when Rose left the mission school for the Indian school, a clear compromise between her Omani father and Baluchi mother. Ironically, it was the "Indianness" she inherited from her mother, who objected to her education, that made it possible for her to continue her studies.

In contrast to Shamsa, Fatma, and Rose, Lucie Machi faced no significant obstacle in attending school. Born in 1950, Lucie grew up in the Taita Hills, inland from Mombasa. Her father was a pastor, a product of the mission school. Not surprisingly, he was "very keen for [her] to go to the missionary schools."[51] Lucie began at a coeducational school and then went on to a girls' boarding high school named after Miss Murray, a CMS missionary heavily engaged in girls' education in the area. Although the CMS Manyimbo School for girls in Mombasa lasted only a few years and the Buxton School had limited female enrolment, CMS's work in the Taita Hills did much to encourage the spread of African girls' education in the 1940s and 1950s.[52] Unlike Rose's family, Lucie's mother and father did not argue about her mission education. Racial and religious restrictions did not come into play for Lucie in the same way they did for Rose, but only because Lucie came from a Christian Taita family living outside of Mombasa's urban center at a time and place in which Christianity and missionary education were widely accepted.

In each of these stories, the fathers wishing to send their girls to school had themselves received some form of Western education as children.[53] As a result, they had a unique idea about the structure and purpose of childhood and its accompanying gendered expectations. The curriculum of Western schools was built on "a linear, graded set of stages."[54] As Michel Foucault describes, Western correctional and educational institutions were based on a "division of time [that] became increasingly minute." The effect was that "it is this disciplinary time that was gradually imposed on pedagogical practice—specializing the time of training and detaching it from the adult time, from the time of mastery; arranging different stages, separated from one another by graded examinations; drawing up programmes, each of which must take place during a particular stage and which involves exercises of increasing difficulty; qualifying individuals according to the way in which they progress through these series."[55] Students at such institutions were to be disciplined into reevaluating their hours, days, months, and years in terms of the school's timetable and calendar. Furthermore, although the content of the curriculum in colonial East Africa was gendered, the educational system was in theory designed for all children, boys and girls alike.

In contrast, indigenous forms of education in East Africa, according to East African specialists Ali A. Mazrui and T. Wagaw, are "not formal in a Euro-modern sense. . . . [There exists] no elaborate grading system to measure performance and progress." They further explain that "there is no sharp distinction between education and socialization, between school and family." Mazrui and Wagaw argue that the imposition of Western education on East Africans sparked a process of "desocialization," which "has tended to divorce children from the norms and values of their parents."[56] The physical and temporal distance between schoolgirls and their mothers in Mombasa had an effect on the socialization process, but not in the way the authors describe. Had they not attended school, girls certainly would have formed stronger bonds with their mothers while staying at home, learning the "norms and values" of womanhood. At the same time, they would have had less in common with their fathers. Education created distance between girls and their mothers, as evidenced by the fact that many mothers and grandmothers disagreed with fathers about educating their girls, and the childhood experience of schooling made these girls more able to relate to their educated fathers. Furthermore, in struggling to break down colonial barriers along the way, fathers and daughters formed a political bond reinforced by this shared educational experience.

The historical transformation was both generational and gendered. Anthropologist Gabrielle O'Malley states that in colonial Zanzibar, "while one member of [a girl's] family may have thought schooling was a good idea (often fathers), there was more often than not another person in the family who forbade them from going (often times grandmothers)." She explains that the biggest concern for those family members who opposed schooling was maintenance of the girls' *heshima*, or honor. Female family members worried that girls would "become 'spoiled' (lose their virginity before marriage)" if they went to school.[57] Most of the women I interviewed were among the first generation of females in their families to attend Western schools in Mombasa. Their conflicts with mothers and grandmothers accentuate that position. As such, and as daughters who identified more with their fathers, they were also among the first generation of girls faced with a new set of options at the age of puberty, some of which had little to do with menstruation and marriage.

Stretching the Limits of Girlhood

Shamsa's father organized her wedding before he died, at which time she was "near puberty." As expected, she received instruction from a *somo* before the marriage, the "beginning of [her] adult life." Shamsa's transition into womanhood accorded with Muslim traditions in Mombasa. Although obeying the wishes of his in-laws in this respect, Shamsa's father made sure his voice was heard through his selection of her husband. He searched for someone educated, "sophisticated," and financially stable in "his own work." Unfortunately, after a couple of years she became discontent with the marriage. She eventually got her husband to divorce her, and then she found someone "smarter" to marry. She seemed to appreciate her father's efforts but ultimately wanted a marriage on her own terms. After announcing her "conditions," Shamsa married her second husband in spite of disapproval from her brothers and friends.[58] No doubt Shamsa's unique childhood played into her determination to make her own decisions, even against the advice of those around her.

At the age of nineteen Fatma finally got her wish to return to Mombasa, this time for teacher training at the Mbaraki School (formerly the Arab Girls' School). The government planned to train her and her sister, Zena, and send them back to Lamu to open the girls' school their father had demanded years before.[59] During a 1956 meeting, the Lamu Arab School Committee urged "the Department to send immediately those girls [Fatma and Zena] in order to open a separate girls' school," a matter that was "urgent and most important."[60] Fatma passed the Kenya Asian Primary Examination and entered formal teacher training the following year.[61] By the time she returned to Lamu in 1961, the conflict over girls' education had waned. "Everyone sent their girls to school," she explained, even though no separate girls' school existed there.[62] The tide had apparently turned.

Meanwhile, Rose graduated from the Coast Girls' High School. After graduation, she hoped to study nursing, but her father lost another battle in the war with his wife's mother; Rose was to be married instead. When asked if she was happy about the marriage, she replied:

> No, no I wasn't happy. Even my father wasn't happy. But . . . [in] those times, grandmas had power. If she says something is "Yes," [then it is] yes. If she says "No," [then] no. . . . She [said,] "No. . . . She's grown up. She's not allowed to stay like this. She has to go to her house." My father really wanted to take me to Nairobi to study nursing. I was very interested in nursing because I started [at the Coast Girls' High School] in school activities I studied nursing. We were going to Coast General every week to study. And then if you finished there, the exam, then you were sent to Nairobi. So I couldn't go to Nairobi.[63]

The Coast Girls' High School cooperated with the Coast General Hospital to provide extra training in nursing for girls who were interested. This was in the early 1960s, by which time the colonial government had instituted programs to encourage women to become the teachers and nurses necessary for Kenya's economic advancement. Rose had passed all the necessary exams and was ready to go to Nairobi for the full nursing course when her grandmother refused. Instead, she married a man "old like [her] father" and moved to Tanzania. After having six children, she left him and returned to Mombasa. She completed a two-year clerical course and then married a man who allowed her to pursue her studies, work as a clerk, and volunteer in schools. Her second husband, Rose explained, "is educated" and "understands the rights of a human being," meaning he allowed her to work and volunteer.[64] Rose's initiative in leaving her first husband and finding a second one who suited her sensibilities is not so uncommon. Shamsa had done the same. In both cases, it was important that the new husband was "smart" or "educated," their code words for a man who allowed his wife to pursue work outside the home. Both Shamsa and Rose seemed to think of their second marriages as the next step in their personal "progress."

After completing secondary school, Lucie began teacher training in the late 1960s. By this time, Kenya had gained independence, the new government had put an end to racial segregation and discrimination in schools, and teacher-training programs existed for women of all backgrounds. When asked what her parents thought of her decision to become a teacher, she replied, "At that time teachers were really honored."[65] When I pressed her further, asking if her postsecondary studies had "any effect on a personal life, especially in terms of marriage," she explained that marriage came later, after college. For Lucie, no conflict emerged between family expectations and career preparation. Both her father and mother encouraged her to delay marriage to continue her education.

Lucie's account appears in contrast with those of Shamsa, Rose, and other schoolgirls who came of age during the colonial period. The historian Tabitha Kanogo stated that girls in colonial Kenya generally married by the age of sixteen. Kanogo relays the story of one young woman, who, like Rose, "was not ready" for marriage because of her commitment to her education and career in nursing. Kanogo demonstrates how such personal histories "serve as roadmaps of the extremely contested terrain of formal education."[66] It is at this moment in the lives of these educated young women, in the years after the onset of puberty, when major decisions about their future surface. Increasingly in the late colonial period, the cap of girlhood was no longer defined by the moment a girl began menstruating or completed the initiation process. In contrast to Shamsa, who attended school when it was still largely unheard of among both boys and girls, the end of girlhood for daughters in late-colonial Mombasa was increasingly defined as the year they graduated from high school or earned their teaching certificate. Even Rose finished secondary school before getting married. As with their fathers, educated daughters began to understand their childhood in terms of the increments of school grades rather than the path toward initiation. The limits of girlhood, previously bound by the onset of menstruation, were gradually stretched to accommodate academic or vocational opportunities. This period was one of tension among competing notions of the limits of childhood. For the fathers, this conflict may not have been so pronounced. Education was thought to lead to better employment and greater financial stability, and nothing like menstruation definitively marked the end of boyhood. For girls, though, the drive to move forth through each stage of schooling came into direct conflict with the apparent biological termination of girlhood. If puberty no longer necessarily indicated the end of girlhood, what, then, was the new marker for entry into womanhood?

Becoming Teachers, Becoming Women

The headmistress of Mombasa's Aga Khan High School, Mariam Lovingia, herself a product of colonial education, aptly describes one effect of the spread of girls' education in the twentieth century: "Some girls have become doctors, dentists, teachers, etc. Things have changed a lot for Muslim girls."[67] Although the variety of professions women have entered since obtaining their education is extensive, one stands out above all others in terms of its impact on girls' education—teaching. Colonial officials often blamed the lack of girls' schools on the lack of female teachers. The real problem was the lack of government willingness to train girls for teaching professions. Officials agreed that "women teachers are better able to handle the junior classes," but in their judgment "the average teaching life of a woman teacher is between two and three years," compared to fifteen years for a man. Therefore the cost of training women was considered too high.[68] Although marriage and pregnancy interrupted a woman's teaching career, officials underestimated the length of a woman's "teaching life." As teaching became a popular profession for female graduates, it became inseparable from the way in which teachers defined their entry into womanhood.

Grace Nzaka, a primary school teacher from Tanganyika, moved to Mombasa with her husband in 1944 at the age of twenty-two. She, along with three other teachers, opened the first municipal nursery school, the Tononoka Nursery School, in 1946. Both Christian and Muslim children attended the school. After Independence, Grace attended Matuga Training Center to obtain her Kenyan teacher's certificate. She taught a total of twelve years, not including the seven years she worked as a cleaner at a nursery school.[69] A longtime advocate of Indian girls' education in Mombasa recruited another teacher, Olinda De Souza Fernandez, from Goa, India, in 1951.[70] Olinda built a community school that "adopted" Indian girls too old to continue at the government school.[71] The girls' parents soon demanded she take their boys too. Today, more than fifty years after her arrival in Mombasa, she continues to work in education as headmistress of the Valentine's School.

By the 1950s and 1960s, women such as Grace and Olinda were in high demand. Local teacher training for women was still in its infancy, but the government's commitment to girls' education was growing. Many women began training to become teachers at this time, and places like the Arab Girls' School initiated new programs for women. Fatma and her sister were among those who took advantage of such opportunities. After 1963, the new independent state of Kenya introduced another layer of options for advanced schoolgirls whose families could not pay for them to continue their schooling. One such government institution was the Municipal Council Girls' Youth Center. Asmah explained, "You go to the [Girls' Youth] Center. The children [there] are taught many things. Mostly they are taught English because many go to finish their studies. They are taught English, then how to type these papers, then sewing, and baking cakes, things like that."[72] Asmah Abdalla and Eunice Wanjika Muriuki both received this training as teenagers at the Girls' Youth Center in the mid- to late 1960s. The center provided much of the same instruction offered at mission schools for African girls during the colonial period. The difference was that those who went to the center to "finish their studies" came upon new opportunities for government employment.

Eunice attended the Buxton Primary School for Standard I and II (first and second grades) in 1956 and 1957, lived in Kirinyaka District north of Nairobi until 1962, and then returned to Mombasa at the age of thirteen to finish school. She spent five years at the Girls' Youth Center. Her uncle, with whom she and her siblings were living, encouraged her to go to the center not only for education and training but also because the center provided food and supplies for her and her siblings. During her four years at the Girls' Youth Center, Eunice learned handicrafts and other domestic and academic skills. At the age of eighteen, she was recruited from the center to work as a nursery school teacher to help support her family. As a teenager, she had worked odd jobs from time to time to help out the family, but the Youth Center provided assistance, allowing her to continue studying until her first teaching job began on October 1, 1967.[73]

Asmah came to the Girls' Youth Center just after Eunice left. The director of the center was her father's friend. After finishing Form II (tenth grade) at the Coast Girls' High School, her family encouraged her to continue her studies at the center. It made sense for her family to stop paying fees to the secondary school and send her for free training instead. She did not get the chance to complete her studies because she was chosen for a teaching job at Tononoka Nursery School within four days of arriving at the center. Asmah explained how the center provided employment placement for young teachers: "Now [in] these Nursery Schools of the Municipal Council, there were few teachers. It was perhaps when a teacher goes on maternity leave, the Council knows [that we are available], so the older girls at the Center were used [as substitutes]. . . . They went with the children and if your disposition was good, you got on well, then you were given a contract and you went to work." For Asmah, who wanted to continue her studies but could not because of lack of funds, becoming a teacher meant access to both further studies (teacher training) and income.[74] The center took advantage of the interruptions for pregnancy or childcare that occurred in a woman's work life to recruit new teachers who began as substitutes.

As the government's commitment to girls' education broadened in the 1950s and 1960s, the professionalization of educated women began to increase. The special need for female teachers fueled this process. Just as the end of secondary school or teacher training began to mark the end of childhood, employment became one of the many characteristics of womanhood. Entry into womanhood continued to rest on marriage, but a woman might see her first job as initiation into a different kind of adulthood based on financial independence. L. Lloys Frates argues that although increased access to education and employment during the colonial period brought Swahili-speaking women into the public sphere, the "lessening of the patriarchal controls [such as purdah] associated with Islam resulted from an erosion of economic status" rather than direct influence of colonial culture.[75] As families became more financially desperate, women left the confines of the home in search of work. An income, regardless of its origin, either bolstered the household economy or served as insurance in case of divorce. A woman's financial independence, whether for cultural or economic reasons, added another layer of meaning to her sense of herself as a woman better equipped to take care of herself and her family. Self-reliance became as important as, and often determined, domestic respectability (*heshima*).

Conclusion

The women I interviewed saw themselves and their fathers as "historical actors" in the same way Shamsa did. Fatma opened the interview by explaining that her father was one of the first in Lamu to send his girls to school. Rose understands her education as crucial to her family's transition from a "primitive" to a "progressive" stage of development. Grace underscored the significance of her involvement in the establishment of the first nursery school in Mombasa. Eunice's emphasis on the date October 1, 1967, demonstrates how she conceptualizes her entry into the teaching profession as an important moment in history. These major events and processes in the history of girls' education in Mombasa coincided with notable events for the individual's passage from girlhood into womanhood. The contested moments, especially debates about secondary school, teacher training, employment, and marriage, arrived for girls during a period when they were no longer children but not yet women. Cultural markers of the end of girlhood changed as new options came to girls

entering puberty. Girls began to identify less with mothers and grandmothers reluctant to support academic and career ambitions and more with
fathers, who seemed to be on their side. Formal schooling, though, did not
supplant local indigenous forms of education such as Qur'an schools or initiation systems, and secondary school, teacher training, and employment
never replaced marriage. Yet these new options certainly delayed marriage
and gradually displaced its centrality in the transition from girlhood to
womanhood, reshaping the relationships daughters had with mothers and
fathers. As a result of these gendered and generational shifts in coming of
age, women recount their education and employment as markers not only
of their own maturation, but also of important stages in Mombasa's "modernization." Their personal stories, sometimes hidden behind the words of
fathers and sometimes standing boldly on their own, nevertheless add new
dimensions to the global history of girlhood.

NOTES

This chapter is based on archival research conducted at the Kenya National Archives (KNA),
the National Museums of Kenya Library at Fort Jesus, Mombasa, the Public Record Office
(PRO) in Surrey, UK, and oral interviews carried out in Mombasa in 2005. I am indebted to the
women who shared their stories and to Zubeida Issa, who directed me to them. The Fulbright
Institute of International Education (2004–2005), the Spencer Foundation (2005–2006), the University of California, Berkeley's Department of History (2004–2005), and UC Berkeley's Center
for African Studies' Andrew and Mary Thompson Rocca Scholarship provided generous support for this project. I thank Colleen Vasconcellos, Jennifer Helgren, Elisabeth McMahon,
Michelle King, Kalil Oldham, Mouna Albakry, Abdulaziz Albakry, and the anonymous
reviewer for providing fruitful comments on drafts.

1. Eunice Wanjika Muriuki, interview with author, Mombasa, May 23, 2006, tape recording,
collection of the author.

2. Asia (pseudonym), interview with author, Mombasa, May 28, 2006, transcription, collection of the author.

3. I use the phrase "modern girls" in the way the Modern Girl Around the World
researchers at the University of Washington do in reference to "schoolgirls or graduates with
panache for fashion and for choosing their own lovers" who emerged in Africa in the 1930s. See
Tani E. Barlow, Madeleine Dong, Uta Poiger, Priti Ramamurthy, Lynn Thomas, and Alys Eve
Weinbaum, "The Modern Girl around the World: A Research Agenda and Preliminary Findings," *Gender and History* 17, no. 2 (August 2005): 249. With regard to the "modern girl" culture
in Kenya and South Africa, see Lynn Thomas, "Schoolgirl Pregnancies, Letter-Writing, and
'Modern' Persons in Late Colonial East Africa," in *Africa's Hidden Histories: Everyday Literacy and
Making the Self*, ed. Karin Barber (Bloomington: Indiana University Press, 2006), 180–207; and
Lynn Thomas, "The Modern Girl and Racial Respectability in 1930s South Africa," in *The Modern Girl Around the World: Consumption, Modernity, and Globalization*, ed. Modern Girl Around
the World Research Group (Alys Eve Weinbaum, Lynn M. Thomas, Priti Ramamurthy, Uta G.
Poiger, Madeleine Yue Dong, and Tani E. Barlow) (Durham, NC: Duke University Press, 2008),
96–119.

4. One of the main issues threatening the social order was the emergence of women's
voices in the public sphere. Susan Hirsch details how Muslim women in Kenya successfully
navigate legal spheres and other public spaces in which they are expected to silently "persevere." Just as Hirsch demonstrates women's agency in Islamic courts in spite of this culture of
female silence, I point to the ways in which girls' entry into and expressed advocacy of Western
schools transformed the culture and experience of girlhood in late colonial Mombasa. See

Susan F. Hirsch, *Pronouncing and Persevering: Gender and the Discourses of Disputing in an African Islamic Court* (Chicago: University of Chicago Press, 1998).

5. Michel Foucault, *Discipline and Punish: The Birth of the Prison* (New York: Vintage, 1979), 150. See also Kathryn M. Anderson-Levitt, "The Schoolyard Gate: Schooling and Childhood in Global Perspective," *Journal of Social History* 38, no. 4 (2005): 997.

6. Anderson-Levitt, "Schoolyard Gate," 992.

7. Ibid.

8. Gertrude Mianda, "Colonialism, Education and Gender Relations in the Belgian Congo: The Évolué Case," in *Women in African Colonial Histories*, ed. Susan Geiger, Jean Marie Allman, and Nakanyike Musisi (Bloomington: Indiana University Press, 2002), 148.

9. See also Tsitsi Dangarembga, *Nervous Conditions* (Seattle: Seal Press, 1988), which beautifully illustrates the struggles of a Shona girl caught between "modern" ambitions associated with exposure to Western education and the overlap of indigenous and Christian forms of male domination in 1960s Rhodesia.

10. In contrast, évolués in the Belgian Congo discouraged women from working in order to keep them dependent on their husbands; Mianda, "Colonialism, Education and Gender Relations in the Belgian Congo," 150–151.

11. A. I. Salim, *The Swahili-Speaking Peoples of Kenya's Coast, 1895–1965* (Nairobi: East African Publishing House, 1973), 100–115. See also Patricia Romero, "Where Have All the Slaves Gone? Emancipation and Post-Emancipation in Lamu, Kenya," *Journal of African History* 27, no. 3 (1986): 497–512; Frederick Cooper, *From Slaves to Squatters: Plantation Labor and Agriculture in Zanzibar and Coastal Kenya, 1890–1925* (New Haven: Yale University Press, 1981); and Bruce Berman and John Londsdale, *Unhappy Valley: Conflict in Kenya and Africa, Book One: State and Class* (London: J. Currey, 1992).

12. Salim, *Swahili-Speaking Peoples*, 71; and George D. Namaswa, "Education and Nation Building," in *Kenya: The Making of a Nation: 1895–1995*, ed. B. A. Ogot and W. R. Ochieng' (Maseno, Kenya: Institute of Research and Postgraduate Studies, Maseno University, 2000), 132–133.

13. Robert W. Strayer, *The Making of Mission Communities in East Africa: Anglicans and Africans in Colonial Kenya, 1875–1935* (London: Heinemann, 1978), 14.

14. Sarah Mirza and Margaret Strobel, eds., *Three Swahili Women: Life Histories from Mombasa, Kenya* (Bloomington: Indiana University Press, 1989), 9. See also Jonathon Glassman, "Slower Than a Massacre: The Multiple Sources of Racial Thought in Colonial Africa," *American Historical Review* 109, no. 3 (2004).

15. Salim, *Swahili-Speaking Peoples*, 91, 188, 193–194. See also Ali A. Mazrui, "Arab and Swahili Dreams and Fears: 1939–1963," in Ogot and Ochieng, *Kenya*; and Alamin M. Mazrui and Ibrahim Noor Shariff, *The Swahili: Idiom and Identity of an African People* (Trenton, NJ: Africa World Press, 1994). The terms "African" and "native" were vague categories that, in Mombasa, sometimes referred to "Swahili" and other times pointed to persons of other ethnic groups on the coast and inland.

16. Thomas Jesse Jones, *Education in Africa: A Study of West, South, and Equatorial Africa by the African Education Commission* (New York: Praeger, 1922), 39–40, 84.

17. In 1928, for example, the Coast Education Committee split into separate committees for Arab education and African education, hardening the distinction between the two categories. See Education Department Central Committee on Arab Education, 1925–28, KNA AV/2/76.

18. Kenya Colony and Protectorate, *Annual Report of the Education Department for 1928* (Nairobi: Government Printer, 1928), 15.

19. Salim, *Swahili-Speaking Peoples*, 163. The Zanzibar Islands made up a British Protectorate about two hundred kilometers south of Mombasa. For more on girls' education in Zanzibar, see Corrie Decker, "Investing in Ideas: Girls' Education in Colonial Zanzibar" (Ph.D. diss., University of California, Berkeley, 2007).

20. Margaret Strobel, *Muslim Women in Mombasa, 1890–1975* (New Haven: Yale University Press, 1979), 104.

21. Sorobea Nyachieo Bogonko, *A History of Modern Education in Kenya (1895–1991)* (London: Evans Brothers, 1992), 1–3.

22. Ali A. Mazrui and T. Wagaw, "Towards Decolonizing Modernity: Education and Culture Conflict in East Africa," in *The Educational Process and Historiography in Africa* (Paris: UNESCO, 1985), 49. Private Islamic education often included instruction in religion, reading, writing, mathematics, and science. Fatma Mahmoud Albakry, interview with author, Mombasa, May 26, 2005, transcription, collection of the author.

23. Families were often mixed religiously, as in Asmah's case. Her grandfather was Muslim, but of his seven boys, four were Muslim and three Christian. Asmah Abdalla, interview with author, Mombasa, May 23, 2006, tape recording, collection of the author.

24. Mirza and Strobel, *Three Swahili Women*, 71, 82–84. A *somo* taught individual "freeborn" girls as part of their wedding ceremonies, whereas the *ukungwi* tradition among slave descendents involved collective initiation of girls. Sexual instruction included instruction in hygiene and beauty, as well as performance of songs and dances simulating the sexual act. See J.W.T. Allen, ed., *Customs of the Swahili People: The Desturi za Waswahili of Mtoro bin Mwinyi Bakar and Other Swahili Persons* (Berkeley: University of California Press, 1981), 55–58.

25. Great Britain Colonial Office, *Closer Union in East Africa* (London: His Majesty's Stationary Office, 1931), 435. Hinawy was Mombasa's *liwali*, or local governor recognized by the colonial state. J. Byrne to Philip Cunliffe-Lister, December 24, 1932, KNA AV/12/148. Parents and officials came into conflict over the location of the Government Indian Girls' School in the mid-1930s.

26. *Mombasa Times* clipping in file, June 5, 1931, KNA/AV/12/245. Girls began attending the Arab Boys' School in 1936, a year after the Ghazali School admitted girls.

27. These ethnic terms are colonial categories. The "Twelve Tribes" were labeled "Swahili" but petitioned for "Arab" status. "Bajuni" was an ethnic distinction within Swahili. "Asians" indicated people of Indian or Pakistani descent.

28. Mary Ann Porter, "Swahili Identity in Post-Colonial Kenya: The Reproduction of Gender in Educational Discourses" (Ph.D. diss., University of Washington, 1992), 137, 142–143, 147–148; see also Strobel, *Muslim Women in Mombasa*, 107–109.

29. Kenya Colony and Protectorate, *Annual Report of the Education Department for 1935* (Nairobi: Government Printer, 1935), 71–72, 75; *Mombasa District Annual Report for 1935*, 29–30, KNA/DC/MSA/1/4. In 1935, only 6 of the 5,815 girls attending CMS schools were pupils in Mombasa.

30. The school turned away more than three hundred children in 1947. Buxton School, Mombasa, CMS, Historical Notes, 1931, KNA MSS/61/251.

31. Most students were "Indian, Goan, or English." Rose Ali Noormohamed, interview with author, Mombasa, May 9, 2005, tape recording, collection of the author. Arab girls like the daughters of Mbarak Ali Hinawy also attended the school. Porter, "Swahili Identity in Post-Colonial Kenya," 255.

32. Provincial Commissioner Coast, African Education Mombasa, 1947–60, KNA CA/3/55.

33. Fathers sent their daughters to school in part to make them attractive as wives for the emerging educated elite. See Strobel, *Muslim Women in Mombasa*, 109.

34. Extract from draft Minutes of the Advisory Committee for Education in the Colonies Meeting held on January 30, 1941, PRO CO 859/42/2. See also Africa, Education of Women and Girls, 1939, PRO CO 847/17/13.

35. Provincial Education Officer, Coast, Mr. Hattfield to Director of Education, January 16, 1960, KNA CA/3/55.

36. Coast Education, 1946–48, KNA MSS/61/291; Education, Arab Schools, 1946–59, KNA AV/12/3. Lucie trained at the Ribe school in the 1960s. Lucie Machi, interview with author, Mombasa, May 17, 2005, tape recording, collection of the author.

37. The Matuga Training Center is one example. District Commissioner, Kilifi to Provincial Commissioner, Coast, March 4, 1957, KNA CA/3/53.

38. Mirza and Strobel, *Three Swahili Women*, 97, 91–97.

39. Mansoor Moaddel, "Conditions for Ideological Production: The Origins of Islamic Modernism in Indian, Egypt, and Iran," *Theory and Society* 30 (2001): 670. Randall L. Pouwels, "Sheikh al-Amin b. Ali Mazrui and Islamic Modernism in East Africa 1875–1947," *International Journal of Middle East Studies* 13, no. 3 (August 1981): 330.

40. Pouwels, "Sheikh al-Amin b. Ali Mazrui," 341.

41. Qasim Amin preached against purdah, gendered divorce laws, and the lack of education for women. Moaddel, "Conditions for Ideological Production," 120–124.

42. Porter, "Swahili Identity in Post-Colonial Kenya," 141, 137–140. See also Strobel, *Muslim Women in Mombasa*, 108. "Madrasa" (also spelled "madarasa" and "madrassa") refers to any school.

43. The day school closed in 1931. Kenya Colony and Protectorate, *Annual Report of the Education Department for 1933* (Nairobi: Government Printer, 1933), 3.

44. It is possible that, as with Rose, Fatma's extended family objected to the Star of the Sea because it was a Catholic school.

45. Fatma Mahmoud Albakry, interview with author.

46. Abdulaziz Mahmoud Fadil Albakry (Fatma's brother) to Corrie Decker, e-mail, September 29, 2006.

47. Fatma Mahmoud Albakry, interview with author.

48. Fifteen Lamu men to the liwali of Lamu, December 1, 1951, KNA DC/LAMU/2/14/5.

49. "Baluchi" refers to those from Karachi in present-day Pakistan.

50. Rose Ali Noormohamed, interview with author. Her mother's Baluchi heritage made it possible for her to attend Mbeheni, a private Indian school.

51. Lucie Machi, interview with author.

52. Taita Girls' Work, Wusi Girls' School, 1944–45, KNA MSS/61/200; Coast Education 1946–48, KNA MSS/61/29.

53. Western schools were numerous in Egypt, where Shamsa's father attended school. See Timothy Mitchell, *Colonizing Egypt* (Berkeley: University of California Press, 1998).

54. Anderson-Levitt, "Schoolyard Gate," 997.

55. Foucault, *Discipline and Punish*, 150, 159.

56. Mazrui and Wagaw, "Decolonizing Modernity," 39, 54.

57. Gabrielle E. O'Malley, "Marriage and Morality: Negotiating Gender and Respect in Zanzibar Town" (Ph.D. diss., University of Washington, 2000), 91–92.

58. Mirza and Strobel, *Three Swahili Women*, 98, 99–100.

59. Fatma Mahmoud Albakry, interview with author. The government attempted to send Sherifa binti Seif, daughter of a Lamu businessman, for teacher training in order to establish a girls' school in Lamu in 1937. The file skips from 1937 to 1953, so it is unclear what happened to those plans. KNA DC/LAMU/2/14/5.

60. Minutes of the Lamu Arab School committee, September 10, 1956, KNA CA/3/52 PC COAST.

61. Provincial Education Officer, Coast, to PC, Coast, July 8, 1957, KNA CA/3/52 PC COAST.

62. Fatma Mahmoud Albakry, interview with author.

63. Rose Ali Noormohamed, interview with author.

64. Ibid. Her second husband, however, refused to allow her to accept a job offered her at the Iranian embassy in Nairobi.

65. Lucie Machi, interview with author.

66. Tabitha Kanogo, *African Womanhood in Colonial Kenya, 1900–50* (Oxford: James Currey, 2005), 199, 202.

67. Mariam Lovingia, interview with author, Mombasa, May 20, 2005, transcription, collection of the author.

68. Kenya Colony and Protectorate, *African Education in Kenya: Report of a Committee Appointed to Inquire into the Scope, Content, and Methods of African Education, Its Administration and Finance, and to Make Recommendations* (Nairobi: Government Printer, 1949), 73.

69. Grace Nzaka, interview with author, Mombasa, May 24, 2005, tape recording, collection of the author. Tanganyika was the mainland area that joined Zanzibar in 1964 to become Tanzania.

70. Government Indian Girls' School, Mombasa, 1932–33, KNA AV/12/148.

71. Olinda De Souza Fernandez, interview with author, Mombasa, May 18, 2005, tape recording, collection of the author.

72. Asmah Abdalla, interview with author.

73. Eunice Wanjika Muriuki, interview with author. Muriuki repeated this date several times, emphasizing its importance.

74. Asmah Abdalla, interview with author. In 1969 when Asmah was chosen to teach at Tononoka, she also entered the Matuga teacher-training program as a condition of employment.

75. L. Lloys Frates, "Domestic Space and Gender Relations among the Swahili" (M.A. thesis, University of California, Los Angeles, 1994), 24.

15   *Mothers of Warriors*

GIRLS IN A YOUTH DEBATE
OF INTERWAR IRAQ

PETER WIEN

As I argue in *Iraqi Arab Nationalism: Authoritarian, Totalitarian and Pro-Fascist Inclinations, 1932–1941*, which examines authoritarian, totalitarian, and pro-Fascist trends in Iraq during the 1930s and early 1940s, the Iraqi nationalist press cast youth in the role of reviving the strength of the Arab nation. Most of this debate on youth took place in Baghdad-based Arab nationalist newspapers during the second half of the 1930s. The debate was predominantly about masculinity under threat by effeminization through the temptations of a Western lifestyle. The debate reflected a broad generational conflict inside the growing politicized middle class of Iraqi urban society. In this conflict, young nationalists attacked the founding fathers of the state for not granting room to the younger generation to move up socially and take over influential positions in the state.[1] There are signs, however, that this generational tension also helped to build a form of girls' agency. A redefinition of girls' role in society fell short of an all-out change of paradigm but nevertheless attributed an active part in their nationalist struggle.

The debate was dominated by concerns about Iraqi boys' masculinity. The counterimage to the effeminated male youth was the physically strong and determined young man modeled along the mythical image of the early Arab Muslim warrior, which corresponded with similar depictions of chivalric manliness from a European context in the nineteenth and twentieth centuries. Women were mostly reduced to a reproductive role as caretakers until the first years of World War II, which brought about a remarkable change in perspective. An image evolved that ran counter to the one of a passive and homebound, traditionally secluded woman. The Iraqi national youth movement encouraged girls to picture themselves as homefront warriors. Female nationalists echoed the masculinity debate when they used a language of individual self-sacrifice for the nation, which reminds of the contemporaneous fascist image of the mother's role at the home front, an image that has its roots in nineteenth-century nationalism as a Europe-wide phenomenon as well. I argue that the increased militancy of this image went beyond "patriotic motherhood" and reflected how World

War II added to the militancy of nationalist language in Iraq as a whole. Girls were promoted as an asset for building national strength as much as boys were.

Elizabeth Thompson introduced the concept of "patriotic motherhood" for interwar Syria, which as a neighboring country provides an excellent comparison with the Iraqi case. The concept indicates the increased value attributed to women as mothers and caretakers. In 1930s Syria, the promotion of this concept by women's associations replaced issues such as the demand for suffrage, apparently as a deliberate concession by movement leaders to the priority of the nationalist struggle for independence, but also because the emphasis on this concept gave women a more acceptable public voice. Likewise, the male leaders of the nationalist movement were always quick to sacrifice projects that involved improvement of women's personal status in order to guarantee the support of religious elites.[2] The voices of the Iraqi girls' debate, however, concentrated on the need to imbue girls, as future mothers of warriors, with a sense of national responsibility. As a result, girls started to be integrated in a totalizing state narrative that demanded self-sacrifice for the nation. In the context of Islamic societies' tendencies to hide girls from the public gaze, this change is remarkable.

In this chapter I address the gender aspects of authoritarian and totalitarian trends in Iraq during the 1930s and early 1940s. The Iraqi state-run youth movement al-Futuwwa embodied Iraqi Arab nationalists' visions of strength and prowess for the state. I analyze the gendered role models that Iraqi newspapers applied when their writers wrote about al-Futuwwa. As one might expect, masculinity dominated this debate, but I argue that authoritarian nationalist agitation during the late 1930s and early 1940s gave girls the opportunity to carve out their own space in this masculine vision of the nation. This opportunity, however, must be understood in close relation to the debate's vision of masculinity.

The history of women gaining voices in Middle Eastern and Islamic societies during the first half of the twentieth century is often told as a story of men discovering women's rights out of concerns about the modernization of society, or of early women's movements as charitable institutions that later developed a particular women's agency in the context of nationalist movements, but always as representatives of middle-class bourgeois sections of society. A particular girls' history seems largely absent. Research on the early women's movement in the Arab lands tends to emphasize girls as objects of education, not as agents.[3] In her recent pioneering contribution to the early history of feminism in Iraq, Noga Efrati has shown that the development of a feminist discourse in Iraq followed similar patterns albeit with some differences. For instance, Iraqi women were relatively late in establishing charitable organizations. Women's associations became more politically related in the 1940s and 1950s after women began to participate openly in the struggle for independence. Earlier, women's activities had been confined to the bourgeois middle class. Girls do not feature in Efrati's account other than as objects of education.[4] In a different geographical context, but still within the Islamic realm, Liat Kozma, in her chapter in this volume, shows how complex the impact of the formation of modern societies was on the position of girls and young women in society. There was little room for self-determination. As I show in this chapter, girls, and those who promoted a new image of girlhood in the Iraq of the early 1940s, did not state revolutionary feminist demands but definitely took on a certain militancy in the way they claimed the nationalist state narrative for themselves.

Al-Futuwwa in Perspective

Youth movements of the interwar Arab East have received a lot of attention in the historiography of the modern Middle East. As it seems, they were exclusively described as locations of male bonding, as strike forces of ideological parties, and as schools of paramilitary discipline. Girls generally do not feature in these stories.[5] Thompson's groundbreaking study on subaltern movements in interwar Syria focuses on the role of women in nationalist movements from a perspective of women as a subaltern group. According to her, women, and thus girls too, suffered from a dual subalternity in interwar Syria in that they were subject to men in households but also to the paternal order of the state, which is a concept that can easily be transferred to the Iraqi case as well. In Syria, the "civic order" reflected the paternalistic care of old and well-established state elites who exerted power through mediation between the French authority of the Mandate regime and the wider population. Thompson argues, furthermore, that World War I initiated a "crisis of paternity" in the Middle East that continued into the colonial period and deeply affected patterns of male authority and gender relations. Women acquired new roles on the home front as the political superstructure of the Ottoman Empire collapsed. Many aspects of social life, such as the definition of the nation and its identity, and the place of religion and class, were affected, which brought about violent confrontations. In the course of the interwar period, the paternalistic position of old notable families was gradually transferred to the state, which grew in strength and took over services and responsibilities. This change affected not only the civic order but also the inherited patterns of paternal rule in society at large.[6] The conflict of generations that broke out in Iraq and elsewhere in the Middle East during the same period corresponds with this "crisis of paternity," and the male rituals of the Futuwwa youth movement, which adopted principles of masculinity that were offered by the colonial state, can be interpreted as a reassurance of male dominance.[7] A change in the self-perception of women and girls during the same period was arguably a consequence as well.

Scholarly literature has, however, largely failed so far to take these internal social dynamics of Middle Eastern societies into account when explaining the popularity of youth organizations during the 1930s and 1940s. The fascist outlook of these movements has often been used as proof of pro-Nazi and pro-Fascist inclinations in the Arab world. From a general perspective, youth organizations were a phenomenon that have spread in the Arab world since the 1920s and gained strongly in popularity in the 1930s. Nationalist parties such as al-Katā'ib and the Syrian Social Nationalist Party in Lebanon or Misr al-Fatā' in Egypt all established paramilitary youth branches to promote strong nationalism and physical fitness as well as strength of character. They offered a sense of community and paramilitary training. The common view is that Arab youth movements of the 1930s were a superficial copy of fascist models, which found the strongest expression in the wearing of uniform-like colored shirts. Admiration for German and Italian national strength and recovery after World War I and for discipline and efficiency were in the background. Being pro-German was more a matter of fashion than a serious approach for Arabs, however.[8] Inherent contradictions such as the competing visions of Arab nationalism and Mussolini's plans of imperialist expansion prevented a deeper adoption of fascist politics and its chauvinistic rituals, which were supposed to integrate divergent classes of a nation.[9]

The Iraqi youth movement al-Futuwwa is outstanding among these groups because it was an official state institution. It did not belong to any of the parties and groupings in the Iraqi pseudo-parliamentary system, which concealed politics of personalities and clientelism. The exact founding date of al-Futuwwa is unclear but was probably in the early to mid-1930s.[10] In 1939, it became compulsory for every student attending secondary state schooling to take part in al-Futuwwa's paramilitary training.[11] Past research on al-Futuwwa has not even considered whether the movement was an all-male affair or if girls played a role in it too. This matter was an issue for Iraqi nationalists, a concern that at some point must have resulted in the establishment of female branches of al-Futuwwa.

Iraqi publicists discussed al-Futuwwa as an ideal as much as an organization. The term stood, first of all, for the desired manly and chivalric qualities of the Iraqi young man, so it seemed an appropriate name for the Iraqi youth organization. The term is old, however. It had been used in the Middle Ages to describe the characteristics of a *fatā,'* a young man, as opposed to the *muruwwa* of a grown-up man. Both terms had connotations of bravery and courage. *Futuwwa* was also a name for urban militias in medieval Arab cities. During the late nineteenth century, an image of youth as avant-garde emerged, which attributed a certain authority to youth. The Young Turk movement that stood behind the Ottoman revolution of 1908 and had an impact on later Arab debates was an expression of this trend.[12]

As an Iraqi organization, al-Futuwwa was part of nationalist schooling. Reflecting European trends of character formation and youth education, which had their origin in the nineteenth and early twentieth centuries and drew upon a clear-cut image of true masculinity, Iraqi Arab nationalists saw al-Futuwwa as an important tool for enhancing the state of the nation's youth. Boys were seen as future warriors ready to sacrifice themselves for the nation, girls as future mothers and caretakers.[13] In Iraq, an Arab concept of youth was remodeled according to specific national myths, referring to the warriors of the early Islamic conquests, for instance, but also to the mothers of these warriors as those who raised them and made them strong. As a result, the imagery of youth was part of a historicizing process. The central aim of the Iraqi youth concept was to turn young boys into soldiers ready to sacrifice their lives for the nation. The debate—albeit focused on masculinity—also provided a limited public forum for female voices, such as those of teachers and students from secondary schools. Still, restrictive role models for both sexes, outlined by the male leaders of the movement, shaped the idea of gender relations among the national Arab youth.

Future Warriors and Mothers

In Iraqi nationalism, youth followed gendered scripts. Girls' role in the society is best described by the nationalist military officer Salāh-al-Dīn al-Sabbāgh, who dedicated his memoirs (written after 1941) to "the Arab woman who nourishes her baby with love of the nation and Arabism."[14] For him, the strengthening of the family and women's access to the spheres of interaction in society were preconditions for a true national awakening: "We want to teach woman to bear the burdens of social life because this does not stain her chastity and keep her away from her household duties and her motherly care." She might enjoy her life like man within the limits of Arab morality and culture.[15] Sabbāgh thus conceded a role to women in society and wanted to bring their status closer to that of men, but all within the limits of a supposed Arab nature and not at the expense of women's household duties. Still, the main emphasis of this quote is on teaching what was required to turn women into productive members of the nation. The state therefore needed access to shape the youth of both sexes.

Traces of an Iraqi youth debate appeared during the first half of the 1930s, related to Robert Baden-Powell's ideas about youth organizations. Baden-Powell founded the Boy Scout movement in 1907 on the principles of self-restraint, discipline, and fair play in sports. As an officer in the British army, Baden-Powell imparted his military experience gained in the Boer Wars directly to boys. The counterimage of the true, sporty, and upright Scouting Boy was a weak sort who smoked and had a sloppy physical appearance. The image of the proper Scouting Boy was close to the ideal taught in the British public schools. It was essential that the Scout be trained to obey orders in wartime, to endure, and to show honest chivalry. Discipline was a virtue the British sought to disseminate among male middle-class youth.[16] In that, the Boy Scouts was an institution supporting the established state rather than one of youthful protest.[17]

The Boy Scout movement enjoyed international appeal, and in the Arab world Baden-Powell's ideas of manliness and chivalry materialized into the movement *kashāfa*. Although Boy Scouts had existed in Iraq at least since 1919, the late Ottoman government had introduced a kind of Boy Scout movement in Iraq called Genc Dernekleri.[18] Then in the late 1930s, the Futuwwa movement incorporated many principles of the international Boy Scout movement. As an institution within the framework of a colonial narrative, the Boy Scouts became a model for an Iraqi disciplining institution intended to prepare youth for the struggle against imperialism. The historian George Mosse concurs that the Boy Scouts' "influence was great, and not confined to any one national elite as scouting and organizations modeled upon it became popular in many nations."[19] Moreover, Iraq showed similarities to trends that have been described by historian Mrinalini Sinha for Bengal.[20] The Iraqi establishment tried to channel youthful vigor by pressing it into a disciplining institution with a strict pattern of gender relations and gender ideals. As in the Indian case, the Iraqi youth movement referenced a mythical past and a decline from a historical state of strength and superiority to promote an awakening of youthful spirit to rebuild Iraqi masculinity. The emergence of a masculinity discourse in the British Empire, according to Sinha, "illustrate[s] the essentially interactive process in the deployment of the discursive mechanisms of colonial rule." The "obsessive concern with the emasculation of the Bengalis among the Bengali middle class cannot be attributed solely to the power of British colonial propaganda.... The production of colonial knowledge in India was always a two-way process, constructed out of the contestation and collaboration of certain sections of the Indian elite with the British." As such, it served certain middle-class strata.[21] In addition, colonial disciplining institutions such as the Boy Scouts served as models for the colonized to set up anticolonial movements.[22] In that sense, nationalist education or youth movements provided a disciplining function to promote national spirit. In Iraq, the Futuwwa movement was just such an anticolonial project. It was not, as has often been assumed, a mere product of fascist propaganda and influence, but rather a result of the wider colonial discourse.[23]

In the 1930s, however, *futuwwa* was apparently a male ideal only. I found no reports of Girl Scouting in Iraq during the period, even though its presence in other Arab countries makes it likely that it existed in Iraq as well.[24] The *Iraq Directory*, published in 1936, presented al-Futuwwa as a new system to strengthen students' appreciation for order and obedience. It referred only to males in the graduating classes of middle and secondary schools and their teachers—as well as to male students of engineering academies who had to attend paramilitary training classes.[25] Around the late 1930s, the topic of a manly Iraqi youth developed into an elaborate debate on the formation of Arab youth within al-Futuwwa. The issue of discipline was central. A quote from the Baghdad newspaper *al-Istiqlāl* of late 1939 alluded to the nature of masculinity as a universal concept: "Manhood belongs to the essential requirements of the nation in the present age."[26] This link between nation and manhood, between *watan* and *rujūla*, can be traced through the Iraqi press of the late 1930s. The same newspaper article underlined that the embodiment of the link was al-Futuwwa.

In addition to strength, al-Futuwwa was charged with giving a semblance of modernity to a society that Iraqi intellectuals regarded as backward. For the intellectuals, it was important to be able to cope with the modern nations of the West, and the way to do so was to provide a representation of the potential of the Iraqi Arab nation. Al-Futuwwa represented this potential in the shape of a masculinity that resembled European trends.

For some in Iraq, the fascist states offered an alternative but distant model of modernity that allowed for a tangible symbolism, for a focused and concentrated image of the nation, and for an easily imaginable identity linked to a mythical past.[27] The origin of the Arab nation was dated to the time of Muhammad, who was reinterpreted as the historical arch-leader of the Arab nation. In the process, the youth won a clear-cut masculine model of endurance and devotion: the warriors of the early Islamic conquests.[28] An example of this modeling is found in a speech by Sāmī Shaukat, published in his book *Hādhihī ahdāfunā*.[29] Shaukat, a leading nationalist politician and demagogue, delivered the speech in front of a Futuwwa unit. He opened with a story of 'Amr Ibn al-'Ās, the first Islamic conqueror of Egypt. A Byzantine delegation had approached 'Amr Ibn al-'Ās in Egypt, and when the members of the delegation returned home, they reported that they had encountered a race that regarded death as higher than life and humility as higher than rank. This race, the delegates reported, had no wishes or desires in the world, sat in the dust and ate their meals from their knees, and recognized no difference in rank between the commander and his soldiers. In his speech, Shaukat pointed out that these forefathers' comportment continued in this manner until they had conquered a third of the world for Islam. He encouraged Futuwwa members to raise their eyes and look at these examples. The Arab heroes of former times were looking down from above to see who among the current generation would fill the heroic roles they left behind. Shaukat's speech referred to a sacred generation as a model of military spirit and of the manly virtues of endurance and submission.

Indeed, al-Futuwwa imagery was built around opposites: true masculinity as opposed to effeminate behavior. Some of Sāmī Shaukat's speeches and articles in *Hādhihī ahdāfunā* show how a leading Arab nationalist constructed this opposition. In an article on the aims of al-Futuwwa and the clothing of youth in similar garments,[30] he told boys to beware of effeminate comportment. The present generations, he argued, were in greater need of moral training than previous generations had been because of their increased exposure to luxury, civilization, and amusement. Moreover, Shaukat believed that the young generation was prone to physical fatness and that Western technology and wealth as well as entertainment put proper Arab manliness at risk. Although the young boys' narrative was adopted from a Western context, al-Futuwwa nevertheless constructed proper Arab manliness as anti-Western, as a countermodel to the temptations of Western civilization. Consequently, the chastity of tradition and of the world before corruption should be revived through proper manliness. Shaukat described the main aims of the Futuwwa system: accustoming the youth to enduring the roughness of life, its labors, and sacrifices; and disseminating military spirit and the qualities of manliness and chivalry, which included love of the system and of obedience. These aims were to be achieved through military training.

Shaukat combined virtues that were integral to Arab nationalist discourse: manliness, chivalry, endurance, and sacrifice. The youth should learn to obey god and religion, and to live like the forefathers on the dust and in tents. Love for the nation and its glorious history, combined with the mentioned virtues, would make the nation rise again. The link between masculinity and nationalism could not have been clearer.

In the same article, Shaukat presented girls' place in this concept: the Futuwwa system should not be applied to girls' schools because, in "sanely mature communities," girls should be raised only to become good mothers and housewives; this belief was common during the period, and the curriculum of girls' schools in the Middle East reflected it. Unlike boys, who wore uniforms, girls were to wear dresses, but not luxurious or elegant clothing, and they were to avoid wearing makeup. When rich and poor looked the same, girls would return to their tasks and to obedience to God and the system. Paradoxically, Sāmī Shaukat announced that outstanding physical education teachers from the most famous universities of the West would be hired to train the girls and help form them into healthy mothers and good housewives, apparently to guard against the temptations of what he might have considered Western influence, namely, that the girls would question their restriction to household duties.

Apparently, Shaukat considered this notion of the female role to be modern. He believed that "mature," that is, modern, nations would see women's role in this way; such a role was a redefinition of women's contribution to society and not a liberalization of gender roles. In a speech published in 1939 in al-Istiqlāl, he praised the awakening of Turkish women and underlined his belief that likewise the Iraqi nahda (Arabic for "awakening") was largely rooted in the nahda of the woman in Iraq. The fact that 50,000 young girls were studying in Iraqi schools was for him a sign of nahda.[31] This number, however, equaled just slightly more than 3 percent of the estimated female population.[32] If we take into account as well the likelihood that the greater number of women were below the age of maturity, we see that public education had not yet reached a representative segment of the female population.

In Shaukat's perception, the meaning of modernity through renewal was blurred. Modernity was associated with the achievements of the West. For Iraqi nationalists, however, their idea of modernity drew from the past glory of the Arabs, ridding them of Western dominance. The perception of females was ambivalent too: girls remained subordinate to boys in their function within society, but still they gained access to the public area of state schooling. Schooling for girls followed the aim to separate them from their families through education. The state claimed access to them in order to shape them according to a totalizing vision. Even though Shaukat's ideas provided that girls would be formed according to a model in much the way boys were, still the girls would have entered the public sphere to learn the function attributed to them. Their role was at least in part an adoption of a European narrative of women's role in society. In Germany, this role for women had been shaped during the wars of liberation in the early nineteenth century. During this period, women became the preservers of morality within the domestic nucleus of the nation. The rationale behind such a role was that, without a prospering household, there would be no prospering nation. The woman's task was to take care of the "cultural side" of life, preserve honor, and raise children according to nationalist principles.[33] Education should prepare girls for this role. In Iraq of the 1930s, this role arguably still ran counter to the role of women in preindependence Iraq,[34] and much closer to, for instance, the North American ideals Jennifer Helgren ascribes to Camp Fire Girls in this volume.

In Iraq, as in other Middle Eastern countries, male intellectuals, starting in 1910, advocated that the state invest in girls' education. The 1920s and 1930s, then, witnessed a gradual growth of women's institutions. The first girls' school opened in 1919, the first women's magazine appeared in 1923, and from 1930 onward there was a girls' club in Baghdad (Nādī al-Banāt al-Baghdādiyya).[35] By 1929, the newspaper *al-Bilād* had a special weekly section for women and girls.[36] Another women's journal, *Fatāt al-'Arab* (Arab Girls), edited by Maryam Nazma, appeared in 1936 or 1937, and other magazines followed.[37] In 1937, there were fifteen female students at the Baghdad Medical College.[38] In 1932, the first Arab women's conference took place in Baghdad, and in 1938 an Iraqi delegation took part in the Eastern Women's Conference in Cairo.[39] The nationalist Muthannā Club established a women's committee.[40] All of these changes, however, reflect the role of established, married middle-class women rather than a particular girls' agency. Further evidence of change in women's and girls' role in society is hard to find in current scholarship, however, because Iraq has been marginal in Middle Eastern women's studies.[41] A proper evaluation of women's entry into the public sphere requires much more information on the role of women in Ottoman Baghdad society, for instance.[42]

Girls' Agency

In the context of the concern for Iraqi boys' manliness, and the general scarcity of information about girls in Iraqi sources, the few public female voices that do emerge stand out in the male domain of nationalist politics and publishing. Women would not only be educated in public schools, but in some instances they would find a public voice. For instance, the newspaper al-Bilād published a speech on the topic of Teachers' Day by Sabīha al-Shaikh Dāwud, a student at the law college.[43] Sabīha, from a liberal family, had become the first female student to enter the law college, in 1936. Later she became an important activist in Iraq.[44] In her Teachers' Day speech, however, she did not mention girls. Nor did she discuss the fact that she, as a young woman, accepted public exposure in giving the speech. Instead, she praised teachers and the model they offered as bulwarks of science and truth. She emphasized that her college was the well from which the national awakening spread in Mesopotamia. Her school had prepared the majority of the great men (rijālāt) for their service to the nation, because the graduates of this college belonged to the elite. Even though the task of giving this speech had been conferred on a woman, it seems that only the male graduates' service to the country was recognized in the official discourse of the school.

A different tone emerges in the speech given by another well-educated woman, Lamī'a al-Badrī, a student in the medical college, on the occasion of a festival commemorating the Arab Revolt of World War I. This speech was broadcast on the radio and published in the newspaper al-Istiqlāl.[45] Lamī'a emphasized that young Arab girls and boys were right in boasting. Claiming this was their day, she confirmed the central position of youth in the contemporary discourse on Arab nationalism, but with remarkable, although implicit, stress on gender equality. She encouraged her peers to take up what national duty decreed them to do. In the accomplishment of this duty, they would find fulfillment of their innermost desires. In the climax of her speech, she called out, "Oh you high-aspiring Arab girl, join your brother, the boy, with the force of your capacity to complete what your fathers and grandfathers have started." Although she referred only to the labors of the male forebears, not the female, she went on to explain that it was the woman who rocked the cradle with her right hand and waved the flag with her left.[46] She counseled Arab women to give their children a truly nationalist education. Mothers should tell children stories of Arab history and heroism, of the wars of al-Qādisiya, al-Yarmūk, and Maysalūn, and teach them to hold sacred the name of their honorable Arab forefathers, praising their deeds and conquests, and their lofty and noble characters.

In this speech, Lamī'a achieved two things. On the one hand, she underwrote the conventional Arab nationalist discourse of the time with its strong emphasis on manly heroism and its references to the forefathers' mythical past. Her speech connected the two decisive battles of the early

Islamic conquests in the seventh century—at Qādisīya against the Sassanian Empire and at the Yarmūk River against Byzantium—with the 1920 battle of Maysalūn, the last stand of a Syrian Arab nationalist army, defending the kingdom under King Faysal I against the French and imperialist takeover. On the other hand, Lamī 'a claimed an agency for girls. Girls had their task to fulfill for the nationalist cause, which was to raise a future generation of proud Arabs. There is no sign in the speech that Lamī'a considered this role to be a subordinate one. Moreover, she promoted a totalizing role for the state, in that nationalist narratives should become part of education in school and at home.

Another speech, given by Maryam Nūrī al-Muftī, headmistress of the girls' school of Samarra, on the occasion of Futuwwa day in June 1940, went even further than Lamī'a's speech to reinterpret the mother's role as that of a warrior on the home front.[47] Her approach was radically different from Sāmī Shaukat's, who attributed a passive role to the Iraqi girl. In principle, al-Muftī accepted man's warrior role on the battlefield, but her vision of the girl's role included a strong position in the Futuwwa system. Girls, she said, presented their own kind of Futuwwa.

Al-Muftī stated that the Iraqi girl had wanted for a long time to be equivalent with her brother in the field of service to the nation and in the readiness to sacrifice herself at his side. Now she had found a way to raise her head in al-Futuwwa. As much as the male leaders of the youth emphasized the descent of the *shabāb* (the male youth) from the warriors, the headmistress stressed that the Iraqi girl descended from the toughest kind as well and had inherited the true determination of the faithful women of ancient times. In contrast to this statement, women never appeared in the usual rhetoric by male Iraqi Arab nationalists about the enduring warriors of early Islam. Al-Muftī, however, claimed in her statement that al-Futuwwa offered a field for a girl's drives and desires. Hence, the day when al-Futuwwa was established had been a day of joy for the girls of Iraq. The speech reached its climax when she expressed her certainty that the Futuwwa of girls was the founding stone for the Futuwwa of boys because "she" guarded "him" for the sake of the rising nation. Futuwwa would lend the Iraqi girl strength to approach all difficulties with patience, whether she was running the domestic economy or raising children in the light of nationalism.

Al-Muftī made explicit that in this portrayal, she followed the role of European women during wartime. The Iraqi mothers and grandmothers had taken part proudly in past wars, in the same way that young European women were currently serving their nations in World War II. Indeed, she said, the day of the Iraqi girl was near. Al-Muftī linked female wartime efforts to other kinds of female Futuwwa: caring for the hopeless, the weeping orphans, and the sick was Futuwwa. The girls performing these virtuous tasks would sanctify Arabism.[48]

In contrast to Sāmī Shaukat's refusal to grant a place to the Iraqi girls in al-Futuwwa, al-Muftī's speech provided a picture of a female warrior fighting on the home front and thus laying the true foundations for the nation. This shift had several sources. Most important, rising female self-consciousness through nationalist education had caused this change of paradigm. It is equally possible that news from the European war had influenced the perception of the role of women in society. A trace of this influence appeared in an article by 'Abd-al-Majīd al-Hāshimī, deputy to the director general for propaganda, in January 1941.[49] He wrote about different kinds of mobilization, such as the "mental mobilization" necessary not only in war but also in times of peace. He stressed that under conditions of mobilization, a great contribution by women was possible as well. A woman could work as a substitute for the man who had gone to the front: she could replace him in factories, government offices, and hospitals, as well as in other services that accorded with her physical capacities. This idea of a woman's contribution came closer to al-Muftī's perception but still fell short of the independent "female nahda" she envisaged. Agency for girls and women was limited as long as woman, in her service to the nation, remained in the position of being merely a substitute for a man and not according to her own value.

Conclusion

Although these three articles are not representative of the overwhelmingly masculinist Iraqi Arab nationalist discourse on youth during the 1930s and early 1940s, nevertheless they hint at important changes in the image of girlhood during this time. They may even be the first traces of a conflict over girls' roles in an envisaged nationalist transformation of state and society. As Noga Efratis's previously cited article proves, the Iraqi feminist debate of the period otherwise moved within the limits of the middle class and its charitable and educationalist approach, apparently with no regard to girls' agency. To be sure, nationalist politicians and writers had a paternalistic approach to the formation of a new generation of youth that was to bring the country and the wider Arab nation forward and to defend it against imperialism. Only a few liberal voices wanted to direct the state educational system in Iraq toward promotion of individual qualities instead of streamlining young boys as future warriors and young girls as mothers and caretakers, notions at the heart of authoritarian nationalist imagery.[50] The widespread preference of nationalists for a totalitarian organization of Iraqi youth was surely out of touch with the realities of a society that was religiously and ethnically largely segregated during the 1930s and early 1940s. This holds true for the demand that girls should be turned into useful members of the national community too. Still, the visions of a society modernized along authoritarian lines put into question the restriction of girls to the domestic role in society following inherited models of seclusion from the public sphere. Al-Futuwwa offered girls potential new means of self-expression, albeit in a limited and illiberal fashion.

NOTES

Parts of this chapter appeared in Peter Wien, *Iraqi Arab Nationalism: Authoritarian, Totalitarian and Pro-Fascist Inclinations, 1932–1941* (New York: Routledge, 2006), and are included here with gracious permission of Routledge Press.

1. On generational conflict, see Reinhart Koselleck, "'Erfahrungsraum' und 'Erwartungshorizont': Zwei Historische Kategorien," in *Vergangene Zukunft: Zur Semantik Geschichtlicher Zeiten*, 4th ed., ed. Reinhart Koselleck (Frankfurt: Suhrkamp Taschenbuch Wissenschaft, 2000), 349–375. Cf. also Mark Roseman, "Introduction: Generation Conflict and German History 1770–1968," in *Generations in Conflict: Youth Revolt and Generation Formation in Germany 1770–1968*, ed. Mark Roseman (New York: Cambridge University Press, 1995), 19–20.

2. Elizabeth Thompson, *Colonial Citizens: Republican Rights, Paternal Privilege, and Gender in French Syria and Lebanon* (New York: Columbia University Press, 2000), 141–154.

3. Ibid., 94–99. Cf. also, for instance, Margaret Lee Meriwether and Judith E. Tucker, *Social History of Women and Gender in the Modern Middle East* (Boulder, CO: Westview Press, 1999).

4. Noga Efrati, "The Other 'Awakening' in Iraq: The Women's Movement in the First Half of the Twentieth Century," *British Journal of Middle Eastern Studies* 31 (2004): 153–173.

5. See James P. Jankowski, *Egypt's Young Rebels: "Young Egypt": 1933–1952* (Stanford: Hoover Institution Press, 1975). Cf. also Keith David Watenpaugh, *Being Modern in the Middle East: Revolution, Nationalism, Colonialism, and the Arab Middle Class* (Princeton, NJ: Princeton University Press, 2006), 255–298. He writes about paramilitary youth organizations, but also about Boy and Girl Scouting in Aleppo before and after World War II.

6. See Thompson, *Colonial Citizens.*

7. Peter Wien, *Iraqi Arab Nationalism: Authoritarian, Totalitarian and Pro-Fascist Inclinations, 1932–1941* (New York: Routledge, 2006), 14–51, 88–105.

8. See Haggai Erlich, "The Arab Youth and the Challenge of Fascism," in *Fascism Overseas*, ed. Stein Larsen (New York: Columbia University Press, 2001), 408–423; Gerhard Höpp, "Araber im Zweiten Weltkrieg: Kollaboration oder Patriotismus?" in *Jenseits der Legenden: Araber, Juden, Deutsche*, ed. Wolfgang Schwanitz (Berlin: Dietz, 1994), 91; Gerhard Höpp, "'Nicht 'Ail zuliebe, Sondern aus Hass gegen Mu'āwiya': Zum Ringen um die 'Arabienerklärung' der Achsenmächte 1940–1942," *Asien Afrika Lateinamerika* 27 (1999): 571; Jankowski, *Egypt's Young Rebels*; Elsa Marston, "Fascist Tendencies in Pre-War Arab Politics: A Study of Three Arab Political Movements," *Middle East Forum* 35 (May 1959): 19–22, 33–35; Fritz Steppat, "Das Jahr 1933 und seine Folgen für die Arabischen Länder des Vorderen Orients," in *Die Große Krise der dreißiger Jahre: Vom Niedergang der Weltwirtschaft zum Zweiten Weltkrieg*, ed. Gerhard Schulz (Göttingen, 1985), 272; Watenpaugh, *Being Modern in the Middle East*, 255–278; Stefan Wild, "National Socialism in the Arab Near East between 1933 and 1939," *Die Welt des Islams* 25 (1985):126–173.

9. Erlich, "Arab Youth," 413.

10. Erlich dates its origins to 1931, Simon to 1932, which would have been under Sāmī Shaukat as director general of education. Haggai Erlich, "Youth and Arab Politics: The Political Generation of 1935–1936," in *Alienation or Integration of Arab Youth*, ed. Roel Meijer (London: Routledge, 2000), 61; Reeva S. Simon, *Iraq between the Two World Wars: The Creation and Implementation of a Nationalist Ideology* (New York: Columbia University Press, 1986), 78, 110–114. Buttī attributes the introduction of the Futuwwa system to Sāti' al-Husrī and dates it to 1935. Husrī was director general of public instruction under Prime Minister Yāsīn al-Hāshimī then. Rufā'īl Buttī, *Dhākira 'Irāqīya, 1900–1956*, 2 vols., ed. Fā'iq Buttī (Damascus: Al-Mada, 2000), 1:449.

11. Hayyim J. Cohen, "The Anti-Jewish Farhūd in Baghdad, 1941," *Middle Eastern Studies* 3, no. 1 (1966): 6–7.

12. Claude Cahen, "Mouvements populaires et autonomisme urbain dans l'Asie musulmane du moyen âge, II–III," *Arabica* 6 (1959): 30–56, 233–244; *Encyclopedia of Islam*, s.v. "Futuwwa" (Leiden: Brill, 1991); Bernard Lewis, *The Political Language of Islam* (Chicago: University of Chicago Press, 1988), 16–17.

13. See George Mosse, *The Image of Man: The Creation of Modern Masculinity* (New York: Oxford University Press, 1996); Ute Frevert, "Soldaten, Staatsbürger: Überlegungen zur historischen Konstruktion von Männlichkeit," in *Männergeschichte—Geschlechtergeschischte: Männlichkeit im Wandel der Moderne*, ed. Thomas Kühne, Geschichte und Geschlechter 14 (Frankfurt: Campus, 1996), 73–74, 80–85; Helen Kanitkar, "'Real True Boys': Moulding the Cadets of Imperialism," in *Dislocating Masculinity: Comparative Ethnographies*, ed. Andrea Cornwall and Nancy Lindisfarne (London: Routledge, 1994); Klaus Schmitz, *Militärische Jugenderziehung: Preußliche Kadettenhäuser und Nationalpolitische Erziehungsanstalten zwischen 1807 und 1936*, Studien und Dokumentationen zur deutschen Bildungsgeschichte 67 (Colognc: Boehlau, 1997).

14. Al-Sabbāgh was the unofficial head of the so-called Golden Square, a group of four Iraqi staff officers who controlled Iraqi politics from the late 1930s. In 1941, they staged a coup against the pro-British government and entered a short-lived military alliance with Germany. The British brought them down in a short war during May 1941, which led to the second British occupation of Iraq.

15. Salāh al-Dīn al-Sabbāgh, *Mudhakkirāt al-shahīd al-'aqīd al-rukn Salāh al-Dīn al-Sabbāgh: Fursān al-'urūba fi'l-'Irāq* (Damascus, [1956]), 3, 10.

16. Mosse, *Image of Man*, 135–136.

17. John Springhall, "'Young England, Rise Up, and Listen': The Political Dimensions of Youth Protest and Generation Conflict in Britain," in *Jugendprotest und Generationenkonflikt in Europa im 20. Jahrhundert: Deutschland, England und Italien im Vergleich. Vorträge eines internationalen Symposiums des Instituts für Sozialgeschichte Braunschweig-Bonn und der Friedrich-Ebert-Stiftung vom 17.–19. Juni 1985 in Braunschweig*, ed. Dieter Dowe (Bonn: Verlag Neue Gesellschaft, 1986), 154.

18. Gillian Grant, *Middle Eastern Photographic Collections in the United Kingdom*, Middle East Libraries Committee Research Guides 3 (Durham, NC: Middle East Libraries Committee, 1989), 139. The collection of the Scout Association, Baden-Powell House, Queen's Gate, London contains material on Iraq from 1919 to 1921: a logbook and box of glass slides covering the activities of the Baghdad and District Boy Scouts Association, with special reference to three troops—the 9th Baghdad (Protestant), 11th Baghdad (Armenian School), and 12th Baghdad (Ta'awun School). Walter Björkmann, "Das irakische Bildungswesen und seine Probleme bis zum Zweiten Weltkrieg," *Die Welt des Islams*, n.s. 1 (1951): 175.

19. Mosse, *Image of Man*, 135.

20. Mrinalini Sinha, *Colonial Masculinity: The 'Manly Englishman' and the 'Effeminate Bengali' in the Late Nineteenth Century* (Manchester: Manchester University Press, 1995).

21. Ibid., 21–22.

22. Cf. Timothy Mitchell, *Colonising Egypt* (Berkeley: University of California Press, 1991), xi.

23. Cf. Simon, *Iraq between the Two World Wars*, 112.

24. Elizabeth Thompson affirms there were Girl Scouts and girls participating in pro-fascist activities in Syria and [0]Lebanon. They remained marginal, however. Thompson, *Colonial Citizens*, 195–196. Cf. also Watenpaugh, *Being Modern in the Middle East*, 255–298.

25. *Al-dalīl al-'Irāqī al-rasmī (The Iraq Directory)* (Baghdad, 1936), 618.

26. "Hadīth al-yaum: Harakat al-Futuwwa," *al-Istiqlāl*, November 20, 1939, 3.

27. Cf. George L. Mosse, *The Fascist Revolution: Toward a General Theory of Fascism* (New York: Howard Fertig, 1999).

28. Cf. the emphasis on Islamic history in state education and the founding of Islamic museums as well as the increase in excavations of Islamic sites in Iraq. Amatzia Baram, "A Case of

Imported Identity: The Modernizing Secular Ruling Elites of Iraq and the Concept of Mesopotamian-Inspired Territorial Nationalism, 1922–1992," *Poetics Today* 15 (1994): 290–291.

29. Sāmī Shaukat, *Hādhihī ahdāfunā* (Baghdad: Matba'at al-Tafayyud al-Ahliyya, 1939), 4–6; first published in *al-Istiqlāl*. Shaukat is often presented as the most aggressive promoter of totalitarian tendencies. See, for instance, Phebe Marr, *The Modern History of Iraq* (Boulder, CO: Westview Press, 1985), 79; Simon, *Iraq between the Two World Wars*, 87–88.

30. Sāmī Shaukat, "Ahdāf al-Futuwwa al-'ulyā wa-tauhīd malābis al-fityān," in *Hādhihī ahdāfunā*, 7–14.

31. "'Uyūbunā al-ijtimā'iyya wa-mahāsinuhā," *al-Istiqlāl*, December 5, 1939, 1. In 1935 there were 85 girls' schools as opposed to 365 boys' schools. Girls' education apparently became an important issue of educational policy in 1930s Iraq. Björkmann, "Das irakische Bildungswesen," 182.

32. In 1930, the population of Iraq amounted to around 2,824,000. Mohammad A. Tarbush, *The Role of the Military in Politics: A Case Study of Iraq to 1941* (London: Routledge, 1983), 16.

33. Karin Hagemann, "Heldenmütter, Kriegerbräute und Amazonen. Entwürfe 'patriotischer' Weiblichkeit zur Zeit der Freiheitskriege," in *Militär und Gesellschaft im 19. und 20. Jahrhundert*, ed. Ute Frevert, Industrielle Welt 58 (Stuttgart: Klett-Cotta, 1997), 182, 185.

34. Cf. Liat Kozma's article in this volume on the situation in Egypt.ī

35. *Al-dalīl al-'Irāqī al-rasmī*, 826.

36. Fā'iq Buttī, *A'lām fī sihāfat al-'Irāq* (Baghdad, 1971), 93.

37. Fā'iq Buttī, *Sihāfat al-'Irāq: Tārīkhuhā wa-kifāh ajyālihā* (Baghdad: Matb'at al-Adīb al-Baghdādiyya, 1968), 118. No copies of the journal *Fatāt al-'Arab* were available for this study, unfortunately.

38. Björkmann, "Das irakische Bildungswesen," 183.

39. 'Abbās 'Atīya Jabbār, *Al-'Irāq wa'l-qadīya al-filastīnīya: 1932–1941* (Baghdad: Āfāq 'Arabiyya, 1990), 61.

40. Ibid., 53. For the entire section, see Efrati, "Other 'Awakening,'" 155–173.

41. Cf. Nikki R. Keddie, "Women in the Limelight: Some Recent Books on Middle Eastern Women's History," *International Journal of Middle East Studies* 34 (2002):553–573. Keddie omits references to Iraq almost entirely.

42. An insightful article on that topic is Dina Rizk Khoury, "Drawing Boundaries and Defining Spaces: Women and Space in Ottoman Iraq," in *Women, the Family, and Divorce Laws in Islamic History*, ed. Amira El Azhary Sonbol (Syracuse: Syracuse University Press, 1996).

43. "Kalimat al-fatāt al-huqūqiyya fī takrīm al-asātidha al-judud," *al-Bilād*, December 27, 1939, 5.

44. Efrati, "Other 'Awakening,'" 154–160. The 1936 *Iraq Directory* mentioned that the law college was there to graduate capable men; *Al-dalīl al-'Irāqī al-rasmī*, 557.

45. "Nahdatunā," *al-Istiqlāl*, September 15, 1940, 1, 4.

46. In Arabic, the word for "to rock" and "to wave" is the same (*tahuzzu*), which gives the image more weight.

47. "Yaum al-Futuwwa," *al-Istiqlāl*, June 28, 1940, 2.

48. For similar trends in Syria, see Thompson, *Colonial Citizens*, 124.

49. "Hadīth 'askarī li'l-ra'īs al-rukn 'Abd-al-Majid al-Hāshimī," *al-Bilād*, January 1, 1941, 1, 4.

50. Cf. Peter Wien, "Who Is 'Liberal' in 1930s Iraq? Education as a Contested Terrain in a Nascent Public Sphere," in *Nationalism and Liberal Thought in the Arab East: Political Practice and Experience*, ed. Christoph Schumann (London: Routledge, 2009).

16

"'Homemaker' Can Include the World"

FEMALE CITIZENSHIP AND INTERNATIONALISM IN THE POSTWAR CAMP FIRE GIRLS

JENNIFER HELGREN

Representing the Camp Fire Girls of America, one of the United States' most popular youth organizations, Eleanore Korman of the national programming department declared in the mid-1950s, "Our girls need to increase their understanding of the word 'homemaker' in order to accept positively their future careers. 'Homemaker' can include the world, and a little more, if we only let it."[1] The statement represented a vision of girl citizenship, emerging in the post–World War II era, that both expanded and constrained girls' roles. As the war drew to a close, youth organizations in the United States reevaluated their programs and determined that girls needed a new relation to national and international politics. If American girls extended their feminine role of service to family and community to the nation and the world, then they might help to reshape the postwar world on an American democratic model. Camp Fire leaders optimistically predicted that girls could help secure international peace by thinking like world citizens.

In this chapter I examine the uniquely gendered and youth-specific model of world citizenship that Camp Fire delineated for girls in the postwar era. First, I describe the familial model of female citizenship that Camp Fire promoted, explaining how organization leaders such as Korman and director Martha Allen linked girls' domestic duties to global responsibility. Second, I examine the specific activities that girls undertook as part of Camp Fire's international program along with Camp Fire's attempt to establish clubs in Japan. I argue that this programming imbued domestic activities with a new cosmopolitan spirit but ultimately reified American girls' patriotic identity as they looked inward to define and export American values abroad. After World War II, in the effort to prevent future wars and the spread of communism, local organizations such as Camp Fire complimented federal policies such as the Marshall Plan and aid to Japan. These nation-building programs carried a service ethic consistent with youth citizenship training, even as they promoted the United States' interests abroad. Ordinary girls could serve as political emissaries of a sort, carrying an image of youthful innocence and tolerance as well as American models of education, childhood, and gender roles into the international arena. In the process, despite a cosmopolitan flavor, Camp Fire's actual program promoted an inward-looking, narrow view of female citizenship that fostered patriotic national identity in its girl citizens.

In 1940s America, commitment to global citizenship—broadly defined as awareness of the interconnectedness of people globally; knowledge of different cultures; duty to those beyond national borders; and international cooperation—held strong political currency. According to historians Paul Boyer and Dorothy Robins, in the final years of and immediately following the Second World War, American scientists, scholars, politicians, and citizen groups expressed optimism about the potential for international cooperation through organizations like the United Nations. According to Robins, no mainstream "school or club program was complete without at least one United Nations or world affairs event."[2] Camp Fire shared this enthusiasm. With the aid of religious groups, youth organizations and schools abroad, correspondence societies, and even the military, Camp Fire sponsored global conversations—contact and understanding between girls of different nations. These efforts at internationalism continued into the 1950s and beyond. Even as Cold War tensions escalated in 1949 and the early 1950s, and American popular support for the United Nations lessened, Camp Fire tempered its internationalism only somewhat. As the Soviet Union detonated an atomic bomb, Mao Zedong assumed control of China, and North Korean forces invaded the South, organization leaders turned greater attention to civil defense, anticommunism, and the task of sheltering girls physically and emotionally, but Camp Fire's programming in the 1950s demonstrated an ongoing belief that girls, properly trained to be nurturing, democratic, tolerant women, offered hope for a peaceful future.[3]

The Girl Citizen: Familial Service on a Global Scale

From the start, limits hemmed this new model of girl citizenship as the global responsibilities assigned to girls actually reinforced their responsibilities to the home. Since its founding in 1910 as a feminine corollary to the Boy Scouts of America, Camp Fire formulated a model of female citizenship in which girls' primary responsibility to the home was supplemented by increasing opportunities in civic reform, education, paid employment, and athletics. In the tradition of Progressive Era female reformers, Camp Fire Girls adopted a definition of girl citizenship based on maternalism, although it also validated citizen roles for girls in the present. As historian Molly Ladd Taylor explains, maternalism was "a uniquely feminine value system based on care and nurturance" that recognized a civic responsibility in child rearing, which brought women into public reform.[4] Perceiving girls, at least in part, as future mothers, Camp Fire adapted the model to them. In the postwar era, girls' responsibility to cultivate relationships within the family and community and to serve the nation stretched to the world stage, but girls' primary identification was still the home. In addition to being a conservative version of female activism, this model of girl citizenship fit squarely with American patriotism. Although the act of teaching global citizenship potentially challenges the dominant concept of the nation-state by encouraging young people to identify with others beyond national borders,[5] Camp Fire's brand of internationalism worked to reaffirm American identity as girls studied their own culture in order to share it with girls abroad. Ultimately, Camp Fire taught lessons in national superiority and a sense of the importance of national borders.

Founded by a network of progressive reformers, educators, and youth workers, Camp Fire was the most popular organization for girls in the United States until 1930, when Girl Scout membership surpassed its own. Camp Fire counted approximately 370,000 girl members between the ages of nine and eighteen in 1951. It had a national presence in over 2,600 communities, with especially strong local councils in the Midwest and on the West Coast.[6] The 1940s and 1950s represented a period of growth and popularity for youth organizations in the United States. As folklorist Jay Mechling explains, this "golden age" resulted from the baby boom, the values of American suburban life, and "symbolic demography," or the web of meaning that Americans constructed to identify their values. The Boy Scouts, the Girls Scouts, and the Camp Fire Girls loomed large in American iconography as symbols of citizenship, virtue, and hope for the future. Along with 4-H Clubs, church groups, the YMCA, political organizations, and other institutions, these youth organizations provided a reassuring counternarrative to the stories of juvenile delinquency and teenage rebellion that captured media attention in the 1940s and 1950s. For many Americans, youth organizations embodied civic virtue and patriotism.[7]

Ostensibly open to all girls, Camp Fire drew a predominantly white middle-class leadership and membership. The middle-class status and worldview of participants framed the concept of female citizenship that emerged in the organization. Camp Fire publications targeted the middle-class girls who anticipated futures as housewives and mothers and who would bring their educations to bear on employment before marriage, part-time work, and volunteer work beyond the home. A model based on a cross-class or multiracial vision of female citizenship would have been, of necessity, more complex and would have sought to introduce a broader depiction of maternal values abroad.[8] Instead, in the wake of World War II, when women had served as WACS and WAVES and fueled the nation's defense industry, Camp Fire adhered to a conservative gender ideology and thereby fueled the cultural contradictions that white middle-class women confronted during the period.[9]

Led by its first female national director, Martha Allen, a woman who, with her advanced education, unmarried status, and insistence on conventional gender roles, embodied these cultural contradictions, Camp Fire emphasized homemaking and gender differences even as it offered new opportunities to girls. In the process, it eroded many of the war's gains for women in work and independence, as described by Lisa Ossian in this volume.[10] Adult leaders such as Allen focused attention on "training for democratic living" and helping "girls to develop a greater capacity for sympathy, forbearance, tolerance, understanding, and those virtues upon which all homes must be built."[11] Such statements rooted girls' civic participation in the home. In fact, girls were future "Republican Mothers," to use Linda Kerber's famous phrase for women's political roles after the American Revolution, receiving training in civic virtue and patriotism. Not only would Camp Fire Girls have an important role within national borders as future mothers, but they also would have an important citizenship role in an anxious world as *girls*.

Allen asserted the need for strong youth organizations in times of stress. The best way to fight communism at home and abroad, she argued, was for America and its institutions, including youth organizations, to live up to their highest democratic ideals.[12] Calling on youth organizations to do their part, she warned that "an organization which seeks to train girls for citizenship cannot ignore this struggle or operate on the assumption that if we teach children to tie knots, build a campfire and give service, all will be well." Instead the organization needed to "teach our girls to value human dignity, democratic practices, free inquiry, and truth."[13] "If democracy could be made 100% effective in the United States," she wrote, "I don't believe it would be possible to convert a single American citizen to communism." Leaders and girls could start close to home "by making democracy work at least in our own organization."[14]

At a regional conference of the Camp Fire Girls near Boston, Camp Fire's director of field operations, Mrs. Lou B. Paine, explained the home's centrality in these efforts to train female citizens for the postwar world: "Home will always be the center of woman's life, but it is not her circumference. Women have come to realize that the walls of her home must expand to include the community, that the fences around communities must expand to include the world."[15] In the Camp Fire manual, national staff categorized the various citizenship honors that girls could earn to mirror widening circles of civic responsibility beyond the home. The manual listed eight categories, starting with duties to "Myself, My Family, My Camp Fire Group and Other Friends, My School, My Religion, My Community, My State and Country," and ending with "Our World." "Our World" activities required learning about the customs, holidays, flags, and languages of other nations, following international events in the newspaper, and volunteering with an international aid society. The section also listed a number of ways girls could support the United Nations, such as observing United Nations Day with a group, touring the United Nations headquarters in New York, attending a General Assembly meeting and reporting on it, and reading the preamble of the United Nations charter to explain how Camp Fire "helps to carry out the principles of world friendship."[16] Envisioning a maternal ethic that extended to international relations, Camp Fire charged girls with a civic responsibility to care for and nurture the world.

As for the girls, they learned to express the language and ideals of Camp Fire's internationalism, at least at Camp Fire events. For example, in Roslindale, Massachusetts, junior high Camp Fire Girls recited lines prepared for the closing ceremony at their council fire, or regional meeting. Their ceremony connected girls' duty to the home with international citizenship and traced civic responsibility from the home outward. After lighting four candles to represent the home, the community, the nation, and the world, Karin Gustavsen, the group leader's daughter, indicated the symbolic meaning of the candles:

> These are lights which we cannot extinguish. They burn ever in our hearts.
> The light of homes and all that homes stand for will never perish as long as there are Homemakers.
> The lights of the community burn brightly in the hearts of all who cherish the community.
> The candle lighted to symbolize our nation has been given to us to pass undimmed to others.
> The lights which symbolize our world with malice toward none with charity for all
> These lights in God's will shall never die.
> We are the builders—the light and the hope of the world! [17]

The girls' ceremonial expressed the widening circle of civic responsibility by depicting girls as homemakers and nation builders, the foundation of democratic society. Thus, the real focus of the girls' speech was on what girls did at home and in the community. In fact, girls became "builders—the light and the hope of the world" as good citizens in their families, schools, and Camp Fire clubs.

Moreover, the actual Camp Fire program activities remained little changed even as the organization re-envisioned girlhood as a symbolic beacon of peace. The maternalism on which the Camp Fire philosophy was based offered flexibility. As American political concerns shifted, Camp Fire's program could address those needs, refashioning rhetoric while changing few program activities. During the Second World War, Camp Fire had militarized these activities to boost war morale; now they sowed peace. Indeed the essential maternalism that had characterized the organization's philosophy since 1910 simply found new arenas for expression, depending on American political and social needs.

Camp Fire Girls and Their International Projects

Camp Fire's international outlook was not entirely new after World War II. Outreach to European refugee children during both world wars had laid a foundation for such efforts. After the war, however, Camp Fire framed these endeavors not only as service projects but also as the gateway to world peace. Camp Fire reinforced the idea of global citizenship in multiple ways. Leaders looked to instill an international ethic in girls by celebrating the United Nations in ceremonials and songs and by performing service. Most significant, Camp Fire sponsored "birthday projects" each year in which girls across the nation followed lesson plans and performed service according to themes provided by national headquarters. With titles such as "Hi, Neighbor!" (1945), "At Home in the World" (1946), and "Let's Get Together" (1948), birthday projects asked local councils to prepare activities that stressed community building on both the local and international level. As a result, Camp Fire groups supported the United Nations, imbued feminine training with a cosmopolitan spirit, and developed pen pal friendships with girls in other countries as sources for cross-cultural understanding.

Camp Fire supported the United Nations by increasing girls' awareness of its structure, function, and human rights declaration. United Nations themes were woven into ordinary Camp Fire activities. For instance, camp directors named cabin groups after different nations and asked girls to learn about those nations during their week at camp.[18] At a Norwood, Massachusetts, ceremonial campfire, each cabin unit presented a folk song, story, or dance "from that corner of the world" about which they had learned.[19] Similarly, organization officials promoted the United Nations and their own organization by including girls in United Nations observances. Thousands of Camp Fire Girls across the United States commemorated the opening day of the United Nation's World Security Conference on April 25, 1945, by holding "World Friendship ceremonials . . . to [express] their friendship for the children of other countries and their hopes for a lasting peace."[20] Later Camp Fire Girls gathered signatures for the "Freedom Scroll," a pledge of world peace and freedom that was enclosed in the bell tower on United Nations Day, when the World Freedom Bell was dedicated in Berlin on October 24, 1950.[21]

Camp Fire tried to educate leaders as well as girls. In March 1949, the *Camp Fire Girl*, Camp Fire's official publication for girls and leaders in the postwar era, published a concise version of the Declaration on Human Rights of the United Nations Commission and asked leaders to reflect on how their clubs encouraged the values it outlined.[22] Camp Fire taught that girls' responsibility to work for peace derived from their roles as females but that an understanding of international institutions such as the United Nations was essential for girls to act as conscientious citizens.

Camp Fire brought a global outlook to girls' training in dance, domesticity, and philanthropy. Camp Fire leaders offered folk dance as a way to bring diverse peoples together and to transcend cultural barriers, and organization programmers hoped international friendships would encourage the sharing of folk dances. A 1946 article in the *Camp Fire Girl* by Walter Terry, a dance critic for the *New York Herald Tribune*, advocated folk dance for promoting "the one world ideal," a reference to the potential of world governments to assure peace. Terry argued that "folk dancing affords good citizenship training. . . . It is truly communal for it belongs, as the name implies, to the 'folk.'" Moreover, folk dance advanced the United Nations' call for international understanding. "In learning and taking part in the folk dances of other lands, the Camp Fire Girls are contributing to the program of the United Nations, which calls for the exchange of ideas among nations, a better understanding of the cultures of this world."[23] Camp Fire had celebrated what historian Diana Selig calls the "cultural gifts" of immigrant groups through folk dance since the 1910s.[24] Now girls could promote tolerance and cross-cultural understanding on an international scale.

Playing hostess also took on a global dimension. Camp Fire Girls held progressive dinners where each course represented a different country.[25] In 1946, the *Camp Fire Girl* called for special plans to make "the first Flag Day since the war an occasion of deep international and interracial significance." Camp Fire Girls would host food collection parties for hungry children in Europe. Tiny United States and United Nations flags would top the cupcakes, girls would wear costumes from other countries, and groups would perform folk dances from around the world and act out skits interpreting Franklin D. Roosevelt's "Four Freedoms." To promote tolerance, each girl was encouraged to invite "as her guest someone of another race, creed or nationality background."[26] Combating hate through youth, who, organization officials implied, were not yet corrupted by prejudice, Camp Fire taught girls to turn the traditional role of party hostess into that of world philanthropist.

Although it is impossible to know how many girls held Flag Day parties, Camp Fire scrapbooks and reports indicate that clubs incorporated the international outlook into their planning. Notably, their focus, however, was usually on their own families and communities, a pattern that served to reaffirm American identity. The Roslindale Camp Fire Girls, for example, dressed in folk costumes and held an "international" exhibit that included displays of objects from other countries. Several of the girls brought "foreign" artifacts from their homes and dressed in traditional costumes representing their own Swedish, Norwegian, and Mexican ancestral backgrounds.[27] Such projects simultaneously directed girls' attention abroad and toward their own unique family histories.

Accustomed to helping families and children in need, Camp Fire Girls increasingly thought of service in global terms. In early 1945, as Allied victory in Europe seemed certain, Camp Fire officials directed the program away from war aims of morale building and conservation and toward peacetime concerns. Some wartime service measures such as Victory Gardens blended seamlessly into the postwar context. Lucille Hein, national Camp Fire program specialist, in her essay "Where Hunger Stalks There Can Be No Peace," explained that fighting world hunger would motivate citizens to a deeper concern for all world issues. Girls supported the United Nations Relief and Rehabilitation Administration and the "Eat Less" Campaign of the Famine Emergency Committee, an organization formed by President Truman and chaired by Herbert Hoover to halt the mass starvation brought on by the war in Asia and Europe. Girls reduced wastes by saving fats and cleaning their plates, and they canned homegrown foods, donated canned goods abroad, and reduced the use of wheat products.[28] These specific home-based tasks, Camp Fire officials hoped, would ameliorate suffering and remind girls of their global responsibilities.

Most ambitious among the postwar service projects were the annual birthday projects. Initiated during the First World War, when Camp Fire had concentrated resources nationwide on relieving European children displaced due to the war, these annual projects gave a unified theme and purpose to the year's activities. Most themes before the war promoted personal development, national service, or American history. The postwar projects, developed by C. Frances Loomis (later Wallace), Camp Fire staffer since 1923 and director of the program department from 1945 to 1949, were routinely international in scope. Loomis's birthday projects asked girls to conceive of their citizenship responsibilities extending out from the individual and home to the community and the world stage.

The 1945 "Hi Neighbor" project, for example, was designed to foster community life and to develop appreciation for the diversity in communities both at home and abroad, whereas the 1946 "At Home in the World" project encouraged greater appreciation of other "nationalities, races, and creeds" by teaching girls about people from different backgrounds. Suggesting that girls should feel at "home" beyond their family, the project broadened girls' roles while maintaining their primary connection to the home.[29]

Among Camp Fire's strongest statements on internationalism was the 1948 birthday project "Hello, World, Let's Get Together," which called for girls to forge international relationships and, in the process, foster world peace. The theme was inspired by the UNESCO statement, "Since wars begin in the minds of men, it is in the minds of men that the defenses of peace must be constructed."[30] The project announcement in the *Camp Fire Girl* explained, "'The best of life is people,' yet human beings are having a hard time getting along together. Now we might be celebrating and working on the great promises of atomic energy for an easier and more plentiful life for everyone. Instead there is talk about another war. We know too much about how to destroy people—and too little about how to make friends with people!" "Hello, World" was intended to show the world how to get along, beginning not "in the minds of men" but with girls. Camp Fire projected an image of youth as uniquely free from prejudice and therefore suited to forging international relationships, explaining that "young people everywhere are naturally friendly and eager to know about the young people of other countries." With youth symbolizing the human potential for cooperation, Camp Fire created projects to promote connections between girls internationally.

Central to the "Hello World" campaign were "friendship groups," pen pal networks with girls from different backgrounds, which were designed to tear down stereotypes. Using connections with churches, schools, correspondence societies, and other youth organizations, Camp Fire matched their clubs to groups of girls in other regions, among other religions, or in other countries.[31] For example, Camp Fire's most influential field worker, Edith Kempthorne, was a crucial link in these programs. Always interested in travel, she had also helped begin Camp Fire groups in England, and in 1949 she moved there to work on Camp Fire's international program. She was instrumental in coordinating the pen pal program through national headquarters, matching international pen pals, especially girls in the United States and Great Britain.[32] Camp Fire's friendship groups encouraged American girls to learn about others, but as I argue they also encouraged American girls to reaffirm and export American values abroad.

In early 1948, the *Camp Fire Girl* listed numerous groups that had established pen pal relationships with girls in foreign countries. Camp Fire Girls in El Centro, California, wrote to groups across the United States and "to Camp Fire Girls in the leper colonies in the Philippine Islands," for whom they were establishing a fund to send supplies.[33] A group in Melrose, Massachusetts, sent a party kit to their friendship group in Stourbridge, England. They shipped everything necessary to throw a party: crepe paper, a lollipop-decorated maypole, fudge mix, Crisco, and Kool-Aid. In the Greater Boston Camp Fire Council area alone, girls sent letters and care packages to girls in Norway, Scotland, France, Germany, Belgium, Italy, Ireland, and Israel.[34] One group in eastern Massachusetts had been slow to "warm up to the project," but the leader soon recorded that the girls were busy learning Dutch folk dances, and "practically every girl, or her family, is now sending clothes parcels over seas." Their friendship groups stretched from England to the Netherlands and China.[35] In fact, when Madame Chiang Kai-shek visited the United States in 1943, she met with a group of high-school-aged Camp Fire Girls in Staten Island. The girls presented her with money collected from various Camp Fire clubs for the "adoption" of two Chinese war orphans. Camp Fire Girls in twenty cities including Worcester, Massachusetts, Los Angeles, and Chiloquin, Oregon, had contributed money for Chinese War Relief earmarked for Chinese children.[36]

Before Mao's victory in 1949, Camp Fire likely maintained ties to China through relief agencies connected to Nationalist China and Taiwan.

The content of girls' pen pal letters indicates both the potential for understanding and the inward-looking focus of American outreach during the postwar era. One Camp Fire mother reported to the national office on the pen pal friendship of her daughter Carolyn Morowitz. Like most girls, Carolyn used her letters to explore her own values as she wrote about American institutions such as school, church, and Camp Fire. Yet in addition to endorsing American childhood as democratic, Carolyn's correspondence unexpectedly broke down the villainous stereotypes of the Japanese as carefully crafted by American propaganda during the war. After writing to and exchanging small souvenirs with a Japanese girl, Carolyn decided to help the girl and her family by sending the girl some money, a move no doubt suggested by Camp Fire's custom of gathering contributions for the poor and suffering, but which also displayed her awareness of her cultural privilege. The money, likely in United States denominations and unusable to the girl and her family, was soon returned via post. Carolyn expressed surprise at what she believed was a gesture of honesty, telling her mother, "We call ourselves Christians, yet we listen when we hear people say that the Japanese can't be trusted. I just wonder how many of us would be that honest and considerate."[37] Through this strange interaction, in which Carolyn's assumption of Christian (and American) cultural superiority is a subtext, Carolyn nonetheless glimpsed the falsity of wartime stereotypes. Perhaps in a small way pen friendships did offer a space for girls to embrace tolerance.

At the same time, these letters contributed to a larger exportation of American values. Carolyn's mother reported in 1953 that she too had been writing to Japanese women and that some of them had converted to Christianity. It is not clear if these were women in the same family that Carolyn corresponded with, but the incident shows how girls' pen pal relationships were connected to broader efforts on the part of Americans to transform the religion and customs of people abroad. Mrs. Morowitz had apparently written during an extended illness about how her faith kept her strong. When the Japanese women inquired about her beliefs, Morowitz contacted missionaries she knew in Japan, who promptly went to visit her pen pals. The Japanese women, then, "finally agreed of their own free-will to be baptized in Christ." Although additional factors, among them the Japanese families' proximity to the missionary networks that would have approached them for pen pal correspondence in the first place, likely prompted their change in faith, the example illustrates how pen pal friendships operated within the larger context of Americanization abroad.[38]

Despite Camp Fire's optimism about using girl citizens to inspire international tolerance, Camp Fire's programs were limited by an inward focus. In effect, American girls learned about their own society and had their national identity affirmed. In preparation for the international friendship group, for example, the *Camp Fire Girl* contributor Leah Milkman Rich invited girls to learn about U.S. history and to share it with another group. After reviewing their history, girls could host an "American party where you imagine what you would want to reveal about your country to a person from another country."[39] To get to know girls in France, then, a Bronx Horizon Club, or high-school-age club, sent holiday items depicting a typical American Halloween and wrote to their pen pals about American holidays.[40] Norwood Camp Fire Girls visited historical places in Boston and wrote "to boys and girls in other countries about American customs, schools and traditions." According to a local news release about their activities, the program increased American girls' understanding of democracy: "Democracy becomes something personal and vital to these girls . . . as they share their work and play, as they participate in group decisions, as they learn to respect persons of racial and religious backgrounds unlike their own."[41] In Camp Fire's framing, girls developed international tolerance by describing America to others and deepened their own understanding of democracy and patriotic commitments in the United States in that process.

On closer inspection, the birthday projects encouraged girls to view American democracy as the one viable model for the world. Camp Fire officials developed programs consistent with U.S. foreign policy objectives to spread democracy abroad and counter communism. Bernice Baxter, former president of the National Council of Camp Fire Girls, representative of Camp Fire, the National Education Association, and the Association of Childhood Education at the Women's World Fellowship in Paris, and later U.S. delegate to UNESCO's Fifth General Conference, expressed this mindset. After studying problems in Germany and conditions in Europe with an eye toward what the United States could do to ensure democracy would flourish there, she explained that the United States had "the rare opportunity to share our way of life." In addition to monetary and spiritual support, Europe needed friendship. Girls, she thought, should write to pen pals in Europe about life in America and "share" the Camp Fire Girl program by telling their international friends about Camp Fire activities and ideals. She thought the program particularly suitable for securing peace because of its emphasis on cooperation and citizenship, themes that could be modified to encompass world cooperation and world citizenship.[42]

Camp Fire's president Mrs. James Parker agreed that a focus inward on American values and customs was appropriate to an international outlook. She asserted, "We can uphold the lofty ideals of the United Nations by learning more and more about all the peoples of the earth; but we must not stop there, for we must let them know about us, too; how we live, work and play."[43] Consequently, although the 1949 "Make Mine Democracy" project challenged leaders to recognize that "ours is only one form of democracy," it also recommended that girls continue their pen pals and party kits, "mak[ing] them around an American theme like Lincoln's Birthday."[44]

After Loomis retired in 1949 and Americans became less enchanted with the "one world" concept, the birthday projects came to spotlight personal growth through creative arts, conservation, and individual goals. Still, Camp Fire undertook several more international-themed projects. In 1954 and 1955, to commemorate the ten-year anniversary of the United Nations, the project "Let's Be Different Together" focused on how people around the world satisfied basic needs and how they added beauty and adventure to daily living. Tellingly, a San Bernardino, California, club of sixth and seventh graders invited a college student from Mexico to attend their meeting. She "very charmingly entertained the group with glimpses into the customs of her native country." In return, the Camp Fire Girls shared with her a copy of the Bill of Rights and "the American Creed as well as pictures of the sources from which liberties spring."[45] The Camp Fire meeting with the international guest became a forum for identifying American core values, asserting patriotism, and sharing those values with an international audience. The inward focus could actually subvert the intention of promoting cross-national understanding by implying that such values were superior and unique to the American political system.

Finally, a 1957 project called "Meet the People," which was inspired by President Eisenhower's 1956 People-to People White House Conference, exemplified how Camp Fire's activities exported American values, affirmed patriotic identity, and strengthened distinct gender roles. At the conference, Eisenhower called on American youth organizations directly: "If our American ideology is to win out in the great struggle being waged between opposing ways of life, it must have the active support of thousands of independent private groups and institutions and millions of individual Americans acting through person-to-person communication in foreign lands."[46] Out of the conference came People-to-People International, a nonprofit group founded by Eisenhower to enhance mutual understanding and friendship on local and international levels. It had, in 1956, forty-one committees representing different aspects of American life. The Camp Fire Girls was a member organization of the People-to-People Youth Committee, and Martha Allen had a key role in its formation, chairing an initial workshop that advocated international friendships among youth.[47] Camp Fire's 1957 birthday project, "Meet the People," was designed in line with the People-to-People mission to exchange culture and ideas. It also offered an opportunity to export American democratic ideals abroad. Targeting girls in an international public relations campaign, Camp Fire drew up a project announcement that read, "First, girls will begin by learning about people in their own communities. Girls will then learn about people in faraway places. Ultimately, they can present the United States to people in distant parts of the world. This will be done by means of photographic stories of communities in which Camp Fire Girls live and the stories will be told, quite literally, by the girls themselves." Camp Fire Girls accordingly prepared photographic exhibits to tour different countries and "share information about life in America."[48]

To ensure that the proper image of American democracy was broadcast, Camp Fire established guidelines for the kinds of images girls should send. Project descriptions warned girls not to send "pictures that inspire envy" but instead pictures that present "elements which the girl from abroad would recognize and enjoy through a feeling of sharing." The Camp Fire Girl suggested that "instead of taking a picture of a group of girls in a long, shiny car—or even a hot rod—get a photo of one or two girls (or even a boy and a girl) as follows: on bicycles, on horseback, in a boat, swimming, dancing, helping an old person, praying in church, working in a hospital, taking care of a baby, studying homework."[49] When the Camp Fire Girl published many of the "Meet the People" pictures in late 1957, no doubt influencing other girls to model their own photographs on these images, most showed white, middle-class girls, rural landscapes, families and children, national monuments, and churches.[50] Fifteen nations were selected for the project: Malaysia, Sri Lanka, Turkey, Greece, Sudan, Egypt, Nigeria, Singapore, Pakistan, Union of South Africa, Mexico, Ghana, India, Lebanon, and Israel. Local Camp Fire groups selected which country they would correspond with from this list. Decisions usually followed available resources in the community. For example, the Lawton Council in Oklahoma chose Pakistan because Pakistani army officers trained at Fort Sill, Oklahoma. Greece and Turkey were the two most popular selections. No doubt the appearance of these two nations during the 1940s and 1950s in news reports on the Cold War and American aid promoted their popularity.[51]

The photograph plan was not limited to this particular birthday project. In 1954, a group in the Ponga City Council in Oklahoma "helped thousands of Koreans in the ravaged city of Pusan to learn what life in Oklahoma is like." One member had heard from her father stationed in Korea that photographs effectively "[told] the American story." The Camp Fire Girl and her friends, therefore, collected pictures of Oklahoma children and adults at work and play, an Oklahoma oil well, newspaper plants, cattle ranches, and Indians to send abroad. With U.S. government assistance, the girls displayed their project in Korea. According to the United States Information Service public affairs officer in Korea, who helped with the project, "the exhibit does much to give the true story of American community development and cooperation."[52] Therefore, to defend against communism, Camp Fire used its international program activities to promote girls' identification with American democracy and to promote its influence abroad.

Camp Fire's programming in the late 1940s and 1950s, then, mirrored the U.S. foreign policy objective of promoting democracy abroad through an image of a benevolent American system. Girls in organizations such as Camp Fire could serve as political emissaries as they learned about international agencies such as the United Nations and formed ties with girls in other countries. As girls' responsibilities broadened to include the world, the lessons girls gleaned reinforced their identity as American girls. They learned to see themselves as benevolent, tolerant, and democratic as they followed a particular vision of what a female "homemaker" should be. Meanwhile, Camp Fire's national officials cooperated in extending that gender system to others as the United States participated in campaigns to rebuild postwar societies and spread democracy.

Camp Fire Abroad

Camp Fire never established a definite policy for starting groups abroad, let alone an international body such as the World Association of Girl Guides and Girl Scouts, which was formed in 1928.[53] Camp Fire's earliest leadership, nonetheless, described the group's international expansion as the "unostentatious way Camp Fire plays its part in promoting international understanding." Founder Luther Gulick recommended slow development abroad by experimenting with program activities, "using whatever of our program is fitted to the needs of the country and introducing new features where it may be necessary." Gulick envisioned a system in which each country had its own national council to oversee Camp Fire work. By the 1920s, Camp Fire clubs existed in nearly thirty countries, from Holland to the Philippines.[54]

This loose international system continued into the postwar era. National headquarters offered words of support once new groups were started, but it focused its limited resources on spreading the movement within the United States. Camp Fire's popularity in other countries never swelled, and by the 1950s Camp Fire counted less than 150 non-British foreign members in Germany, Austria, San Salvador, and other countries; in 1942 it had counted 4,649 members in Great Britain.[55] Although Camp Fire never focused on spreading the organization abroad, its limited efforts underscored a belief that building common experiences for girls around the world could foster world peace.

This belief was most apparent in the Camp Fire clubs formed in Occupied Japan in 1949. Although only a handful of clubs were initiated, the clubs demonstrate Camp Fire's efforts both to foster international friendship and to export democracy through a gendered American culture. Heihachiro Suzuki, the director of a correspondence society in Japan dedicated to fostering international goodwill and understanding between youth, started Camp Fire in Japan soon after World War II. He first learned of Camp Fire when he saw a program booklet in a United States Information Service Center in Occupied Japan and felt it was an appropriate program for introducing democratic citizenship to the girls of Japan.[56] He initially contacted Camp Fire for pen pal correspondents in 1948.[57]

Next, Suzuki organized Camp Fire clubs among the Japanese and sought to translate the manual, for which he needed authorization from the Civil Information and Education Section of Allied Command. In explaining his interest in Camp Fire, Suzuki cited a need to promote democracy in Japan and to find a proper educational model for girls. Article 24 of Japan's new constitution offered the promise of equality for women by granting suffrage and guaranteeing equal rights to education. Equal rights would prove to be elusive, however, as traditionalists held to a family system that honored "good wives and wise mothers." Such a system limited the public ambition of individual women while holding them up as national mothers serving the family and nation. Indeed, although Japanese girls had received education before World War II, much of it had been geared toward reproducing the "national mothers" model.[58] Suzuki likely found in Camp Fire's maternalism a model that adapted the "good wife and wise mother" to demands for the increased civic involvement of girls and women. He explained, "It is very helpful to introduce to our Japanese what the Camp Fire Girls are and let them know how the girls education should be."[59]

Suzuki found the Camp Fire model superior to the Girl Scout model. A small number of Girl Scouting clubs had formed in Japan by the time of Suzuki's request, and he was aware of their existence, but the distinction Martha Allen drew between the two groups, particularly Camp Fire's emphasis on women's "special contribution. . . to citizenship and the community welfare," appealed to him. Allen had detailed how Camp Fire built on women's "concern and ability in connection with their homes; their experience in organization and household management; their concern for the health and well-being of their children; [and] their ability to create an atmosphere of charm and graciousness in their homes."[60] Suzuki hoped to import this maternalist model of citizenship, one that emphasized domestic roles, for Japanese girls.

Suzuki's niece soon established a group in Tokyo with the assistance of American women living in Japan. They included teachers, servicemen's wives, and Red Cross and YWCA volunteers with Camp Fire experience. Several other Japanese Camp Fire groups soon followed.[61] Little information is available on the specific activities of these girls, but they appear to have engaged in activities similar to those of Camp Fire Girls in the United States, submitting some of their craft work for display at the 1952 national Camp Fire Girls conference, for example.[62]

Although the Japanese clubs disbanded around 1954, the Camp Fire venture in Japan illustrates how Camp Fire promoted a particular version of democratic girlhood even beyond its borders.[63] For a time, Japanese girls met in Tokyo as part of Camp Fire's global community, sharing with their American counterparts handicraft activities and pen friendships. Camp Fire had hoped to extend its model of girl citizenship as a way of furthering international understanding through shared experience. By exporting its program, including its gender ideology, Camp Fire participated in broader efforts to build the foundation for American-style democracy in other countries.

Conclusion

Camp Fire's internationalism was built on the ordinary Camp Fire activities and on the maternalist ideals of the organization. Through typical Camp Fire programming that began with girls' service to the home and community, Camp Fire articulated a global role for girl citizens. Encouraging girls to bring their feminine natures to bear on world affairs and to learn about democracy, Camp Fire envisioned girls as beacons of world peace even as it continued to constrain girl citizenship within narrow definitions of femininity. Although girls gained from the expansion of their roles into a broader civic arena, Camp Fire never veered far from a gender-differentiated agenda that trained girls to think of themselves as the mothers and homemakers of the nation.

Moreover, girls became participants in the expansion of American values abroad. As American educational institutions, platitudes about tolerance, teenage parties, and the like were exported as the true meaning of American democracy, these beneficent images obscured the growth of American military power abroad. Indeed, Camp Fire, along with myriad other institutions, worked side by side with American militarism in the Cold War to solidify U.S. foreign policy aims abroad. In the process, what girls learned most was to revere and celebrate their own American identity, central to which was a female citizenship that steered girls toward maternal roles as protectors of hearth and home. The message was that girls could help secure peace by sharing this vision of American values and by helping their nation, through their civic participation, maintain a position of national superiority.

NOTES

1. Eleanore Z. Korman, "Being a Homemaker—Plus," *Camp Fire Girl* 36, no. 5 (January 1957): 11.

2. Paul Boyer, *By the Bomb's Early Light: American Thought and Culture at the Dawn of the Atomic Age* (Chapel Hill: University of North Carolina Press, 1994), 34–37; Dorothy B. Robins, *Experiment in Democracy: The Story of U.S. Citizen Organizations in Forging the Charter of the United Nations* (New York: Parkside Press, 1971), xii.

3. On the waning popularity of the United Nations, see Lisa McGirr, *Suburban Warriors: The Origins of the New American Right* (Princeton, NJ: Princeton University Press, 2001); Evan Luard, *A History of the United Nations: The Years of Western Domination, 1945–1955* (New York: St. Martin's Press, 1982), 1:353–354. On American interest in the world government ideal, see Boyer, *Bomb's Early Light*, 38.

4. On Camp Fire's origins, see Jennifer Hillman Helgren, "Inventing American Girlhood: Gender and Citizenship in the Twentieth-Century Camp Fire Girls" (Ph.D. diss., Claremont Graduate University, 2005); Helen Buckler, Mary F. Fiedler, and Martha F. Allen, *Wo-He-Lo: The Story of Camp Fire Girls, 1910–1960* (New York: Holt, Rinehart and Winston, 1961); and Susan A. Miller, *Growing Girls: The Natural Origins of Girls' Organizations in America* (New Brunswick, NJ: Rutgers University Press, 2007). On maternalism, see Molly Ladd-Taylor, *Mother-Work: Women, Child Welfare, and the State, 1890–1930* (Urbana: University of Illinois Press, 1994), 3–11; as well as variations of this theme in, for example, Karen Blair, *The Clubwoman as Feminist: True Womanhood Redefined, 1868–1914* (New York: Holmes and Meier Publishers, 1980).

5. On the potential of internationalism in education, see Martha C. Nussbaum, "Patriotism and Cosmopolitanism," in *For Love of Country: Debating the Limits of Patriotism*, ed. Joshua Cohen (Boston: Beacon Press, 1996), 11.

6. Camp Fire Girls, *Annual Report of the Camp Fire Girls, 1929*, 6, Camp Fire USA (CFUSA), Kansas City, MO; Camp Fire Girls, "Semi-Annual Report of the General Department, 1932," 4–6, CFUSA; Camp Fire Girls, *Annual Report of the Camp Fire Girls, 1951*, CFUSA; Buckler, Fiedler, and Allen, *Wo-He-Lo*, 83. For Girl Scout statistics, see Anne Hyde Choate and Helen Ferris, eds., *Juliette Low and the Girl Scouts* (New York: Doubleday, Doran, 1928), 168; and Rosa Esposito, Information Specialist at Girl Scouts of the U.S.A., to Jennifer Helgren, e-mail correspondence, April 27, 2005.

7. On juvenile delinquency in the 1940s and 1950s, see Grace Palladino, *Teenagers: An American History* (New York: Basic Books, 1997), 81–84, 159–162; and Leerom Medovoi, *Rebels: Youth and the Cold War Origins of Identity* (Durham, NC: Duke University Press), 29–33.

8. On racial ideologies and their impact on images of motherhood and maternalism in the 1950s, see Ruth Feldstein, *Motherhood in Black and White: Race and Sex in American Liberalism* (Ithaca, NY: Cornell University Press, 2000).

9. On women's postwar lives, see Joanne Meyerowitz, "Beyond the Feminine Mystique: A Reassessment of Postwar Mass Culture 1946–1958," in *Not June Cleaver: Women and Gender in Postwar America*, ed. Joanne Meyerowitz (Philadelphia: Temple University Press, 1994), 229–262; Sara Evans, *Personal Politics: The Roots of Women's Liberation in the Civil Rights Movement and the New Left* (New York: Vintage Books, 1979), 5–6; Ruth Rosen, *The World Split Open: How the Modern Women's Movement Changed America* (New York: Penguin Books, 2000), 4–8, 19–27, 40–43; and Jessica Weiss, *To Have and to Hold: Marriage, the Baby Boom, and Social Change* (Chicago: University of Chicago Press, 2000), 53–54, 205.

10. See Martha F. Allen, "What Will She Be When She Grows Up?" *Camp Fire Girl* 36, no. 1 (September 1956): 6; and Camp Fire Girls, *A Great Leader: Tribute to a Great Leader* (New York: Camp Fire Girls, 1966), pamphlet, 5–8, Camp Fire Council for Eastern Massachusetts Records (CFCEMR), carton 1, folder 7, Schlesinger Library, Radcliffe Institute for Advanced Study, Harvard University, Cambridge. See Lisa Ossian, "Fragilities and Failures, Promises and Patriotism: Elements of a Second World War English and American Girlhood, 1939–1945," in this volume.

11. "Camp Fire Girls Postwar Program," *Camp Fire Girl* 24, no. 7 (March 1945): 1.

12. Martha F. Allen, "The Future of Camp Fire," *Camp Fire Girl* 30, no. 7 (March 1951): 2.

13. Martha F. Allen, "Camp Fire Girls in the Second Half Century," *Camp Fire Girl* 42, no. 3 (January–February 1963): 3–4.

14. Allen, "Future of Camp Fire," 1, 2.

15. Mrs. Lou B. Paine, "Characteristics of Camp Fire" (address delivered at Region I Annual Conference, Boston, April 6–7, 1956), CFCEMR, carton 1, folder 6, Schlesinger Library.

16. Camp Fire Girls, *The Book of the Camp Fire Girls* (New York: Camp Fire Girls, 1962), 86–87.

17. Scrapbook and journal of Tankuloka Camp Fire, Roslindale, MA, 1943–1947, March 17, 1946, CFCEMR, carton 2, folder 62, Schlesinger Library.

18. Mrs. Bernard F. Gimbel, "Report on United Nations Contacts," minutes of the Executive Board of the Camp Fire Girls, ca. 1950, CFUSA.

19. *Norwood Messenger*, August 5, 1948, clipping, scrapbook of Norwood, MA, Camp Fire, 1938–1949, CFCEMR, folio box 5, Schlesinger Library.

20. "A Time for Rededication," *Camp Fire Girl* 34, no. 1 (September 1955): 11.

21. "Freedom Crusade Report," *Camp Fire Girl* 30, no. 8 (April 1950): 2.

22. Lucille Hein, "The Declaration of Human Rights," *Camp Fire Girl* 28, no. 7 (March 1949): 1.

23. Walter Terry, "Join Hands and Dance," *Camp Fire Girl* 25, no. 10 (June 1946): 7; UNESCO also supported a folk dance program.

24. Diana Selig, "Cultural Gifts: American Liberals, Childhood, and the Origins of Multiculturalism, 1924–1939" (Ph.D. diss., University of California at Berkeley, 2000).

25. "At Home in the World," *Camp Fire Girl* 25, no. 10 (June 1946): 8–9.

26. Dorothy Gladys Spicer, "Make Flag Day a Food Day," *Camp Fire Girl* 25, no. 10 (June 1946): 13.

27. Scrapbook and journal of Tankuloka Camp Fire, Roslindale, MA, March 17, 1946.

28. Lucille Hein, "Where Hunger Stalks There Can Be No Peace," *Camp Fire Girl* 25, no. 9 (May 1946): 12.

29. Ruth Teichman, "The Story of the Proud Tradition of Camp Fire's Birthday Projects," *Camp Fire Girl* 34, no. 3 (November 1955): 3; "At Home in the World," 8–9.

30. As quoted in Dorothea Love, "Blueprint for Birthday Week," *Camp Fire Girl* 27, no. 6 (February 1948): 3.

31. Leah Milkman Rich, "First Steps in Friendship," *Camp Fire Girl* 27, no. 5 (January 1948): 1, 4.

32. Edith Kempthorne, "Come to My Friendship Party," *Camp Fire Girl* 28, no. 6 (February 1949): 1–2. Pen pal letters were usually written in the child's native language and then Camp Fire or the sponsoring organization abroad found volunteers to translate the letters for the girls. Americans of Japanese descent living in the San Gabriel Valley, who were affiliated with Camp Fire, translated the Japanese letters for American girls. Camp Fire had followed a similar system with letters from French girls.

33. "Friends in Camp Fire," *Camp Fire Girl* 27, no. 7 (March 1948): 9.

34. Doris E. V. Foster, "Hello, World, Let's Get Together," 1948 Record Book, Greater Boston Council, CFCEMR, carton 1, folder 44, Schlesinger Library.

35. Dorothy Maddox to Doris E. V. Foster, Roslindale, March 10, 1948, in "Hello, World, Let's Get Together."

36. Elizabeth Wilde to Executives of Local Councils, CF Public Relations, March 20, 1943, New York; Elizabeth Wilde, 1943 publicity release, New York, CFUSA; and "Camp Fire Girls to the Relief of China Record," 1943, newspaper clipping, Madame Chiang Kai-shek folder, CFUSA.

37. Ruth Morowitz, Detroit, to Elizabeth McStea, December 18, 1950, CFUSA; and Chieko Suda to Carolyn Morowitz, December 26, 1950, CFUSA.

38. Ruth Morowitz, Detroit, to Elizabeth McStea, July 8, 1953, CFUSA. For more on gender and Americanization in postwar Japan, see Mire Koikari, *Pedagogy of Democracy: Feminism and the Cold War in the U.S. Occupation of Japan* (Philadelphia: Temple University Press, 2008).

39. Rich, "First Steps in Friendship," 1–4.

40. Betty Betz, "Parties around the World," *Camp Fire Girl* 27, no. 6 (February 1948): 6.

41. *Norwood Tribune*, March 16, 1949, clipping, scrapbook of Norwood, MA, Camp Fire.

42. "The World Over," *Camp Fire Girl* 27, no. 6 (February 1948): 1.

43. "The Past Ten Years," *Camp Fire Girl* 34, no. 1 (September 1955): 12.

44. Camp Fire Girls, "1949 National Birthday Project," *Camp Fire Girl* 28, no. 2 (October 1948): 2.

45. *Evening Telegram*, March 14, 1955, clipping, scrapbook (1955) of San Andreas Council, San Bernardino, CA.

46. President Dwight Eisenhower, as quoted in "Meet the People: 1957–58 Annual Project," *Camp Fire Girl* 37, no. 1 (September 1957): 12–13.

47. "Current Biography," October 1959, 3–4, CFUSA.

48. "Meet the People: 1957–58 Annual Project," 12–13.

49. "Horizon Clubs 'Meet the People,' " *Camp Fire Girl* 37, no. 5 (January 1958): 8.

50. See *Camp Fire Girl* 37, no. 3 (November 1957).

51. June Hammond, "News and Statistics on 'Meet the People,' " *Camp Fire Girl* 37, no. 5 (January 1958): 11.

52. "Around the Camp Fire," *Camp Fire Girl* 34, no. 3 (November 1954): 5.

53. See Tammy M. Proctor, *On My Honour: Guides and Scouts in Interwar Britain* (Philadelphia: American Philosophical Society, 2002), 133.

54. Camp Fire Girls, *Annual Report of the Camp Fire Girls, 1923*, 3, CFUSA. Buckler, Fiedler, and Allen, *Wo-He-Lo*, 84, 148; "Report of Camp Fire Work for 1913," January 20, 1914, L. Hollingsworth Wood Papers, box 11, folder 3, Haverford College Library, Haverford, PA.

55. Camp Fire Girls, *Annual Report of the Camp Fire Girls, 1942*, CFUSA; and Martha F. Allen, New York, to General Douglas MacArthur, December 9, 1949, CFUSA.

56. "How Camp Fire Was Organized in Japan," unpublished information sheet, probably 1952, CFUSA; and Helen Rowe to James Donovan, Washington, DC, September 3, 1952, CFUSA.

57. Heihachiro Suzuki, Tokyo, to Camp Fire Girls, January 29, 1949, CFUSA; Heihachiro Suzuki, Tokyo, to Ruth Teichman, October 8, 1948, CFUSA; and Heihachiro Suzuki, Tokyo, to Lucille Hein, August 31, 1948, CFUSA.

58. On the "good wife and wise mother," see Kathleen S. Uno, "The Death of 'Good Wife, Wise Mother'?" in *Postwar Japan as History*, ed. Andrew Gordon (Berkeley: University of California Press, 1993), 293–322. On women's role in crafting the constitution, see Ray A. Moore, *Partners for Democracy: Crafting the New Japanese State under MacArthur* (Oxford: Oxford University Press, 2002), 223–238.

59. Heihachiro Suzuki, Tokyo, to Lucille Hein, New York, November 19, 1949, CFUSA.

60. Martha F. Allen to Heihachiro Suzuki, Tokyo, March 9, 1950, CFUSA.

61. Heihachiro Suzuki, Tokyo, to Ruth Teichman, New York, 26 August 1950, CFUSA.

62. Heihachiro Suzuki, Tokyo, to Ruth Teichman, New York, July 11, 1952, CFUSA.

63. Heihachiro Suzuki, Tokyo, to Ruth Teichman, August 28, 1953, CFUSA; Yoshiko Suzuki, Saitama-Ken, to Ruth Teichman, New York, November 28, 1954, CFUSA.

PART IV

GIRLS TO WOMEN
Work, Marriage, and Sexuality

The chapters in the final section of this volume explore a variety of "coming of age" experiences around the world, focusing specifically on challenges to the definition of girlhood. By probing this definition of girlhood in light of the seemingly adult experiences of labor, sexual activity, rape, and marriage, these chapters show how work roles have often been conflated with sexual coercion and stigmatization.

Colleen Vasconcellos, for example, examines how girlhood and slavery influenced and changed each other from 1750 to 1838. Specifically, she examines how the threat of abolition and Jamaican planters' response to that threat jointly affected the status of girlhood within the Jamaican slave community. As Jamaican planters debated the benefits of "buy versus breed," they began purchasing younger Africans and relying on these girls to aid in efforts to increase the slave population on their estates through natural increase. These expectations, combined with the onslaught of sexual assault by their owners, horrible working conditions, hard labor, and harsh punishments, shortened these girls' already brief adolescence considerably. Liat Kozma continues this theme of the confluence of sexual expectations and girls' work roles in her examination of lower-class girls in late nineteenth-century Egypt. Relying heavily on police and court records, Kozma argues that girls' work roles and their sexual activities, whether chosen or not, affected official and unofficial perceptions of what constituted a girl—that is, the point at which childhood ended and adulthood began. Moreover, the expansion of the Egyptian economy and girls' roles in labor outside the home heightened fears among girls' parents, as well as government officials, about sexual promiscuity and vulnerability.

In Kathryn Sloan's chapter, we see girls themselves choosing marriage, and by association, adulthood, in order to escape parental influence, from 1850 to 1920. Arguing that Mexican daughters defied both their parents and the law to elope with their sweethearts, and in effect challenged traditional ideals about parental authority and filial obedience, Sloan shows that these girls acted out a script of seduction—or *rapto*, elopement, abduction, bride stealing—to force their parents' consent. Last, anthropologist Patricia Sloane-White argues that there has been a significant change in the status and representation of Malay Muslim girls in the past forty years as a result of national economic policy, which opened up educational avenues to girls. While the definition of girlhood was dependent on the girls' role as future mothers, Malay girls were configured as "moral proxies" of Malay mothers as the national economic program sought to develop an urban, educated, economically active middle class. As a result, many middle-class Malay Muslim girls gained significant status during the 1970s, and were character-ized as symbolic "sisters" and "helpers" of the modern nation, meeting the needs of the ethnic group and family while serving modern expectations of female improvement without defying traditional expectations of maternal self-sacrifice and family orientation.

Setting these diverse chapters together suggests important comparisons across cultures and borders. Someone considered a girl in one society may not be considered a girl in another. Still, the developing global interconnec-tivity of societies means that any society's definition of girlhood cannot exist separate from others. Reformers and imperialists (often in the same form) have spread both sexual vulnerability (as they have constructed new definitions of feminine danger and practiced rape and sexual coercion) and the notion that childhood is an extended developmental and moral period deserving of and necessitating protection. The coupling of susceptibility to labor and sexual coercion suggests the ways that "modern" childhood is conceived of as a time in which children, and girls in particular, ought to be protected from the influences and responsibilities of the adult world. Such ideas, as these chapters demonstrate, often run counter to traditional cultures.

17

From Chattel to "Breeding Wenches"

ABOLITIONISM, GIRLHOOD, AND JAMAICAN SLAVERY

COLLEEN A. VASCONCELLOS

In 1745, Governor Edward Trelawney of Jamaica published a controversial pamphlet titled *An Essay concerning Slavery*. Much to the consternation of his constituents, he wrote, "I cou'd wish with all my Heart, that Slavery was abolish'd entirely, and I hope in time it may be so." Unlike those who depended on a constant supply of Africans to the island, Governor Trelawney believed that Jamaican planters already owned far too many slaves. Furthermore, Jamaica's planters neglected and mismanaged these slaves. Still, Trelawney realized that ending slavery in the colony would bring ruin not only to an economy dependent on slave-produced sugar but also to his career as governor and to his aspirations of becoming a member of Parliament, so he simply asked for abolition of the slave trade and nothing more. "I shall be content," Trelawney naively wrote, "if no more Slaves be imported, and those we have put under good regulations—Time will do the rest."[1]

Trelawney's essay did more to annoy Jamaican planters and Parliament than it did to end the slave trade to Jamaica. In fact, correspondence and plantation estate books of this period in Atlantic history indicate that Parliamentarians and Jamaican planters were more concerned with production and output than they were with the almost nonexistent antitrade sentiment. Everything changed in 1783, however, when the Quakers presented Parliament with the first petition to abolish the slave trade.[2] As petitions like these increased in number and strength during the late eighteenth century, Jamaican planters gradually comprehended that their labor supply was in danger. Consequently, these planters began to ask themselves: "If Great Britain was to give up the Slave Trade, what would be the consequence?"[3]

The institutions of childhood and slavery influenced and changed each other from 1750 to 1838, with the abolitionist movement standing as the main catalyst for change. In 1750, Jamaican planters disregarded the presence of slave children and youth on their estates, and Jamaica's slaves raised their children without a great deal of planter interference. As English abolitionism gained momentum in the 1780s, Jamaican planters gradually saw children less as burdens and more as economic investments. In this chapter I examine how the threat of abolition as well as Jamaican planter response to that threat subsequently affected the status of "girlhood" within the Jamaican slave community. Specifically, I discuss how the threat of abolition and Jamaican planters' response to that threat jointly affected the status of girlhood within the Jamaican slave community.

Since the publication of two important works on child slavery in the antebellum South by Wilma King and Marie Jenkins Schwartz, historians have begun to focus more directly on children's experiences in the slave community.[4] Whereas King uses a thematic approach to examine the stages of slave childhood through the lenses of family, leisure and play, work expectations, and spirituality, Schwartz examines her subjects from a developmental point of view, acknowledging their progression from birth to early childhood to adolescence and finally adulthood. Caribbean slave studies place children in much larger, quantitative examinations of gender or family in the plantation complex. Caribbeanists such as Barbara Bush, Richard Sheridan, Kenneth Kiple, and Richard Steckel all discuss how the workload, malnutrition, and harsh treatment of slave mothers contributed to the astounding infant and child mortality in the slave community.[5] Barbara Bush as well as Caribbeanists such as Marietta Morrissey, Lucille Mathurin Mair, and Hilary Beckles also examine slave childhood in relation to the complexities of mother–child relationships, within much larger examinations of gender and slavery in the British Caribbean.[6] The historians Barry Higman and Elsa Goveia were the first Caribbeanists to touch on issues more directly related to slave childhood in their studies of slave families in the Caribbean.[7] How girlhood in the Atlantic World changed over time remains unexplored. This study moves beyond the current historiography to discuss the nature of girlhood in the plantation complex, how colonial Jamaican society and the slave community defined girlhood, and how that definition changed over time.

As abolitionist threats to the slave trade, and later slavery, intensified in the Atlantic World, Jamaican planters responded by debating the benefits of a "buy versus breed" economy. While purchasing younger Africans and encouraging natural increase, Jamaican planters eventually tried to improve the quality of life on their estates. Although children's lives changed for the better in social, medical, and quantitative terms, "girlhood" on Jamaican estates suffered. As the "buy versus breed" debate intensified in the Atlantic World, slave owners increasingly relied on young girls to aid in the natural increase efforts on their estates. These expectations, combined with the onslaught of sexual assault from their owners, horrible working conditions, hard labor, and harsh punishments these girls received, shortened their already short adolescence considerably. As a result, "girlhood" in the Jamaican slave community suffered to the point of near extinction.

A Growing Demand for Girls

With the news of an increased number of abolitionist petitions coming before Parliament spreading throughout England and the British Caribbean, Jamaican planters began to hedge their bets. At first, Jamaican planters responded to this impending threat by simply buying more slaves. George Turner urged a fellow planter to invest in slaves "for the benefit of your family hereafter," and many did just that.[8] Although importing more slaves was an immediate solution, many slaves died quickly and had to be replaced. Thomas Thistlewood, overseer of Egypt Estate in the parish of Westmoreland, wrote that planter Sir James Richardson lost 141 of the 190 Africans he purchased between 1767 and 1784.[9] Other estates had similar experiences.[10] Thistlewood spoke for many when he wrote that the ability to keep slaves alive resulted from "a lucky combination of circumstances."[11]

Accordingly, the Jamaican Assembly began to look more closely at the slave population to ascertain the reasons behind its decrease. After a series of investigations and inquiries beginning in 1788, the Assembly concluded that the slave population could not possibly sustain itself with "the disproportion of the sexes" aboard ship and on Jamaican plantations, a situation acerbated by the high mortality among the newly imported.[12] Although the Assembly claimed that Jamaica annually imported three females to every five males, Stephen Fuller, agent for Jamaica, reported that out of the 250,000 slaves on the island, males outnumbered females by 30,000.[13] Furthermore, of those slave women on the island, few were classified as "breeding wenches," or women of childbearing age.[14] "If future importations from Africa be discontinued," Fuller wrote, "there will unavoidably ensue, from the disproportion of the sexes alone, a very great reduction from the present number of our Slaves, before any augmentation can be expected from natural increase by generation."[15]

The term "breeding wenches" appears more regularly in the correspondence and inventories of Jamaica's planters and assemblymen around this time. Before the appearance of abolitionist petitions before Parliament, the term rarely appeared. If used at all, the label merely described the condition of the slave in question. In other words, a "breeding wench" was simply a pregnant female slave. As abolitionist petitions increasingly appeared before Parliament, however, the term began to be used in a different way. Although the word "breeding" still described pregnancy, the label took on an urgency not previously intended. It signified a need and expectation that gave the word "breeding" an entirely different definition. Pregnancy was now the desired result rather than the current condition. "Breeding wenches," or any female slaves above the age of sixteen, the age at which slaves began working at full capacity on the estates, offered a solution to the threat of the outlawed slave trade, and they would now be used as breeders. Before abolitionists petitions threatened slave supply, it was simply cheaper to purchase more slaves from Africa. With the impending threats to the slave supply, however, "breeding wenches" and adolescent girls became a sought-after commodity in the slave markets and on Jamaica's estates.

Consequently, by the late 1780s, many Jamaican planters opted to buy more African "breeding wenches" and young girls in the hopes of evening out the disproportion between the sexes on their estates. "Young Wenches should be yr object" when buying Africans at market, George Turner frequently directed his estate manager, "as they are much wanted."[16] Nathaniel Phillips wrote the same to his estate manager, stipulating that "whenever you can get a good choice of a Cargo of Negroes, I would have you buy about 20 Strong Women Girls, or Young Women, 15 to 20 years old."[17] Meanwhile, Stephen Fuller implored the Assembly to pass a law making it illegal for any British ship to carry a greater number of male slaves than female slaves from Africa after May 1, 1793.[18] Although some ships, such as the *African Queen*, arrived in Jamaica with cargos dominated by women and girls, the majority of the ships arriving in Jamaica before 1790 still carried mostly men.[19]

Any doubts Jamaican planters had about the seriousness of the situation quickly faded in April 1792, when the English House of Commons voted by a large majority to gradually abolish the British slave trade. Shock turned into panic when the House of Commons voted a few weeks later to end the trade by January 1, 1796. Stephen Fuller, exasperated by the decision, immediately offered a viable solution: in addition to purchasing more "breeding wenches," he urged planters to purchase younger slaves as investments, preferably girls. He proposed that after an unassigned date, it should be illegal for ships to carry males above the age of twenty and females above the age of sixteen. Furthermore, additional duties should be levied on slaves exceeding four feet four inches in height, or those deemed to be adults, beginning in October 1797. Although these were merely proposals, Fuller's suggestions show the changing nature of childhood and girlhood within the Atlantic World. Not only were Jamaican planters feeling pressure to purchase younger Africans, but girls below the age of sixteen suddenly found themselves categorized as "breeding wenches."[20] Slave youth, once avoided by the Jamaican plantocracy, was now a prized investment.

Cautious, Jamaican planters debated the feasibility of girls as an investment, while trading houses reconsidered the profitability of carrying young Africans on their ships. As a rule, most English trading companies encouraged their captains to buy adult Africans, preferring to buy young Africans at the last minute before sailing for the Americas, and only if space was available. Young Africans were a risk, and many planters and traders who purchased them lost money. In addition to the high mortality rates they suffered during the Middle Passage because of their susceptibility to disease, young Africans would be unable to perform hard labor or produce offspring for several years because of their age. Planters were reluctant to feed, shelter, and clothe them with only the prospect of future financial returns. As a result, unless a planter or merchant requested a special order, young Africans were extremely hard to sell in West Indian markets. Those who did purchase them in the Jamaican markets preferred the cheaper Creoles, who already spoke English, over those fresh from the Middle Passage. Such Creoles were in short supply, however, and planters opted for prime adult slaves instead.

As Jamaican planters increasingly realized that their slave supply was in danger, they were quick to justify Fuller's remedy and consider girls as a viable solution. Those buyers who were willing to wait for a profit on their investment rationalized that younger slaves, especially girls, were the best choice. Additional rationales emerged. "Their juvenile minds entertain no regrets for the loss of their connections," argued Dr. Collins, an English physician who practiced in Jamaica, allowing for a smoother transition into a life of servitude.[21] As a result, planters would have more control over their younger purchases, who learned English and work skills faster and easier than the adults. Many planters also believed that because younger slaves had been separated from their parents and family, they would form an attachment to their new masters and remain loyal to them for the rest of their lives.[22] Furthermore, although mortality rates were high, younger slaves represented a lower risk than the adult Africans, who were prone to suicide and resistance.[23] Last of all, younger slaves "improve daily in size, understanding, and capacity for labour, so as to afford a good prospect of their lasting, not only in your time, but long after, to render much service to those who are to succeed you."[24]

Although Jamaican planters pondered the large-scale importation of African youth, many slave traders worked to fill the growing demand for girls. In September 1764, for example, Captain Thomas Trader sailed the *African* from Malemba to Kingston with a total of 112 men, 30 women, 85 boys, and 41 girls.[25] Nearly thirty years later, the Bristol schooner *Flora* purchased 70 men, 60 men-boys, 66 boys, 69 women, 66 women-girls, and 64 girls from Sierra Leone.[26] The following year, in 1791, the *Ruby* sold her Biafran cargo of 50 men, 21 women, 36 boys, and 25 girls in Montego Bay.[27] Not only were African girls increasingly crossing the Atlantic, but they often outnumbered women in the inventory rolls.

The Jamaican Assembly also began to support the importation of African youth. Contrary to the wishes of the abolitionists and their Parliamentarian supporters, the Assembly enacted a succession of laws, beginning in 1797, which laid extra duties on all African slaves above twenty-five years of age imported to the island.[28] Although these laws did not require that more ships carry girls, they made it more difficult for slavers to carry an older cargo. Many planters felt that if the age limit had been eighteen or twenty, the regulation would have been even more productive.[29] Other planters felt that the age limitations should be lower still, as those who wished "only to secure recruits for the service of a future day, will find it for his interest to buy only small boys and girls, in equal numbers."[30] So, as abolitionist sentiment progressively threatened their slave supply, Jamaican planters felt they had no choice but to purchase younger Africans, preferably girls, in order to protect their interests.

To Buy or to Breed?

In Governor Trelawney's controversial 1745 pamphlet, he wrote, "It is notorious that in most Plantations more die than are born there." To illustrate his point, Trelawney created a fictional dialogue between a Royal Naval officer and a Jamaican planter. There, Trelawney alleged that harsh treatment, miscarriages, abortions, and promiscuity contributed to the infertility of the slave population. While the planter lamented the failure of his estate to increase naturally, the Royal Naval officer offered him insight and advice. "If a little Linnen, or other Necessaries, were given to every Wench that was brought to Bed, and all the barren ones whipt on a certain Day every Year," the officer suggested, "I fancy the Negroe Ladies would yield better, and at least keep up the present Stock."[31]

Much like his call to end the slave trade to Jamaica, however, Trelawney's ideas about ameliorating the condition of the slaves at first fell on deaf ears. Although the slave population failed to reproduce naturally, Jamaican planters preferred to purchase slaves directly from Africa rather than invest time and money in children and youth who most likely would never reach their full work potential as adults. Once abolitionist threats to the slave trade intensified, however, planters gradually acknowledged the value of slave children, especially slave girls, and took stock in Trelawney's words of warning.

Until the mid-eighteenth century, slave youth were unwanted chattels on Jamaican estates, and planters largely discouraged their female slaves from becoming pregnant. "I am aware that there are many planters who do not wish their women to breed," William Beckford, a prominent Jamaican planter, wrote in 1788, "as there by so much work is lost in their attendance on their infants."[32] Not only did pregnancy reduce productivity, but planters and estate managers were reluctant to lose slave women in childbirth. Instead, planters felt it more rational to use their slave women to their full potential as field laborers, an easily replaceable commodity in this early period. Furthermore, the majority of Jamaica's slave youth did not begin work in the labor gangs until at least age five, and then they performed only minor tasks until their adolescence. Therefore, planters generally viewed those few youths on their estates as financial burdens, because they had to be supported without any substantial reciprocal contribution to the plantation economy. Planters and estate managers discouraged slave women from having children, but the hard labor and harsh treatment made low birth rates endemic on Jamaican plantations and any natural increase impossible. "It is not an unusual thing," James Ramsay, who witnessed slave life firsthand for twenty years, wrote in 1784, "to lose *in one year* . . . *ten, twelve,* nay, as far as *twenty,* by fevers, fluxes, dropsies, the effect of too much work, and too little food and care."[33]

Archival evidence supports Ramsay's claims, showing that any increase on the island's estates during this early period came largely from the purchase of imported Africans. Although 35 children were born on Spring Vale Pen in the parish of St. James between 1791 and 1800, 48 slaves died, motivating the purchase of 70 Africans during this nine-year period.[34] Worthy Park Estate in St. Catherine is an even better example. While 48 children were born on the estate from 1792 to 1796, 137 slaves died. Yet despite this natural decrease, Worthy Park's slave population increased from 357 slaves in 1792 to 470 slaves in 1796.[35] Unfortunately, figures such as these are unavailable for other plantations, as bookkeepers usually only recorded annually the overall number of slaves on their estates. The absence of such figures means we can have little insight into the nature of childbirth or infant and child mortality on Jamaican estates during these early years; their absence also indicates that estate managers and bookkeepers cared little about the birth and death of their young slaves. Although we have seen that planters responded to abolitionist threats by investing in younger slaves and girls, planters rarely gave infant and child mortality a second thought.

Few children during this early period were strong enough at birth to survive beyond their first few months. Life on a plantation was incredibly hard for Jamaica's female slaves, and it took a devastating toll on their bodies. Pregnant or not, slave women and girls worked an average of twelve hours each day in the fields, sharing the same difficult labor as the men. Others performed backbreaking labor as laundresses, weavers, and water carriers either on Jamaican estates or in the urban areas.[36] Whether working in the fields or as domestics, slave women and girls suffered from the general weakness and frailty associated with an inadequate and vitamin-deficient diet, little or no prenatal care, excessive exertion, and physical abuse. Pregnancy and childbirth did not guarantee immunity from their plantation duties, and most worked until a few days before their due dates only to return to work a few days after giving birth.[37] Others gave birth in the fields, as was the case with Ellen on Egypt Estate in Westmoreland. In September 1759, estate overseer Thomas Thistlewood noted that Ellen's child died from "the hurt it rec'd When it fell from her."[38] Pregnancy did not guarantee immunity from harsh punishment either, and it was not until 1826, during the last years of slavery, that Jamaican law lightened punishments and prohibited the flogging of slave women and girls in an effort to improve natural increase.[39]

The absence of pro-natal policies, adequate medical care, work reduction, and a nutritional diet all worked against pregnant slaves and their unborn children. Some mothers died in childbirth or soon after; others miscarried or were forced into an early labor, only to give birth to stillborn children.

Historian Michael Craton has estimated that only one out of every five children born to pregnant slaves in Jamaica was a live birth.[40] If slave mothers experienced successful births, most delivered severely malnourished and unhealthy children who had little chance of survival. According to historian Barry Higman, as many as 50 percent of all children born during this period died in the first nine days of life.[41] Breastfeeding did little to alleviate the situation, as slave children fed only on vitamin-deficient milk for up to three years.[42] Once weaned, a diet high in starch and low in protein further exacerbated their nutritional deficiencies.[43] Therefore, both mother and child often lacked sufficient levels of calcium, magnesium, and thiamin crucial to a healthy diet.[44] Those children who did not die of malnourishment or starvation often succumbed to fevers or respiratory infections. Consequently, only one in two slave children survived past the age of five.[45] Planters maintained a high degree of ambivalence to all of this, preferring to focus more directly on the bottom line and purchase their slaves directly from Africa.

Despite increased investments in younger Africans and girls, Jamaican planters realized that they could not rely on the present condition of the slave population to get them through their anticipated labor crisis. Many planters questioned whether they were on the wrong side of the "buy versus breed" debate. "A step of life is wanting on most Estates," Sir William Young said in 1791 at a meeting of Parliament, "leaving a chasm between childhood and mature man."[46] Young's statement before Parliament shows the changes that were occurring in ideas about slavery in the colonies, not only regarding natural increase but regarding slave youth as well. As abolitionism gained significant ground in England and more planters demanded a rise in the number of women and girls from Africa, they increasingly rationalized their purchases at market. Yes, the girls they purchased as "breeding wenches" were valuable investments, but that supply may not always be available. Perhaps Governor Trelawney *was* right. With these thoughts creeping into their minds, planters began to justify the need for the amelioration of the slave community. Consequently, they focused their attention more fully on the slaves already on their estates in order to close that gap between childhood and adulthood and hopefully render future slave importations unnecessary. Girlhood became an unexpected casualty of this process.

In 1788, the Jamaican Assembly passed the Consolidated Slave Laws, the first of many laws specifically designed to ameliorate the condition of the slaves and promote natural increase. Under these new laws, each slave received an annual clothing allowance, additional land for provision grounds, and additional time to work those grounds. Although laws like these were difficult to enforce among a generation of planters who placed little value on the lives of their slaves, the Assembly made provisions to combat planter resistance by subjecting each estate to a monthly inspection, requiring a report on the condition of the slaves' provision grounds and asking for proof that each slave received the annual clothing allowance. Desperate to increase the slave population by natural means and lessen reliance on the slave trade, the Assembly used these laws in an attempt to force Jamaican planters to assign a higher value to the slaves already laboring on their estates and to rely less on newly purchased Africans.[47]

These laws also forced Jamaican planters to reevaluate the nature of childhood and youth on their estates. Now each plantation had a physician on site, either daily or weekly, monitoring the health of the slave population and the conduct of the estate managers. In order to "more effectually prevent the destruction of Negroes by executive labour and unreasonable punishments," each surgeon annually reported the increase and decrease of the slaves under his care.[48] At the same time, the Consolidated Slave Laws enacted a reward system to provide incentives for natural increase as well as the better treatment of slaves. Each overseer received an award of twenty shillings for written proof of each child born on the estate and kept alive during the time of the report, with estate owners receiving a tax deduction equaling the same amount paid to their overseer.[49] Although Jamaican planters still viewed young slaves as economic liabilities, this law recognized that the only way to delay the abolition of slavery was to acknowledge that children and youth could grow up to be productive adults.

Designed to sustain the current slave population, the Consolidated Slave Laws did not seek to curtail demand for girls in the Jamaican slave markets. In fact, these laws motivated Jamaican planters to enact their own reward system to ensure population and economic growth at the plantation level. Many planters gave a dollar to each woman, girl, and midwife who successfully birthed a live child, "and told them, that for the future they might claim the same sum . . . for every infant which should be brought to the overseer alive and well."[50] Bernard Ezekiel and William Dickenson, owners of several estates in the parish of St. Elizabeth, ordered that each mother receive one pound of fresh meat and extra clothing for herself and every child under ten years of age.[51] Lord Penrhyn periodically increased the rewards given to midwives and mothers on his Jamaican estates, and by 1805, slave children received "a Fowl to commence its little stock in life" on the date of their birth.[52] Although such incentives seemed excessive to some planters, others felt that these rewards were merely sound economic investments for the future.

Ironically, these laws caused irrevocable damage to slave youth, especially girlhood. Although the quality of life for slave children improved, the increased pressure applied to slave girls to breed at younger and younger ages chipped away at their already brief girlhoods. Girls, as children, gained increased provisions and improved health standards, but their status as girls disappeared. With time, Jamaican planters linked girls and women, making gender synonymous with reproductive potential. Therefore, as amelioration worked to create an environment more conducive to natural increase, the boundary between girlhood and womanhood became so blurred that it began to disappear. Just as childhood became the most protected stage of life, girlhood was turning into a myth.

In 1801, the Jamaican Assembly amended the Consolidated Slave Laws of 1788 and decreed that all mothers with six or more children alive receive an exemption from all estate labor.[53] Not only did this stipulation provide an incentive for slave women and girls to have more children, but it also motivated them to keep their children alive. As laws like these laid the foundation for a spark in natural increase, some slaves began to characterize these so-called breeding wenches as "belly-women" by the nineteenth century.[54] Although archival sources do not indicate whether these slaves called these women and girls "belly-women" as a mark of respect or ridicule, labels like these indicate that the slave community came to understand the special significance that "breeding wenches" gained on the island. Planter Matthew "Monk" Lewis argued that even his slaves understood the importance Jamaican planters placed on natural increase. On his arrival at Cornwall Estate in the parish of Westmoreland in 1815, he noted several slave mothers who thrust their children in his face and said, " 'See massa, see! Here nice new neger me bring for work for massa!' "[55] Although Lewis felt that these mothers tried to impress him with their fertility, their actions suggest that Jamaican slaves realized that amelioration was motivated more by economics and abolitionism rather than humanitarianism.

As slave youth became a desired commodity in Jamaica, their population became more visible in the plantation inventories. Instead of merely listing the number of slaves on their estates, bookkeepers organized the slave population into categories such as first gang, second gang, children's gang, invalids, domestics, and children of nonworking age. By 1796, for example, Braco Estate in the parish of St. James devoted an entire page to "children each mother has had and date of their birth."[56] The following year, the Jamaican periodical *Columbian Magazine* began reporting instances of great fertility on the island, in which slave women and girls gave birth to triplets or had over nine children alive.[57] The planters who once had discouraged pregnancy and ignored the young slaves on their estates, now revealed a sense of pride in the natural increase of their slaves, indicating a shift in the perceived value of childhood and youth.

Meanwhile, planters created an environment more conducive to natural increase by providing pre- and postnatal care for their pregnant slaves. On Halse Hall in the parish of Clarendon, for example, owner Henry de la Beche put all pregnant slaves in the second gang as soon as he learned of their condition. "She is not compelled to do even the light work of that gang," de la Beche wrote in 1825, "the intention being merely to keep her in sight, and prevent her from carrying heavy loads for herself."[58] Jamaican planters also hired new estate managers with qualities "as that of taking especial care of the negro children."[59] Charles Gordon Gray replaced his overseer with one he felt was "particularly careful in looking after the sick and raising children."[60] Planters built hospitals on their estates and began inoculating their slaves in an effort to protect them against smallpox.[61] Also, planters consulted the first self-help books of the day, such as *Practical Rules for the Management and Medical Treatment of Negro Slaves, in the Sugar Colonies* and *Practical Remarks on the Management of Breeding Women during Pregnancy, Lying-in, &c*, for advice on how best to manage the children and pregnant slaves on their estates.[62] Suddenly, the slave youth who were once financial burdens became crucial components to the survival of Jamaican slavery. Slave girls, however, became even more important commodities as this shift in planter opinion took shape.

From Chattel to Breeding Wenches

In March 1817, Matthew "Monk" Lewis expressed his distress over the failure of his slaves to reproduce. "It is just as hens will frequently not lay eggs on shipboard," he wrote in his private journal, "because they do not like their situation." He further lamented the fact that out of 150 females on Cornwall Estate, there were only 8 women listed on the breeding list for that year. "How they manage it so ill I know not," he wrote, "but somehow or other certainly the children do not come."[63]

Lewis spoke for many when he complained of the failure of his "breeding wenches" to perform their expected duties. Although other planters noted similar grievances in their correspondence, archival sources list few "breeding wenches" in the estate inventories of the period. Despite the pressure to reproduce, few women were doing so. Incapable of understanding that the conditions under which female slaves toiled were the reason for their inability to reproduce, planters assigned a myriad of causes ranging from abstinence to abortion to old age. Consequently, incentive programs changed to expectation, and Jamaican slave girls found themselves caught in the crossfire.

From birth, slave youth lived in an environment that constantly reinforced their status as slaves. Before the advent of pro-natal policies, slave mothers returned to work a few days after giving birth with their children tied to their backs. With the passage of the Consolidated Slave Laws came the creation of plantation nurseries, where young children spent their days away from their mothers in the care of young girls or female slaves unable to perform any other productive labor on the estate. Other estates preferred to keep the children closer to the fields and their mothers, where the children watched their mothers suffer in the fields and under the whip. Here, the children stayed an average of five years, after which they were branded with the estate's symbol and put under the care of another elderly woman, who supervised their introduction into plantation labor.[64] At this young age, children in the small gang or children's gang performed menial tasks about the plantation not only "to preserve them from habits of idleness" but also to acclimatize them to labor on the estate.[65] Working the same twelve-hour days as the adults, they were anything but idle as they weeded and cleaned cane and coffee pieces, collected food for livestock, carried manure and trash, picked grass, and fertilized crops. Some performed the same labor as the adults while they were in this gang. "By this," Thomas Roughly, a Jamaican planter, wrote, "they will be taught to observe the mode of planting and putting the cane in the ground."[66] This labor also cemented their identity as slaves firmly in their minds.

Their acculturation to a life of slavery continued as Jamaica's slave youth moved out of the children's gang and into the second gang at age ten. Just as the first gang acclimatized them to plantation labor, the second gang prepared them for more strenuous labor and punishment in the fields. Composed mainly of boys and girls between the ages of ten and fifteen, the second gang often performed the same tasks as the adults.[67] "I have now Eighteen able Young people Cutting Canes," J. Fowler, manager of Dundee Estate in St. Mary, wrote; "I Assure you to my own prejudice, as my Cotton Crop at Thatch Hill is losing for want of picking."[68] Most children continued working in this gang until their fifteenth or sixteenth birthday.

Just like the boys who worked alongside them, girls could never escape their identity as slaves. This was impressed on them from the moment of their birth, and they had been working on the estate as slaves for an average of five years. It was at this age, however, that Jamaica's young female slaves encountered a series of definitions of childhood and girlhood. Under slavery, the various stages of slave childhood revolved around plantation labor and economic need. Infants and children did not work on the estate, while boys and girls labored in the third and second gangs. Before abolitionist threats to the slave trade and, later, to slavery, boyhood and girlhood began around age five, only to end within ten years as entrance into the first gang signified the beginning of their adulthood.

With increased threats to the slave supply and the resulting pressures to reproduce, Jamaican planters and estate managers added new stages to slave childhood. Titles like "man-boy" and "woman-girl" began to appear in the estate inventories, as new categorizations that included fourteen- and fifteen-year-olds just on the cusp of puberty. With labels such as these, young girls between the ages of fourteen and fifteen were added to the lists of "breeding wenches" and "belly women." Some planters referred to girls as young as thirteen as "woman-girls." Although this solved Jamaican planters' problem of too few "breeding wenches" on their estates, the new classification chipped away at the already short girlhood experienced by these young slaves.

These shifting definitions of childhood were subjective as well. Some planters categorized slave children between the ages of five and eight working in the third gang as "boys" and "girls" but classified the gang in which they worked as the "children's gang." Interestingly, those same planters categorized all slave children not working on the estate as "children." Other planters classified all slave children not working on the estate as "infants," while the "children" on their estate worked in the children's or third gang, and the "boys" and "girls" on the estate worked in the second gang.

With the onset of puberty, girls' identity as slaves began to change, and the boundary between women and girls blurred even more. Although the white community carefully worked to distance itself from both the free and slave populations, the absence of white women on the island drew many men from the white community to look in the slave villages and urban slave quarters for companionship. What resulted was a form of institutionalized concubinage that became widely accepted and sometimes encouraged in Jamaica and the British West Indies as a whole by the nineteenth century. Unfortunately, slave girls were not exempt from this practice. In 1751, for example, Jamaican planter Thomas Thistlewood had frequent sexual liaisons with at least twelve of the twenty-six women and six of the nine girls belonging to Egypt Estate in the parish of Westmoreland.[69] J. B. Moreton, a Clarendon bookkeeper, wrote that some owners and estate managers provided slave women and girls for friends and visitors to their estates in "a pimp-like action."[70] Jamaican planters, estate managers, bookkeepers, and overseers also visited young girls in the slave villages and fields.

As time passed, actions like these became more commonplace, indicating further shifts in the definition of girlhood. In 1816, the Jamaican Assembly attempted to protect slave girls under the age of ten from white men by enacting a law stipulating that any carnal knowledge of a female slave below that age was punishable by death.[71] Unfortunately, this law was not always enforced or upheld. While working as an overseer of a jobbing gang at Harmony Hall Estate in the parish of St. Thomas in the Vale sometime in the early 1820s, Benjamin M'Mahon realized the appetite of the gang's owner Adam Steele for young girls. According to M'Mahon, "females at the age of ten and eleven fell victims to his brutal lust."[72] M'Mahon does not state whether any of these girls pressed charges against Steele, or if they even knew the nature of the law. When Kingston authorities charged a white man with chaining down a nine-year-old girl and raping her in 1820, he argued that the girl was chattel and had no rights. Because she could not testify against him, Kingston courts transferred the case to English judges, who ruled in favor of the Kingstonian charged with rape.[73]

Although this evidence suggests that the rape of slave girls under the age of ten was so prevalent that the Assembly enacted a law to prohibit it, it also indicates that there was little consideration of "girlhood" on Jamaica's estates before the creation of this law. In fact, this law actually grants a type of silent consent to planters. By defining "children" as anyone below the age of ten, the law also defined "girlhood" as any girl ten or older. Whereas "children" were protected by law, girls were not. Therefore, as this law illustrates, sex with a girl of eleven was perfectly legal. Although Jamaican law recognized the delicacy of youth, English law still maintained that slaves were chattel, no matter their age.

With the passage of the law prohibiting the rape of slave girls younger than ten, boyhood and girlhood, then, existed between the ages of eleven and fifteen. Furthermore, planters often contradicted themselves where children were concerned. Although Jamaican planters and estate managers did not consider the "girls" and "women-girls" who worked in the second gang as adults, we have seen how some planters took these girls as sexual partners. Therefore, despite an acknowledgment of their sexuality and their entrance into adult situations, these girls remained "girls" until they joined the first gang as adults at the age of sixteen. As planters increasingly acknowledged that slave children could grow up to be productive adults, boys quickly matured into laborers and tradesmen, while girls became "breeding wenches" and eventually "belly-women." As a result, their short childhood ended almost as soon as it began, and their girlhood was quickly disappearing.

Conclusion

As we have seen, Jamaican planters came to depend on youth in the same capacity as they were economically dependent on the slave trade. As the abolitionist movement increasingly threatened their slave supply, Jamaican planters adopted the strategy of importing younger slaves into the island. Consequently, youth became an attractive asset on the auction blocks of the Jamaican slave markets. Abolitionist sentiment, therefore, changed eighteenth-century definitions of risk, investment, and profit. As the Jamaican plantocracy purchased more "breeding wenches" and girls in order to save their West Indian interests, traders modified their ideas of profit and risk, and ideas of child worth changed throughout the Atlantic World. In the end, Jamaican planters also revisited the idea of girlhood as it related to plantation management and profit. According to one planter, "the care of Negroes, the causes of increase and decrease, &c., &c., are becoming the subject of common conversation among a description of persons who used only to think of the speediest methods of obtaining labors."[74] As Jamaican planters demanded more children and "breeding wenches" in the slave markets, the nature of supply and demand along the West Coast of Africa changed, and more girls entered the trade.

As abolitionist threats against the slave trade intensified, Jamaican planters changed their strategy again. Accepting that their slave supply would eventually end, Jamaican planters began to think it more profitable to breed slaves rather than buy them. As a result, the nature of girlhood changed within the Jamaican slave community. Jamaican planters increasingly linked gender to reproductive potential, and the boundaries between girlhood and womanhood blurred to the point of nonexistence. While abolitionists worked tirelessly to end the slave trade and eventually slavery, they inadvertently destroyed girlhood in the process. By the time slave girls reached the delicate age of eleven, they were women. More specifically, they were "breeding wenches."

NOTES

1. Edward Trelawney, *An Essay concerning Slavery, and the Danger Jamaica Is Expos'd to from the Too Great Number of Slaves, and the Too Little Care That Is Taken to Manage Them, and a Proposal to Prevent the Further Importation of Negroes into That Island* (London: Charles Corbett, 1745), 4–6.

2. For Quaker involvement in the abolition movement, see Judith Jennings, "The Campaign for the Abolition of the British Slave Trade: The Quaker Contribution, 1757–1807" (Ph.D. diss., University of Kentucky, 1979).

3. Stephen Fuller to Lord Hawksbury, May 4, 1788, Stephen Fuller Papers, 1702–1798, Duke University Special Collections.

4. See Wilma King, *Stolen Childhood: Slave Youth in Nineteenth-Century America* (Bloomington: Indiana University Press, 1995); and Marie Jenkins Schwartz, *Born in Bondage: Growing Up Enslaved in the Antebellum South* (Cambridge: Harvard University Press, 2000).

5. See Kenneth Kiple, *The Caribbean Slave: A Biological History* (Cambridge: Cambridge University Press, 1984); Richard Sheridan, *Doctors and Slaves: A Medical and Demographic History of Slavery in the British West Indies, 1680–1834* (Cambridge: Cambridge University Press, 1985); Richard Steckel, "A Peculiar Population: The Nutrition, Health, and Mortality of American Slaves from Childhood to Maturity," *Journal of Economic History* 46 (1986): 721–741; and Barbara Bush, "Hard Labor: Women, Childbirth, and Resistance in British Slave Societies," in *More Than Chattel: Black Women and Slavery in the Americas*, ed. David Barry Gaspar and Darlene Clark Hine (Bloomington: Indiana University Press, 1996), 194–217. See also Herbert S. Klein and Stanley L. Engerman, "Fertility Differentials between Slaves in the United States and the British West Indies: A Note on Lactation Practices and Their Possible Implications," *William and Mary Quarterly* 35 (1978): 357–374.

6. See Lucille Mathurin Mair, *Women Field Workers in Jamaica during Slavery* (Mona: Department of History, University of the West Indies, 1987); Marietta Morrissey, *Slave Women in the New World: Gender Stratification in the Caribbean* (Lawrence: University Press of Kansas, 1989); Barbara Bush, *Slave Women in Caribbean Society, 1650–1838* (Kingston: Heinemann Publishers [Caribbean], 1990); Hilary Beckles, *Natural Rebels: A Social History of Enslaved Black Women in Barbados* (New Brunswick, NJ: Rutgers University Press, 1989); and Hilary Beckles, *Centering Woman: Gender Discourses in Caribbean Slave Society* (Kingston: Ian Randle, 1999).

7. See Elsa V. Goveia, *Slave Society in the British Leeward Islands at the End of the Eighteenth Century* (Westport, CT: Greenwood Press, 1965); B. W. Higman, "Household Structure and Fertility on Jamaican Slave Plantations: A Nineteenth Century Example," *Population Studies* 27 (1973): 527–550; B. W. Higman, "The Slave Family and Household in the British West Indies, 1800–1834," *Journal of Interdisciplinary History* 6 (1975): 261–287; and B. W. Higman, "African and Creole Slave Family Patterns in Trinidad," *Journal of Family History* 3 (1978): 163–180. See also Michael Craton, "Changing Patterns of Slave Families in the British West Indies," *Journal of Interdisciplinary History* 10 (1979): 1–35; Humphrey E. Lamur, "The Slave Family in Colonial 19th-Century Suriname," *Journal of Black Studies* 23 (1993): 371–381. There is a large historiography on slave families in the United States, which is too extensive to list here, but see the classic works of E. Franklin Frazier, *The Negro Family in the United States* (Chicago: University of Chicago Press, 1966); and Herbert G. Gutman, *The Black Family in Slavery and Freedom, 1750–1925* (New York: Pantheon Books, 1976). For more recent works that pertain directly to this study, see King, *Stolen Childhood*; and Schwartz, *Born in Bondage*.

8. George Turner to Mrs. Rooke Clarke, October 6, 1791, Tweedie Family Papers, no. 4/45/66, Jamaican Archives. According to *The Trans-Atlantic Slave Trade: A Database on CD-ROM*, the number of slaves imported to Jamaica in 1782 totaled 7,254. The following year Jamaica imported 11,508, with 18,350 arriving in 1784. Although island imports averaged only

7,668 Africans between 1785 and 1788, Jamaica imported 11,458 in 1789, with annual imports increasing steadily each year. See *The Trans-Atlantic Slave Trade: A Database on CD-ROM*, ed. David Eltis, Stephen Behrendt, Herbert S. Klein, and David Richardson (Cambridge: Cambridge University Press, 1999), hereafter cited as *TSTD*.

9. Thomas Thistlewood diaries, July 3, 1784, Monson 12/31, University of the West Indies West India Collection; and Douglas Hall, *In Miserable Slavery: Thomas Thistlewood in Jamaica, 1750–86*, 2nd ed. (Mona: University of the West Indies Press, 1999), 299. For more information on Thomas Thistlewood's escapades in Jamaica, see Trevor Burnard, *Mastery, Tyranny, and Desire: The Anglo-Jamaican World of Thomas Thistlewood and His Slaves, 1750–1786* (Mona: University of the West Indies Press, 2004).

10. Although 61 children were born on York Estate between 1776 and 1780, 99 slaves died, which motivated the owner to purchase 73 Africans during this five-year period. See "Negro and Stock Accounts on York Plantation, 1778–1837," Gale-Morant Family Papers, 1731–1925, MS 769, West India Collection University of the West Indies. In 1783, there were 224 slaves on Somerset Plantation; that number dropped to 215 by 1785. See Somerset Plantation, 1782–1796, MS 229, National Library of Jamaica.

11. Thomas Thistlewood diaries, July 3, 1784, Monson 12/31, West India Collection University of the West Indies; and Hall, *In Miserable Slavery*, 299. Hard labor, harsh treatment, and low birth rates made any natural increase impossible. By 1800, Jamaica had nearly 300,000 slaves, but still their number could not increase by natural means. See Trevor Burnard and Kenneth Morgan, "The Dynamics of the Slave Market and Slave Purchasing Patterns in Jamaica," *William and Mary Quarterly* 58 (2001): 205.

12. *Journals of the Assembly of Jamaica*, vol. 8, f. 428. Assemblymen also attributed the natural decrease of the slave population to female promiscuity, abortions, and high infant and child mortality.

13. Ibid.; and Stephen Fuller, *Report, Resolutions, and Remonstrance, of the Honourable the Council and Assembly of Jamaica, at a Joint Committee, on the Subject of the Slave-Trade, in a Session Which Began the 20th of October 1789* (London: B. White and Son, 1790), 9.

14. Alexander McDonnell, *A Letter to Thos. Fowell Buxton, Esq., M.P., in Refutation of His Allegations Respecting the Decrease of the Slaves in the British West India Colonies* (London: Effingham Wilson, 1833), 23. It is not known how many Jamaican slave women were classified as "breeding wenches" during this early period.

15. Fuller, *Report, Resolutions, and Remonstrance*, 9.

16. George Turner to M. D. Hodgson, November 9, 1791, Tweedie Family Papers, no. 4/45/66, Jamaican Archives. See also George Turner to M. D. Hodgson, April 16 and 18, 1792, Tweedie Family Papers, no. 4/45/66, Jamaican Archives.

17. Nathaniel Phillips to Thomas Barrett, October 20, 1789, Slebach Collection, MS 528, West India Collection University of the West Indies. Increasingly the terms "breeding wenches" and "woman girl" are used interchangeably in the correspondence and plantation books of the period. These terms developed in response to abolitionist threats to the slave supply.

18. "Slave Trade," 1792, Stephen Fuller Papers, 1702–1796, Duke University Special Collections. His proposal never passed the Jamaican Assembly.

19. James Rogers Papers, 1760–1790, box 1, Duke University Special Collections; and *TSTD*. Before leaving Calabar, the *African Queen* carried 93 men, 138 women, 10 boys, and 14 girls.

20. "Slave Trade," 1792, Stephen Fuller Papers, 1702–1796, Duke University Special Collections. Although votes like these passed in the House of Commons, the House of Lords, and Parliament, the slave trade was not abolished until 1808.

21. Dr. Collins, *Practical Rules for the Management and Medical Treatment of Negro Slaves, in the Sugar Colonies* (London: J. Barfield, 1811), 42.

22. William Beckford, *Remarks on the Situation of Negroes in Jamaica, Impartially Made from a Local Experience of Nearly Thirteen Years in That Island* (London: T. and J. Egerton, 1788), 13, 14.

23. John Stewart, *An Account of Jamaica and Its Inhabitants* (London: Longman, Hurst, Rees, and Orme, 1808; repr., Freeport, NY: Books for Libraries Press, 1971), 245 (citations are to the reprint edition).

24. Rev. Benjamin Lucock, *Jamaica: Enslaved and Free* (London: Religious Tract Society, 1846), 108.

25. Elizabeth Donnan, *Documents Illustrative of the Slave Trade* (New York: Octagon Books, 1965), 2:524–525; and *TSTD*.

26. James Rogers Papers, 1760–1790, box 5, Duke University Special Collections; and *TSTD*.

27. James Rogers Papers, 1760–1790, box 10; and *TSTD*.

28. *Laws of Jamaica*, 38 George III, c. 18 (1797); and Stewart, *Account of Jamaica*, 244. See also *Laws of Jamaica*, 39 George III, c. 31 (1799), and 42 George III, c. 15 (1801).

29. Stewart, *Account of Jamaica*, 244.

30. Collins, *Practical Rules*, 42. Dr. Collins and William Beckford both suggested that it would be best if Jamaica imported cargoes of slaves aged between fifteen and twenty-five, or younger still, between twelve and sixteen. See Beckford, *Remarks*, 14.

31. Trelawney, *Essay concerning Slavery*, 34–35.

32. Beckford, *Remarks*, 24–25.

33. James Ramsay, *An Essay on the Treatment and Conversion of African Slaves in the British Sugar Colonies* (London: James Phillips, 1784), 97. The emphasis is Ramsay's.

34. Spring Vale Journal and Accounts, 1790–1815, MS 236, National Library of Jamaica.

35. Michael Craton and James Walvin, *A Jamaican Plantation: A History of Worthy Park, 1670–1970* (London: W. H. Allen, 1970), 130.

36. Although women preferred these tasks to working in the fields, their lives as domestic slaves were not as privileged as one may think. Dr. George Pinkard, a visitor to the region in the 1790s, argued that their duties required the same amount of physical exertion as did those of the field women. He also noted their severe punishments. See George Pinkard, *Notes on the West Indies: Written during the Expedition under the Command of the Late General Sir Ralph Abercromby* (London: Longman, Hurst, Rees, and Orme, 1806; reprint, Westport, CT: Negro Universities Press, 1970), 1:258 (citations are to the reprint edition).

37. J. B. Moreton, *Manners and Customs in the West India Islands* (London: W. Richardson, 1790), 152.

38. Thomas Thistlewood diaries, September 22, 1759, Monson 31/10, West India Collection University of the West Indies.

39. In 1816, the Jamaican Assembly limited the number of lashes to a maximum of 39, no matter the age of slave. In 1826, the Jamaican Assembly prohibited the flogging of women. See *Laws of Jamaica*, 57 George III, c. 25 (1816), and 7 George IV, c. 23 (1826).

40. Michael Craton, *Searching for the Invisible Man: Slaves and Plantation Life in Jamaica* (Cambridge: Harvard University Press, 1978), 87.

41. B. W. Higman, *Slave Population and Economy in Jamaica, 1807–1834* (Mona: University of the West Indies Press, 1995), 49.

42. Klein and Engerman, "Fertility Differentials," 370–371.

43. For weaning, see Jerome S. Handler and Robert S. Corruccini, "Weaning among West Indian Slaves: Historical and Bioanthropological Evidence from Barbados," *William and Mary Quarterly* 43 (1986): 111–117.

44. Kiple, *Caribbean Slave*, 123–124.

45. Richard B. Sheridan, "Mortality and the Medical Treatment of Slaves in the British West Indies," in *Caribbean Slave Society and Economy: A Student Reader*, ed. Hilary Beckles and Verene Shepherd (New York: New Press, 1991), 199.

46. *The Speech of Sir William Young, Bart. Delivered in Parliament on the Subject of the Slave Trade* (London: John Stockdale, 1791), 43.

47. *Laws of Jamaica*, 29 George III, c. 2 (1788). The Jamaican Assembly revised these laws every few years, although the majority remained unchanged. See *Laws of Jamaica*, 41 George III, c. 26 (1801); 50 George III, c. 16 (1810); 57 George III, c. 25 (1816); 7 George IV, c. 23 (1826); and 6 George IV, c. 19 (1831).

48. *Journals of the Assembly of Jamaica*, vol. 8, ff. 428, 431. If auditors discovered instances of natural decrease or increase that were not reported, they fined physicians £20 currency for each instance.

49. Jamaica, House of Assembly, *The New Consolidated Act* (London: Printed for Stephen Fuller, Esq., 1789), 9.

50. Matthew Lewis, *Journal of a West Indian Proprietor Kept during a Residence in the Island of Jamaica*, ed. Judith Terry (London: John Murray, 1834; reprint, Oxford: Oxford University Press, 1999), 79 (citations are to the reprint edition).

51. Bernard and William Dickenson to Thomas S. Salmon, December 1, 1792, Dickenson Family Letterbook, 1792–1794, Dickenson Family Papers, 1675–1849, MS 518, West India Collection University of the West Indies.

52. Rowland Fearon to Lord Penrhyn, January 26, 1805, Penrhyn Castle Papers, 1709–1834, MS 1361, West India Collection University of the West Indies.

53. Jamaica, House of Assembly, *An Act for the Better Order and Government of Slaves; and for Other Purposes* (St. Jago de la Vega: Alexander Aikman, 1801), 29; and *Laws of Jamaica*, 41 George III, c. 26 (1801). The law remained in effect until August 1834.

54. Lewis, *Journal of a West Indian Proprietor*, 79.

55. Ibid., 42, 133.

56. Braco Estate, 1795–1797, 4/2, Jamaican Archives.

57. *Columbian Magazine* 2 (1797): 263, 328, C652, National Library of Jamaica.

58. Henry de la Beche, *Notes on the Present Condition of the Negroes in Jamaica* (London: T. Cadell, 1825), 12. "Lying-in" is the term given by Jamaican planters to this four- to six-month maternity leave granted to slave mothers who recently gave birth.

59. Beckford, *Remarks*, 37.

60. Charles Gordon Gray to Father, June 8, 1815, Gray Correspondence, 1809–1818, MS 163, National Library of Jamaica.

61. See Gale-Morant Family Papers, 1731–1925, MS 769, West India Collection University of the West Indies; Slebach Collection, MS 543, West India Collection University of the West Indies; Somerset Plantation, 1782–1796, National Library of Jamaica; Spring Vale Journal and Accounts, 1790–1815, National Library of Jamaica; Peter Marsden, *An Account of the Island of Jamaica; with Reflections on the Treatment, Occupation, and Provisions of the Slaves* (London: n.p., 1788), 39; and Edward Long, *The History of Jamaica, or, A General Survey of the Antient and Modern State of that Island* (London: T. Lowndes, 1770), 2:436.

62. See also Hector M'Neill, *Observations on the Treatment of the Negroes, in the Island of Jamaica* (London: G.G.J. and J. Robinson, 1788); and Thomas Roughly, *The Jamaica Planter's Guide; or, a System for Planting and Managing a Sugar Estate, or Other Plantations in That Island, and Throughout the British West Indies in General* (London: Longman, Hurst, Rees, Orme, and Brown, 1823).

63. Lewis, *Journal of a West Indian Proprietor*, 54, 237. For similar complaints, see Anna Eliza Elletson to John Poole and Edward East, August 5, 1778, Roger Hope Elletson Letterbook, 1773–1780, MS 29, National Library of Jamaica; William Adlam to John Wemyss, February 1, 1820, Letterbook of John Wemyss, 1819–1824, MS 250, National Library of Jamaica; Dickenson Family Papers, MSS 515, 518, 2599–2600, 2950–2653, West India Collection University of the West Indies; and Slebach Collection, MS 527–529, West India Collection University of the West Indies.

64. The 1826 Consolidated Slave Law outlawed the branding of slaves. See *Laws of Jamaica*, 7 George IV, c. 23 (1826).

65. Robert Renny, *An History of Jamaica* (London: J. Cawthorn, 1807), 176. See also Charles Gordon Gray to Father, January 5, 1809, and March 11, 1814, Gray Correspondence, 1809–1818, MS 163, National Library of Jamaica; and Roughly, *Jamaica Planter's Guide*, 105.

66. Roughly, *Jamaica Planter's Guide*, 107.

67. See "List of Slaves on Green Castle Pen with Their Age, Occupation, & Condition on the 1st January 1834," Kelly Family Papers, 4/43/8, Jamaican Archives; Green Park Estate, 1821–1825, 4/8/2–3, Jamaican Archives; Rose Hall Estate, 1817–1822, 1B/26/1–3, Jamaican Archives; and Radnor Plantation, 1822–1826, MS 180, National Library of Jamaica.

68. J. Fowler to John Stothert, January 8, 1789, James Stothert Papers, 1784–1807, Clements Library.

69. Hall, *In Miserable Slavery*, 28.

70. Moreton, *Manners and Customs*, 77, 90. See also the testimony of Reverend J. Barry before the House of Lords Committee on the condition and treatment of slaves in 1832, in Legion, *A Second Letter from Legion to His Grace the Duke of Richmond* (London: S. Bagster, 1833), 39.

71. *Laws of Jamaica*, 57 George III, c. 25 (1816). By 1831, that punishment could be applied to any abuse of a female slave under ten years of age. See *Laws of Jamaica*, 6 George IV, c. 19 (1831).

72. Benjamin M'Mahon, *Jamaica Plantership* (London: Effingham Wilson, 1839), 51.

73. W. J. Gardner, *A History of Jamaica from Its Discovery by Christopher Columbus to the Year 1872* (London: Frank Cass, 1873; reprint, London: Frank Cass, 1971), 264.

74. Gilbert Mathison, *Notices Respecting Jamaica, in 1808–1809–1810* (London: S. Gosnell, 1811), 12.

18 *Girls, Labor, and Sex in Precolonial Egypt, 1850–1882*

LIAT KOZMA

On the night of October 8, 1864, a girl named Sariyya was crushed to death in a cotton press factory in Alexandria. The accident took place after dark, in the female section of the factory. The division of labor in the factory was gendered: while the men were responsible for pressing the cotton on the upper level, the women dealt with the cotton that came out of the shafts of the pressing machine on the lower level. The woman in charge of the female workers, a woman named Imbaraka, sat outside of the factory at the time of the accident. She explained that she usually left the room after helping the workers settle in their positions and did not see her presence there as necessary. Most important for our purpose, the investigation revealed that most of the "women" working in the factory, including Sariyya herself, were ten years old or younger. Alexandria's appellate court found Imbaraka guilty of harmful negligence for failing to supervise her workers in these hazardous after-dark conditions, and the Supreme Court sentenced her to one month's imprisonment. Then, in an edict that displays the complexity of delimiting girlhood and womanhood in precolonial Egypt, the court ordered all government agencies to disallow the work of "women under ten" after dark, in order to prevent the occurrence of such accidents in the future.[1] Establishing its role as the protector of *girls*, the court still conceptualized working females as *women*.

Girlhood is a gendered social construction defined by adults. Girls rarely left their own narratives in writing, and their stories are usually mediated through the perspective of adults: reformers, parents, doctors, educators, judges, and adults narrating their own childhood. In this chapter I examine changing constructions and changing experiences of girlhood during the decades preceding the British occupation of Egypt. I build on existing literature about the history of childhood as well as the history of children.[2] I combine both the viewpoint of adults, who categorize children according to their needs and interests, and that of girls, whose perspectives are necessarily mediated by adult representation.

In addition, I question how the introduction of modern state power in precolonial Egypt changed the ways in which adult society thought of and handled girls and girlhood. Beginning from the mid-1850s, the modern Egyptian state came to intervene in domains that were, until then, the sole responsibility of the family and the community. In this context, child marriage, labor, and slavery became state concerns. Girls in the later decades of the nineteenth century experienced more legal and medical intervention than their mothers had. At the same time, however, this intervention created more room for negotiation. Whereas Islamic law left the definition of girlhood in the hands of learned men, laypersons in late nineteenth-century Egypt came to articulate—through the police, courts, and others—their own definitions of girlhood.

In the first part of this chapter I examine representations of girlhood in Islamic Sunni law, and focus on the Hanafi School of law, which was hegemonic in the Ottoman Empire and Egypt. I examine some of the canonic texts of the Hanafi School, authored between the twelfth and nineteenth centuries, in order to demonstrate the tensions inherent in the Islamic legal definition of girlhood as a social category. Islamic legal discourse on childhood was highly gendered; it marked boys' maturity mainly by their mental capacities, while marking girls' maturity primarily by their sexual and reproductive roles. Islamic courts handled such questions mostly in the context of family disputes, principally over child marriage and child custody. Menarche, defloration, marriage, and chronological age were some of the factors that judges took into account in determining who was a girl and who was not. An adult woman, unlike a girl, was physically capable of assuming adult roles, namely, having sexual intercourse with her husband and bearing children.

Beginning in the mid-nineteenth century, Egyptian state institutions, such as the police stations and courts, increased their intervention in the daily life of non-elite Egyptians. In this process, the state started to assume a new role—one previously accorded to private patriarchs—as the protector of girls. Girlhood was no longer discussed merely in family affairs. Legal discussion of childhood now extended to crimes such as sexual assault. At the same time, state institutions came to rely on modern mechanisms of power, such as medical examinations, to determine who was a girl and who was not.

In the second part of this chapter I examine girls themselves and their gendered experiences as free and bound laborers. Child labor predated the nineteenth century, but police intervention made it more visible to state authorities and, as I show, to present-day historians as well. Egypt's integration into the world economy, and especially the cotton industry, introduced new forms of labor, such as factory labor and public works, that entailed harsher conditions than earlier forms of labor and deprived girls of communal and familial protection. In the process, girlhood emerged as a target for protection and concern, even as the worker herself appeared in legal discourse as an adult.

At the same time, at least until the early 1880s, domestic labor in Egyptian households relied in part on the bond labor of female black slaves. Many of them were first-generation slaves who had been kidnapped and sold as children from their homes in sub-Saharan Africa. Their forced separation from home, their long journey through the desert, and acculturation into their enslavers' households colored the childhood of Egyptian slaves and freed slaves far into the twentieth century. To thousands of Egyptian women, girlhood therefore entailed a violent rupture from home and family.

This chapter is based, first, on Islamic legal writings, especially legal jurisprudence (*fiqh*) and responsa (*fatwa*) literature.[3] Second, it relies on the archives of the police and the court system that operated in Egypt during the decades preceding the 1882 British occupation of Egypt. Finally, it uses travel accounts by foreign travelers to Egypt. Together, these sources demonstrate the multiple, and often contradictory, definitions of girlhood that shaped girls' experiences in precolonial Egypt.

Girlhood under Islamic Law

Even before the courts and police began exerting increased control over the definitions of girlhood, premodern Muslim scholars, generally within the realm of the family and local community, identified childhood as a unique period in human life. Under Islamic law, children did not hold full responsibility for their crimes. They were not considered capable of forming a criminal intent and were therefore neither rewarded nor punished for their deeds.[4] Moreover, Islamic law saw children as vulnerable and dependant beings. Guardians, usually a father or his male relatives, were responsible for children's education and welfare. They also represented them in any economic transactions and conducted their marriage contract.[5]

Medieval Islamic authors saw childhood as a gradual developmental process and identified several stages in it. The main stepping stones in a child's transition to adulthood were the age of discernment (*tamyyiz*) and the onset of puberty (*bulugh*). The age of discernment was the point in life at which children could distinguish between good and evil and could therefore begin their education and start performing their religious duties. For most children, *tamyyiz* arrived around the age of seven, but individual children could reach this stage earlier or later. For legal purposes, the court determined the child's mental age before assessing the validity of legal procedures. In conversion cases, for example, the judge questioned boys and girls between the ages of seven and ten to ascertain their understanding of legal procedure. Judges only approved conversion of children who could show that they were mature enough to understand what their conversion would entail.[6]

The second important transitional point was the onset of puberty—first menstruation for girls and first nocturnal seminal emission for boys—as recognized by the individual's own admission. Islamic law also set the age of nine as the minimum age for maturity; if biological signs were delayed, the maximum age was fifteen (or eighteen in the Maliki School of Legal Jurisprudence). Puberty rendered both boys and girls legally mature and entailed the capacity to handle property and sign contracts. For some legal purposes, however, physical signs of puberty were not sufficient, and a person's mental capacities, particularly her understanding of legal and economic transactions, were also tested.[7]

In more than one sense the transition to adulthood and legal maturity was gendered. Both colloquial and legal discourses defined girls through their relationship with men and through their sexuality, two elements that are almost absent from legal discussions of boys. The Arabic word for a girl, *bint*, demonstrates the multiplicity in Islamic notions of girlhood, as it means a daughter, a female child, a virgin, and a young unmarried woman. The termination of childhood in Islamic law occurred as a result of a social shift, when a girl's primary relationship with a man shifted from that with her father to that with a husband, or with biological development such as chronological age, puberty, or biologically or socially defined defloration. She was no longer a *bint* if she had had sexual experience with a man, was married, or had shown physical signs that rendered her capable of assuming the social roles of an adult woman, namely, having sexual intercourse with a husband and bearing children.[8] The average age of marriage for females in Egypt at this period was twelve to fourteen, and premarital sex was taboo, so defloration, marriage, and puberty occurred at approximately the same time, meaning a young female might be defined simultaneously as girl and woman.[9] The tension between these categories marked the legal discourse on girlhood.

This gendered definition of childhood and its termination can be traced in several legal domains. Take, for example, the question of child custody. According to Islamic law, a divorced mother retained custody (*hadana*) of her minor children and was to hand them over to their father when they were no longer considered minor. According to the Hanafi School of Legal Jurisprudence, a boy remained with his mother until he no longer needed assistance in performing his daily routine, namely, eating, drinking, and cleaning himself, which was around the age of seven. A girl, on the other hand, remained with her mother until menarche. The Maliki School set the end of *hadana* as puberty for boys, and for girls a first marriage, or its consummation if the child was too young to have her marriage consummated. Other scholars set a girl's maturity for this purpose with the appearance of sexual desire, estimated at around the age of eleven.[10]

Nineteenth-century Egyptian legal scholar Ibn 'Abidin explained the gendered Hanafi definition of childhood in the following way. A boy had to be handed to his father's care at the age of seven, he claimed, because a child capable of telling good from evil needed the guidance of his father, who was more capable of socializing and teaching him than a mother. A girl, on the other hand, needed her mother beyond the age of seven, because she needed to learn the manners of women, and a mother was most capable of teaching them to her. After she reached puberty, however, she needed protection, and a father was firmer and a better guide for such a task.[11]

In this example, childhood and parenthood were gendered and mutually constitutive. Childhood was defined in terms of maternal care, and adulthood in terms of paternal guidance; here gender determined which was more appropriate for an individual child and at what age. Maturity, moreover, was differently defined for boys and for girls. A boy's adulthood was defined through his mental capacities, and a girl's adulthood through her sexuality. Thus several competing end-points rendered girls women, including puberty, ability to bear sexual intercourse, the appearance of sexual desire, marriage, and the consummation of marriage. This list reveals a tension between the protection of a girl's welfare and interest, on the one hand, and the wish to subordinate her to male authority and desire on the other.

Legal discussions of child marriage similarly tried to balance a child's welfare against her guardian's and her husband's interests. In a patriarchal society, early marriage guaranteed male control of women in that a woman was handed directly from her father to her husband, ensuring her transition from daughter to wife without an intermediate period of adult independence. A girl could be married at any age, provided that her marriage was consummated only after she reached puberty and was physically capable of tolerating sexual intercourse. Still, marriage did not force the minor bride into full adult responsibilities, and in a sense, she remained a girl even within marriage. Some girls lived with their husbands and in-laws. They assisted the female members of their husbands' families in everyday domestic chores and assumed their sexual duties to their husbands upon puberty. Court verdicts sometimes allowed girls to stay with their families until puberty, which perhaps implies that husbands sometimes tried to impose sexual intercourse on their minor wives. The girls then turned to courts for protection and were allowed to stay in their fathers' households.[12]

According to the Hanafi School, a guardian could negotiate the marriage contract of a prepubescent girl and could also use this power to marry her against her wishes. It did, however, offer a minor bride some protection and recognized her as a child for several purposes. First, marriage could not be consummated until the girl was capable of tolerating sexual intercourse. Second, when the guardian was other than a girl's father or paternal grandfather, whose concern for a girl's interests was not questioned, a girl who was married against her wishes could annul her marriage immediately upon menarche in a process known as *khiyar al-bulugh*, or the "option of puberty."[13] Demonstrating the complexity of Islamic law, however, the Shafi'i school of thought equated maturity, for this purpose, not with puberty but rather with marriage or defloration. Shafiʻi scholars considered an adult virgin as ignorant as an infant with regard to marriage and therefore forbade her to marry without a guardian. A virgin could not marry without a guardian, and a guardian could marry a virgin against her wishes, regardless of age or physical maturity.[14]

Defloration served as a sign of maturity in the Hanafi School as well, but in a subtler way. An adult virgin's silence could be considered consent to marriage. The nonvirgin, on the other hand, had to explicitly voice her consent.[15] Twelfth-century Hanafi jurist ʻAli ibn Abi Bakr al-Marghinani reasoned that a virgin's "assent is rather to be supposed, as she is ashamed to testify her desire," whereas the nonvirgin, "having had connection with men, has not the same pretence to silence or shyness as a virgin," and her silence was therefore not a sufficient sign of consent.[16] It was important to stress that here virginity was referred to as a social rather than biological category. Hanafi scholars maintained that a girl who lost her virginity as a result of an accident, or even as an outcome of secret sexual intercourse, was seen by her social environment as a virgin and was therefore expected to be silent about men and marriage. Her silence confirmed her social role and social expectations, and her silence was therefore a sign of consent.[17]

Finally, and to complicate the question even further, although marriages were not to be consummated before puberty, an Islamic court judge (*qadi*) could allow earlier consummation in certain cases. The judge here had to balance the interests of the husband in consummating marriage with the girl's well-being. In this context, the criterion of neither chronological age nor puberty was applied but rather courts weighed a girl's appearance as physically mature and capable of tolerating sexual intercourse. A *qadi* could call in a midwife to testify about a girl's competence for sexual intercourse or rely on his own judgment.[18]

Although virginity, puberty, and appearance were all biologically based, they served as socially constructed markers of social roles and social expectations. Transition to adulthood entailed a girl's readiness to assume her gendered role as wife and mother. Girls were therefore those females who were not yet capable of assuming women's sexual and reproductive responsibilities. Incapability to marry and reproduce therefore defined girlhood.

Girl's Sexuality in the Precolonial State

By the mid-nineteenth century, as the Egyptian state institutions developed, the definition of girlhood was no longer left to the discretion of a local *qadi* or a girl's own testimony but rather was debated within a hierarchy of legal institutions, between those legal institutions, and among individual litigants. What emerged was an even more complex delimitation of girlhood—one that viewed girls' experiences in terms of public health and vulnerability to crime, and one that medicalized their biological processes.

In the early 1850s, Egypt's rulers founded a new legal system that supplemented the shari'a courts, which adjudicated cases according to Islamic law. This system included an investigating police, a hierarchy of courts, and a new legal code, the Sultanic Code of 1855, based on Ottoman law. At the top of this hierarchy was Majlis al-Ahkam, the Supreme Council of Adjudication. Forensic medicine became central to this legal reform, and virginity examination became a part of legal determination of premarital defloration.[19]

The Egyptian administration started supplementing and even replacing community-based forms of assistance and protection. As community networks were dissolving, people turned to the state for help; state agencies, such as the police station or the hospital, started providing services that previously had been relegated to the communal realm. Non-elite men and women started using the new institutions to seek assistance, which helped to define the role of the state as the protector of the weak, including children.[20]

The state's legal mechanisms now had to balance girls' interests with those of private patriarchs as well as with some nascent notion of public security or public morality. The introduction of medical examinations and the availability of census reports, two manifestations of what Foucault termed "bio-power," medicalized and bureaucratized official discourse on girlhood. These modern forms of power focused on the production of life and on women's bodies and sexuality as means to regulate and control the population.[21] Virginity and capacity for sexual intercourse came to be framed as a public health concern.

By midcentury, Egyptian medical practitioners began to see early consummation of marriage as a health hazard. Medical textbooks specifically cautioned against its risk to a girl's health. Ahmad Al-Rashidi, one of the first teachers at the school of midwives and the translator of its first textbooks (mainly from French), warned that sexual intercourse and pregnancy could be dangerous for young girls or for women who suffered from physical deformities.[22]

The central administration became interested in child marriage after Cairo's police stations and courts began receiving hospital reports of girls who had died as a result of sexual intercourse with their husbands. One hospital report regarding a girl who was severely injured as a result of intercourse, for example, strongly recommended that girls not be married until they reached puberty and were capable of tolerating sexual intercourse.[23] In one case, which took place in February 1864, a twelve-year-old girl died after her first intercourse with her husband, who insisted on consummating his marriage "although she was not yet able to tolerate intercourse." In his defense the husband claimed that he did not mean to cause her death and that "many are married at the age of ten or eleven, and nothing happens to them." He was sentenced to ten months in prison, which he had served while awaiting his trial.[24] As this case illustrates, some refused to accept the correlation between age and readiness for sexual intercourse. The husband insisted that his wife's childhood could be ended simply upon his wish and with his penetration. Her death, to him, was an unfortunate accident that could not have been foreseen.

Most cases involving girls that were recorded in the archives of nineteenth-century Egyptian police stations and courts were not cases of child marriage but rather cases of premarital defloration. This offense was labeled *izalat bikarat al-bint*, literally, the "removal of a girl's virginity." It was considered an offense against a person's honor (*hatq 'ird*). Both parties involved could be held accountable, and the offense normally carried six months' imprisonment. In this context, the court questioned a girl's consent to sexual intercourse, and one who could convince the court that she had not consented could be acquitted. In a literal manifestation of the interventionist gaze of the state, female medical practitioners examined girls' hymens for evidence of premarital defloration. Notably, this practice was not unique to Egypt. As Kathryn Sloan observes in this volume, premarital sex in nineteenth-century Mexico was often adjudicated with evidence derived from medical examinations of girls' hymens as well.[25]

Court cases are interesting for our purpose for several reasons. First, they offer a glimpse of young girls' lives, their involvement in premarital sex, and how society handled such cases. Second, the multiple meanings of girlhood implied by the label *izalat bikarat al-bint* enable us to examine how new state mechanisms handled girls who lost their virginity, including those who were too young to have their defloration render them "women." In this context, the state served as the protector of virginity as a social value and, at the same time, as the protector of young girls. "Age of consent" was never a clear legal category but was implicit to legal handling of defloration cases. Girls younger than ten were rarely seen as active parties in this offense and were more often seen as victims. Girls and their guardians, moreover, could contest and challenge officials' classifications and definitions.

The word *bint* in the labeling of this offense meant both a virgin and an unmarried woman. It was only the unmarried who brought cases of sexual assault to the police station, and the police only investigated cases of alleged sexual misconduct of runaway daughters. It is the absence of marriage that rendered this offense meaningful. At the same time, and powerfully so, the *bint* was the virgin, biologically defined and medically determined. A ruptured hymen served as evidence of the crime, and a medical examination determined this fact. A medical examination, moreover, was also assumed to determine whether loss of virginity had been recent, that is, whether the girl had been a virgin before an alleged assault. If a medical examination concluded that she had not been a virgin, her loss of virginity was her responsibility alone and her alleged assailant had committed no crime—he had not deflowered a girl but rather had had sexual intercourse with a woman. If a medical examination concluded, on the other hand, that a girl had lost her virginity only recently, she could more easily present herself, and not only her hymen, as a victim. In such cases, convictions of men were more frequent. In one case, for example, a man claimed that he believed the woman he was accused of deflowering had not been a virgin. When medical examination concluded that her defloration was recent, he was convicted and further offered to marry the girl to save her reputation.[26]

Another meaning of *bint*, a female child, was implicit in the legal handling of defloration cases, usually when the girls involved were under ten. Young girls were deemed asexual, incapable of consent. Unlike adult women, children did not have to prove that they had not consented, and courts often reasoned that children were not capable of forging a false complaint in such a matter. In one assault case of a five-year-old girl, for example, the court rejected the defendant's denial on the grounds that "it is inconceivable that in her tender age she would make it up herself, or accuse a man although another had committed the act."[27] In a similar case involving a seven-year-old boy, the court reasoned that the boy was "of a tender age, and hence incapable of forging a lie or of accusing any other than the real perpetrator."[28] Unlike older girls, who had to prove their complaint in an atmosphere of mistrust, young children who had been assaulted laid the burden of proof on the assailant.

In addition, childhood was a moment of partial symmetry between boys and girls; when a child was sexually assaulted, the handling of the molester by police and the courts was consistent regardless of the child's gender. The main difference was that assailants of boys were not convicted of assaulting a "person's honor." Honor was embodied in the sexual conduct of women and girls, and premarital defloration could be harmful to the reputation of the extended family. Sexual assault of boys did not impinge on the taboo of virginity, did not carry the potential of illegitimate offspring, and therefore had no formal implications for the victim's future marital prospects or his family's "honor." Sexual penetration by a male did not turn a male child into an adult. Regardless of his age, an assault victim was still a "boy."[29]

Age of consent, a girl's mental and emotional maturity, or even the definition of girlhood itself was grounds for appeal and legal debate. In two cases I found, girls' relatives appealed the girls' conviction for premarital sex, claiming that the girls were too young to be considered capable of consent. In one such case, which was tried in Alexandria in March 1877, a man named Hasan Ghurab accused Sa'd Abu Tajjar of seducing his sister, Hasna, into leaving home and moving in with him. The appellate court convicted Hasna because, according to the medical examination, she was "seventeen years old, and not a minor, who is incapable of understanding what would dishonor her." In response, Hasna's brother appealed to the Supreme Court, claiming that Hasna was not seventeen years old, but younger, and still a minor girl, lacking the mental capacities of an adult woman. She was an innocent victim of a deceitful man who took her virginity by force and lured her with his marriage promises. The Supreme Council ratified Hasna's conviction but considered her brother's appeal and reduced her sentence to three months rather than the usual six-month imprisonment.[30]

The interactions between state authorities and non-elite girls and their families transformed official and unofficial notions of girlhood in two important ways. First, girlhood became medicalized, which turned the legal discourse of girlhood to a functional, biological, rather than a social, category. Second, state authorities took upon themselves a new role in which they acted to protect girls from an early introduction to adult life—through early consummation of marriage, premarital defloration, and harsh labor conditions. We can find here some of the multiple meanings of girlhood noted in our discussion of Islamic law. The child bride, the defloration victim, and the child worker acted as "women" in one respect, but in another they needed the protection and care of "girls."

Girls at Work: Realities of Child Labor

The expanding scope of criminal prosecution was not the only factor in the changing definitions of girlhood in precolonial Egypt. In addition, the entrance of girls into the labor market furthered the state's efforts to define girlhood as a category in need of protection, even as laborers themselves were seen as adults. Toward the end of the century, the state began offering protection to slaves and slave children as well. As the cotton press case that opened this chapter demonstrates, state encounters with child labor forced the authorities to consider their role as the protectors of girls and to question the point at which girlhood ended—the point at which a female was no longer in need of state protection and could be considered an adult. Interestingly, the female workers in this case are consistently labeled "women," in spite of their tender age, which in most other contexts would have rendered them "girls." Nonetheless, like girls, they were seen as needing care and attention in that their employment after dark was banned.

As Sariyya's tragic death demonstrates, moreover, police encounters with girl workers exposed some aspects of the harsh labor conditions. In nineteenth-century Egypt, children worked in factories, in the fields, as domestic servants, and as slaves. Factory work was a new form of labor, fieldwork sometimes entailed new forms of recruitment, and slavery, at least formally, witnessed its last days. These political and economic transformations changed labor conditions for Egyptian girls, but not necessarily for the better.

Child labor, especially in Britain, had been a major concern of nineteenth-century reformers and later historians. According to the historian E. P. Thompson, the decades between 1780 and 1840, the peak years of the industrial revolution, witnessed a drastic increase in the intensity of exploitation of child labor in coalfields, mines, and mills. The number of hours children worked increased, and work itself became more intensive. It included night work in unlit environments and workdays as long as fourteen hours. Although child labor was prevalent before the late eighteenth century, claims Thompson, during this period monotonous factory work replaced labor in the family setting, where parental care, less demanding cycles, errands, and even play were available. At home, the degree of labor changed according to the child's ability. In the mill or factory, it was the machine that dictated speed, regularity, and discipline for children of all ages.[31]

Britain's industrial revolution had a strong impact on the Egyptian economy. During the first half of the nineteenth century, Egypt's ruler Mehmet Ali turned cotton into Egypt's main product for export to European markets. This process transformed the use of most of Egypt's agricultural land and the lives of Egyptian peasants. To process this cotton for export, as many as thirty cotton factories were founded in the 1820s and 1830s. In the early 1860s, the American civil war reduced cotton production in the American South and brought about a cotton boom in Egypt. During this period, 40 percent of the land cultivated in Upper Egypt was dedicated to cotton, a third of which was ginned in steam-ginning factories, which worked night and day to meet demand. Labor conditions in these factories were harsh. Foreign observers reported long hours of work and frequent acts of sabotage.[32]

In a similar vein, the use of forced labor predated the nineteenth century but was intensified during the period under review. Nineteenth-century rulers turned the corvée from a local institution into a national imposition. They used the forced labor of peasants to transform Egypt's irrigation system, to turn more of Egypt's desert into arable land for cotton cultivation, and to dig the Suez Canal. Contemporary observers reported harsh labor conditions, starved workers, high mortality rates, and villages emptied of their male inhabitants, who had been conscripted or had fled conscription. Measures taken to restrict this migration from the villages further attest to the harsh impact of the corvée on communal and family life.[33]

Evidence of child labor and the effects of the industrial revolution on children in the Ottoman Middle East is sparse. According to foreign observers, women and children were integrated into the cotton industry at cleaning, spinning, and weaving factories. In cotton-ginning factories, women and children sorted the cotton, while men tended to the ginning machines. Women worked in cigarette factories and at construction sites. During the cotton boom, factories hired entire families for factory labor. Children learned manual trades and were enlisted in industry.[34]

Historical evidence indicates that child labor, in Egypt as elsewhere, was gendered. Domestic labor, for example, was mainly the domain of girls, who started working in this trade at an early age. Certain forms of labor, such as intensive factory labor and public work projects, were supposedly reserved for men. In practice, however, girls worked in all of these forums. Because they were a small minority, and because these types of labor detached them from the protective fold of the family and the community, the girls were often vulnerable to abuse. Although many labor hazards were common to both genders, such as violence or accidents, girls were uniquely subject to sexual assault.

Laws regulating child labor were passed in Egypt only during the first decades of the twentieth century.[35] Archival records from precolonial Egypt, however, reflect a nascent state awareness of children's plight and some attempts to protect girls against abuse in their work environment. Police and court records include evidence of violence and fatal accidents, as Sariyya's case demonstrates. In another case, which took place in March 1865, for example, a ten-year-old worker named Amna was beaten to death by her supervisor in a factory at Zaqaziq village, on the eastern part of the Nile Delta. Her killer was sentenced to two years' imprisonment.[36] In April 1866, a girl named Halabiyya died as a result of an accident in a French company in Alexandria. Several male workers accidentally dropped a large iron pipe on her leg and broke it. She died three days later at the hospital. The workers were sentenced to six months' imprisonment.[37]

Public works victimized men, women, and children but had specific effects on Egyptian girls. Although such work was officially designed for men alone, contemporary observers and archival sources point to the participation of women and girls as well.[38] In one such case, Sayyid Muhammad 'Ali from Shahata village in al-Minya governorate could not afford to leave his field for his assigned public works service, so he sent his fifteen-year-old daughter Hadiyya in his stead. She worked in sugar cane fields in a nearby village and was raped and murdered by one of her male peers.[39] 'Alwan al-Abyad from Abu Za'bal village at al-Qalyubiya governorate could not perform his public works duties because of his old age and poor eyesight and so sent his two daughters instead. Their supervisor, a man called Sulayman, raped one of them, Ghandura, while she was sleeping with the other girls. As the representative of the village in the public works project, Sulayman was not only punished for the actual assault and murder but also for violating state regulations to send only males to these works. 'Alwan's daughters, it should be emphasized, were not the only girls sent from Abu Za'bal village. Several similar cases indicate, moreover, that officials inconsistently enforced these regulations.[40] Power relations and tensions that might have existed within village communities were extracted here to an alien environment. As illegal workers, moreover, who were not supposed to be working in this male space, the girls were more vulnerable to abuse and less likely to turn to the authorities for assistance.

At the same time that modern forms of labor and Egypt's integration into the world economy took their toll on the lower strata of Egyptian society, other forms of child labor and exploitation persisted within the village or the family itself. The most widespread form of labor for young girls in the Ottoman Middle East was domestic service. It was the most available and socially acceptable trade for lower-class women and girls. Historians of

Ottoman societies have found evidence of poor families who handed over their daughters, sometimes at the tender age of six or seven, to well-to-do families, for whom they worked for little pay or for subsistence only. For girls' parents, the arrangement lessened the burden of another mouth to feed. For the employer's family, it provided cheap labor. For the girls involved, however, domestic labor mimicked the intimacy of the domicile but deprived girls of their own family's protection and care.[41]

Similar evidence is available for nineteenth-century Egypt as well. Egyptian archives include cases of young women and girls who started working as servants at an early age. An eleven-year-old girl named Zanubiyya was adopted by one of the neighborhood's elders after her parents' death. After the passing of the man's wife, however, she had to leave his house and started working as a servant.[42] A girl named Estita was the daughter of a servant. When she was only six years old, her mother remarried and left her with her former employer, where she was still working as a servant ten years later.[43] A young peasant girl named Hanim worked as a servant in the city of Asyut for about eight years before reaching puberty, at which point her father came for her from the village in order to marry her to her cousin.[44] The intimacy of the domestic assignment amid the unequal power relations of age and gender exposed girls to sexual abuse, of which court cases abound.[45]

One cannot write about girlhood, let alone child labor in nineteenth-century Egypt, without mentioning slavery and child slaves, although sources that document child slaves are scarce. When a female slave bore a child to a man other than her owner, the child was legally the master's property, although the child could not be sold separate from the mother. Because a female slave was also her owner's legal concubine, however, most of their offspring were free persons. A child born to a female slave and her enslaver was his or her father's legal heir. This legal reality made the slave trade crucial for maintaining the institution of slavery, and slaves had to be constantly imported from non-Muslim lands, most notably the Sudan, during the nineteenth-century. Slave traders specifically targeted young children, and especially girls. Children were less capable of resisting their captors, could be more easily trained, and had the potential of providing more years of service. Girls were more desirable than boys. They performed domestic chores; they ran outdoor errands for their upper-class mistresses, who could then observe stricter Islamic gender-segregation norms; and at puberty, they served as legal concubines.[46]

Until the abolition of slavery in the late nineteenth century, slaves constituted a part of Egypt's domestic life. About 75 percent of slaves were women, and many of them were first-generation slaves.[47] Girlhood, for these women, meant memories of abduction, forced travel through the desert, and then forced integration into a new family, a new culture, sometimes a new religion, and a new status—as domestic slaves and concubines.[48] Egyptian sources are virtually silent about slaves' childhoods. As historian Eve Troutt Powell argues, our sources usually describe Africans after they had been removed from their homeland, "making them shadow people in the homes, fields and families of their Muslim masters."[49] Slaves' childhoods are often absent from these sources because many slaves spent their childhood elsewhere, mostly in the Sudan. The violence that brought women and girls into Egyptian households is similarly erased. Writing childhood back into the history of slavery allows us a better understanding of childhood and more specifically of girlhood in nineteenth-century Egypt. For this purpose, travel literature fills some of the historical gap.

American traveler Alvan Southworth provides a rare description of the kidnapping of a young girl, whom he bought in Khartoum in 1872, only to manumit immediately afterward. He then registered her life story: sweet childhood memories from home, and a childhood that was brutally ruptured at the age of six, when she was stolen from her father's home while her father was away. "I was playing with the sheep near the door of the house; my back was toward the entrance," she told Southworth. "Suddenly I was grabbed by two big hands. A piece of iron was thrust into my mouth like a horse's bit. I felt very sick and frightened. I was carried out of the house covered up with clothing, so that no one could see me. . . . I was crushed with grief. . . . I became bewildered and prayed to heaven."[50]

British traveler Lady Lucie Duff-Gordon lived in Egypt during the years 1862–1869. Her letters to her family tell the story of one slave girl, eight-year-old Zeynab, whom Duff-Gordon owned for about a year, beginning in March 1863. Throughout the text, Zeynab's former self, as a free Sudanese child, is gradually erased, and a new identity emerges. She becomes a slave, but also an opinionated Muslim and anti-Christian. As a result, Duff-Gordon lost interested in her and handed her over to a Turkish household. Zeynab was originally sent from Khartoum as a present to the American consul general in Cairo, who had no other female servants in his household. The consul invited Duff-Gordon to see the girl, and when she noticed how coarsely his cook and groom treated her she decided to take her. Initially, Zeynab's most visible behavior was fear. When she got used to her mistress, she articulated her fear: "When she first came, she tells me, she thought I should eat her; now her one dread is that I should leave her behind," Duff-Gordon wrote her family on April 13, 1863. She is so "slavish" and so obedient, Duff-Gordon further observed, that she has no will of her own. Alongside this fear, one can find vague traces of Zeynab's past. In her first letter about Zeynab, Duff-Gordon described the girl singing "quaint Kordofan songs all day."[51] Zeynab was apparently spared some form of social erasure in that she was allowed to retain her name and was not forced to convert. Duff-Gordon mentioned, in a May 21 letter, that one of Zeynab's former masters called her Salaam al-Sidi, "but she said that in her own village she used to be Zeyneb, and so we call her."[52]

The few descriptions that follow convey more of Zeynab's process of acculturation into the Egyptian Muslim society and adaptation to her new Christian masters. In two weeks' time she had already learned to use a needle and "sews very neatly and quickly." Duff-Gordon left her for a while with her daughter Janet in Alexandria, and Zeynab quickly picked up the multiple languages spoken in the international community there.[53]

The religious tension, however, led to frequent conflicts between Zeynab and Duff-Gordon's household, and later with Duff-Gordon herself. "Zeyneb is much grown and very active and intelligent, but a little louder and bolder than she was owing to the maids here wanting to christianize her, and taking her out unveiled, and letting her be among the men," Duff-Gordon wrote on October 1, 1863. At the beginning of December of that year, Duff-Gordon wrote to her family that she decided to hand Zeynab to a Muslim household. She explained, in December 1, 1863: "It would seem that the Berberi men have put it into her head that we are inferior beings, and she pretends not to be able to eat because she thinks everything is pig. . . . She is very clever and I am sorry, but to keep a sullen face about me is more than I can endure, as I have shown her every possible kindness."[54] The frightened slave girl turned too opinionated to Duff-Gordon's liking. She resented the Christian elements of her new cultural environment, and Duff-Gordon decided to give her away.

For tens of thousands of Egyptian women, then, girlhood was a part of their lives that they were forced to forget. Girlhood, for them, entailed a forced rupture and erasure. In a new family, a new language, and new status, childhood was but a fading memory of a village that might no longer exist. A black child in late nineteenth-century Egypt was often already a victim of violence, which marked her maturation and later adulthood. Such a childhood was invisible to most Egyptians, who came to know these girls only as they arrived to Egypt—their origins erased, and sometimes forgotten by the girls themselves. Although not explicitly intended to protect Sudanese girls, the abolition of the slave trade during the second half of the nineteenth century also brought an end to this violation of childhood.

Conclusion

Precolonial Egyptian sources demonstrate how the Egyptian administration and shari'a courts saw girls and how they defined girlhood. The Arabic word *bint* reflected some of the complexity of girlhood in this society. Girls deserved the protection of their mothers, their guardians, or the state, but only until their bodies were sexualized, through puberty, defloration, or signs of physical maturity. Biology was employed to determine maturity. The intrusive gaze of female medical practitioners set virgins apart from nonvirgins, young girls from older ones—as deserving of protection or punishment.

In this chapter I examined the impact of Egypt's precolonial modernity on girlhood and on girls themselves. As the state came to define itself as the protector of the poor, its interactions with Egyptian girls forced state institutions to review existing definitions of girlhood and devise their own. State concern with public health made child marriage into a health hazard; new forms of industrial labor forced the state to define girls as those who require protection from abusive and hazardous labor conditions. A dangerous work environment, violence and sexual abuse were indeed among the hazards that lower-class Egyptian girls had to endure in the decades under review.

To slave girls and young domestic servants, the domestic sphere mimicked the intimacy of home but deprived them of family protection and therefore left them vulnerable to abuse. For slaves, childhood was often a fading memory of home, combined with harsh memories of kidnapping, renaming, conversion, and abuse. For these girls, home itself, and not the industrialized work environment, entailed violence; first and foremost, home entailed the denial of freedom.

In these historical texts, the girls themselves are virtually silent. Their guardians represent them; Zeynab's foreign mistress wrote about her; state officials summarize their words; and some of the girls discussed here reached the police station as corpses. We do not know how girls saw their own childhood. We do know, however, that many reached the police station and courts and asked that their assailants be punished. Through dialogue between girls and their investigators, between Zeynab and her mistress, we hear some of their childhood voices.[55]

NOTES

I thank Omri Paz, Mira Tzoreff, and Gady Kozma for their insightful and helpful comments on an early draft of this chapter.

1. Majlis al-Ahkam, S/7/10/15, case no. 277, 27 Dhu al-Hujja 1281 (May 23, 1865), 77.

2. Historians of childhood question how different stages in a person's life were defined, whether childhood and adolescence were considered to be distinct stages in the human life cycle, and how transition to adulthood was perceived in different times and places. French historian Philippe Ariès opened this field of research. See Philippe Ariès, *Centuries of Childhood: A Social History of Family Life* (New York: Vintage Books, 1965). On his impact on the historiography of childhood, see Ilana Krausman-Ben-Amos, "Adolescence as a Cultural Invention: Philippe Ariès and the Sociology of Youth," *History of the Human Sciences* 8, no. 2 (1995): 69–89. Historians of children, on the other hand, trace evidence of children's lives, at work and at play, their interactions with parents, child marriages, and sexual abuse. See, for example, Colin Heywood, *Childhood in Nineteenth-Century France: Work, Health and Education among the "Class Populaires"* (Cambridge: Cambridge University Press, 1988); and Barbara A. Hanawalt, *Growing Up in Medieval London: The Experience of Childhood in History* (New York: Oxford University Press, 1993).

3. A *fatwa* is a legal opinion issued by an Islamic legal scholar regarding a specific legal matter, in a response to a question addressed to him. *Fiqh* is the science of religious law.

4. Avner Giladi, "Saghir," in *Encyclopedia of Islam*, 2d ed. (henceforth *EI*2) (Leiden: Brill, 1995), 8:826a.

5. Ibid., 8:824a.

6. Ibid., 8:822b; Avner Giladi, *Children of Islam: Concepts of Childhood in Medieval Muslim Society* (Houndmills, Basingstoke: Macmillan, in association with St. Antony's College, Oxford, 1992), 23, 52–54; Eyal Ginio, "Childhood, Mental Capacity and Conversion to Islam in the Ottoman State," *Byzantine and Modern Greek Studies*, no. 25 (2001): 99–100, 104.

7. Harald Motzki, "Child Marriage in Seventeenth-Century Palestine," in *Islamic Legal Interpretation: Muftis and Their Fatwas*, ed. Muhammad Khalid Masud, Brinkley Messick, and David S. Powers (Cambridge: Harvard University Press, 1996), 129–130; Giladi, "Saghir," 8:821b.

8. El-Said Badawi and Martin Hinds, "*Bint*," in *A Dictionary of Egyptian Arabic: Arabic-English* (Beirut: Librairie du Liban, 1986), 104. The word for "girl" signifies a virgin in present-day Lebanon, Turkey, and Palestine as well. See Nadera Shalhoub-Kevorkian, "Towards a Cultural Definition of Rape: Dilemmas in Dealing with Rape Victims in Palestinian Society," *Women's Studies International Forum* 22, no. 2 (1999): 163; Ayşe Parla, "The Honor of the State: Virginity Examinations in Turkey," *Feminist Studies* 27, no. 1 (Spring 2001): 79; Samantha Wehbi, "Women with Nothing to Lose—Marriageability and Women's Perceptions of Rape and Consent in Contemporary Beirut," *Women's Studies International Forum* 25, no. 2 (2002): 298n5.

9. Mahmud Yazbak, "Minor Marriages and *Khiyar Al-Bulugh* in Ottoman Palestine: A Note on Women's Strategies in a Patriarchal Society," *Islamic Law and Society* 9, no. 3 (2002): 391; Edward William Lane, *Manners and Customs of the Modern Egyptians* (London: J. M. Dent, [1908]), 161.

10. Muhammad Amin, known as Ibn 'Abidin, *Radd al-Muhtar 'ala al-Durr al-Mukhtar Sharh Tanwir al-Absar* (Beirut: Dar al-Kutub al-'Ilmiyya), 2:640–641; Giladi, *Children of Islam*, 116; de Bellefonds, "*Hadana*," in *EI2*, 3:16b–17a.

11. Ibn 'Abidin, *Radd al-Muhtar*, 2:640–641.

12. Yazbak, "Minor Marriages," 390–392.

13. Ibid., 390.

14. Shaheen Sardar Ali, "Is an Adult Woman *Sui Juris*? Some Reflections on the Concept of 'Consent in Marriage' without a *Wali* (with Particular Reference to the Saima Waheed Case)," *Yearbook of Islamic and Middle Eastern Law* 3 (1996): 165–167; Yazbak, "Minor Marriages," 390; Amira El Azhary Sonbol, "Adults and Minors in Ottoman *Shari'a* Courts and Modern Law," in *Women, the Family, and Divorce Laws in Islamic History*, ed. A. Sonbol (Syracuse: Syracuse University Press, 1996), 242–243; and Ibn 'Abidin, *Radd al-Muhtar*, 4:170.

15. Ibrahim ibn Muhammad Ibn Ibrahim al-Halabi, *Multaqa al-Abhur* (Beirut: Mu'assasat al-Risalah, 1989), 243–244; Ibn 'Abidin, *Radd al-Muhtar*, 1:252–253, 4:164–165. See also Ron Shaham, *Family and the Courts in Modern Egypt: A Study Based on Decisions by the Shari'a Courts, 1900–1955* (Leiden: Brill, 1997), 28.

16. 'Ali ibn Abi Bakr al-Marghinani, *The Hedaya, Guide: A Commentary on the Mussulman Laws*, trans. Charles Hamilton (Lahore: New Book Co., [1957]), 35.

17. Ibid. See also al-Halabi, *Multaqa al-Abhur*, 244; Ibn 'Abidin, *Radd al-Muhtar*, 4:166–167.

18. Ron Shaham, "Women as Expert Witnesses in Pre-Modern Islamic Societies" (paper presented at the Social and Cultural History of the Middle East Group, Tel Aviv University, December 23, 2004), 15. See, for example, Mahkamat Misr—Murafa'at wa-Da'awa, 1/99/3/1430, 6 Jumada Thani 1287 (September 1, 1870), 127. For a *fiqh* reference, see Ibn 'Abidin, *Radd al-Muhtar*, 4:170. For *fatwa* literature, see Muhammad ibn Muhammad Mahdi al-'Abbasi, *Al-Fatawa al-Mahdiyah fi al-Waqa'i' al-Misriyah* (Cairo: al-Matba'ah al-Azhariyah, 1883 or 1884–1887), 15 Safar 1269 (November 26, 1852), 1:45; Muhammad Kamil ibn Mustafa Tarabulusi, *Al-Fatawa al-Kamiliyah fi al-Hawadith al-Tarabulusiyah 'ala Madhhab al-Imam Abi Hanifah al-Nu'man 'alayhi saha'ib al-rahmah wa-al-ridwan* (Cairo: Matba'at Muhammad Afandi Mustafa, 1896), 24.

19. Khaled Fahmy, "The Police and the People in Nineteenth-Century Egypt," *Die Welt des Islams* 39 (1999): 341–377; Khaled Fahmy, "Women, Medicine and Power in Nineteenth-Century Egypt," in *Remaking Women: Feminism and Modernity in the Middle East*, ed. Lila Abu-Lughod (Princeton, NJ: Princeton University Press, 1998), 35–72; Rudolph Peters, "Administrators and Magistrates: The Development of a Secular Judiciary in Egypt, 1842–1871," *Die Welt des Islam* 39, no. 3 (1999): 378–397; Peters, "Islamic and Secular Criminal Law in Nineteenth Century

Egypt: The Role and Function of the Qadi," *Islamic Law and Society* 4, no. 1 (1997): 70–90; Mario M. Ruiz, "Intimate Disputes, Illicit Violence: Gender, Law, and the State in Colonial Egypt, 1849–1923" (Ph.D. diss., University of Michigan, 2004), 30–35; and Liat Kozma, "Women on the Margins and Legal Reform in Late Nineteenth-Century Egypt, 1850–1882" (Ph.D. diss., New York University, 2006), 30–82.

20. Mine Ener, *Managing Egypt's Poor and the Politics of Benevolence, 1800–1952* (Princeton, NJ: Princeton University Press, 2003), 41–47.

21. Michel Foucault, *History of Sexuality*, trans. Robert Hurley (New York: Vintage Books, 1986), 141–143.

22. Ahmad al-Rashidi, *Bahjat al-Ru'asa' fi Amrad al-Nisa'* (Bulaq: Dar al-Tiba'a al-'Amira, 1844), 592–593.

23. Dabtiyyat Misr, L/2/46/4, case no. 10, 22 Rabi' Thani 1282 (September 12, 1865), 2.

24. Majlis al-Ahkam, S/7/10/12, case no. 1143, 15 Rabi' Awwal 1281 (August 17, 1864), 236–237.

25. See further in Ruiz, "Intimate Disputes, Illicit Violence," 98–112; and Mario M. Ruiz, "Virginity Violated: Sexual Assault and Respectability in Mid- to Late-Nineteenth-Century Egypt," *Comparative Studies of South Asia, Africa and the Middle East* 25, no. 1 (2005): 214–227; see also Kozma, "Women on the Margins and Legal Reform," 205–216; and Liat Kozma, "Negotiating Virginity: Narratives of Defloration from Late Nineteenth-Century Egypt," *Comparative Studies of South Asia, Africa and the Middle East* 24, no. 1 (2004): 55–65.

26. Dabtiyyat Iskandriya, L/4/18/11, case no. 750, 28 Rabi' Awwal 1297 (September 22, 1869), 74–75; and see Kozma, "Women on the Margins and Legal Reform," 93–96.

27. Majlis al-Ahkam, S/7/10/218, case no. 491, 8 Rajab 1300 (May 15, 1883), no pagination.

28. Majlis al-Ahkam, S/7/10/217, case no. 425, 15 Jumada Thani 1300 (April 23, 1883), no pagination.

29. Ahmad Fathi Zaghlul, *Muhamah* (Misr: Matba'at al-ma'arif, 1900), 165 (appendixes); see, for example, Majlis al-Ahkam, S/7/10/214, case no. 253, 15 Jumada Awwal 1300 (March 23, 1883), no pagination. On honor in contemporary Islamic societies, see Lama Abu Odeh, "Crimes of Honour and the Construction of Gender in Arab Societies," in *Feminism and Islam: Legal and Literary Perspectives*, ed. Mai Yamani (New York: New York University Press, 1996), 141–194; Lynn Welchman and Sara Hossain, eds., *"Honour": Crimes, Paradigms, and Violence against Women* (New York: Zed Books, 2005).

30. Majlis al-Ahkam, S/7/10/120, case no. 357, 19 Ramadan 1295 (September 16, 1878), 29–30.

31. E. P. Thompson, *The Making of the English Working Class* (London: Gollancz, 1963), 331–347. For a recent discussion of child labor in nineteenth-century England, see Carolyn Tuttle, "A Revival of the Pessimist View: Child Labor and the Industrial Revolution," *Research in Economic History* 18 (1998): 54.

32. E.R.J. Owen, *Cotton and the Egyptian Economy, 1820–1914: A Study in Trade and Development* (Oxford: Clarendon Press, 1969), 45, 105–106.

33. Nathan Brown, "Who Abolished Corvée Labour in Egypt and Why?" *Past and Present*, no. 144 (August 1994): 118–123; Kenneth M. Cuno, *The Pasha's Peasants: Land, Society, and Economy in Lower Egypt, 1740–1858* (Cambridge: Cambridge University Press, 1992), 122–123; Lucie (Austin) Duff-Gordon, *Letters from Egypt, 1862–1869*, reedited with additional letters by Gordon Westfield (New York: Praeger [1969]), 66–67, 85–86, 146, 230–231, 243–244; Judith E. Tucker, *Women in Nineteenth-Century Egypt* (Cambridge: Cambridge University Press, 1985), 27; Ener, *Managing Egypt's Poor*, 34–35.

34. Ener, *Managing Egypt's Poor*, 34.

35. Tucker, *Women in Nineteenth-Century Egypt*, 88–90.

36. Majlis al-Ahkam, S/7/10/15, case no. 313, 20 Muharram 1282 (June 15, 1865), 116.

37. Majlis al-Ahkam, S/7/10/17, case no. 273, 22 Dhu al-Hujja 1282 (May 8, 1866), no pagination.

38. Tucker, *Women in Nineteenth-Century Egypt*, 27.

39. Majlis al-Ahkam, S/7/10/98, case no. 525, 13 Sha'ban 1293 (September 1, 1876), 122–123.

40. Majlis al-Ahkam, S/7/10/109, case no. 398, 4 Sha'ban 1294 (August 13, 1877), 230–231.

41. Eyal Ginio, "Living on the Margins of Charity: Coping with Poverty in an Ottoman Provincial City," in *Poverty and Charity in Middle Eastern Contexts*, ed. Michael Bonner, Mine Ener, and Amy Singer (Albany : State University of New York Press, 2003), 173–176; Abraham Marcus, *The Middle East on the Eve of Modernity: Aleppo in the Eighteenth Century* (New York: Columbia University Press, 1989), 158; Suraiya Faroqhi, *Towns and Townsmen of Ottoman Anatolia: Trade, Crafts, and Food Production in an Urban Setting, 1520–1650* (Cambridge: Cambridge University Press, 1984), 278–279; Tucker, *Women in Nineteenth-Century Egypt*, 92–93.

42. Majlis al-Ahkam, S/7/10/25, case no. 65, 7 Sha'ban 1284 (December 3, 1867), no pagination.

43. Dabtiyyat Misr, L/2/51/7, case no. 441, 14 Rabi' Thani 1295 (April 16, 1878), 131–132.

44. Majlis al-Ahkam, S/7/10/247, case no. 440, 8 Dhu al-Hujja 1301 (September 28, 1884), no pagination.

45. See, for example, Dabtiyat Misr, L/2/51/7, case no. 441, 14 Rabi' Thani 1295 (April 16, 1878), 131–132; Majlis al-Ahkam, S/7/10/5, case no. 279, 28 Jumada Thani 1280 (December 8, 1863), 183–184; Majlis al-Ahkam, S/7/10/6, case no. 516, 11 Ramadan 1280 (February 18, 1864), 168–169; Dabtiyyat Misr, L/2/6/10, case no. 1009, 20 Dhu al-Qa'da 1296 (November 4, 1879), 32–33; Majlis al-Ahkam, S/7/10/247, case no. 440, 8 Dhu al-Hijja 1301 (September 27, 1884), no pagination; Majlis al-Ahkam, S/7/10/1, case no. 218, 14 Rajab 1279 (January 4, 1863), 91.

46. 'Imad Hilal, *Al-Raqiq fi Misr fi al-Qarn al-Tasi' 'Ashar* (Cairo: al-'Arabi, 1999), 196–197; Tucker, *Women in Nineteenth-Century Egypt*, 183–184; Robert Brunschvig, "Abd," in *EI2*, 1:26–28.

47. Hilal, *Al-Raqiq fi Misr*, 343–360; Gabriel Baer, "Slavery in Nineteenth-Century Egypt," *Journal of African History* 8, no. 3 (1967): 430–433; Eve Troutt Powell, *A Different Shade of Colonialism: Egypt, Great Britain, and the Mastery of the Sudan* (Berkeley: University of California Press, 2003), 66–67; Reda Mowafi, *Slavery, Slave Trade, and Abolition Attempts in Egypt and the Sudan, 1820–1882* ([Stockholm]: Esselte Studium, 1981), 54–80; Ehud Toledano, *Slavery and Abolition in the Ottoman Middle East* (Seattle: University of Washington Press, 1998), 205–223.

48. Ehud Toledano, *As if Silent and Absent: Bonds of Enslavement in the Islamic Middle East* (New Haven: Yale University Press, 2007), 24–35.

49. Eve M. Troutt Powell, "The Silence of the Slaves," in *African Diaspora in the Mediterranean Lands of Islam*, ed. John Hunwick and Eve Troutt Powell (Princeton, NJ: Markus Wiener Publishers, 2002), xxx.

50. Alvan S. Southworth, *Four Thousand Miles of African Travel: A Personal Record of a Journey up the Nile and Through the Soudan to the Confines of Central Africa, Embracing a Discussion of the Sources of the Nile, and an Examination of the Slave Trade* (New York : Baker, Pratt, 1875), 217–225.

51. Duff-Gordon, *Letters from Egypt* (1969 ed.), 73–74.

52. Lady Lucie Duff-Gordon, *Letters from Egypt*, rev. ed. with memoir by her daughter Janet Ross; new introduction by George Meredith (London: R. B. Johnson, 1902); transcribed at the Gutenberg Project, http://www.gutenberg.org/files/17816/17816-h/17816-h.htm. This section does not appear in the 1969 edition.

53. Duff-Gordon, *Letters from Egypt* (1969 ed.), 74, 96.

54. Ibid., 91, 98.

55. Carlo Ginzburg, "The Inquisitor as Anthropologist," in *Clues, Myths, and the Historical Method*, trans. John Tedeschi and Anne C. Tedeschi (Baltimore: John Hopkins University Press, 1992), 159–160.

19 Defiant Daughters and the Emancipation of Minors in Nineteenth-Century Mexico

KATHRYN A. SLOAN

Sixteen-year-old Juana Silva ran off with her sweetheart, Melquiadez Barza-lobre, a nineteen-year-old shoemaker, in 1871. Her single mother, María, citing God as her only witness, complained to the court that the young man had seduced her daughter. Court officials initiated an investigation and complaint of *rapto de seducción*, or abduction by seduction, an offense punishable by four years in prison. Police apprehended the star-crossed couple, and court officials lined up participants and witnesses to tell their version of events. Juana testified first. She swore that she packed her meager possessions and voluntarily fled to Melquiadez's house because she loved him and her mother mistreated her. She also emphasized that they agreed to live together, not marry. Melquiadez substantiated her testimony, emphasizing that Juana wanted to live with him because her mother neglected her by not providing the necessary food and clothing. In fact, Juana lived with her sister Adela, not her mother.[1]

This case, housed in the judicial archives of Mexico, embodies the prevalence of family conflict over such issues as marriage, sexual autonomy, and the rights and responsibilities of parents and their children. Daughters sat at the center of these disputes. Indeed, in her testimony, Juana utilized commonly held views about parental power over minor children. In charging that her mother failed to provide her with the basic necessities to live, Juana implied that her mother no longer possessed legitimate authority over her life or her decision to run away with her suitor. In addition, Juana claimed that Melquiadez supported her, providing fabric for clothing, candles, and significantly, food. In essence, she appealed to notions, embedded in the civil codes and norms of nineteenth-century Mexican society, that laid out the parameters of parental authority and filial obedience. Under law, when parents failed to provide *alimentos* (food, clothing, housing, and basic education), their rights over minor children could be invalidated by the court.[2]

Charging child abuse was a common strategy of minor girls, or girls under twenty-one, in these criminal cases. Yet they also professed love as one of the main reasons they eloped with their sweethearts. In this chapter I focus on the experiences of adolescent girls under the age of seventeen who defied parents to run away with their boyfriends, engage in premarital sex, and struggle to earn emancipation from parental authority in nineteenth-century Mexico.[3] The research is based on analysis of 212 cases of *rapto*, or elopement, in the municipal archives of Oaxaca de Juárez, the capital city of the state of Oaxaca, Mexico. Girls are the focus, as I analyze how they parlayed with parents, their suitors, and state authorities to control their futures and negotiate such issues as filial obedience, love, and marriage. Working-class girls, seemingly the most powerless group in Mexican society, displayed a remarkable understanding of their status as minors and used their sexuality and perceived vulnerability to affect that position.

The Social Construction of Childhood and Adolescence

The *Siete partidas*, a body of laws promulgated between 1251 and 1265 by King Alfonso X of Castile, eventually was applied to Spain's colonies in the Americas as well, where it served as the legal basis of parent-child relations until the advent of nineteenth-century civil codes in Spanish America. *Siete partidas* substituted for the seventh-century *Forum judicum* and provided guidelines for everything from knightly behavior to regulations for Jews, marriage, and dowries. The body of law displayed a rudimentary concept of childhood in that it distinguished the degree of reason between adults and children. Specifically it noted that individuals under the age of ten and a half years could not be tried in court, although it considered that children of age seven and older possessed reason. Minors between the ages ten and a half and seventeen who committed crimes could be tried in court but still did not face the same level of punishment as adults. It was in that age range that minors supposedly knew the difference between moral and immoral actions. Islamic law provides a useful contrast. Liat Kozma discusses girlhood in Egypt earlier in this volume and notes that age seven marked the threshold at which children probably knew the difference between good and evil. In the Catholic formula, minors from ages seventeen to twenty-five also required a representative in court, but their penalty could equal that of adult criminals, because courts believed that they possessed the maturity to know right from wrong.[4]

European intellectuals influenced by Jean Jacques Rousseau and his classic work *Émile* believed infants and children to be innocent, born without "ambition or social prejudices."[5] Rousseau set out concrete stages of childhood, noting that children possessed their own way of experiencing the world and that Nature rather than adults ought to guide them. Later, Romantics expanded Rousseau's formulations and depicted the child as a possessor of deep wisdom and morality, an individual whose unadulterated nature could actually teach parents much about life.[6] Late colonial Latin Americans embraced the ideas of Rousseau and the Romantics and considered childhood a distinct stage of life. No longer was the child considered a mini-adult or an apprentice to adulthood. Barbara Potthast and Sandra Carrera confirm this point, arguing that a 1734 Spanish dictionary defined infancy and youth essentially as preparatory stages to adulthood.[7]

Viewing childhood as a distinct phase in an individual's lifecycle was the first step to viewing Mexico's children as individuals worthy of expanded rights. Although a fundamental tension between Crown or State and family always existed, during the colonial period *patria potestad* (parental author-ity) guided family order or relations between a patriarch and his children. This system provided stability for society, and the authors of the *Siete par-tidas* went to great lengths to provide procedures for marriage, inheritance, and other matters of family life.[8] Furthermore, this cultural change mani-fested itself more concretely in action when politicians and jurists ceased to view children as simply minors needing education and protection. Instead, society increasingly viewed children as "capable of actively confronting dif-ficult situations and raising their voices, emphasizing their character as independent people with their own rights."[9] In this scenario, the clear demarcation of childhood as an important stage in the lifecycle coincided with the appreciation of children as actors, not mere receptacles for adult lessons and demands. The nineteenth century became a watershed for new thinking about childhood in Latin America, which significantly affected the sanctity of *patria potestad* in family relationships. As Mexico consolidated into a liberal state after independence in 1821, civil codes had the effect of weakening *patria potestad* and sanctioning the increased intrusion of the state in private life. Family life sometimes became a public arena where sec-ular officials and individuals fought and parlayed over formerly ecclesiasti-cal matters such as marriage, birth, and the parent-child bond. In effect, as state power grew, definitions of childhood were more clearly delineated and more publicly visible. Concurrent with a preoccupation with patriotic motherhood, the Mexican elite viewed childhood as a distinct phase of life and did not hesitate to contravene private home life to act as a surrogate paternal authority.[10] The breaching of the public-private divide especially occurred in families headed by women and working-class parents, because the state viewed these family forms as incompetent and unable to properly control and socialize their children.[11]

Although terminology such as "childhood" and "adolescence" gradually entered the nineteenth-century Mexican lexicon, Rousseau's innocent Émile was nowhere to be seen. Official documents and attention centered on the problematic child: the juvenile delinquent, the abandoned orphan, the sickly child. As Potthast and Carrera argue, "the innocent, happy, healthy, and mentally sound child did not provoke state or social interven-tion."[12] Not coincidently, these "problematic" children derived from the working class, the very social group the liberal state targeted for its various reform and disciplinary programs.[13] In continuity with the colonial period, the secular politicians desired that families be harmonious, corporate entities, and they saw little reason to intervene unless they perceived that children were in danger or unless family conflict jeopardized public order. In fact, many scholars point out that the state's rhetoric spoke to protecting children, but more accurately, state actions and programs reflected its primary concern of defending family honor and state prerogative in citizens' private lives.[14] Not coincidently, this state interference revolved around the sexual and romantic lives of working-class girls.

Civil Codes and the Balance of Family Power

Civil codes provide an interesting view of legal changes to family power over time and a means to measure legal prescriptions for the parent-child relationship. It is especially important to appraise changes over time, as the Mexican politicians replaced ecclesiastical laws with secular legislation that regulated private life, although in the initial decades after independence secular laws resembled their colonial predecessors. Over time the development of a civil code portended important changes between the colonial and modern eras, as childhood emerged increasingly as a distinct stage with jurists championing individual rights, a factor that led judges in the *rapto* cases to acknowledge girls' choices in their conjugal and sexual relationships.

By the second half of the nineteenth century, Carmen Ramos Escandón argues, the civil codes of Mexico heralded the unambiguous intervention of the state in family life. Mexico did not have its first national civil code in practice until 1870, so before that year most Mexican judges relied on colonial-era laws to rule on family and domestic conflicts over inheritance and *patria potestad*. Therefore, between Mexico's independence in 1821 and 1870, "the imparting of justice and resolution of conflicts" in families operated under the same processes of the colonial period.[15]

Nineteenth-century civil codes forged new legal territory in family relationships. Oaxacan jurists created Latin America's first civil code in 1827–1828,[16] which would be followed by a national code in 1870, the *Código civil del distrito federal y territorio de Baja California*. Officials revised the code in 1884, and it stood until 1915. Oaxaca's 1827–1828 civil code continued the Greco-Roman tradition of noting different epochs of childhood: infancy was defined as birth to seven years; ages seven to thirteen constituted a stage labeled *impuberes* (nonpubescent); and from fourteen to twenty-one, the final stage of childhood, was denoted as *puberes* (pubescent).[17] This final stage of childhood, or *puberes*, was in actuality akin to a newly emerging concept of adolescence—not a child but not yet endowed with the full rights and responsibilities of an adult. Individuals who had passed through puberty but had not fully matured in mind and body were still a protected group. As mentioned earlier, they could be prosecuted and held responsible for crimes, but the jurists recognized them as a special category. In fact, the law punishing *rapto* reinforced this notion. Girls under the age of sixteen who were seduced without violence received particular protection under the law. Jurists assumed that the victim's natural weakness and immaturity had led her to be deceived and dishonored. Girls did not break the law; their suitors did. Conversely if the victim was a minor but found not to be a virgin, the state denied her legal safeguard. In essence jurists pushed girls into the category of adult depending on a girl's sexuality, not on the civil rights and autonomy that came with majority. Until the age of twenty-one, girls had to seek parental permission to marry. In many ways, deflowered, minor girls sat in a purgatory between girlhood and full womanhood—womanly in terms of their sexual experience but still not emancipated by their age or marriage. The code also dictated that, although they still needed parental consent, sons could contract marriage at age fourteen and daughters at age twelve. If a child married at such a young age, he or she was propelled to adulthood, because marriage bestowed that distinction. The law recognized a limited level of maturity, or at least the ability for procreation, and children bypassed "adolescence" if they married. Importantly, the law assumed that girls aged twelve and older understood the law and were ready for marriage.[18]

Still, the law gave special consideration to girls between the ages of twelve and sixteen. The *rapto* or seduction laws illustrate this vulnerable stage in a girl's life. *Rapto* laws assumed that seducers deceived girls under age sixteen to elope with them. Jurists argued that if a girl were mature and knowledgeable of the law, she would not endanger her family's honor by choosing the disgraceful step of elopement. Ironically, jurists could not imagine that a girl purposefully risked her honor and encouraged her suitor to break the law in order to achieve her aims of emancipation from parental authority and the right to marry or live with the suitor of her choice. Importantly, the onset of puberty was not the de facto threshold where girlhood ended. And although Mexican jurists did not discuss "age of consent" explicitly, the *rapto* law implicitly recognized that girls sixteen and older could reasonably consent to sexual relations. In fact, a girl older than sixteen had to prove that she was forcibly and violently abducted to win a *rapto* suit. The law did not allow her the assumption of deception or seduction by amorous promises. In sum, the stage of *puberes*, especially between the ages of fourteen and sixteen, presented challenges for court officials, parents, and girls themselves. Capable of tolerating sexual intercourse and forging a marital union but too immature to make marriage choices on their own, these girls, according to the court, were easily deceived by lotharios. Thus the *rapto* laws in theory punished men when they deceived pubescent, adolescent girls of a certain age. Although *rapto* laws protected adolescent girls, they were designed to sanction adolescent boys who eloped with their girlfriends and effectively challenged the dominion of a father or guardian.[19]

The delineation of childhood was further extended by the creation of laws to punish crimes. The Mexican Penal Code of 1871 stated that children under ten years of age could not be punished for crimes they committed, because they were too young to discern right from wrong. If a child-perpetrator was between the ages of ten and thirteen, the judge had latitude to decide whether the child could differentiate between right and wrong and rule on the case accordingly. Nevertheless, if such a child knowingly committed a crime, the penal code dictated that the judge could exact a punishment that was one-third to one-half of what an adult would receive for the same crime. Even older children, from ages fourteen to seventeen, who consciously committed a crime could receive only one-half to two-thirds the punishment adults received. Likewise, juvenile criminals under the age of eighteen could not be jailed with adult criminals.[20] This late nineteenth-century change reflected a cultural shift in how Mexican society viewed childhood. Although colonial laws had issued lesser punishments to young people than to adults, colonial laws viewed seven as the age of reason, at which age the child was "morally responsible for his or her acts."[21] This directive fundamentally changed with the advent of the 1871 Penal Code, which pushed the "age of reason" to at least nine years of age and, furthermore, provided the judge latitude in determining reason or *discernimiento* from ages ten to fourteen.

As evidenced by the civil and penal codes, the nineteenth century ushered in important changes in child-parent relations. The history of civil legislation in Mexico points to liberal politicians' concerns about what constituted legitimate families and the limits of parental authority over their children. The tone and provisions of the codes changed from time to time, but overall they consistently laid out guidelines for the parent-child relationship as well as inheritance, succession, and division by classification of heir. The civil codes coupled with the penal code provided judges and parties to the *rapto* cases with a mutually comprehensible set of norms and values to negotiate parental authority and filial obedience.

Rapto and the Rebellious Youth

Mexican girls generally eloped as an opportunistic strategy. It was understood that parents facing a daughter recently sullied often relented to allow her to marry the boy or man she chose. Some girls merely ran off with their lovers to form a trial marriage or consensual union and found themselves dragged into court to defend and justify their actions.[22] The process of *rapto* or elopement was deceptively straightforward. Having established a romantic relationship with a young man, the girl would leave her parents' home and go with her boyfriend to the house of his friend or relative. Once free of parental surveillance, the couple would usually engage in sexual relations, at which point the man would "take possession" of the young woman's virginity. The couple would then set up conjugal life together and marry at some later date or maintain an *amasiato* (consensual union). The act of running away and the specter of assumed defloration compelled many parents to accede to their daughter's wishes.

Rapto, as defined by the Mexican Penal Code of 1871, occurred when someone abducted a woman against her will by the use of physical or moral violence, deception, or seduction in order to have sexual relations with her or to marry her.[23] Even if the woman was younger than sixteen and accompanied her *raptor* (abductor/seducer) voluntarily, the perpetrator was charged under the assumption that he must have employed seduction to get her to succumb to his nefarious intentions. If marriage resulted or if the doctors determined that the woman had not been a virgin before the event, the case was dropped. *Rapto* was already a well-established social practice among Mexican working people by the nineteenth century. In the eyes of elite society, however, such deviant sexual behavior jeopardized the order and stability of families and ultimately endangered the state's modernization project, which endeavored to extirpate the backward customs the elite associated with the working class. The project to modernize, therefore, played out on the bodies and sexuality of minor girls who had to defend their actions and submit to virginity tests by medical practitioners.

In the eyes of the law, the man had stolen the young virgin's honor and must suffer imprisonment or pay reparations for her lost virginity (honor). These damages repaired family honor as well. In nineteenth-century Oaxaca, parents or guardians filed most complaints of *rapto* in the courts. Single mothers of the working class filed the majority of petitions. Indeed, female-headed households were not an anomaly in Oaxaca or the rest of Mexico at this time.[24] Mothers filed the majority of cases (71 out of 150 cases), but fathers also initiated a significant proportion of complaints (52 out of 150).[25] An overwhelming majority of the parents hailed from the working class (96 percent).[26] Elite families probably dealt with their children's rebellious actions outside the public, scandal-provoking realm of the court. Some parents initiated complaints in order to force a marriage or a promise of one in the future. Other parents rejected the union and demanded a full enforcement of the law and the imprisonment and fining of the perpetrator, who was usually male, although female accomplices could also be found liable for facilitating the seduction.[27] Unlike cases from the United States, the Oaxacan examples do not show parents punishing or incarcerating their runaway daughters in reformatories or convents.[28]

Oaxaca de Juárez: The Emerald City

The *rapto* dramas played out in the courtrooms and the public spaces of the city. The cases under study in this chapter originated in courts of the state capital and its suburbs, including El Marquesado, Trinidad de las Huertas, Jalatlaco, and Xochimilco. Like most Latin American cities, Oaxaca de Juárez was built around a *zócalo* (central plaza) anchored by the cathedral and ecclesiastical offices to the north and secular government buildings and the governor's palace to the south. Under the eastern and western porticos, business establishments sold clothing, food, and other products to residents.

Two blocks southwest of the plaza, an open-air market operated in which both female and male vendors sold goods to customers. Another market-place, named after Porfirio Díaz, opened in 1892 south of the city center.[29] Adjacent to the central plaza, the alameda provided visitors with shade, park benches, and walkways to enjoy a respite from their workday.[30]

Working-class Mexicans lived public lives, and courtship was rarely a private affair between two families. The girls of the *rapto* dramas literally worked on the street, which presented both dangers and opportunities. Many of the young couples chose to rendezvous on church grounds to take the first step of elopement, as attending mass may have been germane to their daily lives. Marketplaces presented other venues where lovers came together to plan their romantic and tactical trysts away from the scrutiny of parents. Yet the marketplace could also pose dangers for women. More than a few criminal cases attested to the violent abduction of young women on errands to buy tortillas for their families. Leisure activities around the city provided young working Oaxacans with other opportunities to mingle and continue their courtship. Although bullfights were outlawed except by special permit in 1826 and were relatively infrequent, card games and dice, as well as cockfights and traveling circuses, entertained lower-class *oaxaqueños*. Indeed one foreign traveler remarked on the mixing of genders among those playing games of chance on the *zócalo*.[31] The various saint-day festi-vals also provided opportunities for young Oaxacans to meet and flirt or exchange notes that might initiate or foster a courtship.

Although the state scrutinized lower-class Oaxacans and endeavored to reform what they saw as their antimodern customs, the working class played an integral part in modernizing the city. In fact, their presence was crucial to the renovation of the capital's built environment. They con-structed new buildings and renovated old structures, including a city orphanage (1896) and a state pawnshop (1882). Girls cleaned the homes of the elite in the city center and plied foodstuffs and handicrafts in the mar-kets. Ironically, their patterns of work contrasted dramatically with the increasing modernization of the city. While city officials strived for ration-alism and modernity in urban spaces and administration, workers toiled in small enterprises that had more in common with their premodern antecedents than their capitalist descendants. Indeed just a handful of work-ers labored in factories in the city and surrounding valley towns. At the turn of the twentieth century, only 1,360 workers from the central valley were employed in textile, beer, cigarette, and shoe factories.[32] The overwhelming majority worked in artisan-based workshops with a few people—an envi-ronment more closely resembling a cottage industry than a factory floor. Several of the adolescent girls of the *rapto* cases worked with their mothers, selling meat or tortillas in the marketplace and sweets on the street, or they worked as domestic servants in middle- and upper-class homes. The adoles-cent males in these cases probably were employed in small workshops, with some noting that they were apprentice shoemakers or weavers. In fact, apprenticeship for working-class youth was akin to education for elite children. It prepared them for a career and provided a period of guidance and guardianship under the tutelage of a male elder or boss. Girls met their boyfriends at the work sites, and often these small artisan shops were jumping-off points for the elopement.[33]

Workers in the capital city sat at a juncture between the traditional and modern. For working-class and elite Oaxacans alike, the late nineteenth century ushered in significant changes in how state and municipal authorities related to their citizenry. Workers suffered increased surveillance and control; businessmen watched the state's economic fortunes wax and wane with the precious metal and commercial markets. One constant, however, was that children continued to defy their parents' wishes and demands, especially when it came to matters of the heart and personal welfare. Some of these family disputes played out in the municipal courts of the Emerald City.

Defiant Daughters

Civil legislation dismantled the absolutism of the patriarch and allowed plenty of space for the political agents to maneuver in the private lives of families. The elopement of minors was one example of the state acting as patriarch in settling family conflict. Children have always defied parental authority, but the characteristics of this rebellion have changed over time. In Oaxaca, minor girls eloped with their sweethearts throughout all historical eras. Maltreatment was a commonly cited reason for elopement, and romantic love also continued to fuel the decision to defy parents. Indeed, Patricia Seed found that colonial-era Mexican girls often stated that they chose their betrothed and defied parental wishes out of love.[34] Among the nineteenth-century Oaxacan cases, maltreatment and love ring constant in the girls' testimonies, but increasingly these same individuals claimed their right to majority and to forge a conjugal contract on their own. To the judges, parental abuse and young love were the perfect mix that provoked them to side with minors in their decision to forge a conjugal relationship. Parents would have none of it. Even when daughters reached majority age (twenty-one), some parents or guardians still felt they could control the daughters' life choices.

"Maltreatment" could mean overwork, regular arguments with a parent, neglect, and physical or sexual abuse. As mentioned previously, a father had the duty to feed, clothe, and educate his children; he also had the right to discipline them and, if they were minors, consent to their plans for marriage.[35] Children had to obey their fathers or legal guardians, but later civil codes left room for maneuvering in that children could charge their parent with excessive abuse, or *maltrato*. Limiting the severity of parental punishment harks back to the medieval *Siete partidas*, which warned that *patria potestad* sanctioned moderate rather than violent punishment.[36] If a child pleaded maltreatment, he or she could gain the court's ear to determine whether the abuse warranted punishment of the alleged abuser or possibly removal of parental authority over the child. Children claimed parental abuse, both honestly and dishonestly, to explain their actions and garner some credibility before court officials. The court attentively listened.

Returning to the saga of sixteen-year-old Juana and Melquiadez, a nineteen-year-old shoemaker, that began this chapter, we find that the judge accepted the preliminary findings of the investigation and proceeded to hear the case. Señora Ramírez felt justified in initiating the case of *rapto* because she possessed *patria potestad* as Juana's only parent. Yet, if we believe the youngsters' testimony, she was an absent and neglectful parent. Juana lived on her earnings as a domestic as well as on the gifts of food and clothing she received from her boyfriend. These necessities she shared with her sister, with whom she also lived. Although her mother felt justified in complaining about the dishonoring of Adela's home, both of her daughters testified to her neglect and absence as a parent. Juana made it clear to the court using mutually comprehensible concepts that her mother had failed in her parental duties. She had failed to provide *alimentos* for Juana and her sister. Proving this statement alone could jeopardize the mother's *patria potestad* over her daughters and gain Juana sympathy and maybe even emancipation from the court. The case file ends with a concluding note that Juana escaped her temporary custody, so we do not know if she moved in with Melquiadez. Her rebellion against her mother and the legal process, however, certainly confirms her mission to make her own decisions regarding her sexual and romantic life.

In court, many daughters detailed the variety of abuses they received at home. Seventeen-year-old Feliciana told the court that she ran away with Pioquinto because her mother threatened to hire her out as a live-in domestic servant. She chose to elope rather than be forced into domestic service. Other young women feared sexual abuse and left home to avoid it.[37] In another case, Rosa justified her elopement with Aurelio by telling the court that she desired him even though he was poor, but her mother wanted her to marry a rich suitor, Ramón, whom she did not love. Aurelio agreed that she should run away from home, so she slipped out of the house at three o'clock in the morning to meet him in front of her house.[38] Eloping was Rosa's strategy to thwart her mother's plan to have her marry a richer suitor. Stepfathers and male relatives posed the greatest risks to young women. Francisca and Anita justified their elopements by citing the *mala vida* (tough life) their mothers gave them and the fact that their stepfathers repeatedly made sexual advances whenever the girls were left in the house with them.[39] One male suitor regaled the court with the story of a nefarious stepfather and claimed that he eloped with Candelaria before her stepfather could deflower her. Candelaria provided scant testimony, but the duo agreed to marriage, which the judge sanctioned. He consequently closed the case.[40]

In these cases of alleged sexual abuse or threats by stepfathers, there is no evidence that the judges initiated investigations into their behavior. Protection of adolescent girls only went so far. Indeed some girls were not so lucky to escape their stepfathers' predations. Fourteen-year-old Narcisa was selling sweets near Oaxaca's cathedral when she opted to elope with fifteen-year-old stone mason José. She told the court that she chose to accept José's offer of marriage after their one and a half month relationship because she wanted to leave her mother's dominion. Almost as an afterthought, or possibly to reinforce her case, she added that she had been maltreated by her mother. José was more forthcoming with his justification of their actions and his recollection of the events leading to their elopement. He told the judge that Narcisa did not want to go home anymore because her mother was frequently inebriated and hit her, forcing her to flee on many occasions. As the case unfolded, Narcisa had to explain to José and the court why she was not a virgin when the couple first had sexual intercourse. She stated simply that her stepfather deflowered her in the patio of their home. In a rare twist, the case ended unsatisfactorily for José. Doctors affirmed that Narcisa had lost her virginity at an earlier date and went to great clinical lengths to describe her vagina's capacity to accept something the size of a man's penis. The fact that doctors determined that Narcisa was not virginal upon her elopement with José should have nullified the case, but the judge still sentenced the young man to one year and four months in prison and a fifty-peso fine with no further comments or justification.[41]

The charge of maltreatment or dereliction of parental duty gained the court's attention. Civil codes advised parents to be moderate in their punishment, and if a parent could not or would not provide *alimentos*, the law allowed the authorities to intervene. Runaway daughters cited mistreatment as one of their chief justifications for eloping with their lovers. In fact, the charge of maltreatment distinguished nineteenth-century cases from their colonial counterparts. Colonial-era couples did not testify that maltreatment propelled them to elope or defy their parents.[42] This difference points to the budding concept of protected childhood and adolescence in the modernizing state. Law had tempered the severity of parental castigation since medieval times. Yet in late nineteenth-century Mexico, an era characterized by various social and economic programs intended to modernize the nation, an abusive or neglectful parent was antithetical to the state's mission to promote healthy, patriotic, and hardworking families, and the civil code provided the justification to abolish, or at least, weaken the authority of an abusive parent.[43] After all, the future of the nation rested on its children and potential workers.

In addition to complaining that they suffered abuse at home, adolescent daughters claimed they ran away for love.[44] Love letters included in many of the cases prove this sentiment.[45] Like maltreatment, love garnered the attention of judges, and they sanctioned the marriage of many minor couples even without parental approval. Testimony by various sweethearts also provides a glimpse of their inner lives as they defended their actions before parents and court officials. Even defense lawyers waxed eloquently about a young man's love for the woman he eloped with, arguably attesting to the cultural respect for love as a basis of marriage and family. Eulalia complained that she had to work too much at home and that because she loved Pedro, she went to the cigar factory where he worked and waited for him. She intended to flee to San Felipe del Agua to the north of the city, where they would have sex and begin their life together, the customary step for constituting a conjugal unit in the face of parental opposition. Pedro corroborated her story. Doctors ruled that she had been deflowered recently, and the defense lawyer prepared his case well. In his brief to the court, Pedro's lawyer wrote about Pedro's grand love for Eulalia and their wish to begin married life together. Nowhere was there a hint of ridicule or the mention of the folly of fickle minors. Convinced, the judge dismissed the case and allowed the couple to plan their marriage.[46] To the court, female minors declared love as their reason for eloping more often than their boyfriends did, mostly because it was up to them to justify their "immoral" actions.

Young male suitors, although less likely to publicly profess love for their girlfriends in front of the judges, pined longingly for love and affection in the private love letters they wrote to their girlfriends. Arcadio gave several letters to his beloved Anastacia in 1875, and the letters became increasingly desperate as he bemoaned her inattention to his desires. He wrote, "My illusion: What I would offer you on this splendid and luminous day is a new life when the angel of glory comes with garlands for your dark [morena] and gracious face. I cannot offer you more than the honey of contentment of my poor heart and the sea of happiness that runs through my veins when I see you smile . . . you know well that I have loved you with all the sentiment of a man that loves honestly."[47] For their parts, parents willingly submitted love letters to the court in order to prove that their daughters' suitors either promised marriage or had involved the daughter in a serious, romantic relationship. Judges viewed letters as *prendas* (love tokens) or evidence of engagement or promises to marry. Other types of *prendas* included gifts such as jewelry, clothing, or portraits.

Yet some parents, even though they provided the letters as evidence, had other intentions. They did not desire the marriage of the youngsters but rather the punishment of their daughter's seducer. In several testimonies, parents bemoaned the youth and inexperience of their daughters, reasoning that they were too immature to make wise choices in matters of love, perhaps attesting to the fickleness and irrationality of youth. Citing immaturity may have also been a plausible way of expressing their distaste for the suitor to an elite judge. Indeed a few girls told the judge that their parents wanted to force them to marry a richer suitor (but still working class to the judge), so they had run off with their boyfriends to avoid such a plight. Parents' pleas of social distance or inequality fell on deaf ears, however, because undoubtedly the judge saw working-class Oaxacans as one undifferentiated group.[48] Other parents refused to accept love as a valid reason to allow the marriage. Even though their daughters had been deflowered and dishonored, some parents still opposed the marriages. Josefa's story illustrates this point. Her mother charged her intended, Manuel, with being a vagrant, a word that could have several meanings, none of them positive.[49] She simply disapproved of him as marriage material for Josefa and attempted to block the relationship first through hints and threats and then through the court, even supplying the necessary love letters as evidence.[50]

Parlaying Family Conflict: The Court Takes Sides

What did the court make of all these protestations and defenses? Judges and defense lawyers usually provided terse comments and judgments when their opinions were recorded at all. In fact, more often than not, judges refrained from providing lengthy justifications for their conclusions, or at least they were not written down for posterity. If no impediments existed and the young couple was willing, judges preferred marriage as the most favorable outcome. In fact, Oaxaca's 1887 penal code dictated that a criminal case would not proceed if "the *raptor* married the offended woman."[51] In effect, the law and its practitioners recognized and even endorsed *rapto* as a strategy for minors hoping to defy parents by choosing when and whom they wanted to marry. Under these circumstances, judges routinely sided with children and their love matches and against parents and their objections.

There is no evidence that judges required documentation that a marriage had taken place. It sufficed that the couple had verbally contracted to a marriage ceremony, which could take place at an indeterminate time in the future. This situation probably more closely reflected the pattern of marriage among lower order Oaxacans. Young couples in nineteenth-century Mexico, like their colonial counterparts, eloped with a view toward marriage, but marriage itself could be preceded by months or years of a consensual union. Marriage rituals and ceremonies were expensive undertakings. Some couples actually testified that they planned to marry as soon as they had saved the necessary resources. The judges' decisions maintained this tradition. By ignoring parents' demands that boys face incarceration and fines, courts instead adjudicated for the marriage of minor daughters and against the restoration of parental authority. The complicating factor was that many of these young women had been deflowered, a fact the court also sought to repair through matrimony. Obviously, officials supported virginity as a normative value, and most youngsters did as well. Yet the young women also knew that, through *rapto* proceedings, virginity could be wielded as a bargaining chip not only with their suitors but also with parents and judges in order to achieve their aims of independence and the desire to forge a new family.

Playing out the script of seduction and elopement, daughters lost virtue not only by running away with their sweethearts but also by vividly brandished this loss of honor to achieve their desired outcome, a new life with their lover and legal emancipation.[52] By siding with the young sweethearts, court officials proved that sexually mature minors could be emancipated from *patria potestad* if they desired to marry and no impediment stood in their way. This reality meshed with the civil codes, which allowed minor children at the age of twelve for females and fourteen for males to marry with parental consent. In essence, judges recognized a transitional stage (later defined as adolescence) between childhood and adulthood, and they felt comfortable emancipating minors from that state who were capable of forging families or had suffered maltreatment from their parents or guardians. Girls received special protection, and judges did not hesitate to allow them to marry their suitors even in the face of parental opposition. Marriage emancipated them, and they became full-fledged adult women. Even girls who chose consensual unions outside of wedlock won a measure of autonomy. The novelty of the nineteenth century was that judges accepted maltreatment as a reason to allow young, rebellious couples to marry. Moreover, the liberal state wished to promote civil marriage, but through leniency in elopement cases, judges perpetuated the traditional practice of elopement as a clandestine courtship practice that could easily lead to marriage and the disregard of parents' opinions. Therein lay the irony. In essence, the court and the adolescent minors recognized their status as individuals with rights and guarantees. Whereas in colonial times young couples sometimes found their ally in the Church, in nineteenth-century Mexico, the State aided and abetted them in forming nuclear families based on civil marriage and the values of liberalism and individualism.

Conclusion

Mexican girls, some undoubtedly indigenous, found themselves at the nexus of family-state conflict over their rights and responsibilities as minor children.[53] For feelings of love or to escape the abuse they experienced at home, minor daughters chose the dramatic step of running away when their parents opposed their wish to marry or live with their sweethearts. Although they may not have seen themselves as rebels, they emerge as protagonists in the elopement dramas.[54] Others in less dramatic fashion simply slipped out of their homes to meet their lovers in a churchyard or at the marketplace. All ran away with the expressed purpose of sexually consummating their relationship because they had received a commitment to marry or live together from their young suitors. Giving up their virginity accomplished two things: it proved their honor to their sweethearts, and it compelled parents to concede to their plan. When mothers or fathers decided to pursue a criminal complaint against the suitors, the young daughters found themselves in court to convince the elite court officials that their motivations and actions were reasonable and warranted. In the process, they complained about the maltreatment they received at home and declared their love for their boyfriends. It was also important to establish that they had a serious romantic relationship as evidenced by the gift of love tokens such as letters or clothing. Moreover, a promise of marriage further substantiated their actions in the eyes of the adjudicator. Armed with this arsenal of rationales, minor daughters hoped to earn the ear of the judge and receive a favorable judgment.

If the minor girls married their sweethearts, they enjoyed freedom from parental authority. Yet their new husbands now had commensurate power over the girls' daily lives. The laws still dictated that the father or husband ruled over his household, including a disproportionate power over his children. Nonetheless, the conjugal bond, or what Steve Stern has coined the "patriarchal pact," like the parent-child contract, could be negotiated.[55] Wives were not powerless to defend their rights before the courts and in their communities. Although a double standard continued to exist in Mexico during a period of expanded rights for children and women, courts regularly intervened as official patriarchs to side occasionally with minor daughters and wives. Freedom from parental authority was not altogether liberating for these girls, because female adulthood could also be rife with violence and abuse. Nonetheless, by emancipating minor girls and allowing them either to marry their suitors or to cohabit with them, judges also curtailed their childhood by shortening the period of adolescence. Now women, these girls lacked the legal protection provided to children but could seek justice as adult women in domestic violence cases. In the end, poor girls embroiled in *rapto* cases were both sexualized at a younger age and deemed women at an earlier age than their elite sisters.

Girls who either chose or accepted a consensual union may have lacked the legal security of an official marriage, but they also were not legally bound to their male partner. In essence, girls who abandoned the family home to live but not marry their lovers escaped paternal guardianship and control but also did not transfer their official tutelage to their male cohabiter. This state placed girls in a unique position. Newly emancipated from parental authority but not yet under the *patria potestad* of a husband, they may have been able to carve out a degree of autonomy not afforded their married sisters. A woman unsatisfied with her common-law husband could dissolve the union more easily and possibly even have more success in censuring abusive partners. Tanja Christiansen, in her study of working-class Peruvians, found that the court stepped in more often in consensual unions to punish abusive spouses.[56]

Were these eloping protagonists children, girls, or women? The civil code denoted their childlike status until the age of twenty-one or marriage. Once they lost their virginity, they became worldly or womanly in the eyes of the court but were not bestowed with the guarantees that came with majority age. It seems that a concept of "girlhood" emerged, but it was one that was complicated by the integrity of their hymen. Girls could be either virgins or sexually experienced minors. In fact, the jurists and politicians tended to sexualize working-class girls at an early age by assuming that they engaged in sexual relations, whether willingly or not, after puberty. This view may be one reason that judges ordered medical exams to determine the existence or absence of virginity. In the few cases of elite daughters extant in the archive, none underwent the humiliating virginity test.[57] In sum, girls eloped with their boyfriends for a plethora of reasons. They composed a social group that was by no means homogenous but one that held little official or cultural power in Mexican society. Remarkably, these girls exhibited a basic knowledge of their rights as minors before the law and often successfully executed their desire for sexual and personal autonomy.

NOTES

Parts of this chapter appeared in Kathryn A. Sloan, "Disobedient Daughters and the Liberal State: Generational Conflicts over Marriage Choice in Working Class Families in Nineteenth-Century Oaxaca, Mexico," *The Americas* 63, no. 4 (April 2007): 615–648, and are included here with gracious permission of the editors at *The Americas*.

1. Contra Melquiadez Barzalobre por rapto en Juana Silva, Oaxaca, 1872, Alcalde Primero Constitucional, Archivo Histórico Municipal de la Ciudad de Oaxaca (AHMCO).

2. *Código civil declarado vigtente por el H. Congreso del estado de Oaxaca el 14 de Diciembre de 1887*, 4th ed., supplement 37 (Oaxaca: Imprenta del Estado, Segunda de Murguía, 1904), no. 9, article 206.

3. The ages of girls in the *rapto* cases ranged from twelve to twenty-two, with a median age of sixteen. The young men ranged from sixteen to twenty-five, with a median age of twenty. The age of majority for females and males in nineteenth-century Mexico was twenty-one. When minors married, they were considered emancipated from parental authority but encouraged to seek their advice in important decisions.

4. Bianca Premo, "Minor Offenses: Youth, Crime, and Law in Eighteenth-Century Lima," in *Minor Omissions: Childhood in Latin American History and Society*, ed. Tobias Hecht (Madison: University of Wisconsin Press, 2002), 116–119.

5. Barbara Potthast and Sandra Carrera, eds., *Entre la familia, la sociedad y el estado: Niños y jóvenes en América Latina (siglos XIX–XX)* (Madrid: Iberoamericana, 2005), 10. See also Jean Jacques Rousseau, *Émile; or, On Education*, trans. Allan Bloom (London: Penguin, 1991).

6. Colin Heywood, *A History of Childhood* (Cambridge: Polity Press, 2001), 24.

7. Potthast and Carrera, *Entre la familia*, 10.

8. Completed in 1263, the *Siete partidas* was a body of law that governed Spain and Hispanic America, including the territories of Texas, California, and Louisiana, until the civil codes of the nineteenth century were written.

9. Potthast and Carrera, *Entre la familia*, 8.

10. Ibid., 9. For a discussion of patriotic motherhood in nineteenth-century Mexico, see William E. French, "Prostitutes and Guardian Angels: Women, Work, and the Family in Porfirian Mexico," *Hispanic American Historical Review* 72 (November 1992): 529–555.

11. Donna J. Guy, "Lower-Class Families, Women, and the Law in Nineteenth-Century Argentina," *Journal of Family History* 10, no. 3 (Fall 1985): 318–331, 328.

12. Potthast and Carrera, *Entre la familia*, 12.

13. Tobias Hecht, "Children and Contemporary Latin America," in Hecht, *Minor Omissions*, 244–247.

14. Potthast and Carrera, *Entre la familia*, 12; Carmen Ramos Escandón, "Entre la ley y el cariño: Normatividad juridical y disputas familiars sobre la patria potesta," in Potthast and Carrera, *Entre la familia*, 115–141; and Ann S. Blum, "Conspicuous Benevolence: Liberalism, Public Welfare, and Private Charity in Porfirian Mexico City, 1877–1910," *The Americas* 58, no. 4 (2001): 7–38.

15. Ramos Escandón, "Entre la ley y el cariño," 116.

16. Raúl Ortiz-Urquidi, *Oaxaca: Cuna de la codificación iberoamericana* (Mexico City: Editorial Porrúa, 1974), 385.

17. Article 246, *Codigo civil para gobierno del Estado Libre de Oajaca* (Oajaca: Imprenta del Gobierno, 1828); reprinted in Ortiz-Urquidi, *Oaxaca*, 385.

18. Silvia M. Arrom, *The Women of Mexico City, 1790–1857* (Stanford, CA: Stanford University Press, 1985), 57.

19. Girls averaged sixteen years of age, and male defendants were twenty-one on average. Only seven male defendants received a court-sanctioned punishment, including a fifteen-year-old boy whose fourteen-year-old girlfriend had voluntarily eloped with him. See Contra José García por rapto y estupro en Narcisa Rafaela Córtes, Oaxaca, 1886, Juzgado Primero Criminal, AHMCO.

20. *Código penal para el distrito federal y territorio de la Baja California sobre delitos del fuero común y para toda La Republica sobre delitos contra La Federación* (Mexico City: Tip. de Flores y Monsalve, 1874).

21. Elizabeth A. Kuznesof, "The House, the Street, Global Society: Latin American Families and Childhood in the Twenty-first Century," *Journal of Social History* 38, no. 4 (Summer 2005): 863.

22. Eileen J. Suárez Findlay also surmises that plebeian *ponceños* (residents of Ponce, Puerto Rico) often chose serial monogamy over marriage. See Findlay, *Imposing Decency: The Politics of Sexuality and Race in Puerto Rico, 1870–1920* (Durham, NC: Duke University Press, 1999), 40.

23. William E. French, "Rapto and Estupro in Porfirian and Revolutionary Chihuahua" (paper presented at "El espacio y el peligro en México, 1750–1930," ninth reunion of Mexican and North American Historians, October 1994), 2.

24. See Arrom, *Women of Mexico City*; Elizabeth Anne Kuznesof, "The History of the Family in Latin America: A Critique of Recent Work," *Latin American Research Review* 24, no. 2 (1989): 168–186; Elizabeth Dore, "The Holy Family: Imagined Households in Latin American History," in *Gender Politics in Latin America: Debates in Theory and Practice*, ed. Elizabeth Dore (New York: Monthly Review Press, 1997), 101–117; and the special issue of *Journal of Family History* 16, no. 3 (1991).

25. Of 212 cases in total, only 150 include the initial document that cites the person who initiated the complaint.

26. I determined social group by occupation and sometimes by the use of titles such as Don and Doña in the *expedientes*.

27. Sonya Lipsett-Rivera's study of rape in early national Mexico found that rape was associated with marriage and encouraged either marriage between perpetrator and victim or monetary reparations when the victim was a virgin. Marriage and dowries served as an acceptable solution to repairing family honor but also as a means to restore the social peace and order. See Sonya Lipsett-Rivera, "The Intersection of Rape and Marriage in Late-Colonial and Early-National Mexico," *Colonial Latin American Historical Review* 6, no. 4 (Fall 1997): 559–590.

28. In the United States, parents sometimes used the courts to manage their daughters' rebellious behavior by asking judges to places them in reformatories. See Mary Odem, *Delinquent*

Daughters: Protecting and Policing Adolescent Female Sexuality in the United States, 1885–1920 (Chapel Hill: University of North Carolina Press, 1995); and Ruth Alexander, "'The Only Thing I Wanted Was Freedom': Wayward Girls in New York, 1900–1930," in *Small Worlds: Children and Adolescents in America, 1850–1950,* ed. Elliott West and Paula Petrik (Lawrence: University of Kansas Press, 1992).

29. Like many streets and other locations, after the Revolution this market lost its connection to Porfirio Díaz. Visitors to Oaxaca today will recognize this market as the Juárez market.

30. Charles Berry, *The Reform in Oaxaca, 1856–76: A Microhistory of the Liberal Revolution* (Lincoln: University of Nebraska Press, 1981), 3.

31. W. E. Carson, *Mexico: Wonderland of the South* (New York: Macmillan, 1914).

32. Mark Overmyer-Velázquez, *Visions of the Emerald City: Modernity, Tradition, and the Formation of Porfirian Oaxaca, Mexico* (Durham, NC: Duke University Press, 2006), 83. Likewise, of the 11,605 textile workers in the state, only 570 worked in factories in 1910 (82). In 1895, the central district had a population of 66,381, whereas the capital city had 32,437 residents in 1896. See Francie R. Chassen-López, *From Liberal to Revolutionary Oaxaca: The View from the South: Mexico, 1867–1911* (University Park: Pennsylvania State University Press, 2004), 241–242.

33. Poor girls worked in a variety of occupations around the city, and their workday often provided them the freedom to socialize with friends and boyfriends. Although Oaxaca did not have the variety of working-class amusements found in New York City, foreign travelers commented on the mixed-gender crowds at games of chance on the central plaza or in the audiences of itinerant circus performers. See Kathy Lee Peiss, *Cheap Amusements: Working Women and Leisure in New York City, 1880 to 1920* (Philadelphia: Temple University Press, 1986).

34. Patricia Seed, *To Love, Honor, and Obey in Colonial Mexico: Conflicts over Marriage Choice, 1574–1821* (Stanford, CA: Stanford University Press, 1988). Mark Szuchman also found that nineteenth-century Argentine couples were often in conflict with parents over their chosen love matches. See Szuchman, "A Challenge to the Patriarchs: Love among the Youth in Nineteenth-Century Argentina," in *The Middle Period in Latin America: Values and Attitudes in the 17th–19th Centuries,* ed. Mark Szuchman (Boulder, CO: Lynne Rienner Publishers, 1989), 141–166.

35. Donna J. Guy, "The State, the Family, and Marginal Children in Latin America," in Hecht, *Minor Omissions,* 141–142.

36. Premo, "Minor Offenses," 116–117.

37. Contra Pioquinto Aguilar por rapto en Feliciana Sánchez, Oaxaca, 1887, Primero Juzgado Criminal, AHMCO.

38. Contra Aurelio García por robo sin violencia, rapto y estupro en perjuicio de Rosa Martínez, Oaxaca, 1880, Juzgado Primero Criminal, AHMCO.

39 Contra Eduardo Ramírez por rapto en Francisca Delgado, Oaxaca, 1887, Juzgado Criminal Segundo, AHMCO; and Averiguación del rapto de que se queja Perfecta Medina perpetrado en su hija Anita Nicólas, Oaxaca, 1870, Juzgado de Letras, AHMCO.

40. Contra José Inés Caballero y accomplices por rapto, Oaxaca, 1873, Juzgado Tercero de la Capital, AHMCO.

41. Contra José García por rapto y estupro en Narcisa Rafaela Cortés, Oaxaca, 1886, Juzgado Primero Criminal, AHMCO.

42. In her introduction, Asunción Lavrin does not cite maltreatment as one of the reasons that minors eloped. See Lavrin, *Sexuality and Marriage in Colonial Latin America* (Lincoln: University of Nebraska Press, 1989), 65–66. Patricia Seed and Ramón Gutiérrez also do not cite maltreatment as a justification for eloping. See Seed, *To Love, Honor, and Obey;* and Gutiérrez, *When Jesus Came, the Corn Mothers Went Away: Marriage, Sexuality, and Power in New Mexico, 1500–1846* (Stanford, CA: Stanford University Press, 1991).

43. French, "Prostitutes and Guardian Angels."

44. Lawrence Stone, *The Family, Sex and Marriage in England, 1500–1800* (New York: Harper and Row, 1977).

45. For a discussion of a *rapto* case and its love letters, see William E. French, " 'Te Amo Muncho': The Love Letters of Pedro and Enriqueta," in *The Human Tradition in Mexico*, ed. Jeffrey M. Pilcher (Wilmington, DE: Scholarly Resources, 2003). French beautifully reconstructs the tragic story of love turned violent as these lovers struggled over notions of honor, deceit, and trust.

46. Contra Pedro Clérin por rapto en Eulalia Vásquez, Oaxaca, 1872, Juzgado de Letras, AHMCO.

47. Love letter contained in the case Contra Arcadio Ortega acusado de fuerza en Anastacia Delgado, Oaxaca, 1875, Juzgado Tercero de la Capital, AHMCO. Arcadio was a student, so I assume he wrote his own love letters to Anastacia. Other working-class lovers may have relied on scribes (whom they paid) or literate associates to pen their words of love.

48. The Royal Pragmatic on Marriage promulgated in 1776 and applied to all Spanish colonies by 1778 allowed church courts to uphold parental rejection of their children's betrothed for reasons of social and economic inequality. This pronouncement circumscribed earlier practices of ecclesiastical courts that promoted free choice and will of individuals to choose their marriage partners. After independence, this prejudice was not codified in law but occurred in practice.

49. "Vagrant" could mean a jobless or homeless person, or the word might simply be used to denigrate someone's reputation. The 1871 Penal Code dealt with "Vagrancy and Begging" under "Crimes against Public Order" and defined vagrants as "lacking property and rents, do not exercise an honest industry, art, or trade for a living, without having a legitimate impediment" (*Código penal para el distrito federal y territorio de la Baja California*). See also Pablo Piccato, *City of Suspects: Crime in Mexico City, 1900–1931* (Durham, NC: Duke University Press, 2001), 171, and his discussion of *rateros* as vagrants before the law.

50. Contra Manuel Vivas por rapto en la jóven, Josefa Calvo, Oaxaca, 1899, Caja Delitos Sexuales 1891–1899, AHMCO.

51. Estado de Oaxaca, *Código penal para el estado de Oaxaca* (Oaxaca: Imprenta del Estado, 1888), article 807.

52. Like nineteenth-century Cuban couples, the Oaxacan examples demonstrate the individuality and rebelliousness of the youth as they dramatically eloped to control their marriage futures. See Verena Martínez-Alier, *Marriage, Class, and Colour in Nineteenth-Century Cuba: A Study of Racial Attitudes and Sexual Values in a Slave Society*, 2nd ed. (Ann Arbor: University of Michigan Press, 1989), 135.

53. Between 1857 and 1891, the state of Oaxaca vacillated between 87 to 77 percent indigenous. See Daniela Traffano, "En torno de la cuestión indígena en Oaxaca: La prensa y el discurso de los politicos," in *Historia, sociedad y literatura: Nuevos enfoques*, ed. Carlos Sánchez Silva (Oaxaca: IEEPO, 2004), 125.

54. Some rebellious girls planned their own elopements and even threatened their boyfriends that if they did not comply, the girls would find another man who would. Kathryn A. Sloan, "Runaway Daughters: Women's Masculine Roles in Elopement Cases in Nineteenth-Century Mexico," in *Mexico Uncut: Performance, Space, and Masculine Sexuality after 1810*, ed. Anne Rubenstein and Victor Macias González (Albuquerque: University of New Mexico Press, 2008).

55. Steve J. Stern, *The Secret History of Gender: Women, Men, and Power in Late Colonial Mexico* (Chapel Hill: University of North Carolina Press, 1995), 97–98.

56. Tanja Christiansen, *Disobedience, Slander, Seduction, and Assault: Women and Men in Cajamarca, Peru, 1862–1900* (Austin: University of Texas Press, 2004).

57. Medical students in Mexico studied the female body and the hymen in particular. They believed that gynecological exams could have an important bearing on sexual assault and *estupro* (deflowering) cases. For the present cases, doctors examined the girls to determine the timing of their deflowering. They looked for an intact hymen as well as for signs of violence or forcible penetration. For a medical student's thesis on the subject, see Francisco A. Flores, *El hímen en México: Estudio hecho con unas observaciones presentadas en la cátedra de medicina legal en la Escuela de Medicina el año de 1882* (Mexico City: Oficina Tip. de la Secretaría de Fomento, 1885). For more discussion of the Oaxacan *rapto* cases and the medical examinations, see Sloan, "Runaway Daughters."

20

The Shifting Status of Middle-Class Malay Girlhood

FROM "SISTERS" TO "SINNERS"
IN ONE GENERATION

PATRICIA SLOANE-WHITE

Twenty-first-century middle-class Malay Muslim girls are often portrayed as "seducers," "sinners," and "material girls," sexualized symbols of global modernity's dystopia, a place where mothers are working and absent, family is dissolving, and children no longer obey. But a generation ago, their mothers—twentieth-century middle-class Malay Muslim girls—were valorized as "sisters to modernity" for contributing to national development, and *their* mothers were valorized for shaping that modernity. In this chapter I hypothesize that the valuing of girls in modern middle-class Malay Muslim society since Independence in 1957 is contingent upon the cultural authority granted to or denied their mothers; in the Malay case, a middle-class girl's status shifts in tandem with her mother's perceived role in social change. By examining how girls become moral proxies of their mothers, we are led to ask a crucial question about girlhood in general: Is girlhood a category of motherhood?

The status and representation of Malay Muslim girls between the 1960s and the present day have changed. Malaysia, a multiethnic nation with a powerful Muslim majority,[1] is today known as one of Asia's "miracle economies." In 1970, many Malaysians were poor, and, according to government leaders, the majority of Malays still lived much as they had in colonial times: traditional in outlook, humble in expectations, and marginalized from modernization.[2] Malay ethnic and class-based resentment of the Malaysian Chinese, who were perceived to have monopolized the post-Independence economy, erupted into violence in 1969. In response, the Malay-dominated government devised a development program known as the New Economic Policy (NEP).[3] NEP—spanning the years from 1970 to 1990—was an interventionist economic and affirmative-action program directed at creating a capitalist class among the Malays. One of its major policy initiatives used tertiary education as a catalyst of change. The university system was expanded dramatically. Thousands of Malay students were given scholarships to study locally and overseas.[4] During the same period, Malays were affected by the increasing power of Islamic conservatism. By the end of the NEP period in 1990, Malaysia was rife with ethno-religious contestation, and dissension was kept under control by the increasingly authoritarian state. Young Malay women figured prominently in all of these transformations.

In the early 1980s, the Malaysian government courted multinationals to increase export-based production, one of NEP's development goals; the multinationals courted "nimble-fingered Asian girls," of whom there was a ready supply in rural Malay villages. As they were famously described by anthropologist Aihwa Ong, Malay girls were "docile bodies" refigured by the unfamiliar time routines and punishments of industrial capitalism, whose labor benefited the extractive capitalist goals of government and parents alike. In response, unable to cope, some girls reportedly fell into episodes of hysteria on the factory floor.[5]

While some lower-class Malay girls were toiling away in Malaysia's new multinational industries, for other girls a different definition of modern girlhood began to take shape. Social scientists describe how, starting in the 1970s, other Malay females, like their Malay brothers, were brought by NEP policies into tertiary education, some with little emotional, social, or academic preparation. Many of these girls became, according to some literature on Malaysian Islamization, *"dakwah* girls" (girls influenced by Islamic missionizing)[6] and were often described as culture-shocked and unable to cope with urban modernity. *Dakwah* girls were swayed by the fundamentalist movement that enveloped Malay student life in the 1970s and 1980s, a vivid symbol of a vast Islamic reconfiguring of modern Malay life that soon reached far beyond universities.

My own anthropological research on Malay girlhood, part of a larger project addressing middle-class socioeconomic transformations among Malays most affected by NEP,[7] grew from my realization that the girlhoods described by nearly fifty Malay women whose contemporary lives and personal histories I studied—whose ages spanned from the early teens to the early twenties during the NEP period—did not parallel the vulnerable, acted-upon factory or *dakwah* girlhoods I had read about in the literature on modern gender and social change in Malay life. Nor did they originate from the rural and impoverished Malay class that NEP was said to benefit. Indeed, as I learned about their lives, it appeared that most of them had emerged from empowered, modern, and middle-class Malay girlhoods that were in place at the start of NEP. What became truly discomfiting in my research was the awareness that in an Islamicized Malaysia, twenty-first-century middle-class girlhood is no longer valorized; in fact, it is increasingly impugned. Who were those dynamic twentieth-century girls? Where did they go?

The Malay Muslim women analyzed here were daughters of parents who had been strongly influenced by colonial attitudes. They were born in the mid- to late 1950s and 1960s in the towns of British Malaya.[8] Their fathers had received secondary education, often in English. Their mothers had received some education and had married quite young. At Independence, their fathers had been employed by the government as clerks and office workers, the salaried professionals of the time. Today these women are civil servants, academics, lawyers, architects, journalists, business executives, and entrepreneurs. Most are married with children. All of them had received NEP-funded tertiary education in Malaysia or overseas and were typical of thousands of young Malays whose educations, then as now, were funded by the government.[9] Secondary education throughout Peninsular Malaysia was significantly improved during the 1970s, but in terms of tertiary education, the greatest resources went to what researchers of the Malaysian scene variously call "the higher social groups," "higher status families," "well-to-do," "professional classes," and "middle income" Malays of the time.[10]

Issues of class and social distinction are discomfiting to Malays, who see themselves as rooted in an egalitarian and communal culture, and who play down much evidence of and concern with status in the historical past. None of the men or women I interviewed believed they had come from a nascent middle class, despite the fact that their fathers (and sometimes their grandfathers) had been salaried office workers. (Elsewhere I address the NEP-era tendency for these urban-oriented Malays to describe themselves as having come from a rural *kampung* or village as a way to justify the disproportionate benefits that NEP gave to those who in actuality did not emerge from the peasantry, and other complexities inherent to the discussion of Malay class and status.) Although the "middle class" has emerged as a category of sociological analysis in contemporary Malaysia, primarily defined in terms of consumption style and by the processes of self-definition and social distinction, there are few scholarly descriptions of an Independence-era Malay middle class, despite some evidence that in terms of attitudes, experience, and ambitions, one had already formed.[11] The girls who emerged from this background became neither "factory girls" nor "*dakwah* girls." They were middle-class girls groomed for success. Their girlhoods have received little or no attention in studies of Malay life.[12]

Traditional Images of the Malay Girl

H. R. Cheeseman, a colonial administrator in Malaya from the early twentieth century, described the British effort to educate Malay girls as a "struggle." Malay parents, he claimed, insisted on maintaining "traditional Muslim seclusion" that would protect daughters' purity.[13] By the mid-twentieth century, anthropologists, like colonial administrators, tended to present the lives of Malay girls in similar, vaguely "Orientalist" terms; they were "restricted" or "secluded" from puberty onward. Lenore Manderson's study of female education in Malaysia documents that from the late nineteenth century until World War II, some Malay girls, whose parents were influenced by British attitudes and who lived within the range of a formal secular school, received some education. Many more colonial educational opportunities were available for boys, and when long distances had to be traveled to reach a local school, parents were more willing to allow boys to attend than girls. But in the towns of the Federated Malay States and the Straits Settlements in which the British presence was most strongly felt, and in the more urbanized colonial outposts within the Unfederated Malay States, female enrollments in schools grew.[14]

According to the life histories I collected from women who had been born in areas under strong colonial control in the 1930s, what constrained their education most was not traditional-minded parents, as colonial administrators claimed in defense of their meager educational system,[15] but the coming of the Japanese in 1941. They spoke of "the time of the Japanese" as a period in which parents were terrified by stories of rapes and abductions of young girls. Girls were abruptly taken out of school and "married off quickly."[16] Still, several women recalled attending Japanese school during the occupation,[17] and one remembered some Japanese words which she recited to me. These stories—rare voices of colonial-era girlhoods—counter the monolithic presentations of Malay life, which imply that in the first half-century of colonial control, Islamic parents were uniformly conservative, retrogressive, and as anxious about their daughters' bodies as they were toward all social change.

Immediately after World War II, schools began enrolling increasing numbers of boys and girls. Several of the mothers (and nearly all of the fathers) of the women I interviewed, whose schooling had been terminated during the war, returned to school. Some of the mothers were reaching marital age (at that time, on average around seventeen to nineteen)[18] and did not continue schooling. Yet pushing toward Independence, Malays knew education had to be dramatically reorganized and structured.[19] Ten years after the war ended, enrollments in primary schools had risen significantly, and, in many parts of the peninsula, girls were attending at nearly the same rate as boys.[20] Malay leaders argued, as did one woman writer, that "Malay girls especially must not be permitted to terminate their studies soon after leaving the Malay school. They must continue their education in English schools where they will be able to obtain a larger perspective of life."[21] The uplifting of girls through education was perceived to be part of an effort that would help bring Malays into deserving ownership of their own country. Born into this world of educational improvement, ethnic empowerment, and social access, the women of my study benefited as they came of age. The shaping and valuing of their identities—and therefore middle-class Malay girlhood of that time—were intimately connected to the shaping and valuing of their mothers' identities.

Middle-Class Motherhood and Girlhood in the 1960s

Virginia Hooker, who has studied twentieth-century Malay literature, states that Malay novels from the Independence era evidence dramatic themes of duty and progress among the groups she characterizes as the modern ethno-nationalist Malays.[22] Focusing on such ideals as the empowerment of the young nation, Malay novels of the period characterized educated youths as carrying the banner of change. In fiction, as in real life, by the 1950s and early 1960s, young Malay men and women spoke boldly about goals to uplift the Malay race. Hooker argues that among the emerging middle class, childhood, associated with all that was new and nascent in the young nation, was invented—for boys and girls alike—as a time to study. Modern childhood emerged in the Malay middle class as a time of vitality, duty, and, most importantly, full engagement with schooling. I contend that traditional Malay motherhood—previously criticized by the colonial power as "indulgent" and "spoiling," and then in the period from 1948 to the 1960s criticized as "neglectful" by a rising Malay political star, Mahathir Mohamad (later to become prime minister)[23]—was being reinvented by the middle class as a time to enforce study.

This theme resonates with meaning in interviews I conducted among today's middle-class Malay men and women who were born into the middle class around the time of Independence. Women reported that their girlhoods were indistinguishable from those of their brothers; girls, like boys, "had to study or be beaten." Childhood was thus remembered as a time of duties. Fathers, rigid and authoritarian, came home every day from a government office for prayers, lunch, and a nap, and checked children's homework. One woman's father insisted on the use of English in the house; her mother knew no English but enforced the rule nonetheless, slapping the hands of a daughter who spoke to her in Malay. But what emerged in all of their memories was a clear picture of the power and authority of the mother. Whereas the civil-service father may have set the standards, it was the Malay mother and often the mother's mother—a widowed grandmother in the house who claimed even more dominance—who maintained what they remembered as enormous control over children's academic studies. Standards of conduct and rules of deportment were enforced by threats and punishments—a back caned with a bamboo switch, or, after talking back, lips smeared with the cut end of a chili pepper.

The now elderly mothers of the men and women I interviewed agreed that they beat their children to make them work harder; one mother, quoting the Malay saying that "you must straighten the bamboo while it is growing," said she did it every day. Another insisted that her girls could be disciplined with one beating a day, whereas her sons were beaten three times a day. One grown daughter spoke without emotion of her "raging mother who flew into a fury at any academic failure." With the results of school exams published in the newspapers, a child's success became the public cornerstone of a postcolonial middle-class maternal identity, which was built on producing "successful children."

Sociologist Gavin W. Jones, examining changing patterns of rural Malay family life such as increased school attendance and the rising marital age for girls, asks how parents "who as recently as the 1950s and 1960s were cloistering young women until they were safely married off, could have so quickly relaxed these controls and permitted, even encouraged their daughters to proceed further in school and to work outside the home before marriage." He finds the answer to be in part the strong official support of both male and female education, but primarily it was the parents' interest in extracting wages from daughters working in multinational factories of the late 1970s.[24] But this portrayal of a modern girlhood that transports girls from rural backgrounds of domestic servitude to a capitalist wage-based one does not address the point of view of either mothers or daughters within the middle-class, civil-service cohort. The mothers of women I studied were not directly intending to extract wages from their educated daughters.[25] To understand what these mothers sought from their girls, we have to look at mothers' interests—the need to establish their ethno-nationalistic identities as good mothers of the postcolonial nation and their personal need to increase family status. Here, the work of the modern middle-class Malay mother first emerges. But it is through her work on *daughters*—perfecting and then protecting them—that the modern middle-class Malay *girl* first emerges as well, the status of each indexed to the other.

Anthropologist Hanna Papanek argues that we must include in our accounting of the unpaid, unacknowledged, and unrewarded domestic work of women the work of status production. Mothers, she said, especially in societies in which their family's elite standing is predicated on them not holding independent jobs, are likely to be the prime investors in family aspiration, shaping children's lives and futures to increase the family's social standing. Mothers' engagement in status production establishes "the family's present status as well as its future status aspirations. . . . It is instrumental in shaping the children's future occupations and marriage opportunities."[26]

Although it is well established in analyses of traditional Malay life that women, under the liberating terms of Malay customs (*adat*), were significant contributors to family economy,[27] 1960s civil-service-sector mothers of the women I studied did not work at wage-paying jobs. Many of them, however, had home-based businesses in the 1960s, selling domestic or feminized products such as Tupperware, jewelry, cosmetics, and fabric.[28] Success at these ventures could be both socially and financially rewarding for the most charismatic and socially networked women. But my interviews of mothers who had performed this kind of work revealed that what was really at stake in such activities was family status. Women who engaged others in their ventures and interests, whether through selling or community activities they characterized as "social work"—assisting the poor, providing support to needy women, and so on—were highly regarded as leaders in small towns and cities during the 1960s. Refashioning the terms of *adat*, which traditionally allowed married Malay women to play public, political, empowered roles in kin and village relations, the middle-class mothers of many of my respondents were immersed in what Papanek calls the "politics of status maintenance."[29]

Although the subject of status reproduction in traditional Malay society has received little attention, Manderson suggests that in the first half of the twentieth century, "aristocratic Malay families" encouraged the education of daughters to enhance family status and ensure "favorable marriage prospects."[30] By the 1960s, when parents were insisting that daughters "study or be beaten," a daughter who had passed her school exams and was on the road to further academic success reflected well on both her civil-service family and her marriage prospects; her academic achievements also strongly aligned her mother with the modern ethno-nationalistic outlook of the time.[31] Ambitious mothers wanted to play key roles in their communities; they wanted to play equally key roles in Malay group advancement vis-à-vis their children. The consequences for their daughters were burdensome in that the girls were both serving the modern expectations of female improvement and responding to traditional expectations of female self-sacrifice and family orientation. But this is precisely what their mothers recall that they *themselves* were doing, as mothers of a changing nation.

Many women remember that girlhood during the 1960s and 1970s also implied a burden not required of boys. They believe that compared to their brothers, they were treated unfairly. One woman told a vivid story from her girlhood—of having to learn to cook rice without the slightest crust sticking to the side of the pot (a challenging task before the advent of electric rice cookers), of repeating the steps day after day, when her homework was done, while her brothers ran outside to play, their taunts audible as she failed to meet her mother's expectation for perfectly made rice. Some women recalled that domestic chores were often used as a punishment; a girl who was falling behind in her lessons was forced to demonstrate obedience and submissiveness through housework. Schooling was thus just one part of what their ambitious, middle-class mothers were socializing daughters for; modern "femininity" and its expectations for confirming future status required establishing an identity in multiple realms. "My mother," one woman told me in a quiet, measured voice, "felt girls earned a special cruelty—and I served out a sentence of obedience that my brothers did not." Clearly girlhood in this period emerges as a complex set of modern and traditional virtues projected on daughters by mothers.

Creating Modern Sisters

When colonial observers and anthropologists noted in traditional and rural Malay life that the childhood of little girls ended abruptly at around age six, they were remarking on the way in which Malay girls took on the responsibility of caring for younger children (as girls likely did in all traditional societies), which freed up the mother for continued childbearing or economic activities. Characterizing them as "little mothers" and implying that their labor was as burdensome as their girlhood was short,[32] such descriptions tended to miss the heightened status girls obtained through this role. In Malay traditional life, deference was due to older siblings by younger siblings, regardless of gender. The eldest sister, or *kak long*, who took on the role of "mother" was accorded a powerful role, and to be *kak* to any younger sibling (*adek*) provided a girl with significant status.[33] An older sister had greater status than her younger brother; if the two were close in age, their status vis-à-vis younger siblings was complementary, not hierarchical.

Many women in contemporary Malaysian life who were the eldest or second-eldest girls maintain the strong role granted to *kak long*. One forty-year-old woman still manages the lives of her adult brothers and sisters by dispensing both aid and criticism, and as her parents aged, she made financial decisions on their behalf that would affect their lives (and their estate) for years to come. She was the consummate *kak long*, the sister whom the others still both feared and loved. Many of the other successful and dynamic women were also eldest or near-to-eldest sisters within their sibling group, and although I know of no study of birth order and personality development in Malay life, it is easy to associate the strength of some women's present-day personalities, and even their success in the world, with the family role they played in girlhood. Unlike females in many Muslim cultures, Malay sisters as a group do not defer to Malay brothers.[34]

Boys of exceptional ability in the 1970s could be granted greater opportunities than their equally outstanding sisters. The ultimate achievement—to be selected to attend the elite Malay College Kuala Kangsar (MCKK) or a similar English-style boarding school—was a privilege available to boys alone.[35] Although its "sister school," Kolej Tunku Kurshiah in Seremban, supposedly offered an equally excellent education to the best female students, there were fewer institutions of its kind—and all with less cachet—than there were for boys. Sending a son to MCKK was every middle-class Malay mother's dream. A teacher at one of Kuala Lumpur's elite girls' schools with an illustrious past said that in her girlhood, mothers of sons at MCKK were held in greatest awe. They were "like Chinese mothers," she said—who were known for pushing their sons toward academic success. She recalled being resentful that girls like herself were expected to do as well as boys, work harder in the home, but could not earn the rewards conferred on boys. She and many of my respondents remember competing ruthlessly with their brothers for high exam scores, claiming they did well in their studies not only because their mothers required it, but because they wanted to prove to their mothers, brothers, and boys at school that they were as good as boys. If in traditional Malay family life, sibling rank provided some girls with an opportunity to claim equality or superiority to boys, the women in modernizing families I interviewed were not, as girls, willing to accede easily to inequality.

Although real brothers and sisters might have felt gendered inequalities, it was in the symbolic extension of the sibling group—where a real sodality of Malay brothers and sisters became identified with the larger Malay "family" or ethnic group—that the ethno-political interests of all converged. It was here that girls of civil-service families could proclaim their worth, where, along with brothers, they became, in effect, the children and siblings of NEP. As proxies of good mothers and, as will be shown, fictive or symbolic "elder sisters" of Malay modernity, girls became actors in their own lives.

Creating Modern Ethnic Sisters

Traditional, village-based Malay social structure is based on what anthropologists have called a metaphor of siblingship, where everyone—kin and nonkin alike—is referred to by kin-based terms and consequently is treated like family.[36] Researchers have documented the contemporary role of fictive Malay siblingship in the development of male cohorts in boarding schools such as MCKK and in the "cult-like" spread of *dakwah* among vulnerable girls in university settings.[37] What has remained unaddressed is the way in which metaphors of siblingship also lie at the foundation of a dynamic Malay girlhood.

As daughters of a post-Independence middle-class society that valued female education, all of the women I interviewed believed they would go to a university.[38] With the advent of NEP in 1970, however, Malays of all social classes began to associate tertiary education with ethnic responsibility.[39] To capture their experiences as beneficiaries of NEP scholarship funds—which became widely available to qualified Malay students beginning in 1971—I asked them to describe their feelings as they left their homes for higher education. Many of the women, when recalling their identities on the eve of departure to tertiary education in Kuala Lumpur or overseas, described themselves as the "cream of the crop," ready to show themselves capable of modernization and achievement on behalf of what was now perceived to be their "victimized" ethnic group. Highly motivated, competitive, and imbued with female self-esteem, Malay girls became, in their own minds, soldiers for their ethnic group. To catch up with the Chinese and reclaim the nation from their unworthy, greedy hands, one woman told me, meant you couldn't think about yourself as an individual; you thought about the role you had to play in the Malay future.

Group ideology was exaggerated by the way in which NEP education policies began to structure choices of its first student cohorts. The government channeled Malay students into underrepresented fields such as sciences and mathematics and filled new Malay-only institutions such as Institut

Teknologi MARA (ITM) with students in technical and preprofessional fields. Students had little say regarding their field of study. One woman I interviewed and all of her friends were sent to teacher-training programs in the mid-1970s. She wanted to be a journalist, and her friends wanted to be lawyers, and psychologists, and architects, but, as she told me, "you did what the government told you to do." "They needed teachers," she said, "and what right did you have to turn it down?" To do so would be "disloyal and ungrateful." The only thing that mattered to them and to their parents, she emphasized, "was to be picked. After that, you did what was best for *everyone*—not *yourself.*" Other women echoed these sentiments, describing NEP educational policies as "a gift to Malays" or "a contract" that you were obligated to repay. These ideals sustained and empowered the young students, who increasingly saw themselves as ethnic siblings charged with meeting the expectations of the larger Malay family.

On the day of the students' departure from their hometowns, Malays celebrated the theme of belonging to a whole greater than oneself. Because sometimes dozens of Malay girls and boys were leaving at the same time to go to Kuala Lumpur or overseas, parents, younger siblings, cousins, aunts and uncles, and neighbors went to the train station or the airport to see them off. One woman remembered the students from her secondary school coming with banners to congratulate the departing students. Like soldiers going off to battle, the girls of the NEP cohort, like their brothers—both real and fictive—perceived themselves to have responded bravely and boldly. Where members of the middle-class generation before them had seen themselves as brothers and sisters of the Independence movement,[40] members of this fictive sibling group saw themselves as the brothers and sisters of ethnic development. Mothers who had monitored their daughters' behavior and chastity now would have to trust the girls to live on their own for the first time in their lives. How could they be trusted? Sent off confidently as "proxies" of their good mothers, they were also moral "sister-proxies" to the larger Malay family.

By its very nature, "siblingship" in the bilateral kinship system of Malay Muslim life implies that girls are not exclusively defined, as they are in many patrilineal Muslim societies, as sexualized beings.[41] Emphasis on the non-sexual and "sisterly" nature of females within domestic settings deemphasizes or mitigates the sharp gendering of Malay females.[42] I argue that the "sisterly" nature of siblingship was extended to the middle-class girls who left their parents' houses for university dormitories in Kuala Lumpur and overseas. Anthropologist Susan Ackerman claims that rural Malay society sees young, unmarried females as sexually threatening and "dangerous," and Ong argues that Malay females in general are perceived as sexually and spiritually "vulnerable,"[43] but the "proxified" daughters of powerful middle-class mothers were being given, for want of a better description, a special dispensation from sexuality and sexualization that some girls were not.

Many authors claim that in confronting modernity, Malay Muslim parents had no choice but to comply helplessly with changing times. Anthropologist Maila Stivens notes that by the 1970s, girls in Malay society were less restricted than they had been in the past, and they could be seen shopping and traveling under supervision to Kuala Lumpur or Singapore on the train.[44] Researchers who focus on the Malay rural sector describe a dramatic break between "modern girls" and their "traditional mothers," in a changing Malay society where, by the early 1970s,[45] the identities and expectations of both fell into disorder. Indeed, this is the basis for the hypothesis of "vulnerability" that underlies the emergence of both hysterical Malay factory girls and *dakwah* girls. But it is here, among the civil-service, urban-oriented middle class, that there was less chaotic and disruptive dislocation of female identity. Middle-class Malay mothers in the 1960s and 1970s embodied their social and moral value in daughters who became, then, proxies of valorized modern mothers. No mother I spoke to characterized a daughter who had successfully passed her secondary-school exams and was heading off to higher education as vulnerable or endangered. In fact, to her, the opposite was true.

Modern teenage daughters on their way to universities and colleges in the 1970s and 1980s knew what their parents expected. One woman told me that if she had failed her exams at University of Malaya, her mother would have been "as ashamed as if I had returned home pregnant." The expectation was clear: girls would succeed and would remain chaste—like sisters.[46] One elderly mother, who sent five girls and three boys to universities in Malaysia and overseas, said that one of the reasons she had been so harsh and cruel with her daughters as she raised them was to "build up their strengths." "They knew right from wrong and knew the price of their mistakes," she told me proudly; "I beat it into them." Clearly more than knowing how to cook rice was being taught to little girls—all the modern expectations of female duty and self-control were being emphasized when they were denied the same childhood playtime granted to boys.

Sent off as chaste good "sisters" to Malay development alongside their real and fictive brothers, these middle-class girls enjoyed surprising autonomy in Kuala Lumpur and overseas (a condition that has not been sustained in either their or their daughters' lives). Quite a few of them enjoyed freedoms their mothers would have never imagined. Of the women whom I knew well enough to broach the subject, approximately half admitted to me that they had lost their virginity during the years of higher education. Those who said they did not nonetheless reported engaging in all sorts of forbidden, or *haram*, activities, which they could have never revealed to their parents: dancing at discos with boys, drinking alcohol, and neglecting their studies over long, carefree days.[47]

Their experiences stand in sharp contrast to those of university girls who became *dakwah* followers in the 1970s and 1980s, whose experiences are much better documented. The three most widely read accounts of the sociological emergence of *dakwah*—those by Zainah Anwar, Chandra Muzzafar, and Judith Nagata—focus almost exclusively on recruitment of the vulnerable *dakwah* girl in Malaysia and overseas educational settings. Despite the uniformity of female compliance with *dakwah as* described in these books, none of the women I interviewed had been *dakwah* girls. None of them had attended *dakwah*-style meetings or sermons, nor had they begun wearing the veil during their university days.[48] *Dakwah* may have exerted profound and intractable peer pressure on some Malay girls, but not on all.

The majority of my respondents had managed to elude the *dakwah* movement's rigid social and behavioral controls because they attended Malaysian universities in the early and mid-1970s or had gone overseas, where they were not subject to the peer pressure of the late 1970s and early 1980s. Many of my respondents had received their higher education at ITM, where veils and other symbols of *dakwah* were not allowed. Mostly, however, they were able to resist *dakwah* pressure because they were, in their own minds, different from the girls who became involved in it. *Dakwah* girls were, many women claimed, "insecure and self-doubting." They didn't have "strong personalities." They were "followers, not leaders." Other women made more subtle distinctions between themselves and *dakwah* girls, stating: "They were less qualified than we were as students," "Our English was better," and "We were more exposed to Western ideas and experiences."

Although my respondents did not describe the differences between themselves and *dakwah* girls in class-based terms, clearly class and social origin mattered. As NEP policies began to guide more and more Malay youths toward higher education, the population of students who were, according to many critics, ill-prepared for it increased. More and more students from rural backgrounds were sent to Kuala Lumpur and overseas universities. Practiced in academic success, speakers of English from families whose fathers had insisted upon it, aggressively competitive with their brothers and other girls, and proxified—as I have shown, by powerful, ambitious mothers with modern outlooks, yet experimenting privately with social and sexual choices—the middle-class daughters and sisters set themselves apart from the *dakwah* girls. Every woman I interviewed recalled her days in higher education as a time of freedom.

To the women in my study, the end of girlhood coincided with the end of higher education. With schooling finished, work and marriage waited, and adulthood began. Insulated from or resistant to the rigid pressures and repressions of *dakwah* in the 1970s and 1980s, the "sisters" are now working women, wives, and mothers, whose role in an increasingly Islamicized Malaysia is subject to criticism by both the state and its religious institutions. By the 1990s, Islamic intensification had moved from the universities into everyday life. The freedoms my female respondents had enjoyed were undergoing vast transformation. Much had changed for today's girls *and* their mothers.

Mothers, Daughters, and Girls in Contemporary Malay Life

When the first cohorts of the daughters and sisters of Malay NEP-era development returned home from overseas and local universities in the 1980s, they did not return to the small towns of their childhood. They came to Kuala Lumpur, where jobs and opportunities awaited them. Many of them were already married or soon would be, having found spouses during the period of tertiary education or just after. At the time I interviewed them as mature women a decade or more later, only five of the nearly fifty women were still unmarried, and two were divorced.[49] All of the married or divorced women had, on average, three or four children. They had full-time jobs and domestic help at home.[50] Their economic and consumption choices place them among what others have called the two-income "new rich of Asia."[51] In reality, however, the commitment women make to their careers is more complicated than the need to reproduce a middle-class lifestyle.

Although many of the women in my study characterized their NEP-sponsored education as a "gift" that should be returned, in reality, the majority of scholarship students were, upon graduation, "bonded"[52]—which meant that they had to work for a fixed number of years (generally seven) for the state as civil servants or employees of state-owned corporations. Those entering jobs in the private sector had to repay or (as was more common) have the company "buy out" the bond. Although many of the women I interviewed had already fulfilled the terms of their bonds, concerns other than "dutifulness" kept them focused on their careers.

Malay men are obligated by the terms of Muslim marriage to provide material support to a wife and children, and women are allowed to maintain their own savings. Elsewhere I have argued that this longstanding Islamic tradition of women's autonomy over their own money (and men's autonomy over theirs) is not always empowering. Most Malay husbands and wives do not pool their money but maintain separate bank accounts, keeping the balances private from one another. The women I interviewed were concerned to protect their savings; today, as in traditional times, a woman's money was her defense against a husband with undesirable qualities or a roving eye. In contemporary Kuala Lumpur, many Malay wives have a more legitimate fear that their husbands will take a second wife than their own mothers ever did. Polygyny, once rare in Malaysia, is today on the rise among economically successful Muslim men. Many women revealed that they worked to ensure that they were not too dependent on men, who are required by Muslim law to provide a wife and children with only basic support. And they worked to maintain financial autonomy in an atmosphere that increasingly allows greater freedoms to Muslim men. Although the women I interviewed felt that the Islamization of Malay lives was a good thing, making them better Muslims in the service of Allah, they believed they had to accept the new patriarchal thrust of Malaysian Islam. In their attempts to be more doctrinal Muslims, Malays are transforming what has been described as a gendered complementarity of traditional Malay life into gendered hierarchy.

The dynamic "sisters" who had pursued educational success for the development and modernity of the "Malay family" in the 1970s and 1980s, by the 1990s were, as wives and mothers, falling under increasing pressure about the role they were playing in their real families. When I first arrived in Malaysia in the early 1990s, the media reported endlessly on the tragic state of Malay children, who, government and religious leaders declared, were "unsupervised," "lonely and unloved," and unschooled in "traditional values" and Islamic morality.[53] Highly educated and career-focused Malay mothers have increasingly become the target of Islamic groups, which claim that these mothers no longer understand their primary role as Muslim females, are too liberated and autonomous in their careers and lifestyles, and consequently have brought harm to the Muslim family and the larger Malay community.[54]

When prominent Muslim leaders declared that women should not work outside the home,[55] my respondents, men and women alike, were increasingly receptive to their authority. All of the women I interviewed accepted as "Muslim law" that if a woman's job proved harmful to her husband or children in any way, her husband could demand that she stay home, because her primary role is that of preserver of the family. Most of the married women I met were anxious about their multiple roles. They felt a growing pressure from their husbands and society to be uncomplaining, supplicating Muslim wives. They worried about polygyny and husbands to whom Islam has granted greater social, sexual, and economic freedoms. They worried about the costs of providing what they believed was a "good childhood" to their children and resisting the punishing methods of their mothers; they focused not on educational discipline but on "enrichment."[56] Most of all, however, they worried about the effect that the long hours they spent commuting and working had on the lives of their children. Increasingly these women are blamed for the crises of industrialized modernity that NEP sought to create, and the ones I spoke with felt guilty for transgressing the neo-Islamic maternal ideal. The contemporary lives of these married, middle-class Malay women—and the pressures they are under to contribute to national economic development and comply with a more forceful Islam—have been the focus of a significant body of work by anthropologists.[57] What has not received attention from students of Malay contemporary culture is the moralizing, scrutinizing connection—a kind of mother-to-daughter contagion—between today's middle-class Malay motherhood and girlhood. Government and Islamic leaders may present endangered teenagers as the Malay mother's innocent victims, but what appears clear in the ongoing Islamization of the Malay worldview is that more often than not, Malay girls are not perceived as "innocent" parties. I contend that Malay girls are still the moral proxies of their mothers—"bad girls"—now that their mothers are no longer "good."

Malay Girlhoods of the Twenty-First Century—Sexualized and Sinful Girls

The Malay girl today, reportedly neglected by her working mother, is portrayed as a girl gone wild. At once the victim and purveyor of sin, she is both in danger and dangerous. In the popular imagination and in the media, the Malay girl is increasingly believed to be in danger—highly vulnerable to rapists, Internet pornographers, pedophiles, and other modern predators, as well as to the materialism of Western culture. Among the increasingly doctrinal Muslim population of Malaysia, young Malay girls at and before puberty are more and more portrayed as sexually dangerous, especially as some Malaysian states have sought, from the early 1990s onward, to refine and implement Islamic law or shari'a for the Muslim population. Shifting definitions of female sexual potency are common in Malay Muslim culture, but in the present atmosphere, the debate increasingly focuses on—and demonizes—young girls. While unsupervised Malay boys fell victim to such social ills as "loafing," cults, and drug use, Malay girls as young as fourteen were arrested by Islamic police or charged in shari'a courts for seducing prominent Malay politicians, selling sexual favors to businessmen in return for fashionable clothes, and committing indecent behavior as they danced in discos and clubs.[58]

It is not new that modern Malay girls are regarded with sexual ambivalence and moral concern, for indeed, this image is precisely the one that Malay "factory girls" and "*dakwah* girls" confronted in the 1970s and 1980s, when, in the dislocations of modernity from rural to urban lifestyles, they came under increasing social and moral control. What I am drawing attention to here is the reprieve from sexualization that some girls enjoyed during the same period, when as middle-class "sisters" they served the development of the bigger Malay "family." No longer familialized as "sisters" to modernity, middle-class Malay girls are increasingly portrayed as "seducers," sexualized symbols of urban modernity whom today's mothers no longer can or do monitor.

The post-Independence civil-service middle class willingly granted to its girls bravery and duty in the role of the powerful sister. Gender did not inhibit the dynamic reach of Malay girlhood in the cohort I studied; instead, empowered "sisters" were crucial actors in economic and social change from Malaysian Independence onward. So, too, their mothers were valued for their role in producing good daughters and sons who could contribute to Malay ethnic success. Starting out as girls with valor, these daughters went far in Malay life—their careers as business executives, teachers, and government servants attest to this. Now themselves mothers and wives, they are increasingly seen by government and Islamic leaders as disruptive within their own middle-class families and to the larger Malay group. Their duties as women are being called into question. So, too, have their daughters become suspect. The remedy suggested by the powerful Malay *ulama* (scholars), by the husbands of the women I interviewed, and—as Islamic conservatism pulls at them—by the women themselves, is that today's women and girls should fall under greater male social control. Mothers have lost status. So, too, have girls.

A generation ago, however, middle-class Malay Muslim girls were virtuous sisters to modernity, not sinners in modernity, and their mothers were modernity's valued creators. Clarifying the history of the emergence and shifting of modern middle-class Malay girlhood and motherhood serves several crucial purposes. First, it provides an image of a group of Malay girls during the period from the 1960s to the 1980s who participated in the creation of their own identities, rather than showing them, as other portrayals do, merely as "acted upon" bodies and minds. Second, it reveals the crucial role of post-Independence middle-class Malay parents—but more specifically the mothers of my respondents—in the "work" of social class and the key role that girls played in confirming it. Third, by positing that middle-class Malay girls were (and remain) what I call the "moral proxies" of middle-class Malay mothers, it reconnects Malay girls with their mothers, rather than presenting, as the scant work on Malay girls often does, a dramatic break between "modern girls" and their "traditional mothers" in the post-Independence period. Finally, and perhaps most importantly, clarifying the nature of a once-empowered girlhood suggests a way to measure how much status and value contemporary middle-class Malay girls and their mothers have lost in the current period of Islamic conservatism. Only then can we comprehend how Malay girls have gone from "sisters" to "sinners" in one generation.

NOTES

1. All Malays by constitutional definition are Muslims. I use the term "Malay Muslims" in this essay to emphasize the importance of Islam in establishing Malay social and ethnic identity. The current population of Malaysia is approximately twenty-five million, with three major ethnic groups: 61.1 percent are ethnic Malays, or *bumiputra*; 27.4 percent are ethnic Chinese; and 9.4 percent are Indians. *Population and Housing Census of Malaysia 2000* (Putra Jaya, Malaysia: Department of Statistics, 2001).

2. See, for example, Mahathir Mohamad, *The Malay Dilemma* (Singapore: Times Books, 1970).

3. The Malaysian Constitution crafted upon independence from the British in 1957 granted special privileges to *bumiputras*. These provisions became the basis for the increase in Malay privileges and educational policies after 1969.

4. Between 1970 and 1985, the number of Malay students in tertiary education in Malaysia increased by over 300 percent. The Majlis Amanah Raayat (MARA), a government body set up to promote Malay interests, built new universities, residential schools, junior colleges, and professional training institutes for Malays only. For statistics on NEP educational expenditure, see Viswanathan Selvaratnam, "Ethnicity, Inequality, and Higher Education in Malaysia," *Comparative Education Review* 32, no. 2 (1988): 173–196; and Ozay Mehmet and Yip Yat Hoong, *Human Capital Formation in Malaysian Universities: A Socio-Economic Profile of the 1983 Graduates* (Kuala Lumpur: University of Malaya, 1986).

5. See Aihwa Ong, *Spirits of Resistance and Capitalist Discipline* (Albany: State University of New York Press, 1987); and Susan E. Ackerman, "Dakwah and Minah Karan: Class Formation and Ideological Conflict in Malay Society," *Bijdragen Tot De TLV* 147, nos. 2 and 3 (1991): 193–215.

6. The term *dakwah*, which literally means "to respond to a call," refers to the proselytizing activities of Islamic revivalists. The *dakwah* movement swept through the campus of the University of Malaya beginning in 1969. For its history, see Shamsul A. B., "Identity Construction, Nation Formation, and Islamic Revivalism in Malaysia," in *Islam in an Era of Nation-States: Politics and Religious Renewal in Muslim Southeast Asia*, ed. Robert W. Hefner and Patricia Horvatich (Honolulu: University of Hawai'i Press, 1997). For its effects on young women, see Zainah Anwar, *Islamic Revivalism in Malaysia* (Kuala Lumpur: Pelanduk Publications, 1987); Chandra Muzaffar, *Islamic Resurgence in Malaysia* (Petaling Jaya, Malaysia: Perebit Fajar Bakti, 1987); and Judith A. Nagata, *The Reflowering of Malaysian Islam: Modern Religious Radicals and Their Roots* (Vancouver: University of British Columbia Press, 1984).

7. During three research trips made between 1993 and 1998, I conducted anthropological fieldwork in Kuala Lumpur, Malaysia. My research focused on the Malay men and women who were the early beneficiaries of NEP and today make up the urban Malay middle class in Kuala Lumpur. This chapter focuses on a subset of my larger project.

8. Although the British were present in the Malay states from the early nineteenth century, the beginning of the colonial period in Malaysia (known then as Malaya) is usually given as 1874, when a formal relationship was struck between some Malay rulers and the British. Colonial control was not uniform across the Malay Peninsula. Some states were under strong administrative control or directly ruled by British governors; others maintained their own systems of governance. This setup remained until World War II, when Malaya was occupied by the Japanese. For the history of the colonial period, see Barbara Watson Andaya and Leonard Y. Andaya, *A History of Malaysia* (Basingstoke: Macmillan Press, 1982).

9. For NEP educational expenditures, see Selvaratnam, "Ethnicity, Inequality, and Higher Education in Malaysia."

10. See Charles Hirschman, "Educational Patterns in Colonial Malaya," *Comparative Educational Review* 16, no. 3 (1972): 486–502; and Hirschman, "Political Independence and Educational Opportunity in Peninsular Malaysia," *Sociology of Education* 52, no. 2 (1979): 67–83, for a review of colonial education policies and of the successes of the post-Independence Malaysian school system. "Higher social groups": Zafiris Tzannatos, "Reverse Racial Discrimination in Higher Education in Malaysia: Has It Reduced Inequality and at What Cost to the Poor?" *International Journal of Educational Development* 11, no. 3 (1991): 177; "higher status families": Bee-Lan Chan Wang, "Sex and Ethnic Differences in Educational Investment in Malaysia: The Effect of Reward Structures," *Comparative Educational Review* 24, no. 2, part 2 (1980): 143; "well-to-do": Suet-ling Pong, "Preferential Policies and Secondary School Attainment in Peninsular Malaysia," *Sociology of Education* 66, no. 4 (1993): 251; "professional classes": Selvaratnam, "Ethnicity, Inequality, and Higher Education in Malaysia"; and "middle income": Mehmet and Yip, *Human Capital Formation in Malaysian Universities*.

11. Descriptions of the Independence-era middle class can be found, for example, in Shamsul A. B., "From Orang Kaya Baru to Melayu Baru: Cultural Constructions of the Malay 'New Rich,'" in *Culture and Privilege in Capitalist Asia*, ed. Michael Pinches (London: Routledge, 1999). Elite or aristocratic Malay society and Malays in the upper levels of colonial service have been well documented. See, for example, Khasnor Johan, *The Emergence of the Modern Malay*

Administrative Elite (Singapore: Oxford University Press, 1984); and Lenore Manderson, "The Development and Direction of Female Education in Peninsular Malaysia," *Journal of the Malaysian Branch of the Royal Asiatic Society* 51, pt. 2 (1978): 100–121. Few anthropologists in the past addressed the question of class in Malay life; see, however, B.A.R. Mokhzani, "The Study of Social Stratification and Social Mobility in Malaysia," *East Asian Cultural Studies* 4, no.1 (1965): 138–161. In my study, I was able to establish that the women had come from a colonial-era middle-class background because nearly all of them had salaried fathers (or in some cases uncles or other inspirational family members) working in the civil service. They spoke of a socially or economically "exceptional person" or people in the family history, which reflected, at around the end of the nineteenth century, a certain earlier "eliteness." Men in my study were more likely to have *kampung* backgrounds. See Wang, "Sex and Ethnic Differences in Educational Investment in Malaysia," for gender and status mobility under NEP policy.

For middle-class lifestyles and ideology, see Patricia Sloane, *Islam, Modernity and Entrepreneurship among the Malays* (Basingstoke: Macmillan, 1999); Patricia Sloane-White, "Why Malays Travel: Middle-Class Malay Tourism and the Creation of Social Difference and Global Belonging," *Crossroads: An Interdisciplinary Journal of Southeast Asian Studies* 18, no. 2 (2007); Sloane-White, "The Ethnography of Failure: Middle-Class Malays Producing Capitalism in an 'Asian Miracle' Economy," *Journal of Southeast Asian Studies* 39, no. 3 (2008): 455–482; Maila Stivens, "Sex, Gender, and the Making of the New Malay Middle Classes," in *Gender and Power in Affluent Asia*, ed. Krishna Sen and Maila Stivens (New York: Routledge, 1998); Abdul Rahman Embong, "Social Transformation, the State, and the Middle Classes in Post-Independence Malaysia," in *Cultural Contestations: Mediating Identities in a Changing Malaysian Society*, ed. Zawawi Ibrahim (London: ASEAN Academic Press, 1999); and Ibrahim, *State-Led Modernization and the New Middle Class in Malaysia* (Basingstoke: Palgrave, 2002).

12. See Wazir Jahan Karim, *Women and Culture: Between Malay "Adat" and Islam* (Boulder, CO: Westview, 1992), 214–215.

13. H. R. Cheeseman, "Education in Malaya, 1900–1941," *Malayan Historical Journal* 2, no. 1 (1955): 41–42. See Lenore Manderson, "Shaping Reproduction: Maternity in Early Twentieth-Century Malaya," in *Maternities and Modernities: Colonial and Post-Colonial Experiences in Asia and the Pacific*, ed. Kalpana Ram and Margaret Jolly (Cambridge: Cambridge University Press, 1998), for a description of how Europeans viewed Malay women. For a description of Malay girls' "confinement," see M. G. Swift, *Malay Peasant Society in Jelebu* (London: Athlone Press, 1965), 107.

14. See Manderson, "Development and Direction of Female Education," 111; and Leonore Manderson, *Women, Politics, and Change: The Kaum Ibu UMNO, Malaysia, 1945–1972* (Kuala Lumpur: Oxford University Press, 1980). For boys, see Khasnor, *Emergence of the Malay Administrative Elite*.

15. Hirschman, in "Political Independence and Educational Opportunity," argues that the "problem" with the Malays who did not seek education for their children, boys or girls, was never primarily one of attitude but access.

16. Many schools may have closed as well. See Cheeseman, "Education in Malaya."

17. On Japanese-language schools, see Manderson, "Development and Direction of Female Education," 112.

18. Gavin W. Jones, *Marriage and Divorce in Islamic Southeast Asia* (Kuala Lumpur: Oxford University Press, 1994), 145.

19. See Hirschman, "Political Independence and Educational Opportunity," on the "education-mindedness" of nationalists; also Virginia Matheson Hooker, *Writing a New Society: Social Change through the Novel in Malay* (Sydney: Allen and Unwin, 2000).

20. Manderson, "Development and Direction of Female Education," 112.

21. Cik Halimah binti Haji Lajis, *Malay Mail*, January 3, 1948, as quoted ibid., 113.

22. Hooker, *Writing a New Society*.

23. Mahathir Mohamad critiqued the poor mothering techniques of Malays in *Malay Dilemma*. The theme of bad parenting first appears in articles he wrote between 1948 and 1950 in the

Singapore Sunday Times. See Khoo Boo Teik, *Paradoxes of Mahathirism* (Kuala Lumpur: Oxford University Press, 1995).

24. Jones, *Marriage and Divorce in Islamic Southeast Asia*, 146.

25. See Sloane, *Islam, Modernity and Entrepreneurship*, for a discussion of the material demands made by mothers on Malay professionals.

26. Hanna Papanek, "Family Status Production: The 'Work' and 'Non-Work' of Women," *Signs* 4, no. 4 (1979): 777.

27. See the definitive study by Rosemary Firth, *Housekeeping among Malay Peasants*, 2nd ed. (London: Athlone Press, 1966).

28. Many of them also organized revolving credit societies. For this phenomenon in Malaya, see Shirley Ardener, "The Comparative Study of Rotating Credit Associations," *Man* 94, no. 2 (1964): 201–228.

29. Papanek, "Family Status Production," 778.

30. For an example of status-oriented strategies in the past, see S. Husin Ali, *Malay Peasant Society and Leadership* (Kuala Lumpur: Oxford University Press, 1975). Manderson, "Development and Direction of Female Education," 110. I question Manderson's use of the term "aristocratic," by which she implies families of the very elite or royalty. One of the elderly, educated women I interviewed did not belong to the "aristocracy," but had a father and uncle who, as clerks in Penang, "had a love of education" and pushed their daughters into school.

31. For Malay women's role in nationalism, see Manderson, *Women, Politics, and Change*.

32. See Judith Djamour, *Malay Kinship and Marriage in Singapore* (London: Athlone Press, 1959), 35, for a standard description of the way in which the young Malay girl is a "mother" to her younger siblings.

33. For the traditional authority of the elder sister, see Swift, *Malay Peasant Society*, 109.

34. See Suad Joseph, "Brother/Sister Relationships: Connectivity, Love, and Power in the Reproduction of Patriarchy in Lebanon," *American Ethnologist* 21, no. 1 (1994): 50–73, for a discussion of sisterly deference in Arab Muslim societies elsewhere.

35. See Khasnor, *Emergence of the Malay Administrative Elite*, for the history and influence of MCKK in the NEP era; and Khasnor, *Leadership but What's Next?* (Singapore: Times Publishing, Miles Cavendish, 2005).

36. Janet Carsten, *After Kinship* (Cambridge: Cambridge University Press, 2004).

37. For boarding school "siblingship," see Khasnor, *Leadership but What's Next?* For university "siblingship," see Nagata, *Reflowering of Malaysian Islam*, 130–157; and Wazir, *Women and Culture*, 188–194.

38. Two studies of West Malaysian nonrural students in the final years of their secondary education, conducted during the period 1968–1969 and 1972, reveal the optimism of Malay students. See Yoshimitsu Takei, John C. Bock, and Rex H. Warland, "Aspirations and Expectations of West Malaysian Youth: Two Models of Social Class Values," *Comparative Education Review* 17, no. 2 (1973): 216–230; and Wang, "Sex and Ethnic Differences in Educational Investment in Malaysia."

39. Ironically, NEP policies granted scholarships to Malay students from better-off families that in all likelihood could have funded, at least in part, their children's educations. See Tzannatos, "Reverse Racial Discrimination in Higher Education in Malaysia"; and Selvaratnam, "Ethnicity, Inequality, and Higher Education in Malaysia."

40. See Hooker, *Writing a New Society*, 359–363.

41. See Joseph, "Brother/Sister Relationships," for the sexualized nature of Arab Muslim brother/sister roles.

42. For siblinghood and gender, see Michael G. Peletz, *A Share of the Harvest: Kinship, Property, and Social History among the Malays of Rembau* (Berkeley: University of California Press, 1988).

43. Ackerman, "Dakwah and Minah Karan," 203; Ong, *Spirits of Resistance and Capitalist Discipline*, 87–89.

44. Maila Stivens, *Matriliny and Modernity: Sexual Politics and Social Change in Rural Malaysia* (New South Wales: Allen and Unwin, 1996), 213.

45. For discussions of traditional versus modern dislocations in mother/daughter relations, see Ong, *Spirits of Resistance and Capitalist Discipline*, 85–113; Heather Strange, "Continuity and Change: Patterns of Mate Selection and Marriage Ritual in a Malay Village," *Journal of Marriage and the Family* 38, no. 3 (1976): 561–571; and Jones, *Marriage and Divorce in Islamic Southeast Asia*, 145–149.

46. See Michael G. Peletz, *Reason and Passion: Representations of Gender in a Malay Society* (Berkeley: University of California Press, 1996), for discussion of sexuality, self-control, and gender in Malay Muslim culture.

47. Ironically, these were the same behaviors of which many "factory girls" were accused. See Ackerman, "Dakwah and Minah Karan." Lower-class Malay girls enjoyed no dispensation from sexualization.

48. For veiling and its class dimensions in Malaysia, see Judith Nagata, "Modern Malay Women and the Message of the 'Veil,'" in *"Male" and "Female" in Developing Southeast Asia*, ed. Wazir Jahan Karim (Oxford: Berg, 1995).

49. The single women in my study were not necessarily single by choice. See Sloane, *Islam, Modernity and Entrepreneurship*, 30, for concern among parents and Islamic leaders about "bachelor girls" in contemporary Malay life.

50. See Christine B. N. Chin, *In Service and Servitude: Foreign Female Domestic Workers and the Malaysian "Modernity" Project* (New York: Columbia University Press, 1998), for a study of foreign domestic workers in Malaysia.

51. See essays in Richard Robison and David S. G. Goodman, eds., *The New Rich in Asia* (New York: Routledge, 1996).

52. In their survey of the 1983 graduating class of the University of Malaya, Mehmet and Yip report that 75.6 percent of Malay scholarship students were bonded (*Human Capital Formation in Malaysian Universities*, 75).

53. On undisciplined children and teens, see Maila Stivens, "The Hope of the Nation: Moral Panics and the Construction of Teenagerhood in Contemporary Malaysia," in *Coming of Age in South and Southeast Asia: Youth, Courtship and Sexuality*, ed. Lenore Manderson and Pranee Liamputtong (Richmond, Surrey: Curzon Press, 2002); and Aihwa Ong, "Sisterly Solidarity in the Malaysian Public Sphere," in *Religion, Ethnicity and Modernity in Southeast Asia*, ed. Oh Myung-Seok and Kim Hyung-Jun (Seoul: Seoul National University Press, 1998). The descriptions came from speeches made by government officials in the 1990s; see Zeenath Kausar, *Social Ills in Malaysia: Causes and Remedies* (Kuala Lumpur: International Islamic University Malaysia, 2005), chap. 2.

54. For a conservative definition of the ideal Muslim female for modern Malaysia, see Yusof Ismail, ed., *Muslim Women in Organizations: A Malaysian Perspective* (Kuala Lumpur: A. S. Noordeen, 1994).

55. For a discussion of the controversial comments made in 1999 by Nik Aziz, chief minister of the state of Kelantan, on Malay women's proper place, see Maznah Mohamed, "Men Foil as Women Toil," *Aliran Monthly*, April 19, 1999.

56. They want to enrich their children's lives with private tutors, English classes, and so on.

57. See, for example, Stivens, "Hope of the Nation"; Maila Stivens, "Modernizing the Malay Mother," in Ram and Jolly, *Maternities and Modernities*; and Stivens, "Becoming Modern in Malaysia: Women at the End of the Twentieth Century," in *Women in Asia: Tradition, Modernity, and Globalization*, ed. Louise Edwards and Mina Roces (Ann Arbor: University of Michigan Press, 2000).

58. See articles such as "Rapists Now Targeting Girls under 16," *New Straits Times*, December 8, 1996. For the case involving the Malay politician and the fourteen-year-old Malay girl, see "Tamby Chik Case Should Not Be Kept Confidential," *Straits Times* (Singapore), September 1, 1994. For legal cases in shari'a courts brought against young Malay women but not against

Malay men, see Sisters in Islam, http://www.sistersinislam.org.my. Other concerns include "cyberporn" found on Malay girls' mobile phones: "Malaysia Targets Mobile Phone Sex," BBC News, August 29, 2005, http://news.bbc.co.uk. During my trip to Kuala Lumpur in 2007, young middle-class Malay girls were carted off in police wagons, after a raid on a popular nightclub, for drinking, while Malay boys were not.

Contributors

LENIE BROUWER is an assistant professor in ethnic studies at the Department of Social and Cultural Anthropology at Vrije Universiteit, Amsterdam. She has conducted research on Turkish families and on Turkish and Moroccan runaway girls in the Netherlands. Her current research explores immigrant youth and their use of new media.

CHRISTINE CHEATER has a Ph.D. in the history of anthropology in Africa and Australia and teaches the history of childhood, comparative colonial history, and gender studies at the Ourimbah Campus of the University of Newcastle. She has published two local histories, an edited guide for historians working on Australian native title cases, and numerous papers on child labor, nineteenth-century science and popular culture, and women in anthropology.

CORRIE DECKER is an assistant professor in the African and African American Studies Department at Lehman College, City University of New York. She received her Ph.D. in African history from the University of California, Berkeley. Her work addresses questions of gender, education, adolescence, colonialism, and development in twentieth-century East Africa.

S. E. DUFF is completing a Ph.D. at Birkbeck College, University of London. Her dissertation investigates the impact of Dutch Reformed evangelicalism on childhood in the nineteenth-century Cape Colony. She completed her undergraduate and M.A. degrees in history at Stellenbosch University, South Africa.

E. THOMAS EWING is an associate professor in the Department of History at Virginia Tech. He teaches courses in European and world history, women's history, and historical methods. His publications include *The Teachers of Stalinism: Policy, Practice, and Power in Soviet Schools in the 1930s* and articles in *Gender and History, American Educational Research Journal, History of Education Quarterly, Russian Review,* and *Journal of Women's History.* He is editor of *Revolution and Pedagogy: Transnational Perspectives on the Social Foundations of Education* and coeditor of *Education and the Great Depression: Lessons from a Global History.* His current research is on coeducational and single-sex schooling in modern Russian history.

MIRIAM FORMAN-BRUNELL, a professor of history at the University of Missouri–Kansas City, is the author of *The Babysitter: A History* and *Made to Play House: Dolls and the Commercialization of American Girlhood, 1830–1930.* She is editor of *The Girls History and Culture Reader, Girlhood in America, An Encyclopedia,* and *The Story of Rose O'Neill.* She is also the codirector of Children and Youth in History, an online educational resource for history instructors and students.

JESSAMY HARVEY lectures in modern Spanish literature and cultural studies, with a special focus on childhood and youth, particularly girlhood. She researches questions related to children's participation and visibility in Spanish culture, the cultural output aimed at child consumers, and the place of children's culture in adult memory.

JENNIFER HELGREN is a visiting assistant professor of history at the University of the Pacific. She earned her doctorate in U.S. women's history at Claremont Graduate University in 2005. Her article "Gender and Generational Identity: Camp Fire Girls and Cultural Production in the Interwar Years" appears in *Essays on Women's Artistic and Cultural Contributions, 1919–1939*. She is also the author of an encyclopedia entry on the Camp Fire Girls in *Girl Culture: An Encyclopedia* and several book reviews.

JESSE HINGSON is an assistant professor of Latin American history at Jacksonville University, Florida. In 2003 he earned his doctorate in history at Florida International University, where he wrote a dissertation on state violence and the politics of restitution in nineteenth-century Argentina. He has received numerous grants from the Fulbright Institute of International Education, the U.S. Department of Education, and the Mellon Foundation.

CHRISTA JONES is an assistant professor of French at Utah State University. Her research interests focus on postcolonial Francophone literature, particularly Maghrebian literature and women writers in exile. She has published articles in *Problématiques identitaires et discours de l'exil dans les littératures francophones*, *Dalhousie French Studies*, and *International Journal of the Humanities*. She is working on a book about North African fiction and has forthcoming articles in *Al-Raida*, *MIFLC Review*, *Expressions Maghrébines*, and *Francofonia*.

JACKIE KIRK was an adjunct professor in the Department of Integrated Studies in Education at McGill University and a senior advisor to the Child and Youth Protection and Development Unit of the International Rescue Committee, providing technical support to education and child protection programs in conflict-affected areas of the globe. She was killed while engaged in this work in Afghanistan in August 2008. In addition to being the founding coeditor of *Girlhood Studies: An Interdisciplinary Journal*, she was the author of many books and articles, including *Women Teaching in South Asia*, "Addressing Gender-Based Exclusion in Afghanistan: Home-Based Schooling for Girls," and "Menstruation, Marginalization and Girls' Exclusion from Education." She was a committed advocate for gender equality and educational access.

MELISSA R. KLAPPER is an associate professor of history at Rowan University in Glassboro, New Jersey. She is the author of *Jewish Girls Coming of Age in America, 1860–1920* and *Small Strangers: The Experiences of Immigrant Children in the United States, 1880–1925*.

ANN KORDAS received her Ph.D. in history from Temple University in 2002. She is an assistant professor in the Department of Humanities at Johnson and Wales University in Providence, Rhode Island.

LIAT KOZMA is a lecturer at the Department of Middle Eastern Studies at the Hebrew University of Jerusalem. She wrote her Ph.D. dissertation, "Women on the Margins and Legal Reform in Pre-Colonial Egypt, 1852–1882," at New York University. She is revising it for publication.

FRAN MARTIN lectures in cultural studies at the University of Melbourne. She is author of *Backward Glances: Contemporary Chinese Cultures and the Female Homoerotic Imaginary* and *Situating Sexualities: Queer Representation in Taiwanese Fiction, Film and Public Culture*; editor of *Interpreting Everyday Culture*; coeditor, with Peter Jackson, Mark McLelland, and Audrey Yue, of *AsiaPacifiQueer: Rethinking Genders and Sexualities*, and coeditor with Larissa Heinrich of *Embodied Modernities: Corporeality, Representation and Chinese Cultures*. She also edited and translated *Angelwings: Contemporary Queer Fiction from Taiwan*.

CLAUDIA MITCHELL is a James McGill Professor in the Faculty of Education, McGill University, and an Honorary Professor in the Faculty of Education, University of KwaZulu–Natal. Her research focuses on visual and other participatory methodologies, particularly in addressing gender and HIV and AIDS, teacher identity and gender, and the culture of girlhood within broader studies of children and popular culture and media studies. She is the coauthor or coeditor of twelve books, including *Combating Gender Violence in and around Schools*, *Putting People in the Picture: Visual Methodologies for Social Change*, and *Methodologies for Mapping a Southern African Girlhood*. She is a cofounding editor (with J. Kirk and J. Reid-Walsh) of *Girlhood Studies: An Interdisciplinary Journal*. In 2008, the Canadian Bureau for International Education honored her for her work in innovation in international education.

LISA L. OSSIAN is an assistant professor of history at Des Moines Area Community College in central Iowa and earned her doctorate at Iowa State University in agricultural history and rural studies. Ossian has conducted research on Iowa during the early Depression era and the World War II home front years; she has also conducted a national survey of American children's experiences during the Second World War. She serves on the National Education Association's review panel for its academic journal *Thought and Action* as well as the Organization of American Historians' speakers bureau and its Committee on Community Colleges.

JACQUELINE REID-WALSH of McGill University has research interests that include historical children's literature and culture, children's and youth popular culture, comparative media literacy, and girlhood studies. A literary historian working with theoretical lenses drawn from cultural studies, children's studies, and feminist studies, she has coedited and coauthored several books. Her most recent book is *Girl Culture: An Encyclopedia* (2007). She is a founding editor of a new journal titled *Girlhood Studies: An Interdisciplinary Journal*. She holds a joint appointment in Education and Women's Studies.

KATHRYN A. SLOAN is an assistant professor of Latin American history at the University of Arkansas. She is the author of *Runaway Daughters: Seduction, Elopement, and Honor in Nineteenth-Century Mexico*.

PATRICIA SLOANE-WHITE is an anthropologist specializing in Malaysia. She holds a doctorate from Oxford University. Her interests include the Malay Muslim middle class, and Islam and business. Her current research is on "corporate Islam" and the Islamic workplace in Malaysia.

NANCY L. STOCKDALE is an assistant professor of Middle Eastern history at the University of North Texas. She is the author of *Colonial Encounters among English and Palestinian Women, 1800–1948*. A gender historian and expert in Western representations of the Middle East, she has published articles in journals such as the *American Journal of Islamic Social Sciences* and *Women's History Review* and in collections produced by Brill and LIT-Verlag.

MARION DEN UYL is an assistant professor in the Department of Social and Cultural Anthropology, at Vrije Universiteit, Amsterdam. Her Ph.D. thesis, "Invisible Barriers: Gender, Caste and Kinship in a Southern Indian Village," addressed changing gender relations. She has published work on dowry and gender inequality in India and on the anthropology of sexuality. Her current research is on single mothers in multicultural Amsterdam.

COLLEEN A. VASCONCELLOS is a Fulbright scholar and visiting assistant professor at the University of West Georgia. While her teaching focuses on the areas of comparative slavery and emancipation and the history of the Atlantic World, her research examines English abolitionism and the childhood experiences of Jamaican slave children and girls. She is revising her dissertation for publication.

JAN VOOGD, formerly a librarian at Harvard University for ten years, is author of *Race Riots and Resistance: The Red Summer of 1919* and *Maynard, Massachusetts: A House in the Village*. She was awarded a Bryant Fellowship in 2004 and has also contributed articles to several encyclopedias, including the *Encyclopedia of American Race Riots*.

PETER WIEN is an assistant professor of Middle Eastern history at the University of Maryland. He studied at the Universities of Bonn and Heidelberg in Germany, and at Oxford University in Great Britain. He taught at Al-Akhawayn University in Ifrane, Morocco, and was a fellow of the Centre for Modern Oriental Studies in Berlin.

Index

Abidin, Ibn, 347

abolitionism, 3, 323; and "breeding wenches,"
336; and girlhood, 336; and planter purchase
preferences, 328, 334, 335, 339–340n8; and
slave classifications, 336–338

Aboriginal girls, xiii, 9, 11, 215–216, 250–267;
abuse of, 262; age of, 254, 256; assimilation
of, 257–264; and assimilation schools, 252,
253, 254, 255, 257, 258, 259–264; and British
assimilation policies, 250, 251, 252–253, 259,
264; and British welfare policies, 252, 253,
255, 259, 264; and child removal policies,
250, 251, 253, 255, 257–259, 260, 264;
Christianization of, 252; and cultural
identity, 251, 255, 257, 258, 260; and colonial
eugenics, 253, 254, 255, 264; as defined as
by the state, 250–251, 253; as domestic
laborers, 251, 253, 256, 257, 260, 263–264;
and domestic training, 251, 253, 256, 257,
259, 264; friendships of, 251, 260–261, 264,
265; as "half castes," 9, 216, 251, 252, 253,
255, 264; as indentured labor, 256, 263;
innocence of, 257; kidnappings, 254; and
loss of girlhood, 257, 264; and marriage,
254, 255, 257; and matrifocality, 257; and
miscegenation, 252, 253, 264; and
missionaries, 252, 254; and oral history,
251; and parents, 250, 251, 252, 253, 255, 256,
259, 265; passing as boys, 254; perceived
childlike attributes, 256; and pregnancy,
256; punishment of, 261–262; and racial
classifications, 253, 264; and resistance, 251,
252, 262–263, 265; as runaways, 253, 262–263;
segregation of, 255, 259; sexual behavior of,
251, 252, 254, 256, 257; sexual vulnerability
of, 253, 254; and socialization, 254, 255, 257;
as tools of colonialism, 251, 256; and
weekend freedom, 259–260, 261; and white
men, 253, 254, 255, 256. See also Australia

abortion, 173

Académie française, 49

acculturation. See assimilation

Ackerman, Susan, 391

Addams, Jane, 46n11

adolescence, 6, 9, 23, 31, 35, 36, 37, 39, 40, 42,
43, 51, 83, 106, 109, 142, 143, 145, 150, 153–154,
156, 243, 323, 364, 367, 376, 377. See also
teenagers; youth cultures

adoption, 173

Africa, 346; current state of education in, 270;
girls in, 3, 7, 8, 9, 49–64, 234–249, 268–288,
344–362; patriarchy in, 270

African American girls, xii, 9, 31, 66–67, 103,
124, 125; and beauty, 82n25; boarding
houses for, 130; and egg candling, 9,
124–125, 130, 131, 133, 134, 138, 139;
"expressing blackness," 67; independence,
125; and prostitution, 128–129; relationships
with mothers, 67, 72, 81n25; sexuality,
82n30; "street" versus "decent" culture,
67; as strike breakers, 134–136; working
conditions, 125, 126–127

African American press: Broad Ax, 135;
Defender, 134, 135; Negro Advocate, 135

age. See generation

age disaggregation, 17–18

agricultural revolution, 6

Ahkam, Majlis al-, 350

AIDS and HIV, 18, 19, 20, 21

Air Raid Precaution Services Dispatch
Riders, 175

Alba, Father P., 189

alcohol, 77, 128, 171, 172, 392

Alcott, Louisa May, Little Women, 39

Alfonso X of Castile, 364

al-Futuwwa, 2, 10; boys in, 293; and fascism,
294; female branches, 292; and future
warriors, 293, 296; and gender, 290, 295;
and girls' agency, 290, 299; girls in, 216,
290, 295, 299, 300, 301; as an ideal, 292,
295; and Iraqi historical traditions, 295,
298; and loyalty, 296; and male
dominance, 291; and masculinity, 289, 290,
291, 292, 293, 295, 296; and the media, 292,
294, 295; and modernity, 295, 296; and
nationalism, 290, 292, 293, 294, 295, 296,
299; and national schooling, 293; and
paramilitary training, 292, 294; and
paternalism, 291, 296; and socialization,
294, 298; as a tool of the nation-state, 292,
294, 295, 296, 298–299

Algeria, 8, 11, 49–64; decolonization, 49;
and French colonization, 49; and sex-
segregated space, 58, 59; girlhood in, 49,
50, 51, 53–54, 58–64; history from woman's
point of view, 49, 64n24

Algerian War of Liberation, 49, 64n21, 64n24; and freedom fighters (*maquisardes*), 50–51, 53; and rape, 51; and torture, 51
Ali, Mehmet, 354
Allen, Amelia, 39, 47n12
Allen, Fannie, 39, 47n12
Allen, Martha, 304, 306, 315, 318
Allied Commission of Food, 137–138
Allied Provisions Export Commission, 136
Alvarez, Olalla, 105–119; restitution lawsuit, 103, 105–106, 113, 115–118
Amalgamated Meat Cutters, Local 598, 133
American Federation of Labor (AFL), 124, 131, 132, 134, 138
American Girl Dolls, 18
Americanization abroad, 305, 312–313, 315–317
American Railway Union, 134
American Red Cross, 165, 170, 318
Amin, Qasim, 275
Amsterdam, 8, 31, 36; compared to urban African American cultures, 67; cultural diversity in the Bijlmer, 65–67, 68–70, 77–80, 81n11, 81n12; and ethnic stereotypes, 68; family life in the Bijlmer, 70–72; migrant girls in, 8, 31, 36, 65–80; native Dutch in, 68–69; neighborhood pride in the Bijlmer, 70, 79; and religious diversity, 69; and superdiversity, 8, 66, 68–69, 77–80
Anderson, Laurie, 89
Anderson-Levitt, Kathryn, 270
Andréu, Luis María, 188
Anwar, Zainah, 393
anticommunism, 194n48, 305, 307, 314
the Antilles, 70
Apolito, Paolo, 180, 181
apparition scripts, 180, 181
Appel, René, 76
anarchy, 40
Arab girls, xii, xiii, 8, 50, 53; and al-Futuwwa, 290, 295, 299; education of, 54; and female enclosure, 51, 54; and letter writing, 59–60, 72; and patriarchal social structure, 54; and relations with boys and men, 60
Arab women, 50, 54, 58
Argentina, xii, 9, 103, 105–114, 380n34; and civil war, 109, 114, 117–118; girls in, xiii, 9, 107, 109, 111–112, 115–116; local judges, role and duties of, 109, 110–111, 115, 117, 118–119; patriarchal social structure in, 109, 112, 118; role of the state in family, 112, 121n38. *See also* post-Rosas era; Rosas, Juan Manuel de
Ariès, Philippe, 185
Arnstein, Helen, 38, 46n8
Asia, girls in, 7, 25, 83–102, 382–402
assimilation, 9, 10, 36, 38, 39, 41, 44, 54, 58, 215, 250–267, 358

athletics, 9, 56, 195–213, 240, 241, 305; and femininity, 241–242; and susceptibility to illness, 242. *See also* gymnasts
Augustine, Saint, 64n24
Australia, 9, 11, 191, 215–216; Aboriginal Protection Boards, 250, 256, 263; and British colonization policies, 250; child removal policies in, 250, 251; girls in, 7, 250–267. *See also* Aboriginal girls
Austria, 317; girls in, 250–267
autobiography, 49–64, 250

Baff, Bernard, 131
Barbie, 23
Barzalobre, Meliquiadez, 363, 372
Baxter, Bernice, 314
Beecham, Justin, 202, 203
Belgian Congo, 270
Belgium, 312
Bellamy, Edward, *Looking Backward*, 39
Bellinger, Eleanor, 165–166
Bellinger, Patricia, 165–166
Benninghaus, Christina, 6, 146
Berbers, 50, 54
Berlant, Lauren, 196
Bingham, Marjorie, 5
bint, 347, 351–352, 358
blogging, 19
Bolivia, 113
Bollywood, 25
Bottum, Joseph, 179
Bowen, Louise de Koven, 128, 129
Boyer, Paul, 305
boyfriends, 73–75, 371, 378. *See also* courtship
boys, 3, 4, 7, 19, 24, 31, 35, 36, 42, 69, 107, 185, 240, 268, 269, 272, 276, 277, 281, 293, 345, 346, 347, 352, 367, 385, 392, 397; and chivalry, 293; and the fight against imperialism, 294; as future warriors, 293; girls' attitudes toward, 74, 75, 236; girls' interest in, 67, 73, 236; images of, 72, 293; and masculinity, 289, 293
Boy Scouts of America, 293–294, 305
Bratmobile, 87
Brezhnev, Leonid, 198
British Food Ministry, 124, 133, 136, 137–138
Brouwer, Lenie, 7, 8, 31, 35
Brown, Lyn Mikel, 18
Brumberg, Joan Jacobs, 7, 147
Bryn Mawr College, 241
Buckingham, David, 19
Butler, Margaret, 171

cabarets, 128
Camp Fire Girls, 10, 196, 216, 304–319; and Americanization abroad, 305, 312–313, 315–317; citizenship roles of, 216, 304, 307,

319; conservative gender ideology, 306–307, 315, 319; and homemaking (domestic responsibilities), 304, 305, 307, 308, 310; in Japan, 304, 317–318; and internationalism, 216, 304–306, 308, 309–312, 317–319; leaders, 306; and maternalism, 305–308, 318; middle-class membership, 306; and patriotism, 216, 304, 305, 310, 312–315, 316, 319; as peacemakers, 216; as penpals, 309, 312–314, 317, 321n32; and relationship to the nation-state, 216, 308; service projects, 309, 310–312, 314

Canada, 24

Cape Colony, 215, 234–249

Carey, Archibald J., 135

Carrera, Sandra, 365

Carter, Jimmy, 203, 209

Catholic Church, 104, 112, 114, 189, 191n7; culture of, 180, 181, 182, 186, 190–191, 364; and education, 185–186

Catholic girls, 179

Cavanaugh, F., 138

Central Federated Union, 132

Chan, Sandee, 31, 83, 84, 87, 88–91, 92–94, 98; "Beautiful Girl," 94–96; "Café Inn," 88; fans of, 84, 90–91, 92–96, 101n37; and feminism in her songs, 84, 88–93, 94; *Four Seasons*, 88; *Girls Going Forward*, 90, 92; "Girls Going Forward," 90–91; lesbian significance, 92–98; Material Girls, 88; "Perfect," 88; *Perfect Moan*, 88; "Recycling," 88; "Speed," 88; "Surveillance/Violating Vision," 88–89; *When We All Wept in Silence*, 88

Chauncey, George, 85

Cheater, Christine, 9, 11, 215–216

Cheeseman, H. R., 384

Chiang Kai-shek, Madame, 312

Chicago, 9, 33, 34, 38, 40, 41, 43, 44, 124, 126, 127, 128–130, 132–133, 135, 138

Chicago Commission on Race Relations (CCRR), 125, 127, 133–134

Chicago Federation of Labor, 124, 133, 135–136, 138–139

Chicago Hebrew Master Butchers Beneficial Association, 133

Chicago Teachers' Federation, 136

Chicago Women's Club, 40

child-centered family, 6

childhood: and age of discernment, 346–348, 364; definitions of, 6, 23, 324, 348, 364–366, 368, 373, 376; history of, xi, 4, 5–6, 107, 145; modern childhood, 6, 324, 386; rushed, 23, 323; as social construct, 6, 145

children, xi, 4, 6, 52; abuse of, 371, 372–373, 376, 377; and agency, 4, 159n17; as adults (miniature), 4, 365; as burdens, 326; and

custody, 347; expectations of, 4, 326; as investments, 326, 328, 329, 330–335; and prejudice, 312; property rights of, 121n36; rights of, 365; sexual exploitation of, 22; as slaves, 325, 326, 328, 329, 330–335, 336, 337, 338; and the slave trade, 328–329; socialization of, 4; as warriors, 22; writings of, 4

Children's Overseas Reception Board (CORB), 165

Chile, 105, 113

China, 136, 305, 312–313; music industry in, 93

Chisholm, Ann, 196

Christian, William A., 180, 181, 182, 183, 184, 186, 187

Christiansen, Tanja, 377

church groups, 306

Chu T'ien-hsin, 97

citizenship, xi, 2, 8, 10, 21, 39, 103, 107, 305, 307

City of Benares (ship), 165

civic reform, 305

civil defense, 305

Civil War, U.S., 33–34

Clarke, Blake, 166

Clark, E. M., 244

class, social, xi, 8, 26, 36, 38, 43, 44

Claudel, Paul, 56

Clifford, James, 85

Clinton, Bill, 18

clothing, xi, 22–23, 36, 38, 56, 61–62, 67, 73, 76, 79, 97, 200, 242. *See also* veils

code-switching. *See* cultural fluency

Código civil del distrito federal y territorio de Baja California, 366

Cohen, Andrew, 131, 133,

Cohn, Rose, 38, 46n9

Cold War, 103, 179, 195–213, 305, 307, 319

college girls, 3, 51, 236, 240, 243–247. *See also* education

colonialism, xiii, 2, 5, 9, 10; Aboriginal Protection Boards, 250, 256, 263; and British assimilation policies, 250, 251, 252–253, 259, 264; British colonialism, 218–231, 268–288, 325–343; British colonial schools, 218, 231, 252, 253, 254, 255, 257, 258, 259–264; and British welfare policies, 252, 253, 255, 259, 264; and child removal policies, 250, 251, 253, 255, 259, 264; and education, xii, 8, 9, 10, 51, 53, 54, 55–59, 215, 217, 218, 219–231, 234–249, 271–274, 277; and eugenic ambitions, 253, 254, 255, 264; French colonialism, xii, 8, 49–64; French colonial schools, xii, 8, 51, 53, 54, 55–59; and girlhood, 9, 49, 50, 51, 53–54, 58–64, 215, 218–231, 234, 235, 236, 250–251, 253, 256, 257, 259, 264, 270, 271; and language, 274; and modernity, 275; and slavery, 325–343; and socialization, 218, 219, 230–231, 238, 239,

colonialism (*continued*)
254, 255, 257, 269, 270; and westernization, 218, 230–231, 251, 254, 255, 256, 257, 269, 270, 271, 275
communism, 143, 145, 307, 314; in Russia, 143, 145. *See also* Soviet Union
communist youth organizations, 145
community, 37, 40, 42, 44, 45, 51, 65, 66; community clubs and centers, xi, 39, 42; community support, 19, 42
Congregation Mikveh Israel, 47n12
Connell, R. W., 238
consumer culture, 2, 5, 18, 87; and marketing to children and youth, 6, 22–23, 24, 84
Coordinating Council of Women Historians, 5
Córdoba, Argentina, 105, 106, 107, 108–109, 111, 112, 114, 117, 118
courtship, 37, 42, 44, 56, 60, 245, 370–371. *See also* boyfriends.
Court of Domestic Relations, 130
Cuban refugees, 194n48
cultural fluency, 69, 76, 79–80, 82n36, 250
cultural fusion, 38, 60–61, 69
cultural identity, 33–48, 50, 60, 62, 67, 76, 250
culture, xi, 2, 6, 7, 8, 16, 19, 31, 35, 36, 38, 45, 50, 224, 230–231
Curtin, Michael, 93
Cybergirls, 83

Dailey Commission, 131
dakwah girls, 383, 384, 390, 392–393, 396, 398n6
dance halls, 128, 200
dances, xi, 8, 36, 38–39, 58, 61, 73, 77, 170, 171, 172, 200, 392, 396
Davies Company, 124, 132, 133, 136, 138
death rates, 6
Debs, Eugene V., 134
Decker, Corrie, 3, 10, 216, 250
de Gaulle, Charles, 64n21
Déjeux, Jean, 51
delinquency, 11, 171–172, 306, 365
democracy, 10, 307, 314, 317
de Ras, Marion, 172
détente, 198
developmental stages, 145, 150, 153–154, 162, 169; significance of, 4, 6
diaries, xi, xiii, 4, 9, 11, 19, 33, 34, 38, 39, 44, 51, 103, 145, 147, 156, 161n48, 186–187
Difranco, Ani, 89
Ding Xiao-qin, 90
Djebar, Assia, xii, 8, 31, 49–62, 62n1; adolescence of, 51, 56; and arranged marriage, 60; assimilation to Western values, 54, 58; athletics, 56; authorial voice of, 51, 52; and Berber ancestry, 54; bicultural identity, 50, 53, 60–61, 62;

bilingual (Arabic and French) upbringing, 49, 50, 54, 56, 61–62; clothing, 56, 61; compared to female cousins, 57, 58; dance, 58, 61; desire to join Freedom Fighters, 53; and double consciousness, 50; early childhood of, 54–55; education of, 53, 54, 55–57; and female enclosure, 51; girlhood in colonial and wartime Algeria, 49; family social status, 53; father (Tahar), 54–55, 60, 62; in France, 50, 57; and French language and culture, 53, 61; French boarding school, 56; French colonial schooling of, 51, 53, 54, 55–59; friendships of, 56, 59; *L'amour, la fantasia*, 49–57, 59–62; *La soif*, 51; *Les impatients*, 51; and letter writing, 59–60; and modernity, 57; mother (Bahia), 57, 59, 62; and Muslim education (Koranic school), 53, 54; Muslim influence on, 53; parents' support of Western education, 57, 59, 60; and physical and sexual liberation, 51, 53, 55; puberty, 55, 56; reading, 56; and refusal to wear a veil, 56, 57, 58, 59, 61; and relations with boys and men, 57, 58, 59, 60, 63n11; and sense of freedom, 51, 56–57, 60, 61; and strained relationship with female community, 51, 52, 53, 56–57, 58, 61–62; and spatial boundaries, 55, 58–60; and transnational writing, 50; in Tunisia, 57; in the United States, 50, 57; and virginity ideal, 57, 60; *Vaste est la prison*, 49, 50–54, 57, 61, 62; and writing, 49–54, 61, 62, 63n5
domestic training, 9, 182–183, 218, 219, 220
donanción, 112, 121
Donlan, P. F., 131–132, 133, 137, 138
dos Santos, Lucia, 179, 182, 183, 184; compared to Garabandal visionaries, 186
Dotson, Doris, 172
dowries, 109, 111, 112, 118, 364
dress. *See* clothing
Driscoll, Catherine, 24, 87, 91, 181
drugs, 67, 68, 77
Du Bois, W.E.B., 136; double consciousness, 50
Duff, Hilary, fashions, 23
Duff, S. E., 3, 9, 35, 215
Duff-Gordon, Lady Lucie, 357–358
Dutch Afrikaner girls, 9, 215, 234–249; and Christianity, 237; and education, 234–249; as educators, 236; empowerment of, 237; and ideas of femininity, 236, 237–240; and the New Woman, 235; as professionals, 236; as role models, 236–237; and self-reporting, 236–237; societal expectations, 235, 236

economics, 5, 7, 107, 167–169
education, xi, 7, 346; as agent of the state, 9, 185, 215, 239; and assimilation, 9, 218,

230–231; boarding schools, xi, 11, 56, 203, 215, 234–249; as challenge to patriarchy, 60; and colonialism, xii, 8, 9, 10, 51, 53, 54, 55–59, 215, 217, 218, 219–231, 234–249, 252, 253, 254, 255, 257, 258, 259–264, 271–274, 277; and domestic training, 9, 218, 219, 227–228, 231; and empowerment, 9, 10, 60, 72, 75, 215, 227, 228, 229–230, 240; and establishment of schools, 2, 107; expansion of, 6, 35, 305, 324, 383, 385; and French colonial schools, 51, 53, 54, 55–57; and gender roles, 317–318; girls', compared to boys', 35, 185, 385, 386, 389; girls in policy-making, 24, 26; and girls' rights, 107, 203; globalization of, 185; importance of for girls, 75, 77, 78, 79, 240, 390–393; limited by gender, 3, 58, 185; as mark of modern childhood, 6, 184–185; and matriculation as end to childhood, 3, 37, 393; and maternalism, 240; by mother, 113, 118, 122n44, 182–183, 348; and nation-state, 185, 238, 239; religious, 53, 54; and sex segregation, 185; and socialization, 9, 10, 37, 38, 65, 67, 75, 107, 114, 203, 215, 218, 219, 230–231, 238, 239, 240; as time of freedom, 392, 393; university, 79, 240. *See also* college girls; schoolgirl; schools
The Educational Alliance, 38
Efrati, Noga, 290, 291
Egypt, 3, 275, 276, 292, 295, 316, 323, 344–359, 364; boys and girls compared, 345, 346–347, 352; child custody, 347; court system, 346, 351; definitions of girlhood, 344–353, 358–359; education, 346; growth of the state, 344–345; health, 349, 359; homemaking (domestic responsibilities), 348; and Islamic law, 345–350, 353, 364; labor of girls, 344, 345, 353–356, 359; marriage, 347–349, 350–351; and medicalization of girlhood, 345, 349–350, 351, 353; menarche, 345, 346, 347, 348; physical maturity, 350–351; puberty, 346–348, 350, 358; religious duties, 346; role of state in family life, 351; sexual assault, 351, 352, 356; sexuality, 345, 347–352; slavery in, 346, 353–354, 356–359; state's role as protector, 350, 351, 353, 358–359; travel literature, 346, 357
egg candlers' strike, 136, 138
Egg Inspectors Union, Chicago, 124, 131–132, 133–134, 135–136, 138
Eisenhower, Dwight, 315
Eliot, George, *Daniel Deronda*, 40
elopement, 10, 122n40, 323. *See also rapto de seducción*
emancipation: from colonialism, 269; from minor status, 10, 51, 58, 153, 154, 156
Eminem, 76

employment and careers, xi, xii, 3, 9, 10, 39, 51, 215, 218, 236, 239, 247, 305, 370–371, 394–395, 397; cigar factory workers, 39; clerical work, 280; domestic service, 256, 353, 355–356, 359, 370, 372; egg candlers, 9, 124–125, 130–132; as end of childhood, 3; factory work, 344, 353–355, 383–384, 392, 396; farm work, 168; gymnasts, 196–213; indentured laborers, 256; missionaries, 239; and professionalism, 240–243, 247, 281; social workers, 76; teachers, 10, 239, 247, 274, 280, 281–283; and World War II, 163, 168–169. *See also* labor
England, 9, 191, 312
Escanciano, Margarita, 186
Escandón, Carmen Ramos, 366
ethnicity, xi, xiii, 8, 22, 37, 43, 54, 84
Europe, girls in, 6–7, 65–82, 112, 118, 142–194, 182
Evans, Gwen, 198
Ewing, E. Thomas, 4, 6, 8, 103, 118

family, xi, xiii, 2, 8, 10, 11, 18, 23, 33, 34, 36, 42, 44, 45, 50, 218; in Bijlmer, 70–72; division of labor in, 184; economic responsibility of children to, 36, 107, 183; in Malaysia, 387; service of girls to, 2, 10, 21, 112, 218, 304, 324, 388; status, 36, 387; structure of, 70–72
fashion. *See* clothing
Fass, Paula, 3, 5
fathers, girls' relationships with, 10, 54–55, 60, 62, 72, 110, 143, 145, 147, 148–151, 154, 155, 156, 216, 218, 268, 270, 271, 272, 274–278, 279
Fatima, Portugal, 179
Federation of Jewish Trade Unions, 132
Fem Books (*Nüshudian*), 85, 88
femininity, 9, 35, 56, 215, 216, 234–249; hegemonic, 236, 237–239
feminism, xii, 2, 5, 7, 8, 15, 22, 24, 31, 83, 85–86, 88, 186; and mapping, 15–16
Ferber, Edna, 37, 46n6
fertility (birth) rates, 6, 23, 172
Filipovic, Zlata, diary of, 147
Fink, Leon, 131, 138
Fitzpatrick, John, 133, 136, 137, 138
folk dance, 310, 312
Ford, Henry, factories, 166
Forman-Brunell, Miriam, 7
Forum judicum, 364
Foucault, Michel, 84, 277, 350
4-H Clubs, 306
Fournier, Alain, 56
Fox, Lucy, 39, 47n14
France, 50, 312, 314
Frank, Anne, diary of, 147, 156
Frankenstein, Emily, 33, 37, 40, 43, 45n2
Franklin, Jennie, 41, 47n20

Frenna, Mary, 169
Friendly Dogs, 90
friends and peers, xi, xiii, 33, 34, 35, 41, 42,
    56, 65, 75, 76–77, 78, 245; cross-cultural,
    56, 77, 78
Fung, Anthony, 93
Fyson, Nancy, 168

Gafaïti, Hafid, 50, 60
gangs, 68
Gannett, Cinthia, 19
Garabandal, Spain, 179, 186, 190–191
Garabandal centers, 180, 191
Garabandal movement, 180, 187, 188, 189,
    190, 191; as reactionary, 189–190
Garabandal visionaries: attention from
    adults, 188; compared to Lucia dos Santos,
    186; girlhoods of, 184–187, 188; and media,
    188, 193n38. See also González, Jacinta;
    González, María Concepción (Conchita);
    González, Mari Cruz; Mazón, María
    Dolores (Loli)
Garabandal visions, 179, 181, 184, 186,
    187–188, 190
Garrigue, Sheila, 163
Garrow, Stephanie, 25
gay rights movements, 2, 8, 85–86, 95
gender: as category of analysis, 1, 5, 14, 17, 35,
    36, 45, 156, 183, 238; and equity, 21, 22; and
    identity, 234, 237–238; ideology, 306; as
    issue in Taiwan, 85–86
generation, 3, 17, 112; as category of analysis,
    1, 5, 6, 145, 147, 156, 235
genital mutilation, 21
geography (space) and gender, 58, 59, 188
German U-Boats, 165
Germany, 312, 314, 317
Ghana, 69, 70, 316; girlhood in, 78–79
Ghurab, Hasan, 352
Ghurab, Hasna, 352–353
Gibson Girl, 244
Gide, André, 56
Giraud, Maximin, 182
Giraudoux, Jean, 56
Girl Guides, 219, 317
girlhood: and age, xi, 17, 18, 112, 139n2, 156,
    235, 345; autonomy of, xii; as biological
    category, 23, 353, 358; boundaries of,
    14–29, 35, 84, 218, 242, 269, 290, 293–297,
    299, 300; categorization of, 16, 18, 19, 83,
    84; challenges of, xii; as compressed
    (rushed), 163, 172, 257; construction of, xi,
    xii, 2, 3, 8, 10, 11, 23, 35, 36, 61, 62, 83–84, 181,
    218, 269; contestations of, xi, 8, 11, 36, 42,
    230–231, 242, 257; critical politics of, 93;
    definitions of, 3, 6, 7, 8, 10, 14, 15, 17–18, 23,
    35, 36, 53, 54, 56, 57, 58, 61, 83–84, 97, 98, 112,

116, 118, 139n2, 152, 162, 163, 170, 173, 175,
    181, 185, 190, 196, 206, 207, 215, 216, 235, 236,
    238, 242, 243, 244, 245, 246, 247, 256, 269,
    270, 274, 278, 279–281, 290, 293–297, 299,
    300, 323, 324, 326, 333, 334, 335, 336–338,
    340n17, 344–353, 358–359, 378; early
    childhood as relatively free, 54–55; and
    feminism, 15, 31; globalization of, xiii, 8, 9,
    10, 14, 270; global study of, 1, 5, 6, 7, 8, 15;
    histories of, 11, 14, 17; as an imperialist
    possession, 230–231; imposition of, 3, 11;
    independence of, xiii, 4; and legal
    definitions of, 116, 345–349; limitations of,
    xiii, 3, 42, 55, 61, 98, 118, 148, 152, 153, 154,
    155, 163, 173, 185, 190, 196, 206, 207, 216, 218,
    239, 242, 244, 245, 246, 247, 257, 269, 270,
    278, 280, 290, 293–297, 299, 300; mapping
    of, 14–29; marginalization of, xiii, 3, 10, 11,
    17, 36, 239; matriculation of, 3;
    medicalization of, 345, 349–350, 351, 353, 358;
    modernization of, 5, 244, 269, 270, 290, 295,
    296–297, 298, 300; pathologizing of, 20–22,
    25; politicization of, xii, 7, 8, 16; as
    preparatory stage, 182–183; representations
    of, xi, 3, 14, 36, 38, 382, 396; subcultures of,
    xii, xiii, 14; symbolism of, 9, 103, 179, 180,
    181–182, 190; as universal, 181
girl power, 23, 24, 25, 31, 83, 87, 90, 91, 98
girl rock, 83, 87, 90, 98
girls: and agency, xii–xiii, 3, 4–5, 6, 7, 9, 11, 15,
    16, 20, 24, 25, 32, 40, 45, 53, 66, 78, 79, 96,
    103–104, 106, 118, 145–146, 154, 156, 162, 163,
    171, 173, 180, 181, 183–184, 186, 188, 189, 190,
    196, 215, 239, 262–263, 265; attitudes toward
    boys and men, 72, 74, 75, 77; and boys,
    interest in, 67, 73, 77; and their bodies, 15,
    21, 36, 56, 220, 224, 242, 250; as citizens, xi,
    10, 39, 195, 305; coming-of-age experiences,
    10, 198, 323; and conflicting cultural
    messages, 66, 77, 80, 224; as consumers, 20,
    22–23, 39, 40, 243; cultural identity, 2, 8,
    16, 19, 31, 36, 38, 45, 224, 230–231; as culture
    producers, 8; defiance of, xiii, 371; in
    developing countries, 14, 16, 20–22, 25;
    empowerment of, xii, 3, 9, 10, 21, 23, 25, 31,
    36, 51, 52, 87, 88, 97, 169, 170, 188, 189, 190,
    215, 236–237, 239, 262–263, 265; and ethnic
    values, 77; as family leaders, 18, 23, 42, 43,
    109, 186, 215, 221, 223, 238; and female
    relatives, 51, 52, 53, 56–57, 58, 61–62, 74,
    81n23, 221; in the "first" world, 22, 25; as
    future wives and mothers, 3, 10, 21, 23, 39,
    42, 43, 54, 72, 152, 153, 183, 186, 215, 217, 218,
    220, 221, 223, 224–230, 235, 236, 238, 240, 243,
    247, 268, 271, 273, 278, 281, 289, 293–297,
    300, 306, 318, 324, 325, 327, 328, 332, 334–335,
    336, 338, 339; and going out, 77; images of,

7, 8, 162, 170, 173, 175, 181–182, 196–213; individuality, xii, 6, 7, 8, 35, 44, 51; indoctrination of, xiii; legal representations of, xii, 8, 9, 10, 85; and legal proceedings/ strategies, 105–107, 109, 116, 118–119, 363–364; legal rights of, 106, 107, 109, 115–116, 118–119; marginalization of, xiii, 3, 4, 11, 14, 17, 32, 107, 151, 162, 218; as modern women, 244; as moral proxies of their mother, 382, 390–392, 396–397; and participation in policy making, xi, 24, 26; patriotism of, 2, 36, 37, 143, 169, 170, 195, 196, 198, 201, 203; and personal empowerment, xii, 3, 9, 10, 21, 23, 25, 215; as political agents, 3, 9, 10, 15, 26, 40, 106, 143, 154, 162, 169, 186, 195, 197–198, 200–201, 210, 230–231; and political structures, 154, 156; and resistance, xiii, 9, 103, 144; responses to cultural diversity, 79–80; and same-sex love, 97–98, 102n43; sexual exploitation of, 10, 21, 326, 337–338; sexualization of, 358, 369, 377, 391; social roles of, xii, 18, 34, 37, 38, 39, 218, 239, 240, 242, 344, 349, 353, 392; and spatial boundaries, 55; subjectivity of, 181, 182; submission of, 9, 43; voices of, 3, 4, 7, 15, 18, 21, 24, 49, 50, 51, 52, 53, 66, 96, 107, 189, 308, 344, 359; as vulnerable, 104, 151, 154, 169, 174, 253, 254; as warriors, 10, 197–198; welfare of, 7, 11, 15, 224, 239

Girl Scouts, 306, 317, 318

girls' cultures, xii–xiii, 7, 10, 31; devaluation of, 19; as global, 83, 89, 90–91; musical, 87, 89, 91, 93; "street" versus "decent" culture, xi, 8, 65–68, 73, 76, 77, 79–80

Girls' Literary Society, 41

girls' studies, xi, xiii, 3, 14–16, 20, 22–23, 26–27, 181–182; and children's history, 4, 107; funding, 16–17; global character, xii, 1, 5, 6, 7, 8, 14, 156, 159n17, 284; and history, 1, 4, 6–7, 26, 107, 145, 156–157, 284; as interdisciplinary, 1, 4, 15; methods, 17–19, 25, 66, 68, 79–80, 180; and sexuality, 13n13; and women's history, 4, 21

global citizenship, 305

globalization, xi, xiii, 1, 6, 7, 8, 9, 10, 11, 14, 25, 80, 83, 89–91, 185, 270

Goldman, Emma, 47n14

Gompers, Samuel, 47n14

González, Jacinta, 179, 186, 187

González, María Concepción (Conchita), 179, 186–189; diary of, 186–187, 187–190

González, Mari Cruz, 179, 186, 187

Goodall, Heather, 251, 254

Goodman, Janis Lynn, 66, 72, 73, 79

Gorbachev, Mikhail, 179

Gordon, Kim, 89

Gottlieb, Joanne, 87

Gratz, Rebecca, 47n12

Greece, 316

Green, Ann, 39, 47n13

Greenebaum, Hannah, 40, 47n17

Grossman, James, 135

gulag, 155

Gulick, Luther, 317

Guzmán, Alejo, 114–115

gymnasts, xii, 103, 179, 195–213; and abuse by Soviet Union, 202–206; and Americanization, 199–202, 206; and American propaganda, 206–209, 210; and the Cold War, 195–213; Ginny Coco, 207; Nadia Comaneci, 202, 203, 204, 205; Dominique Dawes, 210; diet of, 203, 204, 205; Nina Dronova, 205; and education, 203, 207; and girlish play, 203, 208; Béla Karolyi, 205, 208; Olga Korbut, 197–202, 203, 204, 205; Renald Knysh, 203; the Magnificent Seven, 210; and the media, 197, 198–202, 203, 204, 205, 206, 207, 210; as members of the Soviet army, 197–198; Shannon Miller, 210; and the Olympics, 197–210; physical training of, 203–206, 208; Mary Lou Retton, 200, 206–209; Cathy Rigby, 206–209; and Soviet propaganda, 196, 199, 200, 201, 202, 203; Kerri Strug, 210; as tools of the nation-state, 196, 199, 201, 202, 203, 204, 208, 209, 210; and western portrayals, 203, 204, 205, 206, 209, 210; as wholesome, 206–209, 210

Haley, Margaret, 136

Hall, George, 129

Halperin, David, 84

Hanafi School of Law, 345, 347–349. *See also* Islam

harems, 56, 58

Harris, Anita, 7, 24

Harris, Ruth, 182, 183

Harvey, Jessamy, 9, 17, 103

Havel, Vaclav, 179

health, 6, 7, 15, 224, 349, 359, 365

Hebrew Literary Society, 41

Hein, Lucille, 311

Helgren, Jennifer, 2, 10, 196, 216, 297

Henry, Ed, 138

Hersh, Kristin, 89

Hilton, Paris, 18

Hinaway, Mbarak Ali, 273

Hingson, Jesse, 9, 103

hip-hop, 75, 76, 79

Hole, 87

Holocaust, 147

holy children, 180; authority of, 180

holy girls, 182, 183, 185, 187; agency of, 181, 183; authority of, 183, 186, 188; as divine messengers, 189; educational backgrounds, 183, 184–186; subjectivity of, 181; submission of, 183; symbolic significance of, 182, 190; as visionaries, 182

Holy Land, 215, 217

homemaking (domestic responsibilities), 78, 163, 169, 305, 308, 310, 348, 388

homework, 67, 71, 75, 77, 79

homosexual subcultures, 86, 98. *See also* lesbian (*nütongzhi*) identity

Hong Yun-hui, 90

honor, 352, 366–367, 369, 376

Hooker, Virginia, 386

Hoover, Herbert, 137, 311

Horrocks, Mr., 133, 137

Hsia Yu, 88

Huang Xiao-zhen, 90

Huang Yun-ling, 90

Hubbard, Vesta Lou, 166

Huguenot Seminary, 9, 215, 234–249

Hull House, 38, 39, 46n11

humanitarianism, 21–22

human rights movements, 6

Hunter, Jane, 147

hymen, 351, 352, 378, 381n57. *See also* medical examinations

identity, xii, 2, 7, 9, 19, 32, 40, 45, 98, 143, 145, 184, 201; bicultural, 50, 53, 54, 60–61, 62, 80; and cultural scripts, 66; and familial relationships, 53, 145, 385, 397; gender, 66, 70, 79, 84, 144, 152–153, 156; and generation, 144, 152–153, 156; and history, 53; as intersectional, xii, 8, 31; personal, 60, 77, 143, 145, 151–152, 201, 203; sexual, 84–85, 98. *See also* cultural identity; lesbian (*nütongzhi*) identity; national identity

illegitimacy, 173

Imalayène, Fatma Zohra. *See* Djebar, Assia

immigration, xii, 36, 38, 39, 43, 44, 45

imperialism, 5, 6, 10, 215, 294, 324

India, xiii, 7, 25, 191, 275, 316

industrialization, 6

Industrial Revolution, 353–354

inheritance, and girls' rights, 107, 111, 118

Inness, Sherrie A., 6, 181

Institut Teknologi MARA (ITM), 390–391, 393

integration (social), 33–45

intermarriage, 42

internationalism, 216, 304–306, 308, 309–312, 317–319

international politics, 103, 124, 125, 137, 139, 179

Internet, 78, 92, 180, 191

Iraq, xiii, 2, 10, 216, 289–303; al-Futuwwa, 2, 10, 216, 289, 290, 291–293, 294, 295, 296, 298, 299; Arab Revolt, 298; and authoritarianism, 289, 300; boys in, 289, 298, 299; education in, 298, 299; and fascism, 289, 292, 294, 295; femininity in, 216; Genc Dernekleri, 294; gender categorizations in, 216; gender restrictions in, 216; girls' schools in, 297, 299, 300; and ideas of girlhood, 291, 296–297, 298, 299; and imperialism, 294; masculinity in, 216, 289, 291; and the media, 294, 298, 300; and nationalism, 290, 292, 295, 298–299, 300; and the Ottoman Empire, 291, 294; and patriotic motherhood, 289, 290, 298, 300; role of women in, 216, 289, 290–291, 298, 299, 300; and totalitarianism, 289; and World War I, 298; and World War II, 289, 290; youth organizations in, 216, 290, 291–293, 294

Iraqi girls, 216, 289–303; agency of, 289, 290, 291, 297, 298–300, 301; and al-Futuwwa, 216, 290, 299, 300, 301; chastity of, 293; dress, 296; and domesticity, 300; education, 296–297, 300; and feminism, 291; as future caretakers of the nation-state, 293, 296, 299, 300; as future mothers of warriors, 289, 293–297, 299, 300; and girl scouting, 294; and the Iraqi media, 290, 298, 299–300; and male dominance, 291; and the media, 297, 300; militancy of, 291; and modernization, 290, 295, 296–297, 298, 300; and *nahda* (awakening), 296–297, 300; and nationalism, 290, 299, 300; and the preservation of honor, 297, 300; as providers of strength and masculinity, 216, 290, 298, 299; role in society, 293, 296, 297, 299, 300; and self-determination, 291, 299, 301; as a tool of the nation-state, 290, 293–297, 299, 300; voices of, 290, 298; and western influence, 296, 297

Iraqi youth: and feminism, 291; as future warriors, 289; and masculinity, 291; and national identity, 290, 293, 295; and the struggle against imperialism, 294; and traditionalism, 295

Ireland, 312

Islam, 216, 217, 345–350, 353, 364, 383, 393, 394, 395, 397. *See also* Muslim society

Israel, 312, 316

Italy, 312

Jackson, Carlton, 164

Jacobus, Helen, 40

Jamaica, 3, 323; slavery in, 325–343

Japan, 304, 313, 317–318, 385

Jewish Foster Home, Philadelphia, 41

Jewish girls (Europe), 147

Jewish girls (U.S.), 9, 196; as agents of acculturation, 37, 45; and American girl culture, 36, 45; and assimilation, 35, 36, 38, 39, 41, 44; and class status, 38; clothing, 36, 38; clubs and societies, 36, 40; and conflict between tradition and modernity, 43; and cultural retention, 35; and dance, 36, 38–39; dating, 37, 42, 44; diaries of, 38; education, 36; and ethnic divisions, 43; ethnic identity, 40; ethnic traditions, 37; and exercise, 36; and family social status, 36, 40; and identity, 31, 34, 35–45; immigrants, 36; as keepers of tradition, 37, 45; and Jewish community's importance, 37, 41; and Jewish social circles, 34, 41–42; literary societies, 40, 41; and low intermarriage rates, 42; and marriage, 41, 43–44; meeting men, 39, 41; modernization, 35, 42, 44; and non-Jewish social organizations, 40; parents' influence on marriage choice, 43; peer identification, 37, 40; publishing, 40; and piano playing, 36, 38; and radical ideologies, 39–40; and reading, 36, 39–40; and relationship with parents, 36; religious identity, 40, 44; and religious practice, 34, 37; and school life, 35, 36, 37; shared concerns across generations, 33–34, 44; and social class divisions, 36, 40, 43–44; social roles, 35; views of gender equality, 43; working class, 41
Jewish immigrant communities, 125, 132–133
Jewish press in U.S., 39
Jews, 364
Jones, Christa, 4, 8, 11, 17, 31, 118
Jones, Gavin W., 387
Jones, Roy, 128
journals. *See* diaries
Judaism, 8, 9, 31, 33–48, 221
Juno, Andrea, 89
juvenile courts, 130
Juvenile Protective Association (JPA), 128, 129

Kakimonto, Aiko, 167
Kanogo, Tabitha, 280
Kaplan, Gisela, 184
Kato, Helen, 167
Kazakhstan, 151
Kearney, Mary Celeste, 189
Kempthorne, Edith, 312
Kerber, Linda, 307
Kessler-Harris, Alice, 5
Khaldun, Ibn, 64n24
Khrushchev, Nikita, 157
kidnapping, 230
Kirk, Jackie, 3, 4, 11, 25
Kirk, Robert, 168

Klapper, Melissa, 8, 31, 126, 196
Kleinbaum, Nancy M., 210, 213n75
Knupfer, Anne Meis, 134
Kolej Tunku Kurshiah in Seremban, 389
Kordas, Ann, 9, 103, 179
Korman, Eleanore, 304
Kozma, Liat, 3, 10, 17, 130, 323, 364
Kuala Lumpur, Malaysia, 389, 391, 392, 393, 394

labor, 1, 5, 6, 7, 10, 39, 103, 105, 124–127, 139n2, 183, 323, 324, 344, 345, 353–356, 359; child labor, 168–169, 345, 353–356, 359; history of, 125; and injury to girls, 344, 355; indentured, 256; rural, 183. *See also* employment and careers; slavery
labor union movement: and African Americans, 134–136; in Britain, 131; corruption of in U.S., 130–131; in Jewish community (U.S.), 132–133; in the U.S., 103, 125, 130, 132–133, 134–136; and women, 135–136
Lancastria (ship), 165
Larkin, June, 22
Lather, Patti, 22
Latin America, 366, 369; and childhood, 364, 365; and children's history, 107; civil wars, 107; girls in, 7, 105–123, 325–343, 363–381; independence movements, 108; nation building, 107; political repression, 108, 118
Leach, Fiona, 22
League of Mercy, 165
League of Nations, 219
Lebanon, 316
Lee, Jennifer, 6
Lee, Veronica, 88
lesbian (*nütongzhi*) identity, xiii, 2, 8, 31, 83, 86–87, 92–99
letter writing, 4, 59–60, 72, 188–189
Lewinsky, Monica, 18
Liberty Belles, 171
Lin Shao-pei, 90
literacy, 6, 39, 41, 51, 183, 186, 189
Little Women (Alcott), 39
Lomangino, Joey, 187, 188, 189
London Jews' Society, 219, 220, 221, 222, 230
Loomis, C. Frances, 311, 315
López, Manuel, 108–109, 110, 111, 112, 114
Lourdes, France, 182
love, xi, 68, 73–75, 363–364, 371, 373–375, 377, 378
love letters, 373–375, 378, 381n47
Lowenburg, Clara, 43, 48n27
L7, 87
Lugovskaya, Evgenia, 148–149, 155, 157
Lugovskaya, Lyubov, 148, 152–154, 157; arrest of, 149, 155; and devotion to family, 153–154

Lugovskaya, Nina, 142–157; adolescence, 142–143, 150, 153–154; agency of, 145–146, 156; arrest and exile of, 148, 149, 155, 157; childhood of, 154; conviction overturned, 157; diary of, 142–143, 144, 146, 148, 149–153, 155, 156, 157–158n1; disappointments of, 143, 144, 148; family relations, 148–155; identity, 143, 144, 149, 151–152, 154, 156; marriage of, 157; political views of, 150, 151, 155; political vulnerability, 151, 155; relationship with father, 143, 147, 148–151, 154, 155, 156; relationship with mother, 143, 147, 148–149, 151–155, 156; relationship with sisters, 149; search for "higher purpose," 152–153, 155; in Stalinist Russia, 143, 144, 146, 148, 150–156; views of gender roles, 147, 152, 152–155; as youngest daughter, 148
Lugovskaya, Olga, 148–149, 155, 157
Lunenberg, Mieke, 172

MacTaggert, Agnes, 171
Mahmood, Saba, 183–184
Makanaonalani, Dorinda, 176
makeup, 67, 73, 167
Malay College Kuala Kangsar (MCKK), 389, 390
Malaysia (Malay), xi, 11, 316; boys compared to girls in, 385, 386, 388, 389, 392, 396; colonial era, 384–385, 398n8; communal culture, 384; corporal punishment, 386, 392; dakwah girls, 383, 384, 390, 392–393, 396, 398n6; education, 382–385, 389, 390–393, 398n4; egalitarian culture, 384; employment, 394–395, 397; ethnic Chinese in, 382, 390; ethno-nationalism in, 386, 387, 391; factory girls, 383–384, 392, 396; family life, 387; girls as moral proxies of their mother, 382, 390–392, 396–397; girls as sexualized, 391; homemaking (domestic responsibilities), 388; importance of education for girls, 386, 390–393; independence, 382, 385, 386, 396; Islamic conservatism in, 383, 395, 397; and Malay girls, 11, 323–324, 382–397; marriage, 387, 394; maternal ideal, 395; middle class, 383–384, 386–387, 391, 396, 399n11; and modern childhood, 386; and modern girlhood, 383, 388, 390; modernity, 382, 386, 390, 392, 395, 396; mothers, 385–387, 395; multinational factories in, 383, 387; New Economic Policy (NEP), 382–384, 390, 391, 393, 394–395; polygyny in, 394; representations of girls, 382, 396; seclusion of girls, 387; sexuality, 391, 392; sibling relationships, 389; siblingship in, 390–391; sisters to the state, 391, 396, 397; and World War II, 385
Malik, Farah, 25

Maliki School of Law, 347. See also Islam
Manderson, Lenore, 384, 388
Mann, Sally, 18
Mao Zedong, 305
Marghinani, 'Ali ibn Abi Bakr al-, 349
Marian visions/apparitions, 103, 179–181, 182, 190
Marquardt, Marie, 180
marriage, 10, 18, 21, 35, 38, 41, 42–45, 323, 363–364, 375; age of, 122n39, 347, 367; annulment, 348; choice of partner, 381n48; consummation of, 348–349, 353; early, 20, 347, 348, 350, 353, 359; as emancipation, 376–377; as end of childhood, 3, 345, 347–349; as end of female same-sex love, 97; expectations for, 183; and family conflict, 363, 380n34; and girls' rights, 107, 109, 364, 367, 371; options, 10, 112; and parental consent, 367, 371; and sexual assault, 351. See also elopement
Marshall Plan, 304
Martin, Fran, 2, 8, 18, 31
Marto, Francisco, 182
Marto, Jacinta de Jesus, 182
masculinity, 70, 132, 238, 289, 290, 291, 292, 293, 295, 296; media images of, 295; and the nation-state, 289, 290, 291, 292, 293, 295, 296
mass culture, 186. See also popular culture
Massey, Victoria, 163, 165, 170, 173
maternalism, 305–308, 318, 324
Matthieu, Melanie, 182, 183, 184
Maynes, Mary Jo, 6
Mazón, María Dolores (Loli), 179, 186, 187, 188, 191n2
Mazrui, Ali A., 278
McGregor, Russell, 250, 255
McRobbie, Angela, 24
medical examinations, 345, 350, 351, 358, 369, 373, 378
Medovi, Leerom, 201
Melissa Ann Elam Club Home for Girls, 130
memory, 107
menarche, 345, 346, 347, 348
Meng Ting-wei, 90
menstruation, 21, 23, 278, 280; as end of childhood, 3; knowledge about, 74
Mexican Penal Code of 1871, 367, 369
Mexico, xi, 316, 351, 363–378; abuse in, 371, 372–373, 376, 377; adolescence in, 364, 367, 376, 377; boys compared to girls in, 367; childhood in, 364–366, 368, 373, 376; children's rights, 365; civil law, 363–368, 373, 376; courtship, 370–371; definition of girlhood, 378; delinquency, 365; dowries, 364; emancipation from parental authority, 364, 367, 372, 376–377; employment, 370–371, 372; filial responsibility, 364;

girls in, 363–378; health, 365; Jews in, 364; love, 363–364, 371, 373–375, 377, 378; marriage, 363–364, 367, 368, 371, 375, 376; modernization, 369–370, 373, 376; motherhood, 365; orphans, 365; parental responsibilities, 371–373; patriarchal social structure in, 365, 366, 371–372, 376, 377; puberty, 366–367, 378; *rapto de seducción*, 323, 363, 366–378; relationship between state and family, 365–366, 371, 376; relationships with parents, 363, 366, 368; sexual abuse, 372; sexuality, 363–364, 366, 367, 368–369, 375–378; working class in, 364, 365, 369, 370–371, 375, 378

Mianda, Gertrude, 270

Middle East, girls in, 217–233, 289–303

migrant communities, 6, 65–66; and superdiversity, 8, 66, 68–69, 77–80

migrations, 2, 5, 7, 8, 68–69, 70, 186; and Jewish diaspora, 8

military conflict. *See specific wars*

Miller, Glenn, 170, 171

Mills, C. Wright, 131

Min Zhou, 6

Mirza, Sarah, 271–272, 275

missionaries, xiii, 9, 215, 216, 217–233, 269, 272, 313; as agents of the nation-state, 231, 238, 239; and assimilation, 218, 230–231; and deathbed conversion narratives, 224–230; and domestic training, 218, 219, 227–228, 231; and education, 218, 219–221, 273–274, 275; and evangelicalism, 218; and Islam, 273; as socializing force, 218, 219, 230–231, 238, 239; and traditionalism, 218; and westernization, 218, 231; and youth organizations, 219, 231

Mitchell, Claudia, 3, 4, 7, 11

Mitchell, Sally, 185

mobility, 126

modern girlhood, 383, 388, 390

Modern Girl Research Group, 5

modernity, 31, 184, 359, 382, 390, 392, 395, 396; and family life, 185; as "Western," 57, 60, 61

modernization, 2, 3, 6, 9, 10, 31, 35, 42, 43, 44, 186, 216, 344, 369–370, 373, 376

Mohamad, Mahathir, 386

Mokeddem, Malika, 58

Mombasa, Kenya, xiii, 3, 10, 216, 264; African Girls Primary School, 274; Arab Girls' School, 273; boys in, 268, 269, 272; British colonial period, 268–288; Christian schools in, 273; Church Missionary Society's Buxton School, 273, 277; Coast Girls' High School, 279–280, 282; colonial educational policies, 271–274, 277; colonial schools in, 268–288; cultural diversity in, 269, 271, 272, 277; cultural identity in, 272; Ghazali Muslim School, 273; Girls Youth Center, 282, 283; indigenous education in, 268; and Islam, 269, 283; Mbaraki School, 279; missionaries in, 269, 272; mission schools in, 272, 274, 275; Muslim schools in, 273; Mvita Primary School, 273; Qur'an schools in, 271–272; and racial character of colonial schools, 274; slavery in, 271; trade in, 271; Western schools in, 269–271, 277

Mombasan girls: agency of, 268, 275, 283–284; career goals, 270–271, 272, 280, 281–283, 284; and colonial education, 268–288; and community expectations, 269, 270, 284; cultural identity of, 268, 272, 274, 281, 283, 284; domestic training of, 268, 270, 272; empowerment of, 268, 284; familial relationships, 269, 283; as future wives and mothers, 268, 271, 273, 278, 281; and gender ideals, 269, 270, 271, 283–284; and Islam, 272–273; and marriage, 269, 273, 278–279, 281, 283, 284; and "the modern girl," 269, 270, 284; and modernization, 269; and patriarchy, 270; and relationship with their fathers, 268, 270, 271, 272, 274–278, 279; and relationship with their mothers, 268; and resistance, 268; and sexuality, 269, 278–279; socialization of, 270, 271, 278, 284; as a tool of the nation-state, 270, 271, 280, 281–283, 284; and westernization, 269, 270

Mooney, Tom, 47n14

Morelos, Father Gustavo, 189

Morlock, Maud, 173

Morowitz, Carolyn, 313

Morris, William, *News from Nowhere*, 39–40

Mortimer, Mildred, 49–50, 51

Mosse, George, 294

motherhood, 3, 10, 18, 21, 23, 280, 289, 365; expectations for, 3, 10, 21, 23, 39, 42, 43, 54, 72, 152, 153, 183, 186, 215, 217, 218, 220, 221, 223, 224–230, 235, 236, 238, 240, 243, 247, 268, 271, 273, 278, 281, 289

mothers, 70; girls' relationships with, 67, 71–72, 79, 80, 81n25, 143, 145, 147, 148–149, 151–155, 156, 218, 268, 382, 390–392, 396–397; and matrifocal family structure, 70–71; as role models for daughters, 71, 80; and socialization to middle-class culture, 65–66

Mount Holyoke Seminary, 235, 236

movies, 128, 173, 186

multinational factories, 383, 387

music, xi, 2, 18, 22, 23, 36, 38, 78. *See also* hip-hop; popular music; singing

Muslim girls, 9, 11, 51, 54, 224, 225, 228, 230, 282, 283, 323–324; early childhood as relatively free, 54–55; and education, 272–273; and female enclosure, 51, 384,

Muslim girls (*continued*)
387; puberty, 55, 56; as sexualized, 391; and spatial boundaries, 55
Muslim society: and female enclosure, 51; as holistic, 51; patriarchal social structure in, 50, 348. *See also* Islam
Muzzafar, Chandra, 393
mysticism, 183

Nagata, Judith, 393
Nancy Drew, 23
Nash, Ilana, 172
Natchez, Mississippi, 43, 44
National Council of Jewish Women, 47n17
National Council of Women, 47n20
national identity, 8, 31, 37, 40, 53, 62, 71, 103, 147, 201, 203
nationalism, 5, 8, 37, 53–54, 62
nation-states, 1, 2, 185, 306; and education, 217–233; girls as agents of, 3, 10, 36, 37, 103, 114, 143, 154, 185, 186, 195–213, 293, 296, 299, 300; girls' relationships to, 3, 8, 9, 10, 36, 37, 103, 109, 118–119, 143, 154, 195–213, 216, 238, 239, 293, 296, 299, 300, 308, 324, 359; power of, 345; relationship between state and family, 351, 365, 371
Nayak, Anoop, 7
Nazis, 165
Nelson, Claudia, 7
Netherlands, 7, 31, 36, 82n34, 136, 312, 317
Nevelson, Louise, 46n10
Newell, Barbara Warne, 136
New Orleans, 33, 34
New York, 38
Nicholson, H. V., 165
Nigeria, 316
Nixon, Richard M., 198, 199, 209
North America, girls in, 25, 118. *See also specific nations*
North Korea, 305
Norway, 312

Oaxaca, Mexico, 364, 366, 369–371, 375
Oaxaca de Juárez, Mexico, 369–371, 373
Odriozola, Canon Francisco, 188
Olympics, 197–210; Atlanta (1996), 209–210; Helsinki (1952), 197; Los Angeles (1984), 206, 208, 209; Mexico City (1968), 206; Montreal (1976), 202, 204; Moscow (1980), 203; Munich (1972), 198, 199, 202, 206
O'Malley, Gabrielle, 278
O'Neill, William, 168
Ong, Aihwa, 383, 391
orientalism, 217
orphans, 18, 217, 225–228, 365
Ortner, Sherry, 66, 79
Ossian, Lisa, 2, 9, 103, 129, 307

Ottoman Empire, 217, 218, 220, 229, 230, 231, 345, 350, 354–356
Ouled Riah tribe, 52
Overy, Richard, 166
Oxhandler, Leopold, 138

Paine, Mrs. Lou B., 307
Pakistan, 25, 316
Palestine, xiii, 9, 215, 217–233, 264; British Mandate era, 217, 219–231; Christian girls in, 218, 221; Church Missionary Society/Society for the Promotion of Female Education, 218, 219, 230; colonial education in, 215, 217, 218–231; cultural diversity in, 218, 224, 225, 228, 231; Diocesan Schools for Girls in Jerusalem, 218; East Mission's English High School for Girls, 219, 222; East School in Nazareth, 218; Female Education Society, 220, 223, 224, 226, 227, 228, 230; girls' education in, 218–233; girls' empowerment in, 227, 228, 229–230; girls in, 218–233; Jerusalem Girls' College, 228; Jewish girls in, 220, 221, 222, 228, 230; missionaries in, 217–233; Muslim girls in, 224, 225, 228, 230; orphaned girls in, 217, 225–228; orphaned girls and physical labor, 226–228; Ottoman era, 217, 218, 220, 229, 230, 231; Scottish Mission School, 223
Papanek, Hanna, 387
Paraguay, 113
parents, 4, 6, 10, 33, 34, 35, 36, 37, 42, 43, 44, 218, 221, 226, 238, 243; girls' relationships with, 363, 366, 368; parental abuse, 226, 371, 372–373, 376, 377; parental responsibilities, 363, 371–373; parental restrictions, 55, 218; and socialization, 67. *See also* family; fathers; mothers
Parker, Mrs. James, 314
parties, xi, 41, 73, 167, 245, 310, 312
Pascal, Blaise, 56
patria potestad. *See* Argentina: patriarchal social structure in; Mexico: patriarchal social structure in
patriarchal social structures, 50, 54, 60, 109, 112, 118, 348, 365, 366, 371–372, 377
Paulle, Bowen, 68, 77
Pearl Harbor, 165–166
Pélissier, General, 52
Pelletier, Father Joseph A., 187, 189
penpals, 309, 312–314, 317, 321n32
Pentecostalism, 74, 77
People-to-People International, 315
Pepper, Claude, 167
Pérez, Celestino Ortiz, 288
Pérez, Jesús, 105, 110, 112
Peru, 377
Peterson, Linda, 175

petitions, girls' and women's use of, 109, 111–112, 118

Petrik, Paula, 4

Phelps-Stokes Fund, 272

Philadelphia, 41

Philippines, 317

Philomathians, Chicago, 41

Phyllis Wheatley Home, Chicago, 130

Piercy, William, 137

Pipher, Mary, 145

planters, 3; and amelioration policies, 333–334, 335; and dependency on "breeding wenches," 333, 334, 335; demand for girls, 328, 334, 339–340n8; and destruction of girlhood, 333–334; ideas of girlhood, 3, 333, 334, 335; purchase preferences, 328, 334, 335, 339–340n8; and pro-natal policies, 331, 333, 334–336; and rewards for natural increase, 333–334; and sexual assault of young slave girls, 326, 337–338

play, 19, 54, 150, 163, 188, 354, 392; swinging as challenge to boundaries, 59, 60

political repression, 2, 108, 118, 142, 148, 151, 154–157

political unrest, 103, 106–107, 156

popular culture, 16, 19, 22, 23, 26, 31, 75, 76, 78, 79, 170, 186; global, 83

popular feminism, 83, 84, 86–87, 90–92, 98

popular music, 83; and feminism, 86, 87–88, 91; and globalization, 89–90, 91

Porter, Mary Ann, 275

post-Rosas era (Argentina), 105, 114; and restitution petitions, 103, 105–106, 113, 114, 115–118

Potthast, Barbara, 365

poverty, 21, 25, 51, 70

Povinelli, Elizabeth A., 85

Powell, Christine, 163

pregnancy, 23, 72, 82n29, 171, 172–173, 350

Progressive Era reform, 305, 306

property rights of girls and women, 109, 111–112, 118, 120n22, 121n30, 121n31

prostitution, 20, 72, 82n29, 128–129, 172

puberty, 23, 55, 56, 280, 346–348, 350, 358, 366–367, 378

Puchol, Vicente, 189

Quakers, 165

race, xi, 8, 26, 41, 67, 68, 250–267

rape, 10, 51, 323, 379n27

rapto de seducción, 323, 363, 366–378. *See also* elopement

Rashidi, Ahmad al-, 350

Read, Peter, 251

reading, 36, 39, 40

Reagan, Ronald, 179, 207–208, 209

reformers, 324

refugee and exiled girls, 18, 25, 107, 110, 113

Reid, Robert, 136

Reid-Walsh, Jacqueline, 3, 4, 7, 11

religion, xi, 5, 6, 8, 9, 22, 43, 50, 79, 183, 346; as transnational, 179–180; women's roles in, 193n36. *See also specific religions*

Republican Motherhood, 307

revolution, xii

Rice, Carla, 22

Rich, Leah Milkman, 314

Riot Grrrl, 83, 87

Rivière, Jacques, 56

Robertson, John Dill, 131

Robins, Dorothy B., 305

Rogers, Rebecca, 146

Romania, 103

romanticism, 364

Rosas, Juan Manuel de, 9, 103, 105–114, 118, 119n2; and children's rights, 111; confiscation policy, 105, 110, 111, 114, 115; and Federalism, 105, 108–109, 110, 118, 119n2; political repression, 106, 107, 108–109, 111, 114, 118; restitution petitions, 121n29; and Unitarians, 105, 108–109, 110, 115–117, 118, 119n2. *See also* post-Rosas regime

Rosie the Riveter, 168

Rousseau, Jean Jacques, 364–365; *Émile*, 364, 365

Ruskay, Sophie, 40, 47n15

Russia, 136, 143

Rybim-Lugovskoi, Sergei, 148, 157; arrest and exile, 148, 149, 151, 154, 155; gender prejudice of, 150–151; in prison, 151; politics of, 148, 150, 154. *See also* Lugovskaya, Nina: relationship with father

Sacrosanctum Concilium, 190

Salvatore, Ricardo, 107

San Francisco, 41, 42

San Salvador, 317

Santander, Diocese of, 180, 188, 191n6, 194n48

Saraco, Maria, 187, 188

Sariyya, 344, 353, 355

Satt, Hilda, 38, 46n11

schoolgirl, 184–185, 193n29

schools: and decent cultural messages, 75; French boarding, 146; girl-friendly, 24, 234–249; street culture in, 75, 78; as unsafe places, 20, 22; and women's roles, 240; during World War II, 164, 167, 168–169

Schools at War Program, 168–169

Scotland, 312

Second Vatican Council, 190

Seed, Patricia, 371

Seidman, Harold, 131

segregation: by age, 257, 259; by gender, 55, 217, 259, 300; by race, 280

Selig, Diana, 310

7 Year Bitch, 87

sex education, 74; and religious instruction, 74

sexual activity, 10, 74–75, 82n27, 82n32, 323, 347–348, 378; age of consent, 351, 367; and autonomy, 363, 366; and birth control, 74, 171; and defloration as end of childhood, 3, 345, 347, 349, 350–353, 358, 367, 368, 373, 375, 381n57; as duty to husband, 348; and group sex, 73; and injury, 350; physical capacity for, 348, 350–351, 367; premarital, 347, 351, 364, 368; and promiscuity, 72, 172, 323. *See also* delinquency

sexual abuse and exploitation, 18, 19, 20, 21, 22, 73, 82n29, 323–324, 351–352, 355–356, 359, 372–373, 381n57; and rape, 10, 73; and slave breeding, 10

sexuality, xi, 3, 8, 9, 10, 11, 18, 19, 23, 44, 68, 72–75, 77, 82n30, 82n33, 84–85, 345, 347–352, 363–364, 366, 367, 368–369, 375–378; and double-standard, 74, 171, 172; global queering, 84–85; and maternalism, 240; mothers' ambivalent attitudes toward, 75, 80; and perceived prudishness, 56; representations of, 10–11, 23, 66, 72; and reproductive role, 345, 347, 349; as threatening, 391; as transnational, 84–85, 86; and World War II, 169–174. *See also* lesbian (*nutongzhi*) identity

Shafi'i school of law, 348. *See also* Islam

Shakespeare, Sir Geoffrey, 165

Shakespeare, William, 39

shari'a courts, 350, 358, 396. *See also* Islam

Shelton, Margaret, 162

shopping, 18, 73

Shortt, Rupert, 190

Siete partidas, 364, 365, 371

Silva, Juana, 363, 372

Simon, Bryant, 132

Simonton, Deborah L., 182

Singapore, 316, 392

singing, 58, 77, 357

Sinha, Mrinalini, 294

slave girls: amelioration of conditions for, 333–334; as "belly women," 334, 336, 338; as "breeding wenches," 3, 10, 325, 327, 328, 332, 334–335, 336, 338, 339; and the buy vs. breed debate, 326, 330–335, 338; as chattel, 337, 338; in colonial Jamaica, 325–343; and colonial natural increase efforts, 326, 334–335, 338; as commodities, 328, 335, 338; and compressed girlhood, 326, 332, 334, 336–337, 338–339; as defined by planters, 326, 333, 336–338, 340n17; as defined by the slave community, 326, 338; demand for, 328, 329, 332, 338; as

an economic risk, 328–329; identity as slaves, 336, 337–338; as investments, 327, 328–329, 332, 333, 334–335, 336–338, 339–340n8; and perceived loyalty of, 329; and planter purchase preferences, 328–329, 336–338, 339–340n8; punishment of, 326, 336; and pressure to breed, 334, 335; and pro-natal policies, 335–336; and reproductive potential, 333–335; and sexual assault, 326, 337–338; and the slave trade, 326; socialization of, 329; treatment of, 326; working conditions for, 326, 335–336

slavery, xiii, 3, 10, 70, 323, 325–343, 346, 353, 356–359; abolitionist threats against, 326; and amelioration, 326, 330, 332–334; buy vs. breed debate, 326, 330–335, 338; and childhood, 326, 337–338; and colonial natural increase efforts, 326, 327, 330, 333–335, 340n11; and compressed girlhood, 333, 334; Consolidated Slave Laws, 332–334, 335; and dependency on slave girls, 333, 334, 336–339; and dependency on slave youth, 333, 336–338, 339; diet, 331–332; gender imbalance in, 327, 336–338; and girlhood, 326, 333, 334, 337–339; and graduated labor gang system, 330, 331, 334, 335–336; and harsh treatment of slaves, 326, 330; and infant and child mortality, 326, 330–332, 335, 340n12; medical care, 331, 335; mortality rates, 327, 330–331, 335; and nutritional deficiency, 332; and punishment, 326, 330, 331; and pro-natal policies, 331, 333, 334–335; working conditions, 326, 330, 331, 335–336

slave trade, 3, 325, 356, 358; abolitionist threats against, 325, 326, 327–328, 330, 331, 336, 338; age restrictions, 328; 329, 332, 341n30; and buy vs. breed debate, 330–335, 338; and changing nature of girlhood, 324, 328, 338; and children, 326; demand for girls, 327, 332, 338, 339–340n8; gender imbalance in, 327, 328, 332; gender restrictions, 328, 332; and girls, 326, 327, 338; and the Middle Passage, 329; mortality rates, 327; and planter purchase preferences, 326, 327–330, 332, 338, 339–340n8

Sloane-White, Patricia, 2, 10, 11, 323

Sloan, Kathryn, 10, 17, 128, 323, 351

Smith, Bonnie G., 5

Smith, Patti, 89

Spanish America, 364, 381n48

Socialist Revolutionary Party, 148

socialization, 10, 37, 38, 39, 41, 42, 154, 155, 329; and family, 65–67; and institutions, xiii, 9, 10, 254, 255, 257, 294, 298, 304–307; and media, 66, 75; and peers, 66–67; and schools, 65, 66–67, 75, 107, 114, 203, 215, 218, 219, 230–231, 238–240, 254, 255, 257, 269, 270–271, 278, 284

Society of Friends, 165

Søland, Birgitte, 6
Solomon, Clara, 33, 45n1
Solzhenitsyn, Aleksandr, 179
Soubirous, Bernadette, 182, 183, 184
South Africa, 3, 9, 18, 24, 35, 191, 234–249,
   316; Boer Republic, 234; Boer Wars, 293;
   British Republic, 234; Dutch Afrikaners in,
   235; and elitism, 235; gendered identities in,
   234, 236; girls in, 234–249; Good Hope
   Seminary, 238; Huguenot Seminary and
   College, 234–249; independence in, 234;
   media in, 235; missionaries in, 235, 236;
   mining in, 234; middle class in, 234, 235;
   National Council of Women, 234; and the
   New Woman, 235, 243–247
South African War, 234
South Korea, 305, 316
Southworth, Alvan, 357
Soviet Union, xii, 9, 103, 305; and abuse of
   gymnasts, 202–206; and childhood, 148,
   154; collapse of, 209; and education of
   ideological values, 145; Five-Year Plan, 148;
   girls in, 143, 144, 146, 154; gymnasts from,
   196–213; Iron Curtain, 200; New Economic
   Policy, 143, 148; political repression, 142, 148,
   151, 154–157; security police, 155; Stalinist
   dictatorship in, 143–148, 150–156; women in,
   144, 147, 150–151, 152–153, 155; youth in, 145
Spain: Franco era in, 180, 184, 185; girls in, 9,
   103; modernization, 186; National-Catholic
   curriculum, 185–186; rural, 179, 184, 186
Special Food Mission to the United States, 137
Spice Girls, 83, 87, 91; Sporty Spice Mel C, 91
Sri Lanka, 316
Stalcup, Ann, 167, 168, 175
Stalin, Joseph, 157, 195. *See also* Soviet Union:
   Stalinist dictatorship in
Stanton, Connie, 170
status production, 387–388, 397
Stearns, Peter N., 5, 6, 10, 184–185
Steedman, Carolyn, 189
Steinhart, Amy, 41, 47n22
stepfathers, 372–373
Stern, Steve, 377
Stivens, Maila, 392
Stockdale, Nancy, 9, 125, 215, 250, 269
Strobel, Margaret, 5, 271–272, 275
Stromquist, Nellie, 14, 15
Sudan, 316, 357, 358
Sueldo, Pedro, 106, 109, 110, 111, 112, 115–117, 118
Sultanic Code of 1855, 350
Sunni law, 345. *See also* Islam
Suriname, 69, 70
Suzuki, Heihachiro, 317–318
Swaziland, 20
Syria, 290, 291; and fascism, 292; Mandate
   Regime in, 291; and masculinity, 291; and
   the Ottoman Empire, 291; paramilitary

youth organizations in, 292; and
   paternalism, 291; Syrian Social Nationalist
   Party, 292; and World War I, 291, 292

Taiwan, xiii, 2, 8, 31, 83–84, 85–87, 88–90, 97
Tajjar, Sa'd Abu, 352
Taliban, 3
Tang Na, 90
Taylor, Molly Ladd, 305
teenagers, 2, 23, 168, 196–213, 306. *See also*
   adolescence; pregnancy; youth cultures
Templin, Vikto, 157
Terkel, Studs, 166
Terry, Walter, 310
Thatcher, Margaret, 179
Thompson, E. P., 353–354
Thompson, Elizabeth, 290, 291
Thursie, O. E., 131
Tilly, Louise, 5
toys, 18, 19, 22–23, 162
Trabish, David, 133
transnational history, xi, 1, 146, 156; and
   children's history, 5; and women's
   history, 5
transnationalism, 2, 25, 31, 50, 146; and music,
   90, 91; religious communities as, 179–180;
   and sexuality, 84–85
trauma, 107, 110, 113, 115, 143, 157, 165
Travelers' Aid, 130
Troutt, Eve, 357
Truman, Harry, 311
Tsui Hark, 88
Turkey, 316
Tuttle, William, 134, 135
tweens, 17, 22, 23, 25
Two Bob Mermaid (film), 250

Uganda, 25, 26
UNESCO, 311, 314
United Kingdom, xii, 9, 11, 25, 69, 317;
   girls in, 103
United States, 9, 10, 165, 304–317, 319; girls in,
   xi, xii, 6–7, 11, 33–48, 103, 112, 124–141, 145,
   147, 162–178, 195–213, 304–322, 369; military,
   316, 318; perceptions of, 76; women's roles
   in nineteenth century, 46n5. *See also*
   African American girls
U.S. Department of Labor, 124, 133–134
U.S. Food Administration, 137
United States girls' cultures, 35–42, 173;
   changing views of, 35; characteristics of, 35;
   clothing, 36, 38; and dance, 36; dating, 37,
   42; and exercise, 36; and literary societies,
   41; and piano playing, 36; and reading, 36,
   39; and school life, 36; social roles, 35
University of Malaya, 392
Unkerholz, I., 131
Upsico, Mary, 42

Urquiza, Justo José de, 114
Uruguay, 113
Ussher, Jane M., 181
Uyl, Marion den, 7, 8, 31, 35

Vallone, Lynne, 7
Vasconcellos, Colleen, 3, 10, 17, 323
Vásquez, Manuel, 180
Vedel, Georges, 49
veils, 11, 56, 57, 58, 59, 61, 393
venereal disease, 171, 172
Vertovec, Steven, 69, 80
vice committees, 128–129
Victoria, Queen, 227
Victory Girls, 172
violence, 271n2. See also sexual abuse and
    exploitation
virginity, 57, 60, 349, 350, 351–352, 358, 367,
    368, 375–378, 392. See also sexual activity:
    and defloration as end of childhood
Voogd, Jan, 2, 9, 103

Wachtel, Rosa, 43
Wagaw, T., 28
Wald, Gayle, 87
Walesa, Lech, 179
Walkerdine, Valerie, 24
Wallerstein, Bertha, 135
Wang Song-en, 90
war, 2, 7, 8, 9, 103, 107, 118, 163, 174.
    See also specific wars
Weller, Irene, 163
Weller, Jacob, 133
West, Elliott, 4
westernization, 54, 55, 60, 71
Wien, Peter, 10, 216, 289
Wiesner-Hanks, Merry, 5
Wojtyla, Karol, 179
Women's Awakening Foundation (Funü
    Xinzhi Jijinhui), 85
women's bodies, 89, 350
Women's Christian Temperance Union, 234
Women's Enfranchisement League, 234
women's history, 5, 24. See also girls' studies
women's suffrage, 243
Wong, Faye, 93
Wong Kar-wai, 88
Workers of Garabandal, 180
World Association of Girl Guides and Girl
    Scouts, 317
World War I, 298; and daily life, 33–34; and
    food shortages, 124; and labor shortages,
    125, 129, 137; and patriotism, 37; in the U.K.,
    136–137; in the U.S., 33–34, 37, 103, 124, 125,
    128, 136, 309, 311
World War II, 9, 11, 23, 61, 103, 129, 289, 290,
    305; air raid alerts, 163; and Asian children,
    168; bomb shelters, 163, 170; "boom"

communities, 166; and British girls,
    162–165, 167–168, 170–171, 173–176; and
    changing social roles, 163, 171; civilian
    deaths, 174; contributions of girls to, 162,
    168–169, 174–175; and delinquency, 171–172,
    174; employment of girls, 163, 168–169, 174;
    employment of women, 168; end of war,
    173, 174, 176; and European children, 168;
    evacuation of British children, 162, 164–165,
    174, 175–176; family disruption, 166, 168;
    homemaking (domestic responsibilities),
    163, 169, 174; and illegitimacy, 173, 174;
    images of girls, 162, 170, 173, 175; Japanese
    internment, 167; and Malay girls, 385;
    memoirs, 174; mixed messages to girls,
    162–163; orphans, 174; patriotism, 172, 175;
    Pearl Harbor, 165–166; rationing, 167–168;
    relationships with GIs, 170–172, 174; and
    restrictions on girls, 163; and schools, 164,
    167, 168–169, 174; and sexuality, 169–173;
    teenage pregnancy, 171, 172–173; and U.S.
    girls, 162–163, 165–169, 171–176, 308–309;
    and vulnerability, 169, 174; women's roles
    during, 306
writings of children, xiii, 4, 189; adult
    mediation in, 189
Wu Pei-wen, 90

Yalta Conference, 195
YMCA, 306
Young Women's Union, 47n12
youth, xi, xiii, 8, 10, 23, 144, 300, 365
youth cultures, 2, 9, 35, 40, 42, 45; in the
    Bijlmer, 75–77, 79–80; and crime, 69, 72,
    367–368, 396; ethnic stereotypes, 68;
    formation of, 2, 9, 35–36; gender in, 35;
    globalizing, 79–80; hip-hop, 75, 76, 79;
    language, 69, 75–76, 78–80; music, 87;
    street culture, 65, 67, 68, 72–73, 75, 80;
    and violence, 68, 69, 72
youth meetings, xi, 24, 26, 37, 40, 42, 219
youth movements and organizations, 2, 9,
    10, 24, 26, 37, 40, 42, 219, 292, 304, 306, 307;
    Arab youth movements, 292; and the
    promotion of national spirit, 294, 298; as
    a socializing force, 10, 37, 40, 219, 290, 292,
    294, 295, 296, 298–299, 304–307; as a tool
    of the nation-state, 292, 294, 295, 296,
    298–299, 308. See also al-Futuwwa; Boy
    Scouts; Camp Fire Girls; communist youth
    organizations; 4-H Club; Girl Guides; Girl
    Scouts; YMCA; YWCA
YWCA, 318

Zanzibar, 272, 276, 278
Zeynab, 357–358, 359
Zimbabwe, xii
Zimdars-Swartz, Sandra, 181, 187